Service and Repair Manual
for MINI

Martynn Randall

Models covered
(4904 - 320)

MINI 'second generation'/'Mk 2' Hatchback & Clubman (Estate), and Convertible from 2009
First, One, Cooper and Cooper S

Petrol: 1.4 litre (1397cc) & 1.6 litre (1598cc), inc. turbo

Turbo-diesel: 1.6 litre (1560cc & 1597cc) & 2.0 litre (1995cc)

Does NOT cover Countryman, Paceman, Clubvan, Roadster, Coupe or John Cooper Works (JCW) versions

© Haynes Publishing 2013

ABCDE
FGHIJ
KLMNO
PQ

A book in the **Haynes Owners Workshop Manual Series**

ISBN **978 1 78521 364 9**

British Library Cataloguing in Publication Data
A catalogue record for this book is available from the British Library.

Printed in Malaysia

Haynes Publishing
Sparkford, Yeovil, Somerset BA22 7JJ, England

Haynes North America, Inc
861 Lawrence Drive, Newbury Park, California 91320, USA

Printed using NORBRITE BOOK 48.8gsm (CODE: 40N6533) from NORPAC; procurement system certified under Sustainable Forestry Initiative standard. Paper produced is certified to the SFI Certified Fiber Sourcing Standard (CERT - 0094271)

Contents

LIVING WITH YOUR MINI

Roadside Repairs

Weekly Checks

Lubricants, fluids and tyre pressures

MAINTENANCE

Contents

Building on the success of the 'new' MINI introduced in July 2002, the 'MkII' MINI covered by this manual, was introduced in petrol hatchback form (model designation R56) in August 2006. A PSA (Peugeot/Citroen) diesel engine (W16) model was introduced in March 2007, replaced by a BMW diesel engine (N47) in August 2010.

The hatchback model range was joined by the Clubman (R55) in August 2007, and the Convertible (R57) model in December 2008 (the previous 'MkI' Convertible model remained in production until this date).

Over the years, the range was has been improved with minor cosmetic/mechanical revisions and variants, but the same 'wheel on each corner' driving fun has remained.

All models have fully-independent front and rear suspension, with anti-roll bars fitted both to the front and rear assemblies.

A wide range of standard and optional equipment is available within the MINI range to suit most tastes, including central locking, electric windows, air conditioning, an electric sunroof, an anti-lock braking system, a traction control system, a dynamic stability control system, and numerous air bags.

Provided that regular servicing is carried out in accordance with the manufacturer's recommendations, the MINI should prove reliable and very economical. The engine compartment is well-designed, and most of the items requiring frequent attention are easily accessible.

Your MINI manual

The aim of this manual is to help you get the best value from your vehicle. It can do so in several ways. It can help you decide what work must be done (even should you choose to get it done by a garage). It will also provide information on routine maintenance and servicing, and give a logical course of action and diagnosis when random faults occur. However, it is hoped that you will use the manual by tackling the work yourself. On simpler jobs it may even be quicker than booking the car into a garage and going there twice, to leave and collect it. Perhaps most important, a lot of money can be saved by avoiding the costs a garage must charge to cover its labour and overheads.

The manual has drawings and descriptions to show the function of the various components so that their layout can be understood. Tasks are described and photographed in a clear step-by-step sequence.

References to the 'left' and 'right' of the vehicle are in the sense of a person in the driver's seat facing forward.

Acknowledgements

Thanks are due to Draper Tools Limited, who provided some of the workshop tools, and to all those people at Sparkford who helped in the production of this manual.

We take great pride in the accuracy of information given in this manual, but vehicle manufacturers make alterations and design changes during the production run of a particular vehicle of which they do not inform us. No liability can be accepted by the authors or publishers for loss, damage or injury caused by any errors in, or omissions from, the information given.

Working on your car can be dangerous. This page shows just some of the potential risks and hazards, with the aim of creating a safety-conscious attitude.

General hazards

Scalding

• Don't remove the radiator or expansion tank cap while the engine is hot.

• Engine oil, transmission fluid or power steering fluid may also be dangerously hot if the engine has recently been running.

Burning

• Beware of burns from the exhaust system and from any part of the engine. Brake discs and drums can also be extremely hot immediately after use.

Crushing

• When working under or near a raised vehicle, always supplement the jack with axle stands, or use drive-on ramps.
Never venture under a car which is only supported by a jack.

• Take care if loosening or tightening high-torque nuts when the vehicle is on stands. Initial loosening and final tightening should be done with the wheels on the ground.

Fire

• Fuel is highly flammable; fuel vapour is explosive.

• Don't let fuel spill onto a hot engine.

• Do not smoke or allow naked lights (including pilot lights) anywhere near a vehicle being worked on. Also beware of creating sparks (electrically or by use of tools).

• Fuel vapour is heavier than air, so don't work on the fuel system with the vehicle over an inspection pit.

• Another cause of fire is an electrical overload or short-circuit. Take care when repairing or modifying the vehicle wiring.

• Keep a fire extinguisher handy, of a type suitable for use on fuel and electrical fires.

Electric shock

• Ignition HT and Xenon headlight voltages can be dangerous, especially to people with heart problems or a pacemaker. Don't work on or near these systems with the engine running or the ignition switched on.

• Mains voltage is also dangerous. Make sure that any mains-operated equipment is correctly earthed. Mains power points should be protected by a residual current device (RCD) circuit breaker.

Fume or gas intoxication

• Exhaust fumes are poisonous; they can contain carbon monoxide, which is rapidly fatal if inhaled. Never run the engine in a confined space such as a garage with the doors shut.

• Fuel vapour is also poisonous, as are the vapours from some cleaning solvents and paint thinners.

Poisonous or irritant substances

• Avoid skin contact with battery acid and with any fuel, fluid or lubricant, especially antifreeze, brake hydraulic fluid and Diesel fuel. Don't syphon them by mouth. If such a substance is swallowed or gets into the eyes, seek medical advice.

• Prolonged contact with used engine oil can cause skin cancer. Wear gloves or use a barrier cream if necessary. Change out of oil-soaked clothes and do not keep oily rags in your pocket.

• Air conditioning refrigerant forms a poisonous gas if exposed to a naked flame (including a cigarette). It can also cause skin burns on contact.

Asbestos

• Asbestos dust can cause cancer if inhaled or swallowed. Asbestos may be found in gaskets and in brake and clutch linings. When dealing with such components it is safest to assume that they contain asbestos.

Special hazards

Hydrofluoric acid

• This extremely corrosive acid is formed when certain types of synthetic rubber, found in some O-rings, oil seals, fuel hoses etc, are exposed to temperatures above 4000C. The rubber changes into a charred or sticky substance containing the acid. *Once formed, the acid remains dangerous for years. If it gets onto the skin, it may be necessary to amputate the limb concerned.*

• When dealing with a vehicle which has suffered a fire, or with components salvaged from such a vehicle, wear protective gloves and discard them after use.

The battery

• Batteries contain sulphuric acid, which attacks clothing, eyes and skin. Take care when topping-up or carrying the battery.

• The hydrogen gas given off by the battery is highly explosive. Never cause a spark or allow a naked light nearby. Be careful when connecting and disconnecting battery chargers or jump leads.

Air bags

• Air bags can cause injury if they go off accidentally. Take care when removing the steering wheel and trim panels. Special storage instructions may apply.

Diesel injection equipment

• Diesel injection pumps supply fuel at very high pressure. Take care when working on the fuel injectors and fuel pipes.

Warning: Never expose the hands, face or any other part of the body to injector spray; the fuel can penetrate the skin with potentially fatal results.

Remember...

DO

• Do use eye protection when using power tools, and when working under the vehicle.

• Do wear gloves or use barrier cream to protect your hands when necessary.

• Do get someone to check periodically that all is well when working alone on the vehicle.

• Do keep loose clothing and long hair well out of the way of moving mechanical parts.

• Do remove rings, wristwatch etc, before working on the vehicle – especially the electrical system.

• Do ensure that any lifting or jacking equipment has a safe working load rating adequate for the job.

DON'T

• Don't attempt to lift a heavy component which may be beyond your capability – get assistance.

• Don't rush to finish a job, or take unverified short cuts.

• Don't use ill-fitting tools which may slip and cause injury.

• Don't leave tools or parts lying around where someone can trip over them. Mop up oil and fuel spills at once.

• Don't allow children or pets to play in or near a vehicle being worked on.

The following pages are intended to help in dealing with common roadside emergencies and breakdowns. You will find more detailed fault finding information at the back of the manual, and repair information in the main chapters.

If your car won't start and the starter motor doesn't turn

☐ Lift the bonnet, unclip and remove the battery cover. Make sure that the battery terminals are clean and tight.

☐ Switch on the headlights and try to start the engine. If the headlights go very dim when you're trying to start, the battery is probably flat. Get out of trouble by jump starting (see next page) using a friend's car.

If your car won't start even though the starter motor turns as normal

☐ Is there fuel in the tank?

☐ Is there moisture on electrical components under the bonnet? Switch off the ignition, then wipe off any obvious dampness with a dry cloth. Spray a water-repellent aerosol product (WD-40 or equivalent) on ignition and fuel system electrical connectors like those shown in the photos.

A Check the security of the ignition coil harness connectors.

B Check the throttle body wiring connector with the ignition switched off.

Check that electrical connections are secure (with the ignition switched off) and spray them with a water-dispersant spray like WD-40 if you suspect a problem due to damp.

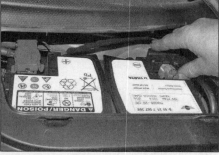

C Check the security and condition of the battery terminals.

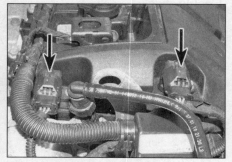

D Check the security of the camshaft position sensors.

Jump starting

When jump-starting a car using a booster battery, observe the following precautions:

✔ Before connecting the booster battery, make sure that the ignition is switched off.

✔ Ensure that all electrical equipment (lights, heater, wipers, etc) is switched off.

✔ Take note of any special precautions printed on the battery case.

✔ Make sure that the booster battery is the same voltage as the discharged one in the vehicle.

✔ If the battery is being jump-started from the battery in another vehicle, the two vehicles MUST NOT TOUCH each other.

✔ Make sure that the transmission is in neutral (or PARK, in the case of automatic transmission).

 Jump starting will get you out of trouble, but you must correct whatever made the battery go flat in the first place. There are three possibilities:

1 *The battery has been drained by repeated attempts to start, or by leaving the lights on.*

2 *The charging system is not working properly (alternator drivebelt slack or broken, alternator wiring fault or alternator itself faulty).*

3 *The battery itself is at fault (electrolyte low, or battery worn out).*

1 Open the bonnet, unclip and remove the battery cover, then connect the red jump lead to the terminal positive (+) terminal.

2 Connect the other end of the red lead to the positive (+) terminal of the booster battery.

3 Connect one end of the black jump lead to the negative (-) terminal of the booster battery.

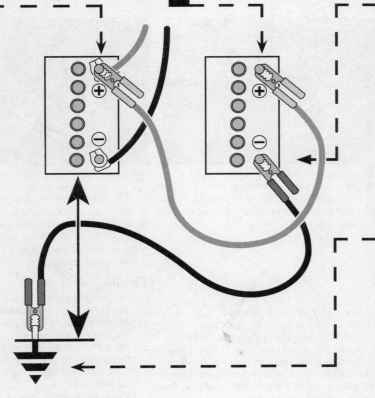

4 Connect the other end of the black jump lead to the battery negative terminal or metal bracket in the engine compartment.

5 Make sure that the jump leads will not come into contact with the cooling fan drivebelts or other moving parts on the engine.

6 Start the engine, then with the engine running at fast idle speed, disconnect the jump leads in the reverse order of connection, ie. negative (black) lead first. Securely refit the plastic cover to the jump start positive terminal where applicable.

Wheel changing

⚠️ **Warning: Do not change a wheel in a situation where you risk being hit by other traffic. On busy roads, try to stop in a lay-by or a gateway. Be wary of passing traffic while changing the wheel – it is easy to become distracted by the job in hand.**

Note: *Your MINI maybe equipped with special 'Run Flat' tyres, the MINI Mobility System, or a Compact spare wheel.*

Preparation

- ☐ When a puncture occurs, stop as soon as it is safe to do so.
- ☐ Park on firm level ground, if possible, and well out of the way of other traffic.
- ☐ Use hazard warning lights if necessary.

- ☐ If you have one, use a warning triangle to alert other drivers of your presence.
- ☐ Apply the handbrake and engage first or reverse gear.
- ☐ Chock the wheel diagonally opposite the

one being removed – a chock is located beneath the jack under the luggage compartment lid.
- ☐ If the ground is soft, use a flat piece of wood to spread the load under the jack.

Vehicles with the Compact spare wheel

Changing the wheel

1 The spare wheel is stored in under the floor of the luggage compartment. The tools are stored in the luggage compartment floor. Lift the luggage compartment floor and remove the jack, wheel chock and special spanner. Lift out the wheel-changing set assembly, then undo the plastic retaining nut and lift out the spare wheel.

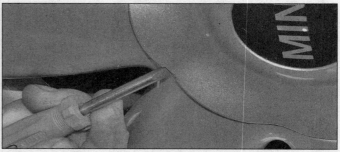

2 Using the screwdriver provided in the toolkit, remove the wheel trim/hub cap (as applicable) then, using the wheel brace from the toolkit, slacken each wheel bolt by a half turn.

3 If anti-theft wheel bolts are fitted, slacken them using the adapter supplied in the tool kit.

4 Locate the jack head under the jacking point nearest to the wheel that is to be removed. As the jack is raised, the head must enter the rectangular recess in the jacking point.

5 Make sure the jack is located on firm ground then turn the jack handle clockwise until the wheel is raised clear of the ground. Unscrew the wheel bolts and remove the wheel. Fit the spare wheel and screw in the wheel bolts. Lightly tighten the bolts with the wheelbrace then lower the vehicle to the ground.

Finally . . .

- ☐ Remove the wheel chocks.
- ☐ Stow the jack, chock and tools in the correct locations in the car.
- ☐ Check the tyre pressure on the wheel just fitted. If it is low, or if you don't have a pressure gauge with you, drive slowly to the next garage and inflate the tyre to the correct pressure.
- ☐ Have the damaged tyre or wheel repaired as soon as possible, or another puncture will leave you stranded.

6 Securely tighten the wheel bolts in a diagonal pattern then refit the wheel trim/hub cap (as applicable). Stow the punctured wheel and tools back in the luggage compartment and secure them in position. Note that the wheel bolts should be slackened and retightened to the specified torque at the earliest possible opportunity.

Vehicles with MINI Mobility System

1 The MINI Mobility System consists of a bottle of puncture sealant and a compressor. Rather than change the punctured wheel, the system allows the tyre to be sealed, enabling the journey to be resumed, albeit at a reduced speed. **Note:** *MINI insist that the sealant bottle be renewed every 4 years if it's not been used.*

2 The system is stored beneath the floor of the luggage compartment.

3 Remove the sealant bottle from the luggage compartment, and shake the contents well. Screw the filler hose onto the bottle.

4 Unscrew the valve cap from the punctured wheel, and using the valve removal tool (stored with the filler hose) unscrew the core from the valve.

5 Pull the stopper from the filler hose, insert the hose into the valve, and holding the bottle upside down, squeeze the entire contents into the tyre.

6 Remove the filler hose, and screw the core back into the valve.

7 Retrieve the compressor from the toolkit, and insert the power plug into the vehicle's cigarette lighter/power outlet socket.

8 Connect the compressor hose to the tyre valve, and with the ignition switch turned to position I, turn the compressor on and inflate the tyre to a pressure of between 1.8 and 2.5 bar (26 to 36 psi). If this pressure is not achieved within 6 minutes, turn off the compressor, disconnect it from the valve, and drive the vehicle forwards about 10 m, then reverse back to place to redistribute the sealant, and repeat the inflation process. With the correct pressure achieved, disconnect the compressor and stow it in the tool kit.

9 Immediately drive the vehicle for approximately 10 minutes at a speed of between 12 and 37 mph to redistribute the sealant.

10 Stop the vehicle, connect the compressor, and check the tyre pressure. If the pressure is less than 1.3 bar (19 psi), it's not safe to continue your journey, and the vehicle must be recovered. If the pressure is above this, turn on the compressor and inflate the tyre to the normal pressure for the vehicle, as specified on the sticker in the driver's door aperture.

11 With the tyre inflated to the correct pressure, do not exceed the maximum speed of 50 mph. Have the tyre repaired or replaced at the earliest opportunity.

Vehicles with Run Flat tyres

1 These tyres can be identified by the letters 'RSC' moulded into the tyre sidewall.

2 When used in conjunction with the special wheel rims, these tyres are able to support the vehicle even when they are completely deflated. In the event of a puncture, the vehicles road behaviour will change (braking distance increase, directional stability diminish) but the journey can continue, albeit at a reduced pace of 50 mph.

3 If the vehicle is lightly loaded (1 to 2 persons without luggage), maximum range with the tyre deflated is 150 miles.

4 If the vehicle has a medium load (2 persons with full luggage, or 4 persons without luggage), maximum range is 90 miles.

5 If the vehicle is fully loaded (4 persons plus luggage), maximum range is 30 miles.

6 It's not possible to repair Run Flat tyres.

Towing

When all else fails, you may find yourself having to get a tow home – or of course you may be helping somebody else. Long-distance recovery should only be done by a garage or breakdown service. For shorter distances, DIY towing using another car is easy enough, but observe the following points:

☐ MINI insist that vehicles with automatic transmission must not be towed with the front wheels on the ground. Consequently, a recovery truck cable of lifting the front of the vehicle must be used.

☐ Use a proper tow-rope – they are not expensive. The vehicle being towed must display an ON TOW sign in its rear window.

☐ Always turn the ignition key to the 'on' position when the vehicle is being towed, so that the steering lock is released, and that the direction indicator and brake lights work. Note that as an electrically operated steering lock is fitted, if the vehicle's electrical system fails, the vehicle cannot be towed.

☐ Only attach the tow-rope to the towing eyes provided. The towing eye is supplied as part of the tool kit which is fitted under the luggage compartment lid or floor. To fit the eye, prise out the access cover from the front/rear bumper (as applicable). Screw the eye into position and tighten it securely **(see illustration)**.

☐ Before being towed, release the handbrake and select neutral on the transmission.

☐ Note that greater-than-usual pedal pressure will be required to operate the brakes, since the vacuum servo unit is only operational with the engine running.

☐ The driver of the car being towed must keep the tow-rope taut at all times to avoid snatching.

☐ Make sure that both drivers know the route before setting off.

☐ Only drive at moderate speeds and keep the distance towed to a minimum. Drive smoothly and allow plenty of time for slowing down at junctions.

Identifying leaks

Puddles on the garage floor or drive, or obvious wetness under the bonnet or underneath the car, suggest a leak that needs investigating. It can sometimes be difficult to decide where the leak is coming from, especially if an engine undershield is fitted. Leaking oil or fluid can also be blown rearwards by the passage of air under the car, giving a false impression of where the problem lies.

 Warning: Most automotive oils and fluids are poisonous. Wash them off skin, and change out of contaminated clothing, without delay.

 The smell of a fluid leaking from the car may provide a clue to what's leaking. Some fluids are distinctively coloured. It may help to remove the engine undershield, clean the car carefully and to park it over some clean paper overnight as an aid to locating the source of the leak.
Remember that some leaks may only occur while the engine is running.

Sump oil

Engine oil may leak from the drain plug...

Oil from filter

...or from the base of the oil filter.

Gearbox oil

Gearbox oil can leak from the seals at the inboard ends of the driveshafts.

Antifreeze

Leaking antifreeze often leaves a crystalline deposit like this.

Brake fluid

A leak occurring at a wheel is almost certainly brake fluid.

Power steering fluid

Power steering fluid may leak from the pipe connectors on the steering rack.

Introduction

There are some very simple checks which need only take a few minutes to carry out, but which could save you a lot of inconvenience and expense.

These *Weekly checks* require no great skill or special tools, and the small amount of time they take to perform could prove to be very well spent, for example:

☐ Keeping an eye on tyre condition and pressures, will not only help to stop them wearing out prematurely, but could also save your life.

☐ Many breakdowns are caused by electrical problems. Battery-related faults are particularly common, and a quick check on a regular basis will often prevent the majority of these.

☐ If your car develops a brake fluid leak, the first time you might know about it is when your brakes don't work properly. Checking the level regularly will give advance warning of this kind of problem.

☐ If the oil or coolant levels run low, the cost of repairing any engine damage will be far greater than fixing the leak, for example.

Underbonnet check points

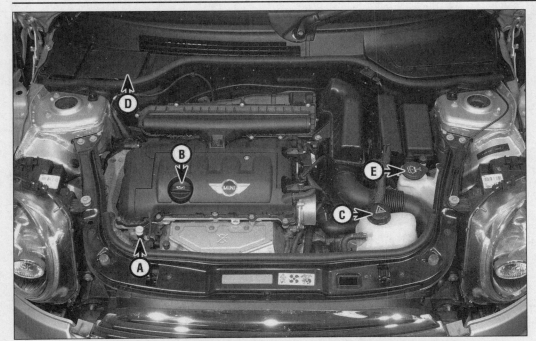

◀ MINI Cooper – petrol

A *Engine oil level dipstick*

B *Engine oil filler cap*

C *Coolant expansion tank*

D *Brake and clutch fluid reservoir*

E *Screen washer fluid reservoir*

◀ MINI Cooper – diesel

A *Engine oil level dipstick*

B *Engine oil filler cap*

C *Coolant expansion tank*

D *Screen washer fluid reservoir*

E *Brake and clutch fluid reservoir*

Engine oil level

Before you start

✔ Make sure that the car is on level ground.
✔ Check the oil level before the car is driven, or at least 5 minutes after the engine has been switched off.

HAYNES HINT *If the oil is checked immediately after driving the vehicle, some of the oil will remain in the upper engine components, resulting in an inaccurate reading on the dipstick.*

The correct oil

Modern engines place great demands on their oil. It is very important that the correct oil for your car is used (see *Lubricants and fluids*).

Car care

● If you have to add oil frequently, you should check whether you have any oil leaks. Place some clean paper under the car overnight, and check for stains in the morning. If there are no leaks, then the engine may be burning oil.

● Always maintain the level between the upper and lower dipstick marks. If the level is too low, severe engine damage may occur. Oil seal failure may result if the engine is overfilled by adding too much oil.

1 The dipstick top is often brightly coloured for easy identification (see *Underbonnet check points* for exact location). Withdraw the dipstick.

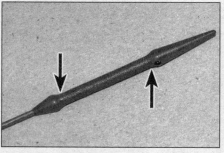

3 Note the oil level on the end of the dipstick, which should be between the upper maximum mark and lower minimum mark. Approximately 1.0 litre (petrol models) or 1.5 litres (diesel models) of oil will raise the level from the lower mark to the upper mark.

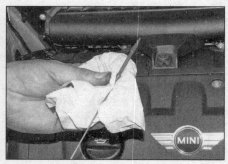

2 Using a clean rag or paper towel remove all oil from the dipstick. Insert the clean dipstick into the tube as far as it will go, then withdraw it again.

4 Oil is added through the filler cap. Unscrew the cap and top-up the level; a funnel may help to reduce spillage. Add the oil slowly, checking the level on the dipstick often. Don't overfill (see *Car care*).

Coolant level

Warning: Do not attempt to remove the expansion tank pressure cap when the engine is hot, as there is a very great risk of scalding. Do not leave open containers of coolant about, as it is poisonous.

Car care

● With a sealed-type cooling system, adding coolant should not be necessary on a regular basis. If frequent topping-up is required, it is likely there is a leak. Check the radiator, all hoses and joint faces for signs of staining or wetness, and rectify as necessary.

● It is important that antifreeze is used in the cooling system all year round, not just during the winter months. Don't top up with water alone, as the antifreeze will become diluted.

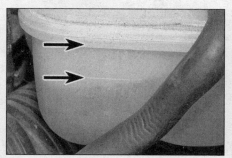

1 The coolant level is indicated by the minimum and maximum marks on the side of the expansion tank at the rear of the engine compartment.

2 If topping-up is necessary, **wait until the engine is cold**. Slowly remove the expansion tank cap, to release any pressure present in the cooling system, and remove it.

3 Add a mixture of water and antifreeze to the expansion tank until the level of the coolant is just below the 'Max' mark on the expansion tank. Refit the cap securely.

Brake and clutch fluid level

⚠️ **Warning:**
* **Brake fluid can harm your eyes and damage painted surfaces, so use extreme caution when handling and pouring it.**
* **Do not use fluid that has been standing open for some time, as it absorbs moisture from the air, which can cause a dangerous loss of braking effectiveness.**

The fluid level in the reservoir will drop slightly as the brake pads wear down, but the fluid level must never be allowed to drop below the MIN mark.

Before you start

✔ Make sure that the car is on level ground.

Safety first!

● If the reservoir requires repeated topping-up this is an indication of a fluid leak somewhere in the system, which should be investigated immediately.

● If a leak is suspected, the car should not be driven until the braking system has been checked. Never take any risks where brakes are concerned

1 Unclip and open the reservoir cover from right-hand side of the engine compartment.

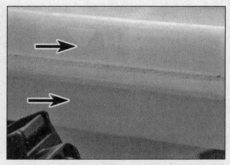

2 The MAX and MIN marks are indicated on the side of the reservoir. The fluid level must be kept between the marks at all times.

3 If topping-up is necessary, first wipe clean the area around the filler cap to prevent dirt entering the hydraulic system. Unscrew the reservoir cap and carefully lift it out of position, taking care not to damage the level switch float. Inspect the reservoir, if the fluid is dirty the hydraulic system should be drained and refilled (see Chapter 1).

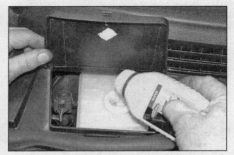

4 Carefully add fluid taking care not to spill it onto the surrounding components. Use only the specified fluid; mixing different types can cause damage to the system. After topping-up to the correct level, securely refit the cap and wipe off any spilt fluid.

Screen washer fluid level

● Screenwash additives not only keep the windscreen clean during bad weather, they also prevent the washer system freezing in cold weather – which is when you are likely to need it most. Don't top-up using plain water, as the screenwash will become diluted, and will freeze in cold weather.

⚠️ **Warning: On no account use engine coolant antifreeze in the screen washer system – this may damage the paintwork.**

1 The screen washer fluid reservoir is located on the left-hand side of the engine compartment, and the headlight washers are supplied from the same reservoir.

2 When topping-up, add a screenwash additive in the quantities recommended by the manufacturer.

Tyre condition and pressure

It is very important that tyres are in good condition, and at the correct pressure - having a tyre failure at any speed is highly dangerous. Tyre wear is influenced by driving style - harsh braking and acceleration, or fast cornering, will all produce more rapid tyre wear. As a general rule, the front tyres wear out faster than the rears. Interchanging the tyres from front to rear ("rotating" the tyres) may result in more even wear. However, if this is completely effective, you may have the expense of replacing all four tyres at once!

Remove any nails or stones embedded in the tread before they penetrate the tyre to cause deflation. If removal of a nail does reveal that the tyre has been punctured, refit the nail so that its point of penetration is marked. Then immediately change the wheel, and have the tyre repaired by a tyre dealer.

Regularly check the tyres for damage in the form of cuts or bulges, especially in the sidewalls. Periodically remove the wheels, and clean any dirt or mud from the inside and outside surfaces. Examine the wheel rims for signs of rusting, corrosion or other damage. Light alloy wheels are easily damaged by "kerbing" whilst parking; steel wheels may also become dented or buckled. A new wheel is very often the only way to overcome severe damage.

New tyres should be balanced when they are fitted, but it may become necessary to re-balance them as they wear, or if the balance weights fitted to the wheel rim should fall off. Unbalanced tyres will wear more quickly, as will the steering and suspension components. Wheel imbalance is normally signified by vibration, particularly at a certain speed (typically around 50 mph). If this vibration is felt only through the steering, then it is likely that just the front wheels need balancing. If, however, the vibration is felt through the whole car, the rear wheels could be out of balance. Wheel balancing should be carried out by a tyre dealer or garage.

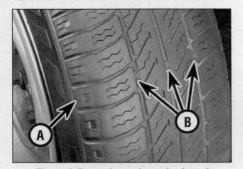

1 *Tread Depth - visual check*
The original tyres have tread wear safety bands (B), which will appear when the tread depth reaches approximately 1.6 mm. The band positions are indicated by a triangular mark on the tyre sidewall (A).

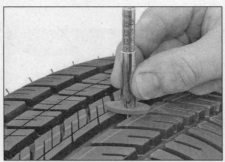

2 *Tread Depth - manual check*
Alternatively, tread wear can be monitored with a simple, inexpensive device known as a tread depth indicator gauge.

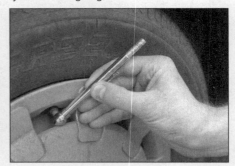

3 *Tyre Pressure Check*
Check the tyre pressures regularly with the tyres cold. Do not adjust the tyre pressures immediately after the vehicle has been used, or an inaccurate setting will result.

Tyre tread wear patterns

Shoulder Wear

Underinflation (wear on both sides)
Under-inflation will cause overheating of the tyre, because the tyre will flex too much, and the tread will not sit correctly on the road surface. This will cause a loss of grip and excessive wear, not to mention the danger of sudden tyre failure due to heat build-up.
Check and adjust pressures
Incorrect wheel camber (wear on one side)
Repair or renew suspension parts
Hard cornering
Reduce speed!

Centre Wear

Overinflation
Over-inflation will cause rapid wear of the centre part of the tyre tread, coupled with reduced grip, harsher ride, and the danger of shock damage occurring in the tyre casing.
Check and adjust pressures

If you sometimes have to inflate your car's tyres to the higher pressures specified for maximum load or sustained high speed, don't forget to reduce the pressures to normal afterwards.

Uneven Wear

Front tyres may wear unevenly as a result of wheel misalignment. Most tyre dealers and garages can check and adjust the wheel alignment (or "tracking") for a modest charge.
Incorrect camber or castor
Repair or renew suspension parts
Malfunctioning suspension
Repair or renew suspension parts
Unbalanced wheel
Balance tyres
Incorrect toe setting
Adjust front wheel alignment
Note: *The feathered edge of the tread which typifies toe wear is best checked by feel.*

Wiper blades

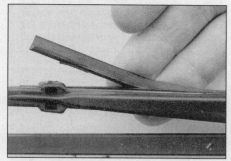  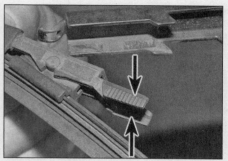

1 Check the condition of the wiper blades; if they are cracked or show any signs of deterioration, or if the glass swept area is smeared, renew them. Wiper blades should be renewed annually.

2 To remove a front wiper blade, pull the arm away from the screen, turn the blade 90° to the arm, depress the clip and slide the blade down the arm.

3 To remove a rear wiper blade, pull the arm away from the screen, squeeze together the catches, swing the blade out, and remove the blade from the catch.

Battery

Caution: Before carrying out any work on the vehicle battery, read the precautions given in 'Safety first!' at the start of this manual.

✔ Make sure that the battery tray is in good condition, and that the clamp is tight. Corrosion on the tray, retaining clamp and the battery itself can be removed with a solution of water and baking soda. Thoroughly rinse all cleaned areas with water. Any metal parts damaged by corrosion should be covered with a zinc-based primer, then painted.

✔ Periodically (approximately every three months), check the charge condition of the battery as described in Chapter 5A.

✔ If the battery is flat, and you need to jump start your vehicle, see *Roadside Repairs*.

HAYNES HINT

Battery corrosion can be kept to a minimum by applying a layer of petroleum jelly to the clamps and terminals after they are reconnected.

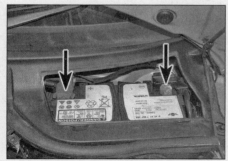  

1 The battery is located under a cover on the left-hand side of the engine compartment. Remove the cover to access the battery.

2 If corrosion (white, fluffy deposits) is evident, remove the cables from the battery terminals, clean them with a small wire brush, then refit them. Automotive stores sell a tool for cleaning the battery post

3 .. as well as the battery cable clamps

Electrical systems

✔ Check all external lights and the horn. Refer to the appropriate Sections of Chapter 12 for details if any of the circuits are found to be inoperative.

✔ Visually check all accessible wiring connectors, harnesses and retaining clips for security, and for signs of chafing or damage.

HAYNES HiNT *If you need to check your brake lights and indicators unaided, back up to a wall or garage door and operate the lights. The reflected light should show if they are working properly.*

1 If a single indicator light, stop-light or headlight has failed, it is likely that a bulb has blown and will need to be renewed. Refer to Chapter 12 for details. If both stop-lights have failed, it is possible that the switch has failed (see Chapter 9).

2 If more than one indicator light or tail light has failed, check that a fuse has not blown or that there is a fault in the circuit (see Chapter 12). The fuses are located in the fuse-box behind a cover in the drivers side footwell kick panel, and in the engine compartment adjacent to the left-hand suspension turret. Details of the circuits protected by the fuses are shown on the inside of the fusebox cover.

3 To renew a blown fuse, simply pull it out and fit a new fuse of the correct rating (see Chapter 12). If the fuse blows again, it is important that you find out why – a complete checking procedure is given in Chapter 12.

Lubricants and fluids

Engine (petrol and diesel)	MINI Long-life 04 (eg. Castrol Edge Professional). SAE 0W-30 or SAE 5W-30 (fully synthetic) to ACEA A3 may be used for topping up only.
Cooling system	Long-life ethylene glycol based antifreeze*
Manual transmission:	
Turbocharged petrol and diesel models	MTF94 Lifetime transmission oil*
Other models	MTF-LT-4 Lifetime transmission oil
Automatic transmission	ATF JWS-3309*
Braking system	Hydraulic fluid to DOT 4

*Refer to your MINI dealer for brand name and type recommendations

Tyre pressures

The tyre pressures are given on a label affixed to the driver's door aperture.

Chapter 1 Part A
Routine maintenance & servicing – petrol models

Contents

Degrees of difficulty

Easy, suitable for novice with little experience	**Fairly easy,** suitable for beginner with some experience	**Fairly difficult,** suitable for competent DIY mechanic	**Difficult,** suitable for experienced DIY mechanic	**Very difficult,** suitable for expert DIY or professional

Lubricants and fluids

Refer to *Weekly checks* on page 0•16

Capacities

Engine oil (including filter)
All engines . . . . 4.25 litres

Cooling system
All engines . . . . 5.2 litres

Fuel tank
All except turbo models (approximate) . . . . 40 litres
Turbo models (approximate). . . . . 50 litres

Cooling system

Antifreeze mixture:
  50% antifreeze . . . . Protection down to –30°C (–22°F)
Note: *Refer to antifreeze manufacturer for latest recommendations.*

Ignition system

Spark plugs:
  N12, N14 and N16 engines . . . . NGK PLZKBR7A–G
  N18 engines . . . . Beru 12ZR6SPP2–1*
Spark plug electrode gap. . . . . Not adjustable
* Check with your dealer for the latest specification

Brakes

Brake pad friction material minimum thickness . . . . 3.7 mm

Torque wrench settings

	Nm	lbf ft
Engine oil filter cover	25	18
Engine sump oil drain plug.	30	22
Roadwheel bolts.	140	103
Spark plugs	23	17

Condition based service

The service intervals are tailored according to the operating conditions, driving style, time elapsed and mileage covered, instead of set distance/time limits. These factors are taken into account, and the maintenance requirements are calculated by the vehicles on-board systems, then a symbol representing the item requiring attention is displayed in the instrument cluster. Consequently, the intervals listed below are guidelines, starting values/interval forecasts, or our recommendations. For more details, refer to the Owners Handbook supplied with the vehicle.

Every 250 miles (400 km) or weekly
☐ Refer to *Weekly checks*

The following items have a flexible interval dependant on conditions etc. The maximum recommend mileage/time interval (where applicable) is also given.
☐ Engine oil service (Section 3) – at least every 15 000 miles or 2 years (whichever comes first). This includes handbrake check, and pollen filter renewal. On every 2nd oil change, renew the air filter element and spark plugs.
☐ Vehicle check (Section 7) – at least every 30 000 miles or 4 years (whichever comes first)
☐ Front brake service (Section 5) – at least every 30 000 miles
☐ Rear brake service (Section 6) – at least every 30 000 miles
☐ Renew the brake fluid (Section 8) – every 2 years
☐ Reset the service interval display (Section 4) – after each item above has been serviced

The following items have no specific recommendation concerning their inspection or renewal. However, we consider it prudent to carry out these tasks at least every 4 years.
☐ Check the condition of the auxiliary drivebelt(s), and adjust/renew if necessary (Section 9)
☐ Coolant renewal (Section 10)
☐ Remote control battery renewal (Section 11)

Front underbonnet view of a non-turbo model

1 Engine oil filler cap
2 Engine oil level dipstick
3 Air filter housing
4 Battery location
5 Brake and clutch fluid reservoir
6 Engine management ECU
7 Resonator box
8 Fuse box
9 Coolant expansion tank
10 Screenwash fluid reservoir

Front underbonnet view of a turbocharged model

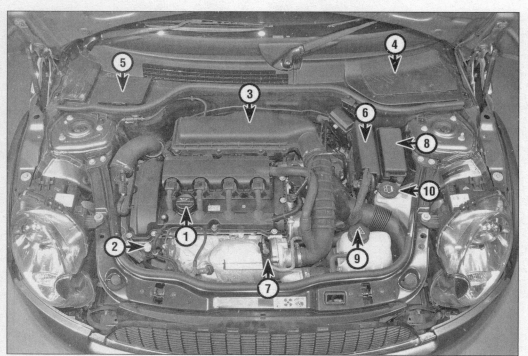

1 Engine oil filler cap
2 Engine oil level dipstick
3 Air filter housing
4 Battery location
5 Brake and clutch fluid reservoir
6 Engine management ECU
7 Turbocharger
8 Fuse box
9 Coolant expansion tank
10 Screenwash fluid reservoir

Front underbody view

1 Engine oil drain plug
2 Gearbox drain plug
3 Steering trackrod
4 Lower suspension arm/
  wishbone
5 Air conditioning
  compressor
6 Catalytic converter
7 Clutch slave cylinder
8 Subframe
9 Rear engine mounting
  tie-rod/link

Rear underbody view (Convertible model shown – others similar)

1 Rear silencer box
2 Fuel tank
3 Trailing arm
4 Shock absorber
5 Lower control arm
6 Handbrake cable
7 Cross reinforcement
  frame (Convertible
  models only)
8 Charcoal canister

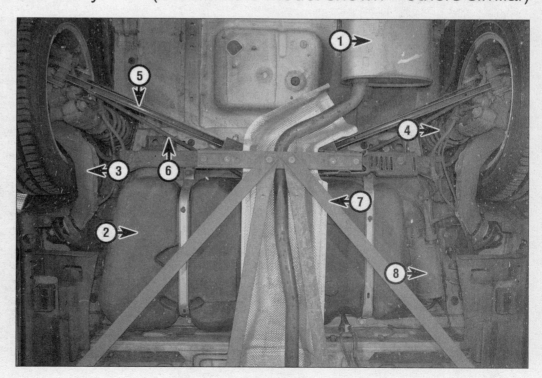

1 Introduction

1 This Chapter is designed to help the home mechanic maintain his/her vehicle for safety, economy, long life and peak performance.

2 The Chapter contains a master maintenance schedule, followed by Sections dealing specifically with each task in the schedule. Visual checks, adjustments, component renewal and other helpful items are included. Refer to the accompanying illustrations of the engine compartment and the underside of the vehicle for the locations of the various components.

3 Servicing your vehicle in accordance with the service indicator display and the following Sections will provide a planned maintenance programme, which should result in a long and reliable service life. This is a comprehensive plan, so maintaining some items but not others at the specified service intervals, will not produce the same results.

4 As you service your vehicle, you will discover that many of the procedures can – and should – be grouped together, because of the particular procedure being performed, or because of the proximity of two otherwise-unrelated components to one another. For example, if the vehicle is raised for any reason, the exhaust can be inspected at the same time as the suspension and steering components.

5 The first step in this maintenance programme is to prepare yourself before the actual work begins. Read through all the Sections relevant to the work to be carried out, then make a list and gather all the parts and tools required. If a problem is encountered, seek advice from a parts specialist, or a dealer service department.

2 Intensive maintenance

1 If, from the time the vehicle is new, the routine maintenance schedule is followed closely, and frequent checks are made of fluid levels and high-wear items, as suggested throughout this manual, the engine will be kept in relatively good running condition, and the need for additional work will be minimised.

2 It is possible that there will be times when the engine is running poorly due to the lack of regular maintenance. This is even more likely if a used vehicle, which has not received regular and frequent maintenance checks, is purchased. In such cases, additional work may need to be carried out, outside of the regular maintenance intervals.

3 If engine wear is suspected, a compression test (refer Chapter 2A) will provide valuable information regarding the overall performance of the main internal components. Such a test can be used as a basis to decide on the extent of the work to be carried out. If, for example, a compression test indicates serious internal engine wear, conventional maintenance as described in this Chapter will not greatly improve the performance of the engine, and may prove a waste of time and money, unless extensive overhaul work is carried out first.

4 The following series of operations are those most often required to improve the performance of a generally poor-running engine:

Primary operations

a) Clean, inspect and test the battery (See 'Weekly checks').
b) Check all the engine-related fluids (See 'Weekly checks').
c) Renew the spark plugs (Section 3).
d) Check the condition of the air filter, and renew if necessary (Section 3).
e) Check the condition of all hoses, and check for fluid leaks (Section 7).

5 If the above operations do not prove fully effective, carry out the following secondary operations:

Secondary operations

All items listed under *Primary operations*, plus the following:

a) Check the charging system (see Chapter 5A).
b) Check the ignition system (see Chapter 5B).
c) Check the fuel system (see Chapter 4A).

3 Engine oil service

Engine oil and filter change

1 Frequent oil and filter changes are the most important preventative maintenance work which can be undertaken by the DIY owner. As engine oil ages, it becomes diluted and contaminated, which leads to premature engine wear.

2 Before starting this procedure, gather together all the necessary tools and materials. Also make sure you have plenty of clean rags and newspapers handy, to mop up any spills. Ideally, the engine oil should be warm, as it will drain better, and more built-up sludge will be removed with it. Take care, however, not to touch the exhaust or any other hot parts of the engine when working under the car. To avoid any possibility of scalding, and to protect yourself from possible skin irritants and other harmful contaminants in used engine oils, it is advisable to wear gloves. Access to the underside of the car will be improved if it can be raised on a lift, driven onto ramps, or jacked up and supported on axle stands (see *Jacking and vehicle support*). Whichever method is chosen, make sure the car remains level, or if it is at an angle, so that the drain plug is at the lowest point. Where necessary remove the under shield from under the engine.

3 Working in the engine compartment, locate the oil filter housing on front of the engine at the left-hand end. On turbocharged models, undo the retaining bolt and move the coolant expansion tank to one side **(see illustration)**.

4 Place a wad of rag around the bottom of the housing to absorb any spilt oil.

5 Using a socket, unscrew and remove the cover, and lift the filter cartridge out **(see illustrations)**. The oil will drain from the housing back into the sump as the cover is removed.

6 Recover the O-ring from the cover.

7 Using a clean rag, wipe the mating faces of the housing and cover.

8 Fit a new O-ring to the cover **(see illustration)**.

3.3 Undo the bolt (arrowed) and move the coolant expansion tank to one side

3.5a Unscrew the oil filter cover (arrowed)...

3.5b ...and lift it out complete with filter element

9 Fit the new element into the cover **(see illustration)**.

10 Smear a little clean engine oil on the O-ring, refit the cover and tighten to the specified torque. Note that some force will be required to push the element far enough into the housing to engage the cover threads.

11 Working under the car, slacken the sump drain plug about half a turn. Position the draining container under the drain plug, then remove the plug completely **(see illustration)**. If possible, try to keep the plug pressed into the sump while unscrewing it by hand the last couple of turns.

12 Discard the drain plug sealing ring, a new one must be used.

13 Allow some time for the old oil to drain, noting that it may be necessary to reposition the container as the oil flow slows to a trickle.

14 After all the oil has drained, clean the area around the drain plug opening, then fit and tighten the plug with its new sealing washer **(see illustration)**.

15 Remove the old oil and all tools from under the car, then lower the car to the ground (if applicable).

16 Remove the dipstick then unscrew the oil filler cap. Fill the engine, using the correct grade and type of oil (see *Weekly checks*). An oil can spout or funnel may help to reduce spillage. Pour in half the specified quantity of oil first, then wait a few minutes for the oil to fall to the sump. Continue adding oil a small quantity at a time until the level is up to the lower mark on the dipstick. Finally, bring the level up to the upper mark on the dipstick. Insert the dipstick, and refit the filler cap. Note that the difference between the lower and upper marks on the dipstick is approximately 1.0L.

17 Start the engine and run it for a few minutes; check for leaks around the oil filter seal and the sump drain plug. Note that there may be a delay of a few seconds before the oil pressure warning light goes out when the engine is first started, as the oil circulates through the engine oil galleries and the new oil filter, before the pressure builds up.

18 Switch off the engine, and wait a few minutes for the oil to settle in the sump once more. With the new oil circulated and the

3.8 Renew the filter cover O-ring seal

3.9 Locate the new filter element into the cover

3.11 Undo the plug and allow the oil to drain. Wearing of gloves is recommended

3.14 Renew the drain plug sealing ring

filter completely full, recheck the level on the dipstick, and add more oil as necessary.

19 Dispose of the used engine oil safely, with reference to *General repair procedures* in the *Reference* section of this manual.

Handbrake check

20 Check and, if necessary, adjust the handbrake as described in Chapter 9. Check that the handbrake cables are free to move easily and lubricate all exposed linkages/cable pivots.

Pollen filter renewal

21 Working in the passengers side footwell, unclip the plastic cover from the cabin air filter. On some models, the plastic cover may be retained by screws **(see illustration)**.

22 Pull down the lower end of the filter

element, and slide it from the housing **(see illustration)**.

23 Install the new filter element into the housing, noting how it curves around to fit in the guide slots.

24 Install the filter cover, and secure it in place with the retaining clips. If the clips break, it is possible to secure the cover using self-tapping screws through the holes provided in the cover.

Air filter element renewal

25 On turbo models, loosen the clamp and remove the intake outlet duct from the air filter housing **(see illustration)**. Also unplug the electrical connector from the Mass Airflow (MAF) sensor (where fitted).

26 Remove the filter housing cover screws. On non-turbo models, there are 7 screws securing

3.21 Pull the cover edge (arrowed) rearwards to unclip it

3.22 Slide the pollen filter element from the housing

3.25 Slacken the clamp (arrowed) and disconnect the air outlet duct

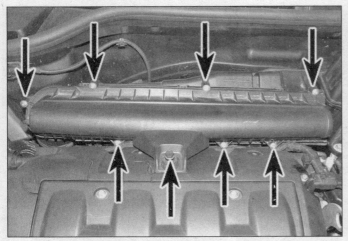

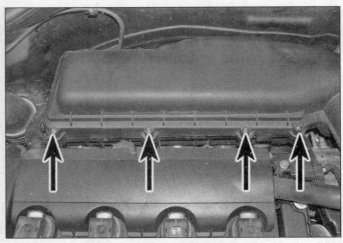

3.26a **Air filter cover retaining screws (arrowed) – non-turbo models...**

3.26b **...and turbo models (arrowed)**

the cover to the housing, plus one holding the cover to the valve cover **(see illustration)**. On turbo models, there are 4 screws along the front edge of the housing **(see illustration)**.

27 Lift the cover up and remove the old filter.

28 Clean the air filter housing, removing all debris.

29 Install the new filter element, making sure it seats in the housing **(see illustration)**.

30 The remainder of refitting is the reverse of removal.

Spark plugs

31 The correct functioning of the spark plugs is vital for the correct running and efficiency of the engine. It is essential that the plugs fitted are appropriate for the engine (the suitable type is specified at the beginning of this Chapter). If this type is used, and the engine is in good condition, the spark plugs should not need attention between scheduled replacement intervals. Spark plug cleaning is rarely necessary, and should not be attempted unless specialised equipment is available, as damage can easily be caused to the firing ends.

32 The spark plugs are located in the top of the cylinder head. Remove the ignition coils (see Chapter 5B).

33 It is advisable to remove the dirt from the spark plug recesses, using a clean brush,

vacuum cleaner or compressed air before removing the plugs, to prevent dirt dropping into the cylinders.

34 Unscrew the plugs using a spark plug socket and extension bar **(see illustration)**. Keep the socket aligned with the spark plug – if it is forcibly moved to one side, the ceramic insulator may be broken off. As each plug is removed, examine it as follows.

35 Examination of the spark plugs will give a good indication of the condition of the engine. If the insulator nose of the spark plug is clean and white, with no deposits, this is indicative of a weak mixture or too hot a plug (a hot plug transfers heat away from the electrode slowly, a cold plug transfers heat away quickly).

36 If the tip and insulator nose are covered with hard black-looking deposits, then this is indicative that the mixture is too rich. Should the plug be black and oily, then it is likely that the engine is fairly worn, as well as the mixture being too rich.

37 If the insulator nose is covered with light tan to greyish-brown deposits, then the mixture is correct, and it is likely that the engine is in good condition. See the inside back cover of this manual for more spark plug conditions.

38 The recommended spark plugs are of the multi-electrode type, and the gap between the centre electrode and the ground electrodes cannot be adjusted.

39 Before installing the spark plugs, check that the plug exterior surfaces and threads are clean. It is very often difficult to insert spark plugs into their holes without cross-threading them. To avoid this possibility, fit a short length of hose over the end of the spark plug **(see illustration)**. Do not apply any lubricant to the spark plug threads.

40 Remove the rubber hose (if used), and tighten the plug to the specified torque using the spark plug socket and a torque wrench. Fit the remaining plugs in the same way.

41 The remainder of refitting is a reversal of removal.

4	Resetting the service interval display

1 Ensure that all electrical items are switched off then turn on the ignition switch. **Note:** *Do not start the engine.*

2 Ensure the on-board time and date are correctly set in accordance with the instructions in the owners handbook.

3 Each service item that appears on the instrument cluster display can be reset. Note that it is only possible to reset an item if the service life of the item is below 80%.

3.29 **Fit the new element into the housing**

3.34 **Unscrew the spark plugs using a long socket or extension bar**

3.39 **Install the spark plugs using a length of rubber hose to prevent cross-threading**

4 Press the trip odometer button for approximately 10 seconds until the first CBS (Condition Based Service) item appears in the instrument cluster display. The upper display in the speedometer is illuminated by a service symbol. The lower display indicated the time or distance remaining until the next service. Scroll through the items by repeatedly pressing the on-board computer button.

5 When the required item is selected, press the on-board computer button (end of indicator stalk/switch) until Reset? appears in the display. Note that the reset process is cancelled by not pressing the button to confirm, and waiting for the display to return to its normal state.

6 Press the button again for approximately 3 seconds to confirm the reset. A clock symbol will be displayed as the reset is being performed. Upon successful resetting, a tick symbol will be displayed. Note that it is only possible to reset the brake pad display if the pad sensors are working properly.

7 In order for the CBS display to function correctly, the on-board time and date must be correct. Refer to the owners handbook for details of how to set these values.

8 Turn off the ignition switch.

5 Front brake service

Front brake pads

1 When this CBS item is displayed, the thickness of the front brake pads friction material should be checked, and if any are approaching the minimum thickness, *all* four front pads should be renewed.

2 Firmly apply the handbrake, then jack up the front of the car and support it securely on axle stands (see *Jacking and vehicle support*). Remove the front roadwheels.

3 The brake pad warning symbol in the CBS display indicates that the pad friction material thickness is worn such that the pads require replacement. However, the warning will also be given if the wiring to and from each pads sensor is damaged or the connections are poor, dirty, etc. Check the wiring to and from the sensor for poor connections/breaks before replacing the pads.

4 The thickness of friction material remaining on each brake pad can be measured through the top of the caliper body. If any pads friction material is worn to the specified thickness or less, all four pads must be renewed as a set. Pad replacement is described in Chapter 9

Front brake disc check

5 Check the front brake disc condition, and measure the thickness of the disc as described in Chapter 9. Replace both front discs if necessary.

6 Reset the CBS display as described in Section 4.

6 Rear brake service

Rear brake pads

1 When this CBS item is displayed, the thickness of the rear brake pads friction material should be checked, and if any are approaching the minimum thickness, *all* four rear pads should be renewed.

2 Chock the front wheels, then jack up the rear of the car and support it on axle stands (see *Jacking and vehicle support*). Remove the rear roadwheels.

3 The thickness of friction material remaining on each brake pad can be measured through the top of the caliper body. If any pads friction material is worn to the specified thickness or less, *all* four pads must be renewed as a set. Pad replacement is described in Chapter 9.

Rear brake disc check

4 Check the front brake disc condition, and measure the thickness of the disc as described in Chapter 9. Replace both front discs if necessary.

5 Reset the CBS display as described in Section 4.

7 Vehicle check

1 The vehicle check consists of several tasks. Before the CBS display can be reset, *all* of the following tasks must be complete.

Instruments and electrical equipment

2 Check the operation of all instruments and electrical equipment.

3 Make sure that all instruments read correctly, and switch on all electrical equipment in turn, to check that it functions properly.

Seat belt check

4 Carefully examine the seat belt webbing for cuts or any signs of serious fraying or deterioration. Pull the belt all the way out, and examine the full extent of the webbing.

5 Fasten and unfasten the belt, ensuring that the locking mechanism holds securely and releases properly when intended. Check also that the retracting mechanism operates correctly when the belt is released.

6 Check the security of all seat belt mountings and attachments which are accessible, without removing any trim or other components, from inside the car.

Windscreen wash/ wipe system check

7 Check that each of the washer jet nozzles are clear and that each nozzle provides a strong jet of washer fluid. Replace as necessary – refer to Chapter 12.

7.12 Use a hydrometer to check the anti-freeze concentration

8 Check the condition of each wiper blade for damage of wear. As time passes the blades will become hardened, wipe performance will deteriorate, and noise will increase. Replace the blades as necessary – see *Weekly checks*.

Bodywork corrosion check

9 This work should be carried out by a MINI dealer in order to validate the vehicle warranty. The work includes a thorough inspection of the vehicle paintwork and underbody for damage and corrosion.

Tyre check

10 Check the tread depth, external condition and inflation pressure of the tyres. See *Weekly checks* for details of the procedures and tyre pressure information.

Battery check

11 Check the condition of the battery, and recharge if necessary – refer to Chapter 5A.

Coolant concentration check

12 Use a hydrometer to check the strength of the antifreeze **(see illustration)**. Follow the instructions provided with your hydrometer. The antifreeze strength should be approximately 50%. If it is significantly less than this, drain a little coolant from the radiator (see this Chapter), add antifreeze to the coolant expansion tank, then re-check the strength.

Hose and fluid leak check

13 Visually inspect the engine joint faces, gaskets and seals for any signs of water or oil leaks. Pay particular attention to the areas around the camshaft cover, cylinder head, oil filter and sump joint faces. Bear in mind that, over a period of time, some very slight seepage from these areas is to be expected – what you are really looking for is any indication of a serious leak **(see Haynes Hint)**. Should a leak be found, renew the offending gasket or oil seal by referring to the appropriate Chapters in this manual.

14 Also check the security and condition of all the engine-related pipes and hoses. Ensure that all cable-ties or securing clips are in place and in good condition. Clips which are broken or missing can lead to chafing of the hoses,

A leak in the cooling system will usually show up as white- of anti-freeze coloured deposits on the area adjoining the leak.

pipes or wiring, which could cause more serious problems in the future.

15 Carefully check the radiator hoses and heater hoses along their entire length. Renew any hose which is cracked, swollen or deteriorated. Cracks will show up better if the hose is squeezed. Pay close attention to the hose clips that secure the hoses to the cooling system components. Hose clips can pinch and puncture hoses, resulting in cooling system leaks.

16 Inspect all the cooling system components (hoses, joint faces etc.) for leaks. A leak in the cooling system will usually show up as white- or rust-coloured deposits on the area adjoining the leak. Where any problems of this nature are found on system components, renew the component or gasket with reference to Chapter 3.

17 Where applicable, inspect the automatic transmission fluid cooler hoses for leaks or deterioration.

18 With the car raised, inspect the petrol tank and filler neck for punctures, cracks and other damage. The connection between the filler neck and tank is especially critical. Sometimes a rubber filler neck or connecting hose will leak due to loose retaining clamps or deteriorated rubber.

19 Carefully check all rubber hoses and metal fuel lines leading away from the petrol tank. Check for loose connections, deteriorated hoses, crimped lines, and other damage. Pay particular attention to the vent pipes and

hoses, which often loop up around the filler neck and can become blocked or crimped. Follow the lines to the front of the car, carefully inspecting them all the way. Renew damaged sections as necessary.

20 Closely inspect the metal brake pipes which run along the car underbody. If they show signs of excessive corrosion or damage they must be renewed.

21 From within the engine compartment, check the security of all fuel hose attachments and pipe unions, and inspect the fuel hoses and vacuum hoses for kinks, chafing and deterioration.

22 Check the condition of the power steering fluid hoses and pipes.

Front suspension and steering check

23 Raise the front of the car, and securely support it on axle stands (see *Jacking and vehicle support*).

24 Visually inspect the balljoint dust covers and the steering rack-and-pinion gaiters for splits, chafing or deterioration. Any wear of these components will cause loss of lubricant, then dirt and water entry, resulting in rapid deterioration of the balljoints or steering gear.

25 Check the power steering fluid hoses for chafing or deterioration, and the pipe and hose unions for fluid leaks. Also check for signs of fluid leakage under pressure from the steering gear rubber gaiters, which would indicate failed fluid seals within the steering gear.

26 Grasp the roadwheel at the 12 o-clock and 6 o-clock positions, and try to rock it **(see illustration)**. Very slight free play may be felt, but if the movement is appreciable, further investigation is necessary to determine the source. Continue rocking the wheel while an assistant depresses the footbrake. If the movement is now eliminated or significantly reduced, it is likely that the hub bearings are at fault. If the free play is still evident with the footbrake depressed, then there is wear in the suspension joints or mountings.

27 Now grasp the wheel at the 9 o-clock and 3 o-clock positions, and try to rock it as before. Any movement felt now may again be caused by wear in the hub bearings or the

steering track-rod balljoints. If the inner or outer balljoint is worn, the visual movement will be obvious.

28 Using a large screwdriver or flat bar, check for wear in the suspension mounting bushes by levering between the relevant suspension component and its attachment point. Some movement is to be expected as the mountings are made of rubber, but excessive wear should be obvious. Also check the condition of any visible rubber bushes, looking for splits, cracks or contamination of the rubber.

29 With the car standing on its wheels, have an assistant turn the steering wheel back and forth about an eighth of a turn each way. There should be very little, if any, lost movement between the steering wheel and roadwheels. If this is not the case, closely observe the joints and mountings previously described, but in addition, check the steering column universal joints for wear, and the rack-and-pinion steering gear itself.

Suspension strut/ shock absorber check

30 Check for any signs of fluid leakage around the suspension strut/shock absorber body, or from the rubber gaiter around the piston rod. Should any fluid be noticed, the suspension strut/shock absorber is defective internally, and should be renewed. **Note:** *Suspension struts/shock absorbers should always be renewed in pairs on the same axle.*

31 The efficiency of the suspension strut/ shock absorber may be checked by bouncing the car at each corner. Generally speaking, the body will return to its normal position and stop after being depressed. If it rises and returns on a rebound, the suspension strut/shock absorber is probably suspect. Examine also the suspension strut/shock absorber upper and lower mountings for any signs of wear.

Exhaust system check

32 With the engine cold (at least an hour after the car has been driven), check the complete exhaust system from the engine to the end of the tailpipe. The exhaust system is most easily checked with the car raised on a hoist, or suitably supported on axle stands, so that the exhaust components are readily visible and accessible.

33 Check the exhaust pipes and connections for evidence of leaks, severe corrosion and damage. Make sure that all brackets and mountings are in good condition, and that all relevant nuts and bolts are tight **(see illustration)**. Leakage at any of the joints or in other parts of the system will usually show up as a black sooty stain in the vicinity of the leak.

34 Rattles and other noises can often be traced to the exhaust system, especially the brackets and mountings. Try to move the pipes and silencers. If the components are able to come into contact with the body or suspension parts, secure the system with new mountings. Otherwise separate the joints (if

7.26 Check for wear in the hub/wheel bearings by grasping the wheel and trying to rock it

7.33 Check the condition of the exhaust rubber mountings

possible) and twist the pipes as necessary to provide additional clearance.

Hinge and lock lubrication

35 Lubricate the hinges of the bonnet, doors and tailgate with a light general-purpose oil. Similarly, lubricate all latches, locks and lock strikers. At the same time, check the security and operation of all the locks, adjusting them if necessary (see Chapter 11). Lightly lubricate the bonnet release mechanism and cable with suitable grease.

Road test

Instruments and electrical equipment

36 Check the operation of all instruments and electrical equipment.
37 Make sure that all instruments read correctly, and switch on all electrical equipment in turn, to check that it functions properly.

Steering and suspension

38 Check for any abnormalities in the steering, suspension, handling or road feel.
39 Drive the car, and check that there are no unusual vibrations or noises.
40 Check that the steering feels positive, with no excessive sloppiness, or roughness, and check for any suspension noises when cornering and driving over bumps.

Drivetrain

41 Check the performance of the engine, clutch (where applicable), gearbox/transmission and driveshafts.
42 Listen for any unusual noises from the engine, clutch and gearbox/transmission.
43 Make sure that the engine runs smoothly when idling, and that there is no hesitation when accelerating.
44 Check that, where applicable, the clutch action is smooth and progressive, that the drive is taken up smoothly, and that the pedal travel is not excessive. Also listen for any noises when the clutch pedal is depressed.
45 On manual gearbox models, check that all gears can be engaged smoothly without noise, and that the gear lever action is not abnormally vague or notchy.
46 On automatic transmission models, make sure that all gearchanges occur smoothly, without snatching, and without an increase in engine speed between changes. Check that all the gear positions can be selected with the car at rest. If any problems are found, they should be referred to a MINI dealer or suitably equipped specialist.

Check the braking system

47 Make sure that the car does not pull to one side when braking, and that the wheels do not lock prematurely when braking hard.
48 Check that there is no vibration through the steering when braking.
49 Check that the handbrake operates correctly without excessive movement of the lever, and that it holds the car stationary on a slope.

50 Test the operation of the brake servo unit as follows. With the engine off, depress the footbrake four or five times to exhaust the vacuum. Hold the brake pedal depressed, then start the engine. As the engine starts, there should be a noticeable give in the brake pedal as vacuum builds up. Allow the engine to run for at least two minutes, and then switch it off. If the brake pedal is depressed now, it should be possible to detect a hiss from the servo as the pedal is depressed. After about four or five applications, no further hissing should be heard, and the pedal should feel much harder.
51 Reset the CBS display as described in Section 4.

8 Brake fluid renewal

⚠️ *Warning: Brake hydraulic fluid can harm your eyes and damage painted surfaces, so use extreme caution when handling and pouring it. Do not use fluid that has been standing open for some time, as it absorbs moisture from the air. Excess moisture can cause a dangerous loss of braking effectiveness.*

1 The procedure is similar to that for the bleeding of the hydraulic system as described in Chapter 9, except that the brake fluid reservoir should be emptied by siphoning, using a clean poultry baster or similar before starting, and allowance should be made for the old fluid to be expelled when bleeding a section of the circuit.
2 Working as described in Chapter 9, open the first bleed screw in the sequence, and pump the brake pedal gently until nearly all the old fluid has been emptied from the master cylinder reservoir.
3 Top-up to the MAX level with new fluid, and continue pumping until only the new fluid remains in the reservoir, and new fluid can be seen emerging from the bleed screw. Tighten the screw, and top the reservoir level up to the MAX level line.
4 Work through all remaining bleed screws in the sequence until new fluid can be seen at all of them. Be careful to keep the master

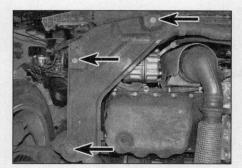

9.3 Undo the screws and remove the auxiliary drivebelt cover (arrowed)

cylinder reservoir topped-up to above the MIN level at all times, or air may enter the system and increase the length of the task.

> **HAYNES HiNT**
> *Old hydraulic fluid is usually much darker in colour than the new, making it easy to distinguish the two.*

5 When the operation is complete, check that all bleed screws are securely tightened, and that their dust caps are refitted. Wash off all traces of spilt fluid, and recheck the master cylinder reservoir fluid level.
6 Check the operation of the brakes before taking the car on the road.

9 Auxiliary drivebelt(s) check and renewal

Drivebelt checking – general

1 Due to their function and construction, the belts are prone to failure after a period of time, and should be inspected periodically to prevent problems.
2 The number of belts used on a particular car depends on the accessories fitted. Drivebelts are used to drive the coolant pump, alternator, and air conditioning compressor (where applicable).
3 To improve access for belt inspection, remove the right-hand front wheelarch liner as described in Chapter 11, then undo the screws and remove the belt pulley cover **(see illustration)**.
4 With the engine stopped, using your fingers (and a torch if necessary), move along the belts, checking for cracks and separation of the belt plies. Also check for fraying and glazing, which gives the belt a shiny appearance. Both sides of the belts should be inspected, which means the belt will have to be twisted to check the underside. If necessary turn the engine using a spanner or socket on the crankshaft pulley bolt to that the whole of the belt can be inspected.

Drivebelt renewal

5 Remove the right-hand front wheelarch liner as described in Chapter 11, then undo the screws and remove the belt pulley cover **(see illustration 9.3)**.
6 If the drivebelt is to be re-used, mark the running direction of the belt before removal.
7 Using a spanner or socket, rotate the tensioner pulley (clockwise) to compress the tensioner, and secure it in position by pressing in the locking pin **(see illustrations)**.
8 In order to set the friction drive into the service position, pull the handle out until the friction gear is away from the belt pulley, and clip it into position on the housing **(see illustrations)**.
9 Slip the belt from the pulleys.

9.7a Rotate the tensioner clockwise...

9.7b ...and lock it in place by pressing-in the pin

9.8a Pull out the handle...

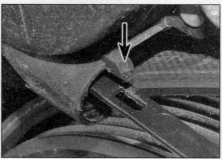

9.8b ...and secure it over the locking pin

10 If the tensioner has not been locked in position, compress the tensioner, and engage the belt with the pulleys, ensuring that it is routed as noted before removal **(see illustration)**. Make sure that the belt engages correctly with the grooves in the pulleys.

11 Where applicable, compress the tensioner until the locking rod can be removed, then withdraw the rod and release the tensioner.

12 Release the friction drive handle.

13 The remainder of refitting is a reversal of removal.

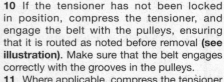

10 Coolant renewal

Cooling system draining

⚠️ *Warning: Wait until the engine is cold before starting this procedure. Do not allow antifreeze to come in contact with your skin, or with the painted surfaces of the car. Rinse off spills immediately with plenty of water. Never leave antifreeze lying around in an open container, or in a puddle in the driveway or on the garage floor. Children and pets are attracted by its sweet smell, but antifreeze can be fatal if ingested.*

Note: *There is no requirement in the MINI service schedule to renew the coolant. However, we consider it prudent to change the coolant every 4 years regardless of mileage.*

1 With the engine completely cold, cover the expansion tank cap with a wad of rag, and slowly turn the cap anti-clockwise to relieve the pressure in the cooling system (a hissing sound may be heard). Wait until any pressure in the system is released, then continue to turn the cap until it can be removed.

2 Undo the retaining screws/clips and remove the undershields from beneath the engine and radiator **(see illustration 9.3)**.

3 Position a suitable container beneath the radiator, release the clamp and disconnect the radiator lower hose.

4 Once drained, the coolant must not be re-used.

5 Once all the coolant has drained, reconnect the radiator lower hose.

Cooling system flushing

6 If coolant renewal has been neglected, or if the antifreeze mixture has become diluted, then in time, the cooling system may gradually lose efficiency, as the coolant passages become restricted due to rust, scale deposits, and other sediment. The cooling system efficiency can be restored by flushing the system clean.

7 The radiator should be flushed independently of the engine, to avoid unnecessary contamination. Refer to Chapter 3.

Cooling system filling

8 Before attempting to fill the cooling system,

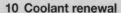

H46898

9.10 Auxiliary drivebelt routing

1 Automatic tensioner	*3 Auxiliary drivebelt*	*6 Driving friction wheel*
2 Alternator	*4 Compressor pulley*	*7 Coolant pump pulley*
	5 Crankshaft pulley	

10.9a The coolant bleed screw (arrowed) is accessible…

10.9b …with a long flat-bladed screwdriver

make sure that all hoses and clips are in good condition, and that the clips are tight and the radiator and cylinder block drain plugs are securely tightened. Note that an antifreeze mixture must be used all year round, to prevent corrosion of the engine components (see following sub-Section).

9 Use a long screwdriver to slacken the bleed screw on the thermostat housing **(see illustrations)**.

10 Turn on the ignition (without starting the engine), and set the heater control to maximum temperature, with the fan speed set to low. This opens the heating valves.

11 Remove the expansion tank filler cap. Fill the system by slowly pouring the coolant into the expansion tank to prevent airlocks from forming.

12 Begin by pouring in a couple of litres of water, followed by the correct quantity of antifreeze, then top-up with more water.

13 Where applicable, tighten the bleed screw on the thermostat housing.

14 Once the level in the expansion tank starts to rise, squeeze the radiator top and bottom hoses to help expel any trapped air in the system. Once all the air is expelled, top-up the coolant level to the maximum mark on the expansion tank. Tighten the expansion tank cap.

Turbocharged models

15 As these models are fitted with an additional electric cooling pump, further bleeding of the system must be carried out as follows:

a) *Connect a battery charger as described in Chapter 5A.*

b) *Switch the ignition on (dont start the engine), then turn on the headlights (dipped beam).* **Note:** *The headlights must be illuminated to prevent the ignition system from automatically switching off.*

c) *Set the heater controls to maximum heat, and the blower motor to the lowest speed.*

d) *Press the accelerator pedal fully for 10 seconds.*

e) *The pump venting procedure should now start, and lasts for approximately 12 minutes. Do not open the expansion tank cap during this procedure.*

f) *Turn off the headlights, and the ignition, and top up the expansion tank to the maximum mark. Disconnect the charger.* **Note:** *If its necessary to repeat this bleeding procedure, remove the ignition key for at least 3 minutes to de-activate the engine management system.*

16 Start the engine and run it until it reaches normal operating temperature, then stop the engine and allow it to cool.

17 Check for leaks, particularly around disturbed components. Check the coolant level in the expansion tank, and top-up if necessary. Note that the system must be cold before an accurate level is indicated in the expansion tank. If the expansion tank cap is removed while the engine is still warm, cover the cap with a thick cloth, and unscrew the cap slowly to gradually relieve the system pressure (a hissing sound will normally be heard). Wait until any pressure remaining in the system is released, then continue to turn the cap until it can be removed.

Antifreeze mixture

18 The antifreeze should always be renewed at the specified intervals. This is necessary not only to maintain the antifreeze properties, but also to prevent corrosion which would otherwise occur as the corrosion inhibitors become progressively less effective.

19 Always use an ethylene-glycol based antifreeze which is suitable for use in mixed-metal cooling systems. The quantity of antifreeze and levels of protection are indicated in the Specifications.

20 Before adding antifreeze, the cooling system should be completely drained, preferably flushed, and all hoses checked for condition and security.

21 After filling with antifreeze, a label should be attached to the expansion tank, stating the type and concentration of antifreeze used, and the date installed. Any subsequent topping-up should be made with the same type and concentration of antifreeze.

22 Do not use engine antifreeze in the windscreen/tailgate washer system, as it will damage the vehicle paintwork. A screenwash additive should be added to the washer system in the quantities stated on the bottle.

11 Remote control battery – renewal

1 On models with the Convenience Access system, the battery in the remote control is replaceable. There is no fixed period for battery replacement, and although a warning message is displayed in the instrument panel when battery power is depleted, we consider it prudent to replace it every 4 years, or when the control range decreases. On all other models, the remote control battery is recharged everytime its inserted into the ignition switch.

2 Prise up the cover from the remote control.

3 Note its fitted position, then remove the old battery.

4 Press the new battery into place, positive (+) side upwards. Try not to touch the battery surfaces with bare skin, as this could reduce battery life.

5 Refit the cover, and check the remote control for correct operation.

Chapter 1 Part B
Routine maintenance & servicing – diesel models

Contents

Degrees of difficulty

Easy, suitable for novice with little experience	**Fairly easy,** suitable for beginner with some experience	**Fairly difficult,** suitable for competent DIY mechanic

Difficult, suitable for experienced DIY mechanic	**Very difficult,** suitable for expert DIY or professional

Lubricants and fluids

Refer to *Weekly checks* on page 0•16

Capacities

Engine oil (including filter)

W16 engines	3.7 litres
N47 engines	5.2 litres

Cooling system

All engines	5.4 litres

Fuel tank

All engines (approximate)	40 litres

Cooling system

Antifreeze mixture:

50% antifreeze	Protection down to –30°C (–22°F)

Note: *Refer to antifreeze manufacturer for latest recommendations.*

Brakes

Brake pad friction material minimum thickness	3.7 mm

Torque wrench settings

	Nm	lbf ft
Engine oil filter cover	25	18
Engine sump oil drain plug:		
W16 engine	30	22
N47 engine	25	18
Roadwheel bolts	140	103

Condition based service

The service intervals are tailored according to the operating conditions, driving style, time elapsed and mileage covered, instead of set distance/time limits. These factors are taken into account, and the maintenance requirements are calculated by the vehicles on-board systems, then a symbol representing the item requiring attention is displayed in the instrument cluster. Consequently, the intervals listed below are guidelines, starting values/ interval forecasts, or our recommendations. For more details, refer to the Owners Handbook supplied with the vehicle.

Every 250 miles (400 km) or weekly
☐ Refer to *Weekly checks*

The following items have a flexible interval dependant on conditions etc. The maximum recommend mileage/time interval (where applicable) is also given.

☐ Engine oil service (Section 3) – at least every 12 000 miles or 2 years (whichever comes first). This includes handbrake check, and pollen filter renewal. On every 2nd oil change, renew the air filter element and fuel filter element.
☐ Vehicle check (Section 7) – at least every 30 000 miles or 4 years (whichever comes first)
☐ Front brake service (Section 5) – at least every 30 000 miles
☐ Rear brake service (Section 6) – at least every 30 000 miles
☐ Renew the brake fluid (Section 8) – every 2 years
☐ Reset the service interval display (Section 4) – after each item above has been serviced
☐ Replenish the diesel fuel additive (Section 13) – every 125 000 miles
☐ Renew the timing belt (Section 12) – every 60 000 miles or 5 years

Note: *Although the MINI interval for timing belt renewal is 125 000 miles, it is strongly recommended that the timing belt renewal interval is reduced to 60 000 miles. The actual renewal interval is therefore upto the individual driver, but bear in mind that severe engine damage will result if the belt brakes.*

The following items have no specific recommendation concerning their inspection or renewal. However, we consider it prudent to carry out these tasks at least every 4 years.

☐ Check the condition of the auxiliary drivebelt(s), and adjust/renew if necessary (Section 9)
☐ Coolant renewal (Section 10)
☐ Remote control battery renewal (Section 11)

Underbonnet view of a W16 diesel model

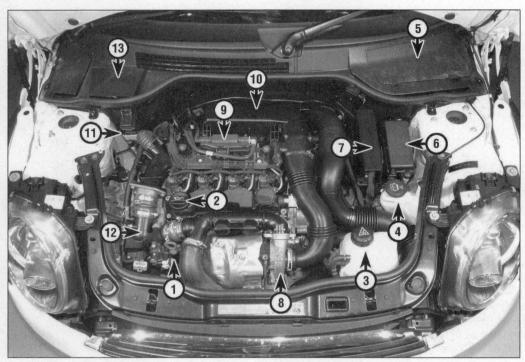

1 Engine oil level dipstick
2 Engine oil filler cap
3 Coolant expansion tank
4 Screenwash reservoir
5 Battery (under cover)
6 Fuse/relay box
7 Engine management ECU
8 Turbocharger
9 Fuel priming hand pump
10 Air cleaner housing
11 Glow plug control unit
12 Throttle body
13 Brake and clutch fluid
reservoir (under cover)

Underbonnet view of an N47 diesel model

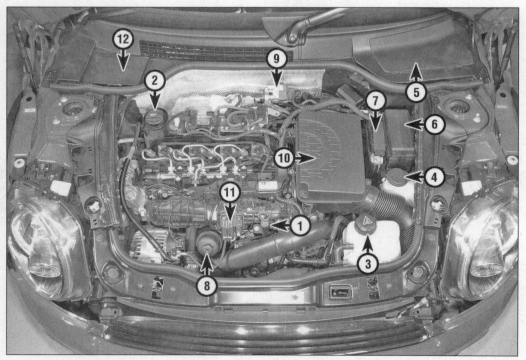

1 Engine oil level dipstick
2 Engine oil filler cap
3 Coolant expansion tank
4 Screenwash reservoir
5 Battery (under cover)
6 Fuse/relay box
7 Engine management ECU
8 Oil filter housing
9 Turbocharger boost
control motor
10 Air cleaner housing
11 Glow plug control unit
12 Brake and clutch fluid
reservoir (under cover)

Front under body view

1 Engine oil drain plug
2 Transmission oil drain plug
3 Catalytic converter/ particulate filter
4 Intercooler hoses
5 Rear engine mounting/link rod
6 Driveshaft
7 Lower suspension arm/ wishbone
8 Steering trackrod end
9 Front subframe
10 Air conditioning compressor
11 Lower radiator hose

Rear underbody view

1 Rear exhaust silencer
2 Suspension trailing arm
3 Suspension lower link arm
4 Shock absorber
5 Handbrake cable
6 Fuel tank
7 Underbody panelling
8 Brake hose

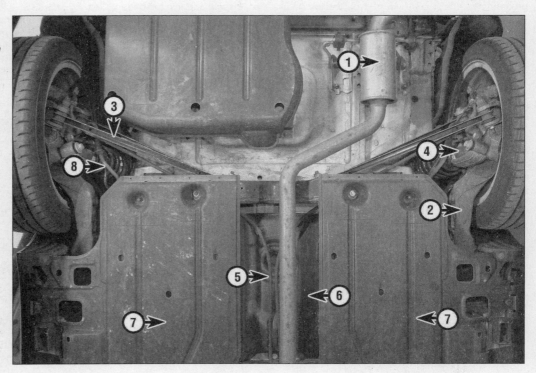

1 Introduction

1 This Chapter is designed to help the home mechanic maintain his/her vehicle for safety, economy, long life and peak performance.

2 The Chapter contains a master maintenance schedule, followed by Sections dealing specifically with each task in the schedule. Visual checks, adjustments, component renewal and other helpful items are included. Refer to the accompanying illustrations of the engine compartment and the underside of the vehicle for the locations of the various components.

3 Servicing your vehicle in accordance with the service indicator display and the following Sections will provide a planned maintenance programme, which should result in a long and reliable service life. This is a comprehensive plan, so maintaining some items but not others at the specified service intervals, will not produce the same results.

4 As you service your vehicle, you will discover that many of the procedures can – and should – be grouped together, because of the particular procedure being performed, or because of the proximity of two otherwise-unrelated components to one another. For example, if the vehicle is raised for any reason, the exhaust can be inspected at the same time as the suspension and steering components.

5 The first step in this maintenance programme is to prepare yourself before the actual work begins. Read through all the Sections relevant to the work to be carried out, then make a list and gather all the parts and tools required. If a problem is encountered, seek advice from a parts specialist, or a dealer service department.

2 Intensive maintenance

1 If, from the time the vehicle is new, the routine maintenance schedule is followed closely, and frequent checks are made of fluid levels and high-wear items, as suggested throughout this manual, the engine will be kept in relatively good running condition, and the need for additional work will be minimised.

2 It is possible that there will be times when the engine is running poorly due to the lack of regular maintenance. This is even more likely if a used vehicle, which has not received regular and frequent maintenance checks, is purchased. In such cases, additional work may need to be carried out, outside of the regular maintenance intervals.

3 If engine wear is suspected, a compression test (refer to Part B or C of Chapter 2) will provide valuable information regarding the overall performance of the main internal components. Such a test can be used as a basis to decide on the extent of the work to be carried out. If, for example, a compression test indicates serious internal engine wear, conventional maintenance as described in this Chapter will not greatly improve the performance of the engine, and may prove a waste of time and money, unless extensive overhaul work is carried out first.

4 The following series of operations are those most often required to improve the performance of a generally poor-running engine:

Primary operations

a) Clean, inspect and test the battery (See 'Weekly checks').
b) Check all the engine-related fluids (See 'Weekly checks').
c) Renew the fuel filter (Section 3).
d) Check the condition of the air filter, and renew if necessary (Section 3).

e) Check the condition of all hoses, and check for fluid leaks (Section 7).

5 If the above operations do not prove fully effective, carry out the following secondary operations:

Secondary operations

All items listed under Primary operations, plus the following:
a) Check the charging system (see Chapter 5A).
b) Check the fuel system (see Chapter 4B).

3 Engine oil service

Engine oil and filter change

1 Frequent oil and filter changes are the most important preventative maintenance work which can be undertaken by the DIY owner. As engine oil ages, it becomes diluted and contaminated, which leads to premature engine wear.

2 Before starting this procedure, gather together all the necessary tools and materials. Also make sure you have plenty of clean rags and newspapers handy, to mop up any spills. Ideally, the engine oil should be warm, as it will drain better, and more built-up sludge will be removed with it. Take care, however, not to touch the exhaust or any other hot parts of the engine when working under the car. To avoid any possibility of scalding, and to protect yourself from possible skin irritants and other harmful contaminants in used engine oils, it is advisable to wear gloves. Access to the underside of the car will be improved if it can be raised on a lift, driven onto ramps, or jacked up and supported on axle stands (see Jacking and vehicle support). Whichever method is chosen, make sure the car remains level, or if it is at an angle, so that the drain plug is at the lowest point. Where fitted, remove the undershield from under the engine (see illustration).

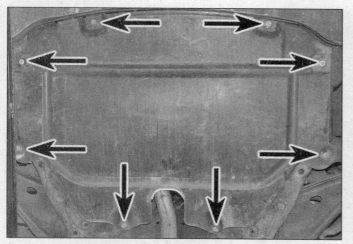

3.2 Engine undershield fasteners (arrowed)

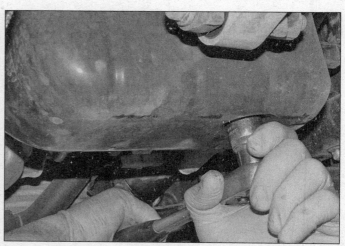

3.3 It's advisable to wear protective gloves when handling used engine oil

3.5a Pull the plastic cover on top of the engine upwards from the mountings – W16 diesel models...

3.5b ...and N47 diesel models

3.6 Coolant expansion tank retaining bolt (arrowed)

3.7a On W16 diesel engines, the oil filter (arrowed) is located at the left-hand end of the engine

3.7b Oil filter location (arrowed) – N47 engines

3.10 Renew the drain plug sealing washer

3 Working under the car, slacken the sump drain plug about half a turn. Position the draining container under the drain plug, then remove the plug completely **(see illustration)**. If possible, try to keep the plug pressed into the sump while unscrewing it by hand the last couple of turns.

4 Discard the drain plug sealing ring, a new one must be used.

5 Pull the plastic cover on top of the engine upwards from its mountings **(see illustrations)**.

6 On W16 engines, undo the retaining bolt and move the coolant expansion tank to one side **(see illustration)**.

7 The oil filter housing is located on the front of the engine, at the left-hand end (W16 engines) or right-hand end (N47 engines) **(see illustrations)**. Place a wad of rag around the bottom of the housing to absorb any spilt oil.

8 Using a socket, unscrew and remove the cover, and lift the filter cartridge out. The oil will drain from the housing back into the sump as the cover is removed.

9 Allow some time for the old oil to drain, noting that it may be necessary to reposition the container as the oil flow slows to a trickle.

10 After all the oil has drained, clean the area around the drain plug opening, then fit and tighten the plug with its new sealing washer **(see illustration)**.

11 Remove the old oil and all tools from under the car, then lower the car to the ground (if applicable).

12 Remove the O-ring from the filter cover, and clean the mating faces of the housing and cover.

13 Fit a new O-ring to the filter cover **(see illustration)**.

14 Smear a little clean engine oil on the cover O-ring, and the O-ring at the base of the filter element **(see illustrations)**.

15 Align the lug on the base of the filter element with the corresponding hole in the housing, then push the filter into place **(see illustrations)**.

16 Locate the cover in the end of the filter and tighten it to the specified torque.

All engines

17 Remove the dipstick then unscrew the oil filler cap. Fill the engine, using the correct grade and type of oil (see *Weekly checks*). An

3.13 Renew the filter cover O-ring seal (arrowed)

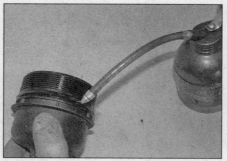

3.14a Apply a little oil to the oil filter cover O-ring seal...

3.14b ...and the O-ring seal at the base of the filter element (arrowed)

3.15a Align the lug on the base of the filter element with the hole in the housing (arrowed) – W16 engines...

3.15b ...and N47 engines (arrowed)

oil can spout or funnel may help to reduce spillage. Pour in half the specified quantity of oil first, then wait a few minutes for the oil to fall to the sump. Continue adding oil a small quantity at a time until the level is up to the lower mark on the dipstick. Finally, bring the level up to the upper mark on the dipstick. Insert the dipstick, and refit the filler cap. Note that the difference between the lower and upper marks on the dipstick is approximately 1.5L

18 Start the engine and run it for a few minutes; check for leaks around the oil filter seal and the sump drain plug. Note that there may be a delay of a few seconds before the oil pressure warning light goes out when the engine is first started, as the oil circulates through the engine oil galleries and the new oil filter, before the pressure builds up.

19 Switch off the engine, and wait a few minutes for the oil to settle in the sump once more. With the new oil circulated and the filter completely full, recheck the level on the dipstick, and add more oil as necessary.

20 Dispose of the used engine oil safely, with reference to *General repair procedures* in the *Reference* section of this manual.

Handbrake check

21 Check and, if necessary, adjust the handbrake as described in Chapter 9. Check that the handbrake cables are free to move easily and lubricate all exposed linkages/cable pivots.

Pollen filter renewal

22 Working in the passenger's side footwell, unclip the plastic cover from the cabin air

filter. On some models, the plastic cover may be retained by screws (see illustration).

23 Pull down the lower end of the filter element, and slide it from the housing.

24 Install the new filter element into the housing, noting how it curves around to fit in the guide slots (see illustration).

25 Install the filter cover, and secure it in place with the retaining clips. If the clips break, it is possible to secure the cover using self-tapping screws through the holes provided in the cover.

Air filter element renewal

26 Undo the air filter housing cover screws (see illustrations).

27 Lift the cover up and remove the old filter.

28 Clean the air filter housing, removing all debris.

29 Install the new filter element, making sure it seats in the housing (see illustrations).

30 The remainder of refitting is the reverse of removal.

Fuel filter

W16 engines

31 Pull the plastic cover on the top of the engine upwards from its mountings, then disconnect the mass airflow sensor wiring plug, release the clamps/clips, undo the screws and remove the air filter cover (see illustration 3.26a) along with the intake duct (see illustration).

32 Note their fitted positions, and disconnect the fuel pipes and wiring plugs from the fuel

3.22 Pull the cover edge (arrowed) rearwards to unclip it

3.24 Slide the pollen filter element from the housing

3.26a Air filter cover screws (arrowed) – W16 engines

3.26b Air filter cover screws (arrowed) – N47 engines

3.29a Install the air filter with the seal uppermost – W16 engines

3.29b On N47 engines, the lug at the front of the filter (arrowed) aligns with a slot in the housing

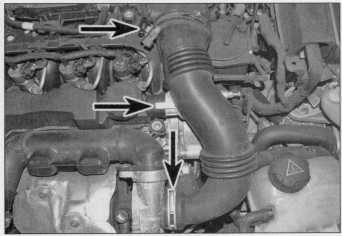

3.31 Disconnect the mass air flow sensor wiring plug, release the clamp, and breather clips (arrowed) then remove the air filter cover, along with the duct

3.32 Depress the release buttons (arrowed) and disconnect the fuel pipes from the filter

filter **(see illustration)**. Be prepared for fuel spillage.

33 Release the catch and slide the fuel filter upwards from place **(see illustration)**. Disconnect any wiring plugs as the filter is withdrawn.

34 Slide the new filter into place and reconnect the fuel pipes/wiring plugs.

35 Prime and bleed the fuel system as described in Chapter 4B.

N47 engines

36 Raise the rear of the vehicle and support

it securely on axle stands (see *Jacking and vehicle support*). On Hatchback and Clubman models, undo the fasteners and remove the right-hand underbody panelling, in front of the rear wheel **(see illustration)**.

37 Place a workshop jack under the fuel tank, and raise it to take the weight of the tank. Use a block of wood to spread the load of the tank.

38 On Convertible models, unclip the cover under the fuel filter.

39 Remove the expansion rivets, undo the

retaining bolts and remove the fuel tank support strap **(see illustration)**.

40 Release the clamps and detach the fuel filter assembly from the fuel tank **(see illustrations)**.

41 Prise out the retaining clip and detach the fuel pre-heater from the end of the filter **(see illustration)**. Be prepared for fuel spillage.

42 Release the clamp and disconnect the remaining fuel hose from the filter **(see illustration)**. If necessary replace the hose clamp.

3.33 Release the clip and slide the filter upwards from place

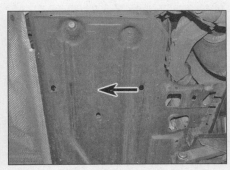

3.36 Undo the fasteners and remove the right-hand underbody panelling (arrowed)

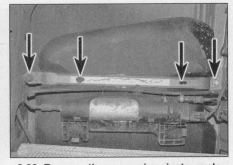

3.39 Remove the expansion rivets, undo the bolts and remove the fuel tank strap

3.40 Pull down the clips a little, then slide the filter outwards and rearwards (arrowed)

3.41 Prise out the clip (arrowed) and pull the heater from the filter

3.42 Cut the clamp and pull the hose from the end of the filter

3.44a Align the lug on the pre-heater (arrowed)...

3.44b ...with the slot in the filter (arrowed)

43 Detach the fuel filter from the housing.
44 Refitting is a reversal of removal. Examine the heater O-ring seal and renew if necessary, and ensure the lug on the pre-heater aligns with the slot in the new filter **(see illustrations)**. Prime and bleed the fuel system as described in Chapter 4B.

4 Resetting the service interval display

1 Ensure that all electrical items are switched off then turn on the ignition switch. **Note:** *Do not start the engine.*
2 Ensure the on-board time and date are correctly set in accordance with the instructions in the owners handbook.
3 Each service item that appears on the instrument cluster display can be reset. Note that it is only possible to reset an item if the service life of the item is below 80%.
4 Press the trip odometer button for approximately 10 seconds until the first CBS (Condition Based Service) item appears in the instrument cluster display. The upper display in the speedometer is illuminated by a service symbol. The lower display indicated the time or distance remaining until the next service. Scroll through the items by repeatedly pressing the on-board computer button.
5 When the required item is selected, press the on-board computer button (end of indicator stalk/switch) until 'Reset?' appears in the display. Note that the reset process is cancelled by not pressing the button to confirm, and waiting for the display to return to its normal state.
6 Press the button again for approximately 3 seconds to confirm the reset. A clock symbol will be displayed as the reset is being performed. Upon successful resetting, a 'tick' symbol will be displayed. Note that it is only possible to reset the brake pad display if the pad sensors are working properly.
7 In order for the CBS display to function correctly, the on-board time and date must be correct. Refer to the owners handbook for details of how to set these values.
8 Turn off the ignition switch.

5 Front brake service

Front brake pads

1 When this CBS item is displayed, the thickness of the front brake pads friction material should be checked, and if any are approaching the minimum thickness, *all* four front pads should be renewed.
2 Firmly apply the handbrake, then jack up the front of the car and support it securely on axle stands (see *Jacking and vehicle support*). Remove the front roadwheels.
3 The brake pad warning symbol in the CBS display indicates that the pad friction material thickness is worn such that the pads require replacement. However, the warning will also be given if the wiring to and from each pads sensor is damaged or the connections are poor, dirty, etc. Check the wiring to and from the sensor for poor connections/breaks before replacing the pads.
4 The thickness of friction material remaining on each brake pad can be measured through the top of the caliper body. If any pad's friction material is worn to the specified thickness or less, all four pads must be renewed as a set. Pad replacement is described in Chapter 9

Front brake disc check

5 Check the front brake disc condition, and measure the thickness of the disc as described in Chapter 9. Replace both front discs if necessary.
6 Reset the CBS display as described in Section 4.

6 Rear brake service

Rear brake pads

1 When this CBS item is displayed, the thickness of the rear brake pads friction material should be checked, and if any are approaching the minimum thickness, *all* four rear pads should be renewed.

2 Chock the front wheels, then jack up the rear of the car and support it on axle stands (see *Jacking and vehicle support*). Remove the rear roadwheels.
3 The thickness of friction material remaining on each brake pad can be measured through the top of the caliper body. If any pad's friction material is worn to the specified thickness or less, *all* four pads must be renewed as a set. Pad replacement is described in Chapter 9.

Rear brake disc check

4 Check the front brake disc condition, and measure the thickness of the disc as described in Chapter 9. Replace both front discs if necessary.
5 Reset the CBS display as described in Section 4.

7 Vehicle check

1 The vehicle check consists of several tasks. Before the CBS display can be reset, *all* of the following tasks must be complete.

Instruments and electrical equipment

2 Check the operation of all instruments and electrical equipment.
3 Make sure that all instruments read correctly, and switch on all electrical equipment in turn, to check that it functions properly.

Seat belt check

4 Carefully examine the seat belt webbing for cuts or any signs of serious fraying or deterioration. Pull the belt all the way out, and examine the full extent of the webbing.
5 Fasten and unfasten the belt, ensuring that the locking mechanism holds securely and releases properly when intended. Check also that the retracting mechanism operates correctly when the belt is released.
6 Check the security of all seat belt mountings and attachments which are accessible, without removing any trim or other components, from inside the car.

Windscreen wash/ wipe system check

7 Check that each of the washer jet nozzles are clear and that each nozzle provides a strong jet of washer fluid. Replace as necessary – refer to Chapter 12.
8 Check the condition of each wiper blade for damage of wear. As time passes the blades will become hardened, wipe performance will deteriorate, and noise will increase. Replace the blades as necessary – see *Weekly checks*.

Bodywork corrosion check

9 This work should be carried out by a MINI dealer in order to validate the vehicle warranty. The work includes a thorough inspection of the vehicle paintwork and underbody for damage and corrosion.

Tyre check

10 Check the tread depth, external condition and inflation pressure of the tyres. See *Weekly checks* for details of the procedures and tyre pressure information.

Battery check

11 Check the condition of the battery, and recharge if necessary – refer to Chapter 5A.

Coolant concentration check

12 Use a hydrometer to check the strength of the antifreeze (see illustration). Follow the instructions provided with your hydrometer. The antifreeze strength should be approximately 50%. If it is significantly less than this, drain a little coolant from the radiator (see this Chapter), add antifreeze to the coolant expansion tank, then re-check the strength.

Hose and fluid leak check

13 Visually inspect the engine joint faces, gaskets and seals for any signs of water or oil leaks. Pay particular attention to the areas around the camshaft cover, cylinder head, oil filter and sump joint faces. Bear in mind that, over a period of time, some very slight seepage from these areas is to be expected – what you are really looking for is any indication of a serious leak (see Haynes Hint). Should a leak be found, renew the offending gasket or oil seal by referring to the appropriate Chapters in this manual.

14 Also check the security and condition of all the engine-related pipes and hoses. Ensure that all cable-ties or securing clips are in place and in good condition. Clips which are broken or missing can lead to chafing of the hoses, pipes or wiring, which could cause more serious problems in the future.

15 Carefully check the radiator hoses and heater hoses along their entire length. Renew any hose which is cracked, swollen or deteriorated. Cracks will show up better if the hose is squeezed. Pay close attention to the hose clips that secure the hoses to the cooling system components. Hose clips can pinch and puncture hoses, resulting in cooling system leaks.

16 Inspect all the cooling system components (hoses, joint faces etc.) for leaks. A leak in the cooling system will usually show up as white- or rust-coloured deposits on the area adjoining the leak. Where any problems of this nature are found on system components, renew the component or gasket with reference to Chapter 3.

17 Where applicable, inspect the automatic transmission fluid cooler hoses for leaks or deterioration.

18 With the car raised, inspect the petrol tank and filler neck for punctures, cracks and other damage. The connection between the filler neck and tank is especially critical. Sometimes a rubber filler neck or connecting hose will leak due to loose retaining clamps or deteriorated rubber.

19 Carefully check all rubber hoses and metal fuel lines leading away from the petrol tank.

7.12 Use an hydrometer to check the anti-freeze concentration

Check for loose connections, deteriorated hoses, crimped lines, and other damage. Pay particular attention to the vent pipes and hoses, which often loop up around the filler neck and can become blocked or crimped. Follow the lines to the front of the car, carefully inspecting them all the way. Renew damaged sections as necessary.

20 Closely inspect the metal brake pipes which run along the car underbody. If they show signs of excessive corrosion or damage they must be renewed.

21 From within the engine compartment, check the security of all fuel hose attachments and pipe unions, and inspect the fuel hoses and vacuum hoses for kinks, chafing and deterioration.

22 Check the condition of the power steering fluid hoses and pipes.

Front suspension and steering check

23 Raise the front of the car, and securely support it on axle stands (see *Jacking and vehicle support*).

24 Visually inspect the balljoint dust covers and the steering rack-and-pinion gaiters for splits, chafing or deterioration. Any wear of these components will cause loss of lubricant, then dirt and water entry, resulting in rapid deterioration of the balljoints or steering gear.

25 Check the power steering fluid hoses for chafing or deterioration, and the pipe and hose unions for fluid leaks. Also check for signs of fluid leakage under pressure from the steering gear rubber gaiters, which would indicate failed fluid seals within the steering gear.

26 Grasp the roadwheel at the 12 o'clock and 6 o'clock positions, and try to rock it (see illustration). Very slight free play may be felt, but if the movement is appreciable, further investigation is necessary to determine the source. Continue rocking the wheel while an assistant depresses the footbrake. If the movement is now eliminated or significantly reduced, it is likely that the hub bearings are at fault. If the free play is still evident with the footbrake depressed, then there is wear in the suspension joints or mountings.

27 Now grasp the wheel at the 9 o'clock and 3 o'clock positions, and try to rock it as before. Any movement felt now may again

A leak in the cooling system will usually show up as white- of anti-freeze coloured deposits on the area adjoining the leak.

be caused by wear in the hub bearings or the steering track-rod balljoints. If the inner or outer balljoint is worn, the visual movement will be obvious.

28 Using a large screwdriver or flat bar, check for wear in the suspension mounting bushes by levering between the relevant suspension component and its attachment point. Some movement is to be expected as the mountings are made of rubber, but excessive wear should be obvious. Also check the condition of any visible rubber bushes, looking for splits, cracks or contamination of the rubber.

29 With the car standing on its wheels, have an assistant turn the steering wheel back and forth about an eighth of a turn each way. There should be very little, if any, lost movement between the steering wheel and roadwheels. If this is not the case, closely observe the joints and mountings previously described, but in addition, check the steering column universal joints for wear, and the rack-and-pinion steering gear itself.

Suspension strut/ shock absorber check

30 Check for any signs of fluid leakage around the suspension strut/shock absorber body, or from the rubber gaiter around the piston rod. Should any fluid be noticed, the suspension strut/shock absorber is defective internally, and should be renewed. **Note:** *Suspension struts/shock absorbers should always be renewed in pairs on the same axle.*

7.26 Check for wear in the hub/wheel bearings by grasping the wheel and trying to rock it

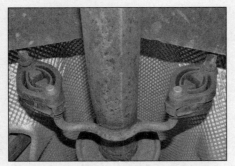

7.33 Check the condition of the exhaust rubber mountings

31 The efficiency of the suspension strut/shock absorber may be checked by bouncing the car at each corner. Generally speaking, the body will return to its normal position and stop after being depressed. If it rises and returns on a rebound, the suspension strut/shock absorber is probably suspect. Examine also the suspension strut/shock absorber upper and lower mountings for any signs of wear.

Exhaust system check

32 With the engine cold (at least an hour after the car has been driven), check the complete exhaust system from the engine to the end of the tailpipe. The exhaust system is most easily checked with the car raised on a hoist, or suitably supported on axle stands, so that the exhaust components are readily visible and accessible.
33 Check the exhaust pipes and connections for evidence of leaks, severe corrosion and damage. Make sure that all brackets and mountings are in good condition, and that all relevant nuts and bolts are tight **(see illustration)**. Leakage at any of the joints or in other parts of the system will usually show up as a black sooty stain in the vicinity of the leak.
34 Rattles and other noises can often be traced to the exhaust system, especially the brackets and mountings. Try to move the pipes and silencers. If the components are able to come into contact with the body or suspension parts, secure the system with new mountings. Otherwise separate the joints (if possible) and twist the pipes as necessary to provide additional clearance.

Hinge and lock lubrication

35 Lubricate the hinges of the bonnet, doors and tailgate with a light general-purpose oil. Similarly, lubricate all latches, locks and lock strikers. At the same time, check the security and operation of all the locks, adjusting them if necessary (see Chapter 11). Lightly lubricate the bonnet release mechanism and cable with a suitable grease.

Road test

Instruments and electrical equipment

36 Check the operation of all instruments and electrical equipment.

37 Make sure that all instruments read correctly, and switch on all electrical equipment in turn, to check that it functions properly.

Steering and suspension

38 Check for any abnormalities in the steering, suspension, handling or road feel .
39 Drive the car, and check that there are no unusual vibrations or noises.
40 Check that the steering feels positive, with no excessive sloppiness , or roughness, and check for any suspension noises when cornering and driving over bumps.

Drivetrain

41 Check the performance of the engine, clutch (where applicable), gearbox/transmission and driveshafts.
42 Listen for any unusual noises from the engine, clutch and gearbox/transmission.
43 Make sure that the engine runs smoothly when idling, and that there is no hesitation when accelerating.
44 Check that, where applicable, the clutch action is smooth and progressive, that the drive is taken up smoothly, and that the pedal travel is not excessive. Also listen for any noises when the clutch pedal is depressed.
45 On manual gearbox models, check that all gears can be engaged smoothly without noise, and that the gear lever action is not abnormally vague or notchy .
46 On automatic transmission models, make sure that all gearchanges occur smoothly, without snatching, and without an increase in engine speed between changes. Check that all the gear positions can be selected with the car at rest. If any problems are found, they should be referred to a MINI dealer or suitably equipped specialist.

Check the braking system

47 Make sure that the car does not pull to one side when braking, and that the wheels do not lock prematurely when braking hard.
48 Check that there is no vibration through the steering when braking.
49 Check that the handbrake operates correctly without excessive movement of the lever, and that it holds the car stationary on a slope.
50 Test the operation of the brake servo unit as follows. With the engine off, depress the footbrake four or five times to exhaust the vacuum. Hold the brake pedal depressed, then start the engine. As the engine starts, there should be a noticeable give in the brake pedal as vacuum builds up. Allow the engine to run for at least two minutes, and then switch it off. If the brake pedal is depressed now, it should be possible to detect a hiss from the servo as the pedal is depressed. After about four or five applications, no further hissing should be heard, and the pedal should feel much harder.
51 Reset the CBS display as described in Section 4.

8 Brake fluid renewal

⚠ **Warning: Brake hydraulic fluid can harm your eyes and damage painted surfaces, so use extreme caution when handling and pouring it. Do not use fluid that has been standing open for some time, as it absorbs moisture from the air. Excess moisture can cause a dangerous loss of braking effectiveness.**

1 The procedure is similar to that for the bleeding of the hydraulic system as described in Chapter 9, except that the brake fluid reservoir should be emptied by siphoning, using a clean poultry baster or similar before starting, and allowance should be made for the old fluid to be expelled when bleeding a section of the circuit.
2 Working as described in Chapter 9, open the first bleed screw in the sequence, and pump the brake pedal gently until nearly all the old fluid has been emptied from the master cylinder reservoir.
3 Top-up to the MAX level with new fluid, and continue pumping until only the new fluid remains in the reservoir, and new fluid can be seen emerging from the bleed screw. Tighten the screw, and top the reservoir level up to the MAX level line.
4 Work through all remaining bleed screws in the sequence until new fluid can be seen at all of them. Be careful to keep the master cylinder reservoir topped-up to above the MIN level at all times, or air may enter the system and increase the length of the task. Note that old hydraulic fluid is usually much darker in colour than the new, making it easy to distinguish the two.
5 When the operation is complete, check that all bleed screws are securely tightened, and that their dust caps are refitted. Wash off all traces of spilt fluid, and recheck the master cylinder reservoir fluid level.
6 Check the operation of the brakes before taking the car on the road.

9 Auxiliary drivebelt(s) – check and renewal

Drivebelt checking – general

1 Due to their function and construction, the belts are prone to failure after a period of time, and should be inspected periodically to prevent problems.
2 The number of belts used on a particular car depends on the accessories fitted. Drivebelts are used to drive the coolant pump (N47 engines only), alternator, and air conditioning compressor (where applicable).
3 To improve access for belt inspection, remove the right-hand front wheelarch liner as described in Chapter 11.
4 With the engine stopped, using your fingers

9.7 Undo the bolt (arrowed) and move the charge pressure sensor to one side

9.9 Use an open-ended spanner to rotate the tensioner arm clockwise, then lock it in place by inserting a 4 mm drill bit/rod into the hole in the tensioner body (arrowed)

(and a torch if necessary), move along the belts, checking for cracks and separation of the belt plies. Also check for fraying and glazing, which gives the belt a shiny appearance. Both sides of the belts should be inspected, which means the belt will have to be twisted to check the underside. If necessary turn the engine using a spanner or socket on the crankshaft pulley bolt to that the whole of the belt can be inspected.

Drivebelt renewal

5 Remove the right-hand front wheelarch liner as described in Chapter 11.

W16 engines

6 Remove the right-hand headlight as described in Chapter 12.
7 Undo the retaining screw, and move the charge pressure sensor to one side **(see illustration)**.
8 If the drivebelt is to be re-used, mark the running direction of the belt before removal.
9 Using an open-ended spanner, reach down and rotate the tensioner arm clockwise to release the belt tension. Insert a short 4 mm drill bit or rod into the hole in the tensioner body, so that the tensioner arm rests against it, and locks it in position **(see illustration)**. It's useful to have a small mirror available to enable the alignment of the locking holes to be more easily seen in the limited space available.

N47 engines

10 Undo the fasteners and remove the engine undershield **(see illustration 3.2)**.
11 If the drivebelt is to be re-used, mark the running direction of the belt before removal.
12 Using a 21 mm spanner, rotate the belt tensioner clockwise until the holes in the tensioner body and bracket align, then insert a 4 mm drill bit or rod into the holes to lock the tensioner in place **(see illustration)**.

All engines

13 Slip the belt from the pulleys.

14 Fit the belt around the pulleys, ensuring that the ribs on the belt are correctly engages with the grooves in the pulleys, and the drivebelt is correctly routed **(see illustrations)**. If refitting a used belt, use the mark made on removal to ensure it's fitted the correct way around.
15 Compress the tensioner until the locking rod can be removed, then withdraw the rod and release the tensioner.
16 The remainder of refitting is a reversal of removal.

10 Coolant renewal

Cooling system draining

⚠️ **Warning: Wait until the engine is cold before starting this procedure. Do not allow antifreeze**

9.12 Rotate the tensioner clockwise and insert a 4 mm drill bit to lock it in place (arrowed)

to come in contact with your skin, or with the painted surfaces of the car. Rinse off spills immediately with plenty of water. Never leave antifreeze lying around in an open container, or in a puddle in the driveway or on the garage floor. Children

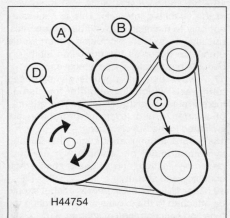

9.14a Auxiliary drivebelt routing – W 16 diesel engines

A Tensioner	C Compressor
B Alternator	D Crankshaft

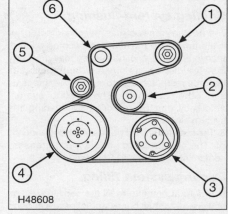

9.14b Auxiliary drivebelt routing – N47 diesel engines

1 Alternator	4 Crankshaft
2 Coolant pump	5 Tensioner
3 Compressor	6 Idler pulley

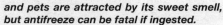

10.3a Disconnect the lower hose at the connection (arrowed) beneath the cooling fan – W16 diesel engines

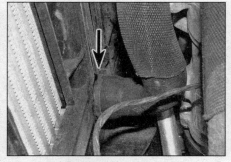

10.3b Radiator lower hose clamp (arrowed) – N47 engines

10.4 Coolant bleed screw (arrowed) – N47 engines

and pets are attracted by its sweet smell, but antifreeze can be fatal if ingested.
Note: *There is no requirement in the MINI service schedule to renew the coolant. However, we consider it prudent to change the coolant every 4 years regardless of mileage.*
1 With the engine completely cold, cover the expansion tank cap with a wad of rag, and slowly turn the cap anti-clockwise to relieve the pressure in the cooling system (a hissing sound may be heard). Wait until any pressure in the system is released, then continue to turn the cap until it can be removed.
2 Undo the retaining screws/clips and remove the undershield from beneath the engine (see illustration 3.2).
3 Position a suitable container beneath the radiator, release the clamp and disconnect the radiator lower hose at the connection beneath the cooling fan (W16 engines) or at the lower right-hand corner of the radiator (N47 engines) (see illustrations).
4 On N47 engines, slacken the coolant bleed screw in the heater hose at the left-hand side of the engine compartment (see illustration).
5 Once drained, the coolant must not be re-used.
6 Once all the coolant has drained, reconnect the radiator lower hose.

Cooling system flushing

7 If coolant renewal has been neglected, or if the antifreeze mixture has become diluted, then in time, the cooling system may gradually lose efficiency, as the coolant passages become restricted due to rust, scale deposits, and other sediment. The cooling system efficiency can be restored by flushing the system clean.
8 The radiator should be flushed independently of the engine, to avoid unnecessary contamination. Refer to Chapter 3.

Cooling system filling

9 Before attempting to fill the cooling system, make sure that all hoses and clips are in good condition, and that the clips are tight and the radiator and cylinder block drain plugs are securely tightened. Note that an antifreeze mixture must be used all year round, to

prevent corrosion of the engine components (see following sub-Section).
10 Turn on the ignition (without starting the engine), and set the heater control to maximum temperature, with the fan speed set to 'low'. This opens the heating valves.
11 Remove the expansion tank filler cap. Fill the system by slowly pouring the coolant into the expansion tank to prevent airlocks from forming.
12 Begin by pouring in a couple of litres of water, followed by the correct quantity of antifreeze, then top-up with more water.
13 On N47 engines, as soon as bubble-free coolant begins to emerge from the heater hose, close the bleed screw.
14 Once the level in the expansion tank starts to rise, squeeze the radiator top and bottom hoses to help expel any trapped air in the system. Once all the air is expelled, top-up the coolant level to the maximum mark on the expansion tank. Tighten the expansion tank cap.
15 Run the engine at a fast idle speed, until it reaches normal operating temperature, keeping an eye on the coolant level in the expansion tank, and topping up as necessary.

Antifreeze mixture

16 The antifreeze should always be renewed at the specified intervals. This is necessary not only to maintain the antifreeze properties, but also to prevent corrosion which would otherwise occur as the corrosion inhibitors become progressively less effective.
17 Always use an ethylene-glycol based antifreeze which is suitable for use in mixed-metal cooling systems. The quantity of antifreeze and levels of protection are indicated in the Specifications.
18 Before adding antifreeze, the cooling system should be completely drained, preferably flushed, and all hoses checked for condition and security.
19 After filling with antifreeze, a label should be attached to the expansion tank, stating the type and concentration of antifreeze used, and the date installed. Any subsequent topping-up should be made with the same type and concentration of antifreeze.
20 Do not use engine antifreeze in the

windscreen/tailgate washer system, as it will damage the vehicle paintwork. A screenwash additive should be added to the washer system in the quantities stated on the bottle.

11 Remote control battery renewal

1 On models with the Convenience Access system, the battery in the remote control is replaceable. There is no fixed period for battery replacement, and although a warning message is displayed in the instrument panel when battery power is depleted, we consider it prudent to replace it every 4 years, or when the control range decreases. On all other models, the remote control battery is recharged everytime it's inserted into the ignition switch.
2 Prise up the cover from the remote control.
3 Note its fitted position, then remove the old battery.
4 Press the new battery into place, positive (+) side upwards. Try not to touch the battery surfaces with bare skin, as this could reduce battery life.
5 Refit the cover, and check the remote control for correct operation.

12 Timing belt renewal

Only models fitted with the W16 1.6L diesel engines are equipped with a timing belt. Timing belt renewal is described in Chapter 2B.

13 Diesel fuel additive renewal

The actual interval for replacing the additive 'bag' is determined by driving style/conditions, but MINI suggest that the bag may need replacing at approximately 125 000 miles. Replacement of the additive bag is described in Setion 12 of Chapter 4B.

Chapter 2 Part A:
Petrol engine in-car repair procedures

Contents

Degrees of difficulty

Easy, suitable for novice with little experience	**Fairly easy,** suitable for beginner with some experience	**Fairly difficult,** suitable for competent DIY mechanic	**Difficult,** suitable for experienced DIY mechanic	**Very difficult,** suitable for expert DIY or professional

Specifications

Engine (general)

Capacity:
    1.4 litre engine 1397cc
    1.6 litre engine 1598cc
Designation:
    1.4 litre engine N12B14
    1.6 litre engine:
        Non-turbo (up to 2010). N12B16
        Non-turbo (2010-on) N16B16
        Turbo (2010 – 2012 173 and 208 bhp) N14B16
        Turbo (2010-on 181 bhp) N18B16
Bore:
    1.4 litre engine . . . .   77.00 mm
    1.6 litre engine . . . .   77.00 mm
Stroke:
    1.4 litre engine . . . .   75.00 mm
    1.6 litre engine . . . .   85.80 mm
Direction of crankshaft rotation . . . .   Clockwise (viewed from the right-hand side of vehicle)
Compression ratio:
    1.4 litre engine . . . .   11.0 : 1
    1.6 litre engine:
        N16 . . . .   11.0 : 1
        N14 . . . .   10.5 : 1
        N18 . . . .   10.5 : 1
Compression:
    Pressure . . . .   8.0 – 12.0 bar
    Maximum difference between cylinders.   3.0 bar

* *The engine code is stamped on a plate attached to the front right-hand end of the cylinder block, below the right-hand branch of the exhaust manifold. The code is the first 3-digits on the first line, and this is the code most often used by MINI.*

Camshafts

Drive . . . .   Chain

Lubrication system

Oil pump type. . . . .   Gear type, chain-driven off the crankshaft
Minimum oil pressure at 80°C (with correct oil level):
    1000 rpm . . . .   2.0 bars
    2000 rpm . . . .   2.9 bars
    4000 rpm . . . .   3.3 bars
Oil pressure warning switch operating pressure . . . .   0.5 bars

Torque wrench settings

	Nm	lbf ft
Acoustic cover	8	6
Big-end bearing bolts:*		
Stage 1	5	4
Stage 2	10	7
Stage 3	Angle-tighten a further 130°	
Camshaft bearing cap	10	7
Camshaft sprocket centre bolts (inlet and exhaust)*:		
Stage 1	20	15
Stage 2	Angle-tighten a further 180°	
Crankshaft pulley centre hub bolt*:		
Stage 1	50	37
Stage 2	Angle-tighten a further 180°	
Crankshaft pulley-to-centre hub bolts (3)	28	21
Cylinder head bolts*:		
M10 x 145 mm:		
Stage 1	30	22
Stage 2	Angle-tighten a further 90°	
Stage 3	Angle-tighten a further 90°	
M8 x 95 mm:		
Stage 1	15	11
Stage 2	Angle-tighten a further 90°	
Stage 3	Angle-tighten a further 90°	
M8 x 35 mm	30	
Cylinder head cover bolts	10	7
Eccentric shaft bearing block-to-cylinder head	10	7
Engine-to-transmission fixing bolts	55	41
Flywheel/driveplate retaining bolts:*		
Stage 1	8	6
Stage 2	30	22
Stage 3	Angle-tighten a further 90°	
Left-hand engine/transmission mounting:		
Mounting bracket-to-body bolts (see text)	56	41
Mounting bracket-to-mounting nut:		
Stage 1	40	30
Stage 2	Angle-tighten a further 105°	
Mounting bracket to transmission	38	28
Main bearing outer housing/ladder bolts*	9	7
Main bearing bolts*:		
Stage 1	30	22
Stage 2	Angle-tighten a further 150°	
Oil filter cap	25	18
Oil filter housing-to-cylinder block	10	7
Oil pressure warning switch:		
N12 engine	20	15
N16 and N18 engine	25	18
Oil pump-to-engine bolts	25	18
Oil pump sprocket bolt*:		
Stage 1	5	3
Stage 2	Angle-tighten a further 90°	
Rear engine/transmission mounting:		
Connecting link-to-mounting bracket bolt	108	80
Connecting link-to-subframe bolt	108	80
Mounting bracket-to-engine	38	28
Right-hand engine/transmission mounting:		
Mounting bracket-to-support bracket/mounting:		
M12 nut	100	74
M10 bolt (8.8 grade)	38	28
M10 bolt (10.9 grade)	56	41
Rubber mounting-to-body	68	50
Support bracket-to-engine	41	30
Sump retaining bolts	12	9
Sump baffle plate bolts	10	7
Sump drain plug	30	22
Timing chain guide securing bolts	25	18
Timing chain tensioner	65	48
Timing control solenoid valves (2) securing bolts	9	7
Variable timing actuator	8	6

* Do not re-use

1   General information

How to use this Chapter

This Part of Chapter 2 describes those repair procedures that can reasonably be carried out on the engine while it remains in the car. If the engine has been removed from the car and is being dismantled as described in Part D, any preliminary dismantling procedures can be ignored.

Note that, while it may be possible physically to overhaul items such as the piston/connecting rod assemblies while the engine is in the car, such tasks are not usually carried out as separate operations. Usually, several additional procedures (not to mention the cleaning of components and oilways) have to be carried out. For this reason, all such tasks are classed as major overhaul procedures, and are described in Part D of this Chapter.

Part D describes the removal of the engine/transmission unit from the vehicle, and the full overhaul procedures that can then be carried out.

The engine is of in-line four-cylinder, double-overhead camshaft, 16-valve type, mounted transversely at the front of the car. The clutch and transmission are attached to its left-hand end.

The engine is of conventional 'dry-liner' type, and the cylinder block is cast in aluminium.

The crankshaft runs in five main bearings. Thrustwashers are fitted to No 2 main bearing cap, to control crankshaft endfloat.

The connecting rods rotate on horizontally-split bearing shells at their big-ends. The pistons are attached to the connecting rods by gudgeon pins. The gudgeon pins are an interference fit in the connecting rod small-end eyes. The aluminium alloy pistons are fitted with three piston rings – two compression rings and an oil control ring.

The camshafts are driven by a chain, and operate sixteen valves by rocker arms located beneath each cam lobe. The valve clearances are self-adjusting by means of hydraulic followers in the cylinder head. The camshafts run in bearing cap housings, which are bolted to the top of the cylinder head. The inlet and exhaust valves are each closed by coil springs, and operate in guides pressed into the cylinder head. All engines except the N14 incorporate a VANOS (variable valve timing) unit on the end of each camshaft. The N14 engine has a VANOS unit on the intake camshaft and a conventional sprocket on the exhaust camshaft. Additionally, all engines except N14, are equipped with Valvetronic, which is an electric motor-controlled variable valve lift apparatus that alters intake valve lift during varying operating conditions to maximize performance, minimize pumping losses, and increase fuel efficiency.

The coolant pump is driven by the auxiliary belt and located in the right-hand end, at the rear of the cylinder block.

Lubrication is by means of an oil pump, which is chain driven off the crankshaft right-hand end. It draws oil through a strainer located in the sump, and then forces it through an externally-mounted filter into galleries in the cylinder block/crankcase. From there, the oil is distributed to the crankshaft (main bearings) and camshaft. The big-end bearings are supplied with oil via internal drillings in the crankshaft; the camshaft bearings also receive a pressurised supply. The camshaft lobes and valves are lubricated by splash, as are all other engine components.

Throughout the manual, it is often necessary to identify the engines not only by their cubic capacity, but also by their engine code. The engine code consists of three digits (eg, N12). The code is stamped on a plate attached to the front, left-hand end of the cylinder block, or stamped directly onto the front face of the cylinder block, on the machined surface located just to the left of the oil filter (next to the crankcase vent hose union).

Operations with engine in the car

The following work can be carried out with the engine in the car:

a) Compression pressure – testing.
b) Cylinder head covers – removal and refitting.
c) Crankshaft pulley – removal and refitting.
d) Timing chain – removal, refitting and adjustment.
e) Timing chain tensioner and sprockets – removal and refitting.
f) Cylinder head – removal and refitting.
g) Cylinder head and pistons – decarbonising.
h) Sump – removal and refitting.
i) Oil pump – removal, overhaul and refitting.
j) Crankshaft oil seals – renewal.
k) Engine/transmission mountings – inspection and renewal.
l) Flywheel/driveplate – removal, inspection and refitting.

2   Compression test – description and interpretation

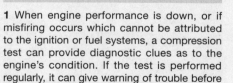

1 When engine performance is down, or if misfiring occurs which cannot be attributed to the ignition or fuel systems, a compression test can provide diagnostic clues as to the engine's condition. If the test is performed regularly, it can give warning of trouble before any other symptoms become apparent.

2 The engine must be fully warmed-up to normal operating temperature, the battery must be fully-charged. The aid of an assistant will also be required.

3 Remove the spark plugs (see Chapter 1A).

4 Fit a compression tester to the No 1 cylinder spark plug hole – the type of tester which screws into the plug thread is to be preferred.

5 Have the assistant hold the throttle wide open, and crank the engine on the starter motor; after one or two revolutions, the compression pressure should build-up to a maximum figure, and then stabilise. Record the highest reading obtained.

6 Repeat the test on the remaining cylinders, recording the pressure in each.

7 All cylinders should produce very similar pressures; a difference of more than 3 bars between any two cylinders indicates a fault. Note that the compression should build-up quickly in a healthy engine; low compression on the first stroke, followed by gradually increasing pressure on successive strokes, indicates worn piston rings. A low compression reading on the first stroke, which does not build-up during successive strokes, indicates leaking valves or a blown head gasket (a cracked head could also be the cause). Deposits on the undersides of the valve heads can also cause low compression.

8 As a guide, any cylinder pressure of below 10 bars can be considered as less than healthy. Refer to a MINI dealer or other specialist if in doubt as to whether a particular pressure reading is acceptable.

9 If the pressure in any cylinder is low, carry out the following test to isolate the cause. Introduce a teaspoonful of clean oil into that cylinder through its spark plug hole, and repeat the test.

10 If the addition of oil temporarily improves the compression pressure, this indicates that bore or piston wear is responsible for the pressure loss. No improvement suggests that leaking or burnt valves, or a blown head gasket, may be to blame.

11 A low reading from two adjacent cylinders is almost certainly due to the head gasket having blown between them; the presence of coolant in the engine oil will confirm this.

12 If one cylinder is about 20 percent lower than the others and the engine has a slightly rough idle; a worn camshaft lobe could be the cause.

13 If the compression reading is unusually high, the combustion chambers are probably coated with carbon deposits. If this is the case, the cylinder head should be removed and decarbonised.

14 On completion of the test, refit the spark plugs (see Chapter 1A).

3   Engine assembly/ valve timing holes – general information and usage

1 This procedure positions the crankshaft in the '90-degree' position so that the pistons are all half-way down in their cylinder bores. This ensures that there will be no valve-to-piston contact when removing the VANOS units, timing chain, or cylinder head. Special tools are required to perform this task (see

3.1 Special tools like these from Auto Service Tools ltd. are needed to set the engine in the reference position

3.3a Rotate the crankshaft until the IN mark on the intake camshaft...

3.3b ...and the EX mark on the exhaust camshaft are pointing upwards

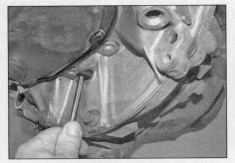

3.4 When the timing hole is aligned with the hole in the flywheel/driveplate, the pin can be inserted to lock the crankshaft in position

3.5a The special camshaft holding tools are bolted in place – N14 engine...

3.5b ...and an N12 engine with Valvetronic

illustration). The special tools include a pin that locks the crankshaft in position and fixtures that are bolted down to the top of the cylinder head, engaging flats on the camshafts, locking them in position.

2 Disconnect the cable from the negative terminal of the battery (see Chapter 5A), then remove the cylinder head cover (see Section 4).

3 Using the crankshaft pulley centre bolt, rotate the engine clockwise until the IN and EX markings at the centre of each camshaft become visible (see illustrations).

4 Locate the hole in the lower cylinder block near the left end of the oil sump (see illustration). Insert MINI special tool no. 11 9 950 through the hole and into its corresponding hole in the flywheel/driveplate. If it won't go in, try turning the crankshaft back and forth a little until the tool can be inserted (it shouldn't take much movement of the crankshaft).

5 At this point, the camshafts must be locked securely in position. While there is no danger of the valves contacting the pistons, there is a danger of intake valves and exhaust valves contacting each other if the VANOS unit(s)/camshaft sprocket are loosened. Also, any procedure requiring the engine to be set at this position will also require the camshafts to be timed to each other and to the crankshaft.

a) If you're working on an N12 or N16 engine, MINI special tool no. 11 9 540 will be required.

b) If you're working on an N14 engine, MINI special tool nos. 11 9 551 and 11 9 552 will be required.

c) If you're working on an N18 engine, MINI special tool no. 11 7 440 will be required.

These tools fit over machined flats near the left ends of the camshaft and bolt to the cylinder head to retain the camshafts in their proper positions (see illustrations). Bolt the camshaft holding tools to the cylinder head.

6 If the camshaft holding tool cannot be installed over one or both camshafts, the VANOS unit or camshaft sprocket bolt at the front of the camshaft will have to be loosened and the camshaft turned slightly so the tool fits. To do this, place a 27 mm open-end spanner on the hex at the left end of the camshaft to counterhold the camshaft while the bolt is being loosened, then turn the camshaft with the spanner until the holding tool engages with the flats on the camshaft (see illustration 6.8).

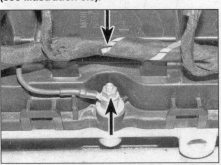

4.3 Unclip the wiring harness and unbolt the earth lead (arrowed)

Caution: Whenever a VANOS unit/camshaft sprocket bolt is loosened, it must be replaced with a new one.

7 Work can now be performed without worry of valve or piston damage, and the camshafts are in proper phasing in relation to the crankshaft. This is the ONLY way to properly set the valve timing for these engines, and if not done correctly, severe and costly engine damage will result. **Note:** *Do not attempt to rotate the engine while the crankshaft/ camshafts are locked in position. If the engine is to be left in this state for a long period of time, it is a good idea to place suitable warning notices inside the vehicle, and in the engine compartment. This will reduce the possibility of the engine being accidentally cranked on the starter motor, which is likely to cause damage with the locking rods/tool in place.*

4 Cylinder head cover – removal and refitting

Removal

1 Remove the air cleaner assembly as described in Chapter 4A.

2 Remove the ignition coils (see Chapter 5B).

Non-turbo engines

3 Unclip the ignition coils wiring harness, and undo the bolt securing the earth lead **(see illustration)**. Position the harness to one side.

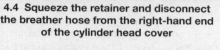

4.4 Squeeze the retainer and disconnect the breather hose from the right-hand end of the cylinder head cover

4.5 Slide the wiring harness guide upwards and place it to one side

4.6 Squeeze the collar (arrowed) and disconnect the crankcase breather hose

4 Detach the crankcase breather hose from the cylinder head cover (**see illustration**).

5 Remove the Camshaft Position (CMP) sensor(s) from the cylinder head cover (see Chapter 4A), then slide up the wiring harness guide at the left-hand end of the cylinder head, and position it to one side (**see illustration**).

Turbocharged engines

6 Disconnect the crankcase breather hose from the cylinder head cover (**see illustration**).

7 Slacken the clamps at each end of the turbo air inlet ducting, disconnect the vacuum hose (**see illustration**).

8 Squeeze together the sides of the locking clip then lift it from place, and pull the breather hose from the cylinder head cover (**see illustration**). Remove the turbo air intake

ducting assembly, disconnecting any wiring plugs as the assembly is withdrawn.

All engines

9 Detach any other wiring harnesses or hoses from the cylinder head cover and disconnect any electrical connectors that would interfere with removal of the cover.

10 Starting at the centre of the cylinder head cover and working outwards, remove the cover retaining fasteners. Note the location of any earth connections. Remove the cover from the cylinder head.

Refitting

11 Thoroughly clean the gasket faces on the cover and the cylinder head, then renew the cover sealing gaskets (**see illustrations**).

12 Apply a thin coat of RTV sealant at the left-hand corners of the cylinder head (**see illustration**).

13 Install the cylinder head cover and bolts. Tighten the bolts a little at a time, in sequence (**see illustration**), to the Specified torque.

14 The remainder of installation is the reverse of removal.

---

5 Crankshaft pulley – removal and refitting

Removal

Caution: This procedure is only for removing the vibration damper/pulley. DO

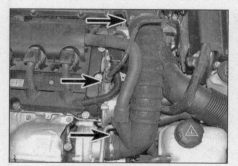

4.7 Depress the release button, disconnect the vacuum hose, and slacken the air duct clamps (arrowed)

4.8 Lift the clip, pull the breather hose from the cylinder head cover (arrowed) and remove the intake ducting assembly

4.11a Renew the cylinder head cover gasket/seals...

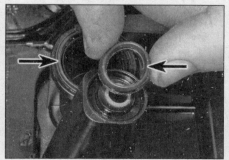

4.11b ...including the small circular seals (arrowed)

4.12 Apply a little sealant a the left-hand corners of the cylinder head surface (arrowed)

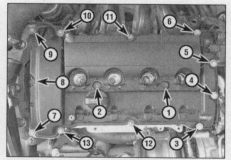

4.13 Cylinder head cover bolt tightening sequence

5.3a Unscrew the retaining bolts...

NOT loosen the crankshaft pulley hub bolt unless the timing chain is to be removed, as crankshaft/camshaft timing will be disturbed and will have to be reset as described in Section 3.

1 Remove the auxiliary drivebelt (Chapter 1A)

2 If required, to prevent the crankshaft turning whilst the pulley retaining bolts are being slackened on manual transmission models, select top gear and have an assistant apply the brakes firmly. On automatic transmission models it will be necessary to remove the starter motor (Chapter 5A) and lock the driveplate with a suitable tool. If the engine has been removed from the vehicle, lock the flywheel ring gear as described in Section 12. *Do not* attempt to lock the pulley by inserting a bolt/drill through the timing hole. If the locking pin is in position, temporarily remove it prior to slackening the pulley bolt, then refit it once the bolt has been slackened.

3 Undo the three crankshaft pulley retaining

6.4a Insert the tool into the cylinder head where the chain tensioner fits

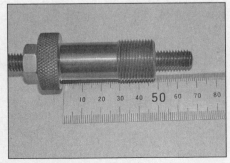

6.4c Make sure the length doesn't exceed 68 mm

5.3b ...and remove the crankshaft pulley

bolts and remove the pulley from the centre hub on the end of the crankshaft (see illustrations).

Refitting

4 Locate the pulley on the hub on the end of the crankshaft, refit the three retaining bolts and tighten them to the specified torque.

5 Refit and tension the auxiliary drivebelt as described in Chapter 1A.

---

6 Timing chain, VANOS unit(s)/ sprocket and tensioner – general information, removal and refitting

General information

1 The timing chain drives the camshafts from a toothed sprocket on the end of the crankshaft.

2 The chain should be replaced if a sprocket or chain is worn, indicated by excessive lateral

6.4b Screw the threaded centre part of the tool in until it contacts the timing chain guide and hand-tighten

6.8 Hold the camshafts in position and slacken the camshaft sprocket/VANOS unit retaining bolts

play between the links and excessive noise in operation. It is wise to replace the chain in any case if the engine is to be disassembled for overhaul. Note that the rollers on a very badly worn chain may be slightly grooved. To avoid future problems, if there is any doubt at all about the condition of the chain, replace it.

3 The timing chain and guides are removed as a complete assembly and are withdrawn out through the top of the cylinder head.

4 To check the wear of the timing chain, a special tool is required. Insert the tool into the cylinder head where the tensioner fits, and tighten the outer part. Run the threaded centre part of the tool in until it contacts the timing chain guide and tighten it hand-tight. Lock the nut on the centre thread and remove the special tool. Check the length of the tool to make sure that it does not exceed 68 mm (see illustrations).

Removal

5 Remove the cylinder head cover (see Section 4).

6 Set the engine in the reference position for the crankshaft and camshaft (see Section 3).

7 Loosen the crankshaft pulley centre hub retaining bolt. To prevent the crankshaft turning while the bolt is being loosened on manual transmission models, select top gear and have an assistant apply the brakes firmly. On automatic transmission models it will be necessary to remove the starter motor (see Chapter 5A) and lock the driveplate with a suitable tool. If the engine has been removed from the vehicle, lock the flywheel ring gear as described in Section 12. Do not attempt to lock the pulley by inserting a bolt/drill through the timing hole. If the locking pin is in position (as shown in illustration 3.4), temporarily remove it prior to loosening the bolt, then install it once the bolt has been loosened. **Note:** *If the crankshaft pulley hub bolt is extremely tight, it will be necessary to obtain a special holding tool with a long handle that bolts in place of the pulley.*

8 Holding the camshafts in position with an open-ended spanner on the flats on the camshaft, loosen the camshaft sprocket/ VANOS unit retaining bolts **(see illustration)**. *Caution: Obtain new VANOS unit/camshaft sprocket bolts; the old ones must NOT be reused.*

9 Remove the crankshaft pulley (see Section 5).

10 Remove the throttle body (see Chapter 4A).

11 Remove the timing chain tensioner from the right-rear corner of the cylinder head (see illustration). Before the tensioner is removed, make sure the camshafts and crankshaft are locked in position as described in Section 3.

12 Undo the bolts and remove the auxiliary drivebelt friction drive **(see illustration)**.

13 Remove the chain guide rail from the top of the cylinder head **(see illustration)**.

14 The front panel must now be moved into the 'assembly' position as follows:

a) Remove the front bumper as described in Chapter 11.

6.11 Unscrew the timing chain tensioner

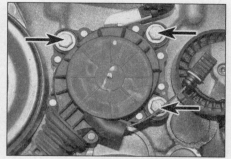

6.12 Undo the bolts (arrowed) and remove the belt friction drive device

6.13 Remove the guide rail from the cylinder head

b) Unplug the air conditioning compressor wiring plug, and release the harness from any clips.
c) Undo the 2 bolts each side securing the front panel to the subframe (see illustration).
d) Remove the bolt each side securing the front panel to the wing (see illustration).
e) Release the coolant pipe from the retaining clips on the front panel.
f) Undo the retaining bolt and move the coolant expansion tank to one side.
g) Detach the air intake ducting gaiter from the front panel.
h) Prise open the junction box on the left-hand support, and disconnect the bonnet release cable (see illustration).
i) Undo the 3 bolts each side securing the front panel/headlight to the suspension turret/front wing (see illustration).
j) On turbocharged models, release the

clamps and disconnect the charge pressure hoses from the intercooler (see illustration).
k) Disconnect the right-hand headlight wiring plug.
l) Screw special tool No. 00 2 271 into the

left-, and right-hand front panel/chassis member sleeve. In the absence of these tools, use 2 lengths of tube, 19 mm outside diameter, at least 120 mm long, with two 8 mm threaded rods at least 150 mm long, and two 8 mm nuts (see illustration).

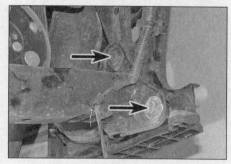

6.14a Front panel-to-subframe bolts (arrowed)

6.14b Undo the bolt (arrowed) securing the front panel to the wing each side

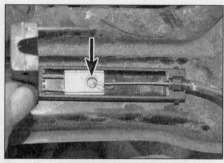

6.14c Open the junction box and disconnect the bonnet release cable (arrowed)

6.14d Remove the headlight bolt, and the panel support-to-suspension turret bolts (arrowed)

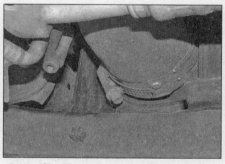

6.14e Slacken the clamp and disconnect the intercooler hose each side

6.14f Screw the tubes/rods through the front panel into the threaded holes in the chassis members

6.14g Undo the 3 nuts (arrowed) each side...

6.14h ...and slide the panel forwards on the tubes

6.15 Remove the engine mounting bracket

6.17a Remove the upper guide securing bolts…

6.17b …and the two lower securing bolts

6.18a Remove the crankshaft hub retaining bolt…

6.18b …and withdraw the hub

16 Remove the alternator as described in Chapter 5A.

17 Remove the timing chain guide retaining bolts **(see illustrations)**.

18 Remove the crankshaft pulley centre bolt and hub **(see illustrations)**.

19 Withdraw the dipstick and remove it from the dipstick tube. The dipstick goes down through the chain guide; if this is not removed, it will prevent the timing chain assembly from being withdrawn out through the cylinder head.

20 Remove the camshaft sprocket/VANOS units from the ends of the camshafts, keeping the timing chain held in position **(see illustrations)**.

Caution: Do not mix-up the VANOS units.
Note: N14 engines only have a VANOS unit on the intake camshaft. The exhaust camshaft uses a traditional timing sprocket.

21 Lift the timing chain and guide assembly out through the top of the cylinder head, complete with crankshaft sprocket **(see illustrations)**.

22 Check the timing chain assembly carefully for any signs of wear. Replace it if there is the slightest doubt about its condition. If the engine is undergoing an overhaul, it is advisable to replace the chain as a matter of course, regardless of its apparent condition.

Refitting

23 Before installing, thoroughly clean the crankshaft and camshaft sprockets/VANOS units; they are a compression fit. The mating faces need to be clean and free from any oil when assembling. Remove all traces of oil with brake system cleaner.

m) Undo the 3 nuts each side, and slide the front panel assembly approximately 10 cm forwards **(see illustrations)**. Take care to ensure no strain is placed on any wiring/hoses.

15 Position a floor jack under the engine, placing a block of wood between the jack head and the oil sump. Take up the weight of the engine, remove the bolts/nuts and remove the right-hand engine mount and bracket **(see illustration)**.

6.20a Remove the retaining bolts…

6.20b …then remove the intake…

6.20c …and exhaust camshaft VANOS units

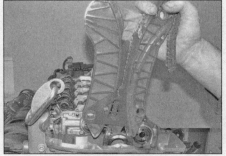

6.21a Withdraw the timing chain guide assembly…

6.21b …complete with crankshaft sprocket

24 Check that the VANOS units are in the rest position **(see illustration)**. If these are not aligned they will have to be replaced.

25 Lower the timing chain assembly down through the top of the cylinder head, complete with crankshaft sprocket **(see illustration)**.

26 Install the crankshaft pulley hub; making sure it engages correctly with the crankshaft timing chain and oil pump sprockets. Tighten the bolt to the torque listed in this Chapter's Specifications, preventing the crankshaft from turning as carried out for removal. If the pin was removed from the lower crankcase/flywheel, reinstall it.

27 Install the timing chain guide retaining bolts and replace the seals/washer.

28 Check that the camshafts and crankshaft are still locked in correct position as described in Section 3.

29 Install the camshaft sprocket/VANOS units to the ends of the camshafts, install the NEW bolts and tighten to the correct torque setting. Make sure the timing chain is located correctly around the sprockets **(see illustration)**. **Note:** *The camshaft sprockets are marked IN for intake and EX for exhaust.*

30 Install the chain guide rail to the top of the cylinder head **(see illustration)**.

31 Install the timing chain tensioner and tighten it to the torque listed in this Chapter's Specifications.

32 Remove the camshaft and crankshaft locking tools, and rotate the crankshaft four complete revolutions clockwise (viewed from the right-hand end of the engine). Realign the engine and install the locking tools to confirm that the timing is still aligned. If not, refer to Section 3. When correct, remove the timing locking tools from the engine.

Caution: Do not attempt to rotate the engine while the locking tools are in position.

33 The remainder of refitting is a reversal of removal.

7 Camshafts and valve assembly – general information

Numerous special tools are required to remove the camshafts or Valvetronic variable valve opening assembly. Consequently, we recommend that this task be entrusted to a MINI dealer or suitably equipped repairer.

Caution: Work on the inlet valve spring mechanism is prohibited as a considerable risk of injury may occur.

8 Cylinder head – removal and refitting

Note: *The cylinder head cannot be stripped (see Section 7); this procedure is for just the removal and refitting of the cylinder head.*

Removal

1 Disconnect the battery (see Chapter 5A).

6.24 Check that the alignment marks are in position

6.25 Lower the crankshaft sprocket (arrowed) and chain into position

6.29 Install the camshaft VANOS units/ sprockets

6.30 Refit the guide rail and bolts (arrowed)

8.5 Depress the release button (arrowed) and disconnect the vacuum hose

Note: *Wait 15 minutes after switching off the ignition before disconnecting the battery, to ensure that the ECU's memory is stored.*

2 Apply the handbrake, then jack up the front of the vehicle and support it on axle stands (see *Jacking and vehicle support*). Undo the screws and remove the engine undershield. For improved access, remove the bonnet as described in Chapter 11.

3 Drain the cooling system as described in Chapter 1A.

4 The front panel must now be moved into the 'assembly' position as follows **(see illustrations 6.14a to 6.14h):**

a) Remove the front bumper as described in Chapter 11.

b) Unplug the air conditioning compressor wiring plug, and release the harness from any clips.

c) Undo the 2 bolts each side securing the front panel to the subframe.

d) Remove the bolt each side securing the front panel to the wing.

e) Release the coolant pipe from the retaining clips on the front panel.

f) Undo the retaining bolt and move the coolant expansion tank to one side.

g) Detach the air intake ducting gaiter from the front panel.

h) Prise open the junction box on the left-hand support, and disconnect the bonnet release cable.

i) Undo the 3 bolts each side securing the front panel/headlight to the suspension turret/front wing.

j) On turbocharged models, slacken the clamps and disconnect the charge pressure hoses from the intercooler.

k) Disconnect the right-hand headlight wiring plug.

l) Screw special tool No. 00 2 271 into the left-, and right-hand front panel/chassis member sleeve. In the absence of these tools, use 2 lengths of tube, 19 mm outside diameter, at least 120 mm long, with two 8 mm threaded rods at least 150 mm long, and two 8 mm nuts.

m) Undo the 3 nuts each side, and slide the front panel assembly approximately 10 cm forwards. Take care to ensure no strain is placed on any wiring/hoses.

5 Disconnect the pipe from the vacuum pump, release the securing clip and move the pipe to one side **(see illustration)**.

6 Disconnect the wiring connectors from the thermostat, temperature sensor and oil pressure sensor on the end of the cylinder head.

8.8 Slide up the wiring harness bracket/ guide

8.9 Disconnect the coolant hoses from the thermostat housing

8.10 Release the wire retaining clip at the rear of the housing

8.11 Detach the thermostat housing from the cylinder head

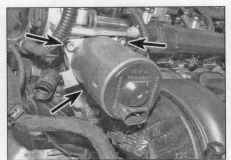

8.12a Undo the retaining bolts (arrowed and),...

8.12b ...using an Allen key, withdraw the Valvetronic actuator from the cylinder head

7 Disconnect the wiring connectors from the camshaft position sensors in the transmission end of the cylinder head cover.

8 Slide the wiring loom bracket upwards from the end of the cylinder head cover and move it to one side (see illustration).

9 Disconnect the four coolant hoses from the thermostat housing (see illustration).

10 Release the retaining clip at the rear of the cylinder head, where the thermostat housing joins the pipe to the coolant pump (see illustration).

11 Undo the retaining bolts and remove the

thermostat housing from the cylinder head and withdraw it from the coolant pump feed pipe (see illustration).

12 Disconnect the wiring connector from the eccentric shaft actuator at the left-hand rear of the cylinder head. Undo the actuator retaining bolts and then remove it from the cylinder head by using a 4 mm Allen key, and turning the centre shaft anti-clockwise, while withdrawing the actuator from the cylinder head (see illustrations).

13 Remove the intake and exhaust manifolds, with reference to Chapter 4A.

14 Remove the timing chain assembly, as described in Section 6.

15 If not already done, undo the retaining bolts and remove the mounting bracket from the right-hand end of the cylinder head. Release the wiring loom and fuel pipes from the securing clips where required (see illustration 6.15).

16 Disconnect the wiring connectors from the inlet and exhaust variable timing electrovalve at the front and rear of the cylinder head at the timing chain end (see illustrations).

17 Slacken and remove the bolt at the right-hand rear of the cylinder head (see illustration).

18 Slacken and remove the two cylinder head bolts at the timing chain end of the cylinder head (see illustration).

19 Progressively slacken and remove the remaining ten cylinder head bolts starting from the middle and spiralling outwards.

20 With all the cylinder head bolts removed, the joint between the cylinder head and gasket, and the cylinder block/crankcase must

8.16a Disconnect the wiring plug from the exhaust VANOS solenoid...

8.16b ...and the intake VANOS solenoid

8.17 Right-hand rear cylinder head bolt (arrowed)

8.18 Cylinder head securing bolts (arrowed)

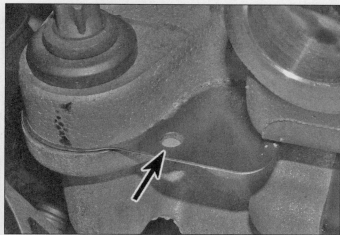

8.23 Cylinder head gasket thickness markings (arrowed)

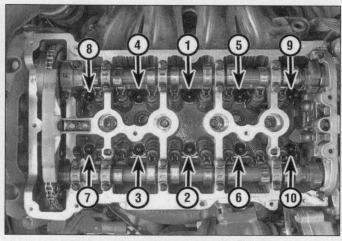

8.31 Cylinder head bolt tightening sequence

now be broken. Carefully 'rock' the cylinder head free towards the front of the car. *Do not try to swivel the head on the cylinder block/crankcase; it is located by dowels*. When the joint is broken, lift the cylinder head away. Use a hoist or seek assistance if possible, as it is a heavy assembly. Remove the gasket from the top of the block, noting the two locating dowels. If the locating dowels are a loose fit, remove them and store them with the head for safe-keeping. Do not discard the gasket; it will be needed for identification purposes.

Preparation for refitting

21 The mating faces of the cylinder head and cylinder block/crankcase must be perfectly clean before refitting the head. Use a hard plastic or wooden scraper to remove all traces of gasket and carbon and also clean the piston crowns. Make sure that the carbon is not allowed to enter the oil and water passages – this is particularly important for the lubrication system, as carbon could block the oil supply to the engine's components. Using adhesive tape and paper, seal the water, oil and bolt holes in the cylinder block/crankcase. To prevent carbon entering the gap between the pistons and bores, smear a little grease in the gap. After cleaning each piston, use a small brush to remove all traces of grease and carbon from the gap, and then wipe away the remainder with a clean rag. Clean all the pistons in the same way.

22 Check the mating surfaces of the cylinder block/crankcase and the cylinder head for nicks, deep scratches and other damage. If slight, they may be removed carefully with a file, but if excessive, machining may be the only alternative to renewal. If warpage of the cylinder head gasket surface is suspected, use a straight-edge to check it for distortion. Refer to Part D of this Chapter if necessary.

23 Obtain a new cylinder head gasket before starting the refitting procedure. There are different thicknesses available – check the old head gasket for markings on the

rear right-hand side of the gasket **(see illustration)**. Note that modifications to the cylinder head gasket material, type, and manufacturer are constantly taking place; seek the advice of a MINI dealer as to the latest recommendations.

24 Due to the stress that the cylinder head bolts are under, it is highly recommended that they be renewed along with the washers, regardless of their apparent condition.

Refitting

25 Wipe clean the mating surfaces of the cylinder head and cylinder block/crankcase. Check that the two locating dowels are in position at each end of the cylinder block/crankcase surface.

26 Position a new gasket on the cylinder block/crankcase surface.

27 Check that the crankshaft pulley and camshaft sprockets are still at their locked positions (see Section 3).

28 With the aid of an assistant, carefully lower the cylinder head assembly onto the block, aligning it with the locating dowels.

29 Apply a smear of grease to the threads, and to the underside of the heads, of the cylinder head bolts. MINI recommend the use of Molykote G Rapid Plus (available from your MINI dealer); in the absence of the specified grease, any good-quality high melting-point grease may be used.

30 Carefully enter each of the new bolts and washers into the relevant hole (*do not drop them in*) and then screw them in finger-tight.

31 Working progressively tighten the main ten cylinder head bolts starting from the middle and spiraling outwards **(see illustration)**. Then tighten the two bolts at the timing chain end of the cylinder head and the one at the rear of the head. Tighten all the cylinder head bolts to their Stage 1 torque setting.

32 Once all the bolts have been tightened to their Stage 1 torque setting, proceed to tighten them through the remaining stages as given in the Specifications. It is recommended that an

angle-measuring gauge be used for the angle-tightening stages, however, if a gauge is not available, use white paint to make alignment marks between the bolt head and cylinder head prior to tightening; the marks can then be used to check that the bolt has rotated sufficiently. Each step must be completed in one movement without stopping.

33 The remainder of the refitting procedure is a reversal of removal, referring to the relevant Chapters or Sections as required. On completion, refill the cooling system as described in Chapter 1A. Initialise the engine management ECU as follows. Start the engine and run to normal temperature. Carry out a road test during which the following procedure should be made. Engage third gear and stabilise the engine at 1000 rpm. Now accelerate fully to 3500 rpm.

9 Sump – removal and refitting

Removal

1 Apply the handbrake, then jack up the front of the vehicle and support it on axle stands (see *Jacking and vehicle support*). Undo the screws and remove the engine undershield (if fitted).

2 Drain the engine oil then clean and refit the engine oil drain plug, tightening it securely. If the engine is nearing its service interval when the oil and filter are due for renewal, it is recommended that the filter is also removed, and a new one fitted. After reassembly, the engine can then be refilled with fresh oil. Refer to Chapter 1A for further information.

3 Withdraw the engine oil dipstick from the guide tube.

4 Undo the two retaining bolts and remove the mounting plate (where fitted) from the rear of the sump **(see illustration)**.

5 Progressively slacken and remove all of the sump retaining bolts. Make a note of the fitting

9.4 Remove the bolts (arrowed) at the rear of the sump

9.6 Remove the oil sump

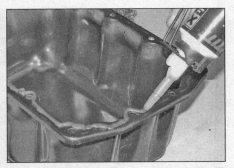

9.10 Apply a thin bead of sealant to the oil sump mating surface

position of the bolts, as they may be different lengths. This will avoid the possibility of installing the bolts in the wrong locations on refitting.

6 Break the joint by striking the sump with the palm of your hand. Lower the sump, and withdraw it from underneath the vehicle **(see illustration)**. While the sump is removed, take the opportunity to check the oil pump pick-up/strainer for signs of clogging or splitting. If necessary, remove the pump as described in Section 10, and clean or renew the strainer. If required, unbolt the oil baffle plate from the bottom of the main bearing ladder, noting which way round it is fitted.

Refitting

7 Where removed, refit the baffle plate to the main bearing ladder and tighten the bolts securely.

8 Where removed, refit the oil pump and pick-up/strainer with reference to Section 10.

9 Clean all traces of sealant/gasket from the mating surfaces of the main bearing ladder and sump, and then use a clean rag to wipe out the sump and the engine's interior.

10 Ensure that the sump mating surfaces are clean and dry, and then apply a thin coating of suitable sealant (MINI part No. 83 19 0 404 517 or Loctite 5970 liquid gasket) to the sump mating surface **(see illustration)**.

11 Refit the sump onto the main bearing ladder and insert the bolts and finger-tighten them at this stage, so that it is still possible to move the sump. Make sure the bolts are refitted in their correct locations.

12 Refit the mounting plate to the rear of the sump and tighten all the retaining bolts.

13 Check that the oil drain plug is tightened securely, then refit the engine undershield (where applicable) and lower the vehicle to the ground.

14 Refit the dipstick and refill the engine with oil as described in Chapter 1A.

10 Oil pump – removal, inspection and refitting

Removal

1 Remove the sump as described in Section 9.

2 Unclip the cover from the oil pump drive sprocket **(see illustration)**.

3 Slacken and remove the drive sprocket retaining bolt, withdraw the sprocket from the drive chain **(see illustration)**.

4 On N16 and N18 engines, disconnect the wiring plug, unclip the harness, undo the retaining screw, remove the sealing plate and feed the harness and centre plate through the hole in the cylinder block.

5 Undo the oil pump retaining bolts and withdraw the pump from the bottom of main bearing ladder **(see illustration)**.

Inspection

6 At the time of writing, checking specifications for the oil pump were not available, however, clean the pump and inspect it for damage and excessive wear.

7 Thoroughly clean the oil pump strainer with a suitable solvent, and check it for signs of clogging or splitting. If the strainer is damaged, the strainer and cover assembly must be renewed.

8 If the oil pump drive chain needs renewing, the timing chain assembly will need to be removed first as described in Section 6. The chain is around a sprocket on the end of the crankshaft, at the rear of the crankshaft sprocket for the timing chain **(see illustration)**.

Refitting

9 Clean the mating surfaces of the oil pump and main bearing ladder/cylinder block and fit the retaining bolts. Tighten to the specified torque setting.

10 Locate the sprocket onto the pump making sure it is located correctly in the drive chain. Tighten the sprocket retaining bolt securely.

11 The remainder of refitting is a reversal of removal. Before starting the engine, prime the oil pump as follows. Disconnect the fuel injector wiring connectors, and then turn the engine over on the starter motor until the oil

10.2 Unclip the cover...

10.3 ...and remove the sprocket retaining bolt (arrowed)

10.5 Undo the oil pump housing retaining bolts

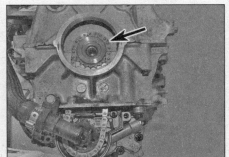

10.8 Oil pump drive chain sprocket (arrowed)

11.2 Check the depth of the fitted oil seal

11.5 Locate the oil seal and fitting sleeve over the end of the crankshaft

11.6 Tap the seal squarely into position

pressure warning light goes out. Reconnect the injector wiring on completion.

11 Crankshaft oil seals – renewal

Right-hand oil seal

1 Remove the crankshaft pulley, with reference to Section 5.
2 Check the depth of the seal in the engine casing before removing **(see illustration)**.
3 Punch or drill two small holes opposite each other in the seal. Screw a self-tapping screw into each, and pull on the screws with pliers to extract the seal **(see illustrations 11.10a and 11.10b)**. Alternatively, the seal can be levered out of position. Use a flat-bladed screwdriver, and take great care not to damage the crankshaft shoulder or seal housing.

4 Clean the seal housing, and polish off any burrs or raised edges which may have caused the seal to fail in the first place.
5 Lubricate the lips of the new seal with clean engine oil, and carefully locate the seal on the end of the crankshaft. The new seal will normally be supplied with a plastic fitting sleeve to protect the seal lips as the seal is fitted. If so, lubricate the fitting sleeve and locate it over the end of the crankshaft **(see illustration)**.
6 Fit the new seal using a suitable tubular drift, which bears only on the hard outer edge of the seal. Tap the seal into position, to the same depth in the housing as the original was prior to removal **(see illustration)**.
7 Wash off any traces of oil, then refit the crankshaft pulley as described in Section 5.

Left-hand oil seal

8 Remove the flywheel/driveplate and

crankshaft timing plate, as described in Section 12.
9 Make a note of the correct fitted depth of the seal in its housing **(see illustration 11.2)**.
10 Punch or drill two small holes opposite each other in the seal. Screw a self-tapping screw into each, and pull on the screws with pliers to extract the seal **(see illustrations)**.
11 Clean the seal housing, and polish off any burrs or raised edges which may have caused the seal to fail in the first place **(see illustration)**.
12 Lubricate the lips of the new seal with clean engine oil, and carefully locate the seal on the end of the crankshaft. The new seal will normally be supplied with a plastic fitting sleeve to protect the seal lips as the seal is fitted. If so, lubricate the fitting sleeve and locate it over the end of the crankshaft **(see illustrations)**.
13 Before driving the seal fully into position, put a small amount of sealer at each side

11.10a Drill a hole...

11.10b ...then use a self-tapping screw and pliers to extract the oil seal

11.11 Clean out the recess

11.12a The new oil seal comes with a protective sleeve...

11.12b ...which fits over the end of the crankshaft

11.13 Apply a small amount of sealant at the casing joints

12.2 Use a tool to lock the flywheel ring gear and prevent rotation

12.3b ...and remove the flywheel

12.3a Slacken the retaining bolts...

12.4 Remove the TDC timing plate from the crankshaft

check the torque converter driveplate carefully for signs of distortion. Look for any hairline cracks around the bolt holes or radiating outwards from the centre, and inspect the ring gear teeth for signs of wear or chipping. If any sign of wear or damage is found, the driveplate must be renewed.

11 Check the crankshaft TDC timing plate for any damage; make sure that none of the teeth around the circumference of the disc are bent.

Refitting

Flywheel

12 Clean the mating surfaces of the flywheel and crankshaft. Remove any remaining locking compound from the threads of the crankshaft holes, using the correct-size tap, if available.

13 If the new flywheel retaining bolts are not supplied with their threads already pre-coated, apply a suitable thread-locking compound to the threads of each bolt.

14 If removed, refit the crankshaft TDC timing plate to the end of the crankshaft.

15 Ensure the locating dowel is in position. Offer up the flywheel, locating it on the dowel, and fit the new retaining bolts.

16 Lock the flywheel using the method employed on dismantling, and tighten the retaining bolts to the specified torque and angle.

17 Refit the clutch as described in Chapter 6. Remove the flywheel locking tool, and refit the transmission as described in Chapter 7A.

Driveplate

18 Carry out the operations described above in paragraphs 12 and 13, substituting 'driveplate' for all references to the flywheel.

19 If removed, refit the crankshaft TDC timing plate to the end of the crankshaft.

20 Locate the driveplate on its locating dowel.

21 Offer up the torque converter plate, with the thinner shim positioned behind the plate and the thicker shim on the outside, and align the marks made prior to removal.

22 Fit the new retaining bolts, then lock the driveplate using the method employed on dismantling. Tighten the retaining bolts to the specified torque wrench setting and angle.

23 Remove the driveplate locking tool, and refit the transmission as described in Chapter 7B.

13 Engine/transmission mountings – inspection and renewal

Inspection

1 If improved access is required, raise the front of the car and support it on axle stands (see *Jacking and vehicle support*).

2 Check the mounting rubber to see if it is cracked, hardened or separated from the metal at any point; renew the mounting if any such damage or deterioration is evident.

of the seal, where the upper and lower crankcases meet **(see illustration)**. Drive the seal into position, to the same depth in the housing as the original was prior to removal.

14 Clean off any excess sealer or oil and then refit the crankshaft timing plate and flywheel/driveplate as described in Section 12.

12 Flywheel/driveplate – removal, inspection and refitting

Removal

Flywheel

1 Remove the transmission as described in Chapter 7A, then remove the clutch assembly as described in Chapter 6.

2 Prevent the crankshaft from turning by locking the flywheel with a wide-bladed screwdriver between the ring gear teeth and the transmission casing. Alternatively, bolt a strap between the flywheel and the cylinder block/crankcase **(see illustration)**. *Do not* attempt to lock the flywheel in position using the crankshaft pulley locking pin described in Section 3.

3 Slacken and remove the flywheel retaining bolts, and remove the flywheel from the end of the crankshaft **(see illustrations)**. Be careful not to drop it; it is heavy. If the flywheel locating dowel is a loose fit in the crankshaft end, remove it and store it with the flywheel for safe-keeping. Discard the flywheel bolts; new ones must be used on refitting.

4 If required, remove the crankshaft TDC

timing plate from the end of the crankshaft **(see illustration)**.

Driveplate

5 Remove the transmission as described in Chapter 7B. Lock the driveplate as described in paragraph 2. Mark the relationship between the torque converter plate and the driveplate, and slacken all the driveplate retaining bolts.

6 Remove the retaining bolts, along with the torque converter plate and (where fitted) the two shims (one fitted on each side of the torque converter plate). Note that the shims are of different thickness, the thicker one being on the outside of the torque converter plate. Discard the driveplate retaining bolts; new ones must be used on refitting.

7 Remove the driveplate from the end of the crankshaft. If the locating dowel is a loose fit in the crankshaft end, remove it and store it with the driveplate for safe-keeping.

8 If required remove the crankshaft TDC timing plate from the end of the crankshaft.

Inspection

9 On models with manual transmission, examine the flywheel for scoring of the clutch face, and for wear or chipping of the ring gear teeth. If the clutch face is scored, the flywheel may be surface-ground, but renewal is preferable. Seek the advice of a MINI dealer or engine reconditioning specialist to see if machining is possible. If the ring gear is worn or damaged, the flywheel must be renewed, as it is not possible to renew the ring gear separately.

10 On models with automatic transmission,

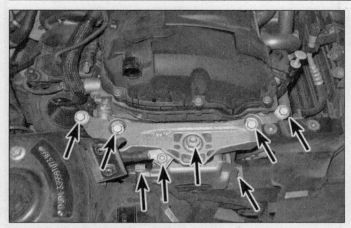

13.6a Undo the nut/bolts securing the mounting bracket. Note the earth lead (arrowed)

13.6b Right-hand engine mounting retaining bolts (arrowed)

3 Check that all the mounting's fasteners are securely tightened; use a torque wrench to check if possible.

4 Using a large screwdriver or a crowbar, check for wear in the mounting by carefully levering against it to check for free play. Where this is not possible, enlist the aid of an assistant to move the engine/transmission back-and-forth, or from side-to-side, while you watch the mounting. While some free play is to be expected even from new components, excessive wear should be obvious. If excessive free play is found, check first that the fasteners are secure, and then renew any worn components as described below.

Renewal

Right-hand mounting

5 Place a jack beneath the engine, with a block of wood on the jack head. Raise the jack until it is supporting the weight of the engine. On turbocharged models, remove the right-hand side charge air duct.

6 Slacken and remove the bolts/nuts securing the mounting bracket, then remove mounting from the body (see illustrations).

7 If required, undo the bolts and remove the bracket from the cylinder head (see illustration). Release the wiring loom and fuel lines from the retaining clips as it is removed.

8 Check for signs of wear or damage on all components, and renew as necessary.

9 On reassembly, refit the bracket to the cylinder head, tightening the bolts to the specified torque.

10 Install the mounting and mounting bracket and tighten its retaining bolts to the specified torque setting.

11 Remove the jack from under the engine.

Left-hand mounting

12 Remove the engine control unit as described in Chapter 4A, then unbolt and reposition the underbonnet fuse and relay box.

13 Place a jack beneath the transmission, with a block of wood on the jack head. Raise

the jack until it is supporting the weight of the transmission.

14 Remove the mounting bracket-to-body bolts, the refrigerant pipe bracket and the bracket-to-mounting nut (see illustration). Note: The mounting bracket-to-body bolts may be either grade 8.8 or 10.9 (cast into the head of the bolt). MINI insist that the grade 8.8 bolts must be replaced with grade 10.9 bolts.

15 Undo the four retaining bolts from the mounting bracket on the body and remove the mounting from the engine compartment (see illustration).

16 Check carefully for signs of wear or damage on all components, and renew them where necessary.

13.7 Remove the mounting bracket from the cylinder head

13.15 Mounting-to-transmission bolts (arrowed)

17 Fit the mounting bolts to the bracket on the transmission and tighten the retaining bolts to the specified torque.

18 Refit the mounting bracket to the vehicle body and tighten its bolts/nut to the specified torque.

19 The remainder of refitting is a reversal of removal.

Rear lower mounting

20 If not already done, firmly apply the handbrake, then jack up the front of the vehicle and support it securely on axle stands (see Jacking and vehicle support).

21 Unscrew and remove the bolt securing the rear mounting link to the bracket on the engine (see illustration).

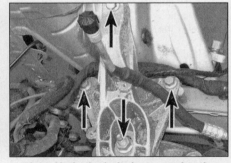

13.14 Undo the bolts/nut securing the left-hand mounting bracket (arrowed)

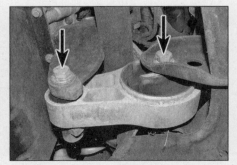

13.21 Rear lower mounting bolts (arrowed)

14.3 Oil pressure warning switch (arrowed) – N12 and N14 engines

14.8 Oil pressure warning switch (arrowed) – N16 and N18 engines

22 Remove the bolt securing the rear mounting link to the subframe and remove the mounting torque reaction link.

23 To remove the mounting bracket, remove the right-hand driveshaft (Chapter 8), then undo the retaining bolts and remove the mounting bracket from the rear of the engine.

24 Check carefully for signs of wear or damage on all components, and renew them where necessary.

25 On reassembly, fit the rear mounting bracket to the transmission, and tighten its retaining bolts to the specified torque.

26 Refit the rear mounting torque reaction link, and tighten both its bolts to their specified torque settings.

27 Lower the vehicle to the ground.

14 Oil pressure warning light switch – removal and refitting

Removal

N12 engine

1 Remove the air intake duct from the left-hand end of the cylinder head.

2 Disconnect the camshaft position sensors

wiring plugs, unlock and disconnect the vacuum hose, then pull the wiring harness duct upwards **(see illustration 8.8)**. Disconnect any other wiring plugs as necessary to gain access to the switch.

3 Unscrew the switch from the cylinder block, and recover the sealing washer **(see illustration)**. Be prepared for oil spillage, and if the switch is to be left removed from the engine for any length of time, plug the hole in the cylinder head.

N14 engine

4 The switch is fitted to the left-hand end of the cylinder head. Release the clamps and move the turbocharger air intake hose to one side.

5 Disconnect the camshaft position sensor wiring plug, unlock and disconnect the vacuum hose, then pull the wiring harness duct upwards **(see illustration 8.8)**. Disconnect any other wiring plugs as necessary to gain access to the switch.

6 Unscrew the switch from the cylinder block, and recover the sealing washer **(see illustration 14.3)**. Be prepared for oil spillage, and if the switch is to be left removed from the engine for any length of time, plug the hole in the cylinder head.

N16 engine

7 The switch is fitted to the oil filter housing

at the front of the engine. Undo the retaining bolts and remove the heat shield above the exhaust manifold.

8 Disconnect the wiring plug, and unscrew the switch **(see illustration)**. Recover the sealing washer. Be prepared for fluid spillage, and if the switch is to be left removed from the engine for any length of time, plug the hole.

N18 engine

9 The switch is fitted to the oil filter housing at the front of the engine. Remove the radiator cooling fan as described in Chapter 3.

10 Disconnect the wiring plug, then unscrew the switch **(see illustration 14.8)**. Recover the sealing washer. Be prepared for fluid spillage, and if the switch is to be left removed from the engine for any length of time, plug the hole.

Refitting

11 Examine the sealing washer for signs of damage or deterioration and if necessary renew.

12 Refit the switch, complete with washer, and tighten it to the specified torque. Reconnect the wiring connector.

13 The remainder of refitting is a reversal of removal. Top up the engine oil as described in *Weekly checks*.

Chapter 2 Part B:
W16 diesel engine in-car repair procedures

Contents

Degrees of difficulty

Easy, suitable for novice with little experience	Fairly easy, suitable for beginner with some experience	Fairly difficult, suitable for competent DIY mechanic	Difficult, suitable for experienced DIY mechanic	Very difficult, suitable for expert DIY or professional

Specifications

General

Engine code*	W16
Capacity	1560 cc
Bore	75.0 mm
Stroke	88.3 mm
Direction of crankshaft rotation	Clockwise (viewed from the right-hand side of vehicle)
Maximum power output	81 kW @ 4000 rpm
Maximum torque output	245 Nm @ 2000 rpm
Compression ratio	18.0 :1

* The engine code is stamped on a plate attached to the front of the cylinder block, next to the oil filter.

Compression pressures (engine hot, at cranking speed)

Normal	20 ± 5 bar
Minimum.	15 bar
Maximum difference between any two cylinders.	4 bar

Camshaft

Drive:	
Inlet camshaft.	Toothed belt from crankshaft
Exhaust camshaft.	Chain-drive from inlet camshaft
Number of teeth	19
Length:	
Inlet camshaft.	401.0 ± 0.15 mm
Exhaust camshaft.	389.0 ± 0.5 mm
Endfloat	0.195 to 0.300 mm

Lubrication system

Oil pump type.	Gear-type, driven directly by the right-hand end of the crankshaft, by two flats machined along the crankshaft journal
Minimum oil pressure at 80°C:	
1000 rpm	1.3 bar
4000 rpm	3.5 bar

Torque wrench settings

	Nm	lbf ft
Ancillary drivebelt tensioner roller	20	15
Big-end bolts:*		
Stage 1.	10	7
Stage 2.	Slacken 180°	
Stage 3.	30	22
Stage 4.	Angle-tighten a further 140°	
Bonnet slam panel-to-body	22	17

Torque wrench settings (continued)

	Nm	lbf ft
Camshaft bearing caps	10	7
Camshaft cover/bearing ladder:		
Studs	10	7
Bolts	10	7
Camshaft position sensor bolt	5	4
Camshaft sprocket:		
Stage 1	20	15
Stage 2	Angle-tighten a further 50°	
Coolant outlet housing bolts	7	5
Crankshaft position/speed sensor bolt	5	4
Crankshaft pulley/sprocket bolt*:		
Stage 1	35	26
Stage 2	Angle-tighten a further 190 °	
Cylinder head bolts*:		
Stage 1	20	15
Stage 2	40	30
Stage 3	Angle-tighten a further 260°	
Cylinder head cover/manifold	10	7
Driveplate bolts*:		
Stage 1	8	6
Stage 2	17	13
Stage 3	Angle-tighten a further 75°	
EGR valve	10	7
Engine-to-transmission fixing bolts	60	44
Flywheel bolt:*		
Stage 1	8	6
Stage 2	30	22
Stage 3	Angle-tighten a further 90°	
Fuel pump sprocket	50	37
Left-hand engine/transmission mounting:		
Mounting bracket to transmission	55	41
Mounting to bracket	60	44
Main bearing ladder outer seam bolts:		
Stage 1	5	4
Stage 2	10	7
Main bearing ladder to cylinder block:		
Stage 1	10	7
Stage 2	Slacken 180°	
Stage 3	30	22
Stage 4	Angle-tighten a further 140°	
Piston oil jet spray tube bolt	20	15
Oil filter cover	25	18
Oil pick-up pipe	10	7
Oil pressure switch	20	15
Oil pump to cylinder block	10	7
Rear engine/transmission mounting:		
Connecting link to mounting assembly	60	44
Connecting link-to-subframe nut/bolt	60	44
Mounting to engine	55	41
Right-hand engine mounting:		
Bracket-to-mounting M12 nut	100	74
Mounting bracket-to-support bracket:		
M10 grade 8.8	38	27
M10 grade 10.9	56	41
Support bracket-to-engine	41	30
Mounting-to-body:		
M12	68	50
M10	68	50
Sump drain plug	30	22
Sump bolts/nuts	12	9
Timing belt idler pulley	35	26
Timing belt tensioner pulley	30	22
Timing chain tensioner	10	7
Vacuum pump:		
Stage 1	18	13
Stage 2	Angle-tighten a further 5°	

Do not re-use

1 General information

How to use this Chapter

This Part of Chapter 2 describes the repair procedures that can reasonably be carried out on the engine whilst it remains in the vehicle. If the engine has been removed from the vehicle and is being dismantled as described in Part D, any preliminary dismantling procedures can be ignored.

Note that, while it may be possible physically to overhaul items such as the piston/connecting rod assemblies while the engine is in the car, such tasks are not usually carried out as separate operations. Usually, several additional procedures are required (not to mention the cleaning of components and oilways); for this reason, all such tasks are classed as major overhaul procedures, and are described in Part D of this Chapter.

Part D describes the removal of the engine/transmission from the car, and the full overhaul procedures that can then be carried out.

W16 series engines

The W16 series engine (fitted from 2007 to 2010) is the result of development collaboration between MINI/Citroën and MINI/BMW. The engine is of double overhead camshaft (DOHC) 16-valve design. The direct injection, turbocharged, four-cylinder engine is mounted transversely, with the transmission mounted on the left-hand side.

A toothed timing belt drives the inlet camshaft, high-pressure fuel pump and coolant pump. The inlet camshaft drives the exhaust camshaft via a chain. The camshafts operate the inlet and exhaust valves via rocker arms, which are supported at their pivot ends by hydraulic self-adjusting followers. The camshafts are supported by bearings machined directly in the cylinder head and camshaft bearing housing.

The high-pressure fuel pump supplies fuel to the fuel rail, and subsequently to the electronically-controlled injectors that inject the fuel direct into the combustion chambers. This design differs from the previous type where an injection pump supplies the fuel at high pressure to each injector. The earlier, conventional type injection pump required fine calibration and timing, and these functions are now completed by the high-pressure pump, electronic injectors and engine management ECM.

The crankshaft runs in five main bearings of the usual shell type. Endfloat is controlled by thrustwashers either side of No 2 main bearing.

The pistons are selected to be of matching weight, and incorporate fully floating gudgeon pins retained by circlips.

Repair operations precaution

The engine is a complex unit with numerous accessories and ancillary components. The design of the engine compartment is such that every conceivable space has been utilised, and access to virtually all of the engine components is extremely limited. In many cases, ancillary components will have to be removed, or moved to one side, and wiring, pipes and hoses will have to be disconnected or removed from various cable clips and support brackets.

When working on this engine, read through the entire procedure first, look at the car and engine at the same time, and establish whether you have the necessary tools, equipment, skill and patience to proceed. Allow considerable time for any operation, and be prepared for the unexpected.

Because of the limited access, many of the engine photographs appearing in this Chapter were, by necessity, taken with the engine removed from the vehicle.

> ⚠ **Warning: It is essential to observe strict precautions when working on the fuel system components of the engine, particularly the high-pressure side of the system. Before carrying out any engine operations that entail working on, or near, any part of the fuel system, refer to the special information given in Chapter 4B.**

Operations with engine in vehicle

a) *Compression pressure – testing.*
b) *Cylinder head cover – removal and refitting.*
c) *Crankshaft pulley – removal and refitting.*
d) *Timing belt covers – removal and refitting.*
e) *Timing belt – removal, refitting and adjustment.*
f) *Timing belt tensioner and sprockets – removal and refitting.*
g) *Camshaft oil seal – renewal.*
h) *Camshaft, rocker arms and hydraulic followers – removal, inspection and refitting.*
i) *Sump – removal and refitting.*
j) *Oil pump – removal and refitting.*
k) *Crankshaft oil seals – renewal.*
l) *Engine/transmission mountings – inspection and renewal.*
m) *Flywheel – removal, inspection and refitting.*

2 Compression and leakdown tests – description and interpretation

Compression test

Note: *A compression tester specifically designed for diesel engines must be used for this test.*

1 When engine performance is down, or if misfiring occurs which cannot be attributed to the fuel system, a compression test can provide diagnostic clues as to the engine's condition. If the test is performed regularly, it can give warning of trouble before any other symptoms become apparent. **Note:** *Carrying out this test as described may result in fault codes being stored in the engine management ECU. These codes must be erased using dedicated test equipment/fault code scanner. Consult a MINI dealer or suitably equipped repairer.*

2 A compression tester specifically intended for diesel engines must be used, because of the higher pressures involved. The tester is connected to an adapter, which screws into the glow plug or injector hole. On this engine, an adapter suitable for use in the glow plug holes will be required, so as not to disturb the fuel system components. It is unlikely to be worthwhile buying such a tester for occasional use, but it may be possible to borrow or hire one – if not, have the test performed by a garage.

3 Unless specific instructions to the contrary are supplied with the tester, observe the following points:

a) *The battery must be in a good state of charge, the air filter must be clean, and the engine should be at normal operating temperature.*
b) *All the glow plugs should be removed as described in Chapter 5C before starting the test.*
c) *The fuel injector wiring plugs must be disconnected (see Chapter 4B).*

4 The compression pressures measured are not so important as the balance between cylinders. Values are given in the Specifications.

5 The cause of poor compression is less easy to establish on a diesel engine than on a petrol engine. The effect of introducing oil into the cylinders ('wet' testing) is not conclusive, because there is a risk that the oil will sit in the swirl chamber or in the recess on the piston crown instead of passing to the rings. However, the following can be used as a rough guide to diagnosis.

6 All cylinders should produce very similar pressures; any difference greater than that specified indicates the existence of a fault. Note that the compression should build-up quickly in a healthy engine; low compression on the first stroke, followed by gradually increasing pressure on successive strokes, indicates worn piston rings. A low compression reading on the first stroke, which does not build-up during successive strokes, indicates leaking valves or a blown head gasket (a cracked head could also be the cause). Deposits on the undersides of the valve heads can also cause low compression.

7 A low reading from two adjacent cylinders is almost certainly due to the head gasket having blown between them; the presence of coolant in the engine oil will confirm this.

8 If the compression reading is unusually high, the cylinder head surfaces, valves and pistons are probably coated with carbon deposits. If this is the case, the cylinder head should be removed and decarbonised (see Part D of this Chapter).

3.8 Insert a 5.0 mm drill bit/rod through the round hole in the sprocket flange into the hole in the oil pump housing (timing cover removed for clarity)

3.9 Insert an 8.0 mm drill bit/rod through the hole in the camshaft sprocket into the hole in the cylinder head

3.10 Insert a 5.0 mm drill bit/rod through the hole in the fuel pump sprocket into the hole in the cylinder block (arrowed)

Leakdown test

9 A leakdown test measures the rate at which compressed air fed into the cylinder is lost. It is an alternative to a compression test, and in many ways it is better, since the escaping air provides easy identification of where pressure loss is occurring (piston rings, valves or head gasket).

10 The equipment needed for leakdown testing is unlikely to be available to the home mechanic. If poor compression is suspected, have the test performed by a suitably-equipped garage.

3 Engine assembly/ valve timing holes – general information and usage

Note: *Do not attempt to rotate the engine whilst the crankshaft and camshaft are locked in position. If the engine is to be left in this state for a long period of time, it is a good idea to place suitable warning notices inside the vehicle, and in the engine compartment. This will reduce the possibility of the engine being accidentally cranked on the starter motor, which is likely to cause damage with the locking pins in place.*

1 Timing holes or slots are located only in the crankshaft pulley flange and camshaft sprocket hub. The holes/slots are used to position the pistons halfway up the cylinder bores. This will ensure that the valve timing is maintained during operations that require

removal and refitting of the timing belt. When the holes/slots are aligned with their corresponding holes in the cylinder block and cylinder head, suitable diameter bolts/pins can be inserted to lock the crankshaft in position, preventing rotation.

2 Note that the fuel system used on these engines does not have a conventional diesel injection pump, but instead uses a high-pressure fuel pump. Although it may be argued that timing of the fuel pump is irrelevant because it merely pressurises the fuel in the fuel rail, MINI include this procedure, using the same timing rod/pin used for crankshaft sprocket timing. In addition, note that the hole in the fuel pump sprocket only aligns correctly with the hole in the mounting bracket every 12 revolutions of the crankshaft (or every 6 revolutions of the camshaft sprocket).

3 To align the engine assembly/valve timing holes, proceed as follows.

4 Chock the rear wheels then jack up the front of the vehicle and support it on axle stands (see *Jacking and vehicle support*). Remove the right-hand front roadwheel.

5 Remove the crankshaft pulley as described in Section 5.

6 Remove the upper and lower timing belt covers as described in Section 6.

7 Temporarily refit the crankshaft pulley bolt, remove the crankshaft locking tool, and then turn the crankshaft until the timing hole in the camshaft sprocket hub is aligned with the corresponding hole in the cylinder head. Note that the crankshaft must always be turned

in a clockwise direction (viewed from the right-hand side of vehicle). Use a small mirror so that the position of the sprocket hub timing slot can be observed. When the slot is aligned with the corresponding hole in the cylinder head, the camshaft is positioned correctly.

8 Insert a 5 mm diameter bolt, rod or drill through the hole in the crankshaft sprocket flange and into the corresponding hole in the oil pump **(see illustration)**, if necessary, carefully turn the crankshaft either way until the rod enters the hole in the block.

9 Insert an 8 mm bolt, rod or drill through the hole in the camshaft sprocket hub and into engagement with the cylinder head **(see illustration)**.

10 If using this procedure during refitting of the timing belt, insert a 5 mm diameter bolt, rod or drill through the hole in the fuel pump sprocket and into the corresponding hole in the cylinder head **(see illustration)**. Note the comment in paragraph 2 – if the fuel pump sprocket holes are not aligned during removal of the timing belt, it is of no consequence, however it is important to align the holes during the refitting procedure. If timing alignment alone is being checked there is no need to check alignment of the pump sprocket.

11 The crankshaft and camshaft are now locked in position, preventing unnecessary rotation.

4 Cylinder head cover/ manifold – removal and refitting

Removal

1 Pull the plastic cover upwards from the top of the engine.

2 Disconnect the wiring plug from the mass airflow meter **(see illustration)**.

3 Remove the inlet and outlet air ducting from the air filter housing **(see illustrations)**.

4 Unscrew the air filter housing cover bolts, then remove the cover and filter element – refer to Chapter 4B **(see illustration)**. Unclip the hoses and pull the air filter housing from its mountings.

5 Disconnect the wiring plugs from the top of

4.2 Depress the catch and disconnect the mass airflow sensor wiring plug (arrowed)

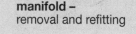

4.3a Release the clamps (arrowed) securing the air outlet ducting…

4.3b ...release the clips each side (arrowed) and remove the outlet ducting

4.3c The intake ducting is secured by a clip (arrowed) each side

4.4 Remove the air filter cover, followed by the filter element and housing

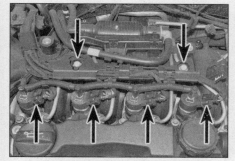

4.5 Injector wiring plugs and harness guide bolts (arrowed)

4.7a Unclip the fuel temperature sensor (arrowed)...

4.7b ...and the fuel priming bulb

each injector, undo the guide bolts, then make sure all wiring harnesses are freed from any retaining brackets on the cylinder head cover/ inlet manifold **(see illustration)**. Disconnect any vacuum pipes as necessary, having first noted their fitted positions.

6 Remove the EGR heat exchanger as described in Chapter 4C.

7 Disconnect the wiring plug, unclip the fuel temperature sensor, then unclip and move the pipe/priming bulb assembly to one side **(see illustrations)**.

8 Release the clamps, undo the bolts and remove the inlet ducting between the turbocharger and the inlet manifold. Make a note of their fitted positions, and then disconnect the various wiring plugs as the assembly is withdrawn **(see illustrations)**.

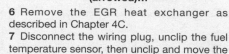

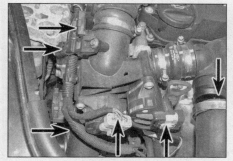

4.8a Release the clamps, disconnect the wiring plugs (arrowed)...

4.8b ...undo the bolts securing the ducting assembly to the intake manifold (arrowed)...

4.8c ...the retaining bolt adjacent to the oil filler cap (arrowed)...

4.8d ...adjacent to the dipstick guide tube (arrowed)...

4.8e ...under the left-hand side of the ducting (arrowed)...

4.8f ...then undo the right-hand duct-to-turbocharger bolt (arrowed)...

4.8g ...pivot the ducting assembly around, disconnect it from the turbocharger...

4.8h ...and manoeuvre it from place

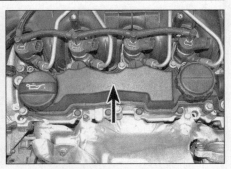

4.9 Undo the bolts and remove the oil separator (arrowed)

4.10a Prise out the clips and pull the fuel return pipes from the top of the injectors

4.10b Undo the pipe unions, counterholding with a second spanner

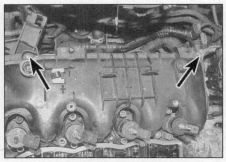

4.11 Undo the 2 bolts (arrowed) and lift the cylinder head cover away

9 Undo the retaining bolts and remove the oil separator from the top of the cylinder head (see illustration). Recover the rubber seal.
10 Prise out the retaining clips and disconnect the fuel return pipes from the injectors, then undo the unions and remove the high-pressure fuel pipes from the injectors and the common fuel rail at the rear of the cylinder head – counterhold the unions with a second spanner (see illustrations). Plug the openings to prevent dirt ingress.
11 Undo the 2 bolts securing the cylinder head cover/inlet manifold. Lift the assembly away (see illustration). Recover the manifold rubber seals.

Refitting

12 Refitting is a reversal of removal, bearing in mind the following points:
a) Examine the seals for signs of damage and deterioration, and renew if necessary. Smear a little clean engine oil on the manifold seals.
b) Renew the fuel injector high-pressure pipes – see Chapter 4B.

5 Crankshaft pulley – removal and refitting

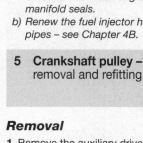

Removal

1 Remove the auxiliary drivebelt as described in Chapter 1B.
2 To lock the crankshaft, working underneath the engine, undo the bolt and remove the

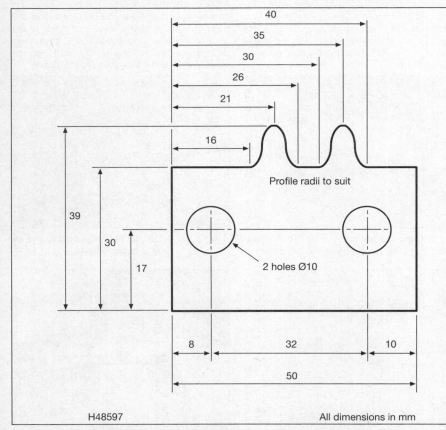

40
35
30
26
21
16
39
30
17
Profile radii to suit
2 holes Ø10
8
32
10
50
H48597
All dimensions in mm

5.2a Flywheel locking tool using 6 mm steel plate. Shape the tool 'teeth' to mesh with the starter ring gear on the circumference of the flywheel

5.2b Engage the teeth of the tool with the starter ring gear, and bolt it to the transmission bellhousing

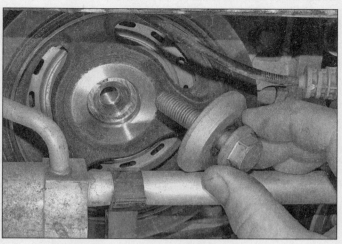

5.3 Slacken and remove the pulley bolt/washer

cover from the rear of the transmission bellhousing/engine block, then attach MINI tool no. 11 9 850 to the housing. This tool engages with the flywheel/driveplate ring gear teeth. In the absence of this tool, fabricate one as shown **(see illustrations)**.

3 Using a suitable socket and extension bar, unscrew the retaining bolt, remove the washer, then slide the pulley off the end of the crankshaft **(see illustration)**. If the pulley is tight fit, it can be drawn off the crankshaft using a suitable puller. If a puller is being used, refit the pulley retaining bolt without the washer to avoid damaging the crankshaft as the puller is tightened. Renew the bolt.

Caution: Do not touch the outer magnetic sensor ring of the sprocket with your fingers, or allow metallic particles to come into contact with it.

4 If necessary, undo the bolt and move the ABS wheel speed sensor connector bracket

to one side so the crankshaft pulley can be manoeuvred from place.

Refitting

5 Refit the pulley to the end of the crankshaft, ensuring the slot in the pulley boss aligns with the corresponding lug on the belt sprocket.

6 Thoroughly clean the threads of the pulley retaining bolt, and then apply a coat of locking compound to the bolt threads. MINI recommend the use of Loctite (available from your MINI dealer); in the absence of this, any good-quality locking compound may be used.

7 Fit the new crankshaft pulley retaining bolt and washer. Tighten the bolt to the specified torque, then through the specified angle, preventing the crankshaft from turning using the method employed on removal.

8 Refit and tension the auxiliary drivebelt as described in Chapter 1B.

6 Timing belt covers – removal and refitting

Removal

Upper cover

1 Raise the front of the vehicle, and support it securely on axle stands (see *Jacking and vehicle support*). Remove the plastic cover from the top of the engine, then undo the fasteners and remove the engine undershield **(see illustrations)**.

2 The front panel must now be moved into the 'assembly' position as follows:

a) Remove the front bumper as described in Chapter 11.

b) Unplug the air conditioning compressor wiring plug, and release the harness from any clips.

6.1a Pull the plastic cover upwards from the mountings

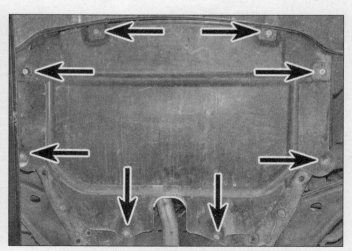

6.1b Engine undershield fasteners (arrowed)

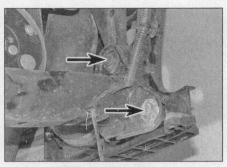

6.2a Front panel-to-subframe bolts (arrowed)

6.2b Undo the bolt (arrowed) securing the front panel to the wing each side

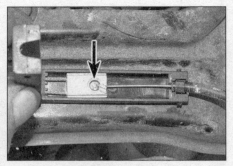

6.2c Open the junction box and disconnect the bonnet release cable (arrowed)

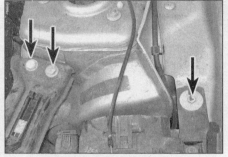

6.2d Remove the headlight bolt, and the panel support-to-suspension turret bolts (arrowed)

6.2e Disconnect the right-hand intercooler hose (arrowed)…

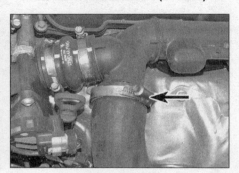

6.2f …and the turbocharger outlet hose (arrowed)

c) Undo the 2 bolts each side securing the front panel to the subframe (see illustration).
d) Remove the bolt each side securing the front panel to the wing (see illustration).

e) Release the coolant pipe from the retaining clips on the front panel.
f) Undo the retaining bolt and move the coolant expansion tank to one side.

g) Detach the air intake ducting gaiter from the front panel.
h) Prise open the junction box on the left-hand support, and disconnect the bonnet release cable (see illustration).
i) Undo the 3 bolts each side securing the front panel/headlight to the suspension turret/front wing (see illustration).
j) Slacken the clamp and disconnect the right-hand charge pressure hose from the intercooler, then disconnect the air hose from the turbocharger outlet ducting (see illustrations).
k) Disconnect the right-hand headlight wiring plug.
l) Screw special tool No. 00 2 271 into the left-, and right-hand front panel/chassis member sleeve. In the absence of these tools, use 2 lengths of tube, 19 mm outside diameter, at least 120 mm long, with two 8 mm threaded rods at least 150 mm long, and two 8 mm nuts (see illustration).
m) Undo the 3 nuts each side, and slide the front panel assembly approximately 10 cm forwards (see illustrations). Take care to ensure no strain is placed on any wiring/ hoses.

6.2g Screw the tubes/rods through the front panel into the threaded holes in the chassis members

6.2h Undo the 3 nuts (arrowed) each side…

3 Position a jack under the engine, and take the weight. Protect the engine with a block of wood on the jack head.

4 Undo the bolts/nuts and remove the mounting bracket between the right-hand engine mounting and the support bracket on the engine. Note the position of the earth strap (see illustration).

6.2i …and slide the panel forwards on the tubes

6.4 Note the earth lead (arrowed) attached to the engine mounting bracket

6.5 Unclip the pipe (arrowed) and the wiring harness

6.6 Upper timing belt cover screws (arrowed)

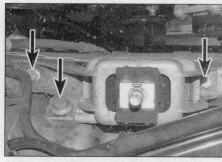

6.9 Right-hand engine mounting bolts (arrowed)

6.10 Lower timing cover bolts (arrowed)

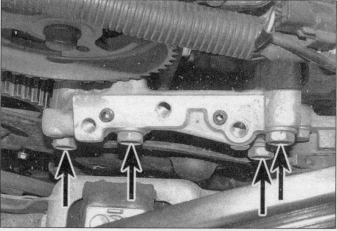

6.11 Undo the bolts (arrowed) and remove the mounting bracket

5 Release the wiring harness and refrigerant pipe from the upper cover **(see illustration)**.

6 Undo the 5 screws and remove the timing belt upper cover **(see illustration)**.

Lower cover

7 Remove the upper cover as described previously.

8 Remove the crankshaft pulley as described in Section 5.

9 Undo the bolts and remove the right-hand engine mounting from the vehicle body **(see illustration)**.

10 Remove the auxiliary drivebelt tensioner locking tool (where applicable), unclip the crankshaft position sensor wiring harness, then undo the 5 bolts securing the lower cover **(see illustration)**. Note that the bolts are retained in the cover.

11 Undo the bolts and remove the engine mounting bracket from the right-hand side of the cylinder head, then manoeuvre the timing belt cover from place **(see illustration)**.

Refitting

12 Refitting of all the covers is a reversal of the relevant removal procedure, ensuring that each cover section is correctly located, and that the cover retaining bolts are securely

tightened. Ensure that all disturbed hoses are reconnected and retained by their relevant clips.

---

7 Timing belt –
removal, inspection, refitting and tensioning

General

1 The timing belt drives the inlet camshaft, high-pressure fuel pump, and coolant pump from a toothed sprocket on the end of the crankshaft. If the belt breaks or

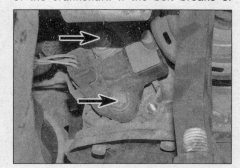

7.7 Crankshaft position sensor bolts (arrowed)

slips in service, the pistons are likely to hit the valve heads, resulting in expensive damage.

2 The timing belt should be renewed at the specified intervals, or earlier if it is contaminated with oil or at all noisy in operation (a 'scraping' noise due to uneven wear).

3 If the timing belt is being removed, we recommend the tensioner, idler pulley and coolant pump be renewed at the same time. This may avoid the need to remove the timing belt again at a later stage should these components fail.

Removal

4 Chock the rear wheels then jack up the front of the vehicle and support it on axle stands (see *Jacking and vehicle support*). Remove the front right-hand roadwheel, wheel arch liner (to expose the crankshaft pulley), and the engine undershield.

5 Remove the auxiliary drivebelt as described in Chapter 1B.

6 Remove the upper and lower timing belt covers, as described in Section 6.

7 Undo the screw and remove the crankshaft position sensor adjacent to the crankshaft sprocket flange, and move it to one side **(see illustration)**.

7.8 Undo the bolt (arrowed) and remove the belt protection bracket

7.10 Slacken the bolt and allow the tensioner to rotate

8 Undo the retaining screw and remove the timing belt protection bracket, again adjacent to the crankshaft sprocket flange (see illustration).

9 Lock the crankshaft and camshaft in the correct position as described in Section 3. If necessary, temporarily refit the crankshaft pulley bolt to enable the crankshaft to be rotated. At this stage, it is of no consequence that the fuel pump sprocket aligns correctly with the hole in the pump mounting bracket.

10 Insert a hexagon key into the belt tensioner pulley centre, slacken the pulley bolt, and allow the tensioner to rotate, relieving the belt tension (see illustration). With the belt slack, temporarily tighten the pulley bolt.

11 Note its routing, and then remove the timing belt from the sprockets.

Inspection

12 Renew the belt as a matter of course, regardless of its apparent condition. The cost of a new belt is nothing compared with the cost of repairs should the belt break in service. If signs of oil contamination are found, trace the source of the oil leak and rectify it. Wash down the engine timing belt area and all related components, to remove all traces of oil. Check that the tensioner and idler pulleys rotate freely without any sign of roughness,

and also check that the coolant pump pulley rotates freely. It is recommended that the tensioner, idler pulley and coolant pump as renewed as a matter course.

Refitting and tensioning

13 Commence refitting by ensuring that the crankshaft and camshaft timing pins are still in position correctly. Also, locate and lock the fuel pump sprocket in its correct position as described in Section 3.

14 Locate the timing belt on the crankshaft sprocket, then keeping it taunt, locate it around the idler pulley, camshaft sprocket, high-pressure pump sprocket, coolant pump sprocket, and the tensioner pulley (see illustration). If the timing belt has directional arrows on it, make sure that they point in the direction of normal engine rotation.

15 Refit the timing belt protection bracket and tighten the retaining bolt securely.

16 Slacken the tensioner pulley bolt, and using a hexagonal key, rotate the tensioner anti-clockwise, which moves the index arm clockwise, until the index arm is aligned as shown (see illustration).

17 Remove the camshaft and crankshaft and fuel pump timing pins and, using a socket on the crankshaft pulley bolt, crankshaft clockwise 10 complete revolutions. Align the

camshaft and crankshaft timing holes and check that the timing pins can be inserted, then remove them. There is no requirement to check the fuel pump sprocket alignment, as it will only be aligned after 12 complete revolutions.

18 Check that the tensioner index arm is still aligned between the edges of the area shown (see illustration 7.16). If it is not, remove the belt and begin the refitting process again, starting at Paragraph 14.

19 The remainder of refitting is a reversal of removal. Tighten all fasteners to the specified torque where given.

8 Timing belt sprockets and tensioner – removal and refitting

Camshaft sprocket

Removal

1 Remove the timing belt as described in Section 7.

2 Remove the locking tool from the camshaft sprocket/hub. Slacken the sprocket hub retaining bolt. To prevent the camshaft rotating as the bolt is slackened, a sprocket holding tool will be required. In the absence of the special MINI tool, an acceptable substitute can be fabricated at home (see Tool Tip 1). Do not attempt to use the engine assembly/valve timing locking tool to prevent the sprocket from rotating whilst the bolt is slackened.

3 Remove the sprocket hub retaining bolt, and slide the sprocket and hub off the end of the camshaft.

4 Clean the camshaft sprocket thoroughly, and renew it if there are any signs of wear, damage or cracks.

Refitting

5 Refit the camshaft sprocket to the camshaft (see illustration).

7.14 Timing belt routing

7.16 The index arm must align with the lug (arrowed)

Tool tip 1: A sprocket holding tool can be made from 2 lengths of steel strip bolted together to form a forked end. Drill holes and insert bolts in the ends of the fork to engage with the sprocket spokes

8.5 Ensure the lug on the sprocket hub engages with the slot on the end of the camshaft (arrowed)

8.11a Slide the sprocket from the crankshaft…

8.11b …and recover the Woodruff key

8.17 Insert a suitable drill bit/rod through the sprocket into the hole in the backplate

6 Refit the sprocket hub retaining bolt. Tighten the bolt to the specified torque, preventing the camshaft from turning as during removal.

7 Align the engine assembly/valve timing slot in the camshaft sprocket hub with the hole in the cylinder head and refit the timing pin to lock the camshaft in position.

8 Fit the timing belt around the pump sprocket and camshaft sprocket, and tension the timing belt as described in Section 7.

Crankshaft sprocket

Removal

9 Remove the timing belt as described in Section 7.

10 Check that the engine assembly/valve timing holes are still aligned as described in Section 3, and the camshaft sprocket and flywheel are locked in position.

11 Slide the sprocket off the end of the crankshaft and collect the Woodruff key **(see illustrations)**.

12 Examine the crankshaft oil seal for signs of oil leakage and, if necessary, renew it as described in Section 14.

13 Clean the crankshaft sprocket thoroughly, and renew it if there are any signs of wear, damage or cracks. Recover the crankshaft locating key.

Refitting

14 Refit the key to the end of the crankshaft, then refit the crankshaft sprocket (with the flange facing the crankshaft pulley).

15 Fit the timing belt around the crankshaft sprocket, and tension the timing belt as described in Section 7.

Fuel pump sprocket

Removal

16 Remove the timing belt as described in Section 7.

17 Using a suitable socket, undo the pump sprocket retaining nut. The sprocket can be held stationary by inserting a suitably-sized locking pin, drill or rod through the hole in the sprocket, and into the corresponding hole in the backplate **(see illustration)**, or by using a suitable forked tool engaged with the holes in the sprocket **(see Tool Tip 1 in paragraph 2)**. **Note:** *On some engines, a hole is provided at the 5 o'clock position for locking purposes only, and the timing position hole is at the 12 o'clock position.*

18 The pump sprocket is a taper fit on the pump shaft and it will be necessary to make up another tool to release it from the taper **(see Tool Tip 2)**.

19 Unscrew the retaining nut and remove the sprocket, then recover the Woodruff key. Prevent the sprocket from rotating as before, and unscrew the sprocket retaining nut. The nut will bear against the tool as it is undone, forcing the sprocket off the shaft taper. Once the taper is released, remove the tool, unscrew the nut fully, and remove the sprocket from the pump shaft.

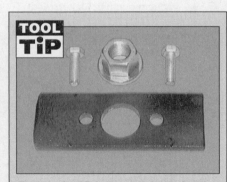

Tool tip 2: Make a sprocket releasing tool from a short strip of steel. Drill 2 holes in the strip to correspond with the 2 holes in the sprocket. Drill a 3rd hole just large enough to accept the flats of the sprocket retaining nut.

20 Clean the sprocket thoroughly, and renew it if there are any signs of wear, damage or cracks.

Refitting

21 Refit the Woodruff key then refit the pump sprocket and retaining nut, and tighten the nut to the specified torque. Prevent the sprocket rotating as the nut is tightened using the sprocket holding tool.

22 Fit the timing belt around the pump sprocket, and tension the timing belt as described in Section 7.

Coolant pump sprocket

23 The coolant pump sprocket is integral with the pump, and cannot be removed. Coolant pump removal is described in Chapter 3.

Tensioner pulley

Removal

24 Remove the timing belt as described in Section 7.

25 Remove the tensioner pulley retaining bolt, and slide the pulley off its mounting stud.

26 Clean the tensioner pulley, but do not use any strong solvent, which may enter the pulley bearings. Check that the pulley rotates freely, with no sign of stiffness or free play. Renew the pulley if there is any doubt about its condition, or if there are any obvious signs of wear or damage.

27 Examine the pulley mounting stud for signs of damage and if necessary, renew it.

8.31 Timing belt idler pulley retaining nut (arrowed)

Refitting

28 Refit the tensioner pulley to its mounting stud, and fit the retaining bolt.

29 Refit the timing belt as described in Section 7.

Idler pulley

Removal

30 Remove the timing belt as described in Section 7.

31 Undo the retaining bolt/nut and withdraw the idler pulley from the engine **(see illustration)**.

32 Clean the idler pulley, but do not use any strong solvent, which may enter the bearings. Check that the pulley rotates freely, with no sign of stiffness or free play. Renew the idler pulley if there is any doubt about its condition,

or if there are any obvious signs of wear or damage.

Refitting

33 Locate the idler pulley on the engine, and fit the retaining bolt/nut. Tighten the bolt/nut to the specified torque.

34 Refit the timing belt as described in Section 7.

9 Camshafts, rocker arms and hydraulic followers – removal, inspection and refitting

Removal

1 Remove the cylinder head cover/manifold as described in Section 4.

2 Remove the injectors as described in Chapter 4B.

3 Remove the camshaft sprocket as described in Section 8.

4 Refit the right-hand engine mounting, but only tighten the bolts moderately; this will keep the engine supported during the camshaft removal.

5 Undo the bolts and remove the vacuum pump. Recover the pump O-ring seals **(see illustration)**.

6 Remove the fuel filter (see Chapter 1B), then undo the bolts and remove the fuel filter mounting bracket.

7 Release the wiring harness clips, then undo the 3 bolts and remove the timing belt inner, upper cover **(see illustration)**.

8 Disconnect the wiring plug, unscrew the retaining bolt, and remove the camshaft position sensor from the camshaft cover/bearing ladder.

9 Undo the bolts securing the turbocharger upper heat shield **(see illustration)**, then working gradually and evenly, slacken and remove the bolts securing the camshaft cover/bearing ladder to the cylinder head in the reverse of the sequence shown in paragraph 26. Lift the cover/ladder from position complete with the camshafts.

10 Undo the retaining bolts and remove the bearing caps. Note their fitted positions, as they must be refitted into their original positions **(see illustration)**. Note that the

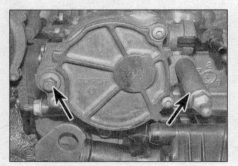

9.5 Vacuum pump bolts (arrowed)

9.7 Timing belt inner/upper cover bolts (2-arrowed)

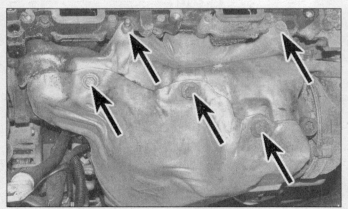

9.9 Undo the bolts (arrowed) and remove the heatshield

9.10 The camshaft bearing caps are numbered 1 to 4 from the flywheel end – A for inlet, and E for exhaust (arrowed)

bearing caps are marked A for inlet, and E for exhaust, and 1 to 4 from the flywheel end of the cylinder head.

11 Undo the bolts securing the chain tensioner assembly to the camshaft cover/ bearing ladder, and then lift the camshafts, chain and tensioner from place **(see illustrations)**. Discard the camshaft oil seal.

12 Obtain 16 small, clean plastic containers, and number them 1 to 8 inlet and 1 to 8 exhaust; alternatively, divide a larger container into 16 compartments.

13 Lift out each rocker arm. Place the rocker arms in their respective positions in the box or containers.

14 A compartmentalised container filled with engine oil is now required to retain the hydraulic followers while they are removed from the cylinder head. Withdraw each hydraulic follower and place it in the container, keeping them each identified for correct refitting. The followers must be totally submerged in the oil to prevent air entering them.

Inspection

15 Inspect the cam lobes and the camshaft bearing journals for scoring or other visible evidence of wear. Once the surface hardening of the cam lobes has been eroded, wear will occur at an accelerated rate. **Note:** *If these symptoms are visible on the tips of the camshaft lobes, check the corresponding rocker arm, as it will probably be worn as well.*

16 Examine the condition of the bearing surfaces in the cylinder head and camshaft bearing housing. If wear is evident, the cylinder head and bearing housing will both have to be renewed, as they are a matched assembly.

17 Inspect the rocker arms and followers for scuffing, cracking or other damage and renew any components as necessary. Also check the condition of the follower bores in the cylinder head. As with the camshafts, any wear in this area will necessitate cylinder head renewal.

Refitting

18 Thoroughly clean the sealant from the mating surfaces of the cylinder head and camshaft bearing housing. Use a suitable

9.11a Undo the tensioner bolts (arrowed)…

9.11b …then lift the camshafts, chain and tensioner from place

9.21 Refit the hydraulic tappets…

9.22 …and rocker arms to their original positions

liquid gasket-dissolving agent (available from MINI dealers) together with a soft putty knife; do not use a metal scraper or the faces will be damaged. As there is no conventional gasket used, the cleanliness of the mating faces is of the utmost importance. Prise out the oil injector oil seals from the camshaft bearing housing.

19 Clean off any oil, dirt or grease from both components and dry with a clean lint-free cloth. Ensure that all the oilways are completely clean.

20 Liberally lubricate the hydraulic follower bores in the cylinder head with clean engine oil.

21 Insert the hydraulic followers into their original bores in the cylinder head unless they have been renewed **(see illustration)**.

22 Lubricate the rocker arms and place them over their respective followers and valve stems **(see illustration)**.

23 Engage the timing chain around the camshaft sprockets, aligning the black/ copper-coloured links with the marked teeth on the camshaft sprockets **(see illustration)**. If the black colouring has been lost, there must be 12 chain link pins between the marks on the sprockets.

24 Fit the chain tensioner between the upper and lower runs of the chain, then lubricate the bearing surfaces with clean engine oil, and fit the camshafts into position on the underside of the camshaft cover/bearing ladder. Refit the bearing caps to their original positions and tighten the retaining bolts to the specified torque **(see illustrations)**. Tighten

9.23 Align the marks on the sprockets with the centre of the block-coloured chain links (arrowed). There must be 12 link pins between the sprocket marks

9.24a Assemble the chain tensioner between the upper and lower runs of the chain…

9.24b ...then lower the camshaft, chain and tensioner into position

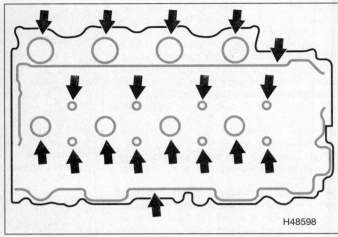

9.25 Apply sealant to the black-line areas arrowed

the tensioner retaining bolts to the specified torque.

25 Apply a thin bead of sealant to the mating surface of the camshaft cover/bearing ladder as shown **(see illustration)**. MINI recommend the use of Drei Bond 2210. Do not allow the sealant to obstruct the oil channels for the hydraulic chain tensioner.

26 Check that the black/copper-coloured links on the chain are still aligned with the marks on the camshaft sprockets, then refit the camshaft cover/bearing ladder, using MINI tools No. 11 9 870 to align the ladder with the head, gradually and evenly tighten the retaining bolts until the

cover/ladder is in contact with the cylinder head, then tighten the bolts to the specified torque in sequence **(see illustration)**. **Note:** *In the absence of the special tools, ensure the cover/ladder is correctly located by checking the bores of the vacuum pump and camshaft oil seal at each end of the cover/ladder.*

27 Fit a new camshaft oil seal as described in Section 14.

28 Refit the camshaft sprocket, and tighten the retaining bolt finger-tight.

29 Using a spanner on the camshaft sprocket bolt, rotate the camshafts approximately 40 complete revolutions clockwise. Check the

black-coloured links on the chain still align with the marks on the camshaft sprockets.

30 If the marks still align, refit the camshaft sprocket as described in Section 8.

31 Refit and adjust the camshaft position sensor as described in Chapter 4B.

32 Press the new oil seals into the bearing housing, using a tube/socket of approximately 20 mm outside diameter, ensuring the inner lip of the seal fits around the injector guide tube **(see illustrations)**. Refit the injectors as described in Chapter 4B.

33 Refit the cylinder head cover/manifold as described in Section 4.

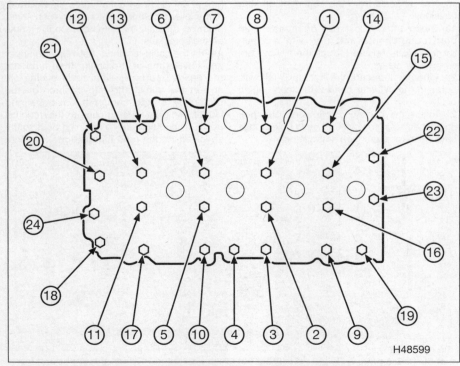

9.26 Camshaft cover/bearing ladder bolt tightening sequence

9.32a Fit the new seal around a 20 mm outside diameter socket...

9.32b ...and push it into place

10 Cylinder head –
removal and refitting

Removal

1 Chock the rear wheels then jack up the front of the vehicle and support it on axle stands (see *Jacking and vehicle support*). Remove the front right-hand roadwheel, the engine undershield, and the front wheel arch liner.

2 Disconnect the battery as described in Chapter 5A.

3 Drain the cooling system as described in Chapter 1B.

4 Remove the camshafts, rocker arms and hydraulic followers as described in Section 9.

5 Remove the turbocharger as described in Chapter 4B.

6 Remove the glow plugs as described in Chapter 5C.

7 Undo the upper mounting bolts, and pivot the alternator away from the engine, undo the oil dipstick guide tube bolt, then undo the bolts securing the alternator mounting bracket to the cylinder head/block **(see illustration)**.

8 Undo the coolant outlet housing (left-hand end of the cylinder head) retaining bolts, slacken the two bolts securing the housing support bracket to the top of the transmission bellhousing, and move the outlet housing away from the cylinder head a little **(see illustration)**. There is no need to disconnect the hoses.

9 Disconnect the high-pressure fuel pipe from the common rail to the pump, and disconnect the fuel supply and return hoses. Remove the bracket at the rear of the pump, then undo the bolt/nut and remove the pump and mounting bracket as an assembly **(see illustrations)**. Note that a new high-pressure pipe must be fitted – see Chapter 4B.

10 Working in the **reverse** of the sequence shown **(see illustration 10.31)** undo the cylinder head bolts.

11 Release the cylinder head from the cylinder block and location dowels by rocking it. The MINI tool for doing this consists simply of two metal rods with 90-degree angled ends **(see illustration)**. Do not prise between the mating faces of the cylinder head and block, as this may damage the gasket faces.

12 Lift the cylinder head from the block, and recover the gasket.

13 If necessary, remove the exhaust manifold with reference to Chapter 4B.

Preparation for refitting

14 The mating faces of the cylinder head and cylinder block must be perfectly clean before refitting the head. MINI recommend the use of a scouring agent for this purpose, but acceptable results can be achieved by using a hard plastic or wood scraper to remove all traces of gasket and carbon. The same method can be used to clean the piston crowns. Take particular care to avoid scoring or gouging the

10.7 Alternator mounting bracket bolts (arrowed)

cylinder head/cylinder block mating surfaces during the cleaning operations, as aluminium alloy is easily damaged. Make sure that the carbon is not allowed to enter the oil and water passages – this is particularly important for the lubrication system, as carbon could block the oil supply to the engine's components. Using adhesive tape and paper, seal the water, oil and bolt holes in the cylinder block. To prevent carbon entering the gap between the pistons and bores, smear a little grease in the gap. After cleaning each piston, use a small brush to remove all traces of grease and carbon from the gap, then wipe away the remainder with a clean rag.

15 Check the mating surfaces of the cylinder block and the cylinder head for nicks, deep scratches and other damage. If slight, they may be removed carefully with a file, but if excessive, machining may be the only

10.9a Remove the high-pressure pipe (arrowed)…

10.9c Pump mounting bracket upper nut and lower bolt (arrowed)

10.8 Undo the coolant outlet housing bolts (arrowed)

alternative to renewal. If warpage of the cylinder head gasket surface is suspected, use a straight-edge to check it for distortion. Refer to Part D of this Chapter if necessary.

16 Thoroughly clean the threads of the cylinder head bolt holes in the cylinder block. Ensure that the bolts run freely in their threads, and that all traces of oil and water are removed from each bolt hole. If required, pull the oil feed non-return valve from the cylinder head, and check the ball moves freely. Push a new valve into place if necessary **(see illustrations)**.

Gasket selection

17 Remove the crankshaft timing pin, then turn the crankshaft until pistons 1 and 4 are at TDC (Top Dead Centre). Position a dial test indicator (dial gauge) on the cylinder block adjacent to the rear of No 1 piston, and zero it on the block

10.9b …and the bracket (arrowed)

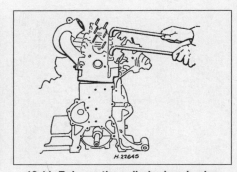

10.11 Release the cylinder head using angled rods

10.16a Pull the non-return valve from the cylinder head...

10.16b ...and push a new one into place

10.20 Measure the piston protrusion using a DTI gauge

10.22 Cylinder head identification notches (arrowed)

face. Transfer the probe to the crown of No 1 piston (10.0 mm in from the rear edge), and then slowly turn the crankshaft back-and-forth past TDC, noting the highest reading on the indicator. Record this reading as protrusion A.

18 Repeat the check described in paragraph 17, this time 10.0 mm in from the front edge of the No 1 piston crown. Record this reading as protrusion B.

19 Add protrusion A to protrusion B, then divide the result by 2 to obtain an average reading for piston No 1.

20 Repeat the procedure described in paragraphs 17 to 19 on piston 4, then turn the crankshaft through 180° and carry out the procedure on the piston Nos 2 and 3 **(see illustration)**. Check that there is a maximum difference of 0.07 mm protrusion between any two pistons.

21 If a dial test indicator is not available, piston protrusion may be measured using

a straight-edge and feeler blades or Vernier calipers. However, this is much less accurate, and cannot therefore be recommended.

22 Note the greatest piston protrusion measurement, and use this to determine the correct cylinder head gasket from the following table. The series of notches/holes on the side of the gasket are used for thickness identification **(see illustration)**.

Piston protrusion	Gasket identification
0.611 to 0.720 mm	2 notches
0.721 to 0.770 mm	3 notches
0.771 to 0.820 mm	1 notches
0.821 to 0.870 mm	4 notches
0.871 to 0.977 mm	5 notches

23 MINI insist that the cylinder head bolts must be renewed, regardless of their apparent condition.

Refitting

24 Turn the crankshaft and position Nos 1

and 4 pistons at TDC, then turn the crankshaft a quarter turn (90°) anti-clockwise.

25 Thoroughly clean the surfaces of the cylinder head and block.

26 Make sure that the locating dowels are in place, then fit the correct gasket the right way round on the cylinder block **(see illustration)**.

27 If necessary, refit the exhaust manifold to the cylinder head as described in Chapter 4B.

28 Carefully lower the cylinder head onto the gasket and block, making sure that it locates correctly onto the dowels.

29 Do not wash the coating from the new cylinder head bolts, or apply any additional lubrication.

30 Carefully insert the cylinder head bolts into their holes (do not drop them in) and initially finger-tighten them.

31 Working progressively and in sequence, tighten the cylinder head bolts to their Stage 1 torque setting, using a torque wrench and suitable socket **(see illustration)**.

32 Once all the bolts have been tightened to their Stage 1 torque setting, working again in the specified sequence, tighten each bolt to the specified Stage 2 setting. Finally, angle-tighten the bolts through the specified Stage 3 angle. It is recommended that an angle-measuring gauge is used during this stage of tightening, to ensure accuracy. **Note:** *Retightening of the cylinder head bolts after running the engine is not required.*

33 Refit the hydraulic followers, rocker arms, and camshaft housing (complete with camshafts) as described in Section 9.

34 Refit the timing belt as described in Section 7.

35 The remainder of refitting is a reversal of removal, noting the following points.

a) *Use a new seal when refitting the coolant outlet housing.*

b) *When refitting a cylinder head, it is good practice to renew the thermostat.*

c) *Refit the camshaft position sensor and set the air gap with reference to Chapter 4B.*

d) *Tighten all fasteners to the specified torque where given.*

e) *Refill the cooling system as described in Chapter 1B.*

f) *The engine may run erratically for the first few miles, until the engine management ECM relearns its stored values.*

11 Sump – removal and refitting

Removal

1 Drain the engine oil, then clean and refit the engine oil drain plug, tightening it securely. If the engine is nearing the service interval when the oil and filter are due for renewal, it is recommended that the filter is also removed, and a new one fitted. After reassembly, the engine can then be refilled with fresh oil. Refer to Chapter 1B for further information.

10.26 Ensure the gasket locates over the dowels (arrowed)

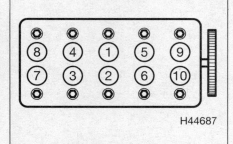

10.31 Cylinder head bolt tightening sequence

H44687

11.8 Apply a bead of sealant to the sump or crankcase mating surface. Ensure the sealant is applied to the inside of the retaining bolt holes

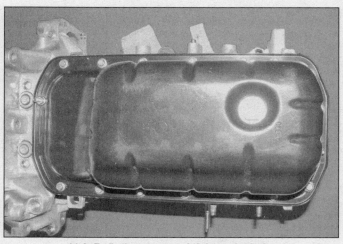

11.9 Refit the sump and tighten the bolts

2 Chock the rear wheels then jack up the front of the vehicle and support it on axle stands (see *Jacking and vehicle support*). Undo the screws and remove the engine undershield.

3 Remove the exhaust system as described in Chapter 4B.

4 Where necessary, disconnect the wiring connector from the oil temperature sender unit, which is screwed into the sump.

5 Progressively slacken and remove all the sump retaining bolts/nuts. Since the sump bolts vary in length, remove each bolt in turn, and store it in its correct fitted order by pushing it through a clearly marked cardboard template. This will avoid the possibility of installing the bolts in the wrong locations on refitting.

6 Try to break the joint by striking the sump with the palm of your hand, then lower and withdraw the sump from under the car. If the sump is stuck (which is quite likely) use a putty knife or similar, carefully inserted between the sump and block. Ease the knife along the joint until the sump is released. While the sump is removed, take the opportunity to check the oil pump pick-up/strainer for signs of clogging or splitting. If necessary, remove the pump as described in Section 12, and clean or renew the strainer.

Refitting

7 Clean all traces of sealant from the mating surfaces of the cylinder block/crankcase and sump, and then use a clean rag to wipe out the sump and the engine's interior.

8 Ensure that the sump mating surfaces are clean and dry, then apply a thin coating of Drei Bond 2210 sealant to the sump or crankcase mating surface **(see illustration)**. Note that the sump must be installed within 5 minutes of applying the sealant.

9 Offer up the sump to the cylinder block/crankcase. Refit its retaining bolts/nuts, ensuring that each bolt is screwed into its original location. Tighten the bolts evenly and progressively to the specified torque setting **(see illustration)**.

10 The remainder of refitting is a reversal of removal.

12 Oil pump –
removal, inspection
and refitting

Removal

1 Remove the sump as described in Section 11.

2 Remove the crankshaft sprocket as described in Section 8. Recover the locating key from the crankshaft.

3 Disconnect the wiring plug, undo the bolts and remove the crankshaft position sensor, located on the right-hand end of the cylinder block.

4 Undo the three Allen screws and remove the oil pump pick-up tube from the pump/block **(see illustration)**. Discard the oil seal; a new one must be fitted.

5 Undo the 8 bolts, and remove the oil pump **(see illustration)**.

Inspection

6 Undo and remove the Torx bolts securing the cover to the oil pump **(see illustration)**. Examine the pump rotors and body for signs of wear and damage. If worn, the complete pump must be renewed.

7 Remove the circlip, and extract the cap, valve piston and spring, noting which way around they are fitted **(see illustrations)**. The condition of the relief valve spring can only be measured by comparing it with a new one; if there is any doubt about its condition, it should also be renewed.

8 Refit the relief valve piston and spring, and then secure them in place with the circlip.

12.4 Oil pick-up tube Allen screws (arrowed)

12.5 Oil pump retaining bolts (arrowed)

12.6 Undo the Torx bolts and remove the pump cover

12.7a Remove the circlip...

12.7b ...cap...

12.7c ...spring...

12.7d ...and piston

9 Refit the cover to the oil pump, and tighten the Torx bolts securely.

Refitting

10 Remove all traces of sealant, and thoroughly clean the mating surfaces of the oil pump and cylinder block.

11 Apply a thin bead of Drei Bond 2210 sealant to the mating face of the cylinder block (see illustration). Ensure that no sealant enters any of the holes in the block. Note that the pump must be installed within 5 minutes of applying the sealant.

12 With a new oil seal fitted, refit the oil pump over the end of the crankshaft, aligning the flats in the pump drivegear with the flats machined in the crankshaft (see illustrations). Note that new oil pumps are supplied with the oil seal already fitted, and a seal protector sleeve. The sleeve fits over the end of the crankshaft to protect the seal as the pump is fitted.

13 Install the oil pump bolts and tighten them to the specified torque.

14 Refit the oil pick-up tube to the pump/ cylinder block using a new O-ring seal. Ensure the oil dipstick guide tube is correctly refitted.

15 Refit the Woodruff key to the crankshaft, and slide the crankshaft sprocket into place.

16 The remainder of refitting is a reversal of removal.

13 Oil cooler – removal and refitting

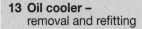

Removal

1 Remove the diesel particulate filter as described in Chapter 4C.

2 The oil cooler is fitted to the front of the oil filter housing. Drain the coolant as described in Chapter 1B.

3 Drain the engine oil as described in Chapter 1B.

4 Undo the 5 bolts/stud and remove the oil cooler. Recover the O-ring seals (see illustrations).

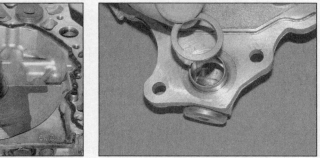

12.11 Apply a bead of sealant to the cylinder block mating surface

12.12a Fit a new seal...

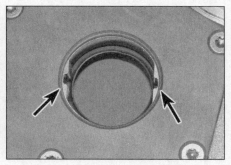

12.12b ...align the pump gear flats (arrowed)...

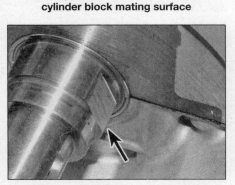

12.12c ...with those of the crankshaft (arrowed)

13.4a Undo the oil cooler bolts/stud (arrowed)

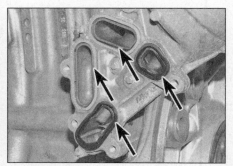

13.4b Renew the O-ring seals (arrowed)

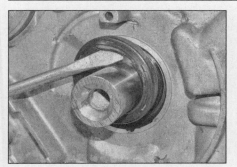

14.3 Take care not to mark the crankshaft whilst levering out the oil seal

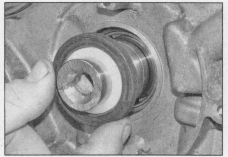

14.5a Slide the seal and protective sleeve over the end of the crankshaft...

14.5b ...and press the seal into place

Refitting

5 Fit new O-ring seals into the recesses in the oil filter housing, and refit the cooler. Tighten the bolts securely.

6 Refill or top-up the cooling system and engine oil level as described in Chapter 1B or *Weekly checks* (as applicable). Start the engine, and check the oil cooler for signs of leakage.

14 Oil seals – renewal

Crankshaft

Right-hand oil seal

1 Remove the crankshaft sprocket and Woodruff key as described in Section 8.

2 Measure and note the fitted depth of the oil seal.

3 Pull the oil seal from the housing using a screwdriver. Alternatively, drill a small hole in the oil seal, and use a self-tapping screw and a pair of pliers to remove it **(see illustration)**.

4 Clean the oil seal housing and the crankshaft sealing surface.

5 Smear a little clean engine oil on the crankshaft running surface. The new seal should be supplied with a protector sleeve, which fits over the end of the crankshaft to prevent any damage to the seal lip. With the sleeve in place, press the seal (open end first) into the pump to the previously-noted

depth, using a suitable tube or socket **(see illustrations)**.

6 Where applicable, remove the plastic sleeve from the end of the crankshaft.

7 Refit the timing belt crankshaft sprocket as described in Section 8.

Left-hand oil seal

8 Remove the flywheel, as described in Section 16.

9 Measure and note the fitted depth of the oil seal.

10 Pull the oil seal from the housing using a screwdriver. Alternatively, drill a small hole in the oil seal, and use a self-tapping screw and a pair of pliers to remove it **(see illustration 14.3)**.

11 Clean the oil seal housing and the crankshaft sealing surface.

12 Apply a little clean engine oil to the crankshaft running surface. The new seal should be supplied with a protector sleeve, which fits over the end of the crankshaft to prevent any damage to the seal lip **(see illustration)**. With the sleeve in place, press the seal (open end first) into the housing to the previously-noted depth, using a suitable tube or socket.

13 Where applicable, remove the plastic sleeve from the end of the crankshaft.

14 Refit the flywheel, as described in Section 16.

Camshaft

15 Remove the camshaft sprocket as described in Section 8. In principle there is

no need to remove the timing belt completely, but remember that if the belt has been contaminated with oil, it must be renewed.

16 Pull the oil seal from the housing using a hooked instrument. Alternatively, drill a small hole in the oil seal and use a self-tapping screw and a pair of pliers to remove it **(see illustration)**.

17 Clean the oil seal housing and the camshaft sealing surface.

18 The seal has a Teflon lip and must not be oiled or marked. The new seal should be supplied with a protector sleeve, which fits over the end of the camshaft to prevent any damage to the seal lip **(see illustration)**. With the sleeve in place, press the seal (open end first) into the housing, using a suitable tube or socket that bears only of the outer edge of the seal.

19 Refit the camshaft sprocket as described in Section 8.

20 Where necessary, fit a new timing belt with reference to Section 7.

15 Oil pressure switch and level sensor – removal and refitting

Oil pressure switch

Removal

1 The oil pressure switch is located at the front of the cylinder block, adjacent to the oil dipstick guide tube. Remove the alternator as described in Chapter 5A.

14.12 Slide the seal and protective sleeve over the left-hand end of the crankshaft

14.16 Drill a hole, insert a self-tapping screw, and pull the seal from place using pliers

14.18 Fit the protective sleeve and seal over the end of the camshaft

15.3 The oil pressure switch is located on the front face of the cylinder block (arrowed)

2 Remove the protective sleeve from the wiring plug (where applicable), and then disconnect the wiring from the switch.

3 Unscrew the switch from the cylinder block, and recover the sealing washer **(see illustration)**. Be prepared for oil spillage, and if the switch is to be left removed from the engine for any length of time, plug the hole in the cylinder block.

Refitting

4 Examine the sealing washer for any signs of damage or deterioration, and if necessary renew.

5 Refit the switch, complete with washer, and tighten it to the specified torque.

6 Refit the alternator

Oil level sensor

Removal

7 The oil level sensor (where fitted) is located at the rear of the cylinder block **(see illustration)**. Jack up the front of the vehicle and support it securely on axle stands (see *Jacking and vehicle support*). Undo the screws and remove the engine undershield.

8 Reach up between the driveshaft and the cylinder block and disconnect the wiring plug from the sensor.

9 Using an open-ended spanner, unscrew the sensor and withdraw it from position.

Refitting

10 Smear a little silicone sealant on the threads and refit the sensor to the cylinder block, tightening it securely.

16.8 Flywheel retaining Torx bolts

15.7 The oil level sensor is located on the rear face of the cylinder block (arrowed)

11 Reconnect the wiring plug to the sensor.
12 Refit the engine undershield, and lower the vehicle to the ground.

16 Flywheel – removal, inspection and refitting

Removal

1 Remove the transmission as described in Chapter 7A, then remove the clutch assembly as described in Chapter 6.

2 Prevent the flywheel from turning by locking the ring gear teeth. Alternatively, bolt a strap between the flywheel and the cylinder block/crankcase. Do not attempt to lock the flywheel in position using the crankshaft pulley locking tool described in Section 3.

3 Make alignment marks between the flywheel and crankshaft to aid refitting. Slacken and remove the flywheel retaining bolts, and remove the flywheel from the end of the crankshaft. Be careful not to drop it; it is heavy. If the flywheel locating dowel (where fitted) is a loose fit in the crankshaft end, remove it and store it with the flywheel for safe-keeping. Discard the flywheel bolts; new ones must be used on refitting.

Inspection

4 Examine the flywheel for scoring of the clutch face, and for wear or chipping of the ring gear teeth. If the clutch face is scored, the flywheel may be surface-ground, but renewal is preferable. Seek the advice of a MINI dealer or engine-reconditioning specialist to see if machining is possible. If the ring gear is worn or damaged, the flywheel must be renewed, as it is not possible to renew the ring gear separately.

Refitting

5 Clean the mating surfaces of the flywheel and crankshaft. Remove any remaining locking compound from the threads of the crankshaft holes, using the correct size of tap, if available.

6 If the new flywheel retaining bolts are not supplied with their threads already pre-coated, apply a suitable thread-locking compound to the threads of each bolt.

7 Ensure that the locating dowel(s) is in position. Offer up the flywheel, locating it on the dowel(s) (where fitted), and fit the new retaining bolts. Where no locating dowel is fitted, align the previously-made marks to ensure the flywheel is refitted in its original position.

8 Lock the flywheel using the method employed on dismantling, and tighten the retaining bolts to the specified torque **(see illustration)**.

9 Refit the clutch as described in Chapter 6. Remove the flywheel locking tool, and refit the transmission as described in Chapter 7A.

17 Engine/transmission mountings – inspection and renewal

Inspection

1 If improved access is required, chock the rear wheels then jack up the front of the car and support it on axle stands (see *Jacking and vehicle support*). Undo the screws and remove the engine undershield.

2 Check the mounting rubbers to see if they are cracked, hardened or separated from the metal at any point; renew the mounting if any such damage or deterioration is evident.

3 Check that all the mountings' fasteners are securely tightened; use a torque wrench to check if possible.

4 Using a large screwdriver or a crowbar, check for wear in each mounting by carefully levering against it to check for free play. Where this is not possible, enlist the aid of an assistant to move the engine/transmission back-and-forth, or from side-to-side, while you watch the mounting. While some free play is to be expected even from new components, excessive wear should be obvious. If excessive free play is found, check first that the fasteners are correctly secured, and then renew any worn components as described below.

Renewal

Right-hand mounting

5 Remove the engine undershield, then place a jack beneath the engine, with a block of wood on the jack head. Raise the jack until it is supporting the weight of the engine.

6 In order to access the engine mounting, the front panel must be moved forwards as described in Section 6.

7 Slacken and remove the bolts/nut securing the mounting bracket to the mounting and the bracket bolted to the cylinder head **(see illustration 6.4)**. Disconnect the earth lead as the bracket is withdrawn.

8 If required, undo the bolts and remove the bracket from the cylinder head **(see illustration 6.11)**. Release the wiring loom and fuel lines from the retaining clips as it is removed.

9 Undo the bolts and remove the mounting.

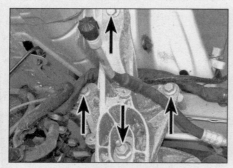

17.14 Left-hand mounting bracket-to-mounting nut and bracket-to-body bolts (arrowed)

17.15 Left-hand mounting-to-transmission bolts (arrowed)

17.21 Rear lower mounting reaction link bolts (arrowed)

10 Check for signs of wear or damage on all components, and renew as necessary.

11 Refitting is a reversal of removal.

Left-hand mounting

12 Remove the engine control unit as described in Chapter 4B, then unbolt and reposition the underbonnet fuse and relay box.

13 Place a jack beneath the transmission, with a block of wood on the jack head. Raise the jack until it is supporting the weight of the transmission.

14 Remove the mounting bracket-to-body bolts, the refrigerant pipe bracket and the bracket-to-mounting nut **(see illustration).** **Note:** *The mounting bracket-to-body bolts may be either grade 8.8 or 10.9 (cast into the head of the bolt). MINI insist that the grade 8.8 bolts must be replaced with grade 10.9 bolts.*

15 Undo the four retaining bolts from the mounting bracket on the transmission and remove the mounting from the engine compartment **(see illustration).**

16 Check carefully for signs of wear or damage on all components, and renew them where necessary.

17 Fit the mounting bolts to the bracket on the transmission and tighten the retaining bolts to the specified torque.

18 Refit the mounting bracket to the vehicle body and tighten its bolts/nut to the specified torque.

19 The remainder of refitting is a reversal of removal.

Rear lower mounting

20 If not already done, firmly apply the handbrake, then jack up the front of the vehicle and support it securely on axle stands (see *Jacking and vehicle support*).

21 Unscrew and remove the bolt securing the rear mounting link to the bracket on the engine **(see illustration).**

22 Remove the bolt securing the rear mounting link to the subframe and remove the mounting torque reaction link.

23 To remove the mounting bracket, remove the right-hand driveshaft (Chapter 8), then undo the retaining bolts and remove the mounting bracket from the rear of the engine.

24 Check carefully for signs of wear or damage on all components, and renew them where necessary.

25 On reassembly, fit the rear mounting bracket to the transmission, and tighten its retaining bolts to the specified torque.

26 Refit the rear mounting torque reaction link, and tighten both its bolts to their specified torque settings.

27 Lower the vehicle to the ground.

Chapter 2 Part C:
N47 diesel engine in-car repair procedures

Contents

Degrees of difficulty

Easy, suitable for novice with little experience	⚒	**Fairly easy,** suitable for beginner with some experience	⚒	**Fairly difficult,** suitable for competent DIY mechanic	⚒	**Difficult,** suitable for experienced DIY mechanic	⚒	**Very difficult,** suitable for expert DIY or professional	⚒

Specifications

General

Engine code*:
  1.6 litre N47 C16
  2.0 litre N47 C20
Capacity:
  1.6 litre . . . . 1597 cc
  2.0 litre . . . . 1995 cc
Bore:
  1.6 litre . . . . 78.0 mm
  2.0 litre . . . . 84.0 mm
Stroke:
  1.6 litre . . . . 83.6 mm
  2.0 litre . . . . 90.0 mm
Direction of crankshaft rotation . . . . Clockwise (viewed from the right-hand side of vehicle)
Maximum power output:
  1.6 litre:
    C16 U1 . . . . 82 kW
    C16 K1 . . . . 66 kW
  2.0 litre:
    C20 U1 . . . . 105 kW
    C20 K1 . . . . 82 kW
Compression ratio . . . . 16.5 :1

* The engine code is stamped on a plate attached to the front of the cylinder block, to the left of the oil filter.

Compression pressures (engine hot, at cranking speed)

Normal . . . . 20 ± 5 bar
Minimum. . . . . 16 bar
Maximum difference between any two cylinders. . . . . 2 bar

Lubrication system

Minimum system pressure:
  Idle speed (hot) . . . . 1.3 bar
  3500 rpm (hot) . . . . 4.0 to 6.0 bar

Torque wrench settings

	Nm	lbf ft
Camshaft bearing cap bolts.	10	7
Camshaft carrier-to-cylinder head	13	9
Camshaft cover bolts:		
M6.	10	7
M7.	15	10

Torque wrench settings (continued)

	Nm	lbf ft
Camshaft sprocket-to-gearwheel – intake camshaft	14	10
Connecting rod big-end bearing cap bolts*:		
Stage 1	5	3
Stage 2	20	15
Stage 3	Angle-tighten a further 70°	
Crankshaft pulley/vibration damper bolts*		
Stage 1	40	30
Stage 2	Angle-tighten a further 120°	
Cylinder head bolts*:		
Stage 1	70	52
Stage 2	Slacken 180°	
Stage 3	50	37
Stage 4	Angle-tighten a further 120°	
Stage 5	Angle-tighten a further 120°	
Cylinder head-to-timing cover bolts:		
M7	15	11
M8	20	15
Engine mountings:		
Right-hand mounting:		
Mounting bracket-to-mounting	100	74
Mounting bracket-to-engine support bracket:		
M10 8.8 grade	38	28
M10 10.9 grade	56	41
Mounting-to-body	68	49
Left-hand mounting:		
Mounting-to-transmission	38	28
Mounting bracket-to-body	56	41
Mounting bracket-to-mounting:		
Stage 1	40	30
Stage 2	Angle-tighten a further 105°	
Rear reaction/stabilizer link:		
Link-to-subframe and mounting bracket	108	80
Mounting bracket-to-engine	38	28
Flywheel/driveplate bolts*	120	88
Fuel injection pump sprocket retaining bolt	65	48
Main bearing cap bolts*:		
Stage 1	25	18
Stage 2	50	37
Stage 3	Angle-tighten a further 60°	
Stage 4	Angle-tighten a further 60°	
Oil cooler-to-cylinder block	10	7
Oil filter cap	25	18
Oil filter housing bolts	25	18
Oil level sensor	8	6
Oil pressure sensor	28	19
Oil pump	20	15
Oil pump sprocket - Left-hand thread:		
Stage 1	5	3
Stage 2	Angle-tighten a further 90°	
Oil pump intake pipe	8	5
Piston oil spray jet bolts	10	7
Sump bolts	20	15
Sump drain plug	25	18
Timing chain cover bolts:		
M6:		
Stage 1	8	5
Stage 2	Angle-tighten a further 90°	
Timing chain cover-to-fuel pump	11	7
M6	10	7
M7	15	11
M8	22	16
Timing chain cover screw plug:		
M34	20	15
M40	30	22
Timing chain guide pins	20	15
Timing chain upper tensioner	70	52
Timing chain lower tensioner bolts	10	7

Do not reuse
Always replace aluminium bolts.

1 General information

How to use this Chapter

This Part of Chapter 2 describes the repair procedures that can reasonably be carried out on the engine whilst it remains in the vehicle. If the engine has been removed from the vehicle and is being dismantled as described in Part D, any preliminary dismantling procedures can be ignored.

Note that, while it may be possible physically to overhaul items such as the piston/connecting rod assemblies while the engine is in the car, such tasks are not usually carried out as separate operations. Usually, several additional procedures are required (not to mention the cleaning of components and oilways); for this reason, all such tasks are classed as major overhaul procedures, and are described in Part D of this Chapter.

Part D describes the removal of the engine/transmission from the car, and the full overhaul procedures that can then be carried out.

N47 series engines

The aluminium cylinder block is of the dry-liner type. The crankshaft is supported within the cylinder block on five shell-type main bearings. Thrustwashers are integral with the No.3 main bearing shells to control crankshaft endfloat.

The cylinder head is of the double overhead camshaft, 4-valve per cylinder design – two intake and two exhaust valves per cylinder. The valves are operated by one intake camshaft and one exhaust camshaft, via rocker fingers. One end of each finger acts upon the valve stem, whilst the other end pivots on a support pillar. Valve clearances are maintained automatically by hydraulic compensation elements incorporated within the support pillars. In order to achieve high levels of combustion efficiency, the cylinder head has two intake ports for each cylinder. One port is tangential, whilst the other is helical.

The connecting rods rotate on horizontally-split bearing shells at their big-ends. The pistons are attached to the connecting rods by gudgeon pins which are secured in position with circlips. The aluminium alloy pistons are fitted with three piston rings, comprising two compression rings and an oil control ring.

The intake and exhaust valves are each closed by coil springs and operate in guides pressed into the cylinder head. Valve guides cannot be replaced.

A timing chain at the left-hand end of the engine, driven by the crankshaft, drives the high pressure fuel pump sprocket, which in turn drives the intake camshaft. The camshafts are geared together. The vacuum pump is integral with the oil pump. The coolant pump is driven by the auxiliary drivebelt.

On all engines, lubrication is by means of an eccentric-rotor type pump driven by the crankshaft via a Simplex chain. The pump draws oil through a strainer located in the sump, and then forces it through an externally-mounted full-flow paper element type oil filter into galleries in the cylinder block/crankcase, from where it is distributed to the crankshaft (main bearings), timing chain (sprayed by a jet), and camshafts. The big-end bearings are supplied with oil via internal drillings in the crankshaft, while the camshaft bearings and the followers receive a pressurised supply via drillings in the cylinder head. The camshaft lobes and valves are lubricated by oil splash, as are all other engine components. An oil cooler (integral with the oil filter housing) is fitted to keep the oil temperature stable under arduous operating conditions.

Repair operations possible with the engine in the car

The following work can be carried out with the engine in the vehicle:

a) Compression pressure – testing.
b) Camshaft cover – removal and refitting.
c) Crankshaft pulley – removal and refitting.
d) Camshafts and rocker arms – removal, inspection and refitting.
e) Cylinder head – removal and refitting.
f) Cylinder head and pistons – decarbonising.
g) Sump – removal and refitting.
h) Oil pump – removal, overhaul and refitting.
i) Oil filter housing/cooler – removal and refitting.
j) Crankshaft oil seals – renewal.
k) Engine/transmission mountings – inspection and renewal.
l) Flywheel/driveplate – removal, inspection and refitting.

Note: Although in theory it is possible to remove the timing cover and timing chains with the engine fitted, in practice access is extremely limited, special MINI tools are needed, and the cylinder head and sump must be removed. Consequently, it is recommended that the engine is removed prior to timing cover and chains removal.

2 Compression and leakdown tests – description and interpretation

Compression test

Note: A compression tester specifically designed for diesel engines must be used for this test.

1 When engine performance is down, or if misfiring occurs which cannot be attributed to the fuel system, a compression test can provide diagnostic clues as to the engine's condition. If the test is performed regularly, it can give warning of trouble before any other symptoms become apparent.

2 A compression tester specifically intended for diesel engines must be used, because of the higher pressures involved. The tester is connected to an adaptor which screws into the glow plug or injector hole. It is unlikely to be worthwhile buying such a tester for occasional use, but it may be possible to borrow or hire one – if not, have the test performed by a garage.

3 Unless specific instructions to the contrary are supplied with the tester, observe the following points:

a) The battery must be in a good state of charge, the air filter must be clean, and the engine should be at normal operating temperature.
b) All the glow plugs should be removed before starting the test (see Chapter 5C).
c) Disconnect the wiring plugs from the injectors (see Chapter 4B).

4 There is no need to hold the accelerator pedal down during the test, because the diesel engine air intake is not throttled.

5 Crank the engine on the starter motor; after one or two revolutions, the compression pressure should build up to a maximum figure, and then stabilise. Record the highest reading obtained.

6 Repeat the test on the remaining cylinders, recording the pressure in each.

7 All cylinders should produce very similar pressures; a difference of more than 2 bars between any two cylinders indicates a fault. Note that the compression should build up quickly in a healthy engine; low compression on the first stroke, followed by gradually-increasing pressure on successive strokes, indicates worn piston rings. A low compression reading on the first stroke, which does not build up during successive strokes, indicates leaking valves or a blown head gasket (a cracked head could also be the cause). Deposits on the undersides of the valve heads can also cause low compression.

Note: The cause of poor compression is less easy to establish on a diesel engine than on a petrol one. The effect of introducing oil into the cylinders ('wet' testing) is not conclusive, because there is a risk that the oil will sit in the swirl chamber or in the recess on the piston crown instead of passing to the rings.

8 Refer to a MINI dealer or other specialist if in doubt as to whether a particular pressure reading is acceptable.

9 On completion of the test, refit the glow plugs as described in Chapter 5C, and reconnect the injector wiring plugs.

Leakdown test

10 A leakdown test measures the rate at which compressed air fed into the cylinder is lost. It is an alternative to a compression test, and in many ways it is better, since the escaping air provides easy identification of where pressure loss is occurring (piston rings, valves or head gasket).

11 The equipment needed for leakdown testing is unlikely to be available to the home mechanic. If poor compression is suspected, have the test performed by a suitably-equipped garage.

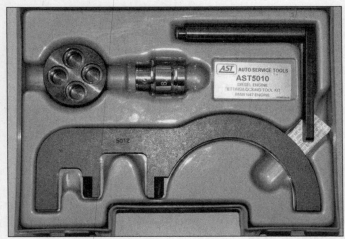

3.1 Kits like this from Auto Service Tools Ltd include crankshaft and camshaft setting tools, along with a tool that fits over the pulley bolts to facilitate crankshaft rotation

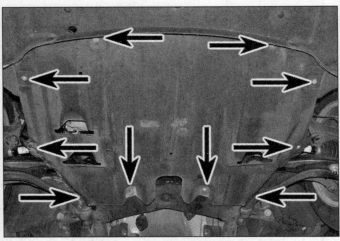

3.3 Engine undershield fasteners (arrowed)

3 Engine assembly/ valve timing settings – general information and usage

Note: *MINI tool No.11 5 320 or suitable equivalent will be required to lock the crankshaft in position, and access to MINI tool No. 11 8 760 or equivalent is required to position the camshafts.*

1 The flywheel is equipped with an indent, which aligns with a hole in the engine block when No.1 piston is at TDC (top dead centre). In this position, if No.1 piston is at TDC on its compression stroke, it must be possible to fit a MINI special tool (No. 11 8 760) or equivalent, over the square sections of the exhaust camshaft (with all four No.1 cylinder camshaft lobes pointing towards the right-hand side). **Note:** *The inexpensive, high quality setting tools featured in this manual were supplied and manufactured by Auto Service Tools ltd (asttools.co.uk)* **(see illustration).**

2 Firmly apply the handbrake then jack up the front of the vehicle and support it securely on axle stands (see *Jacking and vehicle support*).

3 Undo the retaining screws/clips and remove the engine undershield **(see illustration).**

4 Remove the camshaft cover and gasket, as described in Section 4.

5 Pull out the blanking plug from the timing pin hole in the rear side of the engine block **(see illustration).**

6 Using a socket and extension bar on one of the crankshaft pulley centre bolts, turn the crankshaft clockwise whilst keeping an eye on the No.1 cylinder camshaft lobes. MINI tool No. 11 6 480 or equivalent is available to rotate the crankshaft pulley bolts. The tool fits over all 4 bolts **(see illustration). Note:** *Do not turn the engine anti-clockwise.*

7 Rotate the crankshaft clockwise until the No.1 cylinder camshaft lobes approach the point where all four lobes are pointing upwards. Have an assistant insert MINI Tool No. 11 5 320 or equivalent into the timing pin hole, and press the pin gently against the flywheel. Continue to slowly turn the crankshaft slowly until the pin is felt to engage in the indent in the flywheel, and the crankshaft locks **(see illustration).**

8 With the crankshaft in this position, all four camshaft lobes of No.1 cylinder should be pointing to the rear. Check that the 2 marks on the front of the exhaust camshaft sprocket align with the single mark on the front of the intake camshaft sprocket. Fit MINI tool No. 11 8 760 or equivalent over the flats on the

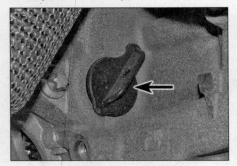

3.5 Pull out the blanking plug (arrowed)

3.6 The tool fits over the heads of the pulley bolts

3.7 Insert the crankshaft timing pin and engage it with the indent in the flywheel

3.8a The marks on the sprocket faces must align

3.8b Fit the setting tool over the flats on the exhaust camshaft collar

exhaust camshaft collar, adjacent to No.1 camshaft bearing cap. If the camshaft is timed correctly, the tool will contact both sides of the camshaft cover gasket face on the cylinder head (see illustrations). Note: *To avoid confusion, bear in mind that the timing chain and sprockets are fitted at the left-hand end of the engine.*

4 Camshaft cover – removal and refitting

4.3 Wiring harness bracket retaining bolts (arrowed)

4.7 Don't forget to renew the seals around the injector apertures

Removal

1 Remove the air cleaner housing as described in Chapter 4B.

2 With reference to Chapter 4B, remove the intake manifold, common rail and fuel injectors.

3 Note their fitted positions and routing, then undo the screws and move the wiring harness and bracket to one side **(see illustration)**. Note that there are 3 bolts securing the bracket on the rear side of the camshaft cover. Disconnect the wiring plugs as necessary, and place the wiring harness assembly over the left-hand side of the engine compartment.

4 Release the clips and detach the engine breather hose from the right-hand rear corner of the camshaft cover, and the glow plug wiring harness from the retaining clips on the cover.

5 Working in from the outside-in, evenly slacken and remove the bolts securing the camshaft cover to the cylinder head.

6 Remove the cover and discard its gaskets.

Refitting

7 Ensure the mating surfaces are clean and dry then fit the new gaskets to the cover **(see illustration)**.

8 Refit the cover to the cylinder head, ensuring that the gaskets remain correctly seated.

9 Insert the cover retaining bolts and tighten them all by hand. Once all bolts are in position, tighten them to the specified torque setting starting from the inside, working outwards.

10 The remainder of refitting is a reversal of removal.

5 Crankshaft pulley/ vibration damper – removal and refitting

1 Firmly apply the handbrake then jack up the front of the vehicle and support it securely on axle stands (see *Jacking and vehicle support*).

2 Remove the auxiliary drivebelt(s) as described in Chapter 1B.

3 If further dismantling is to be carried out (beyond pulley removal), align the engine assembly/valve timing settings as described in Section 3.

4 Slacken the crankshaft pulley retaining bolts. To prevent crankshaft rotation, (the pulley retaining bolts are extremely tight)

special MINI tools No. 11 8 181, 182, 183 and 185 (manual transmission only) are available. This tool fits through the hole in the base of the transmission bellhousing and engages with the starter ring gear. This tool may also be available from automotive tool specialists. In the absence of the tool, remove the starter motor as described in Chapter 5A to expose the flywheel ring gear, and have an assistant insert a wide blade screwdriver between the ring gear teeth and the transmission bellhousing whilst the pulley retaining bolts are slackened. If the engine is removed from the vehicle it will be necessary to lock the flywheel (see Section 12).

Caution: Do not be tempted to use the crankshaft locking pin (see Section 3) to prevent rotation as the centre bolts are slackened.

5 Unscrew the retaining bolts, and remove the pulley from the crankshaft **(see illustration)**. Discard the bolts, new ones must be fitted.

Refitting

6 Fit the pulley to the crankshaft and screw in the new retaining bolts.

7 Lock the crankshaft by the method used on removal, and tighten the pulley retaining bolts to the specified Stage 1 torque setting then angle-tighten the bolt(s) through the specified Stage 2 angle, using a socket and extension bar. It is recommended that an angle-measuring gauge is used during the final stages of the tightening, to ensure accuracy. If a gauge is not available, use paint to make alignment marks between the bolt heads

5.5 Crankshaft pulley retaining bolts

and pulley prior to tightening; the marks can then be used to check that the bolt has been rotated through the correct angle.

8 Refit the auxiliary drivebelt(s) as described in Chapter 1B.

6 Camshafts, rocker arms and hydraulic tappets – removal, inspection and refitting

Removal

1 Remove the camshaft cover as described in Section 4.

2 Firmly apply the handbrake, then jack up the front of the vehicle and support it securely on axle stands (see *Jacking and vehicle support*).

3 Undo the fasteners and remove the engine undershields **(see illustration 3.3)**.

4 Set the engine to TDC on No. 1 cylinder as described in Section 3. Insert the flywheel locking tool, but do not fit the camshaft locking tool.

5 Undo and release the timing chain tensioner **(see illustration)**. Discard the seal, a new one must be fitted.

6 Undo and remove the bolts securing the sprocket to the camshaft. Pull the sprocket from the camshaft, and place the chain in the cylinder head **(see illustrations)**.

7 Identify the camshaft bearing caps, to ensure they are refitted to their original positions. The exhaust camshaft is marked 'A', so mark the exhaust camshaft bearing caps as 'A1, A2, A3' etc starting with the cap

6.5 Unscrew the timing chain tensioner

6.6a Undo the sprocket retaining bolts...

6.6b ...then remove the sprocket and lay the chain to one side

at the front of the engine. The intake camshaft is marked 'E', so repeat the procedure for the intake camshaft starting with 'E1' at the front of the engine (furthest from the timing chain) **(see illustration)**.

8 Evenly and progressively, slacken and remove the retaining bolts, and remove the camshaft bearing caps.

9 Remove the camshafts from the cylinder head.

10 Working from the outside towards the centre, undo the bolts and remove the camshaft carrier **(see illustration)**. Recover the seals between the carrier and the cylinder head.

11 Lift the rocker arms from the cylinder head, and lay them out in order on a clean surface, so that they can be fitted into their original positions – if they are to be reused. Note that the rocker arms are clipped to the tappets – unless required, there is no need to separate the two – lift the rockers and tappets together.

12 Obtain sixteen small, clean plastic containers, and label them for identification. Alternatively, divide a larger container into compartments. Withdraw each hydraulic tappet in turn, and place it in its respective container, which should then be filled with clean engine oil.

Caution: Do not interchange the tappets, and do not allow the tappets to lose oil, as they will take a long time to refill with oil on restarting the engine, which could result in incorrect valve clearances. Absolute cleanliness is essential at all times when handling the tappets.

Inspection

13 Examine the camshaft bearing surfaces and cam lobes for signs of wear ridges and scoring. Renew the camshaft if any of these conditions are apparent. Examine the condition of the bearing surfaces both on the camshaft journals and in the cylinder head. If the head bearing surfaces are worn excessively, the cylinder head will need to be renewed.

14 Examine the rocker bearing surfaces which contact the camshaft lobes for wear ridges and scoring. If the engine's valve clearances have sounded noisy, particularly if the noise persists after initial start-up from cold, then there is reason to suspect a faulty tappet. If any tappet is thought to be faulty or is visibly worn it should be renewed.

Refitting

15 Where removed, lubricate the tappets with clean engine oil and carefully insert each one

into its original location in the cylinder head **(see illustration)**.

16 Refit the rocker arms to their original locations, ensuring that they are correctly orientated, and clipped onto the tappets (if removed).

17 Ensure the mating surfaces of the camshaft carrier and cylinder head are clean, then refit the camshaft carrier using new seals. Tighten the bolts to the specified torque working from the centre to the outside **(see illustration)**.

18 Remove the crankshaft locking tool, and rotate the crankshaft 45° anti-clockwise to prevent any accidental piston-to-valve contact. Ensure the timing chain does not fall into the timing cover, or jam on the crankshaft sprocket.

19 Engage the gear on the exhaust camshaft with the gear on the intake camshaft, so the 2 dots on the front of the intake camshaft gear are each side of the dot on the exhaust camshaft gear, then lay the camshafts in place on the cylinder head so the dots are flush with the upper surface of the cylinder head **(see illustration 3.8a)**.

20 Lubricate the bearing surfaces of the camshaft with clean engine oil, then refit the bearing caps to their original positions.

21 Insert the bearing cap bolts, then evenly and progressively tighten the retaining bolts to draw the bearing caps squarely down into contact with the cylinder head. Once the caps are in contact with the head, tighten the retaining bolts to the specified torque.

Caution: If the bearing caps bolts are carelessly tightened, the caps might break. If the caps are broken then the complete cylinder head assembly must be renewed; the caps are matched to the head and are not available separately.

22 With the camshafts in this position, it should be possible to fit MINI tool No. 11 8 760 (or equivalent) over the square section on the exhaust camshaft, as described in

6.7 The camshaft bearing caps are marked A for exhaust, and E for intake. No. 1 is at the right-hand end of the engine – the timing chain is at the left-hand end

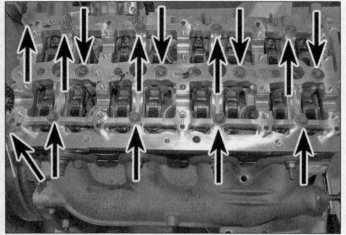

6.10 Working from the outside-in, gradually undo the camshaft carrier bolts (arrowed)

6.15 Refit the hydraulic tappets and rocker arms to their original positions

6.17 Renew the seals between the camshaft carrier and the cylinder head

6.22a Rotate the exhaust camshaft using a 10 mm Allen key/bit...

6.22b ...in the hexagonal section in the centre of the camshaft

6.24 The sprocket bolts holes should be almost in the centre of the slots

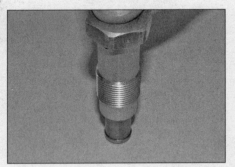

6.26 Compress the tensioner piston to evacuate any oil

Section 3. If not, rotate the camshafts using a 10 mm Allen key in the hexagonal section in the centre of the exhaust camshaft (see illustrations).

23 With the camshafts held in position, rotate the crankshaft 45° clockwise (back to TDC) so the flywheel locking tool can be reinserted. Ensure the timing chain doesn't fall inside the cover, or jam on the crankshaft sprocket.

24 Engage the timing chain with the sprocket, and position the sprocket on the end of the intake camshaft so the bolt holes are in the centre of the slots (see illustration).

25 Fit the sprocket retaining bolts into the holes and tighten them to 10 Nm, then slacken them 90° each.

26 The oil within the chain tensioner must be evacuated. Hold the tensioner on a hard, level surface and slowly compress to squeeze out the oil (see illustration). Repeat this procedure twice. With a new seal fitted, refit the chain tensioner and tighten it to the specified torque.

27 Make a final check to ensure the camshaft and flywheel locking tools are correctly fitted, then tighten the camshaft sprocket bolts to the specified torque.

28 Remove the camshaft and flywheel locking tools, then rotate the crankshaft two complete revolutions clockwise, and check the camshaft and flywheel tools can still be installed. If they cannot, repeat the fitting procedure from paragraph 24 onwards.

29 The remainder of refitting is a reversal of removal.

7 Cylinder head – removal and refitting

Removal

1 Remove the camshafts, rocker arms and tappets as described in Section 6.

2 Drain the cooling system, as described in Chapter 1B.

3 Remove the turbocharger as described in Chapter 4B.

4 Remove the EGR cooler as described in Chapter 4B.

5 Release the retaining clips, and disconnect the various coolant hoses from the cylinder head (see illustration).

6 Undo the plug on the rear of the cylinder

block and drain the coolant (see illustration). Fit a new sealing washer and tighten the drain plug to the specified torque.

7 Position a jack under the engine and take the weight. Place a block of wood on the jack head to prevent damage.

8 Undo the bolts/nut, disconnect the earth strap and remove the right-hand engine mounting bracket.

9 Undo the nut securing the particulate filter upper bracket to the engine.

10 Undo the 2 bolts at the left-hand end of the cylinder head (see illustration).

11 Undo the 3 bolts at the front, left-hand corner or the cylinder head (see illustration).

12 Make a final check to ensure that all relevant hoses, pipes and wires, etc, have been disconnected.

13 Working in the **reverse** of the tightening

7.5 Prise out the clips a little (arrowed) and disconnect the various coolant hoses from the cylinder head

7.6 The cylinder block drain plug (arrowed) is located on the rear of the block

7.10 Undo the 2 bolts (arrowed) at the left-hand end of the cylinder head …

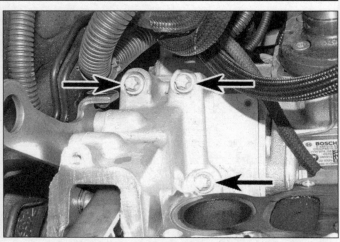

7.11 … and the 3 (arrowed) at the front, left-hand corner

sequence **(see illustration 7.30)**, progressively slacken the cylinder head bolts by a third of a turn at a time until all bolts can be unscrewed by hand. Withdraw and discard the bolts, new ones must be fitted.

14 Lift the cylinder head from the cylinder block. If necessary, tap the cylinder head gently with a soft-faced mallet to free it from the block, but **do not** lever at the mating faces.

15 When the joint is broken, lift the cylinder head away then remove the gasket. Note the fitted positions of the two locating dowels, and remove them for safe-keeping if they are loose. Keep the gasket for identification purposes (see paragraph 21).

Caution: Do not lay the head on its lower mating surface; support the head on wooden blocks, ensuring each block only contacts the head mating surface not the glow plugs. The glow plugs protrude out the bottom of the head and they will be damaged if the head is placed directly onto a bench.

16 If the cylinder head is to be dismantled, refer to the relevant Sections of Part D of this Chapter.

Preparation for refitting

17 The mating faces of the cylinder head and block must be perfectly clean before refitting

the head. Use a scraper to remove all traces of gasket and carbon, and also clean the tops of the pistons. Take particular care with the aluminium surfaces, as the soft metal is damaged easily. Also, make sure that debris is not allowed to enter the oil and water channels – this is particularly important for the oil circuit, as carbon could block the oil supply to the camshaft or crankshaft bearings. Using adhesive tape and paper, seal the water, oil and bolt holes in the cylinder block. To prevent carbon entering the gap between the pistons and bores, smear a little grease in the gap. After cleaning the piston, rotate the crankshaft so that the piston moves down the bore, then wipe out the grease and carbon with a cloth rag. Clean the piston crowns in the same way.

18 Check the block and head for nicks, deep scratches and other damage. If slight, they may be removed carefully with a file. More serious damage may be repaired by machining, but this is a specialist job.

19 If warpage of the cylinder head gasket surface is suspected, use a straight-edge to check it for distortion. Refer to Part D of this Chapter if necessary.

20 Ensure that the cylinder head bolt holes in the crankcase are clean and free of oil. Syringe or soak up any oil left in the bolt holes. This is most important in order that the correct bolt tightening torque can be applied and

to prevent the possibility of the block being cracked by hydraulic pressure when the bolts are tightened.

21 On these engines, the cylinder head to piston clearance is controlled by fitting different thickness head gaskets. The piston protrusion is represented by the number of holes in the gasket next to the timing chain area **(see illustration)**.

Holes in gasket	Largest piston protrusion
One hole	up to 0.92 mm
Two holes	0.92 to 1.03 mm
Three holes	1.03 to 1.18 mm

Select the replacement gasket which has the same thickness/number of holes as the original, unless new piston and connecting rod assemblies have been fitted. In that case, the correct thickness of gasket required is selected by measuring the piston protrusions as follows.

22 Remove the locking pin from the flywheel and mount a dial test indicator securely on the block so that its pointer can be easily pivoted between the piston crown and block mating surface.

23 Ensure the piston is at exactly TDC then zero the dial test indicator on the gasket surface of the cylinder block. Carefully move the indicator over No 1 piston, taking measurements in line with the gudgeon pin axis, measure the protrusion on both the left-hand and right-hand side of the piston **(see illustration)**. **Note:** *When turning the crankshaft, ensure that the timing chain does not jam in the timing cover.*

24 Rotate the crankshaft to bring the remaining pistons to TDC in turn. Ensure the crankshaft is accurately positioned then measure the protrusions of remaining pistons, taking two measurements for each piston. Once both pistons have been measured, rotate the crankshaft to bring No.1 piston back to TDC. Then rotate it 45° anti-clockwise.

25 Use the table in paragraph 21 to select the appropriate gasket.

7.21 Cylinder head gasket identification holes (arrowed – see text)

7.23 Measure the piston protrusion using a DTI gauge

Refitting

26 Wipe clean the mating faces of the head and block and ensure that the two locating dowels are in position on the cylinder block/crankcase surface **(see illustration)**.

27 Apply a little sealant (Drei Bond 1209) to the area where the timing chain cover meets the cylinder block **(see illustration)**, then fit the new gasket to the cylinder block, ensuring that it fits correctly over the locating dowels.

28 Carefully refit the cylinder head, locating it on the dowels. Make sure the timing chain can be pulled up through the cylinder head tunnel.

29 The new cylinder head bolts are supplied pre-coated – do not wash the coating off, or apply grease/oil to them. Carefully enter the main bolts (1 to 10) into the holes and screw them in, by hand only, until finger-tight.
Caution: Do not drop the bolts into their holes.

30 Working progressively and in the sequence shown, first tighten all the cylinder head bolts to the Stage 1 torque setting **(see illustration)**.

31 Slacken all the bolts half a turn (180°), then tighten them in sequence to the Stage 3 setting.

32 Again, in sequence, angle-tighten them to Stage 4, and then Stage 5, using an angle-measuring gauge **(see illustration)**.

33 Refit and tighten the bolts at the corner securing the cylinder head to the timing cover, to the specified torque **(see illustrations 7.10 and 7.11)**.

34 The remainder of refitting is a reversal of removal, noting the following points:
a) Renew all gaskets/seals disturbed during the removal procedure.
b) Tighten all fasteners to their specified torque where given.
c) Refill the cooling system as described in Chapter 1B.

8 Sump – removal and refitting
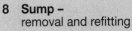

Removal

1 Drain the engine oil as described in Chapter 1B.

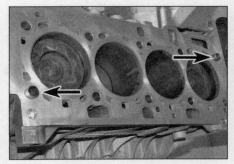

7.26 Ensure the locating dowels (arrowed) are in place

7.27 Apply sealant where the cylinder block meets the timing chain cover (arrowed)

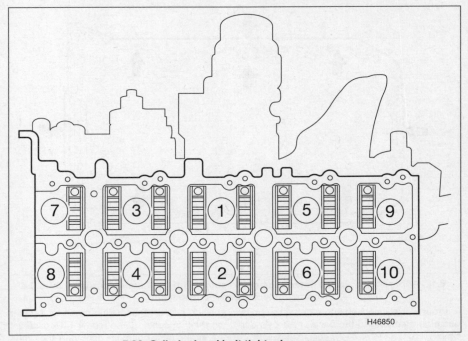

7.30 Cylinder head bolt tightening sequence

2 With reference to Section 13, remove the rear engine link rod/stabilizer bar, then undo the 4 bolts and remove the mounting bracket from the sump.

3 Undo the bolts and detach the fuel pipe support brackets from the sump **(see illustrations)**.

4 Undo the bolt securing the oil level dipstick guide tube and pull the tube from the sump **(see illustration)**. Renew the guide tube O-ring seal.

5 Disconnect the wiring plug from the engine oil level sensor.

6 Slacken and remove the bolts securing the transmission casing to the sump.

7.32 Tighten the cylinder head bolts using and angle-gauge

8.3a Undo the bolt (arrowed) securing the fuel pipe bracket at the rear of the sump...

8.3b ...and at the front (arrowed)

8.4 Oil level dipstick guide tube retaining bolt (arrowed)

8.9 Oil pump intake pipe bolts (arrowed)

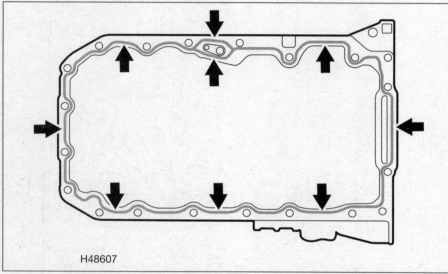

8.12 Apply sealant to the inner edge of the sump. The oil channel (arrowed) must be completely surrounded by sealant

7 Progressively slacken and remove the bolts securing the sump to the base of the cylinder block.

8 Break the sump joint by striking the sump with the palm of the hand, then lower the sump away from the engine.

9 While the sump is removed, take the opportunity to check the oil pump intake pipe for signs of clogging or splitting. If necessary, unbolt the intake pipe, and remove it from the engine along with its gasket **(see illustration)**. The strainer can then be cleaned easily in

8.14 Use a straight-edge to ensure the sump is flush with the cylinder block

solvent. Inspect the strainer mesh for signs of clogging or splitting and renew if necessary. If the intake pipe bolts are damaged they must be renewed.

Refitting

10 Clean all traces of sealant from the mating surfaces of the cylinder block and sump, then use a clean rag to wipe out the sump and the engine interior.

11 Where necessary, fit a new seal to the oil pump intake pipe then carefully refit the pipe. Refit the retaining bolts, and tighten them to the specified torque setting.

12 Apply a bead of suitable sealant (Loctite 5970, available from your MINI dealer) to the sump sealing surface, ensuring the 2.0 to 2.5 mm wide bead runs along the inner edge **(see illustration)**. Note that the sump must be installed within 10 minutes of the sealant being applied.

13 Offer up the sump to the cylinder block/crankcase. Refit the sump retaining bolts, and tighten the bolts finger-tight only.

14 Fit the bolts securing the sump to the gearbox. In order to align the rear sump flange with the gearbox, lightly tighten the bolts, then

slacken them. If the sump is being refitted to the engine with the gearbox removed, use a straight edge to ensure that the sump casting is flush with the end of the cylinder block **(see illustration)**.

15 Tighten the sump-to-engine block bolts, and then the sump-to-transmission bolts to the specified torque.

16 Refit the oil dipstick tube, with a new O-ring, and tighten the bolts securely.

17 The remainder of refitting is a reversal of removal, noting the following points:
 a) Renew all gaskets/seals where disturbed.
 b) Tighten all fasteners to their specified torque where given.
 c) Renew the engine oil and filter as described in Chapter 1B.

9 Oil/Vacuum pump – removal, inspection and refitting

Removal

1 Remove the sump and oil pump intake pipe as described in Section 8.

2 Undo the 4 pump retaining bolts.

3 Lift up the right-hand edge of the pump assembly, and manoeuvre the drive sprocket out from the chain. MINI insist that the drive sprocket is not removed.

Inspection

4 At the time of writing, no replacement parts are available for the oil/vacuum pump. If defective, the complete assembly must be replaced. Consult a MINI dealer or parts specialist.

Refitting

5 Ensure the mating surfaces of the pump and cylinder block are clean and dry. Ensure all mounting holes are clean and free from oil.

6 Engage the pump drive sprocket with the chain and with the pump in place, insert the retaining bolts.

7 Tighten the pump retaining bolts to their specified torque.

8 Refit the sump as described in Section 8.

10 Oil cooler – removal and refitting

Removal

1 Drain the engine coolant, engine oil, and remove the oil filter as described in Chapter 1B.

2 Remove the alternator and starter motor as described in Chapter 5A.

3 Undo the bolts and remove the oil filter housing **(see illustration)**. Discard the sealing gasket.

4 Undo the screws and detach the oil cooler from the oil filter housing. Renew the seals **(see illustrations)**.

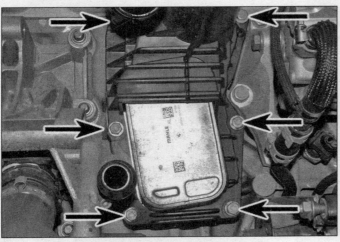

10.3 Oil filter housing bolts (arrowed)

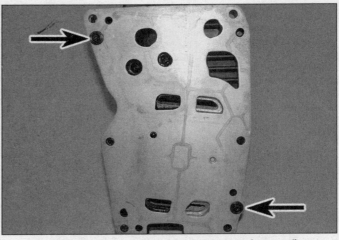

10.4a Oil cooler-to-filter housing screws (arrowed)

Refitting

5 Ensure the mating surfaces of the oil cooler and oil filter housing are clean and dry, and with a new gasket, fit the cooler to the housing. Tighten the screws securely or clip the cooler into the housing as applicable.

6 The remainder of refitting is a reversal of removal.

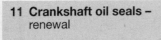

11 Crankshaft oil seals – renewal

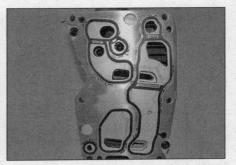

10.4b Renew the seals (arrowed) between the oil filter housing and cooler...

10.4c ...and the gasket/seal between the oil cooler and cylinder block

Right-hand end oil seal

1 Remove the crankshaft pulley/vibration damper as described in Section 5.

2 Lever out the seal using a flat-bladed screwdriver (or similar).

Caution: Great care must be taken to avoid damage to the crankshaft

3 Clean the seal housing and polish off any burrs or raised edges which may have caused the seal to fail in the first place.

4 Do not lubricate the new seal with engine oil or lubricant – the seal must be installed dry. MINI specify a special tool (No. 11 8 801, 802, 803 and 804) to guide the seal over the crankshaft shoulders. However, with care, it is

possible to fit the seal without the tool. Ensure the lips of the seal are around the outer edge of the crankshaft. Press the seal squarely into position until it is flush with the housing. If necessary, a suitable tubular drift, such as a socket, which bears only on the hard outer edge of the seal can be used to tap the seal into position. Take great care not to damage the seal lips during fitting and ensure that the seal lips face inwards.

5 Refit the crankshaft pulley as described in Section 5.

Flywheel/driveplate end oil seal

6 Remove the flywheel or driveplate as

described in Section 12, then remove the end cap (where fitted) **(see illustration)**. Avoid touching the outer edge of the end cap with fingers, as the crankshaft position sensor wheel is embedded in the rubber.

7 Lever out the seal using a flat-bladed screwdriver (or similar) **(see illustration)**.

Caution: Great care must be taken to avoid damage to the crankshaft

8 Do not lubricate the new seal with engine oil or lubricant – the seal must be installed dry. MINI specify a special tool (No. 11 8 815) to guide the seal over the crankshaft shoulders. However, with care, it is possible to fit the seal without the tool **(see illustration)**.

11.6 Remove the end cap from the crankshaft

11.7 Lever out the seal using a hooked tool or screwdriver

11.8 Guide the seal lips over the crankshaft shoulders...

9 Press the seal squarely into position until it is flush with the housing. If possible, a suitable tubular drift, such as a socket, which bears only on the hard outer edge of the seal can be used to tap the seal into position. Take great care not to damage the seal lips during fitting and ensure that the seal lips face inwards **(see illustration)**.

10 Refit the end cap (where fitted), followed by the flywheel/driveplate as described in Section 12.

12 Flywheel/driveplate –
removal, inspection and refitting

Flywheel

Removal

Note: *New flywheel retaining bolts must be used on refitting.*

1 Remove the clutch assembly as described in Chapter 6.

2 Prevent the flywheel from turning by locking the ring gear teeth with a similar arrangement to that shown **(see illustration)**. Alternatively, bolt a strap between the flywheel and the cylinder block/crankcase.

3 Slacken and remove the retaining bolts and remove the flywheel, noting its locating dowel **(see illustrations)**. **Do not** drop it, as it is very heavy. Discard the bolts, they must be renewed whenever they are disturbed.

Inspection

4 If the flywheel-to-clutch mating surface

11.9 ...then press it into place until it's flush with the housing

is deeply scored, cracked or otherwise damaged, then the flywheel must be renewed, unless it is possible to have it surface ground. Seek the advice of a MINI dealer or engine reconditioning specialist.

5 If the ring gear is badly worn or has missing teeth, then it must be renewed. This job is best left to a MINI dealer or engine reconditioning specialist.

6 These vehicles are fitted with dual mass flywheels. Whilst MINI do not publish any checking procedures, rotate the inner mass by hand anti-clockwise, mark its position in relation to the outer mass, then rotate it by hand clockwise and measure the travel. As a general rule, if the movement is more than 30 mm or less than 15 mm, consult a MINI dealer or transmission specialist as to whether a replacement unit is needed.

Refitting

7 Clean the mating surfaces of the flywheel

and crankshaft and remove all traces of locking compound from the crankshaft threaded holes.

8 Fit the flywheel to the crankshaft, engaging it with the crankshaft locating dowel, and fit the new retaining bolts **(see illustrations)**. **Note:** *If the new bolts are not supplied pre-coated with locking compound, apply a few drops prior to fitting the bolts.*

9 Lock the flywheel using the method employed on dismantling, working in a diagonal sequence, tighten all the retaining bolts to the specified torque setting.

10 Refit the clutch assembly as described in Chapter 6.

Driveplate

Removal

Note: *New driveplate retaining bolts must be used on refitting.*

11 Remove the automatic transmission as described in Chapter 7B.

12 Prevent the driveplate from turning by locking the ring gear teeth with a similar arrangement to that shown **(see illustration 12.2)**. Alternatively, bolt a strap between the driveplate and the cylinder block/crankcase.

13 Slacken and remove the retaining bolts and remove the driveplate, noting its locating dowel. Discard the bolts, they must be renewed whenever they are disturbed.

Inspection

14 If the ring gear is badly worn or has missing teeth, then it must be renewed. This job is best left to a MINI dealer or engine reconditioning specialist.

Refitting

15 Clean the mating surfaces of the driveplate and crankshaft and remove all traces of locking compound from the crankshaft threaded holes.

16 Fit the driveplate to the crankshaft, engaging it with the crankshaft locating dowel, and fit the new retaining bolts. **Note:** *If the new bolts are not supplied pre-coated with locking compound, apply a few drops prior to fitting the bolts.*

17 Lock the driveplate using the method employed on dismantling then, working in a diagonal sequence, tighten all the retaining bolts to the specified torque setting.

18 Refit the automatic transmission as described in Chapter 7B.

12.2 Lock the flywheel using a similar tool

12.3a Note the locating dowel (arrowed)...

12.3b ...which locates in the hole (arrowed) in the flywheel

12.8a Clean the crankshaft flywheel bolt threads using an old bolt with a saw cut across it

12.8b The new bolts should be pre-coated with thread-locking compound

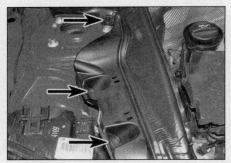

13.7 Undo the 2 scrivets and nut (arrowed) then remove the foam/plastic panel each side

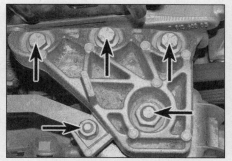

13.8 Engine mounting bracket bolts/nut and earth strap (arrowed)

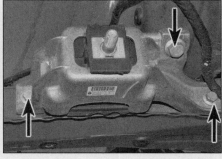

13.9 Right-hand engine mounting bolts (arrowed)

13 Engine/transmission mountings – inspection and renewal

Inspection

1 If improved access is required, chock the rear wheels then jack up the front of the car and support it on axle stands (see *Jacking and vehicle support*). Undo the screws and remove the engine undershield.

2 Check the mounting rubbers to see if they are cracked, hardened or separated from the metal at any point; renew the mounting if any such damage or deterioration is evident.

3 Check that all the mountings' fasteners are securely tightened; use a torque wrench to check if possible.

4 Using a large screwdriver or a crowbar, check for wear in each mounting by carefully levering against it to check for free play. Where this is not possible, enlist the aid of an assistant to move the engine/transmission back-and-forth, or from side-to-side, while you watch the mounting. While some free play is to be expected even from new components, excessive wear should be obvious. If excessive free play is found, check first that the fasteners are correctly secured, and then renew any worn components as described below.

Renewal

Right-hand mounting

5 Remove the engine undershield, then place

a jack beneath the engine, with a block of wood on the jack head. Raise the jack until it is supporting the weight of the engine.

6 Pull up the plastic cover from the top of the engine.

7 In order to access the engine mounting, the bonnet lock slam panel must be moved to one side as follows:

a) *Release the fasteners and remove the foam/plastic panels from the each side of the engine compartment* **(see illustration)**.

b) *Undo the bolts securing both the headlights to the bonnet slam panel, then completely remove the right-hand headlight (Chapter 12).*

c) *Remove the radiator grille as described in Chapter 11.*

d) *Undo the 3 bolts each side at the upper surface and move the slam panel to one side a little.*

8 Slacken and remove the bolts/nut securing the mounting bracket to the mounting and the bracket bolted to the cylinder head **(see illustration)**. Disconnect the earth lead as the bracket is withdrawn.

9 Undo the bolts and remove the mounting **(see illustration)**.

10 Check for signs of wear or damage on all components, and renew as necessary.

11 Refitting is a reversal of removal.

Left-hand mounting

12 Remove the air cleaner housing and engine control unit as described in Chapter 4B, then

unbolt and reposition the underbonnet fuse and relay box.

13 Place a jack beneath the transmission, with a block of wood on the jack head. Raise the jack until it is supporting the weight of the transmission.

14 Remove the mounting bracket-to-body bolts, the refrigerant pipe bracket and the bracket-to-mounting nut **(see illustration)**. **Note:** *The mounting bracket-to-body bolts may be either grade 8.8 or 10.9 (cast into the head of the bolt). MINI insist that the grade 8.8 bolts must be replaced with grade 10.9 bolts.*

15 Undo the four retaining bolts from the mounting on the body and remove it from the engine compartment **(see illustration)**.

16 Check carefully for signs of wear or damage on all components, and renew them where necessary.

17 Fit the mounting bolts to the bracket on the transmission and tighten the retaining bolts to the specified torque.

18 Refit the mounting bracket to the vehicle body and tighten its bolts/nut to the specified torque.

19 The remainder of refitting is a reversal of removal.

Rear lower mounting

20 If not already done, firmly apply the handbrake, then jack up the front of the vehicle and support it securely on axle stands (see *Jacking and vehicle support*).

21 Unscrew and remove the bolt securing the rear mounting link to the bracket on the engine **(see illustration)**.

13.14 Left-hand mounting bracket bolts/nut (arrowed)

13.15 Undo the bolts and remove the left-hand engine/transmission mounting

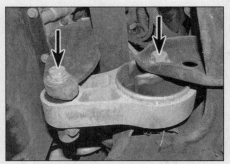

13.21 Rear lower mounting link bolts (arrowed)

14.3 Drive the flywheel pilot bearing out from the engine side

14.4a Position the bearing…

14.4b …then drive it into place using a tubular spacer or socket

22 Remove the bolt securing the rear mounting link to the subframe and remove the link.

23 To remove the mounting bracket, remove the right-hand driveshaft (Chapter 8), then undo the retaining bolts and remove the mounting bracket from the rear of the engine.

24 Check carefully for signs of wear or damage on all components, and renew them where necessary.

25 On reassembly, fit the rear mounting bracket to the transmission, and tighten its retaining bolts to the specified torque.

26 Refit the rear mounting torque reaction link, and tighten both its bolts to their specified torque settings.

27 Lower the vehicle to the ground.

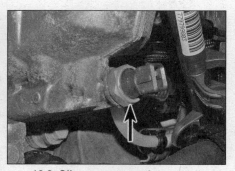

16.2 Oil pressure warning sensor (arrowed)

14 Flywheel pilot bearing – inspection, removal and refitting

Inspection

1 The pilot bearing is fitted into the centre of the dual mass flywheel, and provides support for the free end of the gearbox input shaft on manual transmission vehicles. It can only be examined once the clutch (Chapter 6) has been removed. Using a finger, rotate the inner race of the bearing and check for any roughness, binding or looseness in the bearing. If any of these conditions are evident, the bearing must be replaced.

Removal

2 Remove the flywheel as described in Section 12.

3 The bearing must be pressed out using a hydraulic press, with a drift that bears only on the inner bearing race. The bearing is pressed from the engine side of the flywheel and out of the clutch side **(see illustration)**. Note that the act of pressing the bearing out will render it unusable – it must be replaced.

Refitting

4 Using a suitable tubular spacer that bears only on the hard outer edge of the bearing, press the new bearing into the flywheel until it contacts the shoulder **(see illustrations)**.

5 Refit the flywheel as described in Section 12.

15 Timing chains and cover – general information

On these engines, the timing chains are fitted at the rear of the engine. In order to remove the timing chains or the timing cover, it is necessary to first remove the engine. Consequently, replacement of the timing chain and covers is described in Chapter 2D.

16 Oil pressure sensor – removal and refitting

Oil pressure sensor

1 The oil pressure switch is fitted into the cylinder block beneath the high-pressure pump at the front of the engine.

2 Disconnect the wiring plug, and unscrew the sensor **(see illustration)**. Be prepared for oil spillage.

3 Refitting is a reversal of removal, using a new sealing washer, and tightening the sensor to the specified torque.

Chapter 2 Part D:
Engine removal and overhaul procedures

Contents

Degrees of difficulty

Easy, suitable for novice with little experience	Fairly easy, suitable for beginner with some experience	Fairly difficult, suitable for competent DIY mechanic	Difficult, suitable for experienced DIY mechanic	Very difficult, suitable for expert DIY or professional

Specifications

Engine identification

Petrol engines

1.4 litre engine	N12B14
1.6 litre engine:	
Non-turbo (up to 2010)	N12B16
Non-turbo (2010-on)	N16B16
Turbo (2010 – 2012 173 and 208 bhp)	N14B16
Turbo (2010-on 181 bhp)	N18B16

Diesel engines

1.6 litre up to 2010	W16
1.6 litre from 2010	N47 C16
2.0 litre	N47 C20

Cylinder block

Cylinder bore diameter:

Petrol engines	77.00 mm (nominal)
Diesel engines:	
W16	75.00 mm (nominal)
N47	
1.6 litre	78.00 mm (nominal)
2.0 litre	84.00 mm (nominal)

Cylinder head

Maximum gasket face distortion	0.05 mm
New cylinder head height:	
Petrol engines:	
N12	No refacing permitted
N14, N16 and N18	N/A
Diesel engines:	
W16	124.0 ± 0.05 mm
N47	N/A
Minimum cylinder head height after machining:	
Petrol engines	N/A
Diesel engines	No refacing permitted

Valves

	Inlet	Exhaust
Valve head diameter:		
Petrol engines	N/A	N/A
Diesel engines:		
W16	N/A	N/A
N47:		
1.6 litre	24.8 mm	21.2 mm
2.0 litre	27.2 mm	24.6 mm
Valve stem diameter:		
Petrol engines	4.960 to 4.975 mm	4.952 to 4.967 mm
Diesel engines:		
W16	5.485 +0.0, −0.015 mm	5.475 +0.0, −0.015 mm
N47	4.920 mm	4.920 mm

Pistons

Piston diameter:	
Petrol engines:	
N12 and N14	76.941 mm (nominal)
N16 and N18	76.949 mm (nominal)
Diesel engines:	
W16	N/A
N47:	
1.6 litre	77.95 mm (nominal)
2.0 litre	84.95 mm (nominal)

Check with your MINI dealer or engine specialist regarding piston oversizes

Piston ring end gaps

Petrol engines:	
Top compression ring	0.25 to 0.35 mm
Second compression ring	0.35 to 0.50 mm
Oil control ring	0.10 to 0.35 mm
Diesel engines:	
W16:	
Top compression ring	0.15 to 0.25 mm
Second compression ring	0.30 to 0.50 mm
Oil control ring	0.35 to 0.55 mm
N47:	
Top compression ring	0.15 to 0.25 mm
Second compression ring	0.30 to 0.45 mm
Oil compression ring	N/A

Crankshaft

Endfloat:	
Petrol engines	0.015 to 0.050 mm
Diesel engines:	
W16	0.07 to 0.32 mm (thrustwasher thickness 2.40 ± 0.05 mm)
Main bearing journal diameter:	
Petrol engines	44.984 to 45.000 mm
Diesel engines:	
W16	49.962 to 49.981 mm
N47	54.971 to 54.990 mm
Big-end bearing journal diameter:	
N12 and N14	40.975 to 40.991 mm
N16 and N18	44.975 to 44.991 mm
Diesel engines:	
W16	46.975 to 46.991 mm
N47:	
1.6 litre	45.000 (nominal)
2.0 litre	50.000 (nominal)
Maximum bearing journal out-of-round (all models)	0.007 mm

Torque wrench settings

Petrol engines

Refer to Chapter 2A Specifications

W16 diesel engines

Refer to Chapter 2B Specifications

N47 diesel engines

Refer to Chapter 2C Specifications

1 General information

Included in this Part of Chapter 2 are details of removing the engine/transmission from the car and general overhaul procedures for the cylinder head, cylinder block/crankcase and all other engine internal components.

The information given ranges from advice concerning preparation for an overhaul and the purchase of parts, to detailed step-by-step procedures covering removal, inspection, renovation and refitting of engine internal components.

After Section 5, all instructions are based on the assumption that the engine has been removed from the car. For information concerning in-car engine repair, as well as the removal and refitting of those external components necessary for full overhaul, refer to Part A, B or C of this Chapter, as applicable and to Section 5. Ignore any preliminary dismantling operations that are no longer relevant once the engine has been removed from the car.

Apart from torque wrench settings, which are given at the beginning of Parts A, B and C, all specifications relating to engine overhaul are at the beginning of this Part of Chapter 2.

2 Engine overhaul – general information

1 It is not always easy to determine when, or if, an engine should be completely overhauled, as a number of factors must be considered.

2 High mileage is not necessarily an indication that an overhaul is needed, while low mileage does not preclude the need for an overhaul. Frequency of servicing is probably the most important consideration. An engine, which has had regular and frequent oil and filter changes, as well as other required maintenance, should give many thousands of miles of reliable service. Conversely, a neglected engine may require an overhaul very early in its life.

3 Excessive oil consumption is an indication that piston rings, valve seals and/or valve guides are in need of attention. Make sure that oil leaks are not responsible before deciding that the rings and/or guides are worn. Perform a compression test, as described in Part A, B or C of this Chapter (as applicable), to determine the likely cause of the problem.

4 Check the oil pressure with a gauge fitted in place of the oil pressure switch, and compare it with that specified. If it is extremely low, the main and big-end bearings, and/or the oil pump, are probably worn out.

5 Loss of power, rough running, knocking or metallic engine noises, excessive valve gear noise, and high fuel consumption may also point to the need for an overhaul, especially if they are all present at the same time. If

a complete service does not remedy the situation, major mechanical work is the only solution.

6 A full engine overhaul involves restoring all internal parts to the specification of a new engine. During a complete overhaul, the pistons and the piston rings are renewed. New main and big-end bearings are generally fitted; if necessary, the crankshaft may be reground, to compensate for wear in the journals. The valves are also serviced as well, since they are usually in less-than-perfect condition at this point. While the engine is being overhauled, other components, such as the starter and alternator, can be overhauled as well. Always pay careful attention to the condition of the oil pump when overhauling the engine, and renew it if there is any doubt as to its serviceability. The end result should be an as-new engine that will give many trouble-free miles.

7 Critical cooling system components such as the hoses, thermostat and water pump should be renewed when an engine is overhauled. The radiator should be checked carefully, to ensure that it is not clogged or leaking. Also, it is a good idea to renew the oil pump whenever the engine is overhauled.

8 Before beginning the engine overhaul, read through the entire procedure, to familiarise yourself with the scope and requirements of the job. Overhauling an engine is not difficult if you follow carefully all of the instructions, have the necessary tools and equipment, and pay close attention to all specifications. It can, however, be time-consuming. Plan on the car being off the road for a minimum of two weeks, especially if parts must be taken to an engineering works for repair or reconditioning. Check on the availability of parts and make sure that any necessary special tools and equipment are obtained in advance. Most work can be done with typical hand tools, although a number of precision measuring tools are required for inspecting parts to determine if they must be renewed. Often the engineering works will handle the inspection of parts and offer advice concerning reconditioning and renewal.

9 Always wait until the engine has been completely dismantled, and until all components (especially the cylinder block/crankcase and the crankshaft) have been inspected, before deciding what service and repair operations must be performed by an engineering works. The condition of these components will be the major factor to consider when determining whether to overhaul the original engine, or to buy a reconditioned unit. Do not, therefore, purchase parts or have overhaul work done on other components until they have been thoroughly inspected. As a general rule, time is the primary cost of an overhaul, so it does not pay to fit worn or sub-standard parts.

10 As a final note, to ensure maximum life and minimum trouble from a reconditioned engine, everything must be assembled with care, in a spotlessly clean environment.

3 Engine removal – methods and precautions

1 If you have decided that the engine must be removed for overhaul or major repair work, several preliminary steps should be taken.

2 Locating a suitable place to work is extremely important. Adequate workspace, along with storage space for the car, will be needed. Engine/transmission removal is extremely complicated and involved on these vehicles. It must be stated, that unless the vehicle can be positioned on a ramp, or raised and supported on axle stands over an inspection pit, it will be more difficult to carry out the work involved.

3 Cleaning the engine compartment and engine/transmission before beginning the removal procedure will help keep tools clean and organised.

4 An engine hoist or A-frame will also be necessary. Make sure the equipment is rated in excess of the weight of the engine. Safety is of primary importance, considering the potential hazards involved in lifting the engine/transmission out of the car.

5 The help of an assistant is essential. Apart from the safety aspects involved, there are many instances when one person cannot simultaneously perform all of the operations required during engine/transmission removal.

6 Plan the operation ahead of time. Before starting work, arrange for the hire of or obtain all of the tools and equipment you will need. Some of the equipment necessary to perform engine/transmission removal and installation safely and with relative ease (in addition to an engine hoist) is as follows: a heavy duty trolley jack, complete sets of spanners and sockets (see Tools and working facilities), wooden blocks, and plenty of rags and cleaning solvent for mopping-up spilled oil, coolant and fuel. If the hoist must be hired, make sure that you arrange for it in advance, and perform all of the operations possible without it beforehand. This will save you money and time.

7 Plan for the car to be out of use for quite a while. An engineering machine shop or engine reconditioning specialist will be required to perform some of the work, which cannot be accomplished without special equipment. These places often have a busy schedule, so it would be a good idea to consult them before removing the engine, in order to accurately estimate the amount of time required to rebuild or repair components that may need work.

8 During the engine/transmission removal procedure, it is advisable to make notes of the locations of all brackets, cable ties, earthing points, etc, as well as how the wiring harnesses, hoses and electrical connections are attached and routed around the engine and engine compartment. An effective way of doing this is to take a series of photographs of the various components before they are

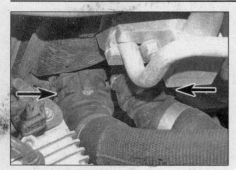

4.11a Prise out the wire clips a little (arrowed) and disconnect the heater hoses at the engine compartment bulkhead

4.11b Move the radiator forwards a little to access the upper hose and expansion tank hose (arrowed)

4.12 Depress the release button (arrowed), and disconnect the servo vacuum hose at the left-hand side of the engine compartment

disconnected or removed; the resulting photographs will prove invaluable when the engine/transmission is refitted.

9 The engine can be removed complete with the transmission as an assembly. Remove the front bumper, crossmember, radiator panel, and then the assembly is removed from the front of the vehicle.

10 Always be extremely careful when removing and refitting the engine/transmission. Serious injury can result from careless actions. Plan ahead and take your time, and a job of this nature, although major, can be accomplished successfully.

Note: *Such is the complexity of the power unit arrangement on these vehicles, and the variations that may be encountered according to model and optional equipment fitted, that the following should be regarded as a guide to the work involved, rather than a step-by-step procedure. Where differences are encountered, or additional component disconnection or removal is necessary, make notes of the work involved as an aid to refitting.*

4	Engine –
	removal and refitting

Note: *Such is the complexity of the power unit arrangement on these vehicles, and the variations that may be encountered according to model and optional equipment fitted, the following should be regarded as a guide to*

the work involved, rather than a step-by-step procedure. Where differences are encountered, or additional component disconnection or removal is necessary, make notes of the work involved as an aid to refitting.

Removal

1 On models with air conditioning, have the refrigerant evacuated by a MINI dealer or suitably equipped repairer.

2 Disconnect the battery negative terminal as described in Chapter 5A.

3 Apply the handbrake, then jack up the front of the vehicle and support it on axle stands (see *Jacking and vehicle support*). Remove both front roadwheels. Undo the screws/fasteners and remove the engine undershield (where fitted).

4 Remove the bonnet, radiator grille and front bumper as described in Chapter 11.

5 Drain the cooling system with reference to Chapter 1A or Chapter 1B.

6 Drain the transmission oil/fluid as described in Chapter 7A or Chapter 7B. Refit the drain and filler plugs, and tighten them to their specified torque settings.

7 If the engine is to be dismantled, drain the engine oil and remove the oil filter as described in Chapter 1A or Chapter 1B. Clean and refit the drain plug, tightening it securely.

8 Refer to Chapter 8 and remove both front driveshafts.

9 Remove the air cleaner assembly and exhaust system as described in Chapter 4A or Chapter 4B.

10 Remove the radiator cooling fan as described in Chapter 3.

11 Make a note of their fitted positions and routing, then disconnect all coolant hoses from the engine and radiator **(see illustrations)**.

12 Disconnect the vacuum hose from the brake servo at the engine compartment bulkhead **(see illustration)**.

13 Remove the engine management ECU as described in Chapter 4A or Chapter 4B.

14 Release the clamp, disconnect the hose from the top of the coolant expansion tank, then undo the retaining bolt, lift the tank slightly, and disconnect the hose from the base of the tank **(see illustration)**.

15 Working under the front, left-hand wheelarch, disconnect the wiring and hoses from the washer pump(s).

16 Disconnect the wiring plug from the air conditioning compressor.

17 On turbocharged models, disconnect the intercooler intake and outlet hoses.

18 Undo the bolts each side securing the front subframe members to the front panel **(see illustration)**.

19 Remove both headlights as described in Chapter 12.

20 On models with air conditioning, unclip the refrigerant pipe from the front panel on the right-hand side (where applicable), then undo the bolts and disconnect the refrigerant pipes at the left-hand end of the front panel **(see illustration)**. Plug the openings to prevent contamination. Renew the pipe O-ring seals.

4.14 Coolant expansion tank retaining bolt (arrowed)

4.18 Undo the bolts/screw each side (arrowed) securing the front panel to the subframe

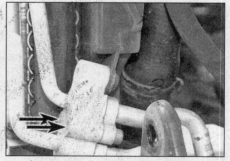

4.20 Undo the bolts (arrowed) and disconnect the condenser refrigerant pipes

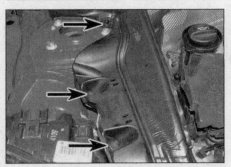

4.21a Undo the nut and scrivets (arrowed), then remove the panel each side

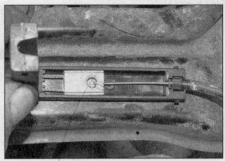

4.21b Prise open the junction box and disconnect the bonnet release cable

4.22a Undo the bolt (arrowed) securing the front panel to the wing each side...

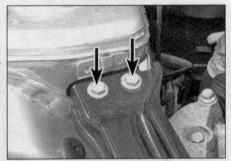

4.22b ...the 2 bolts (arrowed) securing the panel to the suspension turrets...

4.22c ...and the 3 nuts (arrowed) securing the panel to the chassis members

4.23a On petrol models, the fuel feed hose is located at the left-hand end of the cylinder head (arrowed)

21 Remove the padding from each side of the engine compartment (where fitted), then disconnect the bonnet release cable at the junction box on the left-hand side of the engine compartment (see illustrations).

22 With an assistant supporting the front panel, undo the nuts/bolts each side and manoeuvre the front panel forwards a little. Check to ensure all relevant hoses/wiring etc. have been disconnected, then place the front panel to one side (see illustrations).

23 Disconnect the fuel feed and return (where applicable) hoses. On N47 diesel engines, remove the bolt securing the hose bracket to the rear of the sump, then position the hoses to one side and secure them to the subframe with cable ties etc. (see illustrations). Plug the end of the hoses to prevent dirt ingress, then unclip from the rear of the engine.

24 Disconnect the selector cable(s) from the transmission as described in Chapter 7A or Chapter 7B.

25 On manual transmission models, unbolt the clutch slave cylinder, then tie it to one side, without disconnecting the fluid pipe (see Chapter 6). Use an elastic band around the cylinder to prevent the piston from coming out, then unclip the fluid hose from the support bracket on the transmission casing.

26 On all except N47 diesel engines, unclip the auxiliary fuse box from the bulkhead panel at the rear of the engine compartment, undo the nut at each end, and remove the panel.

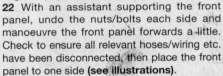

4.23b Press the hose onto the pipe a little, push the collar (arrowed) into the coupling, and pull the hose from the pipe

4.23c Depress the release button (arrowed) and disconnect the fuel hose from the filter – W16 diesel engines

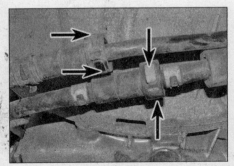

4.23d On N47 diesel engines, depress the release buttons each side (arrowed), disconnect the hoses...

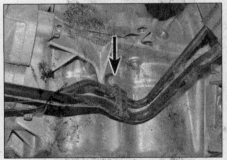

4.23e ...then undo the bolt (arrowed) securing the fuel pipe bracket to the sump

4.26a Unclip the fusebox (arrowed) and disconnect the bonnet switch

4.26b Unclip the wiring harness(s) from the bulkhead panel

4.26c Undo the plastic nut (arrowed) each side...

4.26d ...and lift out the bulkhead panel

4.26e Undo the nuts (arrowed), disconnect the positive leads...

4.26f ...and disconnect the positive lead (arrowed) from the battery's IBS unit

Release any retaining clips as necessary (see illustrations). This will allow the battery positive lead to be disconnected, and removed

with the engine assembly. On N47 engines, disconnect the battery positive lead from the alternator and starter motor (see illustration).

27 Disconnect the air conditioning refrigerant pipe adjacent to the crankshaft pulley, and remove the pipes from the air conditioning compressor where applicable (see illustrations). Plug/cover the openings to prevent contamination.

28 Make a final check to ensure all wiring, hoses and brackets that would prevent the removal of the assembly have been disconnected.

29 Using a hoist attached to the lifting eyes, take the weight of the engine and transmission.

30 If not already done so, undo the 2 retaining bolts, move the engine compartment fusebox to one side, then undo the 3 bolts and remove the support bracket beneath (see illustration). Release any wiring clips as the bracket it withdrawn.

31 Undo the nut securing the right-hand engine mounting bracket to its mounting, then remove the left-hand mounting bracket as described in Chapter 2A, 2B or 2C. Disconnect the earth strap from the right-hand mounting bracket.

32 Lift the right-hand end of the engine so the assembly is clear of the mounting, then move the engine/transmission forwards and out from the front of the vehicle. Enlist the help of an assistant during this procedure, as it may be necessary to tilt and twist the assembly slightly to clear the body panels and adjacent components. Move the unit clear of the car and lower it to the ground (see illustration).

Separation

33 With the engine/transmission assembly

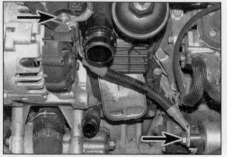

4.26g On N47 diesel engines, undo the nuts (arrowed) and disconnect the positive lead from the alternator and starter motor

4.27a Disconnect the refrigerant pipe adjacent to the crankshaft pulley (arrowed)

4.27b Disconnect the pipe from the compressor and manoeuvre the pipe from place

4.30 Fusebox/ECM support bracket retaining bolts (arrowed)

Engine removal and overhaul procedures 2D•7

removed, support the assembly on suitable blocks of wood on a workbench (or failing that, on a clean area of the workshop floor).

34 Undo the retaining bolts, and remove the flywheel lower cover plate (where fitted) from the transmission.

35 Slacken and remove the retaining bolts, and remove the starter motor from the transmission.

36 Disconnect any remaining wiring connectors at the transmission, then move the main engine wiring harness to one side.

37 On automatic transmission models, turn the crankshaft by means of a socket on the crankshaft pulley bolt, until one of the six torque converter retaining nuts is accessible through the starter motor aperture. Undo the accessible torque converter nut, then turn the crankshaft as necessary and undo the remaining nuts.

38 Ensure that both engine and transmission are adequately supported, then slacken and remove the remaining bolts securing the transmission housing to the engine. Note the correct fitted positions of each bolt (and the relevant brackets) as they are removed, to use as a reference on refitting.

39 Carefully withdraw the transmission from the engine, ensuring that the weight of the transmission is not allowed to hang on the input shaft while it is engaged with the clutch friction disc (manual transmission models) or that the torque converter does not slip from the input shaft (automatic transmission models).

40 If they are loose, remove the locating dowels from the engine or transmission, and keep them in a safe place.

Refitting

41 Refitting is a reversal of removal, noting the following points:

a) *Ensure that the wiring loom is correctly routed and retained by all the relevant retaining clips; all connectors should be correctly and securely reconnected.*

b) *Prior to refitting the driveshafts to the transmission, renew the driveshaft oil seals as described in Chapter 7A or Chapter 7B.*

c) *Do not apply lubricant of any kind to the input shaft splines.*

d) *Ensure that all coolant hoses are correctly reconnected, and securely retained by their retaining clips.*

e) *Refill the engine and transmission with the correct quantity and type of lubricant, as described in Chapter 1A or Chapter 1B, and Chapter 7A or Chapter 7B.*

f) *Refill the cooling system as described in Chapter 1A or Chapter 1B.*

g) *It's likely that after reassembly, fault codes will be stored in the engine management ECU. If the faults are not cleared after a full road test, have the codes read, and erased by a MINI dealer or suitably equipped repairer. If after a further roadtest, the fault codes reappear, investigate and rectify as necessary.*

4.32 Twist the engine/transmission assembly as necessary to clear the chassis members

5 Engine overhaul – dismantling sequence

1 It is much easier to dismantle and work on the engine if it is mounted on a portable engine stand. These stands can often be hired from a tool hire shop. Before the engine is mounted on a stand, the flywheel/driveplate should be removed, so that the stand bolts can be tightened into the end of the cylinder block/crankcase.

2 If a stand is not available, it is possible to dismantle the engine with it blocked up on a sturdy workbench, or on the floor. Be extra careful not to tip or drop the engine when working without a stand.

3 If you are going to obtain a reconditioned engine, all the external components must be removed first, to be transferred to the new engine (just as they will if you are doing a complete engine overhaul yourself). These components include the following:

a) *Ancillary unit mounting brackets (oil filter, starter, alternator, power steering pump, etc)*

b) *Thermostat and housing (Chapter 3).*

c) *Dipstick tube/sensor.*

d) *All electrical switches and sensors.*

e) *Inlet and exhaust manifolds – where applicable (Chapter 4A or Chapter 4B).*

f) *Ignition coils and spark plugs – as applicable (Chapter 5B and Chapter 1A).*

g) *Flywheel/driveplate (Part A, B or C of this Chapter).*

Note: *When removing the external components from the engine, pay close attention to details that may be helpful or important during refitting. Note the fitted position of gaskets, seals, spacers, pins, washers, bolts, and other small items.*

4 If you are obtaining a 'short' engine (which consists of the engine cylinder block/crankcase, crankshaft, pistons and connecting rods all assembled), then the cylinder head, sump, oil pump, and timing belt will have to be removed also.

5 If you are planning a complete overhaul, the engine can be dismantled, and the internal components removed, in the order

given below, referring to Part A, B or C of this Chapter unless otherwise stated.

a) *Inlet and exhaust manifolds – where applicable (Chapter 4A or Chapter 4B).*

b) *Timing belts, chains, sprockets and tensioner(s).*

c) *Cylinder head.*

d) *Flywheel/driveplate.*

e) *Sump.*

f) *Oil pump.*

g) *Piston/connecting rod assemblies (Section 9).*

h) *Crankshaft (Section 11).*

6 Before beginning the dismantling and overhaul procedures, make sure that you have all of the correct tools necessary. Refer to *Tools and working facilities* for further information.

6 Cylinder head – dismantling

Note: *New and reconditioned cylinder heads are available from the manufacturer, and from engine overhaul specialists. Be aware that some specialist tools are required for the dismantling and inspection procedures, and new components may not be readily available. It may therefore be more practical and economical for the home mechanic to purchase a reconditioned head, rather than dismantle, inspect and recondition the original head.*

1 Remove the cylinder head as described in Part A, B or C of this Chapter (as applicable).

2 If not already done, remove the inlet and the exhaust manifolds with reference to Chapters 4A or Chapter 4B. Remove any remaining brackets or housings as required.

3 Remove the camshaft(s), hydraulic followers and rockers (as applicable) as described in Part A, B or C of this Chapter.

4 If not already done on petrol models, remove the spark plugs as described in Chapter 1A.

5 If not already done on diesel models, remove the glow plugs as described in Chapter 5C.

6 On all models, using a valve spring compressor, compress each valve spring in turn until the split collets can be removed. Release the compressor, and lift off the spring retainer and spring. Using a pair of pliers, carefully extract the valve stem oil seal from the top of the guide. The valve stem oil seal also forms the spring seat and is deeply recessed in the cylinder head. It is also a tight fit on the valve guide making it difficult to remove with pliers or a conventional valve stem oil seal removal tool. It can be easily removed, however, using a self-locking nut of suitable diameter screwed onto the end of a bolt and locked with a second nut. Push the nut down onto the top of the seal; the locking portion of the nut will grip the seal allowing it to be withdrawn from the top of the valve guide. Access to the valves is limited, and it may be necessary to make up an adapter out of metal

6.6a Compress the valve spring using a spring compressor…

6.6b …then extract the collets and release the spring compressor

6.6c Remove the spring retainer…

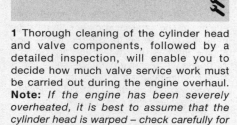

6.6d …followed by the valve spring…

6.6e …and the spring seat (not all models)

tube – cut out a 'window' so that the valve collets can be removed **(see illustrations)**.

7 If, when the valve spring compressor is screwed down, the spring retainer refuses to free and expose the split collets, gently tap the top of the tool, directly over the retainer, with a light hammer. This will free the retainer.

8 Withdraw the valve from the combustion chamber. Remove the valve stem oil seal from the top of the guide, then lift out the spring seat where fitted.

9 It is essential that each valve is stored together with its collets, retainer, spring, and spring seat. The valves should also be kept in their correct sequence, unless they are so badly worn that they are to be renewed. If they are going to be kept and used again, place each valve assembly in a labelled polythene bag or similar small container **(see illustration)**.

7 Cylinder head and valves – cleaning and inspection

1 Thorough cleaning of the cylinder head and valve components, followed by a detailed inspection, will enable you to decide how much valve service work must be carried out during the engine overhaul.
Note: *If the engine has been severely overheated, it is best to assume that the cylinder head is warped – check carefully for signs of this.*

Cleaning

2 Scrape away all traces of old gasket material from the cylinder head.
3 Scrape away the carbon from the combustion chambers and ports, then wash

the cylinder head thoroughly with paraffin or a suitable solvent.
4 Scrape off any heavy carbon deposits that may have formed on the valves, then use a power-operated wire brush to remove deposits from the valve heads and stems.

Inspection

Note: *Be sure to perform all the following inspection procedures before concluding that the services of a machine shop or engine overhaul specialist are required. Make a list of all items that require attention.*

Cylinder head

5 Inspect the head very carefully for cracks, evidence of coolant leakage, and other damage. If cracks are found, a new cylinder head should be obtained. Use a straight-edge and feeler blade to check that the cylinder head gasket surface is not distorted **(see illustration)**. If it is, have the cylinder head inspected by a MINI dealer or automotive engineering specialist. In most cases, MINI insist that the sealing surface of the cylinder head is not re-machined. In this case a new cylinder head must be fitted.
6 Examine the valve seats in each of the combustion chambers. If they are severely pitted, cracked, or burned, they will need to be renewed or recut by an engine overhaul specialist. If they are only slightly pitted, this can be removed by grinding-in the valve heads and seats with fine valve grinding compound, as described below. If in any doubt, have the cylinder head inspected by an engine overhaul specialist.

6.6f Use a pair of pliers to remove the valve stem oil seal. On some models the spring seat is integral with the seal

6.9 Use clearly marked containers to identify components and to keep matched assemblies together

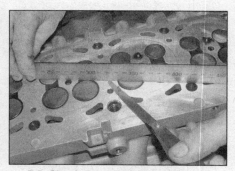

7.5 Check the cylinder head gasket surface for distortion

7 Check the valve guides for wear by inserting the relevant valve, and checking for side-to-side motion of the valve. A very small amount of movement is acceptable. If the movement seems excessive, remove the valve. Measure the valve stem diameter (see below), and renew the valve if it is worn. If the valve stem is not worn, the wear must be in the valve guide, and the guide must be renewed. The renewal of valve guides is best carried out by a MINI dealer or engine overhaul specialist, who will have the necessary tools available. Where no valve stem diameter is specified, seek the advice of a MINI dealer or specialist repairer on the best course of action.

8 If renewing the valve guides, the valve seats should be recut or reground only after the guides have been fitted.

9 Where applicable, examine the camshaft oil supply non-return valve in the oil feed bore at the timing belt end of the cylinder head. Check that the valve is not loose in the cylinder head and that the ball is free to move within the valve body. If the valve is a loose fit in its bore, or if there is any doubt about its condition, it should be renewed. The non-return valve can be removed (assuming it is not loose), using compressed air, such as that generated by a tyre foot pump. Place the pump nozzle over the oil feed bore of the camshaft bearing journal and seal the corresponding oil feed bore with a rag. Apply the compressed air and the valve will be forced out of its location in the underside of the cylinder head **(see illustrations)**. Fit the new non-return valve to its bore on the underside of the head ensuring it is fitted the correct way. Oil should be able to pass upwards through the valve to the camshafts, but the ball in the valve should prevent the oil from returning back to the cylinder block. Use a thin socket or similar to push the valve fully into position.

Valves

10 Examine the head of each valve for pitting, burning, cracks, and general wear. Check the valve stem for scoring and wear ridges. Rotate the valve, and check for any obvious indication that it is bent. Look for pits or excessive wear on the tip of each valve stem. Renew any valve that shows any such signs of wear or damage.

11 If the valve appears satisfactory at this stage, measure the valve stem diameter at several points using a micrometer **(see illustration)**. Any significant difference in the readings obtained indicates wear of the valve stem. Should any of these conditions be apparent, the valve must be renewed.

12 If the valves are in satisfactory condition, they should be ground (lapped) into their respective seats, to ensure a smooth, gas-tight seal. If the seat is only lightly pitted, or if it has been recut, fine grinding compound *only* should be used to produce the required finish. Coarse valve-grinding compound should *not* be used, unless a seat is badly burned or deeply pitted. If this is the case, the cylinder head and valves should be inspected by an

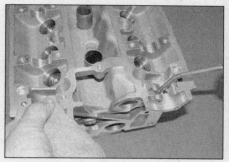

7.9a Apply compressed air to the oil feed bore of the inlet camshaft, seal the bore in the exhaust camshaft bore with a rag...

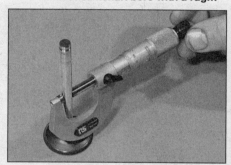

7.11 Measure the valve stem diameter with a micrometer

expert, to decide whether seat recutting, or even the renewal of the valve or seat insert (where possible) is required.

13 Valve grinding is carried out as follows. Place the cylinder head upside-down on a bench.

14 Smear a trace of (the appropriate grade of) valve-grinding compound on the seat face, and press a suction grinding tool onto the valve head **(see illustration)**. With a semi-rotary action, grind the valve head to its seat, lifting the valve occasionally to redistribute the grinding compound. A light spring placed under the valve head will greatly ease this operation.

15 If coarse grinding compound is being used, work only until a dull, matt even surface is produced on both the valve seat and the valve, then wipe off the used compound, and repeat the process with fine compound. When a smooth unbroken ring of light grey matt finish is produced on both the valve and seat, the grinding operation is complete. *Do not* grind-in the valves any further than absolutely necessary, or the seat will be prematurely sunk into the cylinder head.

16 When all the valves have been ground-in, carefully wash off *all* traces of grinding compound using paraffin or a suitable solvent, before reassembling the cylinder head.

Valve components

17 Examine the valve springs for signs of damage and discoloration. No minimum free length is specified by MINI, so the only way of judging valve spring wear is by comparison with a new component.

7.9b ...and the camshaft oil supply non-return valve will be ejected from the underside of the cylinder head

7.14 Grinding-in a valve

18 Stand each spring on a flat surface, and check it for squareness. If any of the springs are damaged, distorted or have lost their tension, obtain a complete new set of springs. It is normal to renew the valve springs as a matter of course if a major overhaul is being carried out.

19 Renew the valve stem oil seals regardless of their apparent condition.

8 Cylinder head – reassembly

1 Working on the first valve assembly, dip the new valve stem oil seal in fresh engine oil. Locate the seal on the valve guide and press the seal firmly onto the guide using a suitable socket **(see illustrations)**.

8.1a Locate the valve stem oil seal on the valve guide...

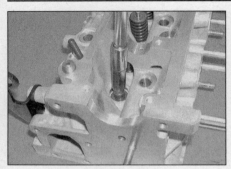

8.1b ...and press the seal firmly onto the guide using a suitable socket

8.1c On some models, the seal is integral with the spring seat

8.2 Lubricate the stem of the valve and insert it into the guide

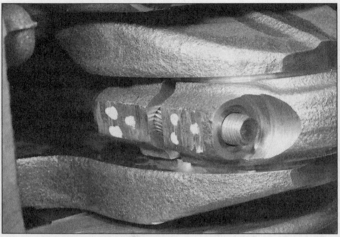

9.3 Connecting rod and big-end bearing cap identification marks (No. 3 shown)

9.5 Remove the big-end bearing shell and cap

2 Lubricate the stem of the first valve, and insert it in the guide **(see illustration)**.

3 Locate the valve spring on top of its seat, and then refit the spring retainer.

4 Compress the valve spring, and locate the split collets in the recess in the valve stem. Release the compressor, then repeat the procedure on the remaining valves. Ensure that each valve is inserted into its original location. If new valves are being fitted, insert them into the locations to which they have been ground.

5 With all the valves installed, support the cylinder head and, using a hammer and interposed block of wood, tap the end of each valve stem to settle the components.

9.6 To protect the crankshaft journals, tape over the connecting rod stud threads

6 The remainder of refitting is a reversal of removal.

9 Piston/connecting rod assembly – removal

1 Remove the cylinder head, sump and oil pump, and baffle plate (where fitted) as described in Part A, B or C of this Chapter.

2 If there is a pronounced wear ridge at the top of any bore, it may be necessary to remove it with a scraper or ridge reamer, to avoid piston damage during removal. Such a ridge indicates excessive wear of the cylinder bore.

3 Using quick-drying paint, mark each connecting rod and big-end bearing cap with its respective cylinder number on the flat machined surface provided; if the engine has been dismantled before, note carefully any identifying marks made previously **(see illustration)**. Note that No 1 cylinder is at the transmission (flywheel) end of the engine.

4 Turn the crankshaft to bring pistons 1 and 4 to BDC (Bottom Dead Centre).

5 Unscrew the nuts or bolts, as applicable, from No 1 piston big-end bearing cap. Take off the cap, and recover the bottom half bearing shell **(see illustration)**. If the bearing shells

are to be re-used, tape the cap and the shell together.

6 Where applicable, to prevent the possibility of damage to the crankshaft bearing journals, tape over the connecting rod stud threads **(see illustration)**.

7 Using a hammer handle, push the piston up through the bore, and remove it from the top of the cylinder block. Recover the bearing shell, and tape it to the connecting rod for safe-keeping.

8 Loosely refit the big-end cap to the connecting rod, and secure with the nuts/bolts – this will help to keep the components in their correct order.

9 Remove number 4 piston assembly in the same way.

10 Turn the crankshaft through 180° to bring pistons 2 and 3 to BDC (Bottom Dead Centre), and remove them in the same way.

10 Timing chains (N47 engine) – removal and refitting

Removal

1 Remove the cylinder head, flywheel and sump as described in Chapter 2A.

2 Undo the bolts and remove the timing

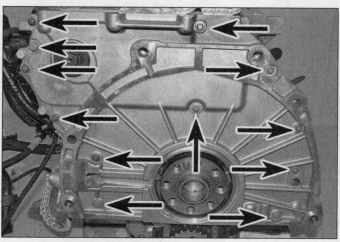

10.2 Timing cover retaining bolts (arrowed)

10.4 The oil pump sprocket bolt has a left-hand thread

cover from the rear of the engine (see illustration).

3 Clean any sealant remains from the mating surfaces. Check the locating dowels are in good condition and correctly located.

4 Undo the bolt securing the sprocket to the oil pump shaft. Note that the bolt has a left-hand thread (see illustration). Pull the sprocket and chain from the shaft.

5 Slide the upper timing chain guide rail from the locating pin (see illustration).

6 Secure the crankshaft against rotation and slacken the fuel pump central bolt (see illustration).

7 Using MINI tool No. 11 8 740 or a suitable puller, release the fuel pump sprocket from the shaft (see illustration).

8 Press-in the chain tensioner piston, and insert a suitable diameter rod/drill bit to lock the piston in place (see illustration).

9 Slide the guide rails from each side of the fuel pump drive chain, as the chain and fuel pump sprocket are removed (see illustration).

Refitting

10 Position the crankshaft so piston No. 1 is 45° after top dead centre (TDC). This can be

verified by measuring the distance from the cylinder block upper gasket surface to the top of the piston. When the crankshaft is correctly positioned, the distance should be 16 mm (see illustration).

11 With the crankshaft correctly positioned, the groove in the fuel pump shaft must be aligned with the mark on the cylinder block (see illustration).

12 Fit the fuel pump sprocket into the chain, then fit the chain around the crankshaft sprocket. Position the sprocket on the fuel pump shaft noting the mark and pin on the sprocket (which aligns with the groove on

10.5 Slide the upper chain guide from the pin (arrowed)

10.6 Slacken the fuel pump sprocket bolt

10.7 Use a puller to remove the fuel pump sprocket

10.8 Push-in the piston, then use a drill bit/rod to secure it in place

10.9 Remove the timing chain, pump sprocket and guide rails together

10.10 When the crankshaft is correctly positioned, the distance from the piston to the gasket surface should be 16 mm

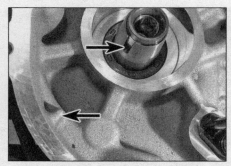

10.11 The groove on the pump shaft must align with the mark on the block (arrowed)

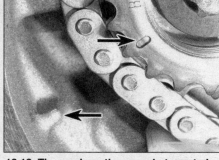

10.12 The mark on the sprocket must also align with the mark on the block (arrowed)

10.15 The flat on the oil pump shaft aligns with the flat in the mounting hole (arrowed)

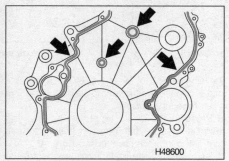

10.17 Apply sealant to the areas indicated

the pump shaft) must align with the mark on the cylinder block **(see illustration)**. Push the sprocket onto the pump shaft, and refit the guide rails at the same time.

13 With the crankshaft held stationary, tighten the fuel pump shaft bolt to the specified torque.

14 Pull out the locking rod/drill bit from the tensioner to release the tensioner piston.

15 Engage the upper timing chain with the fuel pump sprocket, and the lower chain with the oil pump sprocket and crankshaft sprocket. Fit the sprocket to the oil pump, noting that the flat on the pump shaft must align with the flat in the sprocket mounting hole **(see illustration)**.

16 Prevent the crankshaft from rotating, and tighten the oil pump sprocket retaining bolt to the specified torque. Note that the bolt has a left-hand thread.

17 Apply a 1.5 to 2.0 mm thick bead of

11.10 Prise up the two caps to expose the main bearing bolts at the flywheel end

sealant (Loctite 5970) to the timing cover mating surface as shown **(see illustration)**, then refit the timing cover to the rear of the cylinder block. Tighten the retaining bolts to the specified torque. Note that the cover must be installed within 12 minutes of the sealant being applied.

18 The remainder of refitting is a reversal of removal.

11 Crankshaft – removal

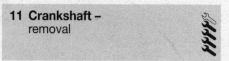

1 Remove the crankshaft sprocket and the oil pump as described in Part A, B or C of this Chapter (as applicable).

2 Remove the pistons and connecting rods, as described in Section 9. If no work is to be done on the pistons and connecting rods, there is no need to remove the cylinder head, or to push the pistons out of the cylinder bores. The pistons should just be pushed far enough up the bores so that they are positioned clear of the crankshaft journals.

3 Check the crankshaft endfloat as described in Section 14, then proceed as follows.

Petrol engine

4 Work around the outside of the cylinder block, and unscrew all the small bolts securing the main bearing ladder to the base of the cylinder block. Note the correct fitted depth of the left-hand crankshaft oil seal in the cylinder block/main bearing ladder.

5 Working in a diagonal sequence, evenly and

progressively slacken the large main bearing ladder retaining bolts by a turn at a time. Once all the bolts are loose, remove them from the ladder. **Note:** *Prise up the two caps at the flywheel end of the ladder to expose the two end main bearing bolts (see illustration 11.10).*

6 With all the retaining bolts removed, carefully lift the main bearing ladder casting away from the base of the cylinder block. Recover the lower main bearing shells, and tape them to their respective locations in the casting. If the two locating dowels are a loose fit, remove them and store them with the casting for safe-keeping.

7 Lift out the crankshaft, and discard both the oil seals.

8 Recover the upper main bearing shells, and store them along with the relevant lower bearing shell. Also recover the two thrustwashers (one fitted either side of No 2 main bearing) from the cylinder block.

W16 diesel engine

9 Work around the outside of the cylinder block, and unscrew all the small bolts securing the main bearing ladder to the base of the cylinder block. Note the correct fitted depth of the left-hand crankshaft oil seal in the cylinder block/main bearing ladder.

10 Working in a diagonal sequence, evenly and progressively slacken the large main bearing ladder retaining bolts by a turn at a time. Once all the bolts are loose, remove them from the ladder. **Note:** *Prise up the two caps at the flywheel end of the ladder to expose the two end main bearing bolts (see illustration).*

11 With all the retaining bolts removed, carefully lift the main bearing ladder casting away from the base of the cylinder block. Recover the lower main bearing shells, and tape them to their respective locations in the casting. If the two locating dowels are a loose fit, remove them and store them with the casting for safe-keeping. Undo the big-end bolts and remove the pistons/connecting rods as described in Section 9.

12 Lift out the crankshaft, and discard both the oil seals.

13 Recover the upper main bearing shells, and store them along with the relevant lower bearing shell. Also recover the two thrustwashers (one fitted either side of No 2 main bearing) from the cylinder block.

N47 diesel engine

14 Remove the timing chain as described in Section 10.

15 The main bearing caps should be numbered 1 to 5 from the right-hand end of the engine (the timing chain is at the left-hand end). If the bearing caps are not marked, mark them accordingly using a centre-punch.

16 Slacken and remove the main bearing cap retaining bolts, and lift off each bearing cap. Recover the lower bearing shells, and tape them to their respective caps for safe-keeping. Note that the main bearing cap bolts must be renewed.

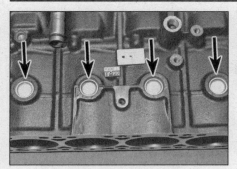

12.1 Cylinder block core plugs (arrowed)

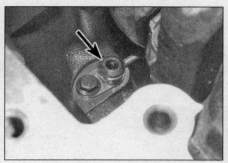

12.3 Piston oil jet spray tube (arrowed) in the cylinder block

12.9 Use a suitable tap to clean the cylinder block threaded holes

17 Note that the thrust bearing shell, which controls crankshaft endfloat, is fitted to No 3 main bearing saddle. The correct location can be identified by the machined area for the thrust bearings to locate.

12 Cylinder block/crankcase – cleaning and inspection

Cleaning

1 Remove all external components and electrical switches/sensors from the block. For complete cleaning, the core plugs should ideally be removed **(see illustration)**.
2 Drill a small hole in the plugs, and then insert a self-tapping screw into the hole. Pull out the plugs by pulling on the screw with a pair of grips, or by using a slide hammer.
3 Where applicable, undo the retaining bolts and remove the piston oil jet spray tubes (there is one for each piston) from inside the cylinder block **(see illustration)**.
4 Scrape all traces of gasket from the cylinder block/crankcase, and from the main bearing ladder/caps (as applicable), taking care not to damage the gasket/sealing surfaces.
5 Remove all oil gallery plugs (where fitted). The plugs are usually very tight – they may have to be drilled out, and the holes re-tapped. Use new plugs when the engine is reassembled.
6 If any of the castings are extremely dirty, all should be steam-cleaned.
7 After the castings are returned, clean all oil holes and oil galleries one more time. Flush all internal passages with warm water until the water runs clear. Dry thoroughly, and apply a light film of oil to all mating surfaces, to prevent rusting. On cast-iron block engines, also oil the cylinder bores. If you have access to compressed air, use it to speed up the drying process, and to blow out all the oil holes and galleries.

⚠️ *Warning: Wear eye protection when using compressed air.*

8 If the castings are not very dirty, you can do an adequate cleaning job with hot (as hot as you can stand), soapy water and a stiff brush. Take plenty of time, and do a thorough job.

Regardless of the cleaning method used, be sure to clean all oil holes and galleries very thoroughly, and to dry all components well. On cast-iron block engines, protect the cylinder bores as described above, to prevent rusting.
9 All threaded holes must be clean, to ensure accurate torque readings during reassembly. To clean the threads, run the correct-size tap into each of the holes to remove rust, corrosion, thread sealant or sludge, and to restore damaged threads **(see illustration)**. If possible, use compressed air to clear the holes of debris produced by this operation.
10 Apply suitable sealant to the new oil gallery plugs, and insert them into the holes in the block. Tighten them securely. Also apply suitable sealant to new core plugs, and drive them into the block using a tube or socket.
11 Where applicable, clean the threads of the piston oil jet retaining bolts, and apply a drop of thread-locking compound to each bolt threads. Refit the piston oil jet spray tubes to the cylinder block, and tighten the retaining bolts to the specified torque setting.
12 If the engine is not going to be reassembled right away, cover it with a large plastic bag to keep it clean; protect all mating surfaces and the cylinder bores as described above, to prevent rusting.

Inspection

13 Visually check the castings for cracks and corrosion. Look for stripped threads in the threaded holes. If there has been any history of internal water leakage, it may be worthwhile having an engine overhaul specialist check

13.2 Remove the piston rings with the aid of a feeler gauge

the cylinder block/crankcase with special equipment. If defects are found, have them repaired if possible, or renew the assembly.
14 Check each cylinder bore for scuffing and scoring. Check for signs of a wear ridge at the top of the cylinder, indicating that the bore is excessively worn.
15 If the necessary measuring equipment is available, measure the bore diameter of each cylinder at the top (just under the wear ridge), centre, and bottom of the cylinder bore, parallel to the crankshaft axis.
16 Next, measure the bore diameter at the same three locations, at right angles to the crankshaft axis. Compare the results with the figures given in the Specifications. If there is any doubt about the condition of the cylinder bores, seek the advice of a MINI dealer or suitable engine reconditioning specialist.
17 At the time of writing, it was not clear whether oversize pistons were available for all models. Consult your MINI dealer or engine specialist for the latest information on piston availability. If oversize pistons are available, then it may be possible to have the cylinder bores rebored and fit the oversize pistons. If oversize pistons are not available, and the bores are worn, renewal of the block seems to be the only option.

13 Piston/connecting rod assembly – inspection

1 Before the inspection process can begin, the piston/connecting rod assemblies must be cleaned, and the original piston rings removed from the pistons.
2 Carefully expand the old rings over the top of the pistons. The use of two or three old feeler blades will be helpful in preventing the rings dropping into empty grooves **(see illustration)**. Be careful not to scratch the piston with the ends of the ring. The rings are brittle, and will snap if they are spread too far. They are also very sharp – protect your hands and fingers. Note that the third ring incorporates an expander. Always remove the rings from the top of the piston. Keep each set of rings with its piston if the old rings are to be re-used.

13.13a Prise out the circlip...

13.13b ...and withdraw the gudgeon pin

3 Scrape away all traces of carbon from the top of the piston. A hand-held wire brush (or a piece of fine emery cloth) can be used, once the majority of the deposits have been scraped away.

4 Remove the carbon from the ring grooves in the piston, using an old ring. Break the ring in half to do this (be careful not to cut your fingers – piston rings are sharp). Be careful to remove only the carbon deposits – do not remove any metal, and do not nick or scratch the sides of the ring grooves.

5 Once the deposits have been removed, clean the piston/connecting rod assembly with paraffin or a suitable solvent, and dry thoroughly. Make sure that the oil return holes in the ring grooves are clear.

6 If the pistons and cylinder bores are not damaged or worn excessively, and if the cylinder block does not need to be re-bored (where possible), the original pistons can be refitted. Normal piston wear shows up as even vertical wear on the piston thrust surfaces, and slight looseness of the top ring in its groove. New piston rings should always be used when the engine is reassembled.

7 Carefully inspect each piston for cracks around the skirt, around the gudgeon pin holes, and at the piston ring 'lands' (between the ring grooves).

8 Look for scoring and scuffing on the piston skirt, holes in the piston crown, and burned areas at the edge of the crown. If the skirt is scored or scuffed, the engine may have been suffering from overheating, and/or abnormal combustion, which caused excessively high operating temperatures. The cooling

and lubrication systems should be checked thoroughly. Scorch marks on the sides of the pistons show that blow-by has occurred. A hole in the piston crown, or burned areas at the edge of the piston crown, indicates that abnormal combustion (pre-ignition, knocking, or detonation) has been occurring. If any of the above problems exist, the causes must be investigated and corrected, or the damage will occur again. The causes may include incorrect ignition/injection pump timing, or a faulty injector (as applicable).

9 Corrosion of the piston, in the form of pitting, indicates that coolant has been leaking into the combustion chamber and/or the crankcase. Again, the cause must be corrected, or the problem may persist in the rebuilt engine.

10 Examine each connecting rod carefully for signs of damage, such as cracks around the big-end and small-end bearings. Check that the rod is not bent or distorted. Damage is highly unlikely, unless the engine has been seized or badly overheated. Detailed checking of the connecting rod assembly can only be carried out by a MINI dealer or engine specialist with the necessary equipment.

11 The connecting rod big-end cap bolts/nuts must be renewed whenever they are disturbed.

12 The gudgeon pins are of the floating type, secured in position by two circlips. On these engines, the pistons and connecting rods can be separated as described in the following paragraphs.

13 Using a small flat-bladed screwdriver, prise out the circlips, and push out the gudgeon

pin **(see illustrations)**. Hand pressure should be sufficient to remove the pin. Identify the piston and rod to ensure correct reassembly. Discard the circlips – new ones must be used on refitting. Note the orientation of the piston in regard to the connecting rod.

14 Examine the gudgeon pin and connecting rod small-end bearing for signs of wear or damage. Wear can be cured by renewing both the pin and bush (where possible) or connecting rod. Bush renewal, however, is a specialist job – press facilities are required, and the new bush must be reamed accurately.

15 The connecting rods themselves should not be in need of renewal, unless seizure or some other major mechanical failure has occurred. Check the alignment of the connecting rods visually, and if the rods are not straight, take them to an engine overhaul specialist for a more detailed check.

16 Examine all components, and obtain any new parts from your MINI dealer. If new pistons are purchased, they will be supplied complete with gudgeon pins and circlips. Circlips can also be purchased individually.

17 Ensure the piston and connecting rod are correctly positioned, then apply a smear of clean engine oil to the gudgeon pin. Slide it into the piston and through the connecting rod small-end. Check that the piston pivots freely on the rod, then secure the gudgeon pin in position with two new circlips. Ensure that each circlip is correctly located in its groove in the piston.

14 Crankshaft – inspection

Checking endfloat

1 If the crankshaft endfloat is to be checked, this must be done when the crankshaft is still installed in the cylinder block/crankcase, but is free to move (see Section 11).

2 Check the endfloat using a dial gauge in contact with the end of the crankshaft. Push the crankshaft fully one way, and then zero the gauge. Push the crankshaft fully the other way, and check the endfloat. The result can be compared with the specified amount, and will give an indication as to whether new thrustwashers are required **(see illustration)**.

3 If a dial gauge is not available, feeler blades can be used. First push the crankshaft fully towards the flywheel end of the engine, and then use feeler blades to measure the gap between the web of No 2 crankpin and the thrustwasher **(see illustration)**.

Inspection

4 Clean the crankshaft using paraffin or a suitable solvent, and dry it, preferably with compressed air if available. Be sure to clean the oil holes with a pipe cleaner or similar probe, to ensure that they are not obstructed.

 Warning: Wear eye protection when using compressed air.

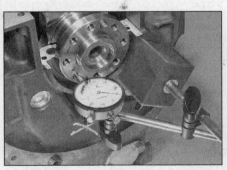

14.2 The crankshaft endfloat can be checked with a DTI gauge...

14.3 ...or with feeler gauges

5 Check the main and big-end bearing journals for uneven wear, scoring, pitting and cracking.

6 Big-end bearing wear is accompanied by distinct metallic knocking when the engine is running (particularly noticeable when the engine is pulling from low speed) and some loss of oil pressure.

7 Main bearing wear is accompanied by severe engine vibration and rumble – getting progressively worse as engine speed increases – and again by loss of oil pressure.

8 Check the bearing journal for roughness by running a finger lightly over the bearing surface. Any roughness (which will be accompanied by obvious bearing wear) indicates that the crankshaft requires regrinding (where possible) or renewal.

9 Check the oil seal contact surfaces at each end of the crankshaft for wear and damage. If the seal has worn a deep groove in the surface of the crankshaft, consult an engine overhaul specialist; repair may be possible, but otherwise a new crankshaft will be required.

10 Take the crankshaft to a MINI dealer or engine reconditioning specialist to have it measured for journal wear. If excessive wear is evident, they will be able to advise you with regard to regrinding the crankshaft and supplying new bearing shells.

11 If the crankshaft has been reground, check for burrs around the crankshaft oil holes (the holes are usually chamfered, so burrs should not be a problem unless regrinding has been carried out carelessly). Remove any burrs with a fine file or scraper, and thoroughly clean the oil holes as described previously.

12 At the time of writing, it was not clear whether MINI produce undersize bearing shells for all of these engines. On some engines, if the crankshaft journals have not already been reground, it may be possible to have the crankshaft reconditioned, and to fit undersize shells. If no undersize shells are available and the crankshaft has worn beyond the specified limits, it will have to be renewed. Consult your MINI dealer or engine specialist for further information on parts availability.

15 Main and big-end bearings – inspection

1 Even though the main and big-end bearings should be renewed during the engine overhaul, the old bearings should be retained for close examination, as they may reveal valuable information about the condition of the engine. The bearing shells are graded by thickness, the grade of each shell being indicated by the colour code marked on it.

2 Bearing failure can occur due to lack of lubrication, the presence of dirt or other foreign particles, overloading the engine, or corrosion (see illustration). Regardless of the cause of bearing failure, the cause must be corrected (where applicable) before the engine

is reassembled, to prevent it from happening again.

3 When examining the bearing shells, remove them from the cylinder block/crankcase, the main bearing ladder/caps (as appropriate), the connecting rods and the connecting rod big-end bearing caps. Lay them out on a clean surface in the same general position as their location in the engine. This will enable you to match any bearing problems with the corresponding crankshaft journal. Do not touch any shell's bearing surface with your fingers while checking it, or the delicate surface may be scratched.

4 Dirt and other foreign matter gets into the engine in a variety of ways. It may be left in the engine during assembly, or it may pass through filters or the crankcase ventilation system. It may get into the oil, and from there into the bearings. Metal chips from machining operations and normal engine wear are often present. Abrasives are sometimes left in engine components after reconditioning, especially when parts are not thoroughly cleaned using the proper cleaning methods. Whatever the source, these foreign objects often end up embedded in the soft bearing material, and are easily recognised. Large particles will not embed in the bearing, and will score or gouge the bearing and journal. The best prevention for this cause of bearing failure is to clean all parts thoroughly, and keep everything spotlessly clean during engine assembly. Frequent and regular engine oil and filter changes are also recommended.

5 Lack of lubrication (or lubrication breakdown) has a number of interrelated causes. Excessive heat (which thins the oil), overloading (which squeezes the oil from the bearing face) and oil leakage (from excessive bearing clearances, worn oil pump or high engine speeds) all contribute to lubrication breakdown. Blocked oil passages, which usually are the result of misaligned oil holes in a bearing shell, will also oil-starve a bearing, and destroy it. When lack of lubrication is the cause of bearing failure, the bearing material is wiped or extruded from the steel backing of the bearing. Temperatures may increase to the point where the steel backing turns blue from overheating.

6 Driving habits can have a definite effect on bearing life. Full-throttle, low-speed operation (labouring the engine) puts very high loads on bearings, tending to squeeze out the oil film. These loads cause the bearings to flex, which produces fine cracks in the bearing face (fatigue failure). Eventually, the bearing material will loosen in pieces, and tear away from the steel backing.

7 Short-distance driving leads to corrosion of bearings, because insufficient engine heat is produced to drive off the condensed water and corrosive gases. These products collect in the engine oil, forming acid and sludge. As the oil is carried to the engine bearings, the acid attacks and corrodes the bearing material.

8 Incorrect bearing installation during engine assembly will lead to bearing failure as

well. Tight-fitting bearings leave insufficient bearing running clearance, and will result in oil starvation. Dirt or foreign particles trapped behind a bearing shell result in high spots on the bearing, which lead to failure.

9 Do not touch any shell's bearing surface with your fingers during reassembly; there is a risk of scratching the delicate surface, or of depositing particles of dirt on it.

10 As mentioned at the beginning of this Section, the bearing shells should be renewed as a matter of course during engine overhaul; to do otherwise is false economy.

16 Engine overhaul – reassembly sequence

1 Before reassembly begins, ensure that all new parts have been obtained, and that all necessary tools are available. Read through the entire procedure to familiarise yourself with the work involved, and to ensure that all items necessary for reassembly of the engine are at hand. In addition to all normal tools and materials, thread-locking compound will be needed. A tube of suitable liquid sealant will also be required for the joint faces that are fitted without gaskets. It is recommended that MINI's own product(s) be used, which are specially formulated for this purpose; the relevant product names are quoted in the text of each Section where they are required.

2 In order to save time and avoid problems, engine reassembly can be carried out in the following order, referring to Part A, B or C of this Chapter unless otherwise stated:

a) Crankshaft (See Section 18).

b) Piston/connecting rod assemblies (See Section 19).

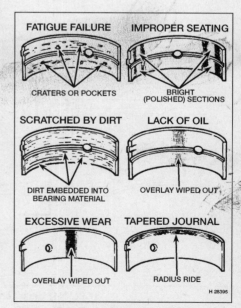

15.2 Typical bearing failures

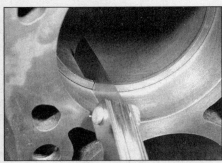

17.5 Measure the piston rings end gaps with a feeler gauge

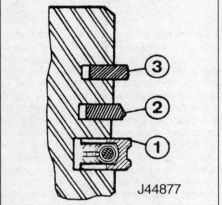

J44877

17.9a Petrol engine piston rings

1 Oil control ring
2 Second compression ring
3 Top compression ring

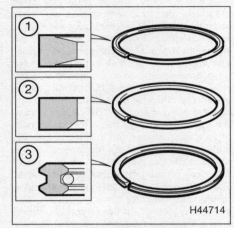

H44714

17.9b W16 diesel engine piston rings

1 Top compression ring
2 Second compression ring
3 Oil control ring

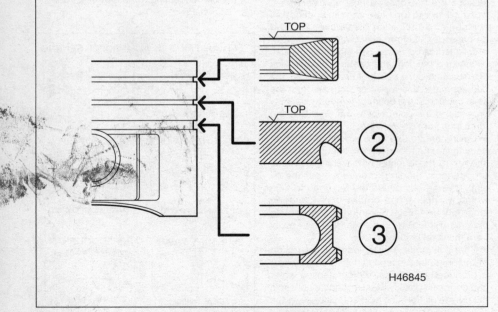

H46845

17.9c N47 diesel engine piston rings

1 Top compression ring
2 Second compression ring
3 Oil control ring

c) Oil pump.
d) Sump.
e) Flywheel/driveplate.
f) Cylinder head.
g) Injection pump and mounting bracket – diesel engine (Chapter 4B).
h) Timing belt/chains, tensioner, pulley(s) and sprockets.
i) Engine external components.

3 At this stage, all engine components should be absolutely clean and dry, with all faults repaired. The components should be laid out (or in individual containers) on a completely clean work surface.

17 Piston rings – refitting

1 Before fitting new piston rings, the ring end gaps must be checked as follows.

2 Lay out the piston/connecting rod assemblies and the new piston ring sets, so that the ring sets will be matched with the same piston and cylinder during the end gap measurement and subsequent engine reassembly.

3 Insert the top ring into the first cylinder, and push it down the bore using the top of the piston. This will ensure that the ring remains square with the cylinder walls. Position the ring near the bottom of the cylinder bore, at the lower limit of ring travel. Note that the top and second compression rings are different. The second ring can be identified by its taper; on petrol engines it also has a step on its lower surface. On diesel engines, the top ring has a chamfer on its upper/outer edge.

4 Measure the end gap using feeler blades.

5 Repeat the procedure with the ring at the top of the cylinder bore, at the upper limit of its travel **(see illustration)**, and compare the measurements with the figures given in the Specifications. If the end gaps are incorrect, check that you have the correct rings for your engine and for the cylinder bore size.

6 Repeat the checking procedure for each ring in the first cylinder, and then for the rings in the remaining cylinders. Remember to keep rings, pistons and cylinders matched up.

7 Once the ring end gaps have been checked and if necessary corrected, the rings can be fitted to the pistons.

8 Fit the oil control ring expander (where fitted) then install the ring. The ring gap should be positioned 180° from the expander gap.

9 The second and top rings are different and can be identified from their cross-sections; the top ring is symmetrical whilst the second ring is tapered. Fit the second ring, ensuring its identification (TOP) marking is facing upwards, and then install the top ring **(see illustrations)**. Arrange the second and top ring end gap so they are equally spaced 120° apart. **Note:** *Always follow any instructions supplied with the new piston ring sets – different manufacturers may specify different procedures. Do not mix up the top and second compression rings, as they have different cross-sections.*

18 Crankshaft – refitting

Selection of bearing shells

1 Have the crankshaft inspected and measured by a MINI dealer or engine reconditioning specialist. They will be able to carry out any regrinding/repairs, and supply suitable main and big-end bearing shells.

Crankshaft refitting

Note: *New main bearing cap/lower crankcase bolts must be used when refitting the crankshaft.*
2 Where applicable, ensure that the oil spray jets are fitted to the bearing locations in the cylinder block.

Petrol engines

3 Clean the backs of the bearing shells in both the cylinder block/crankcase and the main bearing ladder. If new shells are being fitted, ensure that all traces of protective grease are cleaned off using paraffin. Wipe dry the shells with a lint-free cloth.
4 Press the bearing shells into their locations, ensuring that the tab on each shell engages in the notch in the cylinder block/crankcase and bearing ladder. Take care not to touch any shell's bearing surface with your fingers. Note that the upper bearing shells all have a grooved surface, whereas the lower shells have a plain bearing surface.
5 Liberally lubricate each bearing shell in the cylinder block with clean engine oil then lower the crankshaft into position.
6 Insert the thrustwashers to either side of No 2 main bearing upper location and push them around the bearing journal until their edges are horizontal. Ensure that the oilway grooves on each thrustwasher face outwards (away from the cylinder block).
7 Thoroughly degrease the mating surfaces of the cylinder block and the crankshaft bearing cap housing/main bearing ladder. Apply a thin bead of Loctite 5970 sealant to the bearing cap housing mating surface.
8 Lubricate the lower bearing shells with clean engine oil, then refit the bearing cap housing, ensuring that the shells are not displaced, and that the locating dowels engage correctly.
9 Install the large and small crankshaft bearing cap housing/ladder retaining bolts, and screw them in until they are just making contact with the housing.
10 Working in sequence, tighten the main bearing ladder bolts to the torque settings given in the Specifications (see Chapter 2A) **(see illustration)**.
11 With the bearing housing in place, check that the crankshaft rotates freely.
12 Refit the piston/connecting rod assemblies to the crankshaft as described in Section 19.
13 Refit the oil pump and sump as described in Chapter 2B.
14 Fit a new crankshaft left-hand oil seal, then refit the flywheel as described in Chapter 2B.
15 Where removed, refit the crankshaft sprocket and timing belt also as described in Chapter 2B.

Diesel engines

16 Place the bearing shells in their locations. If new shells are being fitted, ensure that all traces of protective grease are cleaned off using paraffin. Wipe dry the shells with a lint-free cloth. On W16 engines, the upper bearing shells all have a grooved surface, whereas the lower shells have a plain surface.

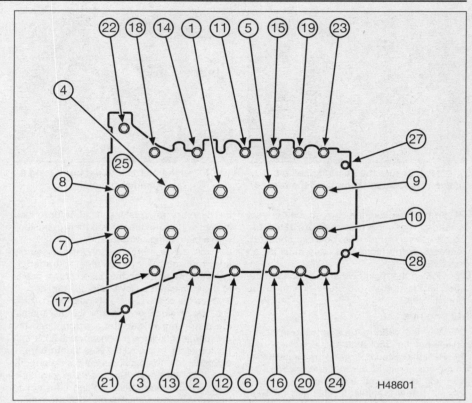

18.10 Main bearing ladder bolt tightening sequence – petrol engines

17 Liberally lubricate each bearing shell in the cylinder block with clean engine oil then lower the crankshaft into position.
18 Insert the thrustwashers to either side of No 2 (W16 engine) or No 4 (N47 engine) main bearing upper location and push them around the bearing journal until their edges are horizontal **(see illustration)**. Ensure that the oilway grooves on each thrustwasher face outwards (away from the bearing journal).

W16 engines

19 Thoroughly degrease the mating surfaces of the cylinder block and the crankshaft bearing cap housing. Apply a thin bead of Loctite 5970 sealant to the bearing cap housing mating surface.
20 Lubricate the lower bearing shells with clean

engine oil, then refit the bearing cap housing, ensuring that the shells are not displaced, and that the locating dowels engage correctly.
21 Install the ten large diameter and sixteen smaller diameter crankshaft bearing cap housing retaining bolts, and screw them in until they are just making contact with the housing.
22 Working in sequence, tighten the bolts to the torque settings given in the Specifications **(see illustration)**.

N47 engines

23 Lubricate the lower bearing shells in the main bearing caps with clean engine oil. Make sure that the locating lugs on the shells engage with the corresponding recesses in the caps.

18.18 Place the thrustwashers each side of the upper bearing shell location

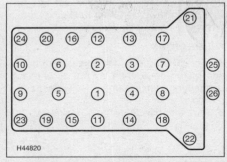

18.22 Main bearing ladder bolts tightening sequence (W16 diesel engine)

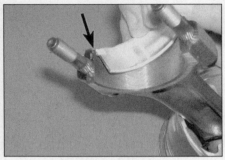

19.3 Ensure the bearing shell tab (arrowed) locates correctly in the recess

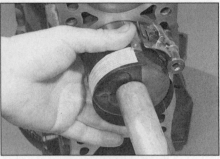

19.7 Tap the piston into the bore using a hammer handle

19.8 Fit the big-end bearing cap, ensuring it is fitted the right way around, and fit the new nuts

24 Fit the main bearing caps to their correct locations, ensuring that they are fitted the correct way round (the bearing shell tab recesses in the block and caps must be on the same side).

25 Tighten the main bearing cap bolts to the specified torque, in the stages given in the Specifications.

All engines

26 With the bearing caps/housing in place, check that the crankshaft rotates freely.

27 Refit the piston/connecting rod assemblies to the crankshaft as described in Section 19.

28 Refit the oil pump and sump.

29 Fit a new crankshaft left-hand oil seal, then refit the flywheel.

30 Refit the cylinder head, crankshaft sprocket and timing belt/chain.

19 Piston/connecting rod assembly – refitting

Note: *New big-end cap nuts/bolts must be used on refitting.*

1 Note that the following procedure assumes that the crankshaft and main bearing ladder/caps are in place.

2 Clean the backs of the bearing shells, and the bearing locations in both the connecting rod and bearing cap.

Petrol engines

3 Press the bearing shells into their locations, ensuring that the tab on each shell engages in the notch in the connecting rod and cap. Take care not to touch any shell's bearing surface with your fingers **(see illustration)**.

All engines

4 Lubricate the cylinder bores, the pistons, and piston rings, then lay out each piston/connecting rod assembly in its respective position.

5 Start with assembly No 1. Make sure that

the piston rings are still spaced as described in Section 17, and then clamp them in position with a piston ring compressor.

6 Insert the piston/connecting rod assembly into the top of cylinder/liner number 1; ensuring the arrow on the piston crown points to the crankshaft pulley end of the engine.

7 Once the piston is correctly positioned, using a block of wood or hammer handle against the piston crown, tap the assembly into the cylinder/liner until the piston crown is flush with the top of the cylinder/liner **(see illustration)**.

8 Ensure that the bearing shell is still correctly installed. Liberally lubricate the crankpin and both bearing shells. Taking care not to mark the cylinder/liner bores, pull the piston/connecting rod assembly down the bore and onto the crankpin. Refit the big-end bearing cap and fit the new nuts, tightening them finger-tight at first **(see illustration)**. Note that the faces with the identification marks must match (which means that the bearing shell locating tabs abut each other).

9 Tighten the bearing cap retaining nuts evenly and progressively to the specified torque setting.

10 Once the bearing cap retaining nuts have been correctly tightened, rotate the crankshaft. Check that it turns freely; some stiffness is to be expected if new components have been fitted, but there should be no signs of binding or tight spots.

11 Refit the cylinder head and oil pump as described in Part A, B or C of this Chapter (as applicable).

20 Engine – initial start-up after overhaul

1 With the engine refitted in the vehicle, double-check the engine oil and coolant levels. Make a final check that everything has been reconnected, and that there are no tools or rags left in the engine compartment.

Petrol engine models

2 Remove the spark plugs and disable the fuel system by disconnecting the wiring connectors from the fuel injectors, referring to Chapter 4A for further information.

3 Turn the engine on the starter until the oil pressure warning light goes out. Refit the spark plugs, and reconnect the wiring.

Diesel engine models

4 On the models covered in this Manual, the oil pressure warning light is linked to the STOP warning light, and is not illuminated when the ignition is initially switched on. Therefore it is not possible to check the oil pressure warning light when turning the engine on the starter motor.

5 Prime the fuel system (refer to Chapter 4B).

6 Fully depress the accelerator pedal, turn the ignition key to position II, and wait for the preheating warning light to go out.

All models

7 Start the engine, noting that this may take a little longer than usual, due to the fuel system components having been disturbed.

8 While the engine is idling, check for fuel, water and oil leaks. Don't be alarmed if there are some odd smells and smoke from parts getting hot and burning off oil deposits.

9 Assuming all is well, keep the engine idling until hot water is felt circulating through the top hose, then switch off the engine.

10 After a few minutes, recheck the oil and coolant levels as described in Weekly checks, and top-up as necessary.

11 Note that there is no need to retighten the cylinder head bolts once the engine has first run after reassembly.

12 If new pistons, rings or crankshaft bearings have been fitted, the engine must be treated as new, and run-in for the first 500 miles. Do not operate the engine at full-throttle, or allow it to labour at low engine speeds in any gear. It is recommended that the oil and filter be changed at the end of this period.

Chapter 3
Cooling, heating and ventilation systems

Contents

Degrees of difficulty

Easy, suitable for novice with little experience 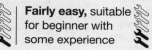	Fairly easy, suitable for beginner with some experience	Fairly difficult, suitable for competent DIY mechanic	Difficult, suitable for experienced DIY mechanic	Very difficult, suitable for expert DIY or professional

Specifications

General

Maximum system pressure	1.4 bars

Thermostat

Start of opening temperature (approximate):
Petrol engines...	82°C
Diesel engine models	83°C

Air conditioning compressor

Compressor oil:
Quantity	135 cc

Refrigerant

Quantity	490 ± 25 g
Type	R134a

Torque wrench settings

	Nm	lbf ft
Air conditioning compressor mounting bolts	25	18
Auxiliary coolant pump	8	6
Coolant outlet housing...................................	10	7
Coolant pump:		
Petrol engines...	10	7
Diesel engines	10	7
Coolant pump pulley (petrol engines only).....................	8	6
Friction drive gear......................................	10	7
Thermostat housing:		
Petrol engines, W16 diesel engines	8	6
N47 diesel engines......................................	10	7

2.5 To release the spring-type clips, squeeze together the clip 'ears' with pliers

1 General information and precautions

1 The cooling system is of pressurised type, comprising a coolant pump driven by the timing belt or auxiliary belt, an aluminium radiator, an expansion tank, an electric cooling fan, a thermostat, a heater matrix, and all associated hoses and switches. On petrol turbo models, an additional electrically powered coolant pump is fitted to circulate coolant through the turbocharger.

2 The system functions as follows. Cold coolant in the bottom of the radiator passes through the bottom hose to the coolant pump, where it is pumped around the cylinder block and head passages. After cooling the cylinder bores, combustion surfaces and valve seats, the coolant reaches the underside of the thermostat, which is initially closed. The coolant passes through the heater, and is returned via the cylinder block to the coolant pump.

3 When the engine is cold, the coolant circulates only through the cylinder block, cylinder head, and heater. When the coolant reaches a predetermined temperature, the thermostat opens, and the coolant passes through the top hose to the radiator. As the coolant passes down through the radiator, it is cooled by the inrush of air when the car is in forward motion. The airflow is supplemented by the action of the electric cooling fan when necessary. Upon reaching the bottom of the

2.12 Where click-fit connectors are used, prise out the wire clip then disconnect the hose

radiator, the coolant has now cooled, and the cycle is repeated.

4 On models with automatic transmission, a proportion of the coolant is recirculated through the transmission fluid cooler mounted on the transmission. On models fitted with an engine oil cooler, the coolant is also passed through the oil cooler.

5 The operation of the electric cooling fan(s) is controlled by the engine management control unit.

⚠️ *Warning: Do not attempt to remove the expansion tank filler cap, or to disturb any part of the cooling system, while the engine is hot, as there is a high risk of scalding. If the expansion tank filler cap must be removed before the engine and radiator have fully cooled (even though this is not recommended), the pressure in the cooling system must first be relieved. Cover the cap with a thick layer of cloth to avoid scalding, and slowly unscrew the filler cap until a hissing sound is heard. When the hissing has stopped, indicating that the pressure has reduced, slowly unscrew the filler cap until it can be removed; if more hissing sounds are heard, wait until they have stopped before unscrewing the cap. At all times keep well away from the filler cap opening, and protect your hands.*

• *Do not allow antifreeze to come into contact with your skin, or with the painted surfaces of the vehicle. Rinse off spills immediately, with plenty of water. Never leave antifreeze lying around in an open container, or in a puddle in the driveway or on the garage floor. Children and pets are attracted by its sweet smell, but antifreeze can be fatal if ingested.*

• *If the engine is hot, the electric cooling fan(s) may start rotating even if the engine is not running. Be careful to keep your hands, hair, and any loose clothing well clear when working in the engine compartment.*

• *Refer to Section 11 for precautions to be observed when working on models equipped with air conditioning.*

2 Cooling system hoses – disconnection and renewal

Note: *Refer to the warnings given in Section 1 of this Chapter before proceeding. Hoses should only be disconnected once the engine has cooled sufficiently to avoid scalding.*

1 If the checks described in the *Hose and fluid leak check* Section in Chapter 1A or Chapter 1B reveal a faulty hose, it must be renewed as follows.

2 First drain the cooling system (see Chapters 1A or Chapter 1B). If the coolant is not due for renewal, it may be re-used, providing it is collected in a clean container.

3 To disconnect a hose, proceed as follows, according to the type of hose connection.

Conventional connections

4 On conventional connections, the clips used to secure the hoses in position may be standard worm-drive (Jubilee) clips, spring clips or disposable crimped types. The crimped type of clip is not designed to be re-used and should be renewed with a worm-drive type on reassembly.

5 To disconnect a hose, release the retaining clips and move them along the hose, clear of the relevant inlet/outlet. Carefully work the hose free. The hoses can be removed with relative ease when new – on an older car; they may have stuck **(see illustration)**.

6 If a hose proves to be difficult to remove, try to release it by rotating its ends before attempting to free it. Gently prise the end of the hose with a blunt instrument (such as a flat-bladed screwdriver), but do not apply too much force, and take care not to damage the pipe stubs or hoses. Note in particular that the radiator inlet stub is fragile; do not use excessive force when attempting to remove the hose. If all else fails, cut the hose with a sharp knife, then slit it so that it can be peeled off in two pieces. Although this may prove expensive if the hose is otherwise undamaged, it is preferable to buying a new radiator. Check first, however, that a new hose is readily available.

7 When fitting a hose, first slide the clips onto the hose, then work the hose into position. If crimped-type clips were originally fitted, use standard worm-drive clips when refitting the hose.

8 Work the hose into position, checking that it is correctly routed, and then slide each clip back along the hose until it passes over the flared end of the relevant inlet/outlet, before tightening the clip securely.

9 Refill the cooling system (see Chapter 1A or Chapter 1B).

10 Check thoroughly for leaks as soon as possible after disturbing any part of the cooling system.

Click-fit connections

Note: *New sealing ring should be used when reconnecting the hose.*

11 On certain models, some cooling system hoses are secured in position with click-fit connectors where the hose is retained by a large circlip.

12 To disconnect this type of hose fitting, carefully prise the wire clip out of position then disconnect the hose connection **(see illustration)**. Once the hose has been disconnected, refit the wire clip to the hose union. Inspect the hose unit sealing ring for signs of damage or deterioration and renew if necessary.

13 On refitting, ensure that the sealing ring is in position and the wire clip is correctly located in the groove in the union **(see illustration)**. Lubricate the sealing ring with a smear of soapy water, to ease installation, and then push the hose into its union until it is heard to click into position.

14 Ensure the hose is securely retained by the wire clip then refill the cooling system as described in Chapter 1A or Chapter 1B.
15 Check thoroughly for leaks as soon as possible after disturbing any part of the cooling system.

3 Coolant expansion tank – removal and refitting

Removal

1 Referring to Chapter 1A or Chapter 1B, drain the cooling system sufficiently to empty the contents of the expansion tank. Do not drain any more coolant than is necessary.
2 Squeeze the clips on the collar of the pipe together, then pull the plastic hose from the top of the expansion tank (see illustration).
3 Undo the retaining bolt, lift the tank upwards a little, then disconnect the hose from the base.

Refitting

4 Refitting is the reverse of removal, ensuring the hoses are securely reconnected. On completion, top-up the coolant level as described in *Weekly checks*.

2.13 Ensure the sealing ring and clip (arrowed) are correctly fitted to the hose union before reconnecting

4 Radiator – removal, inspection and refitting

Note: *If leakage is the reason for removing the radiator, bear in mind that minor leaks can often be cured using a radiator sealant with the radiator still in position.*

Removal

1 Raise the front of the vehicle and support it securely on axle stands (see *Jacking and vehicle*

support). Undo the fasteners and remove the engine undershield (see illustration).
2 Drain the cooling system (see Chapter 1A or Chapter 1B).
3 Remove the front bumper as described in Chapter 11.
4 Screw special tool No. 00 2 271 into the left, and right-hand front panel/chassis member sleeve. In the absence of these tools, use 2 lengths of tube, 19 mm outside diameter, at least 120 mm long, with two 8 mm threaded rods at least 150 mm long, and two 8 mm nuts (see illustration).
5 Undo the bolt, nuts each side and move the bumper support bar forwards on the tools previously inserted (see illustration). Where applicable, unclip the air conditioning compressor wiring harness from the bumper panel as it's withdrawn.

Models with air conditioning

6 Undo the bolt(s) securing the refrigerant pipes to the front panel (see illustration).
7 Undo the 3 mounting bolts tilt the condenser forwards a little (see illustration 12.19).Take great care no to bend the refrigerant pipes.

All models

8 Release the retaining clip/screw at the

3.2 Coolant expansion tank top hose and retaining bolt (arrowed)

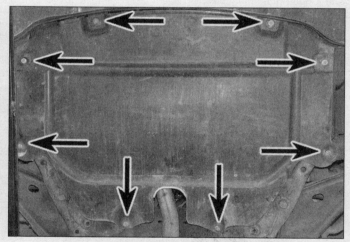

4.1 Engine undershield fasteners (arrowed)

4.4 Screw the tubes/rods through the front panel into the threaded holes in the chassis members

4.5 Undo the nuts/bolt (arrowed) each side, and slide the bumper bar forwards

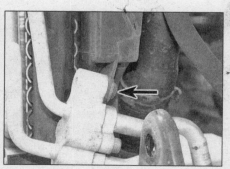

4.6 Undo the bolt (arrowed) securing the refrigerant pipe

4.8 Squeeze together the tangs and release the radiator clips

left-hand, and right-hand corner, and tilt the radiator forwards a little (see illustration).
9 Release the clamps and disconnect the radiator hoses (see illustration).
10 Carefully lift the radiator from place, taking care not to damage the radiator fins.

Inspection

11 Insert a garden hose into the radiator top inlet. Direct a flow of clean water through the radiator, and continue flushing until clean water emerges from the radiator bottom outlet.
12 If after a reasonable period, the water still does not run clear, the radiator can be flushed with a good proprietary cleaning agent. It is important that their manufacturer's instructions are followed carefully. If the contamination is particularly bad, insert the hose in the radiator bottom outlet, and reverse-flush the radiator.
13 Clean dirt and debris from the radiator fins, using an airline (in which case, wear eye

4.9 Pull the radiator forwards a little to access the upper coolant hose and expansion tank hose

protection) or a soft brush. Be careful, as the fins are sharp, and easily damaged.
14 If necessary, a radiator specialist can perform a 'flow test' on the radiator, to establish whether an internal blockage exists.
15 A leaking radiator must be referred to a specialist for permanent repair. Do not attempt to weld or solder a leaking radiator, as damage to the plastic components may result.
16 Inspect the condition of the radiator mounting rubbers, and renew them if necessary.

Refitting

17 Refitting is a reversal of removal, bearing in mind the following points:
 a) Ensure that the lower lugs on the radiator are correctly engaged.
 b) Reconnect the hoses with reference to Section 2.
 c) On completion, refill the cooling system as described in Chapter 1A or Chapter 1B.

5 Thermostat – removal, testing and refitting

Removal

1 Drain the cooling system (see Chapter 1A or Chapter 1B), then remove the plastic cover from the top of the engine (where fitted).

All except N47 diesel engines

2 The thermostat is located in the coolant outlet housing on the left-hand end of the cylinder head. It is integral with the housing, requiring removal of the complete housing.
3 Remove the air cleaner housing as described in Chapter 4B.
4 On W16 diesel models, remove the fuel filter as described in Chapter 1B.
5 On petrol models, disconnect the wiring plugs from the camshaft position sensors, thermostat housing, oxygen sensors, oil pressure sensor, then release the ignition coil wiring harness clips. Slide the wiring loom bracket upwards from the cylinder head cover and move it to one side (see illustrations).
6 Disconnect the wiring connectors from the sensors on the thermostat housing (if not already done so).
7 Disconnect all the hoses from the coolant housing, having noted their fitted locations (see illustration).
8 Unscrew the retaining bolts and remove the housing (see illustrations). Recover the gasket/seals.

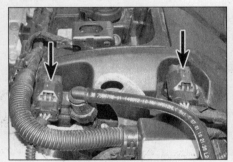

5.5a Camshaft position sensor wiring plugs (arrowed)

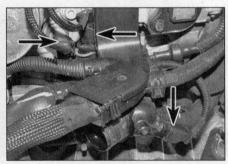

5.5b Oil pressure and thermostat housing wiring plugs (arrowed)

5.5c Slide the wiring harness guide upwards from the bracket

5.7 Disconnect the coolant hoses from the thermostat housing – petrol models shown

5.8a Thermostat housing bolts – W16 diesel engine shown

5.8b Remove the thermostat housing – petrol engines shown

N47 diesel engines

9 Remove the air conditioning compressor (where fitted) as described in Section 12.
10 Release the clamp and disconnect the coolant hose from the thermostat housing **(see illustration)**.
11 Undo the retaining bolts and remove the housing, complete with thermostat **(see illustration)**.
12 Pull the thermostat from the housing, and renew the seal **(see illustration)**.

Testing

13 A rough test of the thermostat may be made by suspending it with a piece of string in a container full of water. Heat the water to bring it to the boil – the thermostat must open by the time the water boils. If not, renew it.
14 If a thermometer is available, the precise opening temperature of the thermostat may be determined; compare with the figures given in the Specifications.
15 A thermostat which fails to close as the water cools, must also be renewed.

Refitting

16 Refitting is a reversal of removal, bearing in mind the following points.
  a) Renew the coolant housing gasket/seal **(see illustration)**.
  b) Examine the sealing ring for damage or deterioration, and if necessary, renew.
  c) On N47 diesel engines, ensure the pin on the end of the thermostat engages with the hole in the housing.
  d) On completion, refill the cooling system as described in Chapter 1A or Chapter 1B.

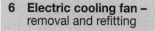

6 Electric cooling fan – removal and refitting

Removal

1 Raise the front of the vehicle and support it securely on axle stands (see *Jacking and vehicle support*). Undo the fasteners and remove the engine undershield (where fitted).

W16 diesel engines

2 Remove the plastic cover from the top of the engine.
3 The front panel must now be moved into the 'assembly' position as follows:
  a) Remove the front bumper as described in Chapter 11.
  b) Unplug the air conditioning compressor wiring plug, and release the harness from any clips.
  c) Undo the 2 bolts each side securing the front panel to the subframe **(see illustration)**.
  d) Remove the bolt each side securing the front panel to the wing **(see illustration)**.
  e) Release the coolant pipe from the retaining clips on the front panel.
  f) Undo the retaining bolt and move the coolant expansion tank to one side.

5.10 Prise out the clip a little and pull the hose from the thermostat housing

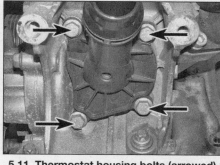

5.11 Thermostat housing bolts (arrowed)

5.12 Renew the housing seal, and ensure the pin on the end of the thermostat engages with the hole in the housing (arrowed)

  g) Detach the air intake ducting gaiter from the front panel.
  h) Prise open the junction box on the left-hand support, and disconnect the bonnet release cable **(see illustration)**.

5.16 Renew the thermostat housing gasket/seal

  i) Undo the 3 bolts each side securing the front panel/headlight to the suspension turret/front wing **(see illustration)**.
  j) Slacken the clamp and disconnect the right-hand charge pressure hose from the

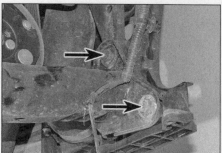

6.3a Front panel-to-subframe bolts (arrowed)

6.3b Undo the bolt (arrowed) securing the front panel to the wing each side

6.3c Open the junction box and disconnect the bonnet release cable (arrowed)

6.3d Remove the headlight bolt, and the panel support-to-suspension turret bolts (arrowed)

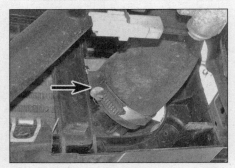

6.3e Disconnect the right-hand intercooler hose (arrowed)…

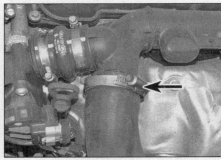

6.3f …and the turbocharger outlet hose (arrowed)

6.3g Screw the tubes/rods through the front panel into the threaded holes in the chassis members

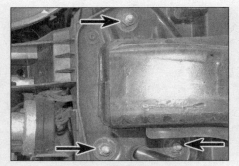

6.3h Undo the 3 nuts (arrowed) each side…

6.3i …and slide the panel forwards on the tubes

intercooler, then disconnect the air hose from the turbocharger outlet ducting **(see illustrations)**.

k) Disconnect the headlight wiring plugs.

l) Screw special tool No. 00 2 271 into the left-, and right-hand front panel/chassis

member sleeve. In the absence of these tools, use 2 lengths of tube, 19 mm outside diameter, at least 120 mm long, with two 8 mm threaded rods at least 150 mm long, and two 8 mm nuts **(see illustration)**.

m) Undo the 3 nuts each side, and slide the front panel assembly approximately 10 cm forwards **(see illustrations)**. Take care to ensure no strain is placed on any wiring/ hoses.

All engines

4 Undo the retaining bolt and move the coolant expansion tank to one side **(see illustration 3.2)**. There's no need to disconnect any coolant hoses.

5 On Cooper S models, slacken the clamps, undo the retaining bolt, and remove the left-hand charge air hose and duct **(see illustrations)**.

6 Disconnect the cooling fan wiring plug, then unclip it from the cowling **(see illustration)**. Ensure any wiring is released from the fan cowling.

7 Undo the upper and lower retaining screws from the cooling fan cowling **(see illustrations)**.

6.5a Slacken the clamp (arrowed) securing the air hose to the turbocharger…

6.5b …and the clamp at the lower end of the intercooler hose (arrowed)

6.5c Undo the bolt (arrowed) securing the intercooler air duct

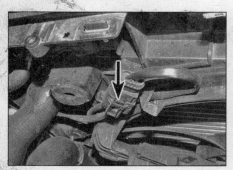

6.6 Cooling fan wiring plug (arrowed)

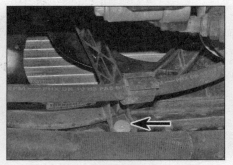

6.7a Cooling fan lower retaining bolt (arrowed)…

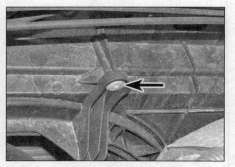

6.7b …and upper retaining bolt (arrowed)

7.1a Coolant temperature sensor (arrowed) – petrol models

7.1b Coolant temperature sensor – W16 diesel models

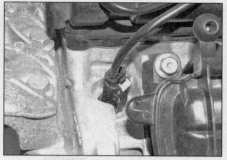

7.1c Coolant temperature sensor – N47 diesel models

7.2 Electrically controlled thermostat (arrowed)

7.8a Prise out the clip...

7.8b ...then pull out the sensor and sealing ring

Rotate the fan anti-clockwise a little, and carefully lower the fan assembly out of position, taking care not to damage the radiator fins.

Refitting

8 Refitting is a reversal of removal.

7 Cooling system electrical sensors – general information, removal and refitting

General information

1 There is only one coolant temperature sensor on most models, which is fitted to the coolant outlet housing on the left-hand end of the cylinder head (all models except N47 diesel), or the front left-hand corner of the cylinder head (N47 diesel models) **(see illustrations)**. The coolant temperature gauge and the cooling fan are all operated by the engine management ECU using the signal supplied by this sensor.

2 On petrol models, there is a second wiring connector on the coolant housing, which is for the electrically-controlled thermostat **(see illustration)**.

Removal

Note: *Ensure the engine is cold before removing a temperature sensor.*

3 Partially drain the cooling system to just below the level of the sensor (as described in Chapter 1A or Chapter 1B). Alternatively, have ready a suitable bung to plug the sensor aperture whilst the sensor is removed. If this

method is used, take great care not to damage the switch aperture or use anything which will allow foreign matter to enter the cooling system.

All models except N47 diesel

4 Remove the air cleaner housing as described in Chapter 4B.

5 On petrol models, disconnect the wiring plugs from the camshaft position sensors, and oil pressure sensor on the end of the cylinder head. Slide the wiring loom bracket upwards from the cylinder head cover and move it to one side **(see illustration 5.5a, 5.5b and 5.5c)**.

6 On turbocharged models, slacken the clamps and remove the turbocharger intake hose from the left-hand end of the cylinder head.

7 Disconnect the wiring connector from the sensor.

8 Prise out the sensor retaining circlip, and then remove the sensor and sealing ring from the housing **(see illustrations)**. If the system has not been drained, plug the sensor aperture to prevent further coolant loss.

N47 diesels

9 Pull the plastic cover on top of the engine upwards to release the mountings.

10 Disconnect the wiring plug, then unscrew the coolant temperature sensor from the cylinder head **(see illustration 7.1c)**. Check the condition of the sealing O-ring, and renew if necessary. If the system has not been drained, plug the sensor aperture to prevent further coolant loss.

Refitting

11 Where the sensor was clipped in place, fit a new sealing ring to the sensor. Push the sensor firmly into the housing and secure it in position with the circlip, ensuring it is correctly located in the housing groove.

12 Where the sensor was screwed into place, check the condition of the O-ring seal, and fit the sensor, tightening it securely.

13 Reconnect the wiring connector then refit any components removed from access. If removed, wiring bracket, plugs and air cleaner housing.

14 Top-up the cooling system as described in *Weekly checks*.

8 Coolant pump – removal and refitting

Primary coolant pump

Removal

1 Drain the cooling system (see Chapter 1A or Chapter 1B).

Petrol models

2 Raise the front of the vehicle and support it securely on axle stands (see *Jacking and vehicle support*). Remove the front right roadwheel.

3 Release the fasteners and remove the right-hand front wheelarch liner.

4 Pull out the belt friction drive gear locking device, and secure it on the locking hook **(see illustration)**.

8.4 Pull out the locking device, and secure it on the hook (arrowed)

8.5 Slacken the coolant pump pulley bolts

8.6 Friction device retaining bolts (arrowed)

8.8 Coolant pump retaining bolts (arrowed) – petrol engines

8.10 Coolant pump retaining bolts (arrowed) – W16 diesel engines

8.18 Coolant pump retaining bolts (arrowed) – N47 engines

5 Slacken the coolant pump pulley retaining bolts (see illustration). Use a strap-wrench to prevent the pulley from rotating.

6 Undo the retaining bolts and remove the belt friction gear (see illustration).

7 Remove the retaining bolts and withdraw the pulley from the coolant pump.

8 Undo the retaining bolts, then withdraw the pump from the cylinder block (see illustration).

W16 diesel engines

9 Remove the timing belt as described in Chapter 2B.

10 Undo the retaining bolts and remove the coolant pump (see illustration).

N47 diesel engines

11 Raise the front of the vehicle and support it securely on axle stands (see *Jacking and vehicle support*). Remove the front right roadwheel.

12 Undo the fasteners and remove the engine undershield.

13 Remove the auxiliary drivebelt as described in Chapter 1B.

14 Remove the right-hand headlight as described in Chapter 12.

15 Position a jack under the engine, and take the weight. Use a block of wood on the jack head to prevent damage.

16 Undo the bolts/nut and remove the right-hand engine mounting (see Chapter 2C).

17 Raise the engine a maximum of 47 mm to access the coolant pump. Do not exceed this dimension or damage to the driveshafts, wiring harnesses, etc. may result.

18 Working from above and below, undo the bolts and remove the coolant pump (see illustration). Manoeuvre the coolant pump upwards from place.

Refitting

19 Ensure that the pump and cylinder block/housing mating surfaces are clean and dry.

20 Fit the new sealing ring/gasket (as applicable) to the pump, and then refit the pump assembly, tightening its retaining bolts securely. Note that on N47 diesel engines, if the pump sealant is damaged, remove all trace of it, then apply a 2.0 mm thick bead of Loctite 5970 sealant to the groove in the pump mating face.

21 The remainder of refitting is a reversal of removal.

22 Refill the cooling system as described in Chapter 1A or Chapter 1B.

Auxiliary coolant pump

23 Cooper S models are fitted with an auxiliary, electrically-powered coolant pump in addition to the primary pump. Remove the cooling fan as described in Section 6.

24 Drain the coolant as described in Chapter 1A.

25 Slacken the clamps, undo the retaining bolt, and remove the left-hand charge air hoses/duct.

26 Disconnect the wiring plug, slacken the clamps, disconnect the hoses, then undo the bolts and remove the pump (see illustrations).

27 Refitting is a reversal of removal. Refill the cooling system as described in Chapter 1A.

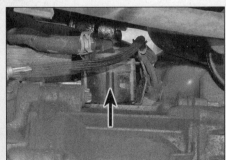

8.26a The auxiliary coolant pump is located on the front of the engine block (arrowed)

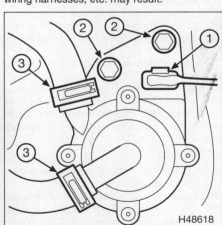

8.26b Auxiliary pump details

1 Wiring plug   3 Hose clamps
2 Retaining bolts

9 Heating and ventilation system – general information

Note: *Refer to Section 11 for information on the air conditioning side of the system.*

Manually-controlled system

1 The heating/ventilation system consists of a variable speed blower motor (housed behind the facia), face level vents in the centre and at each end of the facia, and air ducts to the front footwells.

2 The control unit is located in the facia, and the controls operate flap valves to deflect and mix the air flowing through the various parts of the heating/ventilation system. The flap valves are contained in the air distribution housing, which acts as a central distribution unit, passing air to the various ducts and vents.

3 Cold air enters the system through the grille in the scuttle. If required, the airflow is boosted by the blower, and then flows through the various ducts, according to the settings of the controls. Stale air is expelled through ducts at the rear of the vehicle. If warm air is required, the cold air is passed over the heater matrix, which is heated by the engine coolant.

4 A recirculation lever enables the outside air supply to be closed off, while the air inside the vehicle is recirculated. This can be useful to prevent unpleasant odours entering from outside the vehicle, but should only be used briefly, as the recirculated air inside the vehicle will soon become stale.

5 On some engine models an electric heater is fitted into the heater housing. When the coolant temperature is cold, the heater warms the air before it enters the heater matrix. This quickly increases the temperature of the heater matrix on cold starts, resulting in warm air being available to heat the vehicle interior soon after start-up.

Automatic climate control

6 A fully-automatic electronic climate control system was offered as an option on some models. The main components of the system are exactly the same as those described for the manual system, the only major difference being that the temperature and distribution flaps in the heating/ventilation housing are operated by electric motors rather than cables.

7 The operation of the system is controlled by the electronic control module (which is incorporated in the blower motor assembly) along with the following sensors:

a) *The passenger compartment sensor – informs the control module of the temperature of the air inside the passenger compartment.*

b) *Evaporator temperature sensor – informs the control module of the evaporator temperature.*

c) *Heater matrix temperature sensor – informs the control module of the heater matrix temperature.*

8 Using the information from the above sensors, the control module determines the appropriate settings for the heating/ventilation system housing flaps to maintain the passenger compartment at the desired setting on the control panel.

9 If the system develops a fault, the vehicle should be taken to a MINI dealer. A complete test of the system can then be carried out, using a special electronic diagnostic test unit, which is simply plugged into the system's diagnostic connector (see Chapter 4A or Chapter 4B).

10 Heater/ventilation components – removal and refitting

Control panel

1 Undo the screws and pull down the panel beneath the steering column, and remove the glovebox as described in Chapter 11 **(see illustration)**.

2 Using a blunt, flat-bladed tool, carefully prise away the panel each side of the facia centre panel **(see illustration)**.

3 Remove the tachometer from the steering column as described in Chapter 12.

4 Carefully prise the decorative strip from each side of the facia. On models with a facia storage compartment/CD autochanger, undo the screws and unclip the passengers side decorative strip, then prise rearwards the plastic trim around the facia vent **(see illustrations)**.

5 Unclip the covers from the rear edge of the facia air vent, and undo the screws exposed **(see illustrations)**.

10.1 Undo the screws (arrowed) and remove the panel beneath the steering column

10.2 Prise away the panel each side of the facia

10.4a Pull the decorative strip rearwards to unclip it

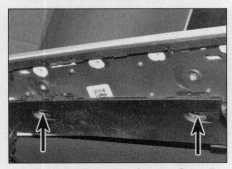

10.4b Undo the screws (arrowed), unclip the storage compartment cover...

10.4c ...and prise rearwards the decorative strip

10.5a Unclip the covers in the corners of the air vent...

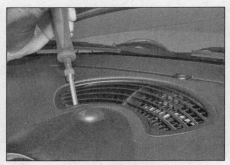

10.5b ...and undo the screws exposed

10.6a Undo the screws (arrowed)...

10.6b ...and remove the central instrument cover

10.7 Pull the panel at the base of the central facia rearwards to release the clips

10.8a Undo the 2 screws each side (arrowed)...

10.8b ...the screw in the centre (arrowed)...

10.8c ...and pull the facia centre panel rearwards at little

10.9 Heater control panel retaining screws (arrowed)

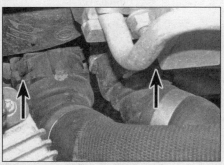

10.12 Prise down the clips (arrowed) and pull the heater hoses from the connections on the engine compartment bulkhead

10.13 Undo the screws (arrowed) and remove the panel in the footwell

6 Undo the 4 retaining screws, and remove the central instrument cover panel (see illustrations). Disconnect the hazard warning switch wiring plug as the panel is withdrawn.

7 Prise the small panel at the base of the facia centre panel from place (see illustration).

8 Undo the 2 screws each side, and the one in the centre, then unclip the facia centre panel by pulling it rearwards a little (see illustrations). Disconnect any wiring plugs as the panel is withdrawn. Note that on models with an integral telephone, an additional retaining screw is located at the centre, lower part of the panel.

9 Undo the 4 retaining screws, and remove the heater/air conditioning control panel (see illustration).

Heater matrix

10 To improve access to the matrix unions on the bulkhead, remove the air cleaner housing and air inlet ducting as described in Chapters 4A or Chapter 4B.

11 Drain the cooling system (see Chapter 1A or Chapter 1B). Alternatively, clamp the heater matrix coolant hoses to minimise coolant loss.

12 Unlock and disconnect the coolant hoses from the heater matrix pipe unions on the engine compartment bulkhead (see illustration).

13 Undo the retaining screws and remove the panel on the side of the console in the passengers footwell (see illustration).

14 Position a container (or rags) beneath the heater matrix pipe union on the left-hand side of the heating/ventilation housing to catch any spilt coolant.

15 Undo the retaining screw and pull the matrix approximately 10 mm from place (see illustration).

16 Remove the single screw, unclip the holder, and carefully pull the pipes from the

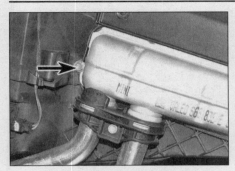

10.15 Heater matrix retaining screws (arrowed)

10.16a Undo the screw (arrowed)…

10.16b …unclip the holder…

matrix (see illustrations). Be prepared for fluid spillage.

17 Pull the matrix from the housing, taking care not to damage the cooling fins (see illustration). Renew the sealing rings on the pipes.

18 Refitting is a reversal of removal.

19 Refill the cooling system as required with reference to Chapter 1A or Chapter 1B.

Heater blower motor

20 The blower motor is fitted to the front of the heating/ventilation housing.

21 On right-hand drive models, remove the complete facia, with crossmember, as described in Chapter 11.

22 On left-hand drive models, remove the panel beneath the steering column, and the panel adjacent to the accelerator pedal.

23 On left-hand drive models with automatic transmission, remove the transmission control module (TCM) as described in Chapter 7B.

24 Disconnect the wiring connector from the blower motor (see illustration).

25 Undo the 3 retaining screws, and manoeuvre the blower motor out of position. If improved access is required, undo the screws and move the distribution flap actuator assembly to one side.

26 Refitting is the reverse of removal.

Heater blower motor resistor

27 The blower motor resistor is fitted to the lower part of the heating/ventilation housing, adjacent to the blower motor. 3 different versions of the resistor may be fitted. Proceed as follows:

28 Undo the retaining screws and remove the passengers side footwell panel (see illustration 10.13).

Version 1

29 Disconnect the wiring plug, rotate the resistor anti-clockwise a little, and pull it from the housing. When refitting the resistor, the arrow on the housing must align with the arrow on the resistor.

Version 2

30 Disconnect the wiring plug, release the locking catch, slide the resistor upwards slightly and manoeuvre it from the housing (see illustration).

10.16c …and pull the pipes from the matrix

Version 3 (models with climate control)

31 Lift the locking clip and pull the resistor from the housing. Disconnect the wiring plug as the resistor is withdrawn.

Heater housing assembly

32 On models with air conditioning, have the refrigerant circuit evacuated by an air conditioning specialist and obtain some plugs to seal the air conditioning pipe unions whilst the system is disconnected.

⚠️ **Warning: Failure to seal the refrigerant pipe unions will result in the dehydrator reservoir become saturated, necessitating its renewal.**

33 To improve access to the matrix unions on the bulkhead, remove the air cleaner housing and air inlet ducting as described in Chapters 4A or Chapter 4B. On models with the N47 diesel

10.17 Pull the matrix from the housing

engines, also remove the right-hand charge air duct.

34 Drain the cooling system (see Chapter 1A or Chapter 1B). Alternatively, working in the engine compartment, clamp the heater matrix coolant hoses to minimise coolant loss.

35 Unlock and disconnect the coolant hoses from the heater matrix pipe unions on the engine compartment bulkhead (see illustration 10.12).

36 Slacken the nut securing the air conditioning pipe unions to the bulkhead (see illustration). Separate the pipes from the evaporator and quickly seal the pipe and evaporator unions to prevent the entry of moisture into the refrigerant circuit. Discard the sealing rings, new ones must be used on refitting.

37 Remove the facia and crossmember assembly as described in Chapter 11.

38 Disconnect the wiring connectors from the

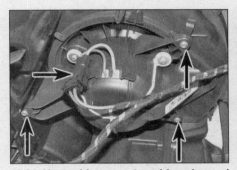

10.24 Heater blower motor wiring plug and retaining screws (arrowed)

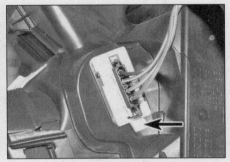

10.30 Heater blower motor resistor locking catch (arrowed)

10.36 Air conditioning pipes connection retaining nut (arrowed)

10.38a Manoeuvre the heater housing from the vehicle

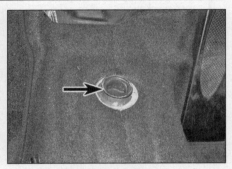

10.38b Evaporator drain tube sealing grommet (arrowed)

heating/ventilation housing components then remove the housing assembly from the vehicle. Keep the heater matrix pipe unions uppermost as the assembly is removed to prevent coolant spillage. On models with air conditioning, note how the evaporator drain tube locates in a rubber grommet in the floor **(see illustrations)**.
39 Refitting is the reverse of removal ensuring the seals are in position on the pipes and housing mounting. On completion, refill the cooling system (see Chapter 1A or Chapter 1B).

Additional heater/resistor – diesel models

40 Remove the centre console and passengers glovebox as described in Chapter 11.
41 Remove the central instrument cluster as described in Chapter 12.
42 Undo the retaining screw and remove the panel at the base of the centre face panel.
43 Note its routing, then disconnect the wiring plugs and unclip the additional heater wiring harness.
44 Undo the 2 retaining screws, and slide the heater from the housing **(see illustration)**.
45 Refitting is the reverse of removal.

Air recirculation/temperature blend/distribution motors

46 Access to the various servo motors controlling the air flow through the heater housing can only be access once the complete facia has been removed as described in Chapter 11.
47 Disconnect the motor wiring plug, undo the bolts, and remove the relevant motor **(see illustration)**.

10.44 Additional heater retaining screws (arrowed)

48 Refitting is a reversal of removal.

Ambient temperature sensor

49 Remove the front bumper as described in Chapter 11.
50 Unclip the sensor and disconnect the wiring plug.
51 Refitting is a reversal of removal.

11 Air conditioning system – general information and precautions

General information

1 An air conditioning system is available on certain models. It enables the temperature of incoming air to be lowered, and also dehumidifies the air, which makes for rapid demisting and increased comfort.
2 The cooling side of the system works in the same way as a domestic refrigerator. Refrigerant gas is drawn into a belt-driven compressor, and passes into a condenser mounted on the front of the radiator, where it loses heat and becomes liquid. The liquid passes through an expansion valve to an evaporator, where it changes from liquid under high pressure to gas under low pressure. This change is accompanied by a drop in temperature, which then cools the evaporator. The refrigerant returns to the compressor, and the cycle begins again.
3 Air blown through the evaporator passes to the heating/ventilation housing, where it is mixed with hot air blown through the heater

10.47 Undo the bolts (arrowed) and remove the relevant motor

matrix to achieve the desired temperature in the passenger compartment.
4 The heating side of the system works in the same way as on models without air conditioning (see Section 9).
5 The operation of the system is controlled electronically by the ECU integral with the control panel. Any problems with the system should be referred to a MINI dealer, or suitably-equipped specialist.

Precautions

6 When an air conditioning system is fitted, it is necessary to observe special precautions whenever dealing with any part of the system, or its associated components. The refrigerant is potentially dangerous, and should only be handled by qualified persons. Uncontrolled discharging of the refrigerant is dangerous and damaging to the environment for the following reasons.
a) *If it is splashed onto the skin, it can cause frostbite.*
b) *The refrigerant is heavier then air and so displaces oxygen. In a confined space, which is not adequately ventilated, this could lead to a risk of suffocation. The gas is odourless and colourless so there is no warning of its presence in the atmosphere.*
c) *Although not poisonous, in the presence of a naked flame (including a cigarette) it forms a noxious gas that causes headaches, nausea, etc.*

⚠ *Warning: Never attempt to open any air conditioning system refrigerant pipe/hose union without first having the system fully discharged by an air conditioning specialist. On completion of work, have the system recharged with the correct type and amount of fresh refrigerant.*

• Always seal disconnected refrigerant pipe/hose unions as soon as they are disconnected. Failure to form an airtight seal on any union will result in the dehydrator reservoir become saturated, necessitating its renewal. Also renew all sealing rings disturbed.

Caution: Do not operate the air conditioning system if it is known to be short of refrigerant as this could damage the compressor.

12 Air conditioning system components – removal and refitting

Warning: Refer to the precautions given in Section 11 and have the system discharged by an air conditioning specialist before carrying out any work on the air conditioning system.

Compressor

Removal

1 Have the air conditioning system fully discharged and evacuated by an air conditioning specialist **(see illustration)**.
2 Raise the front of the vehicle and support it securely on axle stands (see *Jacking and vehicle support*).

All except N47 diesel engines

3 Remove the air conditioning compressor/ auxiliary drivebelt as described in Chapter 1A or Chapter 1B.

N47 diesel engines

4 Slacken the clamps and remove the right-hand charge air duct.
5 Remove the auxiliary drivebelt as described in Chapter 1B.
6 Remove the bolt securing the rear, lower engine mounting link rod to the bracket on the engine. This allows the engine to be swivelled slighty.

All models

7 Disconnect the compressor wiring plug.
8 Unscrew the nuts securing the refrigerant pipes retaining plates to the compressor **(see illustration)**. Separate the pipes from the compressor and quickly seal the pipe and compressor unions to prevent the entry of moisture into the refrigerant circuit. Discard the sealing rings, new ones must be used on refitting. Release the pipes from any retaining clips as necessary.

Warning: Failure to seal the refrigerant pipe unions will result in the dehydrator reservoir become saturated, necessitating its renewal.

9 Unscrew the compressor mounting bolts, then free the compressor from its mounting bracket and remove it from the engine. Take care not to lose the spacers from the compressor rear mountings (where fitted).
10 If the compressor is to be renewed, drain the refrigerant oil from the old compressor. The specialist who recharges the refrigerant system will need to add this amount of oil to the system.

Refitting

11 If a new compressor is being fitted, drain the refrigerant oil.
12 Manoeuvre the compressor into position and fit the mounting bolts. Tighten the compressor front (drivebelt pulley) end mounting bolts to the specified torque first then tighten the rear bolt.

12.1 Refrigerant circuit service ports (arrowed)

13 Lubricate the new refrigerant pipe sealing rings with compressor oil. Remove the plugs and install the sealing rings then quickly fit the refrigerant pipes to the compressor. Ensure the refrigerant pipes are correctly joined then refit the retaining nuts, tighten it securely.
14 The remainder of refitting is a reversal of removal.
15 Have the air conditioning system recharged with the correct type and amount of refrigerant by a specialist before using the system. Remember to inform the specialist which components have been renewed, so they can add the correct amount of oil.

Condenser

Removal

16 Have the air conditioning system fully discharged by an air conditioning specialist.
17 Remove the front bumper as described in Chapter 11.
18 Undo the retaining bolts and disconnect the refrigerant pipes from the left-hand side of the condenser. Recover the O-ring seals **(see illustration)**.

Warning: Failure to seal the refrigerant pipe unions will result in the dehydrator reservoir becoming saturated, necessitating its renewal.

19 Undo the 3 retaining screws and remove the condenser from the front panel **(see illustration)**.

Refitting

20 Refitting is a reversal of removal. Noting the following points:

12.18 Disconnect the refrigerant pipes at the left-hand side of the condenser

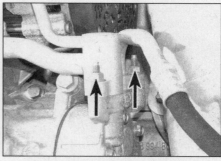

12.8 Compressor refrigerant pipes retaining nuts (arrowed)

a) Ensure the mountings are secure when the condenser is in position in the front panel.
b) Lubricate the sealing rings with compressor oil. Remove the plugs and install the sealing rings then quickly fit the refrigerant pipes to the condenser. Securely tighten the dehydrator pipe union nut and ensure the compressor pipe is correctly joined.
c) Have the air conditioning system recharged with the correct type and amount of refrigerant by a specialist before using the system.

Receiver/drier

21 The receiver/drier is located on the side of the condenser. Remove the condenser as previously described in this Section.
22 Unscrew the protective cap, then remove the circlip and pull the receiver/drier from the condenser. Renew the sealing rings.
23 Refitting is a reversal of removal.

Evaporator

Removal

24 Have the air conditioning system fully discharged and evacuated by an air conditioning specialist.
25 Remove the heating/ventilation housing and matrix as described in Section 10.
26 Disconnect the wiring plug from the evaporator temperature sensor, located on the left-hand side of the housing **(see illustration 12.33)**.
27 On diesel models, remove the additional heater element as described in Section 10.

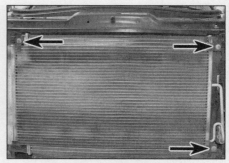

12.19 Condenser retaining screws (arrowed)

12.28a Unclip the rubber cover

12.28b Undo the screws (arrowed) and remove the cover and pipes assembly

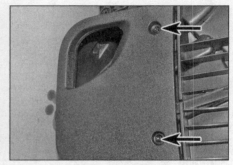

12.29 Right-hand panel retaining screws (arrowed)

12.30 Undo the screws (arrowed), remove the cover…

12.31 …and remove the evaporator with the expansion valve

12.33 Evaporator temperature sensor

28 Unclip the rubber retainer, remove the foam insert, then undo the screws and remove the cover and pipes assembly **(see illustrations)**.
29 Undo the 3 screws and remove the plastic panel from the right-hand side of the housing **(see illustration)**.
30 Undo the retaining screws and remove the cover from the base of the heater housing **(see illustration)**.
31 Slide the evaporator and expansion valve from the housing **(see illustration)**.

Refitting

32 Refitting is a reversal of removal but have the air conditioning system recharged with the correct type and amount of refrigerant by a specialist prior to using the system.

Evaporator sensor

Removal

33 The evaporator sensor is fitted to the lower part of the heating/ventilation housing, at the left-hand side, below the heater matrix coolant pipes **(see illustration)**.
34 Remove the lower trim panel from the left-hand side of the centre console.
35 Trace the wiring back from the sensor and disconnect the wiring connector. **Note:** *If a wiring connector is not available, it may be*

part of the wiring loom. In this case, the wiring will need to be cut approximately 50mm from the sensor.
36 Pull the sensor from the heater housing.

Refitting

37 Refit the sensor into position in the housing and connect the wiring connector. **Note:** *If required, join the wiring where it has been cut.*
38 Refit any components removed for access.

Expansion valve

Removal

39 Have the air conditioning system fully discharged and evacuated by an air conditioning specialist.
40 Remove the air cleaner assembly as described in Chapter 4A or Chapter 4B.
41 On N47 diesel engines, slacken the clamps and remove the right-hand charger air duct to enable access to the engine compartment bulkhead.
42 Slacken the nut, and disconnect the refrigerant pipes at the engine compartment bulkhead **(see illustration 10.36)**. Plug/cover the openings to prevent contamination/saturation. Recover and discard the O-ring seals – new ones must be fitted.

⚠ *Warning: Failure to seal the refrigerant pipe unions will result in the receiver/drier becoming saturated, necessitating its renewal*

43 Undo the upper bolt and insert a piece of threaded rod (or stud), then undo the lower bolt and insert another piece of threaded rod (or stud). The expansion/relief valve can then be withdrawn out from the bulkhead along the length of the threaded rods. **Note:** *If the threaded rods (studs) are not used the spacer at the rear of the expansion/relief valve may drop down behind the heater unit housing. Recover and discard the O-ring seals – new ones must be fitted.*

Refitting

44 Refitting is a reversal of removal but have the air conditioning system recharged with the correct type and amount of refrigerant by a specialist prior to using the system.

Solar sensor

45 The solar sensor (where fitted) is located in the centre of the facia. Using a blunt, flat-bladed tool, carefully prise the sensor from the facia. Disconnect the wiring plug as the sensor is withdrawn.
46 Refitting is a reversal of removal.

Chapter 4 Part A:
Fuel and exhaust systems – petrol models

Contents

Degrees of difficulty

Easy, suitable for novice with little experience	**Fairly easy,** suitable for beginner with some experience	**Fairly difficult,** suitable for competent DIY mechanic	**Difficult,** suitable for experienced DIY mechanic	**Very difficult,** suitable for expert DIY or professional

Specifications

Engine identification

Designation:
  1.4 litre engine . . . .
  1.6 litre engine:
    Non-turbo (up to 2010). . . . .
    Non-turbo (2010-on) . . . .
    Turbo (2010 – 2012 173 and 208 bhp) . . . .
    Turbo (2010-on 181 bhp) . . . .

Engine code

N12B14

N12B16
N16B16
N14B16
N18B16

System type

Non-turbo. . . . . Siemens DME multipoint sequential indirect fuel injection
Turbo . . . . Siemens DME direct sequential injection

Fuel system data

Fuel pump type:
  Non-turbo. . . . . Electric, immersed in tank
  Turbo. . . . . Electric, immersed in tank, and engine driven high-pressure pump
Electric fuel pump regulated constant pressure:
  Non-turbo. . . . . 3.5 ± 0.2 bar
  Turbo. . . . . 5.0 bar
Specified idle speed. . . . . 850 ± 100 rpm (not adjustable – controlled by ECU)
Idle mixture CO content . . . . Less than 1.0% (not adjustable – controlled by ECU)

Recommended fuel

Minimum octane rating. . . . . 95 RON unleaded (UK unleaded premium).
Leaded/lead replacement fuel (LRP) must **not** be used

Torque wrench settings

	Nm	lbf ft
Camshaft position sensor	8	6
Common fuel rail:		
Non-turbo	8	6
Turbo	20	15
Exhaust manifold-to-cylinder head nuts	25	18
High-pressure fuel pipe nuts (turbo models):		
Stage 1	15	11
Stage 2	33	24
Stage 3, after warm-up	33	24
High-pressure fuel pump	10	7
Intake manifold nuts	15	11
Intake manifold bracket	20	15
Oil feed-to-turbocharger	30	22
Oil return-to-turbocharger	8	6
Throttle body	10	7
Turbocharger-to-manifold	20	15
Turbocharger coolant pipes	35	25

1 General information and precautions

1 The fuel supply system consists of a fuel tank, which is mounted under the rear of the car, with an electric fuel pump immersed in it, a fuel filter (depending on model), fuel feed and return pipes. On non-turbo models (indirect injection), the fuel pump supplies fuel to the fuel rail, which acts as a reservoir for the four fuel injectors, which inject fuel into the inlet tracts. Turbocharged models are equipped with a direct injection system, where the tank-immersed electric pump supplies fuel to an engine-driven high-pressure pump. This pump supplies fuel to a common fuel rail, where it is distributed under high-pressure to the injectors. Fuel is then injected directly into the combustion chambers, resulting in lower emissions, higher engine output, for reduced consumption.

2 Refer to Section 5 for further information on the operation of the engine management system, and to Section 15 for information on the exhaust system.

⚠ **Warning: Many of the procedures in this Chapter require the removal of fuel pipes and connections, which may result in some fuel spillage. Before carrying out any operation on the fuel system, refer to the precautions given in 'Safety first!' at the beginning of this manual, and follow them implicitly. Petrol is a highly dangerous and volatile liquid, and the precautions necessary when handling it cannot be overstressed.**

Note: *Residual pressure will remain in the fuel pipes long after the vehicle was last used. When disconnecting any fuel line, first depressurise the fuel system as described in Section 6.*

2 Air cleaner assembly – removal and refitting

Removal

Non-turbo models

1 Release the clip and disconnect the air intake ducting from the resonator box **(see illustration)**.

2 Undo the 2 retaining screws and pull the air cleaner housing and resonator box upwards from the rubber mountings **(see illustrations)**.

3 If required, rotate the resonator box clockwise and detach it from the air cleaner housing **(see illustration)**.

Turbo models

4 Undo the retaining bolt at the right-hand end of the air cleaner housing **(see illustration)**.

2.1 Release the clip each side and disconnect the air intake duct

2.2a Undo the screws (arrowed)...

2.2b ...and pull the air cleaner upwards from the mountings

2.3 Rotate the resonator box clockwise and detach it from the air cleaner

2.4 Undo the screw in the corner of the air cleaner (arrowed)

5 Release the clamp and pull the upper air hose from the housing **(see illustration)**.
6 Depress the catches and pull the lower air hose from the housing **(see illustration)**.
7 Manoeuvre the air cleaner from position, disconnecting any wiring plugs, and unclip any hoses as it's withdrawn.

Refitting

8 Refitting is a reversal of the removal procedure, ensuring that all hoses and ducts are properly reconnected and correctly seated and, where necessary, securely held by their retaining clips. Do not use any grease or lubricant when refitting the air hoses/ducts on turbocharged models – damage to the turbocharger could result.

3 Accelerator pedal – removal and refitting

1 Prise up the plastic cap, and undo the screw exposed **(see illustration)**.
2 Pull the accelerator pedal assembly upwards, then disconnect the position sensor wiring plug **(see illustration)**.
3 Refitting is a reversal of the removal procedure. Note that if a new assembly is fitted, it must be programmed using Mini diagnostic equipment.

4 Unleaded petrol – general information and usage

Note: *The information given in this Chapter is correct at the time of writing. If updated information is thought to be required, check with a MINI dealer. If traveling abroad, consult one of the motoring organisations (or a similar authority) for advice on the fuel available.*

1 The fuel recommended by MINI is given in the Specifications Section of this Chapter, followed by the equivalent petrol currently on sale in the UK.
2 All models are designed to run on fuel with a minimum octane rating of 95 (RON). All models have a catalytic converter, and so must be run on unleaded fuel only. Under no circumstances should leaded/lead replacement fuel (UK 4-star/LRP) be used, as this may damage the converter.
3 Super unleaded petrol (97, 98 or 99 octane) can also be used in all models if wished, though there is no advantage in doing so.

5 Engine management system – general information

Note: *The fuel injection ECU is of the 'self-learning' type, meaning that as it operates, it also monitors and stores the settings, which give optimum engine performance under all operating conditions. When the battery is*

2.5 Slacken the clamp (arrowed) and disconnect the upper hose

disconnected, these settings are lost and the ECU reverts to the base settings programmed into its memory at the factory. On restarting, this may lead to the engine running/idling roughly for a short while, until the ECU has relearned the optimum settings. This process is best accomplished by taking the vehicle on a road test (for approximately 15 minutes), covering all engine speeds and loads, concentrating mainly in the 2500 to 3500 rpm region.

On all engines, the fuel injection and ignition functions are combined into a single engine management system. The system incorporates a closed-loop catalytic converter and an evaporative emission control system, and complies with the latest emission control standards. Refer to Chapter 5B for information on the ignition side of each system; the fuel side of the system operates as follows.

The fuel pump, which is situated in the fuel tank, supplies fuel from the tank to the fuel rail (non-turbo models) or high-pressure fuel pump (turbo models). The pump motor is permanently immersed in fuel, to keep it cool. The fuel rail is mounted directly above the fuel injectors and acts as a fuel reservoir.

Fuel rail supply pressure is controlled by the pressure regulator, also located in the fuel tank. The regulator contains a spring-loaded valve, which lifts to allow excess fuel to recirculate within the tank when the optimum operating pressure of the fuel system is exceeded (eg, during low speed, light load cruising).

The fuel injectors are electromagnetic valves, which spray atomised fuel into the inlet manifold tracts (non-turbo engines) or combustion chambers (turbo model) under

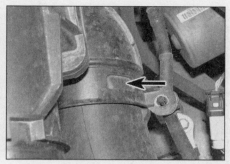

2.6 Depress the catch (arrowed) and disconnect the lower hose

the control of the engine management system ECU. There are four injectors, one per cylinder, mounted in the cylinder head. On non-turbo engines, each injector is mounted at an angle that allows it to spray fuel directly onto the back of the inlet valves. On turbocharged engines, the fuel is injected directly in the top of the combustion chambers. The ECU controls the volume of fuel injected by varying the length of time for which each injector is held open. The fuel injection systems are of the sequential type, whereby each injector operates individually in cylinder sequence.

The electrical control system consists of the ECU, along with the following sensors:

a) *Throttle potentiometer – informs the ECU of the throttle valve position, and the rate of throttle opening/closing.*
b) *Coolant temperature sensor – informs the ECU of engine temperature.*
c) *Inlet air temperature sensor – informs the ECU of the temperature of the air passing through the throttle housing.*
d) *Oxygen sensors – inform the ECU of the oxygen content of the exhaust gases (explained in greater detail in Chapter 4C).*
e) *Manifold pressure sensor – informs the ECU of the load on the engine (expressed in terms of inlet manifold vacuum).*
f) *Crankshaft position sensor – informs the ECU of engine speed and crankshaft angular position.*
g) *Vehicle speed sensor – informs the ECU of the vehicle speed (not all models).*
h) *Knock sensor – informs the ECU of pre-ignition (detonation) within the cylinders (not all models).*

3.1 Prise up the cap and undo the Allen screw beneath

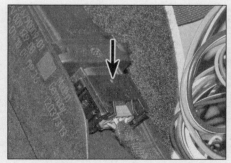

3.2 Disconnect the accelerator pedal position sensor wiring plug (arrowed)

5.1 The diagnostic plug (arrowed) is located under the drivers side of the facia

i) *Camshaft sensor – informs the ECU which cylinder is on the firing stroke on systems with sequential injection.*

j) *Accelerator pedal position sensor – informs the ECU of the pedal position and rate of change.*

k) *Throttle valve positioner motor – allows the ECU to control the throttle valve position.*

l) *Engine oil temperature sensor – informs the ECU of the engine oil temperature (not all models).*

m) *Clutch and brake pedal position sensor – informs the ECU of the pedal positions (not all models).*

Signals from each of the sensors are compared by the ECU and, based on this information, the ECU selects the response appropriate to those values, and controls the fuel injectors (varying the pulse width – the length of time the injectors are held open – to provide a richer or weaker air/fuel mixture, as appropriate). The air/fuel mixture is constantly varied by the ECU, to provide the best settings for cranking, starting (with either a hot or cold engine) and engine warm-up, idle, cruising and acceleration.

The ECU also has full control over the engine idle speed, via a stepper motor (depending on model) fitted to the throttle housing. The stepper motor either controls the amount of air passing through a bypass drilling at the side of the throttle or controls the position of the throttle valve itself, depending on model. A sensor informs the ECU of the position, and rate of change, of the accelerator pedal. The ECU then controls the throttle valve by means

6.2 The fuel pressure relief valve (arrowed) is located at the right-hand end of the fuel rail

of a throttle positioning motor integral with the throttle body – no accelerator cable is fitted. The ECU also carries out 'fine tuning' of the idle speed by varying the ignition timing to increase or reduce the torque of the engine as it is idling. This helps to stabilise the idle speed when electrical or mechanical loads (such as headlights, air conditioning, etc) are switched on and off.

The throttle housing is also fitted with an electric heating element. The heater is supplied with current by the ECU, warming the throttle housing on cold starts to help prevent icing of the throttle valve.

The exhaust and evaporative loss emission control systems are described in more detail in Chapter 4C.

If there is any abnormality in any of the readings obtained from the coolant temperature sensor, the inlet air temperature sensor or the oxygen sensor, the ECU enters its 'back-up' mode. If this happens, the erroneous sensor signal is overridden, and the ECU assumes a pre-programmed 'back-up' value, which will allow the engine to continue running, albeit at reduced efficiency. If the ECU enters this mode, the warning lamp on the instrument panel will be illuminated, and the relevant fault code will be stored in the ECU memory.

If the warning light illuminates, the vehicle should be taken to a MINI dealer or specialist at the earliest opportunity. Once there, a complete test of the engine management system can be carried out, using a special electronic diagnostic test unit, which is plugged into the system's diagnostic connector, located behind the trim panel under the drivers side of the facia **(see illustration)**.

6 Fuel system – depressurisation

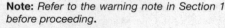

Note: *Refer to the warning note in Section 1 before proceeding.*

Depressurisation

⚠️ *Warning: The following procedure will merely relieve the pressure in the fuel system – remember that fuel will still be present in the system components and take precautions accordingly before disconnecting any of them.*

1 The fuel system referred to in this Section is defined as the tank-mounted fuel pump, the fuel filter (where fitted), the fuel injectors, high-pressure pump (where applicable), the fuel rail and the pipes of the fuel pipes between these components. All these contain fuel, which will be under pressure while the engine is running, and/or while the ignition is switched on. The pressure will remain for some time after the ignition has been switched off, and must be relieved in a controlled fashion when any of these components are disturbed for servicing work.

2 Some models are equipped with a pressure relief valve on the end of the fuel rail **(see illustration)**. On these models, unscrew the cap from the valve and position a container beneath the valve. Hold a wad of rag over the valve and relieve the pressure in the system by depressing the valve core with a suitable screwdriver. Be prepared for the squirt of fuel as the valve core is depressed and catch it with the rag. Hold the valve core down until no more fuel is expelled from the valve. Once the pressure is relieved, securely refit the valve cap.

3 Where no valve is fitted to the fuel rail, it will be necessary to release the pressure as the fuel pipe is disconnected. Place a container beneath the union and position a large rag around the union to catch any fuel spray, which may be expelled. Slowly release and disconnect the fuel pipe and catch any spilt fuel in the container. Plug the pipe/union to minimise fuel loss and prevent the entry of dirt into the fuel system.

7 Fuel pump/level sensors – removal and refitting

Turbocharged models

Note: *There are two level sensors installed in the fuel tank – one in the left side of the tank, and one in the right side. The pump is integral with the left side sensor, and the filter is integral with the right side sensor.*

Removal

1 Relieve the fuel system pressure (see Section 6).

Left-hand sensor/fuel pump

2 Remove the rear seat cushion as described in Chapter 11.

3 Unscrew the nuts/bolts, and remove the access cover from the floor.

4 Remove the gasket.

5 Slide out the locking element to disconnect the electrical connector **(see illustration)**.

6 Unscrew the fuel pump/level sensor unit locking ring and remove it from the tank. Although a MINI tool (16 1 020) is available for this task, suitable alternative tools are available from good tools suppliers. Turn the

7.5 Slide out the locking element and disconnect the wiring plug

7.7 Depress the button (arrowed) and disconnect the fuel hose

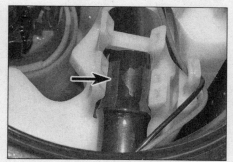

7.8a Unclip the transfer pipe (arrowed)...

7.8b ...and disconnect the wiring plug

7.12 Squeeze the sides of the clip and pull out the fuel pipe

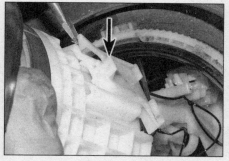

7.14 Lift the clip (arrowed) and slide the fuel hose holder downwards

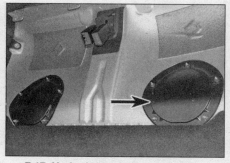

7.17 Undo the nuts and remove the left-hand access cover (arrowed)

ring anti-clockwise until it can be unscrewed by hand (see illustration 7.20).

7 Lift the sensor cover a little, then unclip the keeper from the fuel hose connection, depress the button and disconnect the fuel hose (see illustration).

8 Disconnect the electrical connector, and release the transfer pipe from the clips on the top of the pump unit (see illustrations).

9 Carefully lift the level sensor/pump unit from the tank, taking care not to bend the sensor float arm (gently push the float arm towards the unit if necessary). Remove the sealing ring (see illustration 7.21b). No further disassembly is recommended – at the time of writing, it would appear the pump is not available separately from the level sensor.

Right-hand sensor and filter housing

10 Remove the left-side sensor cover, and

disconnect the fuel hoses/wiring plug as described in paragraphs 2 to 8.

11 Unscrew the nuts/bolts and remove the access cover from over the right-side sensor.

12 Squeeze together the sides of the retaining clip and disconnect the fuel hose (see illustration).

13 Unscrew the locking ring as described in paragraph 6.

14 Lift the sensor a little, pry out the clip and slide the fuel hose holder down and off the sensor assembly (see illustration).

15 Lift the sensor assembly from the tank, complete with fuel hoses. Remove the sealing ring.

Non-turbocharged models

Note: Only 1 sensor is fitted to these models, integral with the pump.

Removal

16 Remove the rear seat cushion as described in Chapter 11.

17 Undo the 5 nuts and remove the left-hand access cover (see illustration).

18 Slide out the locking element and disconnect the wiring plug (see illustration).

19 Push the pipe downwards, squeeze together the clips and disconnect the fuel pipe (see illustration). Be prepared for fuel spillage.

20 Unscrew the fuel pump/level sensor unit locking ring and remove it from the tank. Although a MINI tool (16 1 020) is available for this task, suitable alternative tools are available from good tool suppliers. Turn the ring anti-clockwise until it can be unscrewed by hand (see illustration).

21 Carefully manoeuvre the pump assembly

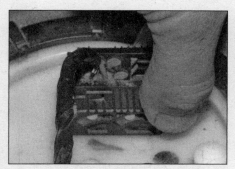

7.18 Slide the locking element outwards to disconnect the wiring plug

7.19 Push the pipe down, and squeeze the clip (arrowed) each side

7.20 Unscrew the sensor unit locking ring

7.21a Take care not to damage the sensor arm

7.21b Renew the sealing ring

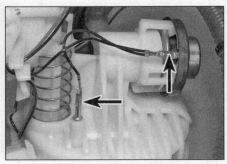

7.22a Disconnect the wiring plugs (arrowed)…

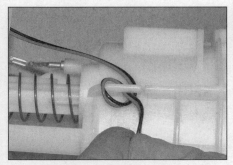

7.22b …and release the wiring from the hooks

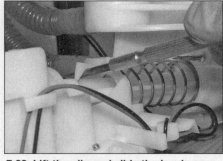

7.23 Lift the clip and slide the level sensor downwards

7.24 Unscrew the cap to access the filter

from the tank, taking care not to damage the level sensor arm **(see illustrations)**. Renew the sealing ring. No further disassembly is recommended – at the time of writing, it would appear the pump is not available separately from the level sensor

Filter replacement (turbo models only)
22 Remove the right-hand sensor/filter assembly as described previously in this Section, then disconnect the wiring plugs, and release the wiring from the small hooks on the side of the housing **(see illustrations)**.

23 Detach the fuel level sensor from the housing **(see illustration)**. Take care not to lose the spring!
24 If equipped with a retaining ring at the top of the housing, unscrew it. On models without a retaining ring, turn the cap anti-clockwise to unlock it. Remove the cap from the housing **(see illustration)**. Note that the cap will only fit in one position.
25 Remove the filter element from the housing **(see illustration)**.
26 Clean all components and replace all O-rings with new ones **(see illustrations)**.
27 Reassembly is the reverse of disassembly.

Refitting
28 Refitting is a reversal of removal, noting the following points:
a) Use a new sensor sealing ring(s).
b) To allow the unit to pass through the opening in the fuel tank, insert the float arm first.

7.25 Lift the filter from the housing

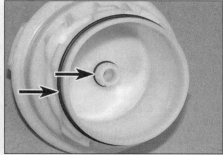

7.26a Renew the O-ring seals in the cap (arrowed)…

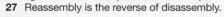

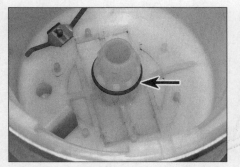

7.26b …and the seal in the cap (arrowed)

7.28a The arrow must align with the marks on the fuel tank (arrowed)

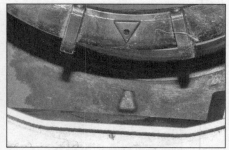

7.28b The arrows indicate the start positions of the thread on the tank and locking ring

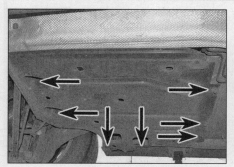

9.4 Undo the fasteners (arrowed) and remove the underbody panelling each side

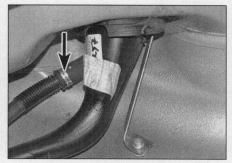

9.8 Disconnect the vent hose from the filler neck (arrowed)

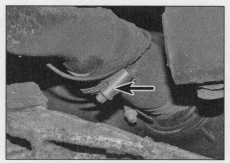

9.9 Slacken the clamp (arrowed) and disconnect the filler neck

c) When the unit is installed, the arrow on the pump/sender unit cover must align with the corresponding marks on the fuel tank *(see illustration)*.

d) Tighten the locking collar securely. Note that the arrow on the collar and tank indicates the start position of the threads *(see illustration)*.

8 Fuel gauge sender unit – removal and refitting

The fuel gauge sender unit is an integral part of the fuel pump assembly and is not available separately. Refer to Section 7 for removal and refitting details.

The resistance of the sender unit we examined is as follows:

Full tank (float at the highest position):
  20 ohms
Empty tank (float in the lowest position):
  Non-turbo models   480 ohms
  Petrol turbo models   300 ohms

9 Fuel tank – removal and refitting

Note: *Refer to the warning note in Section 1 before proceeding.*

Removal

1 Relieve the fuel system pressure (see Section 6), then disconnect the cable from the negative terminal of the battery (see Chapter 5A).

2 Before removing the fuel tank, all fuel should be drained from the tank. Since a fuel tank drain plug is not provided, it is preferable to carry out the removal operation when the tank is nearly empty.

⚠️ **Warning: If it's necessary to siphon the fuel out, use a siphoning kit, available at most automotive parts stores. Never start the siphoning action by mouth.**

3 Raise the rear of the vehicle and support it securely on axle stands (see *Jacking and vehicle support*). Remove both rear roadwheel.

4 On undo the plastic nuts/screw, release

the plastic expansion rivets and remove the underbody panelling **(see illustration)**.

5 Remove the rear section of the exhaust system, and any heat shields that would interfere with removal of the fuel tank.

6 Undo the fasteners and remove the left-hand wheelarch liner.

7 Disconnect the handbrake cables from the rear calipers with reference to Chapter 9, then undo the bolts securing the cable support brackets to the rear axle. Feed the cables out through the axle support, leaving the cables attached to the handbrake lever.

8 Cut the hose clamp and disconnect the fuel vent hose from the filler neck **(see illustration)**.

9 Loosen the clamp and disconnect the fuel filler hose from the tank **(see illustration)**.

10 Remove the rear seat cushion as described in Chapter 11. Unscrew the nuts/bolts and remove the fuel tank access covers. Disconnect the electrical connector from the sensor, and the fuel hose from the right-side sensor (where applicable).

11 Note their fitted positions and disconnect the hoses from the charcoal carbon canister adjacent to the fuel tank **(see illustration)**.

12 On convertible models, remove the cross frame reinforcement supports from under the fuel tank.

13 Support the fuel tank using a floor jack and a wood plank.

14 Remove the retaining bolts securing the tank retaining straps, and the bolt at the centre-front of the tank **(see illustration)**.

15 Lower the tank slightly, and disconnect the vent hose connection above the tank.

16 Lower the tank and manoeuvre it from under the vehicle.

Refitting

17 Refitting is a reversal of removal.

10 Engine management system – testing and adjustment

Testing

1 If a fault appears in the engine management system, first ensure that all the system wiring connectors are securely connected and free of corrosion. Ensure that the fault is not due to poor maintenance; ie, check that the air cleaner filter element is clean, the spark plugs are in good condition and correctly gapped, the cylinder compression pressures are correct and that the engine breather hoses are clear and undamaged, referring to Chapters 1A, 2A and 5B for further information.

2 If these checks fail to reveal the cause of the problem, the vehicle should be taken to a suitably-equipped MINI dealer or specialist for testing using a diagnostic tester, which is connected into the diagnostic socket located behind the trim panel under the drives side of the facia **(see illustration 5.1)**. The tester will locate the fault quickly and simply, alleviating the need to test all the system components individually, which is a time-consuming operation that carries a risk of damaging the ECU.

9.11 Disconnect the hoses from the charcoal canister

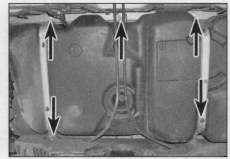

9.14 Fuel tank retaining bolts (arrowed)

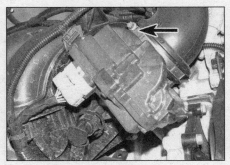

11.1 Slacken the clamp and disconnect the air duct from the throttle body (arrowed)

Adjustment

3 Whilst it is possible to check the exhaust CO level and the idle speed, if these are found to be in need of adjustment, the car must be taken to a suitably-equipped MINI dealer or specialist or further testing. Neither the mixture adjustment (exhaust gas CO level) nor the idle speed is adjustable, and should either be incorrect, a fault must be present in the engine management system.

11 Throttle housing – removal and refitting

Non-turbocharged models

1 Remove the air filter housing as described in Section 2. Also loosen the clamp and remove the duct from the throttle body **(see illustration)**.

12.4a Disconnect the fuel feed hose at the back of the engine (arrowed)...

12.5 Fuel rail retaining bolts (arrowed)

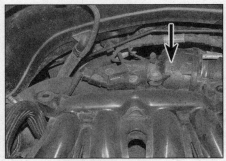

11.6 Remove the 'sound generator' and air hose (arrowed)

2 Remove the throttle body mounting screws.
3 Detach the throttle body from the intake manifold, then disconnect its electrical connector.
4 Refitting is a reversal of removal, but install a new sealing ring. **Note:** *If a new throttle body has been installed, the engine management ECU must be recoded and the throttle body matched using dedicated test equipment – this task must be entrusted to a MINI dealer or specialist.*

Turbocharged models

5 Remove the air filter housing (see Section 9).
6 Remove the sound generator **(see illustration)**.
7 Release the clamps and remove the air hose.
8 Loosen the clamp and disconnect the charge air duct from the throttle body **(see illustration)**.

12.4b ...by pushing the collar (arrowed) into the coupling

12.7a Detach the injectors from the fuel rail

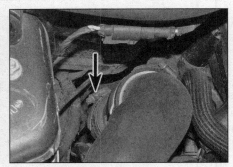

11.8 Slacken the clamp (arrowed) securing the charge air hose

9 Remove the throttle body mounting screws.
10 Detach the throttle body from the intake manifold, then disconnect its electrical connector.
11 Refitting is a reversal of removal, but install a new sealing ring. **Note:** *If a new throttle body has been installed, the engine management ECU must be recoded and the throttle body matched using dedicated test equipment – this task must be entrusted to a MINI dealer or specialist.*

12 Engine management system components – removal and refitting

Note: *Refer to the warning note in Section 1 before proceeding.*
1 Before proceeding with removing any of the engine management system components, disconnect the battery (see Chapter 5A)

Fuel rail and injectors

Note: *If a faulty injector is suspected, before condemning the injector, it is worth trying the effect of one of the proprietary injector cleaning treatments, which are available from car accessory shops.*
2 Remove the air cleaner housing and air ducting as described in Section 2.
3 Before any work is carried out on the fuel system, depressurise the system as described in Section 6.

Non-turbo models

4 Detach the fuel line from the fuel rail **(see illustrations)**.
5 Remove the fuel rail mounting bolts **(see illustration)**.
6 Pull the fuel rail and injectors up, then disconnect the electrical connectors from the injectors.
7 Pry out the retaining clips and remove the injectors from the fuel rail. Replace the injector O-rings **(see illustrations)**.
8 Lightly lubricate the fuel injector O-rings with a little petroleum jelly or a light film of engine oil.
9 Refit the injectors to the fuel rail, and retain them in place with the clips pushed into the grooves.

10 The remainder of refitting is a reversal of removal.

Turbocharged models

⚠️ **Warning: Even after relieving the fuel system pressure on the fuel delivery (low-pressure) side of the system, fuel in the fuel rail remains under extremely high pressure.**

11 Remove the intake manifold as described in Chapter 4A.

12 Unscrew the nuts at each end of the high-pressure fuel pipe (between the fuel rail and the high-pressure fuel pump) (see Section 13).

⚠️ **Warning: Be sure to wear full face protection, long sleeves and thick leather gloves, and cover the fittings with shop rags while slowly loosening them so fuel under pressure in the line bleeds out slowly. Also, the manufacturer states that it is necessary to replace the high-pressure fuel line (between the fuel rail and the high-pressure fuel pump) with a new one whenever it is removed.**

13 Disconnect the electrical connector from the high-pressure fuel sensor.

14 Remove any retainers/tie-wraps and detach the wiring harness from the fuel rail.

15 Depress the tabs and disconnect the electrical connectors from the fuel injectors.

16 Remove the fuel rail mounting bolts, then pull the fuel rail off the fuel injectors.

17 Remove the spring steel retainers from the injectors. Discard the retainers – new ones must be used during installation.

18 Pull the injectors from the cylinder head. Special tools are available to remove injectors that are stuck (MINI special tool nos. 13 0 231 and 13 0 232). Sometimes improvised methods will work, too, but be careful not to damage the injectors.

19 Remove the old combustion chamber Teflon sealing ring and the upper O-ring and support ring from each injector **(see illustration)**.

Caution: Be extremely careful not to damage the groove for the seal or the rib in the floor of the groove. If you damage the groove or the rib, you must replace the injector.

20 Before installing the new Teflon seal on each injector, thoroughly clean the groove for the seal and the injector shaft. Remove all combustion residue and varnish with a clean shop rag.

Teflon seal installation using the special tools

21 The manufacturer recommends that you use the tools included in the special injector tool set to install the Teflon lower seals on the injectors: Install the special seal assembly cone on the injector, install the special sleeve on the injector and use the sleeve to push on the assembly cone, which pushes the Teflon seal into place on its groove. Do NOT use any lubricants to do so.

22 Pushing the Teflon seal into place in its groove expands it slightly. There are three sizing sleeves in the special tool set with progressively smaller inside diameters. Using a clockwise rotating motion of about 180

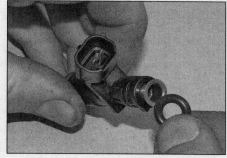

12.7b Renew the O-ring seals at each end of the injector

degrees, install the slightly larger sleeve onto the injector and over the Teflon seal until the sleeve hits its stop, then carefully turn the sleeve anti-clockwise as you pull it off the injector. Use the slightly smaller sizing sleeve the same way, followed by the smallest sizing ring. The seal is now sized. Repeat this step for each injector.

Teflon seal installation without special tools

23 If you don't have the special injector tool set, the Teflon seal can be installed using this method: First, find a socket that is equal or very close in diameter to the diameter of the end of the fuel injector.

24 Work the new Teflon seal onto the end of the socket **(see illustration)**.

25 Place the socket against the end of the injector **(see illustration)** and slide the seal from the socket onto the injector. Do NOT use any lubricants to do so. Continue pushing

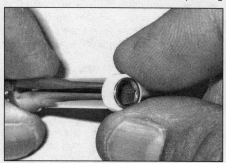

12.24 Slide the new Teflon seal onto the end of a socket that's the same diameter as the end of the fuel injector...

12.26a Use the socket to push a short section of plastic tubing onto the end of the injector and over the new seal...

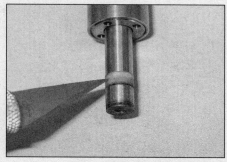

12.19 Remove the Teflon seal with a sharp knife

the seal onto the injector until it seats into its mounting groove.

26 Because the inside diameter of the seal has to be stretched open to fit over the bore of the socket and the injector, its outside diameter is now slightly too large – it is no longer flush with the surface of the injector. It must be shrunk it back to its original size. To do so, push a piece of plastic tubing with an interference fit onto the end of the socket; a plastic straw that fits tightly on the injector will work. After pushing the plastic tubing onto the socket about an inch, snip off the rest of the tubing, then use the socket to push the tubing onto the end of the injector **(see illustration)** and slide it onto the injector until it completely covers the new seal **(see illustration)**. Leave the tubing on for a few hours, then remove it. The seal should now be shrunk back its original outside diameter, or close to it.

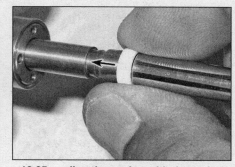

12.25 ...align the socket with the end of the injector and slide the seal onto the injector and into its mounting groove

12.26b ...then leave the plastic tubing in place for several hours to compress the new seal

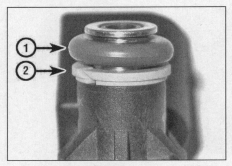

12.27 Note that the upper O-ring (1) is installed above the support ring (2)

12.35 Release the clips, undo the screw and remove the ECU cover (arrowed)

31 Install a new spring steel retainer on each injector, then install the fuel rail, tightening the fasteners to the torque listed in this Chapter's Specifications.
32 Install a *new* high-pressure fuel line, tightening the tube nuts to the torque listed in this Chapter's Specifications.
33 The remainder of refitting is the reverse of removal.

Fuel pressure regulator

34 The fuel pressure regulator is an integral part of the fuel pump assembly and is not available separately. Refer to Section 7 for removal and refitting details.

Electronic Control Unit (ECU)

Note: *Disconnecting the battery will erase any fault codes stored in the PCM. It is strongly recommended that the fault code memory of the unit is interrogated using a code reader or scanner prior to battery disconnection.*
35 Unclip the cover from the ECU **(see illustration)**. Note that on some models, a cover retaining screw is located at the front, left-hand edge.
36 Depress the locking catches, pivot over the release levers and disconnect the wiring plugs from the ECU **(see illustrations)**.
37 Press-in the catches and slide the ECU upwards from place **(see illustration)**.
38 Refitting is a reversal of removal. **Note:** *If a new ECU has been fitted, it will need to be coded using MINI diagnostic equipment. Entrust this task to a MINI dealer or suitably equipped repairer. After reconnection, the vehicle must be driven for several miles so that the ECU can re-learn its basic settings. If the engine still runs erratically, the basic setting may be reinstated by a MINI dealer or suitably equipped repairer.*

12.36a Depress the clip...

12.36b ...then pivot of the release levers and disconnect the ECU wiring plugs

Manifold pressure sensor

39 The MAP sensor is mounted on the inlet manifold. Remove the air cleaner housing as described in Section 2.
40 Disconnect the wiring connector then undo the screw and remove the sensor from the manifold **(see illustrations)**.
41 Refitting is a reversal of the removal procedure ensuring the sensor seal is in good condition.

Injector and fuel rail installation
Note: *There are two different styles of injectors: first generation and second generation. When obtaining replacement parts, you'll need the cylinder head number which is stamped on the front side of the head, just above the exhaust manifold. Cylinder heads with the first six characters 'MCGU10' are of the first generation. Heads with the first six characters 'MCGU15' are of the second generation. First generation injectors have a plastic top where the upper O-ring seats, and use a 'compensation element' with a retaining ring at the bottom, but without a 'stop choc.' Second generation injectors have a metal top where the O-ring seats, and use a 'decoupling' element at the bottom without a retaining ring. Be sure to obtain the correct parts, as they aren't interchangeable.*
27 Install the new support ring at the upper end of the injector. Lubricate the new upper

O-ring with clean engine oil and install it on the injector. Do NOT oil the new Teflon seal. Note that the seal is installed *above* the spacer **(see illustration)**.
28 Thoroughly clean the injector bores with a small nylon brush. If any of the valves are in the way, carefully rotate the engine just enough to provide enough clearance to reach all of the bore.
29 Install the new compensation element and retaining ring, or the new decoupling element, as applicable, to the bottom of each injector.
30 Install the fuel injectors in the cylinder head (NOT in the fuel rail). You should be able to push each assembled injector into its bore in the cylinder head. The bore is tapered, so you will encounter some resistance as the Teflon seal nears the bottom of the bore. Press the injector into its bore until it stops, making sure to align the plastic projection on the injector with the hole in the cylinder head.

12.37 Depress the clip (arrowed) each side and slide up the ECU

12.40a Manifold pressure sensor (arrowed) – non-turbo models

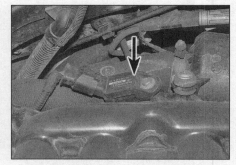

12.40b Manifold pressure sensor (arrowed) – turbo models

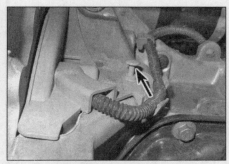

12.44a Remove the plastic fastener (arrowed)...

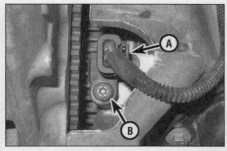

12.44b ...then disconnect the crankshaft position sensor wiring plug (A) and remove the retaining bolt (B)

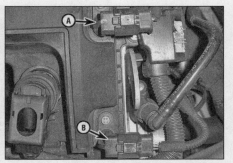

12.48 Intake (A) and exhaust (B) camshaft position sensors

12.49a Disconnect the wiring plug...

12.49b ...undo the bolt and withdraw the sensor

12.50 Renew the sensor seal

Coolant temperature sensor

42 The coolant temperature sensor is either screwed, or secured by a retaining clip, in the coolant outlet housing on the left-hand end of the cylinder head. Refer to Chapter 3, Section 7, for removal and refitting information.

Crankshaft position sensor

43 The crankshaft sensor is situated at the rear of the cylinder block, below the starter motor. Raise the front of the vehicle and support it securely on axle stands (see *Jacking and vehicle support*).
44 Release the securing clips for the wiring loom, remove the plastic fastener, unclip the plastic cover and disconnect the sensor wiring connector. Undo the retaining bolt and remove the sensor from behind the flywheel (see illustrations).
45 Refitting is reverse of the removal procedure.

Vehicle speed sensor

46 The engine management ECU receives vehicle speed data from the wheel speed sensors, via the ABS ECU.

Knock sensor

47 Refer to Chapter 5B.

Camshaft position sensor

48 There are two camshaft position sensors located on the left-hand end of the cylinder head cover (see illustration).
49 Disconnect the wiring plug, then undo the bolt and remove the relevant sensor from the cylinder head cover (see illustrations).

50 Refitting is the reverse of removal ensuring the sensor seal is in good condition (see illustration).

DME master relay

51 Ensure the ignition system is switched off, then open the electronics box on the left-hand side of the engine compartment.
52 The DME master relay is at the front of the box. Pull the relay from the socket (see illustration).
53 Refitting is a reversal of removal.

Accelerator pedal position sensor

54 The sensor is integral with the accelerator pedal assembly – see Section 3.

Charge pressure/ temperature sensor

Turbo models only

55 The sensor is located in the charge air

12.52 DME master relay (arrowed)

duct at the right-hand side of the engine compartment. Disconnect the sensor wiring plug (see illustration).
56 Undo the retaining bolt and remove the sensor.
57 Refitting is a reversal of removal, ensuring the sensor seal is in good condition.

Hot film air mass sensor

N18 turbocharged engines only

58 The sensor is fitted to the air outlet duct from the air cleaner housing. Disconnect the sensor wiring plug.
59 Slacken the clamp and disconnect the air duct from the sensor.
60 Undo the 2 retaining screws and detach the sensor from the air cleaner.
61 Refitting is the reverse of removal. **Note:** *It's essential that when refitting the sensor or the air ducting, no lubrication/grease is used on reassembly. The air passages must be free*

12.55 Charge pressure/temperature sensor (arrowed)

12.62 Oxygen sensors locations (arrowed)

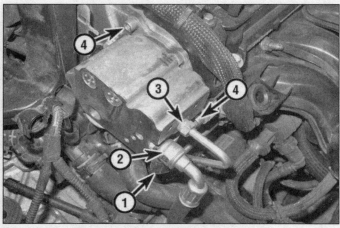

13.7a High-pressure pump details

1 Electrical connector	3 High-pressure fuel pipe fitting
2 Fuel feed pipe fitting	4 Mounting bolts

from oil/grease, or damage to the turbocharger may result.

Oxygen sensor

Note: *The oxygen sensor is delicate and will not work if it is dropped or knocked, if its power supply is disrupted, or if any cleaning materials are used on it.*

62 Trace the wiring back from the oxygen sensor(s), which are located before and after the catalytic converters **(see illustration)**. Disconnect both wiring connectors and free the wiring from any relevant retaining clips or ties.

63 Unscrew the sensor from the exhaust system front pipe/manifold and remove it along with its sealing washer.

64 Refitting is a reverse of the removal procedure using a new sealing washer. Prior to installing the sensor apply a smear of high temperature grease to the sensor threads. Ensure that the sensor is securely tightened and that the wiring is correctly routed and in no danger of contacting either the exhaust system or engine.

---

13 High-pressure pump –
removal and refitting

Note: *The high-pressure pump is only fitted to turbocharged models.*

Removal

1 Disconnect the battery negative lead as described in Chapter 5A.

2 Remove the air cleaner housing as described in Section 2.

3 Relieve the fuel system pressure (see Section 6).

4 Disconnect the fuel feed pipe from the high-pressure pump. This requires MINI tool no. 13 0 250. Install the tool over the line fitting, engaging the lugs of the tool in the openings of the fitting. Tighten the screw on the side of the tool to secure it to the fitting.

5 Cover the fitting with a cloth, push the fuel pipe into the pump, then pull the tool and pipe away from the pump.

6 Remove the tool from the fuel pipe, then plug the pipe and fuel pump opening to prevent the entry of dirt.

7 Unscrew the union nuts at each end of the high-pressure fuel pipe (between the fuel rail and the high-pressure fuel pump) **(see illustrations)**.

⚠ *Warning: Be sure to wear full face protection, long sleeves and thick leather gloves, and cover the fittings with shop rags while slowly loosening them so fuel under pressure in the pipe bleeds out slowly. Also, the manufacturer states that it is necessary to replace the high-pressure fuel pipe (between the fuel rail and the high-pressure fuel pump) with a new one whenever it is removed.*

8 Disconnect the electrical connector from the pump, then remove the mounting screws and detach the pump from the cylinder head.

⚠ *Warning: The manufacturer states that the pump mounting screws must be replaced with new ones whenever they are removed.*

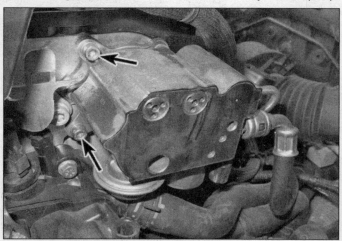

13.7b High-pressure fuel pump front mounting bolts

13.7c High-pressure fuel pipe-to-fuel rail fitting

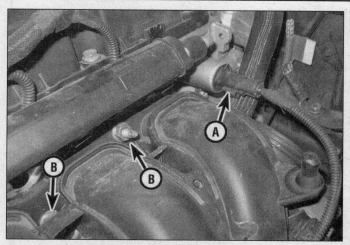

14.3 VANOS solenoid wiring plug (A) and intake manifold mounting nuts (B – two of five shown)

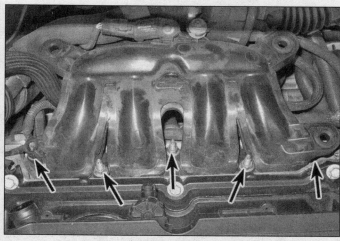

14.13 Intake manifold retaining nuts (arrowed) – Cooper S models

Refitting

9 Clean the mating surfaces of the pump and cylinder head. Install a new O-ring on the pump.

10 Turn the drive rotor on the pump so it's in the proper position to mate with the slots in the end of the camshaft.

11 Install the pump to the cylinder head. Install the new mounting screws and tighten them hand tight at this time, so that the pump can move a little.

12 Install the new high-pressure fuel pipe, first tightening the pipe-to-fuel rail union nut (hand-tight only), then the pipe-to-pump union nut (also only hand-tight).

13 Tighten the pump-to-cylinder head fasteners to the specified torque.

14 Tighten the high-pressure fuel pipe union nuts to the specified torque.

15 The remainder of refitting is the reverse of removal.

14 Intake manifold – removal and refitting

Note: *Refer to the warning note in Section 1 before proceeding.*

Intake manifold

1 Disconnect the cable from the negative terminal of the battery (see Chapter 5A).

2 Remove the air filter housing as described in Section 2.

Non-turbo models

3 Disconnect the electrical connector from the VANOS solenoid at the right-hand side of the cylinder head **(see illustration)**.

4 Disconnect the electrical connector from the throttle body.

5 Raise the vehicle and support it securely on axle stands (see Jacking and vehicle support). Remove the EVAP purge solenoid/fuel tank vent valve (see Chapter 4C).

6 Disconnect the wires from the guide on the Valvetronic actuating motor at the left end of the manifold.

7 Remove the wiring harness bracket from the starter motor.

8 Remove the intake manifold nuts **(see illustration 14.3)** and detach the manifold from the cylinder head.

9 Clean the manifold and cylinder head mating surfaces. Install new seals around the intake manifold runner ports.

10 Refitting is the reverse of removal. Tighten the manifold fasteners to the specified torque.

Cooper S models

11 Disconnect the electrical connector from the intake manifold pressure sensor, as described in Section 12.

13 Remove the intake manifold nuts and detach the manifold from the head **(see illustration)**.

14 Mark and disconnect all hoses and electrical connectors from the underside of the manifold.

15 Clean the manifold and cylinder head mating surfaces. Install new seals around the intake manifold runner ports.

16 Refitting is the reverse of removal. Tighten the manifold fasteners to the specified torque.

15 Exhaust manifold – removal and refitting

Warning: Wait until the engine is completely cool before beginning this procedure.

Note: *Apply penetrating to all exhaust system fasteners and allow it to soak in for a while before attempting to remove them. When reassembling, apply anti-seize compound to the threads of the fasteners.*

1 Disconnect the battery negative terminal as described in Chapter 5A.

2 The front panel must now be moved into the 'assembly' position as follows:

a) Remove the front bumper as described in Chapter 11.

b) Unplug the air conditioning compressor wiring plug, and release the harness from any clips.

c) Undo the 2 bolts each side securing the front panel to the subframe **(see illustration)**.

d) Remove the bolt each side securing the front panel to the wing **(see illustration)**.

e) Release the coolant pipe from the retaining clips on the front panel.

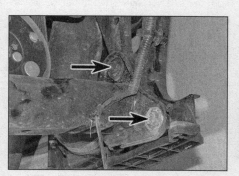

15.2a Front panel-to-subframe bolts (arrowed)

15.2b Undo the bolt (arrowed) securing the front panel to the wing each side

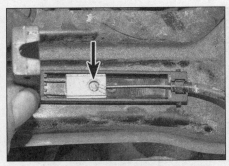

15.2c Open the junction box and disconnect the bonnet release cable (arrowed)

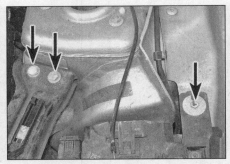

15.2d Remove the headlight bolt, and the panel support-to-suspension turret bolts (arrowed)

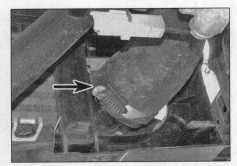

15.2e Disconnect the right-hand intercooler hose (arrowed)...

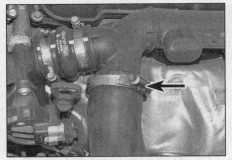

15.2f ...and the turbocharger outlet hose (arrowed)

f) Undo the retaining bolt and move the coolant expansion tank to one side.

g) Detach the air intake ducting gaiter from the front panel.

h) Prise open the junction box on the left-hand support, and disconnect the bonnet release cable **(see illustration)**.

i) Undo the 3 bolts each side securing the front panel/headlight to the suspension turret/front wing **(see illustration)**.

j) Slacken the clamp and disconnect the right-hand charge pressure hose from the intercooler, then disconnect the air hose from the turbocharger outlet ducting **(see illustrations)**.

k) Disconnect the right-hand headlight wiring plug.

l) Screw special tool No. 00 2 271 into the left-, and right-hand front panel/chassis member sleeve. In the absence of these tools, use 2 lengths of tube, 19 mm outside

15.2g Screw the tubes/rods through the front panel into the threaded holes in the chassis members

diameter, at least 120 mm long, with two 8 mm threaded rods at least 150 mm long, and two 8 mm nuts **(see illustration)**.

m) Undo the 3 nuts each side, and slide the front panel assembly approximately 10 cm forwards **(see illustrations)**. Take care to ensure no strain is placed on any wiring/hoses.

Non-turbo models

Note: *On these models, the primary catalytic converter is part of the exhaust manifold.*

3 Remove the upstream oxygen sensor (see Section 12).

4 Remove the exhaust manifold heat shield **(see illustration)**.

5 Raise the front of the vehicle and support it securely on axle stands (see *Jacking and vehicle support*), then remove the downstream oxygen sensor. Detach the exhaust pipe from the catalytic converter, then remove the

15.2h Undo the 3 nuts (arrowed) each side...

fasteners and detach the converter from the engine block.

6 Remove the exhaust manifold nuts and detach the manifold from the cylinder head **(see illustration)**.

7 Remove the old gasket, then clean the manifold and cylinder head mating surfaces.

8 Refitting is the reverse of the removal procedure. Be sure to use a new gasket. If the mounting nuts were difficult to remove, replace them with new ones (also replace the studs if necessary).

Turbocharged models

Note: *This procedure includes removal of the turbocharger.*

9 Drain the cooling system (see Chapter 1A) and remove the coolant expansion tank (see Chapter 3).

10 Remove the (primary) catalytic converter (see Chapter 4C).

15.2i ...and slide the panel forwards on the tubes

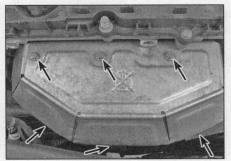

15.4 Exhaust manifold heat shield fasteners (arrowed)

15.6 Exhaust manifold retaining nuts (arrowed)

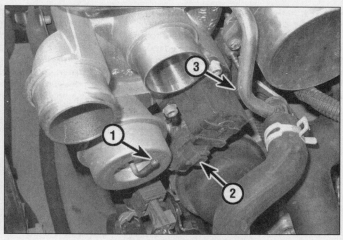

15.13 Turbocharger details

1 Coolant pipe fittings
2 Oil feed pipe fitting (return pipe fitting on the underside of the turbo)

15.14 Turbocharger details

1 Vacuum hose fitting
2 Electrical connector
3 Coolant pipe bracket bolt

11 Loosen the clamps and detach the intake duct and charge air duct from the turbocharger.
12 Detach the radiator hose from the thermostat housing (see Chapter 3).
13 Detach the coolant and oil pipes from the turbocharger **(see illustration)**.
14 Disconnect the vacuum pipe and electrical connector from the left side of the turbocharger. Also remove the bracket bolt for the coolant pipe **(see illustration)**.
15 Remove the support bracket from the underside of the exhaust manifold.
16 Remove the exhaust manifold mounting nuts and detach the manifold and turbocharger assembly from the cylinder head **(see illustration)**.
17 If necessary, remove the nuts and detach the turbocharger from the manifold.
18 Refitting is the reverse of the removal procedure. Be sure to use a new gasket(s). If the mounting nuts were difficult to remove, replace them with new ones (also replace the studs if necessary). When refitting, ensure all air/turbocharger ducts/hoses are free from grease or oil, otherwise turbocharger damage may result.

16 Turbocharger – removal and refitting

Removal and refitting of the turbocharger is described in Section 15 – Exhaust manifold removal and refitting.

17 Intercooler – removal and refitting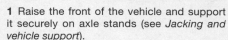

1 Raise the front of the vehicle and support it securely on axle stands (see *Jacking and vehicle support*).
2 Remove the front bumper as described in Chapter 11.
3 Slacken the clamps and disconnect the left-, and right-hand air hoses from the underside of the intercooler **(see illustration)**.
4 Undo the retaining bolts and manoeuvre the intercooler from place **(see illustration)**.
5 Refitting is a reversal of removal. **Note:** *When refitting, ensure all air/intercooler ducts/hoses are free from grease or oil, otherwise turbocharger damage may result.*

18 Exhaust system – general information

General information

Note: *Allow exhaust system components to cool before inspection or repair. Also, when working under the vehicle, make sure it is securely supported on axle stands (see Jacking and vehicle support).*
1 The exhaust system consists of the exhaust manifolds, catalytic converter, muffler, tailpipe and all connecting pipes, flanges and clamps. The exhaust system is isolated from the vehicle body and from chassis components by a series of rubber hangers. Periodically inspect these hangers for cracks or other signs of deterioration, replacing them as necessary.
2 Conduct regular inspections of the exhaust system to keep it safe and quiet. Look for any damaged or bent parts, open seams, holes, loose connections, excessive corrosion or other defects which could allow exhaust fumes to enter the vehicle. Do not repair deteriorated exhaust system components; replace them with new parts.

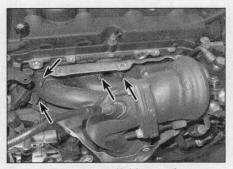

15.16 Exhaust manifold mounting nuts (4 of 10 shown)

17.3 Intercooler duct hose clamps (arrowed)

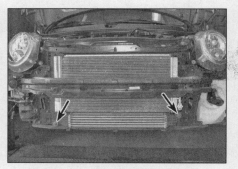

17.4 Intercooler retaining fasteners (arrowed)

3 If the exhaust system components are extremely corroded, or rusted together, a cutting torch is the most convenient tool for removal. Consult a properly-equipped repairer. If a cutting torch is not available, you can use a hacksaw, or if you have compressed air, there are special pneumatic cutting chisels that can also be used. Wear safety goggles to protect your eyes from metal chips and wear work gloves to protect your hands.

4 Here are some simple guidelines to follow when repairing the exhaust system:

a) *Work from the back to the front when removing exhaust system components.*

b) *Apply penetrating oil to the exhaust system component fasteners to make them easier to remove.*

c) *Use new gaskets, hangers and clamps.*

d) *Apply anti-seize compound to the threads of all exhaust system fasteners during reassembly.*

e) *Be sure to allow sufficient clearance between newly installed parts and all points on the underbody to avoid overheating the floor pan and possibly damaging the interior carpet and insulation. Pay particularly close attention to the catalytic converter and heat shield.*

Chapter 4 Part B:
Fuel and exhaust systems – diesel models

Contents

Degrees of difficulty

Easy, suitable for novice with little experience	**Fairly easy,** suitable for beginner with some experience	**Fairly difficult,** suitable for competent DIY mechanic	**Difficult,** suitable for experienced DIY mechanic	**Very difficult,** suitable for expert DIY or professional

Specifications

Engine identification

	Designation
1.6 litre	W16
1.6 litre	N47 C16
2.0 litre	N47 C20

General

System type	High-pressure direct injection with full electronic control, direct injection and turbocharger
Fuel system operating pressure	200 to 1800 bars (according to engine speed)
Idle speed	800 ± 20 rpm (controlled by ECU)
Engine cut-off speed	5000 rpm (controlled by ECU)

Injectors

Type	Electromagnetic or Piezo

Torque wrench settings

	Nm	lbf ft
Accumulator rail mounting bolts	23	17
Accumulator rail-to-fuel injector fuel pipe unions:		
W16 engines*:		
Injector end union:		
Stage 1	25	18
Stage 2	27	20
Rail end union:		
Stage 1	24	18
Stage 2	26	19
N47 engines	24	18
Camshaft position sensor bolt	4	3
Charge air pressure sensor (W16 engine only)	4	3
Crankshaft speed/position sensor	5	4
Exhaust gas/particulate temperature sensor	30	20
Exhaust manifold nuts*:		
W16 engine:		
Short stud	25	18
Long stud	30	20
N47 engine	13	10
Fuel injector clamp bolt:		
W16 engine:		
Stage 1	4	3
Stage 2	Angle-tighten a further 65°	
N47 engine:		
Stage 1	8	6
Stage 2	26	19
Fuel injector clamp stud	7	5
Fuel pressure sensor to accumulator rail	45	33
Fuel pump-to-accumulator rail fuel pipe unions:		
W16 engine*	25	18
N47 engine	24	18
High-pressure fuel pump mounting bolts:		
W16 engine	23	17
N47 engine	20	15
High-pressure fuel pump support bracket (N47 engines)	20	15
High-pressure fuel pump rear mounting bolts/nut (8 mm)	17	13
High-pressure fuel pump sprocket nut:		
W16 engines	50	37
N47 engines	65	48
Inlet manifold bolts (N47 engine only)	10	7
Inlet manifold pressure sensor (N47 engine only)	5	4
Inlet manifold air temperature sensor (W16 engine only)	5	4
Oxygen sensor	50	37
Throttle body (N47 engines)	8	6
Timing cover cap (N47 engines)	20	15
Turbocharger clamp (N47 engines)*	20	15
Turbocharger mounting bolts/nuts	25	18
Turbocharger oil feed pipe banjo bolts	22	17
Turbocharger oil return pipe bracket (N47 engines)	10	7

* Do not re-use

1 General information and system operation

The fuel system consists of a rear-mounted fuel tank and fuel lift pump, a fuel filter with integral water separator, on some models a fuel cooler mounted under the car, and an electronically-controlled high-pressure direct injection system, together with a turbocharger.

The exhaust system is conventional, but to meet the latest emission levels an unregulated catalytic converter and an exhaust gas recirculation system are fitted to all models.

On some models, an exhaust emission particulate filter is fitted – refer to Chapter 4C for further details.

The injection system (generally known as a 'common rail' system) derives its name from the fact that a common rail (referred to as an accumulator rail), or fuel reservoir, is used to supply fuel to all the fuel injectors. Instead of an in-line or distributor type injection pump, which distributes the fuel directly to each injector, a high-pressure pump is used, which generates a very high fuel pressure (1350+ bars at high engine speed) in the accumulator rail. The accumulator rail stores fuel, and maintains a constant fuel pressure, with the aid of a pressure control valve. Each injector is supplied with high-pressure fuel from the accumulator rail, and the injectors are individually controlled via signals from the system electronic control unit (ECU). The injectors are electronically operated.

In addition to the various sensors used on models with a conventional fuel injection pump; common rail systems also have a fuel pressure sensor. The fuel pressure sensor allows the ECU to maintain the required fuel pressure, via the pressure control valve.

System operation

For the purposes of describing the operation of a common rail injection system, the components can be divided into three sub-systems; the low-pressure fuel system, the high-pressure fuel system and the electronic control system.

Low-pressure fuel system

The low-pressure fuel system consists of the following components:

a) *Fuel tank.*
b) *Fuel lift pump.*
c) *Fuel filter/water trap.*
d) *Low-pressure fuel lines.*

The low-pressure system (fuel supply system) is responsible for supplying clean fuel to the high-pressure fuel system.

High-pressure fuel system

The high-pressure fuel system consists of the following components:

a) *High-pressure fuel pump with pressure control valve.*
b) *High-pressure fuel accumulator rail.*
c) *Fuel injectors.*
d) *High-pressure fuel lines.*

After passing through the fuel filter, the fuel reaches the high-pressure pump, which forces it into the accumulator rail. As diesel fuel has certain elasticity, the pressure in the accumulator rail remains constant, even though fuel leaves the rail each time one of the injectors operates. Additionally, a pressure control valve mounted on the high-pressure pump ensures that the fuel pressure is maintained within preset limits.

The pressure control valve is operated by the ECU. When the valve is opened, fuel is returned from the high-pressure pump to the tank, via the fuel return lines, and the pressure in the accumulator rail falls. To enable the ECU to trigger the pressure control valve correctly, a fuel pressure sensor measures the pressure in the accumulator rail.

The electronically-controlled fuel injectors are operated individually, via signals from the ECU, and each injector injects fuel directly into the relevant combustion chamber. The fact that high fuel pressure is always available allows very precise and highly flexible injection in comparison to a conventional injection pump: for example, combustion during the main injection process can be improved considerably by the pre-injection of a very small quantity of fuel.

Electronic control system

The electronic control system consists of the following components:

a) *Electronic control unit (ECU).*
b) *Crankshaft speed/position sensor.*
c) *Camshaft position sensor.*
d) *Accelerator pedal position sensor.*
e) *Coolant temperature sensor.*
f) *Fuel temperature sensor.*
g) *Air mass meter.*
h) *Fuel pressure sensor.*
i) *Fuel injectors.*
j) *Fuel pressure control valve.*
k) *Preheating control unit.*
l) *EGR solenoid valve.*
m) *Air temperature sensor*
n) *Inlet manifold pressure sensor.*

The information from the various sensors is passed to the ECU, which evaluates the signals. The ECU contains electronic 'maps' which enable it to calculate the optimum quantity of fuel to inject, the appropriate start of injection, and even pre- and post-injection fuel quantities, for each individual engine cylinder under any given condition of engine operation.

Additionally, the ECU carries out monitoring and self-diagnostic functions. Any faults in the system are stored in the ECU memory, which enables quick and accurate fault diagnosis using appropriate diagnostic equipment (such as a suitable fault code reader).

System components

Fuel lift pump

The fuel lift pump and integral fuel gauge sender unit/level sensor is electrically operated, and is mounted in the fuel tank.

High-pressure pump

The high-pressure pump is mounted on the engine in the position normally occupied by the conventional distributor fuel injection pump. The pump is driven at half engine speed by the timing belt (W16 engines) or timing chain (N47 engines), and is lubricated by the fuel, which it pumps.

The fuel lift pump forces the fuel into the high-pressure pump chamber, via a safety valve.

The high-pressure pump consists of three radially-mounted pistons and cylinders. The pistons are operated by an eccentric cam mounted on the pump drive spindle. As a piston moves down, fuel enters the cylinder through an inlet valve. When the piston reaches bottom dead centre (BDC), the inlet valve closes, and as the piston moves back up the cylinder, the fuel is compressed. When the pressure in the cylinder reaches the pressure in the accumulator rail, an outlet valve opens, and fuel is forced into the accumulator rail. When the piston reaches top dead centre (TDC), the outlet valve closes, due to the pressure drop, and the pumping cycle is repeated. The use of multiple cylinders provides a steady flow of fuel, minimising pulses and pressure fluctuations.

As the pump needs to be able to supply sufficient fuel under full-load conditions, it will supply excess fuel during idle and part-load conditions. This excess fuel is returned from the high-pressure circuit to the low-pressure circuit (to the tank) via the pressure control valve.

The pump incorporates a facility to effectively switch off one of the cylinders to improve efficiency and reduce fuel consumption when maximum pumping capacity is not required. When this facility is operated, a solenoid-operated needle holds the inlet valve in the relevant cylinder open during the delivery stroke, preventing the fuel from being compressed.

Accumulator rail

As its name suggests, the accumulator rail (also known as common rail) acts as an accumulator, storing fuel and preventing pressure fluctuations. Fuel enters the rail from the high-pressure pump, and each injector has its own connection to the rail. The fuel pressure sensor is mounted in the rail, and the rail also has a connection to the fuel pressure control valve on the pump.

Pressure control valve

The pressure control valve is operated by the ECU, and controls the system pressure. The valve is integral with the high-pressure pump and cannot be separated.

If the fuel pressure is excessive, the valve opens, and fuel flows back to the tank. If the pressure is too low, the valve closes, enabling the high-pressure pump to increase the pressure.

The valve is an electronically-operated ball valve. The ball is forced against its seat, against the fuel pressure, by a powerful spring, and also by the force provided by the electromagnet. The force generated by the electromagnet is directly proportional to the current applied to it by the ECU. The desired pressure can therefore be set by varying the current applied to the electromagnet. Any pressure fluctuations are damped by the spring.

Fuel pressure sensor

The fuel pressure sensor is mounted in the accumulator rail, and provides very precise information on the fuel pressure to the ECU.

Fuel injector

The injectors are mounted on the engine in a similar manner to conventional diesel fuel injectors. The injectors are electronically-operated via signals from the ECU, and fuel is injected at the pressure existing in the accumulator rail. The injectors are high-precision instruments and are manufactured to very high tolerances.

Fuel flows into the injector from the accumulator rail, via an inlet valve and an inlet throttle, and an electromagnet causes the injector nozzle to lift from its seat, allowing injection. Excess fuel is returned from the injectors to the tank via a return line. The injector operates on a hydraulic servo principle: the forces resulting inside the injector due to the fuel pressure effectively amplify the effects of the electromagnet, which does not provide sufficient force to open the injector nozzle directly. The injector functions as follows. Five separate forces are essential to the operation of the injector.

a) *A nozzle spring forces the nozzle needle against the nozzle seat at the bottom of the injector, preventing fuel from entering the combustion chamber.*
b) *In the valve at the top of the injector, the valve spring forces the valve ball against the opening to the valve control chamber. The fuel in the chamber is unable to escape through the fuel return.*

2.4 Typical plastic plug and cap set for sealing disconnected fuel pipes and components

c) When triggered, the electromagnet exerts a force, which overcomes the valve spring force, and moves the valve ball away from its seat. This is the triggering force for the start of injection. When the valve ball moves off its seat, fuel enters the valve control chamber.

d) The pressure of the fuel in the valve control chamber exerts a force on the valve control plunger, which is added to the nozzle spring force.

e) A slight chamfer towards the lower end of the nozzle needle causes the fuel in the control chamber to exert a force on the nozzle needle.

When these forces are in equilibrium, the injector is in its rest (idle) state, but when a voltage is applied to the electromagnet, the forces work to lift the nozzle needle, injecting fuel into the combustion chamber. There are four phases of injector operation as follows:

a) Rest (idle) state – all forces are in equilibrium. The nozzle needle closes off the nozzle opening, and the valve spring forces the valve ball against its seat.

b) Opening – the electromagnet is triggered which opens the nozzle and triggers the injection process. The force from the electromagnet allows the valve ball to leave its seat. The fuel from the valve control chamber flows back to the tank via the fuel return line. When the valve opens, the pressure in the valve control chamber drops, and the force on the valve plunger is reduced. However, due to the effect of the input throttle, the

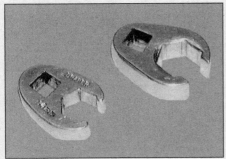

2.7 Two crow-foot adapters will be necessary for tightening the fuel pipe unions

pressure on the nozzle needle remains unchanged. The resulting force in the valve control chamber is sufficient to lift the nozzle from its seat, and the injection process begins.

c) Injection – within a few milliseconds, the triggering current in the electromagnet is reduced to a lower holding current. The nozzle is now fully open, and fuel is injected into the combustion chamber at the pressure present in the accumulator rail.

d) Closing – the electromagnet is switched off, at which point the valve spring forces the valve ball firmly against its seat, and in the valve control chamber, the pressure is the same as that at the nozzle needle. The force at the valve plunger increases, and the nozzle needle closes the nozzle opening. The forces are now in equilibrium once more, and the injector is once more in the idle state, awaiting the next injection sequence.

ECU and sensors

The ECU and sensors are described earlier in this Section – see *Electronic control system*.

Air inlet sensor and turbocharger

An airflow sensor is fitted downstream of the air filter to monitor the quantity of air supplied to the turbocharger. On some models, air from the high-pressure side of the turbocharger is either channelled through the intercooler, or into the manifold without being intercooled, depending on the air temperature. The flow and routing of inlet air is controlled by the engine management ECU. On these models, an engine coolant-heated matrix is fitted to the base of the air cleaner housing to warm the incoming air, which decreases harmful exhaust emissions. The turbochargers are of the variable nozzle geometry type.

2	**High-pressure diesel injection system –** special information

Warnings and precautions

1 It is essential to observe strict precautions when working on the fuel system components, particularly the high-pressure side of the system. Before carrying out any operations on the fuel system, refer to the precautions given in *Safety first!* at the beginning of this manual, and to the following additional information.

• Do not carry out any repair work on the high-pressure fuel system unless you are competent to do so, have all the necessary tools and equipment required, and are aware of the safety implications involved.

• Before starting any repair work on the fuel system, wait at least 30 seconds after switching off the engine to allow the fuel circuit pressure to reduce.

• Never work on the high-pressure fuel system with the engine running.

• Keep well clear of any possible source of fuel leakage, particularly when starting the engine after carrying out repair work. A leak in the system could cause an extremely high pressure jet of fuel to escape, which could result in severe personal injury.

• Never place your hands or any part of your body near to a leak in the high-pressure fuel system.

• Do not use steam cleaning equipment or compressed air to clean the engine or any of the fuel system components.

Procedures and information

2 Strict cleanliness must be observed at all times when working on any part of the fuel system. This applies to the working area in general, the person doing the work, and the components being worked on.

3 Before working on the fuel system components, they must be thoroughly cleaned with a suitable degreasing fluid. Specific cleaning products may be obtained from MINI dealers. Alternatively, a suitable brake cleaning fluid may be used. Cleanliness is particularly important when working on the fuel system connections at the following components:

a) Fuel filter.
b) High-pressure fuel pump.
c) Accumulator rail.
d) Fuel injectors.
e) High-pressure fuel pipes.

4 After disconnecting any fuel pipes or components, the open union or orifice must be immediately sealed to prevent the entry of dirt or foreign material. Plastic plugs and caps in various sizes are available in packs from motor factors and accessory outlets, and are particularly suitable for this application **(see illustration)**. Fingers cut from disposable rubber gloves should be used to protect components such as fuel pipes, fuel injectors and wiring connectors, and can be secured in place using elastic bands. Suitable gloves of this type are available at no cost from most petrol station forecourts.

5 Whenever any of the high-pressure fuel pipes are disconnected or removed, new pipes must be obtained for refitting.

6 On the completion of any repair on the high-pressure fuel system, MINI recommend the use of a leak-detecting compound. This is a powder which is applied to the fuel pipe unions and connections, and turns white when dry. Any leak in the system will cause the product to darken indicating the source of the leak.

7 The torque wrench settings given in the Specifications must be strictly observed when tightening component mountings and connections. This is particularly important when tightening the high-pressure fuel pipe unions. To enable a torque wrench to be used on the fuel pipe unions, two MINI crow-foot adapters are required. Suitable alternatives are available from motor factors and accessory outlets **(see illustration)**.

3.1 Operate the hand priming pump by squeezing it 10 to 15 times

4.2 Disconnect the air mass sensor wiring plug (arrowed)

4.4 Pull the air cleaner housing upwards from its mountings (arrowed)

3 Fuel system – priming and bleeding

W16 engines

1 Should the fuel supply system be disconnected between the fuel tank and high-pressure pump, it is necessary to prime the fuel system. This is achieved by operating the hand-priming pump 10 to 15 times **(see illustration)**. Remove the plastic cover from the top of the engine to access the priming pump.

2 With the system primed, reconnect the hoses, and then operate the starter until the engine starts. If the engine fails to start repeat the priming steps in paragraph 1.

3 If the engine still fails to start, the system must be primed using MINI diagnostic equipment. Entrust this task to a MINI dealer or suitably equipped repairer.

N47 engines

4 The fuel supply system is designed to be self-bleeding. After disturbing the fuel system, proceed as follows.

5 Switch on the ignition, and leave it for approximately 1 minute. Do not attempt to start the engine. During this time the electric fuel pump is activated and the system vented.

6 Depress the accelerator pedal to the floor then start the engine as normal (this may take longer than usual, especially if the fuel system has been allowed to run dry – operate the starter in ten second bursts with 5 seconds rest in between each operation). Run the engine at a fast idle speed for a minute or so to purge any remaining trapped air from the fuel lines. After this time the engine should idle smoothly at a constant speed.

7 If the engine idles roughly, then there is still some air trapped in the fuel system. Increase the engine speed again for another minute or so then recheck the idle speed. Repeat this procedure as necessary until the engine is idling smoothly.

8 If the engine still fails to start, the system must be primed using MINI diagnostic equipment. Entrust this task to a MINI dealer or suitably equipped repairer.

4 Air cleaner assembly – removal and refitting

Removal

1 Pull the plastic engine cover up and remove it.

W16 engines

2 Disconnect the air mass sensor wiring plug **(see illustration)**.

3 Slacken the clamp securing the air outlet hose to the air cleaner.

4 Pull the air cleaner housing upwards from its mountings, and disconnect the air inlet hose **(see illustration)**.

N47 engines

5 Disconnect the hot film air mass sensor wiring plug **(see illustration)**.

6 Unclip the wiring harness from the air cleaner housing.

7 Disconnect the air outlet hose from the housing.

8 Pull the air cleaner housing upwards from its mountings, disconnecting the intake hose as the housing is removed **(see illustration)**.

5 Accelerator pedal – removal and refitting

Refer to Chapter 4A.

4.5 Air mass sensor wiring plug (arrowed) and outlet hose clamp (arrowed)

6 Fuel lift pump – removal and refitting

The diesel fuel lift pump is located in the same position as the conventional fuel pump on petrol models, and the removal and refitting procedures are virtually identical. Refer to Chapter 4A.

7 Fuel gauge sender unit – removal and refitting

The fuel gauge sender unit is integral with the fuel lift pump. Refer to Section 6.

8 Fuel tank – removal and refitting

Refer to Chapter 4A.

9 High-pressure fuel pump – removal and refitting

⚠ **Warning: Refer to the information contained in Section 2 before proceeding.**

Note: A new fuel pump-to-accumulator rail high-pressure fuel pipe will be required for refitting.

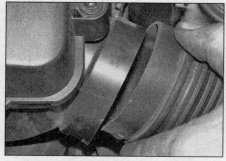

4.8 Disconnect the inlet hose as the air cleaner is removed

9.4a Remove the air filter support bracket (arrowed)…

W16 engine

Removal

1 Disconnect the battery (see Chapter 5A) and remove the timing belt as described in Chapter 2B. After removal of the timing belt, temporarily refit the right-hand engine mounting but do not fully tighten the bolts.
2 Remove the air filter assembly as described in Section 4.
3 Remove the EGR cooler as described in Chapter 4C.
4 Undo the bolts/nuts and remove the 3 support brackets above the fuel accumulator rail and the high-pressure pump **(see illustrations)**.

Tool Tip 1 *A sprocket holding tool can be made from two lengths of steel strip bolted together to form a forked end. Bend the ends of the strip through 90° to form the fork 'prongs'*

9.15 Disconnect the wiring plug, fuel hoses (arrowed) from the metering unit

9.4b …and the brackets around the fuel pump (arrowed)

5 Undo the union nuts and remove the high-pressure fuel pipe between the fuel accumulator rail and the high-pressure pump. Plug the openings to prevent contamination.
6 Disconnect the wiring plug from the high-pressure fuel pump.
7 Depress the release buttons and disconnect the fuel supply and return hoses from the pump. Note that the hoses may have a release button on each side of the fitting. Plug the openings to prevent contamination.
8 Hold the pump sprocket stationary, and loosen the centre nut securing it to the pump shaft **(see Tool Tip 1)**.
9 The fuel pump sprocket is a taper fit on the pump shaft and it will be necessary to make

Tool Tip 2 *Make a sprocket releasing tool from a short strip of steel. Drill two holes in the strip to correspond with the two holes in the sprocket. Drill a third hole just large enough to accept the flats of the sprocket retaining nut.*

9.17 Note the rubber grommets (arrowed) on the high-pressure fuel pipe

up a tool to release it from the taper **(see Tool Tip 2)**. Partially unscrew the sprocket retaining nut, fit the home-made tool, and secure it to the sprocket with two 7.0 mm bolts and nuts. Prevent the sprocket from rotating as before, and screw down the nuts, forcing the sprocket off the shaft taper. Once the taper is released, remove the tool, unscrew the nut fully, and remove the sprocket from the pump shaft.
10 Undo the three bolts, and remove the pump from the mounting bracket.
Caution: The high-pressure fuel pump is manufactured to extremely close tolerances and must not be dismantled in any way. Do not unscrew the fuel pipe male union on the rear of the pump, or attempt to remove the sensor, piston de-activator switch, or the seal on the pump shaft. No parts for the pump are available separately and if the unit is in any way suspect, it must be renewed.

Refitting

11 Refitting is a reversal of removal, noting the following points:
a) *Always renew the pump-to-accumulator rail high-pressure pipe.*
b) *With everything reassembled and reconnected, and observing the precautions listed in Section 2, start the engine and allow it to idle. Check for leaks at the high-pressure fuel pipe unions with the engine idling. If satisfactory, increase the engine speed to 3000 rpm and check again for leaks.*
c) *Take the car for a short road test and check for leaks once again on return. If any leaks are detected, obtain and fit another new high-pressure fuel pipe.* **Do not** *attempt to cure even the slightest leak by further tightening of the pipe unions. During the road test, initialise the engine management ECU as follows – engage third gear and stabilise the engine at 1000 rpm, then accelerate fully up to 3500 rpm.*

N47 engines

Removal

12 Pull up the acoustic cover on the top of the engine.
13 Remove the air intake manifold as described in Section 13.
14 Lock the crankshaft/flywheel at TDC on No. 1 cylinder as described in Chapter 2C.
15 Release the locking catch, and disconnect the wiring plug from the metering unit on the injection pump **(see illustration)**.
16 Slacken the clamps and disconnect the fuel feed and return pipes from the pump. Plug or seal the openings to prevent contamination.
17 Note the fitted locations of the rubber mountings, then undo the union nuts and remove the high-pressure fuel pipe between the injection pump and the common rail **(see illustration)**. MINI state that the pipes may be re-used 3 times, providing they are not damaged. After the 3rd time, and if they show signs of leaking, the pipes must be replaced.

9.18 Unscrew the cap (arrowed) at the left-hand end of the engine

9.19 Screw the special tool into the timing chain cover

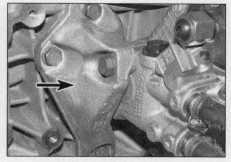

9.20 Remove the support bracket (arrowed) from the pump

9.23 Withdraw the pump from the cylinder block

9.25 Renew the fuel pump O-ring seal

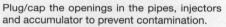
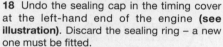
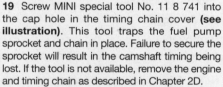

9.28 Finger-tighten the pump bracket bolts in the sequence shown

Plug/cap the openings in the pipes, injectors and accumulator to prevent contamination.

18 Undo the sealing cap in the timing cover at the left-hand end of the engine (see illustration). Discard the sealing ring – a new one must be fitted.

19 Screw MINI special tool No. 11 8 741 into the cap hole in the timing chain cover (see illustration). This tool traps the fuel pump sprocket and chain in place. Failure to secure the sprocket will result in the camshaft timing being lost. If the tool is not available, remove the engine and timing chain as described in Chapter 2D.

20 Undo the retaining bolts and remove the support bracket from the front of the pump (see illustration).

21 Undo the bolts securing the pump to the timing chain cover.

22 Undo the bolt securing the drive chain sprocket to the pump shaft. Note that the bolt remains in place in the sprocket.

23 Remove the pump from position (see illustration).

Refitting

24 Ensure the pump and cylinder block mating surfaces are clean, then align the keyway on the pump shaft with the key in the tapered bore in the pump drive sprocket.

25 Fit a new O-ring seal, then offer the pump into position (see illustration).

26 Engage the shaft with the drive sprocket. Ensure the key and keyway engage correctly.

27 Lightly tighten the bolts securing the pump to the cylinder block/timing chain cover.

28 Refit the pump support bracket, then working in the sequence shown, tighten the

bolts hand-tight, then to their specified torque in the sequence of 2–3–4–1 (see illustration).

29 Tighten the drive sprocket retaining bolt to the specified torque.

30 Unscrew the special tool, then refit the sealing cap with a new seal. Tighten the cap to the specified torque.

31 Remove the crankshaft/flywheel locking tool, with reference to Chapter 2C.

32 Fit the high-pressure fuel pipe between the pump and common rail, tighten the nuts to specified torque, then refit the rubber mounting.

33 The remainder of refitting is a reversal of removal, noting the following points:
a) Tighten all fasteners to their specified torque where given.
b) Reconnect the battery negative lead as described in Chapter 5A.
c) Bleed the fuel system as described in Section 3.

10 Accumulator rail – removal and refitting

⚠ **Warning: Refer to the information contained in Section 2 before proceeding.**

Removal

1 Disconnect the battery (refer to Chapter 5A).
2 Remove the plastic cover from the top of the engine.

W16 engine

Note: *A complete new set of high-pressure fuel pipes will be required for refitting.*

3 Drain the cooling system as described in Chapter 1B.
4 Remove the EGR cooler as described in Chapter 4C.
5 Clean around the pipe, then undo the unions, remove the mounting bolt, and remove the high-pressure pipe from the accumulator rail to the high-pressure pump. Plug the openings to prevent contamination.
6 Unclip the fuel hose from above the injector pressure pipes, then undo the screws, and move the wiring harness duct to one side (see illustration).
7 Clean around the pipes, then slacken the unions and remove the high-pressure pipes between the accumulator and the injectors. Seal/cap the openings to prevent contamination. Note their fitted positions, the pipes are specific to their injectors:

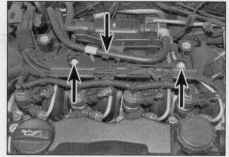

10.6 Unclip the fuel hose/pump, and remove the wiring harness duct retaining screws (arrowed)

10.9 The pressure sensor is located at the end of the accumulator rail (arrowed)

Even final digit of part number =
cylinder 2 or 4
Odd final digit of part number =
cylinder 1 or 3

8 Undo the nut and release the high-pressure pipe holder.

9 Disconnect the pressure sensor wiring plug from the accumulator rail **(see illustration)**.

10 Unscrew the two rail mounting bolts and manoeuvre it from place **(see illustration)**. **Note:** *MINI insist that the fuel pressure sensor on the accumulator rail must not be removed.* **Caution: Do not attempt to remove the four high-pressure fuel pipe male unions from the accumulator rail. These parts are not available separately and if disturbed are likely to result in fuel leakage on reassembly.**

N47 engine

11 Remove the sound insulation material above the injectors.

12 Slacken unions, and remove the high-pressure fuel pipes between the accumulator and the injectors. Take care not to damage/bend the pipes **(see illustration)**. MINI state that the pipes may be re-used 3 times, providing they are not damaged. After the 3rd time, and if they show signs of leaking, the pipes must be replaced. Plug/cap the openings in the pipes, injectors and accumulator to prevent contamination.

13 Remove the intake manifold as described in Section 13.

14 Undo the union nuts, and remove the high pressure fuel pipe between the accumulator and the pump **(see illustration 9.17)**. Note the

10.12 If possible, use a crow-foot adapter to slacken and tighten the high-pressure pipe unions

10.10 Remove the accumulator rail mounting bolts (arrowed)

fitted positions of the rubber mountings. Plug/cap the openings in the pump, accumulator and pipes to prevent contamination.

15 Disconnect the wiring plugs, undo the retaining bolts and remove the accumulator **(see illustration)**.

Refitting

16 Locate the accumulator rail in position, refit and finger-tighten the mounting bolts/nuts.

17 Reconnect the accumulator rail wiring plug(s).

W16 engines

18 Fit the new pump-to-rail high-pressure pipe, and only finger-tighten the unions at first, then tighten the unions to the specified torque setting. Use a second spanner to counterhold the union screwed into the pump body.

19 Fit the new set of rail-to-injector high-pressure pipes, and finger tighten the unions. If it's not possible to fit the new pipes to the injector unions, remove and refit the injectors as described in Section 11, and then try again.

20 Tighten the accumulator rail mounting bolts/nuts to the specified torque.

21 Tighten the rail-to-injector pipe unions to the specified torque setting. Use a second spanner to counterhold the injector unions.

N47 engines

22 Fit the high-pressure pipes to the injectors, accumulator and pump. Only finger-tighten the unions at this stage. Refit the rubber mountings where applicable.

10.15 Accumulator rail clamp bolts (arrowed)

23 Tighten the accumulator mounting bolts to the specified torque.

24 Tighten the high-pressure pipe unions to the specified torque in the following order:
  1) Injectors
  2) Accumulator
  3) Pump

All engines

25 The remainder of refitting is a reversal of removal, noting the following points:
  a) *Ensure all wiring connectors and harnesses are correctly refitting and secured.*
  b) *Reconnect the battery as described in Chapter 5A.*
  c) *Observing the precautions listed in Section 2, start the engine and allow it to idle. Check for leaks at the high-pressure fuel pipe unions with the engine idling. If satisfactory, increase the engine speed to 3000 rpm and check again for leaks. Take the car for a short road test and check for leaks once again on return. If any leaks are detected, obtain and fit additional new high-pressure fuel pipes as required.* **Do not** *attempt to cure even the slightest leak by further tightening of the pipe unions.*

11 Fuel injectors – removal and refitting

Warning: Refer to the information contained in Section 2 before proceeding.

W16 engine

Removal

1 Remove the plastic cover from the top of the engine.
Note: *The following procedure describes the removal and refitting of the injectors as a complete set, although each injector may be removed individually if required. New copper washers, upper seals, and a high-pressure fuel pipe will be required for each disturbed injector when refitting.*

2 Remove the EGR cooler as described in Chapter 4C.

3 Unclip the fuel hose/pump from above the injector pressure pipes, then undo the screws, and move the wiring harness duct to one side **(see illustration 10.6)**.

4 Clean around the pipes, then slacken the unions and remove the high-pressure pipes between the accumulator and the injectors. Seal/cap the openings to prevent contamination. Note their fitted positions, the pipes are specific to their injectors:
  Even final digit of part number =
    cylinder 2 or 4
  Odd final digit of part number =
    cylinder 1 or 3

5 Disconnect the injector wiring plugs.

6 Extract the retaining circlip and disconnect

11.6 Prise out the clip and disconnect the fuel leak-off pipe from each injector

11.7 Use a second spanner to counterhold the high-pressure pipe union nuts

11.8a Injector retaining nuts (arrowed)

the leak-off pipe from each fuel injector **(see illustration)**.

7 Clean the area around the high-pressure fuel pipes between the injectors and the accumulator rail, then unscrew the pipe unions. Use a second spanner to counterhold the union screwed into the injector body **(see illustration)**. The injectors screwed-in unions must not be allowed to move. Remove the bracket above the accumulator rail unions, and then remove the pipes. Plug the openings in the accumulator rail and injectors to prevent dirt ingress.

8 Unscrew the injector retaining nuts, and carefully pull or lever the injector from place. If necessary, use an open-ended spanner and twist the injector to free it from position **(see illustrations)**. Do not lever against or pull on the solenoid housing at the top of the injector. Note down the injectors' position – if the injectors are to be refitted, they must be refitted to their original locations. If improved access is required, undo the bolts and remove the oil separator housing from the front of the cylinder head cover.

9 Remove the copper washer and the upper seal from each injector, or from the cylinder head if they remained in place during injector removal. New copper washers and upper seals will be required for refitting. Cover the injector hole in the cylinder head to prevent dirt ingress.

10 Examine each injector visually for any signs of obvious damage or deterioration. If any defects are apparent, renew the injector(s). Note down the 8-digit injector classification number – this may be needed

11.8b Use a spanner to twist the injector and release it from position

during the refitting procedure if the ECU has been renewed **(see illustration)**.

11 If the injectors are in a satisfactory condition, plug the fuel pipe union (if not already done) and suitably cover the electrical element and the injector nozzle.
Caution: The injectors are manufactured to extremely close tolerances and must not be dismantled in any way. Do not unscrew the fuel pipe union on the side of the injector, or separate any parts of the injector body. Do not attempt to clean carbon deposits from the injector nozzle or carry out any form of ultrasonic or pressure testing.

Refitting

12 Locate a new upper seal on the body of each injector, and place a new copper washer on the injector nozzle **(see illustrations)**.

13 Ensure the injector clamps are in place over their respective circlips on the injector bodies, and then fit the injectors into place in

11.10 Note the injector classification number

the cylinder head. If the original injectors are being refitted, ensure they are fitted into their original positions **(see illustration)**.

14 Fit the injector retaining bolts/nuts, but only finger-tighten them at this stage. When tightening the nuts/bolts, ensure the clamps stay horizontal.

15 Working on one fuel injector at a time, remove the blanking plugs from the fuel pipe unions on the accumulator rail and the relevant injector. Locate a new high-pressure fuel pipe over the unions and screw on the union nuts. Take care not to cross-thread the nuts or strain the fuel pipes as they are fitted. Once the union nut threads have started, finger-tighten the nuts to the ends of the threads.

16 When all the fuel pipes are in place, tighten the injector clamp retaining nuts/bolts to the specified torque (and angle where applicable).

17 Using an open-ended spanner, hold each fuel pipe union in turn and tighten the union nut to

11.12a Locate a new upper seal on the body of the injector...

11.12b ...and place a new copper washer on the injector nozzle

11.13 Fit the injectors into their original locations

11.17 Tighten the high-pressure pipe union nuts using a crow-foot adapter

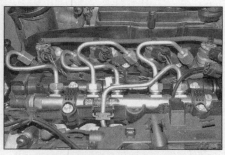

11.21 Remove the high-pressure fuel pipes between the accumulator rail and the injectors

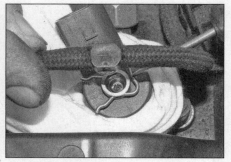

11.22 Push-in the closed end of the clip and pull the return hose upwards

11.24a Undo the injector retaining bolt and remove the clamping jaw

11.24b If necessary, use a spanner to rotate the injector a few degrees…

11.24c …and pull it from place

the specified torque using a torque wrench and crow-foot adapter **(see illustration)**. Tighten all the disturbed union nuts in the same way.

18 If new injectors have been fitted, their classification numbers may need be programmed into the engine management ECU using dedicated diagnostic equipment/ scanner. If this equipment is not available, entrust this task to a MINI dealer or suitably-equipped repairer. Note that it should be possible to drive the vehicle, albeit with reduced performance/increased emissions, to a repairer for the numbers to be programmed.

19 The remainder of refitting is a reversal of removal, noting the following points:
 a) Ensure all wiring connectors and harnesses are correctly refitting and secured.
 b) Reconnect the battery as described in Chapter 5A.
 c) Observing the precautions listed in Section 2, start the engine and allow it to

idle. Check for leaks at the high-pressure fuel pipe unions with the engine idling. If satisfactory, increase the engine speed to 3000 rpm and check again for leaks. Take the car for a short road test and check for leaks once again on return. If any leaks are detected, obtain and fit additional new high-pressure fuel pipes as required. **Do not** attempt to cure even the slightest leak by further tightening of the pipe unions.

N47 engines

Removal

20 Remove the plastic cover from the top of the engine, then remove the sound insulation material above the injectors.

21 Slacken unions, and remove the high-pressure fuel pipes between the accumulator and the injectors. Take care not to damage/bend the pipes **(see illustration)**. MINI state that the pipes may be re-used

3 times, providing they are not damaged. After the 3rd time, and if they show signs of leaking, the pipes must be replaced. Plug/ cap the openings in the pipes, injectors and accumulator to prevent contamination.

22 Push in the closed end of the clips and remove the fuel return hoses from the injectors **(see illustration)**. Plug/cap the openings to prevent contamination.

23 Disconnect the wiring plugs from the injectors.

24 Undo the retaining bolt, remove the clamping jaw and remove the injectors. If the injectors are reluctant to move, rotate them a few degrees each way to release them **(see illustrations)**. Discard the sealing washers – new ones must be fitted. If the injectors are to be refitted, they must be stored upright, and marked/labelled so they can be refitted into their original positions.

Refitting

25 Ensure the injectors and seats in the cylinder head are clean and dry.

26 If any of the injectors are being renewed, make a note of the 7 digit adjustment value engraved on the top of the injector. In order for the injector function at maximum efficiency, this number must be programmed into the engine management ECU using MINI diagnostic equipment. Entrust this task to a MINI dealer or suitably equipped repairer.

27 Fit new sealing washers to the injectors, apply a little high-temperature anti-seize grease (MINI part no. 83 23 0 441 070) to the injector stems and refit them with the clamps **(see illustrations)**. It's absolutely essential

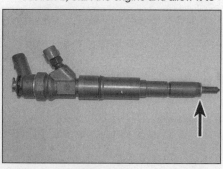

11.27a Renew the injector sealing washers (arrowed)…

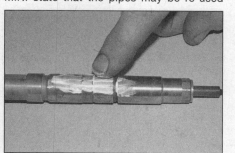

11.27b …and apply a little high-temperature anti-seize grease to the injector stems

12.2 The diagnostic connector is located under the drivers side of the facia (arrowed)

12.5a Release the clips each side (arrowed)…

12.5b …and remove the cover from the ECU

they are fitted to their original positions. Refit the clamping jaw, insert the retaining bolt, and tighten it to the specified torque.

28 Refit the injector pipes, and tighten the unions finger tight, then to the specified torque.

29 Squeeze together the open ends of the retaining clips and refit the fuel return hoses to the injectors. MINI insist that if a return hose O-ring seal is damaged, the complete hoses assembly must be renewed.

30 The remainder of refitting is a reversal of removal, noting the following points:

a) *Ensure all wiring connectors and harnesses are correctly refitting and secured.*

b) *Reconnect the battery as described in Chapter 5A.*

c) *Observing the precautions listed in Section 2, start the engine and allow it to idle. Check for leaks at the high-pressure fuel pipe unions with the engine idling. If satisfactory, increase the engine speed to 3000 rpm and check again for leaks. Take the car for a short road test and check for leaks once again on return. If any leaks are detected, obtain and fit additional new high-pressure fuel pipes as required.* **Do not** *attempt to cure even the slightest leak by further tightening of the pipe unions.*

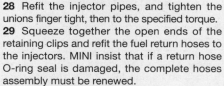

12 Electronic control system components – testing, removal and refitting

Testing

Note: *Before carrying out any of the following procedures, disconnect the battery (refer to Chapter 5A). Reconnect the battery on completion of work.*

1 If a fault is suspected in the electronic control side of the system, first ensure that all the wiring connectors are securely connected and free of corrosion. Ensure that the suspected problem is not of a mechanical nature, or due to poor maintenance; ie, check that the air cleaner filter element is clean, the engine breather hoses are clear and undamaged, and that the cylinder compression pressures are correct, referring to Chapters 1B and 2B or 2C for further information.

12.6 Slide out the locking catches (arrowed) and disconnect the ECU wiring plugs

2 If these checks fail to reveal the cause of the problem, the vehicle should be taken to a MINI dealer or suitably-equipped garage for testing. A diagnostic socket is located behind the trim panel to the right of the steering column, to which a fault code reader or other suitable test equipment can be connected **(see illustration)**. By using the code reader or test equipment, the engine management ECU (and the various other vehicle system ECU's) can be interrogated, and any stored fault codes can be retrieved.

3 This will allow the fault to be quickly and simply traced, alleviating the need to test all the system components individually, which is a time-consuming operation that carries a risk of damaging the ECU.

Electronic control unit (ECU)

Note: *If a new ECU is to be fitted, this work must be entrusted to a MINI dealer or suitably-*

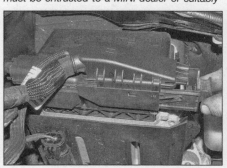

12.9 Slide out the locking catches and disconnect the ECU wiring plugs

12.7 Depress the locking clips (arrowed) and slide the ECU upwards

equipped specialist. It is necessary to initialise the new ECU after installation, which requires the use of dedicated MINI diagnostic equipment.

4 The ECU is located on the left-hand side of the engine compartment.

W16 engine

5 Unclip the plastic ECU cover **(see illustrations)**.

6 Unlock and disconnect the ECU wiring plugs **(see illustration)**.

7 Depress the 2 clips and slide the ECU upwards from place **(see illustration)**.

8 Refitting is a reverse of the removal procedure ensuring the wiring connectors are securely reconnected.

N47 engine

9 Unlock and disconnect the wiring plug(s) from the top of the ECU **(see illustration)**.

10 Release the 2 clamps and slide the ECU upwards from place **(see illustration)**.

12.10 Release the clamps (arrowed) and slide the ECU upwards

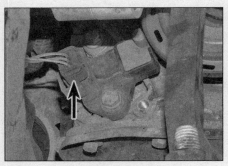

12.15 Disconnect the crankshaft position sensor wiring plug (arrowed) – W16 engines

11 If a new ECU is being fitted, make a note of the units identification number. This will be needed for recoding (see Note above). The fuel injector identification numbers will also be needed (see Section 11).

12 Refitting is a reversal of removal ensuring the wiring plugs are securely reconnected.

Crankshaft speed/ position sensor

W16 engines

13 The crankshaft position sensor is located adjacent to the crankshaft pulley on the right-hand end of the engine.

14 Remove the crankshaft pulley/vibration damper as described in Chapter 2B.

15 Disconnect the sensor wiring plug **(see illustration)**.

16 Undo the bolt and remove the sensor.

17 Refitting is a reversal of removal, tightening the sensor retaining bolt securely.

12.26 The gap between the end of the camshaft sensor and the webs of the signal wheel must be 1.0 mm (used sensor only)

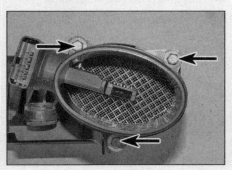

12.37 Air mass meter retaining screws (arrowed) – W16 engines

12.19 Crankshaft position sensor (arrowed) – N47 engines

N47 engines

18 Raise the front of the vehicle and support it securely on axle stands (see *Jacking and vehicle support*). Undo the fasteners and remove the engine undershield.

19 The sensor is located at the rear of the engine, adjacent to the transmission bellhousing **(see illustration)**. Disconnect the sensor wiring plug.

20 Undo the retaining bolt and remove the sensor.

21 Refitting is a reversal of removal, tightening the sensor to the specified torque.

Camshaft position sensor

W16 engine

22 The camshaft position sensor is mounted on the right-hand end of the cylinder head cover, directly behind the camshaft sprocket.

23 Remove the upper timing belt cover, as described in Chapter 2B.

12.28 Camshaft position sensor (arrowed) – N47 engines

12.40 Undo the screws and remove the hot film air mass sensor – N47 engines

24 Unplug the sensor wiring connector.

25 Undo the bolt and pull the sensor from position.

26 Upon refitting, position the sensor so that the air gap between the sensor end and the webs of the signal wheel is 1.0 mm, measured with feeler gauges, for a used sensor. If fitting a new sensor, the small tip of the sensor must be just touching one of the three webs of the signal wheel. Tighten the sensor retaining bolt to the specified torque **(see illustration)**.

27 The remainder of refitting is a reversal of removal.

N47 engine

28 The camshaft position sensor is located at the left-hand end of the cylinder head **(see illustration)**. Pull the plastic cover on the top of the engine upwards from its' mountings, and remove the foam insulation panel.

29 Disconnect the sensor wiring plug.

30 Undo the retaining bolt and remove the sensor.

31 Apply a thin coat of clean engine oil to the sensor sealing ring, install it in the cylinder head, and tighten the bolt to the specified torque.

32 Refit the plastic cover.

Accelerator pedal position sensor

33 On these models, the pedal sensor is integral with the accelerator pedal assembly. Refer to the relevant Section of Chapter 4A for the pedal removal procedure.

Coolant temperature sensor

34 Refer to Chapter 3, Section 7.

Air mass/ Hot film air mass meter

W16 engine

35 Air mass meter is located in the inlet ducting from the air cleaner housing/intercooler. Remove the air cleaner element as described in Chapter 1B.

36 Disconnect the wiring plug connector(s) from the air mass meter.

37 Undo the 3 retaining screws, and remove the sensor from the air cleaner upper cover **(see illustration)**.

38 Refitting is reverse of the removal procedure.

N47 engine

39 Release the wiring harness from the air cleaner housing, and disconnect the sensor wiring plug **(see illustration 4.5)**.

40 Undo the 2 retaining screws, and remove the hot film air mass meter from the air duct **(see illustration)**.

41 Refitting is a reversal of removal. Tighten the retaining screws securely.

Exhaust gas pressure sensor

W16 engine

42 The exhaust gas pressure sensor is located on the engine oil level dipstick guide

tube **(see illustration)**. Disconnect the sensor wiring plug.

43 Undo the retaining bolt and manoeuvre the sensor from place.

44 Note their fitted positions, and disconnect the hoses from the sensor.

45 Refitting is a reversal of removal. Tighten the retaining bolt to the specified torque.

N47 engine

46 Pull the plastic cover on top of the engine upwards from its' mountings.

47 The sensor is located at the rear of the engine **(see illustration)**. Disconnect the sensor wiring plug.

48 Release the clip and pull the sensor forwards from its mounting bracket.

49 Disconnect the hose from the sensor.

50 Refitting is a reversal of removal, noting the following points:

a) Check the pressure hose – replace if hardened.

b) Install the hose without any kinks.

c) If the original hose is being refitted, secure it with a 15 – 19 mm screw-type clamp (Jubilee).

Charge air pressure sensor

W16 engine

51 The charge air pressure sensor is located on the charge air pipe at the right-hand side of the engine **(see illustration)**. Disconnect the sensor wiring plug.

52 Undo the retaining screw and remove the sensor.

53 Refitting is a reversal of removal. Tighten the screw to the specified torque.

N47 engine

54 Pull the plastic cover on the top of the engine upwards from its' mountings.

55 The sensor is located on the inlet manifold **(see illustration)**. Disconnect the sensor wiring plug.

56 Undo the retaining screw and remove the sensor.

57 Apply a thin coat of clean engine oil to the sensor sealing ring, install it in the cylinder head, and tighten the bolt to the specified torque.

58 Refit the plastic cover.

12.42 Exhaust gas pressure sensor (arrowed) – W16 engines

12.51 Charge air pressure sensor (arrowed) – W16 engines

Charge air temperature sensor

W16 engine

59 The charge air temperature sensor is located on the charge air pipe at the right-hand side of the engine **(see illustration)**. Disconnect the sensor wiring plug.

60 Undo the retaining screw and remove the sensor.

61 Refitting is a reversal of removal. Tighten the screw to the specified torque.

N47 engine

62 Remove the electric cooling fan and shroud as described in Chapter 3.

63 Release the clips and remove the air hose from the intercooler to the throttle body.

64 The sensor is located on the underside of the throttle body **(see illustration)**. Disconnect the sensor wiring plug.

12.47 On N47 engines, the exhaust gas pressure sensor (arrowed) is adjacent to the oil filler cap

12.55 Charge air pressure sensor – N47 engines

65 Rotate the sensor 45° anti-clockwise and remove it from the throttle body. Check the condition of the sealing ring, and renew if necessary.

66 Refitting is a reversal of removal.

Exhaust gas temperature sensor(s)

W16 engine

67 The sensor is located at the front of the engine **(see illustration)**. Disconnect the sensor wiring plug.

68 Using a split-type socket, unscrew the sensor from the filter.

69 Refitting is a reversal of removal. Tighten the sensor to the specified torque.

N47 engine

70 Pull the plastic cover on the top of the engine upwards from its' mountings.

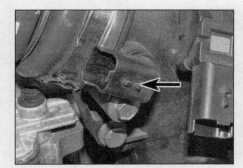

12.59 Charge air temperature sensor (arrowed) – W16 engines

12.64 The charge air temperature sensor is located on the underside of the throttle body – N47 engines

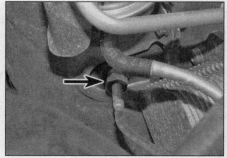

12.67 Temperature sensor on the left-hand side of the particulate filter (arrowed) – W16 engines

12.71 Exhaust gas temperature sensors (arrowed)

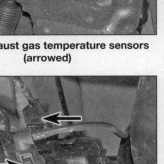

12.78 Disconnect the hose and wiring plug from the tank (arrowed)

71 Two sensors are fitted to this engine. One adjacent to the oxygen sensor before the catalytic converter, and one located in the exhaust pipe between the catalytic converter and the particulate filter **(see illustration)**.

12.82 Tank upper section retaining clips (arrowed)

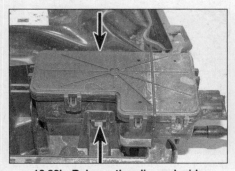

12.83b Release the clip each side (arrowed) and lift out the metering pump

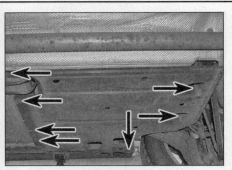

12.77 Right-hand underbody panelling fasteners (arrowed)

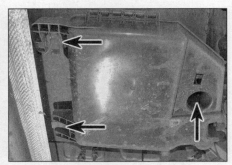

12.79 Additive tank retaining bolt and mounting pins (arrowed)

Trace the wiring back to the wiring plug, and disconnect it.
72 Using a split-type socket, unscrew the sensor **(see illustration 12.95)**.
73 Refitting is a reversal of removal. Check

12.83a Depress the release buttons (arrowed) and disconnect the hose

12.86 Lift out the additive bag

the top of the sensor is not damaged, and tighten it to the specified torque.

Preheating system control unit
74 Refer to Chapter 5C.

Vehicle speed sensor
75 The engine management ECU receives the vehicle speed signal from the wheel speed sensors via the ABS ECU. Refer to Chapter 9 for wheel speed sensor removal.

Fuel additive system

⚠ **Warning: Avoid skin contact with the additive, wear protective clothing, gloves and goggles.**

Additive tank
76 Raise the rear of the vehicle and support it securely on axle stands (see *Jacking and vehicle support*).
77 Undo the plastic nuts, screw and expansion rivets, then remove the right-hand underbody panelling (where fitted) **(see illustration)**.
78 Disconnect the wiring plug and hose connection from the tank **(see illustration)**.
79 Undo the retaining bolt, swing the front of the tank outwards, then slide it rearwards from the mounting pins **(see illustration)**.
80 Refitting is a reversal of removal.

Metering pump
81 Remove the additive tank as described previously in this Section.
82 Release the catches and open the upper section of the tank **(see illustration)**.
83 Unlock the quick-release coupling, release the retaining clip and remove the metering pump **(see illustrations)**.
84 Refitting is a reversal of removal.

Additive bag
85 Remove the metering pump as previously described in this Section.
86 Lift the additive bag from the tank **(see illustration)**.
87 Refitting is a reversal of removal.

Fuel temperature sensor

⚠ **Warning: Refer to the information contained in Section 2 before proceeding.**

W16 engine
88 The sensor is clipped in to the plastic fuel manifold at the right-hand rear end of the cylinder head. To remove the sensor, disconnect the wiring plug, and then unclip the sensor from the manifold. Be prepared for fuel spillage **(see illustration)**.
89 Refitting is a reversal of removal.
90 Observing the precautions listed in Section 2, start the engine and allow it to idle. Check for leaks at the fuel temperature sensor with the engine idling. If satisfactory, increase the engine speed to 4000 rpm and check again for leaks. Take the car for a short road test and check for leaks once again on return. If any leaks are detected, obtain and fit a new sensor.

12.88 Fuel temperature sensor (arrowed) – W16 engines

12.91 The N47 fuel temperature sensor is adjacent to the high-pressure fuel pump (arrowed)

12.95 Use a split-type socket to unscrew the oxygen sensor

N47 engine

91 The fuel temperature sensor is located in the fuel return hose beneath the high pressure pump at the front of the engine (see illustration).

92 Release the clamps, disconnect the fuel hoses, and remove the sensor. Disconnect the wiring plug as the sensor is removed.

Oxygen sensor

N47 engine only

93 Pull the plastic cover on the top of the engine upwards from its' mountings.

94 The sensor is located catalytic converter behind the upstream exhaust gas temperature sensor. Trace the wiring back to the wiring plug, and disconnect it.

95 Using a split-type socket, unscrew the sensor (see illustration).

96 Refitting is a reversal of removal. New sensors have their threads pre-coated with anti-seize compound (Never-Seez – available from MINI dealers). If a sensor is being refitted, apply a little anti-seize compound to the threads. Tighten it to the specified torque.

13 Inlet manifold –
removal and refitting

W16 engine

1 The inlet manifold is an integral part of the cylinder head cover, see Chapter 2B or 2D for the removal of the cylinder head cover.

N47 engine

2 Pull the plastic cover on the top of the engine upwards from its' mountings (see illustration).

3 Disconnect the wiring plugs from the pre-heating control unit (see illustration).

4 Undo the bolts securing the manifold to the throttle body (see illustration).

5 Undo the screws securing the exhaust gas recirculation cooler to the manifold (see illustration).

6 Undo the 5 retaining bolts and manoeuvre the inlet manifold upwards from place.

7 Pull the EGR pipe from the manifold. Renew the O-ring seal.

8 Refitting is a reversal of removal, remembering to renew the manifold seals. Tighten the retaining bolts to the specified torque, working from the centre outwards.

14 Exhaust manifold –
removal and refitting

Removal

1 Remove the turbocharger as described in Section 16.

2 On N47 engines, undo the bolts and detach the EGR pipe from the manifold (see illustration). Renew the gasket.

3 Undo the retaining nuts, recover the spacers (where fitted), and remove the manifold. Recover the gasket.

Refitting

4 Refitting is a reverse of the removal procedure, bearing in mind the following points:
 a) Ensure that the manifold and cylinder

13.2 Pull the engine cover upwards from its' mountings

13.3 Disconnect the wiring plugs from the pre-heating control unit

13.4 Manifold-to-throttle body bolts (arrowed – one hidden)

13.5 EGR cooler-to-manifold bolts (arrowed)

14.2 EGR pipe-to-exhaust manifold bolts (arrowed)

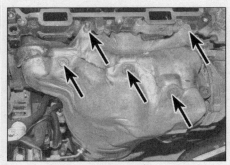

16.4 Undo the bolts and remove the turbocharger heat shield (arrowed)

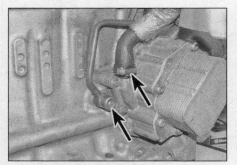

16.6 Turbocharger oil supply and return pipes (arrowed)

16.5 Disconnect the vacuum pipe from the wastegate control assembly (arrowed)

16.8 Undo the nuts (one hidden) and remove the support bracket and turbocharger

head mating faces are clean, with all traces of old gasket removed.
b) Use new gaskets when refitting the manifold to the cylinder head.
c) Tighten the exhaust manifold retaining nuts to the specified torque.

15 Turbocharger –
description and precautions

Description

1 A turbocharger is fitted to increase engine efficiency by raising the pressure in the inlet manifold above atmospheric pressure. Instead of the air simply being sucked into the cylinders, it is forced in.

2 Energy for the operation of the turbocharger comes from the exhaust gas. The gas flows through a specially shaped housing (the turbine housing) and, in so doing, spins the turbine wheel. The turbine wheel is attached to a shaft, at the end of which is another vaned wheel known as the compressor wheel. The compressor wheel spins in its own housing, and compresses the inlet air on the way to the inlet manifold.

3 Boost pressure (the pressure in the inlet manifold) is controlled by a variable inlet nozzle to improve boost pressure at low engine speeds.

4 The turbo shaft is pressure-lubricated by an oil feed pipe from the main oil gallery. The shaft 'floats' on a cushion of oil. A drain pipe returns the oil to the sump.

Precautions

5 The turbocharger operates at extremely high speeds and temperatures. Certain precautions must be observed, to avoid premature failure of the turbo, or injury to the operator.

• Do not operate the turbo with any of its parts exposed, or with any of its hoses removed. Foreign objects falling onto the rotating vanes could cause excessive damage, and (if ejected) personal injury.

• Do not race the engine immediately after start-up, especially if it is cold. Give the oil a few seconds to circulate.

• Always allow the engine to return to idle speed before switching it off – do not blip the throttle and switch off, as this will leave the turbo spinning without lubrication.

• Allow the engine to idle for several minutes before switching off after a high-speed run.

16.12 Undo the fasteners (arrowed) and pull the scuttle panel each side upwards – bonnet removed for clarity

• Observe the recommended intervals for oil and filter changing, and use a reputable oil of the specified quality. Neglect of oil changing, or use of inferior oil, can cause carbon formation on the turbo shaft, leading to subsequent failure.

16 Turbocharger –
removal, inspection and refitting

Removal

1 Apply the handbrake, then jack up the front of the vehicle and support it on axle stands (see *Jacking and vehicle support*). Undo the screws and remove the engine undershield. Disconnect the battery as described in Chapter 5A, Section 4.

W16 engine

2 Remove the catalytic converter/particulate filter as described in Section 18.

3 Slacken the clamps, undo the bolts, and remove the air ducts to and from the turbocharger and inlet manifold. Note their fitted positions and disconnect the various wiring plugs as the assembly is withdrawn.

4 Undo the mounting bolts (see illustration), and remove the heat shield from above turbocharger.

5 Disconnect the vacuum hose from the turbocharger variable nozzle control assembly (see illustration).

6 Undo the oil supply pipe banjo bolts and recover the sealing washers (see illustration). Note: *If the turbocharger is being renewed, also renew the supply pipe banjo bolts – the sealing washers must be replaced in all cases.*

7 Slacken the retaining clips and disconnect the oil return pipe from the turbocharger and cylinder block.

8 Unscrew the four nuts, and the nut securing the support bracket, then remove the turbocharger from the exhaust manifold (see illustration).

N47 engine

Note: *Although it is possible to remove the turbocharger with the engine in situ, access is extremely limited. If greater access is required, remove the engine and transmission unit as described in Chapter 2D.*

9 Pull the plastic acoustic cover from the top of the engine.

10 Remove the air cleaner assembly as described in Section 4.

11 Remove the wiper blades as described in Chapter 12.

12 Pull up the rubber sealing strip, then undo the fasteners and remove the left-, and right-hand scuttle panels (see illustration).

13 Undo the nuts and lift the bulkhead panel from place (see illustrations). Unclip any wiring as the panel is withdrawn.

14 Release the clamps and remove the charge pressure hose between the intercooler

16.13a Lift out the dividing panel (arrowed)…

16.13b …then undo the nuts and lift out the bulkhead panel

16.16a Remove the upper…

16.16b …and lower heatshields

16.17 Remove the turbocharger support bracket (arrowed)

16.19 Slacken the oil return pipe bracket bolt (arrowed) 180°

and the turbocharger. Unclip any coolant and fuel hoses as the hose is withdrawn.

15 Trace the wiring back from the temperature/oxygen sensors and disconnect their wiring plugs, then unscrew the oxygen sensor **(see illustration 12.95)**.

16 Undo the bolts and remove the heatshields from the turbocharger and catalytic converter/particulate filter **(see illustrations)**.

17 Undo the bolts and remove the support bracket to the left of the turbocharger **(see illustration)**.

18 Disconnect the wiring plug from the turbocharger boost control motor.

19 Slacken the bolt securing the turbo oil return pipe support bracket by a maximum of 180° **(see illustration)**. Do not unscrew the bolts securing the pipe flange to the turbo.

20 Undo the banjo bolt and detach the oil feed pipe from the turbocharger **(see illustration)**. Discard the pipe seals, new ones must be fitted. Plug/seal the openings to prevent contamination.

21 Undo the nuts securing the turbo oil feed pipe above the exhaust manifold and pull the brackets from the studs **(see illustration)**. The pipe should now be free to move a little.

22 Release the exhaust gas pressure sensor from its retaining bracket as described in Section 12. There's no need to disconnect the hose from the sensor – position the sensor to one side.

23 Undo the 3 retaining screws and move the carrier plate to one side **(see illustration)**.

24 Undo the retaining bolt and release the clamp securing the turbocharger to the catalytic converter/particulate filter **(see**

illustration). MINI insist that the band is not re-used – fit a new one.

25 Undo the 3 bolts, and manoeuvre the turbocharger from place **(see illustrations)**.

16.20 Undo the oil feed pipe banjo bolt (arrowed)

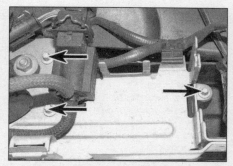

16.23 Undo the bolts (arrowed) and move the carrier plate above the turbocharger to one side

Use a socket, extension and universal joint to access the hidden, inner bolt. Renew the gaskets. Take care not to damage the oil return and feed pipes.

16.21 Remove the nuts (arrowed) and pull the pipe brackets from the studs

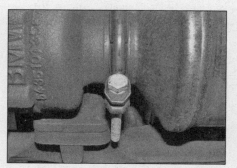

16.24 Remove the bolt securing the turbo-to-cat/filter clamp

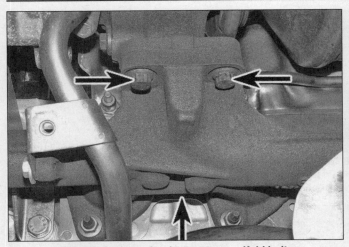

16.25a Undo the turbocharger-to-manifold bolts…

16.25b …then rotate the turbocharger upwards and manoeuvre it from place. Take care not to damage the oil feed and return pipes

16.25c Note how the oil return pipe engages with the flange (arrowed)

16.25d Renew the clamp (arrowed)…

16.25e …turbo-to-manifold gasket…

Inspection

26 With the turbocharger removed, inspect the housing for cracks or other visible damage.

27 Spin the turbine or the compressor wheel, to verify that the shaft is intact and to feel for excessive shake or roughness. Some play is normal, since in use, the shaft is 'floating' on a film of oil. Check that the wheel vanes are undamaged.

28 If oil contamination of the exhaust or induction passages is apparent, it is likely that turbo shaft oil seals have failed.

29 No DIY repair of the turbo is possible and none of the internal or external parts are

16.25f …and turbo-to-cat/filter gasket

available separately. If the turbocharger is suspect in any way a complete new unit must be obtained. Do not attempt to dismantle the turbocharger control assemblies.

Refitting

30 Refitting is a reverse of the removal procedure, bearing in mind the following points:

a) Renew the turbocharger retaining nuts and gaskets (where applicable).

b) If a new turbocharger is being fitted, change the engine oil and filter. Also renew the filter in the oil feed pipe (W16 engines).

c) Prime the turbocharger by injecting clean engine oil through the oil feed pipe union before reconnecting the union.

d) Coat the turbocharger-to-manifold bolts with high-temperature anti-seize grease.

e) Renew the oil return pipe O-ring seals (where fitted).

f) If a new turbocharger is being fitted, remove all traces of oil or grease from all air pipes/ducts. Any such residue could cause premature failure of the turbocharger.

g) On N47 engines, to prevent leaks, refit the turbocharger-to-manifold bolts evenly until they are flush with the manifold, then slacken them 90°. Tighten the turbo-to-

catalytic converter/particulate filter clamp, then the turbo-to-manifold bolts, followed by the support bracket bolts.

17 Intercooler – removal and refitting

Removal

1 Remove the front bumper as described in Chapter 11.

2 Release the clip and disconnect the right-hand charge air pipe from the intercooler (see illustration).

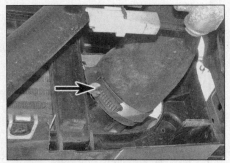

17.2 Intercooler right-hand hose clamp (arrowed)…

3 Slacken the clamp and disconnect the left-hand charge air pipe from the intercooler **(see illustration)**.

4 Undo the 2 retaining bolts and remove the intercooler **(see illustration)**.

Refitting

5 Refitting is a reversal of removal. The charge air pipes must be free from oil, grease and debris. They must be refitted without using oil or grease as a lubricant. Any such residue could cause premature failure of the turbocharger.

18 Exhaust system – general information and component renewal

General information

1 According to model, the exhaust system consists of either two or three sections. Three-section systems consist of a catalytic converter, an intermediate pipe, and a tailpipe. On two-section systems, the intermediate pipe and rear silencer are combined to form a single section.

2 The exhaust joints are of either the spring-loaded ball type (to allow for movement in the exhaust system) or clamp-ring type.

3 The system is suspended throughout its entire length by rubber mountings.

4 To remove the system or part of the system, first jack up the front or rear of the car and support it on axle stands (see *Jacking and vehicle support*). Alternatively, position the car over an inspection pit or on car ramps. Undo the screws and remove the engine undershield.

5 If the intermediate pipe/rear silencer section of the exhaust needs renewing, it is available as a two-part system, check with your local exhaust dealer. The original exhaust will need to be cut, just in front of the rear axle. Before making any cuts, it is advisable to get the new part of the exhaust system; this can then be measured to fit the original.

6 Each section is refitted by reversing the removal sequence, noting the following points:

a) *Ensure that all traces of corrosion have been removed from the flanges and renew all necessary gaskets.*

b) *Inspect the rubber mountings for signs of damage or deterioration, and renew as necessary.*

c) *Where joints are secured together by a clamping ring, apply a smear of exhaust system jointing paste to the flange joint to ensure a gas-tight seal. Insert the bolt through the clamping ring and fit the washer.*

d) *Prior to tightening the exhaust system fasteners, ensure that all rubber mountings are correctly located, and that there is adequate clearance between the exhaust system and vehicle underbody.*

17.3 ...and left-hand hose clamp (arrowed)

e) *On models fitted with a particulate filter, have the additive reservoir filled by your local dealer. If renewing the particulate filter, seal the old filter in the bag of the new filter and dispose of it correctly.*

Catalytic converter removal

W16 engine only

7 Move the front panel into the 'assembly' position as follows:

a) *Remove the front bumper as described in Chapter 11.*

b) *Unplug the air conditioning compressor wiring plug, and release the harness from any clips.*

c) *Undo the 2 bolts each side securing the front panel to the subframe **(see illustration)**.*

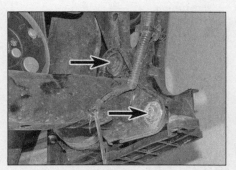

18.7a Front panel-to-subframe bolts (arrowed)

18.7c Open the junction box and disconnect the bonnet release cable (arrowed)

17.4 Intercooler mounting bolts (arrowed)

d) *Remove the bolt each side securing the front panel to the wing **(see illustration)**.*

e) *Release the coolant pipe from the retaining clips on the front panel.*

f) *Undo the retaining bolt and move the coolant expansion tank to one side.*

g) *Detach the air intake ducting gaiter from the front panel.*

h) *Prise open the junction box on the left-hand support, and disconnect the bonnet release cable **(see illustration)**.*

i) *Undo the 3 bolts each side securing the front panel/headlight to the suspension turret/front wing **(see illustration)**.*

j) *Slacken the clamp and disconnect the right-hand charge pressure hose from the intercooler, then disconnect the air hose from the turbocharger outlet ducting **(see illustrations)**.*

18.7b Undo the bolt (arrowed) securing the front panel to the wing each side

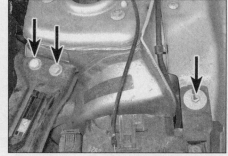

18.7d Remove the headlight bolt, and the panel support-to-suspension turret bolts (arrowed)

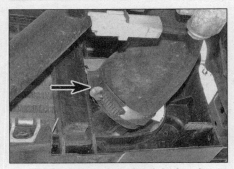

18.7e Disconnect the right-hand intercooler hose (arrowed)...

18.7f ...and the turbocharger outlet hose (arrowed)

18.7g Screw the tubes/rods through the front panel into the threaded holes in the chassis members

18.7h Undo the 3 nuts (arrowed) each side...

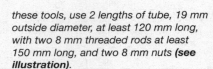

18.7i ...and slide the panel forwards on the tubes

k) Disconnect the right-hand headlight wiring plug.
l) Screw special tool No. 00 2 271 into the left-hand, and right-hand front panel/ chassis member sleeve. In the absence of

these tools, use 2 lengths of tube, 19 mm outside diameter, at least 120 mm long, with two 8 mm threaded rods at least 150 mm long, and two 8 mm nuts **(see illustration)**.

m) Undo the 3 nuts each side, and slide the front panel assembly approximately 10 cm forwards (see illustrations). Take care to ensure no strain is placed on any wiring/ hoses.

8 Disconnect the exhaust gas pressure sensor wiring plug, then using a split-type socket, unscrew the sensor from the filter **(see illustration 12.67)**.

9 Remove the pipe clamp, and unscrew the pressure sensor pipes from the catalytic converter and particulate filter **(see illustration)**.

10 Undo the bolts and remove the heat shield from the catalytic converter/particulate filter.

11 Slacken the retaining clamps joining the catalytic converter to the turbocharger, and exhaust pipe. Take care not to damage the flexible section of the front exhaust pipe **(see illustration)**.

12 Undo the 2 nuts securing the catalytic converter to the cylinder block and manoeuvre it (complete with particulate filter) down and out of the engine compartment **(see illustration)**.

13 If required, note its fitted position, then slacken the clamp and detach the particulate filter from the base of the catalytic converter (see illustration).

Particulate filter removal

W16 engine

14 Move the front panel into the 'assembly' position as described earlier in this Section.

15 Release the clamp securing the particulate filter to the exhaust pipe. Take care not to damage the flexible section of the exhaust pipe.

16 Undo the heat shield retaining bolts and move it forwards a little **(see illustration 16.4)**. Note the retaining bolt behind the alternator and above the oil cooler.

17 Unscrew the pressure sensor pipe from the particulate filter.

18 Support the particulate filter, then release the clamp and detach it from the catalytic converter **(see illustration 18.13)**.

19 Upon refitting, use the gauge supplied in the seal set to align the filter with the sump.

N47 engine

Note: *Access to the particulate filter is*

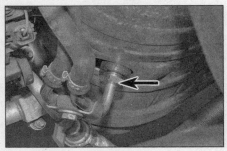

18.9 Unscrew the pressure take-off pipes from the particulate filter/catalytic converter (arrowed)

18.11 Exhaust pipe-to-catalytic converter/ filter clamp (arrowed)

18.12 Catalytic converter mounting nuts (arrowed)

18.13 Undo the clamp (arrowed) and slide the particulate filter from the catalytic converter

extremely limited. We suggest that it may be easier to remove the engine/transmission unit as described in Chapter 2D to facilitate filter removal.

20 Remove the right-hand driveshaft and support bearing block as described in Chapter 8.
21 Remove the engine rear/lower engine mounting/link rod as described in Chapter 2C.
22 Remove the oxygen and exhaust gas temperature sensors as described in Section 12.
23 Undo the retaining nuts, release the plastic expansion rivets, then remove the panels on the left-hand, and right-hand side of the engine compartment, followed by the rear engine bulkhead panel **(see illustrations 16.13a and 16.13b)**.
24 Undo the screws and remove the heat shields from the turbocharger and particulate filter **(see illustrations 16.16a and 16.16b)**.
25 Release the fasteners securing the particulate filter support brackets **(see illustrations)**. Where applicable, remove the support bracket(s) to facilitate filter removal.
26 Pull the pressure sensor hose from the filter **(see illustration)**.
27 Unlock and disconnect the fuel feed and return hoses. Be prepared for fluid spillage. Plug the openings to prevent contamination.
28 Undo the retaining bolt, open the holder, and release the fuel pipes from the sump **(see illustration)**. Move the pipes to one side.
29 Slacken the clamp securing the particulate filter to the turbocharger, and manoeuvre the filter downwards, and out from under the vehicle.

18.25a Remove the support bracket on the right-hand side of the filter...

18.25b ...and the bracket beneath

18.26 Exhaust gas temperature sensors and pressure sensor hose (arrowed)

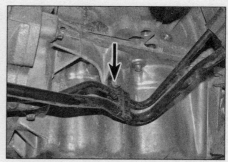

18.28 Undo the bolt (arrowed) securing the fuel pipes to the rear of the sump

30 Refitting is a reversal of removal. If a new particulate filter has been fitted, it will be necessary to have the adaption values within the engine management ECU reset using MINI diagnostic equipment. Entrust this task to a MINI dealer or suitably equipped repairer.

Chapter 4 Part C:
Emission control systems

Contents

Degrees of difficulty

Easy, suitable for novice with little experience	Fairly easy, suitable for beginner with some experience	Fairly difficult, suitable for competent DIY mechanic	Difficult, suitable for experienced DIY mechanic	Very difficult, suitable for expert DIY or professional

---

1 General information

All petrol engines use unleaded petrol and also have various other features built into the fuel system to help minimise harmful emissions. In addition, all engines are equipped with the crankcase emission control system described below. All engines are also equipped with a catalytic converter and an evaporative emission control system.

All diesel engines are also designed to meet the strict emission requirements and are equipped with a crankcase emission control system and a catalytic converter. To further reduce exhaust emissions, all diesel engines are also fitted with an exhaust gas recirculation (EGR) system. Additionally, diesel models may be equipped with a particulate emission filter, which uses porous silicon carbide substrate to trap particulates of carbon as the exhaust gases pass through.

The emission control systems function as follows.

Petrol engines

Crankcase emission control

To reduce the emission of unburned hydrocarbons from the crankcase into the atmosphere, the engine is sealed and the blow-by gases and oil vapour are drawn from inside the crankcase, through a wire mesh oil separator, into the inlet tract to be burned by the engine during normal combustion.

Under all conditions the gases are forced out of the crankcase by the (relatively) higher crankcase pressure; if the engine is worn, the raised crankcase pressure (due to increased blow-by) will cause some of the flow to return under all manifold conditions.

Exhaust emission control

To minimise the amount of pollutants which escape into the atmosphere, a catalytic converter is fitted in the exhaust system. On all models where a catalytic converter is fitted, the system is of the closed-loop type, in which oxygen (lambda) sensors in the exhaust system provides the fuel injection/ignition system ECU with constant feedback, enabling the ECU to adjust the mixture to provide the best possible conditions for the converter to operate.

The oxygen sensors have a heating element built-in that is controlled by the ECU through the oxygen sensor relay to quickly bring the sensor's tip to an efficient operating temperature. The sensor's tip is sensitive to oxygen and sends the ECU a varying voltage depending on the amount of oxygen in the exhaust gases; if the inlet air/fuel mixture is too rich, the exhaust gases are low in oxygen so the sensor sends a low-voltage signal, the voltage rising as the mixture weakens and the amount of oxygen rises in the exhaust gases. Peak conversion efficiency of all major pollutants occurs if the inlet air/fuel mixture is maintained at the chemically correct ratio for the complete combustion of petrol of 14.7 parts (by weight) of air to 1 part of fuel (the 'stoichiometric' ratio). The sensor output voltage alters in a large step at this point, the ECU using the signal change as a reference point and correcting the inlet air/fuel mixture accordingly by altering the fuel injector pulse width.

Evaporative emission control

To minimise the escape into the atmosphere of unburned hydrocarbons, an evaporative emission control system is fitted to models equipped with a catalytic converter. The fuel tank filler cap is sealed and a charcoal canister is mounted behind the wheel arch liner under the right-hand side front wing to collect the petrol vapours generated in the tank when the car is parked. It stores them until they can be cleared from the canister (under the control of the fuel injection/ignition system ECU) via the purge valve into the inlet tract to be burned by the engine during normal combustion.

To ensure that the engine runs correctly when it is cold and/or idling and to protect the catalytic converter from the effects of an over-rich mixture, the purge control valve is not opened by the ECU until the engine has warmed-up, and the engine is under load; the valve solenoid is then modulated on and off to allow the stored vapour to pass into the inlet tract.

Diesel models

Crankcase emission control

Refer to the description for petrol engines.

Exhaust emission control

To minimise the level of exhaust pollutants released into the atmosphere, a catalytic converter is fitted in the exhaust system of all models.

The catalytic converter consists of a canister containing a fine mesh impregnated with a catalyst material, over which the hot exhaust gases pass. The catalyst speeds up the oxidation of harmful carbon monoxide, un-burnt hydrocarbons and soot, effectively reducing the quantity of harmful products released into the atmosphere via the exhaust gases.

Exhaust gas recirculation system

This system is designed to recirculate small quantities of exhaust gas into the inlet tract, and therefore into the combustion process. This process reduces the level of oxides of nitrogen present in the final exhaust gas, which is released into the atmosphere.

The volume of exhaust gas recirculated is controlled by the system electronic control unit.

A vacuum-operated valve is fitted to the exhaust manifold, to regulate the quantity of exhaust gas recirculated. The valve is operated by the vacuum supplied by the solenoid valve, or electrically powered solenoid.

Particulate filter system

The particulate filter is combined with the catalytic converter in the exhaust system, and its purpose it to trap particulates of carbon (soot) as the exhaust gases pass through, in order to comply with latest emission regulations.

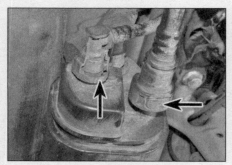

2.4 Depress the quick-release buttons or squeeze together the sides of the collar (arrowed)

2.5 Carbon canister retaining screw (arrowed)

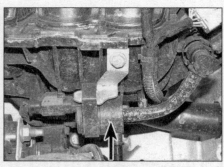

2.7 The purge valve is located at the rear of the engine (arrowed)

The filter can be automatically regenerated (cleaned) by the system's ECU on-board the vehicle. The engine's high-pressure injection system is utilised to inject fuel into the exhaust gases during the post-injection period; this causes the filter temperature to increase sufficiently to oxidise the particulates, leaving an ash residue. The regeneration period is automatically controlled by the on-board ECU. Subsequently, at the correct service interval the filter must be removed from the exhaust system, and renewed.

To assist the combustion of the trapped carbon (soot) during the regeneration process, a fuel additive is automatically mixed with the diesel fuel in the fuel tank. The additive is stored in a container attached to the side of the fuel tank, and the ECU regulates the amount of additive to send to the fuel tank by means of an additive injector located on the top of the fuel tank.

2 Emission control systems – testing and component renewal

Petrol models

Crankcase emission control

1 The components of this system require no attention other than to check that the hose(s) are clear and undamaged at regular intervals.

Evaporative emission control

2 If the system is thought to be faulty,

2.23 EGR valve mounting bolts (arrowed – one hidden)

disconnect the hoses from the charcoal canister and purge control valve and check that they are clear by blowing through them. If the purge control valve or charcoal canister is thought to be faulty, they must be renewed.

Charcoal canister renewal

3 The charcoal canister is located under the wheel arch on the right-hand side. To gain access, slacken the right-hand rear roadwheel bolts, jack up the rear of the car and support it on axle stands (see *Jacking and vehicle support*). Remove the roadwheel, push in the centre pins then prise out the plastic expanding rivets, and remove the wheel arch liner. Where applicable, release the fasteners and remove the under body panelling.

4 Identify the location of the hoses then depress the quick-release button and disconnect hoses from the canister **(see illustration)**.

5 Undo the retaining screw, and remove the canister **(see illustration)**.

6 Refitting is a reverse of the removal procedure ensuring that the hoses are correctly reconnected.

Purge valve renewal

Non-turbo models

7 The purge valve is located on the underside of the inlet manifold **(see illustration)**. Raise the front of the vehicle and support it securely on axle stands (see *Jacking and vehicle support*). Remove the engine undershield.

Turbo models

8 Remove the inlet manifold as described in Chapter 4A.

All models

9 Disconnect the wiring plug from the valve.

10 Unbolt the valve and disconnect the hoses.

11 Refitting is a reversal of removal.

Exhaust emission control

12 The performance of the catalytic converter can be checked only by measuring the exhaust gases using a good-quality, carefully-calibrated exhaust gas analyser.

13 If the CO level at the tailpipe is too high, the vehicle should be taken to a MINI dealer or specialist so that the complete fuel injection and ignition systems, including the

oxygen sensor, can be thoroughly checked using the special diagnostic equipment. Once these have been checked and are known to be free from faults, the fault must be in the catalytic converter, which must be renewed as described in Chapter 4A.

Catalytic converter renewal

14 Refer to Chapter 4A.

Oxygen sensor renewal

15 Refer to Chapter 4A.

Diesel models

Crankcase emission control

16 The components of this system require no attention other than to check that the hose(s) are clear and undamaged at regular intervals.

Exhaust emission control

17 The performance of the catalytic converter and particulate filter can be checked only by measuring the exhaust gases using a good-quality, carefully-calibrated exhaust gas analyser.

18 If the catalytic converter or particulate filter is thought to be faulty, it is worth checking the problem is not due to a faulty injector. Refer to your MINI dealer for further information.

Catalytic converter renewal

19 Refer to Chapter 4B.

Exhaust gas recirculation system

20 Testing of the system should ideally be entrusted to a MINI dealer or suitably equipped repairer.

EGR valve renewal

W16 engine

21 The EGR valve is located on the left-hand rear of the cylinder head. Remove the EGR cooler as described later in this Section. Note there is no need to disconnect the coolant hoses from the cooler – move the cooler to one side.

22 Disconnect the wiring connector from the top of the EGR valve.

23 There are two bolts securing the EGR valve, undo the bolts and remove the valve. Discard the metal gasket from the valve, and the O-ring seal from the pipe – new ones must be fitted **(see illustration)**.

24 Refitting is a reversal of removal.

2.28 Disconnect the EGR cooler coolant hoses (arrowed)

2.32 Disconnect the blue hose, red hose, and wiring plug from the EGR valve (arrowed)

2.33 Remove the EGR pipe bolts (arrowed)

N47 engine

25 The EGR valve is located at the left-hand rear of the engine, and must be removed along with the EGR cooler as described later in this Section.

EGR cooler renewal

W16 engine

26 Drain the cooling system (see Chapter 1B). Alternatively, fit hose clamps to the hoses connected to the EGR heat exchanger.

27 Remove the air cleaner housing as described in Chapter 4B.

28 Loosen the clips and disconnect the coolant hoses from the EGR heat exchanger **(see illustration)**.

29 Release the metal clamps securing the EGR inlet and outlet pipes to the cooler, then undo the retaining nuts and remove the cooler.

30 Refitting is a reversal of removal.

N47 engine

31 Drain the coolant as described in Chapter 1B, then pull the plastic cover on the top of the engine upwards from its mountings, and remove the air cleaner as described in Chapter 4B.

32 Note their fitted positions, then disconnect the blue, and red vacuum hoses, and the wiring plug from the EGR valve and cooler **(see illustration)**.

33 Undo the 2 bolts securing the EGR cooler to the EGR pipe **(see illustration)**.

34 Undo the 2 bolts securing the EGR valve to the exhaust manifold **(see illustration)**.

35 Release the clamp, and disconnect the coolant hose from the EGR cooler **(see illustration)**.

36 Undo the 3 retaining bolts and pull the EGR cooler outwards from the cylinder head, along with the EGR valve **(see illustrations)**.

37 If required, undo the 2 retaining nuts and detach the EGR valve from the cooler.

38 Upon refitting, renew all gaskets and seals, regardless of their apparent condition.

39 The EGR valve must be aligned with the cooler and manifold by tightening the bolts in the following sequence:

a) *Tighten the valve-to-cooler nuts to 5 nm, then release them 90°.*

b) *Apply a little high-temperature snit-seize grease to the threads, then tighten the valve-to-exhaust manifold bolts to 5 nm, and release them 90°*

2.34 EGR valve-to-manifold bolts (arrowed)

2.35 Prise up the clip (arrowed) a little, and pull the hose from the cooler

2.36a The EGR cooler is secured by 2 bolts above (arrowed)…

2.36b …and one below (arrowed)

c) *Now tighten all fasteners securely in the sequence shown (see illustration).*

40 The remainder of refitting is a reversal of removal.

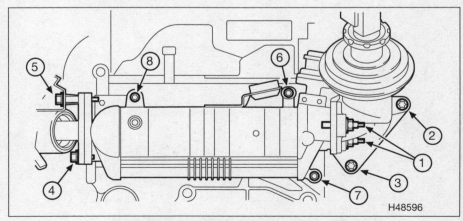

2.39 EGR valve/cooler bolt tightening sequence

Fuel additive reservoir renewal

41 Refer to Chapter 4B.

Particulate filter

42 Renewal of the particulate filter is described in Chapter 4B.

---

3 Catalytic converter –
general information
and precautions

The catalytic converter is a reliable and simple device which needs no maintenance in itself, but there are some facts of which an owner should be aware if the converter is to function properly for its full service life.

Petrol models

a) DO NOT use leaded petrol or LRP – the lead will coat the precious metals, and will eventually destroy the converter.

b) Always keep the ignition and fuel systems well maintained to the service schedule.

c) If the engine develops a misfire, do not drive the car at all (or at least as little as possible) until the fault is cured.

d) DO NOT push- or tow-start the car – this will soak the catalytic converter in unburned fuel, causing it to overheat when the engine does start.

e) DO NOT switch off the ignition at high engine speeds.

f) DO NOT use fuel or engine oil additives – these may contain substances harmful to the catalytic converter.

g) DO NOT continue to use the car if the engine burns oil to the extent of leaving a visible trail of blue smoke.

h) Remember that the catalytic converter operates at very high temperatures. DO NOT, therefore, park the car in dry undergrowth, over long grass or piles of dead leaves after a long run.

i) Remember that the catalytic converter is FRAGILE – do not strike it with tools.

j) In some cases a sulphurous smell (like that of rotten eggs) may be noticed from the exhaust. This is common to many catalytic converter-equipped cars and once the car has covered a few thousand miles the problem should disappear.

k) If the converter is no longer effective it must be renewed.

Diesel models

Refer to parts f, g, h and i of the *petrol models* information given above.

Chapter 5 Part A:
Starting and charging systems

Contents

Degrees of difficulty

Easy, suitable for novice with little experience 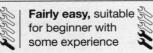	**Fairly easy,** suitable for beginner with some experience 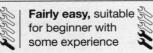	**Fairly difficult,** suitable for competent DIY mechanic 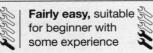	**Difficult,** suitable for experienced DIY mechanic 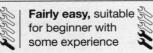	**Very difficult,** suitable for expert DIY or professional

Specifications

System type	12 volt, negative earth

Battery

Type	AGM 'maintenance-free' sealed for life (Absorbent Glass Mat).
Charge condition:	
Poor	12.5 volts
Normal	12.6 volts
Good	12.7 volts

Alternator

Type	Denso, Bosch, Magneti-Marelli, Valeo or Mitsubishi (depending on model)
Rating:	
Petrol models	70, 80, 90 or 120 amp
Diesel models	150 amp

Starter motor

Type	Mitsubishi, Valeo, Ducellier, Iskra, or Bosch (depending on model)

Torque wrench settings	**Nm**	**lbf ft**
Alternator mounting bolts:		
Petrol models	20	15
W16 diesel models	43	32
N47 diesel models	38	28
Auxiliary drivebelt tensioner bolts	20	15
Battery terminals	5	3
Starter motor:		
W16 diesel models	20	15
N47 diesel models	66	48
Petrol models	20	15

3.7 Attach the charger negative clamp to a suitable metal bracket on the engine

1 General information and precautions

General information

The engine electrical system consists mainly of the charging and starting systems. Because of their engine-related functions, these components are covered separately from the body electrical devices such as the lights, instruments, etc (which are covered in Chapter 12). On petrol engine models refer to Part B for information on the ignition system, and on diesel models refer to Chapter 5C for information on the preheating system.

The electrical system is of the 12 volt negative earth type.

The battery is of the low maintenance or 'maintenance-free' (sealed for life) type and is charged by the alternator, which is belt-driven from the crankshaft pulley.

The starter motor is of the pre-engaged type incorporating an integral solenoid. On starting, the solenoid moves the drive pinion into engagement with the flywheel ring gear before the starter motor is energised. Once the engine has started, a one-way clutch prevents the motor armature being driven by the engine.

Precautions

Further details of the various systems are given in the relevant Sections of this Chapter. While some repair procedures are given, the usual course of action is to renew the component concerned.

It is necessary to take extra care when working on the electrical system to avoid damage to semi-conductor devices (diodes and transistors), and to avoid the risk of personal injury. In addition to the precautions given in *Safety first!* at the beginning of this manual, observe the following when working on the system:

• Always remove rings, watches, etc, before working on the electrical system. Even with the battery disconnected, capacitive discharge could occur if a component's live terminal is earthed through a metal object. This could cause a shock or nasty burn.

• Do not reverse the battery connections. Components such as the alternator, electronic control units, or any other components having semi-conductor circuitry could be irreparably damaged.

• If the engine is being started using jump leads and a slave battery, make use of the built-in jump lead connections points (see *Jump starting*, at the beginning of this manual). This also applies when connecting a battery charger.

• Never disconnect the battery terminals, the alternator, any electrical wiring or any test instruments when the engine is running.

• Do not allow the engine to turn the alternator when the alternator is not connected.

• Never 'test' for alternator output by 'flashing' the output lead to earth.

• Never use an ohmmeter of the type incorporating a hand-cranked generator for circuit or continuity testing.

• Always ensure that the battery is disconnected when working on the electrical system.

• Before using electric-arc welding equipment on the car, disconnect the battery, alternator and components such as the fuel injection/ ignition electronic control unit to protect them from the risk of damage.

2 Electrical fault finding – general information

Refer to Chapter 12.

3 Battery – testing and charging

Note: *The following is intended as a guide only. Always refer to the manufacturer's recommendations (often printed on a label attached to the battery) before charging a battery.*

1 All models are fitted with a maintenance-free battery in production, which should require no maintenance under normal operating conditions.
2 In all cases, a 'sealed for life' maintenance-free battery is fitted, and topping-up and testing of the electrolyte in each cell is not possible. The condition of the battery can therefore only be tested using a battery condition indicator or a voltmeter.
3 Models may be fitted with a battery, with a built-in charge condition indicator. The indicator is located in the top of the battery casing, and indicates the condition of the battery from its colour. If the indicator shows green, then the battery is in a good state of charge. If the indicator turns darker, eventually to black, then the battery requires

charging, as described later in this Section. If the indicator shows clear/yellow, then the electrolyte level in the battery is too low to allow further use, and the battery should be renewed. **Do not** attempt to charge, load or jump start a battery when the indicator shows clear/yellow.
4 If testing the battery using a voltmeter, connect the voltmeter across the battery and compare the result with those given in the Specifications under 'charge condition'. The test is only accurate if the battery has not been subjected to any kind of charge for the previous six hours. If this is not the case, switch on the headlights for 30 seconds, then wait four to five minutes before testing the battery after switching off the headlights. All other electrical circuits must be switched off, so check that the doors and tailgate are fully shut when making the test.
5 If testing the battery using a voltmeter, connect the voltmeter across the battery. A fully-charged battery should give a reading of 12.5 volts or higher. The test is only accurate if the battery has not been subjected to any kind of charge for the previous six hours. If this is not the case, switch on the headlights for 30 seconds, then wait four to five minutes before testing the battery after switching off the headlights. All other electrical circuits must be switched off, so check that the doors and tailgate are fully shut when making the test.
6 Generally speaking, if the voltage reading is less than 12.2 volts, then the battery is discharged, whilst a reading of 12.2 to 12.4 volts indicates a partially discharged condition.
7 The battery should be charged by using the position terminal of the battery, and a suitable earth point in the engine compartment – engine mounting/lifting bracket, etc. **(see illustration).** Do not connect a battery charger directly to the battery negative terminal/IBS terminals of a fitted battery. These vehicles may be fitted with an Intelligent Battery Sensor (IBS) incorporated into the battery negative clamp, which monitors the flow of current to and from the battery. If it calculates the state of the battery is getting low, it will ask the CAS (Car Access System) control unit to shut down certain electrical consumers. Eventually, the IBS may decide the battery state is so poor it decides the starting system must be disabled. Consequently, if a battery charger is connected directly to the terminals of the battery, even though the battery may be completely recharged, the IBS may still believe the battery state to be poor, as it has registered no current passing into the battery. Therefore, even though the battery is charged, the starter circuit may still be disabled. Resetting of the CAS battery register must be carried out using MINI diagnostic equipment. Entrust this task to a MINI dealer or suitably equipped specialist.

4 Battery –
disconnection, removal and refitting

Note: *The audio unit fitted as standard equipment by MINI is equipped with an anti-theft system, to deter thieves. If the power source is disconnected, the unit will automatically recode itself as long as it is still fitted to the correct vehicle. If the unit is removed it will not operate in another vehicle.*

Note: *Prior to disconnecting the battery, wait 15 minutes after switching off the ignition to allow the vehicle's ECU's to store all learnt values in their memories.*

Disconnection

1 Prior to disconnecting the battery, close all windows and the sunroof, and ensure that the vehicle alarm system is deactivated (see Owner's Handbook).

⚠ *Warning: Make sure the keys are not left in the car, in case of the vehicle locking system activating and locking all the doors.*

2 The battery is located on the left-hand side of the engine compartment.

3 Unclip the battery cover and slacken the negative lead clamp nut **(see illustrations)**. On models with an IBS (Intelligent Battery Sensor) fitted to the negative lead terminal, take great care handling the IBS unit – they are fragile and easily damaged. The following guidelines should be adhered to:

Do not attach any additional connections to the negative terminal.
Do not modify the earth lead.
Do not use force when disconnecting the earth terminal.
Do not pull the earth cable.
Do not subject the IBS to any levering, pulling, etc.
Do not slacken or tighten the IBS sensor Torx screw.

Removal

4 Disconnect the battery negative terminal as previously described in this Section.

5 Where fitted, release the clips at the sides, and unclip the cover over the positive terminal clamp, then slacken the retaining nut and remove the battery positive terminal clamp **(see illustrations)**.

6 Pull up the rubber weatherstrip at the front edge, undo the screw and nut at the outer edge, and unclip the cowl panel above the battery. Ensure the cowl seals are not damaged **(see illustrations)**.

7 Disconnect the vent pipe from the side of the battery **(see illustration)**.

8 Undo the clamp bolt and lift the battery

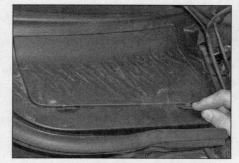

4.3a Release the clips and remove the battery cover

4.3b Battery negative lead clamp nut and IBS sensor (arrowed)

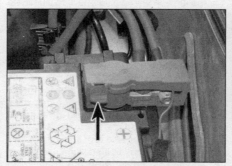

4.5a Release the clip each side (arrowed)…

4.5b …lift the cover and slacken the positive lead clamp nut (arrowed)

4.6a Pull up the rubber weatherstrip…

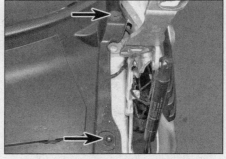

4.6b …undo the screw and nut (arrowed)…

4.6c …pull the cowl panel away from the base of the windscreen

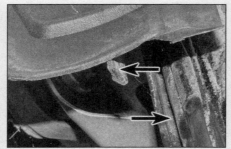

4.6d Note how the cowl panel clips into the moulding at the base of the windscreen (arrowed)

4.7 Pull the vent pipe from the side of the battery

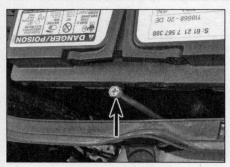

4.8 Undo the battery clamp bolt (arrowed)

from place **(see illustration)**. Take care as the battery is heavy!

Refitting

9 Refitting is a reversal of removal. Always reconnect the positive lead first, and the negative lead last.

10 If a new battery has been fitted, the new unit must be registered with the CAS (Car Access System) control unit, using MINI diagnostic equipment. Entrust this task to a MINI dealer or suitably equipped specialist. Failure to register the battery may cause the IBS to malfunction (where fitted).

11 After reconnecting the battery, several of the vehicles ECMs will require time to relearn certain values. The will normally be complete within a normal driving pattern of 15 miles (approximately). In addition, several systems may require re-initialisation as follows:

Sunroof

1) With the battery reconnected, and the ignition on, press the sunroof operating switch into the 'closed' position and hold it there.

2) The sunroof will move a few centimetres – continue to hold the switch in the 'closed' position for approximately 75 seconds. During this time the roof will open completely, then close completely. Now release the switch.

Electric windows

1) Operate the button to fully open the window, then press the switch into the 'open, one-touch operation' (second

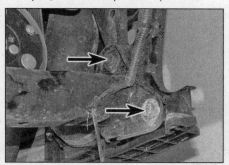

7.2a Front panel-to-subframe bolts (arrowed)

switch position) and hold it there for 20 seconds.

2) Release the switch, then press the switch into the 'close, one-touch operation (second switch position) and hold it there until the window closes completely.

5 Charging system – testing

Note: *Refer to the warnings given in 'Safety first!' and in Section 1 of this Chapter before starting work.*

1 If the ignition warning light fails to illuminate when the ignition is switched on, first check the alternator wiring connections for security. If satisfactory, check that the warning light bulb has not blown, and that the bulbholder is secure in its location in the instrument panel. If the light still fails to illuminate, check the continuity of the warning light feed wire from the alternator to the bulbholder. If all is satisfactory, the alternator is at fault and should be renewed or taken to an auto-electrician for testing and repair.

2 If the ignition warning light illuminates when the engine is running, stop the engine and check that the drivebelt is correctly fitted and tensioned (see Chapter 1A or Chapter 1B) and that the alternator connections are secure. If all is so far satisfactory, have the alternator checked by an auto-electrician for testing and repair.

3 If the alternator output is suspect even though the warning light functions correctly, the regulated voltage may be checked as follows.

4 Connect a voltmeter across the battery terminals and start the engine.

5 Increase the engine speed until the voltmeter reading remains steady; the reading should be approximately 12 to 13 volts, and no more than 14 volts.

6 Switch on as many electrical accessories (eg, the headlights, heated rear window and heater blower) as possible, and check that the alternator maintains the regulated voltage of around 13 to 14 volts.

7 If the regulated voltage is not as stated, the fault may be due to worn brushes, weak

7.2b Undo the bolt (arrowed) securing the front panel to the wing each side

brush springs, a faulty voltage regulator, a faulty diode, a severed phase winding or worn or damaged slip-rings. The alternator should be renewed or taken to an auto-electrician for testing and repair.

6 Alternator drivebelt – removal, refitting and tensioning

Refer to the procedure given for the auxiliary drivebelt in Chapter 1A or Chapter 1B.

7 Alternator – removal and refitting

Removal

1 Disconnect the battery (see Section 4).

2 The front panel must now be moved into the 'assembly' position as follows:

a) Remove the front bumper as described in Chapter 11.

b) Unplug the air conditioning compressor wiring plug, and release the harness from any clips.

c) Undo the 2 bolts each side securing the front panel to the subframe **(see illustration)**.

d) Remove the bolt each side securing the front panel to the wing **(see illustration)**.

e) Release the coolant pipe from the retaining clips on the front panel.

f) Undo the retaining bolt and move the coolant expansion tank to one side.

g) Detach the air intake ducting gaiter from the front panel.

h) Prise open the junction box on the left-hand support, and disconnect the bonnet release cable **(see illustration)**.

i) Undo the 3 bolts each side securing the front panel/headlight to the suspension turret/front wing **(see illustration)**.

j) Slacken the clamp and disconnect the right-hand charge pressure hose from the intercooler, then disconnect the air hose from the turbocharger outlet ducting **(see illustrations)**.

k) Disconnect the right-hand headlight wiring plug.

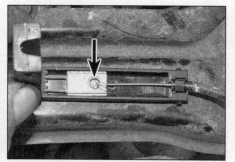

7.2c Open the junction box and disconnect the bonnet release cable (arrowed)

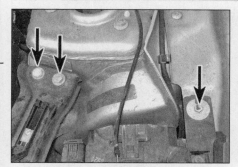

7.2d Remove the headlight bolt, and the panel support-to-suspension turret bolts (arrowed)

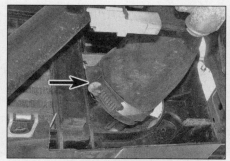

7.2e Disconnect the right-hand intercooler hose (arrowed)...

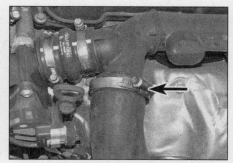

7.2f ...and the turbocharger outlet hose (arrowed) – where fitted

7.2g Screw the tubes/rods through the front panel into the threaded holes in the chassis members

7.2h Undo the 3 nuts (arrowed) each side...

7.2i ...and slide the panel forwards on the tubes

l) Screw special tool No. 00 2 271 into the left-hand, and right-hand front panel/ chassis member sleeve. In the absence of these tools, use 2 lengths of tube, 19 mm outside diameter, at least 120 mm long, with two 8 mm threaded rods at least 150 mm long, and two 8 mm nuts (see illustration).

m) Undo the 3 nuts each side, and slide the front panel assembly approximately 10 cm forwards (see illustrations). Take care to ensure no strain is placed on any wiring/ hoses.

3 Remove the auxiliary drivebelt as described in Chapter 1A or Chapter 1B. W16 diesel models – see Paragraph 8.

Petrol models

4 On turbo engines, undo the bolt and move the harness holder to one side.

5 Disconnect the wiring connector from the rear of the alternator, remove the rubber cover (where fitted) from the alternator terminals, and then unscrew the retaining nut (see illustration).

6 Undo the alternator two upper retaining bolts and remove the auxiliary belt automatic tensioner (see illustration).

7 Undo the alternator lower mounting bolt using a 'wobble drive' type socket extension. Do not disconnect the refrigerant pipes. Manoeuvre the alternator away from its mounting brackets and out from the engine compartment

W16 diesel models

8 Undo the retaining bolts and remove the auxiliary drivebelt tensioner (see illustration).

Note that the lower, rearmost bolt can only be accessed prior to removing the drivebelt.

9 Remove the charge air hose between the intercooler and the throttle body.

7.5 Disconnect the wiring plug, then undo the nut and disconnect the lead (arrowed)

7.8 Undo the auxiliary drivebelt tensioner bolts (arrowed)

10 Prise out the cap, undo the nut securing the positive lead to the alternator, then unlock and disconnect the wiring plug (see illustration).

7.6 Tensioner/alternator upper mounting bolts, and lower mounting bolt (arrowed)

7.10 Prise out the rubber cover, then disconnect the alternator wiring and plug

7.11a Alternator right-hand (arrowed)...

11 Undo the mounting bolts and manoeuvre the alternator from place **(see illustrations)**.

N47 diesel models

12 Undo the bolt securing the air conditioning refrigerant pipe bracket to the alternator.
13 Prise out the cap, undo the nut securing the positive lead to the alternator, then unlock and disconnect the wiring plug **(see illustration)**.
14 Undo the mounting bolts and manoeuvre the alternator from place **(see illustration)**.

All models

15 To remove the alternator pulley on models with an over-running clutch, grip the alternator in a bench vice, prise off the plastic cap, then the pulley can be removed by inserting tool No. 12 7 121 into the pulley centre, and holding the alternator shaft with tool No. 12 7 122 **(see illustrations)**. Slacken the pulley centre whilst holding the alternator shaft stationary.

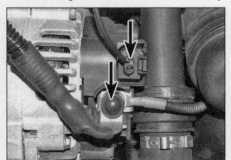

7.13 Prise up the cap, undo the nut and disconnect the wiring plug (arrowed)

7.15a Insert the special tools into the alternator shaft and pulley centre

7.11b ...and left-hand mounting bolts (arrowed)

Suitable alternative tools are available from tool aftermarket tool manufacturers.

Refitting

16 Refitting is a reversal of removal, tensioning the auxiliary drivebelt as described in Chapter 1A or Chapter 1B, and ensuring that the alternator mountings are securely tightened.

8 Alternator –
testing and overhaul

If the alternator is thought to be suspect, it should be removed from the vehicle and taken to an auto-electrician for testing. Most auto-electricians will be able to supply and fit brushes at a reasonable cost. However, check on the cost of repairs before proceeding, as it may prove more economical to obtain a new or exchange alternator.

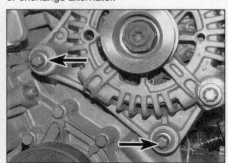

7.14 Alternator mounting bolts (arrowed) – N47 engines

7.15b Hold the alternator shaft and slacken the pulley centre...

9 Starting system –
testing

Note: *Refer to the precautions given in 'Safety first!' and in Section 1 of this Chapter before starting work.*

1 If the starter motor fails to operate when the ignition key is turned to the appropriate position, the following possible causes may be to blame.
   a) *The engine immobiliser is faulty.*
   b) *The battery is faulty.*
   c) *The electrical connections between the switch, solenoid, battery and starter motor are somewhere failing to pass the necessary current from the battery through the starter to earth.*
   d) *The solenoid is faulty.*
   e) *The starter motor is mechanically or electrically defective.*

2 To check the battery, switch on the headlights. If they dim after a few seconds, this indicates that the battery is discharged – recharge (see Section 3) or renew the battery. If the headlights glow brightly, operate the ignition switch and observe the lights. If they dim, then this indicates that current is reaching the starter motor; therefore the fault must lie in the starter motor. If the lights continue to glow brightly (and no clicking sound can be heard from the starter motor solenoid), this indicates that there is a fault in the circuit or solenoid – see following paragraphs. If the starter motor turns slowly when operated, but the battery is in good condition, then this indicates that either the starter motor is faulty, or there is considerable resistance somewhere in the circuit.

3 If a fault in the circuit is suspected, disconnect the battery leads (including the earth connection to the body of the vehicle), the starter/solenoid wiring and the engine earth strap – located on the right-hand engine mounting (see Chapter 12). Thoroughly clean the connections and reconnect the leads and wiring, then use a voltmeter or test lamp to check that full battery voltage is available at the battery positive lead connection to the solenoid, and that the earth is sound. Smear

7.15c ...then slide the pulley from the shaft

petroleum jelly around the battery terminals to prevent corrosion – corroded connections are amongst the most frequent causes of electrical system faults.

4 If the battery and all connections are in good condition, check the circuit by disconnecting the wire from the solenoid blade terminal. Connect a voltmeter or test lamp between the wire end and a good earth (such as the battery negative terminal), and check that the wire is live when the ignition switch is turned to the 'start' position. If it is, then the circuit is sound – if not the circuit wiring can be checked as described in Chapter 12.

5 The contacts inside the solenoid can be checked, by connecting a voltmeter or test lamp between the battery positive feed connection on the starter side of the solenoid and earth. When the ignition switch is turned to the 'start' position, there should be a reading or lighted bulb, as applicable. If there is no reading or lighted bulb, the solenoid is faulty and should be renewed.

6 If the circuit and solenoid are proved sound, the fault must lie in the starter motor. In this event, it may be possible to have the starter motor overhauled by a specialist, but check on the cost of spares before proceeding, as it may prove more economical to obtain a new or exchange motor.

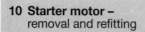

10 Starter motor – removal and refitting

Removal

1 Disconnect the battery (see Section 4).

All except N47 diesel models

2 So that access to the motor can be gained both from above and below, apply the handbrake then jack up the front of the vehicle and support it on axle stands (see *Jacking and vehicle support*). Release the

10.5 Undo the nut and disconnect the lead, then press-up the clip and disconnect the wiring plug (arrowed)

screws and remove the engine undershield (where fitted). Remove the right-hand roadwheel.

3 Remove the air cleaner housing and air ducting as described in Chapter 4A or Chapter 4B.

4 On petrol non-turbo models, remove the purge valve as described in Chapter 4C, then on N14 and N16 engines, undo the 3 bolts and move the vacuum reservoir to one side.

5 Slacken and remove the retaining nut(s) and disconnect the wiring from the starter motor solenoid. Recover the washers under the nuts. Where applicable, release the wiring loom from the retaining clips, then undo the bolt securing the wiring loom support plate above the starter motor **(see illustration)**.

6 On W16 diesel engines, undo the retaining bolts and move the vacuum reservoir from the rear of the cylinder block to access the starter motor bolts, then move the pressure transducer and wiring harness to one side.

7 Undo the three mounting bolts (two at the rear of the motor, and one which comes through from the top of the transmission housing), supporting the motor as the bolts are withdrawn. Recover the washers from

10.7 Starter motor mounting bolts (arrowed)

under the bolt heads and note the locations of any wiring or hose brackets secured by the bolts **(see illustration)**.

8 Manoeuvre the starter motor out from underneath the engine and recover the locating dowel(s) from the motor/transmission (as applicable).

N47 diesel models

9 Remove the air cleaner housing as described in Chapter 4B

10 Release the clip, disconnect the hose from the intercooler, undo the retaining bolts, and move the charge air duct between the intercooler and the turbocharger to one side **(see illustration)**. Check the condition of the duct O-ring seals, and renew if necessary.

11 Undo the retaining bolt and pull the engine oil level dipstick guide tube upwards from the sump **(see illustration)**. Renew the guide tube O-ring seal.

12 Undo the 2 bolts securing the starter motor to the transmission **(see illustration)**.

13 Undo the retaining screw, and pull the vacuum pipe from the engine, and move it to one side. Renew the O-ring seal on the vacuum pipe **(see illustration)**.

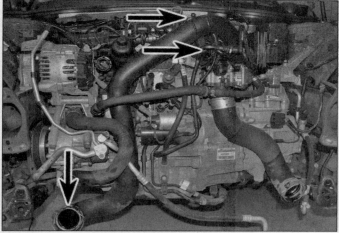

10.10 Release the clip, disconnect the hose, undo the bolts and move the turbocharger-to-intercooler duct/hose to one side (arrowed) – front panel removed for clarity

10.11 Oil level dipstick guide tube bolt (arrowed)

10.12 Starter motor mounting bolts (arrowed)

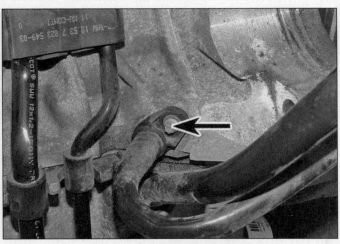

10.13 Undo the bolt and pull the vacuum hose from the engine (arrowed)

14 Slacken and remove the retaining nut(s) and disconnect the wiring from the starter motor solenoid. Recover the washers under the nuts **(see illustration)**.

15 Manoeuvre the starter motor downwards and withdraw it from under the vehicle.

Refitting

16 Refitting is a reversal of removal, ensuring that the locating dowel(s) are correctly positioned. Also make sure that any wiring or hose brackets are in place under the bolt heads as noted prior to removal.

11 Starter motor –
testing and overhaul

If the starter motor is thought to be suspect, it should be removed from the vehicle and taken to an auto-electrician for testing. Most auto-electricians will be able to supply and fit brushes at a reasonable cost. However, check on the cost of repairs before proceeding, as it may prove more economical to obtain a new or exchange motor.

10.14 Starter motor wiring connections – N47 engines

Chapter 5 Part B:
Ignition system – petrol models

Contents

Degrees of difficulty

Easy, suitable for novice with little experience	Fairly easy, suitable for beginner with some experience	Fairly difficult, suitable for competent DIY mechanic 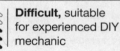	Difficult, suitable for experienced DIY mechanic	Very difficult, suitable for expert DIY or professional

Specifications

General

System type .... Static (distributorless) ignition system controlled by engine management ECU
Spark plugs .... See Chapter 1A Specifications
Ignition timing... Controlled by engine management ECU

Torque wrench setting	Nm	lbf ft
Knock sensor securing bolt	20	15

1 Ignition system – general information

The ignition system is integrated with the fuel injection system to form a combined engine management system under the control of one ECU (see Chapter 4A for further information). The ignition side of the system is of the static (distributorless) type, consisting of the ignition coils and spark plugs. The ignition coils are housed in a single unit mounted directly above the spark plugs. The coils are integral with the spark plug caps and are pushed directly onto the spark plugs, one for each plug. This removes the need for any HT leads connecting the coils to the plugs.

Under the control of the ECU, the ignition coils operate on the 'wasted spark' principle, ie, each plug sparks twice for every cycle of the engine, once during the compression stroke and once during the exhaust stroke. The spark voltage is greatest in the cylinder which is under compression; in the cylinder on its exhaust stroke the compression is low and this produces a very weak spark which has no effect on the exhaust gases.

The ECU uses its inputs from the various sensors to calculate the required ignition advance setting and coil charging time, depending on engine temperature, load and speed. At idle speeds, the ECU varies the ignition timing to alter the torque characteristic of the engine, enabling the idle speed to be controlled.

A knock sensor is also incorporated into the ignition system. Mounted onto the cylinder block, the sensor detects the high-frequency vibrations caused when the engine starts to pre-ignite, or 'pink'. Under these conditions, the knock sensor sends an electrical signal to the ECU, which in turn retards the ignition advance setting in small steps until the 'pinking' ceases.

2 Ignition system – testing

 Warning: Voltages produced by an electronic ignition system are considerably higher than those

2.1 The 16-pin diagnostic connector is located under the drivers side of the facia (arrowed)

3.1 Undo the screws (arrowed) then tilt the cover forwards to release the clips at the front edge

3.2 Lift up the locking lever and disconnect the wiring plug from the top of the coil

produced by conventional ignition systems. Extreme care must be taken when working on the system with the ignition switched on. Persons with surgically implanted cardiac pacemaker devices should keep well clear of the ignition circuits, components and test equipment.

If a fault appears in the engine management (fuel injection/ignition) system, first ensure that the fault is not due to a poor electrical connection or poor maintenance; ie, check that the air cleaner filter element is clean, the spark plugs are in good condition and correctly gapped, that the engine breather hoses are clear and undamaged, referring to Chapter 1A for further information. If the engine is running very roughly, check the compression pressures as described in Chapter 2A.

If these checks fail to reveal the cause of the problem the vehicle should be taken to a suitably-equipped MINI dealer or specialist for testing. A wiring block diagnostic connector is incorporated in the engine management circuit into which a special electronic diagnostic tester can be plugged **(see illustration)**. The tester will locate the fault quickly and simply alleviating the need to test all the system components individually, which is a time-consuming operation that carries a high risk of damaging the ECU.

The only ignition system checks which can be carried out by the home mechanic are those described in Chapter 1A relating to the spark plugs.

3 Ignition coil unit – removal, testing and refitting

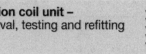

Removal

1 Undo the two retaining screws and unclip the front of the plastic cover from the cylinder head cover **(see illustration)**.
2 Release the locking lever and disconnect the wiring connector from the top of the ignition coil unit **(see illustration)**.
3 Lift the coil unit upwards, off the spark plug and from its location in the cylinder head cover **(see illustration)**. **Note:** *Pull the coil units upwards smoothly and slowly. The silicone tube that engages with the outside of the spark plug are delicate and will easily tear.*

Testing

4 The circuitry arrangement of the ignition coil unit on these engines is such that testing of an individual coil in isolation from the remainder of the engine management system is unlikely to prove effective in diagnosing a particular fault. Should there be any reason to suspect a faulty individual coil, the engine management system should be tested by a MINI dealer or specialist using diagnostic test equipment (see Section 2).

Refitting

5 Refitting is a reversal of the relevant removal

procedure ensuring the wiring connectors are securely reconnected. **Note:** *The silicone tubes that engage with the spark plugs are pre-coated with talcum powder to aid fitting and removal. Under no circumstances should they be lubricated with oil or grease.*

4 Ignition timing – checking and adjustment

There are no timing marks on the flywheel or crankshaft pulley. The timing is constantly being monitored and adjusted by the engine management ECU, and nominal values cannot be given. Therefore, it is not possible for the home mechanic to check the ignition timing.

The only way in which the ignition timing can be checked is using special electronic test equipment, connected to the engine management system diagnostic connector; see Chapter 4A for further information.

5 Knock sensor – removal and refitting

Removal

1 The knock sensor is screwed into the rear face of the cylinder block.
2 Firmly apply the handbrake, and then jack up the front of the vehicle and support it securely on axle stands (see *Jacking and vehicle support*). Undo the screws and remove the engine undershield (where fitted).
3 Depending on type of knock sensor fitted, either trace the wiring back from the sensor to its wiring connector, and disconnect it from the main loom or disconnect the wiring connector directly from the sensor **(see illustration)**.
4 Undo the sensor securing bolt and remove the sensor from the cylinder block.

Refitting

5 Refitting is a reversal of the removal procedure, ensuring that the securing bolt for the knock sensor is tightened to the specified torque, and its mating surface is clean and dry.

3.3 Pull the coil straight-up from the spark plug/cylinder head cover

5.3 The knock sensor (arrowed) is adjacent to the starter motor

Chapter 5 Part C:
Pre/post-heating system – diesel models

Contents

Degrees of difficulty

Easy, suitable for novice with little experience	**Fairly easy,** suitable for beginner with some experience 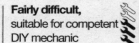	**Fairly difficult,** suitable for competent DIY mechanic	**Difficult,** suitable for experienced DIY mechanic	**Very difficult,** suitable for expert DIY or professional

Specifications

Torque wrench settings	Nm	lbf ft
Glow plugs:		
N47 engine	13	9
W16 engine	10	7

---

1 Pre/post-heating system – description and testing

Description

1 To assist cold starting, diesel engines are fitted with a preheating system, which consists of four of glow plugs (one per cylinder), a glow plug relay unit, a facia-mounted warning lamp, the engine management ECU, and the associated electrical wiring.

2 The glow plugs are miniature electric heating elements, encapsulated in a metal case with a probe at one end and electrical connection at the other. Each combustion chamber has one glow plug threaded into it, with the tip of the glow plug probe positioned directly in line with incoming spray of fuel from the injectors. When the glow plug is energised, it heats up rapidly, causing the fuel passing over the glow plug probe to be heated to its optimum temperature, ready for combustion. In addition, some of the fuel passing over the glow plugs is ignited and this helps to trigger the combustion process.

3 The preheating system begins to operate as soon as the ignition key is switched to the second position, but only if the engine coolant temperature is below 20ºC and the engine is turned at more than 70 rpm for 0.2 seconds. A facia-mounted warning lamp informs the driver that preheating is taking place. The lamp extinguishes when sufficient preheating has taken place to allow the engine to be started, but power will still be supplied to the glow plugs for a further period until the engine

is started. If no attempt is made to start the engine, the power supply to the glow plugs is switched off after 10 seconds to prevent battery drain and glow plug burnout.

4 With the electronically-controlled diesel injection systems fitted to models in this manual, the glow plug relay unit is controlled by the engine management system ECU, which determines the necessary preheating time based on inputs from the various system sensors. The system monitors the temperature of the inlet air, and then alters the preheating time (the length for which the glow plugs are supplied with current) to suit the conditions.

5 Post-heating takes place after the ignition key has been released from the 'start' position, but only if the engine coolant temperature is below 20ºC, the injected fuel flow is less than a certain rate, and the engine speed is less than 2000 rpm. The glow plugs continue to operate for a maximum of 60 seconds, helping to improve fuel combustion whilst the engine is warming-up, resulting in quieter, smoother running and reduced exhaust emissions.

Testing

6 If the system malfunctions, testing is ultimately by substitution of known good units, but some preliminary checks may be made as follows.

7 On W16 engines, remove the air cleaner housing as described in Chapter 4B.

8 On N47 engines, pull the plastic cover on the top of the engine upwards from its mountings, then undo the retaining screw, and move the wiring harness channel to one side **(see illustration)**.

9 Connect a voltmeter or 12 volt test lamp

between the glow plug supply cable and earth (engine or vehicle metal). Make sure that the live connection is kept clear of the engine and bodywork.

10 Have an assistant switch on the ignition, and check that voltage is applied to the glow plugs. Note the time for which the warning light is lit, and the total time for which voltage is applied before the system cuts out. Switch off the ignition.

11 Compare the results with the information given in the Specifications. Warning light time will increase with lower temperatures and decrease with higher temperatures.

12 If there is no supply at all, the control unit or associated wiring is at fault.

13 Disconnect the main supply cable and the interconnecting wire or strap from the top of the glow plugs. Be careful not to drop the nuts and washers.

14 Use a continuity tester, or a 12 volt test lamp connected to the battery positive terminal,

1.8 Wiring harness channel retaining screw (arrowed)

2.2 Undo the nuts securing the glow plug connections (arrowed) – W16 engines

2.3 Squeeze together the sides of the connector and pull it from the glow plug – N47 engines

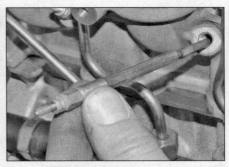

2.5 Unscrew the glow plugs from the cylinder head

to check for continuity between each glow plug terminal and earth. The resistance of a glow plug in good condition is very low (less than 1 ohm), so if the test lamp does not light or the continuity tester shows a high resistance, the glow plug is certainly defective.

15 If an ammeter is available, the current draw of each glow plug can be checked. After an initial surge of 15 to 20 amps, each plug should draw 12 amps. Any plug which draws much more or less than this is probably defective.

16 As a final check, the glow plugs can be removed and inspected as described in the following Section. On completion, refit any components removed for access.

2 Glow plugs –
removal, inspection and refitting

Caution: If the preheating system has just been energised, or if the engine has been running, the glow plugs will be very hot.

Removal

1 Ensure the ignition is turned off. To gain access to the glow plugs, remove the components described in Section 1, according to engine.

W16 engine

2 Unscrew the nuts from the glow plug terminals, and recover the washers. Note that on some models, an interconnecting wire/

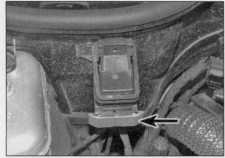

3.2 Pull out the locking catch (arrowed) to disconnect the wiring plug from the glow plug control unit – W 16 engines

shunt is fitted between the four plugs **(see illustration)**.

N47 engine

3 Squeeze together the sides and pull the wiring connector upwards from each glow plug **(see illustration)**.

All engines

4 Where applicable, carefully move any obstructing pipes or wires to one side to enable access to the relevant glow plug(s).
5 Unscrew the glow plug(s) and remove from the cylinder head **(see illustration)**.

Inspection

6 Inspect each glow plug for physical damage. Burnt or eroded glow plug tips can be caused by a bad injector spray pattern. Have the injectors checked if this sort of damage is found.
7 If the glow plugs are in good physical condition, check them electrically using a 12 volt test lamp or continuity tester as described in the previous Section.
8 The glow plugs can be energised by applying 12 volts to them to verify that they heat up evenly and in the required time. Observe the following precautions.
 a) *Support the glow plug by clamping it carefully in a vice or self-locking pliers. Remember it will become red-hot.*
 b) *Make sure that the power supply or test lead incorporates a fuse or overload trip to protect against damage from a short-circuit.*

3.7 Slide down the locking clips (arrowed) and disconnect the control unit wiring plugs – N47 engines

 c) *After testing, allow the glow plug to cool for several minutes before attempting to handle it.*
9 A glow plug in good condition will start to glow red at the tip after drawing current for 5 seconds or so. Any plug, which takes much longer to start glowing, or which starts glowing in the middle instead of at the tip, is defective.

Refitting

10 Refit by reversing the removal operations. Apply a smear of copper-based anti-seize compound to the plug threads and tighten the glow plugs to the specified torque. Do not overtighten, as this can damage the glow plug element.
11 Refit any components removed for access.

3 Pre/post-heating
system relay unit –
removal and refitting

Removal

1 Disconnect the battery (see Chapter 5A).

W16 engine

2 The unit is located on the right-hand side of the engine compartment bulkhead **(see illustration)**.
3 Unlock and disconnect the wiring plug.
4 Remove the unit from the engine compartment.

N47 engine

5 Pull the plastic cover on the top of the engine upwards from its mountings.
6 The unit is located on the front of the engine, adjacent to the oil filter housing.
7 Slide down the locking clips, and disconnect the wiring plugs from the unit **(see illustration)**.
8 Undo the retaining screw, and remove the unit.

Refitting

9 Refitting is a reversal of removal, ensuring that the wiring connectors are correctly connected.

Chapter 6
Clutch

Contents

Degrees of difficulty

Easy, suitable for novice with little experience	**Fairly easy,** suitable for beginner with some experience 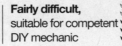	**Fairly difficult,** suitable for competent DIY mechanic	**Difficult,** suitable for experienced DIY mechanic	**Very difficult,** suitable for expert DIY or professional

Specifications

General

Type . . . . Single dry disc with diaphragm spring, hydraulic operation
Lining material thickness above rivet head . . . . 1.0 mm

Friction disc diameter

Petrol engine models:
  Non-turbo models . . . . 200 mm
   Turbo models . . . . 228 mm
Diesel engine models . . . . 228 mm

Torque wrench setting

	Nm	lbf ft
Clutch master cylinder nuts	10	7
Pedal assembly retaining nuts*	21	16
Pressure plate retaining bolts:		
W16 diesel engine*	20	15
All other engines*	23	17
Slave cylinder	21	16

*Do not re-use

1 General information

The clutch consists of a friction disc, a pressure plate assembly, a release bearing and release fork; all of these components are contained in the large cast-aluminium alloy bellhousing, sandwiched between the engine and the transmission. The release mechanism is hydraulic on all models.

The friction disc is fitted between the engine flywheel and the clutch pressure plate, and is allowed to slide on the transmission input shaft splines.

The pressure plate assembly is bolted to the engine flywheel. When the engine is running, drive is transmitted from the crankshaft, via the flywheel, to the friction disc (these components being clamped securely together by the pressure plate assembly) and from the friction disc to the transmission input shaft.

To interrupt the drive, the spring pressure must be relaxed. This is done by means of the clutch release bearing, fitted concentrically around the transmission input shaft. The bearing is pushed onto the pressure plate assembly by means of the release fork actuated by clutch slave cylinder pushrod.

The clutch pedal is connected to the clutch master cylinder by a short pushrod. The master cylinder is mounted on the engine side of the bulkhead in front of the driver and receives its hydraulic fluid supply from the brake master cylinder reservoir. Depressing the clutch pedal moves the piston in the master cylinder forwards, so forcing hydraulic fluid through the clutch hydraulic pipe to the slave cylinder. The piston in the slave cylinder moves forward on the entry of the fluid and actuates the clutch release fork by means of a short pushrod. The release fork pivots on its mounting stud, and the other end of the fork then presses the release bearing against the pressure plate spring fingers. This causes the springs to deform and releases the clamping force on the pressure plate.

On all models the clutch operating mechanism is self-adjusting, and no manual adjustment is required.

2 Clutch hydraulic system – bleeding

⚠ *Warning: Hydraulic fluid is poisonous; wash off immediately and thoroughly in the case of skin contact, and seek immediate medical advice if any fluid is swallowed or gets into the eyes. Certain types of hydraulic fluid are inflammable, and may ignite when allowed into contact with hot components; when servicing any hydraulic system, it is safest to assume that the fluid IS inflammable, and to take precautions against the risk of fire as though it is petrol that is being handled. Hydraulic fluid is also an effective paint stripper, and will attack plastics; if any is spilt, it should be washed off immediately,*

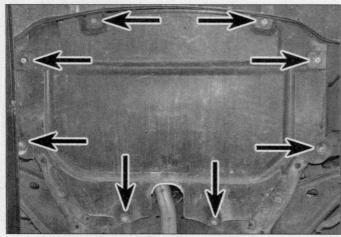

2.2 Engine undershield fasteners (arrowed)

2.4 Clutch slave cylinder bleed screw (arrowed)

using copious quantities of clean water. When topping-up or renewing the fluid, always use the recommended type, and ensure that it comes from a freshly-opened sealed container.

1 Obtain a clean jar, a suitable length of rubber or clear plastic tubing, which is a tight fit over the bleed screw on the clutch slave cylinder, and a tin of the specified hydraulic fluid. The help of an assistant will also be required. (If a one-man do-it-yourself bleeding kit for bleeding the brake hydraulic system is available, this can be used quite satisfactorily for the clutch also. Full information on the use of these kits may be found in Chapter 9.)

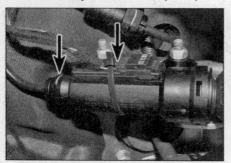

3.2 Clutch master cylinder wiring plug and pipe retaining clip (arrowed)

3.3b ...undo the nut and screw...

2 Raise the front of the vehicle and support it securely on axle stands (see *Jacking and vehicle support*). Release the fasteners and remove the engine undershield (where fitted) **(see illustration)**.
3 Remove the filler cap from the brake master cylinder reservoir, and if necessary top-up the fluid. Keep the reservoir topped-up during subsequent operations.
4 Remove the dust cap from the slave cylinder bleed screw, located on the lower front facing side of the transmission **(see illustration)**.
5 Connect one end of the bleed tube to the bleed screw, and insert the other end of the

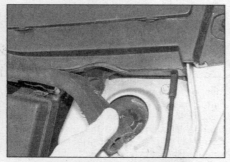

3.3a Pull up the rubber weatherstrip at the rear of the engine compartment...

3.3c ...then pull up the scuttle trim panel above the battery

tube in the jar containing sufficient clean hydraulic fluid to keep the end of the tube submerged.
6 Open the bleed screw half a turn and have your assistant depress the clutch pedal and then slowly release it. Continue this procedure until clean hydraulic fluid, free from air bubbles, emerges from the tube. Now tighten the bleed screw at the end of a downstroke. Make sure that the brake master cylinder reservoir is checked frequently to ensure that the level does not drop too far, allowing air into the system.
7 Check the operation of the clutch pedal. After a few strokes it should feel normal. Any sponginess would indicate air still present in the system.
8 On completion remove the bleed tube and refit the dust cover. Top-up the master cylinder reservoir if necessary and refit the cap. Fluid expelled from the hydraulic system should now be discarded, as it will be contaminated with moisture, air and dirt, making it unsuitable for further use.

3 Clutch master cylinder – removal and refitting

Note: *Before starting work, refer to the note at the beginning of Section 2 concerning the dangers of hydraulic fluid.*

Removal

1 Remove the steering column as described in Chapter 10.
2 Disconnect the wiring plug from the clutch master cylinder, then prise out the clip a little, and disconnect the pressure pipe at the connection **(see illustration)**.
3 Pull up the rubber weatherstrip at the front edge, undo the screw and nut at the outer edge, and unclip the cowl panel above the battery. Ensure the cowl seals are not damaged **(see illustrations)**.

4 Remove both wiper arms as described in Chapter 12.
5 Pull up the rubber weather strip, undo the screw and nut at the outer edge, unclip the right-hand scuttle panel cowl **(see illustrations)**.
6 Remove the brake master cylinder reservoir filler cap, and then tighten it down onto a piece of polythene to obtain an airtight seal. This will minimise hydraulic fluid loss.
7 Release the securing clip and disconnect the hydraulic fluid supply pipe from the brake fluid reservoir **(see illustration)**. Plug or cap the pipe end to prevent further fluid loss and dirt entry.
8 Lift up the edge, slide off the retaining clip securing the master cylinder push rod to the clutch pedal **(see illustration)**.
9 Undo the 2 retaining nuts and withdraw the clutch master cylinder.

Refitting

10 Refitting the master cylinder is the reverse sequence to removal, bearing in mind the following points.
  a) *Ensure all fasteners are tightened to their specified torque where given.*
  b) *On completion, bleed the clutch hydraulic system as described in Section 2.*

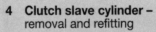
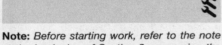

4 Clutch slave cylinder – removal and refitting

Note: *Before starting work, refer to the note at the beginning of Section 2 concerning the dangers of hydraulic fluid.*

Removal

1 Raise the front of the vehicle and support it securely on axle stands (see *Jacking and vehicle support*). Release the fasteners and remove the engine undershield.
2 Pull up the rubber weatherstrip at the front edge, undo the screw and nut at the outer edge, and unclip the cowl panel above the battery. Ensure the cowl seals are not damaged **(see illustrations 3.3a, 3.3b and 3.3c)**.
3 Remove both wiper arms as described in Chapter 12.
4 Pull up the rubber weather strip, undo the screw and nut at the outer edge, unclip the scuttle panel cowl **(see illustration 3.5a and 3.5b)**.
5 To minimise hydraulic fluid loss, remove the brake master cylinder reservoir filler cap then tighten it down onto a piece of polythene to obtain an airtight seal.
6 Release the securing clip and disconnect the hydraulic fluid supply pipe from the brake fluid reservoir **(see illustration 3.7)**. Plug or cap the pipe end to prevent further fluid loss and dirt entry.
7 Place absorbent rags under the clutch slave cylinder located on the lower front facing side of the transmission. Be prepared for hydraulic fluid loss.

3.5a Release the clips (arrowed) at the front edge of the scuttle trim panel

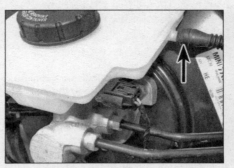
3.7 Disconnect the clutch master cylinder fluid supply hose (arrowed)

8 Lever out the retaining clip a little, and then disconnect the hydraulic pipe from the slave cylinder **(see illustration)**. Suitably plug or cap the pipe end to prevent further fluid loss and dirt entry. **Note:** *Some models may have two retaining clips securing the hydraulic pipe.*
9 Undo the two retaining bolts and remove the cylinder from the transmission housing **(see illustration)**.

Refitting

10 Refitting the slave cylinder is the reverse sequence to removal, bearing in mind the following points.
  a) *Apply a little Molykote BR2 Plus (MINI part no. 83 19 9 407 854) grease to the end of the slave cylinder pushrod.*
  b) *On completion, bleed the clutch hydraulic system as described in Section 2.*

4.8 Lever out the clip (arrowed) and disconnect the fluid pipe

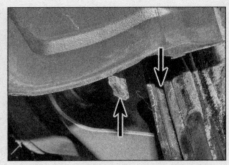
3.5b Note hose the scuttle trim panel engages with the extrusion at the base of the windscreen (arrowed)

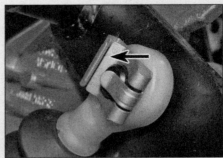
3.8 Lever up the edge (arrowed) and slide the retaining clip from the pin

5 Clutch pedal – removal and refitting

Removal

1 Remove the steering column as described in Chapter 10.
2 Lift up the edge, slide off the clip securing the master cylinder pushrod to the pedal **(see illustration 3.8)**.
3 Undo the 2 retaining nuts and move the master cylinder to the left-hand side, away from the pedal. There's no need to disconnect the fluid pipes.
4 Carefully release the securing clip and remove the clutch pedal from the pedal bracket and recover the bush from the pedal pivot. Disengage the return spring as the pedal is withdrawn.

4.9 Clutch slave cylinder retaining nuts (arrowed)

6.3 Remove the clutch cover retaining bolts (arrowed)

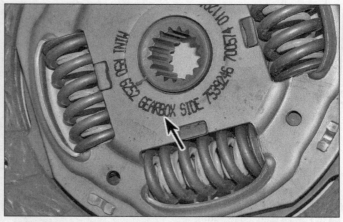

6.13a The clutch friction plate may be marked 'flywheel side' or 'Getriebeseite' (meaning transmission side)

5 Check the condition of the pedal and pivot bush assembly and renew any components as necessary.

Refitting

6 Lubricate the pedal pivot bolt with multipurpose grease, then locate the pedal in the pivot, and secure it with the retaining clip.
7 The remainder of refitting is a reversal of removal.

---

6 Clutch assembly –
removal, inspection and refitting

⚠️ **Warning: Dust created by clutch wear and deposited on the clutch components may contain asbestos, which is a health hazard. DON'T blow it out with compressed air, nor inhale any of it. DO NOT use petrol or petroleum-based solvents to clean off the dust. Brake system cleaner or methylated spirit should be used to flush the dust into a suitable receptacle. After the clutch components are wiped clean with rags, dispose of the contaminated rags and cleaner in a sealed, marked container.**

Note: *Although most friction materials no longer contain asbestos, it is safest to assume that some still do, and to take precautions accordingly.*

6.13b Install the friction disc with the spring hub on the gearbox side

Removal

1 Unless the complete engine/transmission unit is to be removed from the car and separated for major overhaul (see Chapter 2D), the clutch can be reached by removing the transmission as described in Chapter 7A.
2 Once the transmission is separated from the engine, check if there are any marks identifying the relation of the clutch pressure plate to the flywheel. If not, make your own marks using a dab of paint or a scriber. These marks will be used if the original plate is installed, and will help to maintain the balance of the unit. A new plate may be installed in any position allowed by the locating dowels.

Models without a self-adjusting clutch

3 Unscrew the six clutch pressure plate retaining bolts, working in a diagonal sequence, and loosening the bolts only a turn at a time **(see illustration)**. If necessary, the flywheel may be held stationary using a wide-bladed screwdriver, inserted in the teeth of the starter ring gear and resting against part of the cylinder block. The manufacturer states that new pressure plate bolts must be used when installing.
4 Ease the clutch pressure plate off its locating dowels. Be prepared to catch the clutch friction disc, which will drop out as the plate is removed. Note which way the disc is installed.

Models with a self-adjusting clutch

5 If a new pressure plate is to be installed, follow paragraphs 3 and 4 and remove it.
6 If the original pressure plate is to be used, Install MINI special tool no. 21-2-170 (or equivalent) with the arms of the tool engaged with the cutouts in the side of the clutch cover (near where the diaphragm spring is riveted to the clutch cover). Tighten the knob of the tool until the diaphragm spring is depressed about 6.0 mm.
7 Install special tool no. 21-0-010 into the cutout near the curved portion of the cover to relieve the adjustment function.

Inspection

8 Ordinarily, when a problem occurs in the clutch, it can be attributed to wear of the clutch driven plate assembly (clutch disc). However, all components should be inspected at this time. **Note:** *If the clutch components are contaminated with oil, there will be shiny, black glazed spots on the clutch disc lining, which will cause the clutch to slip. Replacing clutch components won't completely solve the problem - be sure to check the crankshaft rear oil seal and the transmission input shaft seal for leaks. If it looks like a seal is leaking, be sure to install a new one to avoid the same problem with the new clutch. Check with your MINI dealer or specialist regarding seal availability.*
9 Check the lining on the clutch disc. There should be at least the minimum amount of lining, listed in this Chapter's Specifications, above the rivet heads. Check for loose rivets, distortion, cracks, broken springs and other obvious damage. As mentioned above, ordinarily the clutch disc is routinely replaced, so if you're in doubt about its condition, replace it.
10 Check the machined surfaces and the diaphragm spring fingers of the pressure plate. If the surface is grooved or otherwise damaged, replace the pressure plate. Also check for obvious damage, distortion, cracks, etc. Light glazing can be removed with medium-grit emery cloth.
11 The release bearing should also be replaced along with the clutch disc (see Section 7).

Refitting

12 Clean the machined surfaces of the flywheel and pressure plate with brake cleaner. It's important that no oil or grease is on these surfaces or the lining of the clutch disc. Handle the parts only with clean hands.
13 Position the clutch disc and pressure plate against the flywheel with the clutch held in place with an alignment tool. Make sure it's installed properly (most replacement clutch plates will be marked "flywheel side" or something similar - if it's not marked, install the clutch disc with the damper springs toward the transmission) **(see illustrations)**.

14 Centre the clutch disc using the type of tool that clamps the friction disc to the clutch pressure plate/cover, as there is no suitable recess in the end of the crankshaft to enable the use of the rod-and-spacer type alignment tool, unless special MINI tools (or equivalent) are available: Tool no. 21 2 290 (Petrol non-turbo), 21 6 110 (Petrol turbo and W16 diesel) or 21 0 00 (N47 diesel).

15 If a new self-adjusting clutch is being installed, install the special tools as described in paragraph 6, but turn the knob on the tool until the diaphragm spring fingers are depressed 10 to 12 mm, but no further.

16 Place the clutch pressure plate over the dowels (see illustration). Install the new retaining bolts, and tighten them finger-tight so that the friction disc is gripped lightly, but can still be moved.

17 Check that the friction disc is still aligned in relation to the pressure plate/cover assembly.

18 Once the clutch is aligned, progressively tighten the cover bolts in a diagonal sequence to the torque listed in this Chapter's Specifications. On models with a self-adjusting clutch, remove the special tools.

19 Ensure that the input shaft splines and friction disc splines are clean. Apply a thin smear of clutch assembly grease to the input shaft splines - do not apply excessively, however, or it may end up on the friction disc, causing the new clutch to slip.

20 Refit the transmission to the engine.

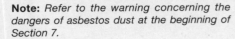

7 Clutch release mechanism – removal, inspection and refitting

Note: *Refer to the warning concerning the dangers of asbestos dust at the beginning of Section 7.*

Removal

1 Remove the transmission as described in Chapter 7A.

6.16 Ensure the clutch cover locates over the dowels in the flywheel

7.3 Unclip the release bearing from the lever

2 Push the end of the retaining clip back through the release lever, and manoeuver the lever and bearing assembly over the end of the input shaft (see illustration).

3 Turn the lever over, and release the clips securing the release bearing to the lever (see illustration).

Inspection

4 Check the bearing for smoothness of operation, and replace it if there is any sign of harshness or roughness as the bearing is spun. Do not attempt to disassemble, clean or lubricate the bearing.

7.2 Push the end of the clip back through the lever

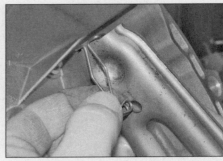

7.7 Fit the retaining clip to the rear of the release lever

5 It is worth replacing the release bearing as a matter of course, unless it is known to be in perfect condition.

Refitting

6 Fit the new release bearing to the lever, ensuring the retaining clips engage fully.

7 Pull the lever retaining clip from the mounting on the transmission casing, and fit it to the rear of the lever (see illustration).

8 Position the lever/bearing assembly over the input shaft, and push the lever retaining clip over the ballstud on the transmission.

9 The remainder of refitting is the reverse of removal.

Chapter 7 Part A:
Manual transmission

Contents

Section number   **Section number**

Degrees of difficulty

Easy, suitable for novice with little experience 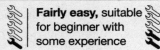	Fairly easy, suitable for beginner with some experience	Fairly difficult, suitable for competent DIY mechanic	Difficult, suitable for experienced DIY mechanic	Very difficult, suitable for expert DIY or professional

Specifications

General

Type	Manual, six forward speeds and reverse. Synchromesh on all forward speeds
Designation:	
N12, N16 petrol engines.	Getrag GS6–55BG
N14, N16, N18 petrol engines	Getrag GS6–53BG
Diesel engines	Getrag GS6–53DG
Capacity.	1.7 litres
Recommended oil type	See *Lubricants and fluids* on page 0•16

Torque wrench settings

	Nm	lbf ft
Front bumper carrier bolts	20	15
Front subframe bolts:		
M12.	100	74
M10 x 60 mm:*		
Stage 1	59	43
Stage 2	Angle-tighten a further 90°	
Engine-to-transmission fixing bolts:		
M12.	66	49
M10 x 1.5	38	27
M10 x 1.75	55	41
M8.	20	15
Neutral switch.	5	3
Oil drain plug	43	32
Oil filler/level plug	43	32
Reversing light switch	16	12
Roadwheel bolts.	140	103
Steering column pinch bolt*	28	20

*Do not re-use

---

1 General information

The transmission is contained in a cast-aluminium alloy casing bolted to the engine's left-hand end, and consists of the gearbox and final drive differential – often called a transaxle.

Drive is transmitted from the crankshaft via the clutch to the input shaft, which has a splined extension to accept the clutch friction plate, and rotates in sealed ball-bearings. From the input shaft, drive is transmitted to the output shaft, which rotates in a roller bearing at its right-hand end, and a sealed ball-bearing at its left-hand end. From the output shaft, the drive is transmitted to the differential crownwheel, which rotates with the differential case and planetary gears, thus driving the sun gears and driveshafts. The rotation of the planetary gears on their shaft allows the inner roadwheel to rotate at a

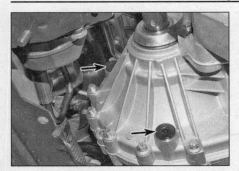

2.3 Transmission oil filler/level and drain plugs (arrowed)

slower speed than the outer roadwheel when the car is cornering.

The input and output shafts are arranged side by side, parallel to the crankshaft and driveshafts, so that their gear pinion teeth are in constant mesh. In the neutral position, the output shaft gear pinions rotate freely, so that drive cannot be transmitted to the crownwheel.

Gear selection is via a floor-mounted lever and cable mechanism. The selector/ gearchange cables causes the appropriate selector fork to move its respective synchro-sleeve along the shaft, to lock the gear pinion to the synchro-hub. Since the synchro-hubs are splined to the output shaft, this locks the pinion to the shaft, so that drive can be transmitted. To ensure that gear-changing can be made quickly and quietly, a synchromesh system is fitted to all forward gears, consisting

of baulk rings and spring-loaded fingers, as well as the gear pinions and synchro-hubs. The synchromesh cones are formed on the mating faces of the baulk rings and gear pinions.

2 Manual transmission – draining and refilling

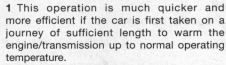

1 This operation is much quicker and more efficient if the car is first taken on a journey of sufficient length to warm the engine/transmission up to normal operating temperature.

2 Park the car on level ground, switch off the ignition and apply the handbrake firmly. For improved access, jack up the front of the car and support it securely on axle stands (see *Jacking and vehicle support*). Note that the car must be level to ensure accuracy when refilling and checking the oil level. Undo the fasteners and remove the engine undershield.

3 Wipe clean the area around the filler/level plug, which is situated above the right-hand driveshaft. Unscrew the filler/level plug from the transmission **(see illustration)**.

4 Position a suitable container under the drain plug and unscrew the plug.

5 Allow the oil to drain completely into the container. If the oil is hot, take precautions against scalding. Clean both the filler/level and the drain plugs.

6 When the oil has finished draining, clean

the drain plug threads and those of the transmission casing, and refit the drain plug, tightening it to the specified torque wrench setting.

7 Refilling the transmission is an extremely awkward operation. Above all, allow plenty of time for the oil level to settle properly before checking it. Note that the car must be parked on flat level ground when checking the oil level.

8 Refill the transmission carefully until oil begins to run out of the filler plug hole, then refit the filler/level plug and tighten it to the specified torque. Take the car on a short journey so that the new oil is distributed fully around the transmission components, then check the level again on your return.

3 Gearchange lever and cables – removal and refitting

1 Firmly apply the handbrake, then jack up the front of the vehicle and support it on axle stands (see *Jacking and vehicle support*).

2 Unclip the gearchange lever gaiter from the centre console **(see illustration)**.

3 Pull the gearchange lever knob sharply upwards and remove it along with the gaiter **(see illustration)**. Do not twist the knob to remove it.

4 Remove the exhaust system as described in Chapter 4A.

5 Undo the nuts and remove the heat shield below the gearchange lever housing.

6 On non-turbo models, remove the air filter housing and fresh air duct (Chapter 4A). On petrol turbo, and diesel models, remove the charge air ducts from above the transmission. To improve access, remove the engine management ECM as described in Chapter 4A, then undo the retaining bolts and move the relay/fusebox and ECM bracket to one side.

7 On all models, slide the retaining clips rearwards (where fitted), then use a pair of thin-nosed pliers to prise the cable ball joints from the levers on the transmission **(see illustrations)**.

8 Release the retaining clips and prise the

3.2 Prise up the gaiter retaining ring

3.3 Pull the gearknob and gaiter sharply upwards

3.7a Lever out the side of the clip...

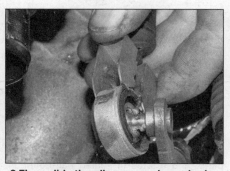

3.7b ...slide the clip rearwards, and prise the balljoint from the lever stud

3.7c On some models, the balljoint just prises from the lever stud

3.8 Spread apart the plastic clips, and pull the cable outer from the bracket

3.9a Undo the screws (arrowed)...

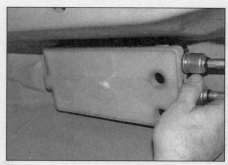

3.9b ...pull the housing rearwards, then lower the front edge...

outer cables upwards from the bracket **(see illustration)**.

9 Working underneath the vehicle, detach the cable grommets from the brackets, undo the four Torx screws, then pull the lever housing rearwards slightly, lower the front edge and manoeuvre the housing from position, complete with cables **(see illustrations)**. Note that the bolts are captive in the housing and will not fully release.

10 With the assembly on a workbench, carefully release the clips securing the cover to the base of the lever housing **(see illustration)**.

11 Lever the cable balljoints from the levers, then slide out the locking plates and pull the cables from the housing **(see illustrations)**.

12 The gearchange lever is integral with the housing, and is not available separately.

Refitting

13 Refitting is a reversal of the removal procedure, noting the following points:
  a) *Apply grease to the ball joints before refitting.*
  b) *No adjustment of the gear change cables is possible.*

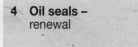

4 Oil seals –
  renewal

Driveshaft oil seals

1 Remove the appropriate driveshaft as described in Chapter 8.

2 Carefully prise the oil seal out of the transmission, using a large flat-bladed screwdriver **(see illustration)**.

3 Remove all traces of dirt from the area around the oil seal aperture. Fit the new seal into its aperture, and drive it squarely into position using a suitable tubular drift (such as a socket) which bears only on the hard outer edge of the seal, until it abuts its locating shoulder **(see illustration)**.

4 Refit the driveshaft as described in Chapter 8.

Input shaft oil seal

5 Remove the transmission as described in Section 6, and the clutch release mechanism as described in Chapter 6.

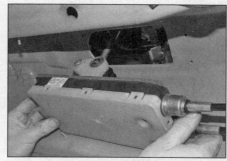

3.9c ...and manoeuvre it from place

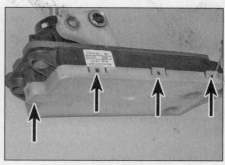

3.10 Release the clips (arrowed) and remove the base

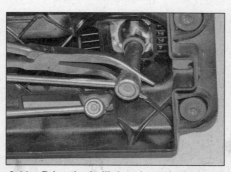

3.11a Prise the balljoints from the base of the levers

3.11b Prise up the clip and pull the cable from the housing

6 Undo the bolts securing the clutch release bearing guide sleeve in position, and slide the guide off the input shaft **(see illustration)**.

7 Screw a slide hammer with a self-tapping screws adapter end into the seal, then

operate the slide hammer to extract the seal. Alternatively, a self-tapping screw can be threaded into the seal and a prybar with a crows-foot end can be used to prise against the screw to dislodge the seal. **Note:** *Either*

4.2 Carefully prise the driveshaft oil seal from the transmission casing

4.3 Drive the new seal into place using a seal driver or large socket

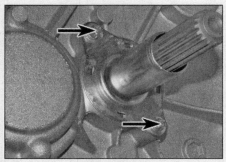

4.6 Undo the bolts (arrowed) and remove the clutch release bearing guide sleeve

method might require drilling a small pilot into the casing of the seal, to allow the screw to thread into the seal case. If so, ensure all metal fragments are cleaned up.

8 Before fitting a new guide seal, check the input shaft's seal rubbing surface for signs of burrs, scratches or other damage, which may have caused the seal to fail in the first place. It may be possible to polish away minor faults of this sort using fine abrasive paper; however, more serious defects will require the renewal of the input shaft.

9 Lubricate the lips of the new seal with clean transmission oil, then use a tubular spacer that bears only on the hard outer edge of the seal, and drive the seal into position in the casing.

10 Slide the guide sleeve over the input shaft and into position.

11 Apply a little thread locking compound to the screws and tighten them securely.

12 The remainder of refitting is a reversal of removal.

5.4 The reversing light switch is on the rear of the lever housing (arrowed)

5.7 Disconnect the neutral light switch wiring plug (arrowed)

5 Reversing light and neutral switches – testing, removal and refitting

Reversing light switch

Testing

1 The reversing light circuit is controlled by a plunger-type switch fitted to the top the transmission casing. If a fault develops, first ensure that the circuit fuse has not blown.

2 To test the switch, disconnect the wiring connector, and use a multimeter (set to the resistance function) or a battery-and-bulb test circuit to check that there is continuity between the switch terminals only when reverse gear is selected. If this is not the case, and there are no obvious breaks or other damage to the wires, the switch is faulty, and must be renewed.

Removal

3 Where necessary, to improve access to the switch, remove the air cleaner housing intake duct assembly (as applicable – see the relevant part of Chapter 4).

4 Disconnect the wiring connector, then unscrew the switch from the transmission casing along with its sealing washer – where fitted **(see illustration)**.

Refitting

5 Fit a new sealing washer to the switch, then screw it back into position in the top of the transmission housing and tighten it to the

5.6 Undo the bolt (arrowed) and move the coolant expansion tank to one side

6.7 Fuse/relay panel retaining bolts (arrowed)

specified torque setting. Refit the wiring plug, and test the operation of the circuit. Refit any components removed for access.

Neutral switch

Removal

6 Undo the retaining bolt and move the coolant expansion tank to one side **(see illustration)**. There's no need to drain the coolant.

7 Disconnect the neutral switch wiring plug **(see illustration)**.

8 Undo the 2 retaining bolts and remove the switch.

9 Refitting is a reversal of removal, tightening the retaining bolts to the specified torque. **Note:** *If a new neutral switch has been fitted, the ECM must 're-learn' the position of the switch. This must be carried out using MINI diagnostic equipment. Entrust this task to a MINI dealer or suitably equipped repairer. Until this is carried out, the Stop-Start system may not function correctly.*

6 Manual transmission – removal and refitting

Removal

1 Disconnect the cable from the negative terminal of the battery as described in Chapter 5A.

2 Remove the air cleaner housing as described in Chapter 4A or Chapter 4B.

3 On Cooper S models, remove the charge air ducts from above the transmission.

4 On diesel models, release the clamps, undo the retaining bolts and remove the charge air ducts to, and from the intercooler as described in Chapter 4B.

5 Install an engine support fixture to the engine, with the chain connected to the engine on the transmission end. If no lifting hook is present, you'll either have to obtain or fabricate one (tool no. 11–8–260 or equivalent) that you can bolt to the left end of the cylinder head. Tighten the support fixture chain screw/nut to remove all slack in the chain.

6 Remove the engine management ECM as described in Chapter 4A or Chapter 4B.

7 Disconnect the battery cable from the underbonnet fuse/relay panel, then remove the fuse/relay panel bolts and move the panel out of the way **(see illustration)**.

8 Remove the transmission-to-inner wing support bracket, followed by the transmission mounting (see Chapter 2A).

9 Detach the gearchange cables from the levers on the transmission, then unbolt the cable bracket (see Section 3).

10 Loosen, but don't remove, the centre nut of the right-side engine mounting **(see illustrations)**.

11 Loosen the front wheel bolts. Chock the rear wheels, then firmly apply the parking brake. Raise the front of the vehicle and securely

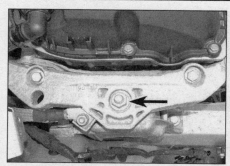

6.10a Right-hand engine mounting centre nut (arrowed) – petrol models...

6.10b ...and diesel models (arrowed)

6.16a Remove the steering column pinch bolt (arrowed)

6.16b Disconnect the wiring plugs (arrowed) from the Electronic Power Steering (EPS) control unit

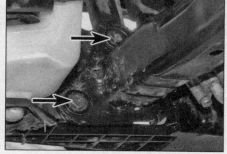

6.16c Remove the subframe mounting bolts each side at the front (arrowed)...

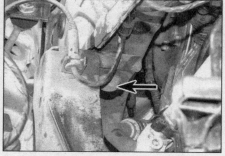

6.16d ...the bolt (arrowed) each side...

support it on axle stands (see *Jacking and vehicle support*). Remove both front wheels, and wheelarch liners (see Chapter 11).

12 Drain the transmission oil as described in Section 2, then refit the drain plug and tighten it to the specified torque.

13 Remove both driveshafts (see Chapter 8).

14 Tighten the screw/nut on the support fixture to raise the engine approximately 10 mm. Remove the lower engine stabiliser link rod/ mounting arm (see Chapter 2A, Chapter 2B or Chapter 2C).

15 Remove the exhaust system (see Chapter 4A or Chapter 4B), and on W16 diesel engines, also remove the catalytic converter.

16 The front subframe must be removed as follows:

a) *Remove the front bumper (see Chapter 11).*

b) *Disconnect the track-rod ends and control arms from the hub carriers (see Chapter 10).*

c) *Disconnect the link rods from the anti-roll bar (see Chapter 10).*

d) *Disconnect the wiring plugs from the left-hand side ride height sensor (where fitted) (Chapter 10).*

e) *Remove the pinch-bolt, slide the steering column joint rearwards, and detach it from the steering gear pinion shaft (see illustration). Discard the pinch bolt – a new one must be fitted. Note that the universal joint will only fit correctly on the pinion in one position.*

f) *Disconnect the wiring plugs from the control unit on the steering rack (see illustration). To improve access to the control unit, remove the air cleaner assembly as described in Chapter 4A or Chapter 4B.*

g) *Ensure all wiring etc. is released from any clips on the subframe.*

h) *Place a floor jack under the subframe to support it.*

i) *Remove the bolts securing the control arm brackets to the vehicle body.*

j) *Remove the bolts securing the subframe to the vehicle body, and lower the subframe with the floor jack, ensuring the steering rack is not damaged, and the pipes below the EPS unit are not damaged by the bulkhead as the assembly is lowered (see illustrations). Enlist the help of an assistant.*

17 Remove the clutch release cylinder from the transmission (see Chapter 6). There is no need to disconnect the fluid line – free the line from its retaining clips and position the cylinder to one side.

18 On N47 diesel models, undo the retaining bolts securing the fuel feed and return pipes to the front and rear of the engine sump, then disconnect the quick-release couplings under the transmission **(see illustration)**. Be prepared for fuel spillage. Plug/cover the openings to prevent contamination.

6.16e ...the bolt (arrowed) at the rear of the lower arms each side...

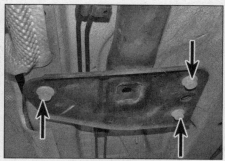

6.16f ...and the 3 bolts (arrowed) at the rear of the subframe each side

6.18 Depress the release buttons (arrowed) and disconnect the fuel hoses

6.20a Prise out the pin (arrowed) and remove the cover…

6.20b …or undo the bolt (arrowed) as applicable

19 On W16 diesel models, unscrew the catalytic converter mounting stud below the oil filter housing.

20 Where fitted, prise out the pin/undo the bolt and remove the small inspection cover between the bell housing and the right-hand driveshaft aperture in the transmission housing **(see illustrations)**.

21 Remove the starter motor as described in Chapter 5A.

22 Noting their locations, disconnect all electrical connectors from the transaxle. Note the harness routing and move the harness to one side.

23 Support the transmission with a jack – preferably one made for this purpose. **Note:** *Transmission jack head adapters are available that replace the round head on a floor jack.* Noting their installed locations, remove the bolts securing the transmission to the engine.

24 Using the jack, and with the help of an assistant, slide the transmission from the engine. **Note:** *It may be necessary to lower the engine, using the support fixture, to facilitate transmission removal.*

Refitting

25 The transmission is refitted by a reversal of the removal procedure, bearing in mind the following points:

a) *Prior to refitting, check the clutch assembly and release mechanism components (see Chapter 6). Do not lubricate the input shaft splines with oil or grease.*

b) *Ensure that the locating dowels are correctly positioned prior to installation.*

c) *Tighten all nuts and bolts to the specified torque (where given).*

d) *Renew the driveshaft oil seals, then refit the driveshafts (see Chapter 8).*

e) *Refit the slave cylinder (see Chapter 6).*

f) *On completion, refill the transmission with the specified type and quantity of lubricant, as described in the relevant part of this Chapter.*

7 Manual transmission overhaul – general information

1 Overhauling a manual transmission is a difficult and involved job for the DIY home mechanic. In addition to dismantling and reassembling many small parts, clearances must be precisely measured and, if necessary, changed by selecting shims and spacers. Internal transmission components are also often difficult to obtain, and in many instances, extremely expensive. Because of this, if the transmission develops a fault or becomes noisy, the best course of action is to have the unit overhauled by a specialist repairer, or to obtain an exchange reconditioned unit.

2 Nevertheless, it is not impossible for the more experienced mechanic to overhaul the transmission, provided the special tools are available, and the job is done in a deliberate step-by-step manner, so that nothing is overlooked.

3 The tools necessary for an overhaul include internal and external circlip pliers, bearing pullers, a slide hammer, a set of pin punches, a dial test indicator, and possibly a hydraulic press. In addition, a large, sturdy workbench and a vice will be required.

4 During dismantling of the transmission, make careful notes of how each component is fitted, to make reassembly easier and more accurate.

5 Before dismantling the transmission, it will help if you have some idea what area is malfunctioning. Certain problems can be closely related to specific areas in the transmission, which can make component examination and replacement easier. Refer to the *Fault Finding* Section for more information.

Chapter 7 Part B:
Automatic transmission

Contents

Degrees of difficulty

Easy, suitable for novice with little experience | **Fairly easy,** suitable for beginner with some experience | **Fairly difficult,** suitable for competent DIY mechanic | **Difficult,** suitable for experienced DIY mechanic | **Very difficult,** suitable for expert DIY or professional

Specifications

General
Type . . . . 6-forward speeds, one reverse, with electronic control.
Designation . . . . Aisin GA6F21 WA

Lubrication
Capacity:
  Refilling after draining. . . . . 4.5 litres
  From dry . . . . 6.0 litres
Recommended fluid. . . . . See *Lubricants and fluids* on page 0•16

Torque wrench settings

	Nm	lbf ft
Engine-to-transmission fixing bolts:		
M12.	66	49
M10.	38	28
M8.	19	15
Fluid cooler centre bolt.	35	26
Fluid drain plug.	25	18
Fluid filler plug.	25	18
Gear position switch:		
Bolt M6.	8	6
Nut M8.	10	7
Roadwheel bolts.	140	103
Torque converter-to-driveplate nuts:		
All except W16 diesel models.	53	40
W16 diesel models.	45	33

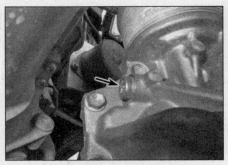

2.3 Transmission filler plug (arrowed)

2.4 Transmission inspection plug (arrowed)

1 General information

1 Certain models were offered with the option of a 6-speed electronically-controlled automatic transmission, consisting of a torque converter, an epicyclic geartrain, and hydraulically-operated clutches and brakes. The unit is controlled by the electronic control unit (ECU) via the electrically-operated solenoid valves in the hydraulic block within the transmission unit. The gearchanges can be left completely automatic, or changed using the selector lever or steering wheel controls in Steptronic mode.

2 The torque converter provides a fluid coupling between the engine and transmission, which acts as an automatic clutch, and also provides a degree of torque multiplication when accelerating.

3 The epicyclic geartrain provides either of the four forward or one reverse gear ratios, according to which of its component parts are held stationary or allowed to turn. The components of the geartrain are held or released by brakes and clutches, which are controlled by the ECU via the electrically-operated solenoid valves in the hydraulic unit. A fluid pump within the transmission provides the necessary hydraulic pressure to operate the brakes and clutches.

4 Driver control of the transmission is by a floor mounted selector lever of steering wheel 'paddle' controls (where applicable). The 'drive' position D provides automatic changing

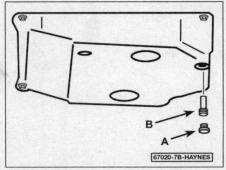

2.16 Transmission inspection plug (A) and fluid overflow tube (B)

throughout the range of all six gear ratios, and is the one to select for normal driving. An automatic kickdown facility shifts the transmission down a gear if the accelerator pedal is fully depressed.

5 On some models, the selector lever is equipped with a shift-lock function. This prevents the selector lever being moved from the P position unless the brake pedal is depressed.

6 When the selector lever is moved to the M/S position, each of the six ratios can be selected sequentially, by moving the lever forwards/backwards, or operating the 'paddle' controls on the steering wheel.

7 Due to the complexity of the automatic transmission, any repair or overhaul work must be left to a MINI dealer with the necessary special equipment for fault diagnosis and repair. The contents of the following Sections are therefore confined to supplying general information, and any service information and instructions that can be used by the owner.

Note: *The automatic transmission unit is of the 'auto-adaptive' type. This means that it takes into account your driving style and modifies the transmission shift points to provide optimum performance and economy to suit. When the battery is disconnected, the transmission will lose its memory and will resort to one of its many base shift programs. The transmission will then relearn the optimum shift points when the vehicle is driven a few miles. During these first few miles of driving, there maybe a noticeable difference in performance whilst the transmission adapts to your individual style.*

2 Automatic transmission fluid – check and renewal

Note: *The following fluid replacement procedures do not include replacing the fluid that remains in the torque converter. For a complete fluid change, inquire at a dealer service department or other properly equipped repair shop for a transaxle fluid flush/replacement.*

Fluid level check

Caution: *To ensure proper refilling/obtaining proper fluid level, a scan tool capable of measuring transmission fluid temperature is required.*

1 Raise the vehicle and support it securely on axle stands (see *Jacking and vehicle support*). **Note:** *The front AND rear of the vehicle must be raised an equal amount.*

2 Remove the engine undershield, then place a drain pan underneath the transmission.

3 Use a Torx T55 bit and remove the filler plug from the bulkhead side of the transmission case **(see illustration)**. Access is limited.

4 Remove the inspection plug from the transmission fluid pan **(see illustration)**.

5 Connect a scan tool to the EOBD diagnostic connector (see Chapter 4A or Chapter 4B).

6 Using a fluid pump from below, or a hose and funnel from above, add the proper type of fluid (see *Lubricants and fluids*) to the filler hole until fluid flows from the inspection hole in the fluid pan.

7 Start the engine and allow it to idle. A little fluid should flow from the inspection hole. If not, add some until it does.

8 Depress the brake pedal and move the selector lever from Park to Drive.

9 Repeat paragraph 8, then return the selector lever to Park.

10 Monitor the transmission fluid temperature with the scan tool. When the temperature reaches 35 to 45°C, check to see if any fluid is flowing from the inspection plug hole. If not, add some until it does.

11 Wait until the fluid stops flowing, then refit the inspection plug (with a new sealing washer), tightening it to the torque listed in this Chapter's Specifications.

Renewal

Note: *Although not required for a routine fluid change, there is a strainer in the transmission that can be removed and cleaned, or replaced. To do so requires suspending the engine/transmission assembly from above and lowering the subframe, then removing the fluid pan and strainer.*

12 Raise the vehicle and support it securely on axle stands (see *Jacking and vehicle support*). **Note:** *The front AND rear of the vehicle must be raised an equal amount.*

13 Remove the engine undershield, then place a drain pan underneath the transmission.

14 Use a Torx T55 bit and remove the filler plug from the bulkhead side of the transmission case **(see illustration 2.3)**. Access is limited.

15 Remove the inspection plug from the transmission fluid pan **(see illustration 2.4)**.

16 Unscrew the fluid overflow tube from the fluid pan **(see illustration)** and allow the fluid to drain.

17 Refit the overflow tube and tighten it securely.

18 Using a fluid pump from below, or a hose and funnel from above, add the proper type of fluid (see *Lubricants and fluids*) to the filler hole until fluid flows from the inspection hole in the fluid pan.

19 Connect a scan tool to the EOBD diagnostic connector (see Chapter 4A or Chapter 4B).

20 Proceed as described in paragraphs 7 to 11 of this Section.

3 Selector cable – adjustment

1 To gain access to the transmission end of the selector cable, remove the air cleaner housing and intake ducts above the transmission (see Chapter 4A or Chapter 4B).
2 Position the selector lever firmly against its detent in the P (park) position.
3 Slacken the clamping nut securing the end of the selector cable at the transmission lever end (see illustration).
4 Rotate the lever on the stop of the transmission fully anti-clockwise, and firmly tighten the clamp nut.
5 Check the operation of the selector lever before refitting the air cleaner and ducting.

4 Selector lever and cable – removal and refitting

Removal

1 Remove the centre console as described in Chapter 11.
2 Remove the air cleaner and intake ducts above the transmission as described in Chapter 4A or Chapter 4B.
3 Remove the rear section of the exhaust system as described in Chapter 4A or Chapter 4B.
4 Undo the fasteners and remove the heat shield below the selector lever housing.
5 Unclip the selector cable from any grommets/bracket on the vehicle underside.
6 Working at the transmission end, pull the outer cable retaining sleeve rearwards and detach the outer cable from the bracket on the transmission (see illustration).
7 Slacken the clamp nut and pull the inner cable from the lever on the transmission. Release the cable from any retaining clips on the transmission.
8 Undo the 4 bolts securing the selector lever housing to the underside of the vehicle.
9 Pull the selector housing rearwards and lower it a little. Disconnect the wiring plug from the upper side of the housing as it's lowered from place.

4.6 Twist the cable outer casing to release it from the bracket

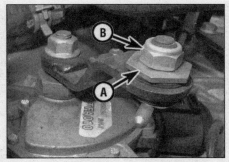

3.3 Hold the clamping sleeve (A) and unscrew the locknut (B)

10 Note its routing, and manoeuvre the selector lever housing and cable assembly from under the vehicle. Note that the cable is integral with the housing, and cannot be renewed separately.

Refitting

11 Refitting is the reverse of removal, adjust the cable as described in Section 3.

5 Oil seals – renewal

Driveshaft oil seals

1 Remove the appropriate driveshaft as described in Chapter 8.
2 Note its fitted depth, then carefully punch two small holes opposite each other into the seal. Screw a self-tapping screw into each hole and pull on the screws to extract the seal.
3 Remove all traces of dirt from the area around the oil seal aperture, then apply a smear of clean transmission fluid to the sealing lip of the new oil seal. Drive the seal squarely into position using a suitable tubular drift (such as a socket), which bears only on the hard outer edge of the seal.
4 Refit the driveshaft as described in Chapter 8.

Selector shaft oil seal

5 Remove the gear position switch as described in Section 7.
6 Screw a seal removing tool (MINI tool no. 24 4 280) into the seal, and pull the seal from the housing.
7 Apply a little clean transmission fluid to the sealing lip, then drive the new seal into place, using a suitable tubular spacer, or MINI tool no. 24 4 290.
8 Refit the gear position switch as described in Section 7.

Torque converter oil seal

9 Remove the transmission unit as described in Section 8.
10 Carefully slide the torque converter off the transmission shaft whilst being prepared for fluid spillage.

11 Note the correct fitted position of the seal in the housing then carefully lever it out of position, taking care not to mark the housing or shaft.
12 Remove all traces of dirt from the area around the oil seal aperture. Apply a little clean transmission fluid to the sealing lips, then ease the new seal into its aperture, ensuring its sealing lip is facing inwards, then press it squarely into position.
13 Engage the torque converter with the transmission shaft splines and slide it into position, taking care not to damage the oil seal.
14 Refit the transmission unit as described in Section 8.

6 Fluid cooler – removal and refitting

Caution: Be careful not to allow dirt into the transmission unit during this procedure.

Removal

1 The fluid cooler is mounted on the rear of the transmission housing. To gain access to the cooler, remove the air cleaner housing and intake ducts above the transmission.
2 Remove all traces of dirt from around the fluid cooler before proceeding.
3 Using a hose clamp or similar, clamp both the fluid cooler coolant hoses to minimise coolant loss during subsequent operations.
4 Release the retaining clips, and disconnect both coolant hoses from the fluid cooler – be prepared for some coolant spillage (see illustration). Wash off any spilt coolant immediately with cold water, and dry the surrounding area before proceeding further.
5 Slacken and remove the fluid cooler centre bolt, and remove the cooler from the transmission. Remove the seals fitted to the cooler, and discard them; new ones must be used on refitting.

Refitting

6 Lubricate the new seals with clean automatic transmission fluid, then fit the new large seal to the underside of the cooler, and the small seal to the retaining bolt aperture.

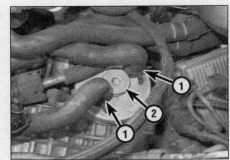

6.4 Transmission fluid cooler details

1 Coolant hoses   2 Mounting bolt

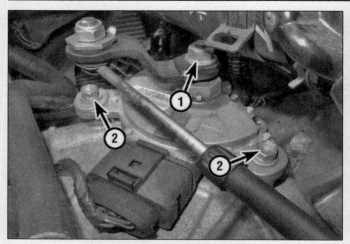

7.9 Gear position switch details

1 *Selector lever nut*   2 *Switch mounting bolts*

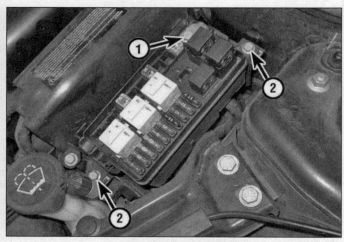

8.5 Fuse/relay panel details

1 *Battery positive cable*
2 *Fuse/relay panel mounting bolts*

7 Locate the fluid cooler on the transmission housing, aligning the cooler lug with the casing, then refit the centre bolt. Ensure the cooler is correctly positioned then tighten the centre bolt to the specified torque setting.

8 Reconnect the coolant hoses to the fluid cooler, and secure them in position with their retaining clips. Remove the hose clamps.

9 The remainder of refitting is a reversal of removal. Check the fluid level as described in Section 2, and top up the cooling system as described in *Weekly checks*.

7 Transmission control system components – removal and refitting

Electronic control unit (ECU)

Note: *The automatic transmission electronic control system relies on accurate communication between the engine management ECU and the automatic transmission ECU. If the ECU is renewed, then both ECUs must be 'initialised'. The initialisation procedure requires access to specialised electronic test equipment and so it is recommended that this operation be entrusted to a suitably-equipped MINI dealer or specialist.*

Removal

1 Disconnect the battery negative terminal as described in Chapter 5A.

2 The ECU is located on the passenger cabin bulkhead, in front of the steering column. Remove the panel beneath the steering column (Chapter 11).

3 Undo the mounting bolt and remove the ECU from the mounting plate.

4 Slide out the locking catch and disconnect the wiring connector from the ECU.

Refitting

5 Refitting is the reverse of removal, ensuring the wiring connector is securely reconnected.

Output shaft speed sensor

6 Removal of the sensor requires the transmission to be partially dismantled and the hydraulic shift unit removed.

Input shaft speed sensor

7 Removal of the sensor requires the transmission to be partially dismantled and the hydraulic shift unit removed.

Gear position switch

Removal

8 Detach the selector cable from the lever on the transmission as described in Section 4.

9 Undo the retaining nut and remove the lever from above the switch (see illustration).

10 Remove the nut, retaining ring and shim from the shaft, then undo the retaining bolts and remove the switch from the housing.

11 Installation is the reverse of removal. Tighten the shift shaft nut to the specified torque.

12 A special tool (MINI tool no. 24 4 270) is available to properly adjust the switch to the neutral position, but with a little patience an alternative method works:

a) *Connect the selector cable, then place the shift lever on the transmission in the Park position (fully anti-clockwise).*

b) *Move the lever to the Reverse position and verify that the reversing lights come on. If they don't, loosen the switch mounting screws and rotate the switch one way or the other until they do, then tighten the bolts. Move the lever to the Neutral position and make sure the back-up lights go off. Also move the shifter back to the Park position and verify that the back-up lights are off.*

c) *With the brake pedal depressed, make sure the engine starts only in Park and Neutral.*

13 When the proper adjustment is achieved, tighten the switch mounting bolts to the torque listed in this Chapter's Specifications.

8 Automatic transmission – removal and refitting

Removal

1 Disconnect the battery negative lead as described in Chapter 5A.

2 Remove the air cleaner housing, and the air ducts above the transmission (see Chapter 4A or Chapter 4B).

3 Install an engine support fixture to the engine, with the chain connected to the engine on the transmission end. If no lifting hook is present, you'll either have to obtain or fabricate one (tool no. 11 8 260 or equivalent) that you can bolt to the left end of the cylinder head. Tighten the support fixture chain screw/nut to remove all slack in the chain.

4 Remove the engine management ECU as described in Chapter 4A or Chapter 4B.

5 Disconnect the battery cable from the underbonnet fuse/relay panel, then remove the fuse/relay panel bolts and move the panel out of the way (see illustration).

6 Unbolt the fuse/relay panel bracket.

7 Detach the coolant hoses from the transmission fluid cooler (see Section 6).

8 Detach the selector cable from the lever on the transmission, then unbolt the cable bracket (see Section 4).

9 Remove the transmission-to-inner wing panel support bracket, followed by the transmission mounting (see Chapter 2A, Chapter 2B or Chapter 2C).

8.10 Slacken the right-hand side engine mounting nut (arrowed)

8.20 Transmission lower bolt locations (arrowed – rear bolts not visible)

10 Loosen, but don't remove, the centre nut of the right-side engine mount (see illustration).

11 Loosen the front wheel bolts. Chock the rear wheels, then firmly apply the parking brake. Loosen both front wheel bolts. Raise the front of the vehicle and securely support it on axle stands (see *Jacking and vehicle support*). Remove both front wheels, and wheelarch liners (see Chapter 11).

12 Drain the transmission fluid as described in Section 2.

13 Remove both driveshafts (see Chapter 8).

14 Remove the starter motor (see Chapter 5A).

15 Tighten the screw/nut on the support fixture to raise the engine approximately 10 mm. Remove the lower engine rear link arm (see Chapter 2A, Chapter 2B or Chapter 2C).

16 Remove the exhaust system (see Chapter 4A or Chapter 4B).

17 The front subframe must now be removed as described in Chapter 7A, Section 6.

18 Noting their locations, disconnect all electrical connectors from the transmission. Note the harness routing and move the harness to one side.

19 Using a socket on the crankshaft pulley bolt, rotate the engine (clockwise while looking at the pulley) until one of the torque converter nuts is visible through the starter opening, then remove the nut. Continue rotating the crankshaft and removing the nuts until all six are removed. When the last nut has been removed, mark the stud and driveplate so balance will be preserved when the transmission is reinstalled.

20 Support the transmission with a jack – preferably one made for this purpose. **Note:** *Transmission jack head adapters are available that replace the round head on a floor jack.* Noting their installed locations, remove the bolts securing the transmission to the engine (see illustration).

21 Using the jack, and with the help of an assistant, slide the transaxle from the engine. **Note:** *It may be necessary to lower the engine, using the support fixture, to facilitate transmission removal.*

Refitting

22 Refitting of the transmission is a reversal of the removal procedure, but note the following points:

a) *As the torque converter is reinstalled, ensure that the drive hub at the center of the torque converter hub engages properly with the recesses in the transmission fluid pump.*

b) *When installing the transmission, make sure the marks on the torque converter and driveplate are in alignment.*

c) *Tighten the transmission-to-engine bolts and torque converter-to-driveplate nuts to the torque listed in this Chapter's Specifications.*

d) *Refill the cooling system (see Chapter 1A or Chapter 1B).*

e) *Refill the transmission (see Section 2).*

f) *Check the selector lever cable adjustment (see Section 4).*

9 Automatic transmission overhaul – general information

In the event of a fault occurring with the transmission, it is first necessary to determine whether it is of an electrical, mechanical or hydraulic nature and, to do this, special test equipment is required. It is therefore essential to have the work carried out by a MINI dealer or specialist if a transmission fault is suspected.

Do not remove the transmission from the car for possible repair before professional fault diagnosis has been carried out, since most tests require the transmission to be in the vehicle.

Chapter 8
Driveshafts

Contents

Degrees of difficulty

Easy, suitable for novice with little experience | **Fairly easy,** suitable for beginner with some experience | **Fairly difficult,** suitable for competent DIY mechanic | **Difficult,** suitable for experienced DIY mechanic | **Very difficult,** suitable for expert DIY or professional

Specifications

Driveshaft grease
Outer constant velocity joint. . . . . 65g max.
Inner tripod joint . . . . 100g max.

Torque wrench settings

	Nm	lbf ft
Anti-roll bar link nut*	56	41
Driveshaft nut*	182	134
Lower arm outer balljoint-to-lower arm*	175	130
Right-hand intermediate shaft bearing housing bolts	38	28
Roadwheel bolts	140	103
Steering track rod end balljoint nut*	65	48

*Do not re-use

2.2 Remove the bolt (arrowed) and withdraw the wheel speed sensor

1 General information

Drive is transmitted from the transmission differential to the front wheels by means of two driveshafts. The right-hand driveshaft is in two sections, and incorporates a support bearing. The inner driveshaft gaiters are made of rubber, and the outer driveshaft gaiters are made of thermoplastic. This gives the outer gaiter a good resistance to external effects, like road chippings and permanent loading when the steering is being turned.

Each driveshaft consists of three main components: the sliding (tripod type) inner joint, the driveshaft itself, and the outer CV (constant velocity) joint. The inner end of the left-hand tripod joint is secured in the differential side gear by the engagement of

2.5 Use an Allen key to counterhold the anti-roll bar link rod balljoint shank

2.9a Remove the rear engine mounting link (arrowed)

2.4a Un-stake the driveshaft nut

a circlip. The inner tripod of the right-hand driveshaft is located in the intermediate shaft tripod housing. The intermediate shaft is held in the transmission by the support bearing, which in turn is supported by a bracket bolted to the rear of the cylinder block. The outer CV joint on both driveshafts is of ball-bearing type, and is secured in the front hub by the driveshaft nut.

2 Driveshafts – removal and refitting

Removal

1 Slacken the relevant front roadwheel bolts, then jack the front of the vehicle up and support it securely on axle stands (see *Jacking and vehicle support*). Remove the relevant roadwheel.

2.8 Carefully prise the driveshaft from the transmission using a large screwdriver of similar (arrowed)

2.9b Right-hand driveshaft intermediate bearing housing retaining bolts (arrowed)

2.4b If necessary, attach a bar to the hub to counterhold the driveshaft nut

2 Undo the bolt and remove the wheel speed sensor from the hub carrier **(see illustration)**. Release the wiring from the bracket on the suspension strut and move to one side.

3 To avoid spillage when the driveshafts are separated from the transmission, drain the transmission fluid, as described in Chapter 7A or Chapter 7B, or use a suitable container to catch the oil/fluid when the driveshaft has been removed.

4 Slacken and remove the nut securing the driveshaft to the hub **(see illustrations)**. Have an assistant depress the brake pedal to prevent the hub from rotating. Discard the nut, a new one must be used.

5 Undo the nut and detach the link rod from the anti-roll bar **(see illustration)**. Use an Allen key in the shank to counterhold the balljoint.

6 Undo the nut and use a universal balljoint separator to detach the steering track rod end balljoint from the hub carrier, then undo the nuts and detach the outer balljoint from the lower arm (see Chapter 10). Discard the nuts – new ones must be fitted.

7 Pull the hub carrier outwards and push the driveshaft outer joint back through the hub at the same time, disengaging it from the hub.

8 On the left-hand driveshaft, use a tyre lever or large flat-bladed screwdriver to prise the inner joint from the transmission **(see illustration)**. Take care not to damage the casing.

9 On the right-hand side driveshaft, remove the lower/rear engine mounting link as described in Chapter 2A, Chapter 2B or Chapter 2C, then undo the 2 bolts securing the driveshaft intermediate bearing housing to the mounting bracket **(see illustrations)**.

10 Carefully pull the right-hand inner driveshaft from the transmission, and manoeuvre it from place.

11 Discard the circlip on the inner end of the left-hand driveshaft – a new one must be fitted **(see illustration)**.

12 Check the condition of the differential oil seals, and if necessary renew them as described in Chapter 7A or Chapter 7B. Check the intermediate bearing. At the time of writing, it would appear that the bearing is not available separately from the driveshaft – check with your Mini dealer or Motor Factor/Specialist.

Refitting

13 Fit a new circlip to the groove on the inner end of the – the 20 mm diameter round circlip is for manual transmission models, and the 25 x 16 mm oval circlip is for automatics.

14 Refit the driveshaft(s) into the transmission. Use a special sleeve to protect the differential oil seal as the driveshaft is inserted. If the sleeve is not used, take great care to avoid damaging the seal. (Installation sleeves are supplied with new oil seals, where required.) Turn the driveshaft until it engages the splines on the differential gears. Make sure the circlip is fully engaged.

15 If refitting the right-hand driveshaft, tighten the bolts securing the support bearing to the bracket on the cylinder block to the specified torque. If removed, refit the power steering pump cooling fan assembly.

16 On either driveshaft, slide the hub carrier/hub assembly over the end of the driveshaft, ensuring the hub splines engage correctly with the splines of the driveshaft.

17 Screw on the driveshaft nut finger-tight.

18 Locate the hub carrier balljoint onto the studs in the control arm and the steering track rod end in the hub carrier, and tighten the new nuts to the specified torque.

19 Apply a little clean oil to the nut/wheel bearing contact surface, then fit the new driveshaft/hub nut, and tighten to the specified torque, whilst an assistant depresses the brake pedal to prevent the hub from rotating. With the nut correctly tightened, use a hammer and punch to 'stake' the nut in position **(see illustration)**.

20 Refit the wheel speed sensor as described in Chapter 9.

21 Fill the transmission with oil or fluid, and check the level as described in the relevant part of Chapter 7A or 7B.

22 Refit the wheel, and lower the vehicle to the ground. Tighten the wheel retaining bolts to the specified torque.

3 Driveshaft inner tripod joint gaiter – renewal

1 Remove the driveshaft, then cut off the gaiter clamps and remove the inner joint housing.

2 Remove the circlip from the end of the shaft, then remove the tripod from the shaft, noting how it's oriented (the flat side faces the end of the shaft). **Note:** *If the tripod is stuck on the shaft, use a three-legged puller to remove it.*

3 Remove the gaiter from the shaft and clean the components.

4 Slide the new small clamp and gaiter onto the shaft, then refit the tripod with the flat side of the spider (centre portion) facing the end of the shaft. Secure the tripod with a new circlip.

5 Fill the housing with the grease supplied in the kit (100g maximum), then install it onto the tripod. Make sure the gaiter sealing area on the housing is clean, then install the

2.11 Renew the circlip at the end of the driveshaft

gaiter over the housing, making sure it seats properly. Install the new large gaiter clamp.

6 Position the joint mid-way through its travel. Ensure that the gaiter is not twisted or distorted, then insert a small screwdriver under the small end of the gaiter. This will allow trapped air to escape.

7 Install the new retaining clamps and tighten them securely **(see illustrations)**.

4 Driveshaft outer CV joint gaiter – renewal

1 Remove the inner CV joint (see Section 3).

2 Cut the clamps from the gaiter, and slide the gaiter off the inner end of the driveshaft. Do not disassemble the outer CV joint.

3 Clean the inner and outer joints. The outer

2.19 Use a hammer and punch to stake the driveshaft nut

joint will be more difficult to clean since it can't be removed, but with an ample supply of solvent or brake system cleaner, and flexing the joint through its range of motion, you should be able to get all of the old grease out. Allow the joint to dry thoroughly (used compressed air, if possible).

4 Slide the new outer gaiter and clamps onto the driveshaft. Fill the gaiter with the grease supplied in the kit (max. 65g). Make sure the outer joint housing is clean where the gaiter fits, then pull the gaiter onto the housing.

5 Make sure the small-diameter end of the gaiter is seated properly in its groove, then insert a small screwdriver under the lip of the gaiter at the housing end to allow any trapped air to escape.

6 Remove the screwdriver, install the retaining clamps in their previously noted positions, and tighten them **(see illustrations)**.

3.7a Tighten the large clamp with thin-nosed pliers...

3.7b ...and the small clamp with boot clamp crimping pliers

4.6a Install the new outer clamp and tighten it with boot clamp crimping pliers...

4.6b ...followed by the inner clamp

5 Driveshafts – inspection and joint renewal

1 If any of the checks described in Chapter 1A or Chapter 1B reveal apparent excessive wear or play in any driveshaft joint, first remove the wheel cover (or centre cover), and check that the driveshaft nut is tightened to the specified torque. Repeat this check on the other side of the vehicle.

2 Road test the vehicle, and listen for a metallic clicking from the front as the vehicle is driven slowly in a circle on full-lock. If a clicking noise is heard, this indicates wear in the outer constant velocity joint, which means that the joint must be renewed; reconditioning is not possible.

3 To renew an outer CV joint, remove the driveshaft as described in Section 2, then separate the joint from the driveshaft with reference to Section 4. In principle, the gaiter can be left on the driveshaft, provided that it is in good condition; in practice, it makes sense to renew the gaiter in any case, having got this far.

4 If vibration, consistent with road speed, is felt through the car when accelerating, there is a possibility of wear in the inner tripod joints.

5 To renew an inner tripod joint, remove the driveshaft as described in Section 2, then separate the joint from the driveshaft with reference to Section 3.

6 Continual noise from the right-hand driveshaft, increasing with road speed, may indicate wear in the support bearing. To renew this bearing, the driveshaft and intermediate shaft must be removed, and the bearing extracted using special tools. Entrust this task to a MINI dealer or suitably equipped specialist.

Chapter 9
Braking system

Contents

Degrees of difficulty

Easy, suitable for novice with little experience	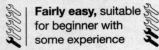	**Fairly easy,** suitable for beginner with some experience		**Fairly difficult,** suitable for competent DIY mechanic		**Difficult,** suitable for experienced DIY mechanic		**Very difficult,** suitable for expert DIY or professional	

Specifications

Front brakes

Type	Ventilated disc, with single-piston sliding caliper
Disc diameter	280, 294 or 316 mm
Disc minimum thickness:	
Drilled discs	20.4 mm
Non-drilled disc	19.6 mm
Maximum disc run-out	0.05 mm
Brake pad friction material minimum	3.7 mm

Rear brakes

Disc diameter	259 or 259 mm
Disc minimum thickness	Cast into the disc outer face
Brake pad friction material minimum thickness	3.7 mm

Torque wrench settings

	Nm	lbf ft
Disc retaining screws*	27	20
DSC yaw rate sensor	8	6
Front brake caliper:		
Guide pin bolts*	35	25
Mounting bracket bolts*	110	81
Handbrake lever	23	17
Hydraulic hose/pipe union nuts	15	11
Master cylinder retaining nuts*	23	17
Rear brake caliper:		
Guide pin bolts*	35	25
Mounting bracket bolts*	65	28
Roadwheel bolts	140	103
Vacuum servo unit mounting nuts*	20	15
Wheel speed sensor retaining bolts	8	6

*Do not reuse.

1 General information

The braking system is of the servo-assisted, dual-circuit hydraulic type. The arrangement of the hydraulic system is such that each circuit operates one front and one rear brake from a tandem master cylinder. Under normal circumstances, both circuits operate in unison. However, in the event of hydraulic failure in one circuit, full braking force will still be available at two wheels.

All models are equipped with disc brakes on all wheels. ABS is fitted as standard (refer to Section 18 for further information on ABS operation).

The disc brakes are actuated by single-piston sliding type calipers, which ensure that equal pressure is applied to each disc pad.

On all models, the handbrake provides an independent mechanical means of rear brake application. All models are fitted with rear brake calipers with an integral handbrake function. The handbrake cable operates a lever on the caliper which forces the piston to press the pad against the disc surface. A self-adjust mechanism is incorporated, to automatically compensate for brake pad wear.

Note: *When servicing any of the system, work carefully and methodically; also observe scrupulous cleanliness when overhauling any of the hydraulic system. Always renew components (in axle sets, where applicable) if in doubt about their condition, and use only genuine MINI replacement parts, or at least those of known good quality. Note the warnings given in 'Safety first!' and at relevant points in this Chapter concerning the dangers of asbestos dust and hydraulic fluid.*

2 Hydraulic system – bleeding

⚠️ *Warning: Hydraulic fluid is poisonous; wash off immediately and thoroughly in the case of skin contact, and seek immediate medical advice if any fluid is swallowed or gets into the eyes. Certain types of hydraulic fluid are inflammable, and may ignite when allowed into contact with hot components; when servicing any hydraulic system, it is safest to assume that the fluid is inflammable, and to take precautions against the risk of fire as though it is petrol that is being handled. Hydraulic fluid is also an effective paint stripper, and will attack plastics; if any is spilt, it should be washed off immediately, using copious quantities of fresh water. Finally, it is hygroscopic (it absorbs moisture from the air) – old fluid may be contaminated and unfit for further use. When topping-up or renewing the* fluid, always use the recommended type, and ensure that it comes from a freshly-opened sealed container.

Note: *If difficulty is experienced in bleeding the braking circuit on models with ABS, this maybe due to air being trapped in the ABS regulator unit. If this is the case then the vehicle should be taken to a MINI dealer or suitably equipped specialist, so that the system can be bled using special electronic test equipment.*

Note: *A hydraulic clutch shares its fluid reservoir with the braking system, and may also need to be bled (see Chapter 6).*

General

1 The correct operation of any hydraulic system is only possible after removing all air from the components and circuit; this is achieved by bleeding the system.

2 During the bleeding procedure, add only clean, unused hydraulic fluid of the recommended type; never re-use fluid that has already been bled from the system. Ensure that sufficient fluid is available before starting work.

3 If there is any possibility of incorrect fluid being already in the system, the brake components and circuit must be flushed completely with uncontaminated, correct fluid, and new seals should be fitted to the various components.

4 If hydraulic fluid has been lost from the system, or air has entered because of a leak, ensure that the fault is cured before proceeding further.

5 Park the vehicle on level ground, switch off the engine and select first or reverse gear, then chock the wheels and release the handbrake.

6 Check that all pipes and hoses are secure, unions tight and bleed screws closed. Clean any dirt from around the bleed screws.

7 Unscrew the master cylinder reservoir cap, and top the master cylinder reservoir up to the MAX level line; refit the cap loosely, and remember to maintain the fluid level at least above the MIN level line throughout the procedure, or there is a risk of further air entering the system.

8 There are a number of one-man, do-it-yourself brake bleeding kits currently available from motor accessory shops. It is recommended that one of these kits is used whenever possible, as they greatly simplify the bleeding operation, and also reduce the risk of expelled air and fluid being drawn back into the system. If such a kit is not available, the basic (two-man) method must be used, which is described in detail below.

9 If a kit is to be used, prepare the vehicle as described previously, and follow the kit manufacturer's instructions, as the procedure may vary slightly according to the type being used; generally, they are as outlined below in the relevant sub-section.

10 Whichever method is used, the same sequence must be followed (paragraphs 11 and 12) to ensure that the removal of all air from the system.

Bleeding

Sequence

11 If the system has been only partially disconnected, and suitable precautions were taken to minimise fluid loss, it should be necessary only to bleed that of the system (ie, the primary or secondary circuit).

12 If the complete system is to be bled, then it should be done working in the following sequence:
a) *Right-hand rear brake.*
b) *Left-hand rear brake.*
c) *Right-hand front brake.*
d) *Left-hand front brake.*

Basic (two-man) method

13 Collect a clean glass jar, a suitable length of plastic or rubber tubing which is a tight fit over the bleed screw, and a ring spanner to fit the screw. The help of an assistant will also be required.

14 Remove the dust cap from the first screw in the sequence. Fit the spanner and tube to the screw, place the other end of the tube in the jar, and pour in sufficient fluid to cover the end of the tube.

15 Ensure that the master cylinder reservoir fluid level is maintained at least above the MIN level line throughout the procedure.

16 Have the assistant fully depress the brake pedal several times to build-up pressure, then maintain it on the final downstroke.

17 While pedal pressure is maintained, unscrew the bleed screw (approximately one turn) and allow the compressed fluid and air to flow into the jar. The assistant should maintain pedal pressure, following it down to the floor if necessary, and should not release it until instructed to do so. When the flow stops, tighten the bleed screw again, have the assistant release the pedal slowly, and recheck the reservoir fluid level.

18 Repeat the steps given in paragraphs 16 and 17 until the fluid emerging from the bleed screw is free from air bubbles. If the master cylinder has been drained and refilled, and air is being bled from the first screw in the sequence, allow approximately five seconds between cycles for the master cylinder passages to refill.

19 When no more air bubbles appear, tighten the bleed screw securely, remove the tube and spanner, and refit the dust cap. Do not overtighten the bleed screw.

20 Repeat the procedure on the remaining screws in the sequence, until all air is removed from the system and the brake pedal feels firm again.

Using a one-way valve kit

21 As their name implies, these kits consist of a length of tubing with a one-way valve fitted, to prevent expelled air and fluid being drawn back into the system; some kits include a translucent container, which can be positioned so that the air bubbles can be more easily seen flowing from the end of the tube.

22 The kit is connected to the bleed screw,

which is then opened **(see illustration)**. The user returns to the driver's seat, depresses the brake pedal with a smooth, steady stroke, and slowly releases it; this is repeated until the expelled fluid is clear of air bubbles.

23 Note that these kits simplify work so much that it is easy to forget the master cylinder reservoir fluid level; ensure that this is maintained at least above the MIN/DANGER level line at all times.

Using a pressure-bleeding kit

24 These kits are usually operated by the reservoir of pressurised air contained in the spare tyre. However, note that it will probably be necessary to reduce the pressure to a lower level than normal; refer to the instructions supplied with the kit.

25 By connecting a pressurised, fluid-filled container to the master cylinder reservoir, bleeding can be carried out simply by opening each screw in turn (in the specified sequence), and allowing the fluid to flow out until no more air bubbles can be seen in the expelled fluid.

26 This method has the advantage that the large reservoir of fluid provides an additional safeguard against air being drawn into the system during bleeding.

27 Pressure-bleeding is particularly effective when bleeding 'difficult' systems, or when bleeding the complete system at the time of routine fluid renewal.

All methods

28 When bleeding is complete, and firm pedal feel is restored, wash off any spilt fluid, tighten the bleed screws securely, and refit their dust caps.

29 Check the hydraulic fluid level in the master cylinder reservoir, and top-up if necessary (see *Weekly checks*).

30 Discard any hydraulic fluid that has been bled from the system; it will not be fit for re-use.

31 Check the feel of the brake pedal. If it feels at all spongy, air must still be present in the system, and further bleeding is required. Failure to bleed satisfactorily after a reasonable repetition of the bleeding procedure may be due to worn master cylinder seals.

3 Hydraulic pipes and hoses – renewal

Caution: Ensure the ignition is switched off before starting the bleeding procedure, to avoid any possibility of voltage being applied to the hydraulic modulator before the bleeding procedure is complete. Ideally, the battery should be disconnected. If voltage is applied to the modulator before the bleeding procedure is complete, this will effectively drain the hydraulic fluid in the modulator, rendering the unit unserviceable. Do not, therefore, attempt to 'run' the modulator in order to bleed the brakes.

2.22 Connect the kit to the bleed screw

Note: *Before starting work, refer to the note at the beginning of Section 2 concerning the dangers of hydraulic fluid.*

1 If any pipe or hose is to be renewed, minimise fluid loss by first removing the master cylinder reservoir cap, then tightening it down onto a piece of polythene to obtain an airtight seal. Alternatively, flexible hoses can be sealed, if required, using a proprietary brake hose clamp; metal brake pipe unions can be plugged (if care is taken not to allow dirt into the system) or capped immediately they are disconnected. Place a wad of rag under any union that is to be disconnected, to catch any spilt fluid.

2 To unscrew the union nuts, it is preferable to obtain a brake pipe spanner of the correct size; these are available from most large motor accessory shops. Failing this, a close-fitting open-ended spanner will be required, though if the nuts are tight or corroded, their flats may be rounded-off if the spanner slips. In such a case, a self-locking wrench is often the only way to unscrew a stubborn union, but it follows that the pipe and the damaged nuts must be renewed on reassembly. Always clean a union and surrounding area before disconnecting it. If disconnecting a component with more than one union, make a careful note of the connections before disturbing any of them.

3 If a brake pipe is to be renewed, it can be obtained, cut to length and with the union nuts and end flares in place, from MINI dealers. All that is then necessary is to bend it to shape, following the line of the original, before fitting it

to the car. Alternatively, most motor accessory shops can make up brake pipes from kits, but this requires very careful measurement of the original, to ensure that the replacement is of the correct length. The safest answer is usually to take the original to the shop as a pattern.

4 On refitting, do not overtighten the union nuts. It is not necessary to exercise brute force to obtain a sound joint.

5 Ensure that the pipes and hoses are correctly routed, with no kinks, and that they are secured in the clips or brackets provided. After fitting, remove the polythene from the reservoir, and bleed the hydraulic system as described in Section 2. Wash off any spilt fluid, and check carefully for fluid leaks.

4 Front brake pads – renewal

![Warning] *Warning: Renew both sets of front brake pads at the same time – never renew the pads on only one wheel, as uneven braking may result. Note that the dust created by wear of the pads may contain asbestos, which is a health hazard. Never blow it out with compressed air, and don't inhale any of it. An approved filtering mask should be worn when working on the brakes. DO NOT use petrol or petroleum-based solvents to clean brake parts; use brake cleaner or methylated spirit only.*

1 Apply the handbrake, then slacken the front roadwheel bolts. Jack up the front of the vehicle and support it on axle stands (see *Jacking and vehicle support*). Remove both front roadwheels.

2 Follow the accompanying photos **(see illustrations 4.2a to 4.2ac)** for the actual pad replacement procedure. Be sure to stay in order and read the caption under each illustration, and note the following points:

a) *New pads may have an adhesive foil on the backplates. Remove this foil prior to installation.*

b) *Thoroughly clean the caliper guide surfaces, and apply a little brake assembly*

4.2a If there's a lip of rust around the edge of the disc, insert a screwdriver into the disc vent holes, and lever the caliper outwards to retract the piston a little

4.2b Pull the pad wear sensor from the inner pad (left-hand caliper only) - a new sensor must be fitted

4.2c Release the wear sensor wiring from the clip on the bleed screw

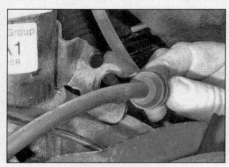

4.2d Unclip the brake hose from the bracket on the suspension strut

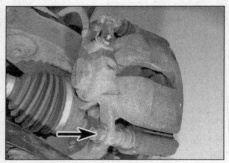

4.2e Remove the lower guide pin bolt (arrowed)...

4.2f ...using a second spanner to counterhold

4.2g Pivot the caliper upwards...

4.2h ...and secure it to the coil spring. Don't strain the brake hose!

4.2i Remove the outer brake pad...

4.2j ...and the inner brake pad

4.2k Remove the upper...

4.2l ...and lower shims

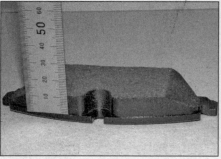

4.2m Measure the thickness of the friction material – if it's less than 3.7 mm, renew all 4 pads

4.2n Use aerosol brake cleaner to remove any brake dust

4.2o Genuine MINI brake kits include new shims. Fit the lower shim...

4.2p ...and upper shim

4.2q If new pads are to be fitted, use a retraction tool to push the piston back into the caliper. Keep an eye on the fluid level in the master cylinder reservoir!

4.2r Apply a thin smear of high-temperature anti-seize grease to the piston face, and inner caliper faces where they press against the pads (arrowed)

4.2s The inner pad has a 'bulge' to accommodate the wear sensor (arrowed)

4.2t Apply a little high-temperature anti-seize grease to the sliding edges of the pad backing plates

4.2u Fit the inner pad...

4.2v ...and the outer pad

4.2w Ensure the pads' friction material is against the disc!

4.2x Pivot the caliper back down...

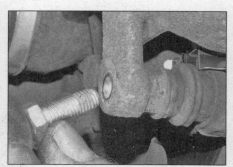

4.2y ...insert the new guide pin bolt...

4.2z ...and tighten it to the specified torque

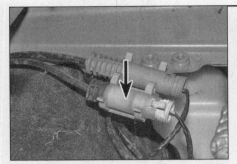

4.2aa Trace the wiring back and disconnect the pad wear sensor wiring plug (arrowed)…

4.2ab …connect the new sensor, clip the wiring into place…

4.2ac …then push the sensor firmly into the slot in the inner brake pad

(MINI pad paste 83 19 2 158 8851) grease.

c) *When pushing the caliper piston back to accommodate new pads, keep a close eye on the fluid level in the reservoir.*

d) *MINI insist that the brake pad wear sensor must be renewed if it's been removed.*

e) *It's recommended that the pad mounting shims are renewed along with the new pads.*

3 Depress the brake pedal repeatedly, until the pads are pressed into firm contact with the brake disc, and normal (non-assisted) pedal pressure is restored.

4 Repeat the above procedure on the remaining front brake caliper.

5 Before refitting the roadwheels, use a wire brush or mildly abrasive cloth (Scotchbrite, etc.) to clean the mating surfaces of the hub and wheel. Apply a little anti-seize grease (Copperslip) to the hub and wheel surface prior to refitting.

6 Refit the roadwheels, then lower the vehicle to the ground and tighten the roadwheel bolts to the specified torque.

7 Check the hydraulic fluid level as described in *Weekly checks*.

Caution: New pads will not give full braking efficiency until they have bedded-in. Be prepared for this, and avoid hard braking as far as possible for the first hundred miles or so after pad renewal.

5 Rear brake pads – renewal

⚠ **Warning: Renew BOTH sets of rear brake pads at the same time – NEVER renew the pads on only one wheel, as uneven braking may result. Note that the dust created by wear of the pads** may contain asbestos, which is a health hazard. Never blow it out with compressed air, and don't inhale any of it. An approved filtering mask should be worn when working on the brakes. DO NOT use petroleum-based solvents to clean brake parts – use brake cleaner or methylated spirit only.**

1 Apply the handbrake, then loosen the rear roadwheel nuts. Jack up the rear of the vehicle and support it securely on axle stands (see *Jacking and vehicle support*). Remove both rear roadwheels.

2 Follow the accompanying photos **(see illustrations 5.2a to 5.2y)** for the actual pad replacement procedure. Be sure to stay in order and read the caption under each illustration, and note the following points:

a) *New pads may have an adhesive foil on the backplates. Remove this foil prior to installation.*

b) *Thoroughly clean the caliper guide surfaces, and apply a little brake assembly (MINI pad paste 83 19 2 158 8851) grease.*

c) *When pushing the caliper piston back to accommodate new pads, keep a close eye on the fluid level in the reservoir.*

d) *MINI insist that the brake pad wear sensor must be renewed if it's been removed.*

e) *If a new sensor is fitted, but the pads not renewed, the thickness of the sensor must be reduced by filing, until it's flush with the pad friction material.*

f) *It's recommended that the pad mounting shims are renewed along with the new pads.*

3 Depress the brake pedal repeatedly, until the pads are pressed into firm contact with the brake disc, and normal (non-assisted) pedal pressure is restored.

4 Repeat the above procedure on the remaining rear brake caliper.

5 Refit the roadwheels, then lower the vehicle to the ground and tighten the roadwheel bolts to the specified torque.

6 Check the hydraulic fluid level as described in *Weekly checks*.

Caution: New pads will not give full braking efficiency until they have bedded-in. Be prepared for this, and avoid hard braking as far as possible for the first hundred miles or so after pad renewal.

5.2a Carefully pull the pad wear sensor from the aperture in the right-hand rear caliper …

5.2b …and unclip the sensor wiring harness

5.2c Pivot down the lever, detach the end of the handbrake cable…

5.2d …slide out the clip, and pull the handbrake cable from the bracket

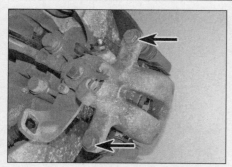

5.2e Remove the caliper guide pin bolts (arrowed)…

5.2f …using a second spanner to counterhold

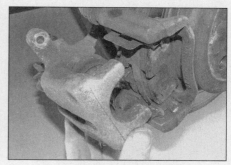

5.2g Slide off the caliper…

5.2h …and support it to prevent straining the hose

5.2i Remove the outer pad…

5.2j …inner pad…

5.2k …upper and lower shims

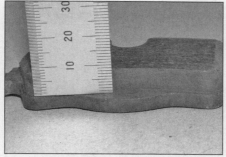

5.2l Measure the thickness of the pad's friction material. If it's less than 3.7 mm, renew all four pads

5.2m Clean the pads mounting surfaces with aerosol brake cleaner

5.2n Refit the upper…

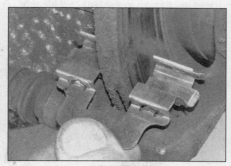

5.2o …and lower shims

5.2p Apply a little high-temperature anti-seize grease to the pad backing and mounting surfaces (arrowed). Take care not to get any grease on the friction material

9•8 Braking system

5.2q Fit the outer pad...

5.2r ...followed by the inner pad. Ensure the friction material is against the disc!

5.2s If new pads are fitted, the caliper piston must be rotated clockwise, at the same time as being pushed back into the housing – use a piston retraction tool. Keep an eye on the fluid level in the master cylinder reservoir

5.2t Slide the caliper back into place without disturbing the pads

5.2u Fit new guide pin bolts, and tighten them to the specified torque

5.2v Slide the handbrake cable into the bracket, and refit the clip

5.2w Lever down the arm, and re-attach the end of the handbrake cable

5.2x Press the new pad wear sensor into the groove in the inner brake pad (arrowed)...

5.2y ...and re-clip the wiring harness to the bleed screw

6 Front brake disc – inspection, removal and refitting

Note: *Before starting work, refer to the note at the beginning of Section 4 concerning the dangers of asbestos dust.*

Inspection

Note: *If either disc requires renewal, BOTH should be renewed at the same time, to ensure even and consistent braking. New brake pads should also be fitted.*

1 Apply the handbrake, slacken the front roadwheel bolts, then jack up the front of the car and support it on axle stands (see *Jacking and vehicle support*). Remove the appropriate front roadwheel.

2 Slowly rotate the brake disc so that the full area of both sides can be checked; remove the brake pads if better access is required to the inboard surface. Light scoring is normal in the area swept by the brake pads, but if heavy scoring or cracks are found, the disc must be renewed.

3 It is normal to find a lip of rust and brake dust around the disc's perimeter; this can be scraped off if required. If, however, a lip has formed due to excessive wear of the brake pad swept area, then the disc's thickness must be measured using a micrometer. Take measurements at several places around the disc, at the inside and outside of the pad swept area; if the disc has worn at any point to the specified minimum thickness or less, the disc must be renewed **(see illustration)**.

4 If the disc is thought to be warped, it can be checked for run-out. Either use a dial gauge mounted on any convenient fixed point, while the disc is slowly rotated, or use feeler blades to measure (at several points all around the disc) the clearance between the disc and a fixed point, such as the caliper mounting bracket. If the measurements obtained are at

6.3 Measure the disc thickness using a micrometer

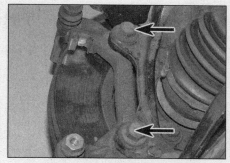

6.6 Caliper mounting bracket bolts (arrowed)

6.7 Front brake disc retaining screw (arrowed)

the specified maximum or beyond, the disc is excessively warped, and must be renewed; however, it is worth checking first that the hub bearing is in good condition (Chapter 1A or Chapter 1B). Also try the effect of removing the disc and turning it through 180°, to reposition it on the hub; if the run-out is still excessive, the disc must be renewed.

5 Check the disc for cracks, especially around the wheel bolt holes, and any other wear or damage, and renew if necessary.

Removal

6 Slacken and remove the two bolts securing the brake caliper mounting bracket to the hub carrier **(see illustration)**. Slide the assembly off the disc and tie it to the coil spring, using a piece of wire or string, to avoid placing any strain on the hydraulic brake hose.

7 Remove the Torx screw securing the brake disc to the hub, and remove the disc **(see illustration)**. If it is tight, lightly tap its rear face with a hide or plastic mallet.

Refitting

8 Refitting is the reverse of the removal procedure, noting the following points:
  a) *Ensure that the mating surfaces of the disc and hub are clean and flat.*
  b) *Tighten the disc retaining screw to the specified torque setting.*
  c) *If a new disc has been fitted, use a suitable solvent to wipe any preservative coating from the disc, before refitting the caliper.*
  d) *Refit the roadwheel then lower the vehicle to the ground and tighten the wheel bolts to the specified torque. Apply the footbrake several times to force the pads back into contact with the disc before driving the vehicle.*

7 Rear brake disc –
inspection, removal and refitting

Note: *Before starting work, refer to the note at the beginning of Section 5 concerning the dangers of asbestos dust.*

Inspection

Note: *If either disc requires renewal, BOTH*

should be renewed at the same time, to ensure even and consistent braking. New brake pads should also be fitted.

1 Firmly chock the front wheels, slacken the appropriate rear roadwheel bolts, then jack up the rear of the car and support it on axle stands (see *Jacking and vehicle support*). Remove the relevant rear roadwheel.

2 Inspect the disc as described in Section 6.

Removal

3 Remove the brake pads as described in Section 5.

4 Undo the two bolts securing the caliper mounting bracket to the stub axle **(see illustration)**. Discard the bolts – new ones must be fitted.

5 Use chalk or paint to mark the relationship of the disc to the hub, then undo the Torx screw securing the disc to the hub. If necessary, gently tap the disc from behind and release it from the hub **(see illustration)**.

Refitting

6 Refitting is the reverse of the removal procedure, noting the following points:
  a) *Ensure that the mating surfaces of the disc and hub are clean and flat.*
  b) *Align (if applicable) the marks made on removal, and tighten the disc retaining screw to the specified torque.*
  c) *If a new disc has been fitted, use a suitable solvent to wipe any preservative coating from the disc, before refitting the caliper.*
  d) *Refit the roadwheel, then lower the vehicle to the ground and tighten the roadwheel bolts to the specified torque.*

7.4 Rear brake caliper mounting bracket bolts (arrowed)

Depress the brake pedal several times to force the pads back into contact with the disc.

8 Front brake caliper –
removal, overhaul and refitting

Caution: Ensure the ignition is switched off before disconnecting any braking system hydraulic union and do not switch it on until after the hydraulic system has been bled. Failure to do this could lead to air entering the regulator unit requiring the unit to be bled using special MINI test equipment (see Section 2).

Note: *Before starting work, refer to the note at the beginning of Section 2 concerning the dangers of hydraulic fluid, and to the warning at the beginning of Section 4 concerning the dangers of asbestos dust.*

Removal

1 Apply the handbrake, slacken the relevant front roadwheel bolts, then jack up the front of the vehicle and support it on axle stands (see *Jacking and vehicle support*). Remove the appropriate roadwheel.

2 Minimise fluid loss by first removing the master cylinder reservoir cap, and then tightening it down onto a piece of polythene, to obtain an airtight seal. Alternatively, use a brake hose clamp, a G-clamp or a similar tool to clamp the flexible hose **(see illustration)**.

3 Clean the area around the caliper hose union, then loosen the union.

7.5 Rear brake disc retaining screw (arrowed)

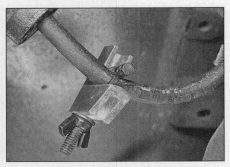

8.2 To minimise fluid loss, fit a brake hose clamp to the flexible hose

4 Slacken and remove the upper and lower caliper guide pins **(see illustration 4.2e)**. Lift the caliper away from the brake disc, then unscrew the caliper from the end of the brake hose. Pull the inner-pad from the caliper piston.

5 If required, the caliper mounting bracket can be unbolted from the hub carrier.

Overhaul

Note: *Check the availability of repair kits for the caliper before dismantling.*

6 With the caliper on the bench, wipe away all traces of dust and dirt, but *avoid inhaling the dust, as it is a health hazard.*

7 Withdraw the partially ejected piston from the caliper body, and remove the dust seal.

 HAYNES HiNT *If the piston cannot be withdrawn by hand, it can be pushed out by applying compressed air to the brake hose union hole. Only low pressure should be required, such as is generated by a foot pump. As the piston is expelled, take great care not to trap your fingers between the piston and caliper.*

8 Using a small screwdriver, extract the piston hydraulic seal, taking great care not to damage the caliper bore.

9 Thoroughly clean all components, using only methylated spirit, isopropyl alcohol or clean hydraulic fluid as a cleaning medium. Never

9.4 Slacken the fluid hose union (arrowed)

use mineral-based solvents such as petrol or paraffin, as they will attack the hydraulic system's rubber components. Dry the components immediately, using compressed air or a clean, lint-free cloth. Use compressed air to blow clear the fluid passages.

10 Check all components, and renew any that are worn or damaged. Check particularly the cylinder bore and piston; these should be renewed (note that this means the renewal of the complete body assembly) if they are scratched, worn or corroded in any way. Similarly check the condition of the guide pins and their gaiters; both pins should be undamaged and (when cleaned) a reasonably tight sliding fit in the caliper bracket. If there is any doubt about the condition of any component, renew it.

11 If the assembly is fit for further use, obtain the appropriate repair kit; the components should be available from MINI dealers in various combinations. All rubber seals should be renewed as a matter of course; these should never be re-used.

12 On reassembly, ensure that all components are clean and dry.

13 Soak the piston and the new piston (fluid) seal in clean brake fluid. Smear clean fluid on the cylinder bore surface.

14 Fit the new piston (fluid) seal, using only your fingers (no tools) to manipulate it into the cylinder bore groove.

15 Fit the new dust seal to the rear of the piston and seat the outer lip of the seal in the caliper body groove. Carefully ease the piston squarely into the cylinder bore using a twisting motion. Press the piston fully into position, and seat the inner lip of the dust seal in the piston groove.

16 If the guide pins are being renewed, lubricate the pin shafts with the special grease supplied in the repair kit. Insert the pins into the caliper bracket.

Refitting

17 If previously removed, refit the caliper mounting bracket to the hub carrier, and tighten the bolts to the specified torque.

18 Screw the caliper body fully onto the flexible hose union.

19 Fit the inner brake pad to the caliper piston, and ensure that the outer brake pad is correctly fitted in the caliper mounting bracket and refit the caliper (see Section 4).

20 Fit the guide pin bolts, and tighten them to the specified torque. Refit the plastic caps.

21 Tighten the brake hose union nut to the specified torque, then remove the brake hose clamp or polythene (where fitted).

22 Bleed the hydraulic system as described in Section 2. Note that, providing the precautions described were taken to minimise brake fluid loss, it should only be necessary to bleed the relevant front brake.

23 Refit the roadwheel, then lower the vehicle to the ground and tighten the roadwheel bolts to the specified torque.

9 Rear brake caliper – removal, overhaul and refitting

Caution: Ensure the ignition is switched off before disconnecting any braking system hydraulic union and do not switch it back on until after the hydraulic system has been bled. Failure to do this could lead to air entering the regulator unit.
Note: *Before starting work, refer to the note at the beginning of Section 2 concerning the dangers of hydraulic fluid, and to the warning at the beginning of Section 5 concerning the dangers of asbestos dust.*

Removal

1 Chock the front wheels, slacken the relevant rear roadwheel bolts, then jack up the rear of the vehicle and support on axle stands (see *Jacking and vehicle support*). Remove the relevant rear wheel.

2 Remove the brake pads as described in Section 5.

3 Minimise fluid loss by first removing the master cylinder reservoir cap, and then tightening it down onto a piece of polythene, to obtain an airtight seal. Alternatively, use a brake hose clamp, a G-clamp or a similar tool to clamp the flexible hose at the nearest convenient point to the brake calliper **(see illustration 8.2)**.

4 Wipe away all traces of dirt around the brake hose union on the caliper, then slacken the hose union **(see illustration)**.

5 Remove the caliper from the vehicle and unscrew it from the hose. If required, the caliper mounting bracket can be unbolted from the hub carrier. Plug the pipe and caliper unions to minimise fluid loss and prevent dirt entry.

Overhaul

6 At the time of writing, no parts were available to recondition the rear caliper assembly, with the excepting of the guide pins. Check the condition of the guide pins; both pins should be undamaged and (when cleaned) a reasonably tight sliding fit in the caliper bracket. If there is any doubt about the condition of any component, renew it.

Refitting

7 If previously removed, refit the caliper mounting bracket to the hub carrier, and tighten the bolts to the specified torque.

8 Refit the caliper and insert the guide pins, tightening them to the specified torque settings.

9 Reconnect the brake pipe to the caliper, and tighten the brake hose union nut to the specified torque. Remove the brake hose clamp or polythene (where fitted).

10 Refit the brake pads as described in Section 5.

11 Bleed the hydraulic system as described in Section 2. Note that, providing the precautions described were taken to minimise brake fluid

10.1a Pull up the rubber weatherstrip at the rear of the engine compartment...

10.1b ...undo the nut and screw...

10.1c ...then pull up the scuttle trim panel above the battery

loss, it should only be necessary to bleed the relevant front brake.

12 Refit the roadwheel, then lower the vehicle to the ground and tighten the roadwheel bolts to the specified torque.

10 Master cylinder – removal, overhaul and refitting

Caution: Ensure the ignition is switched off before disconnecting any braking system hydraulic union and do not switch it back on until after the hydraulic system has been bled. Failure to do this could lead to air entering the regulator unit requiring the unit to be bled using special MINI test equipment (see Section 2).
Note: *Before starting work, refer to the warning at the beginning of Section 2 concerning the dangers of hydraulic fluid.*

Removal

1 Pull up the rubber weatherstrip, undo the retaining nut and screw, then pull the left-hand scuttle panel upwards **(see illustrations)**.
2 Remove both wiper arms as described in Chapter 12, then undo the nut and screw, pull up the rubber weatherstrip and remove the right-hand scuttle panel **(see illustrations)**.
3 Remove the master cylinder reservoir cap, and siphon the hydraulic fluid from the reservoir. **Note:** *Do not siphon the fluid by mouth, as it is poisonous; use a syringe or an old antifreeze tester.* Alternatively, open any convenient bleed screw in the system, and gently pump the brake pedal to expel the fluid through a plastic tube connected to the screw until the reservoir is emptied (see Section 2).
4 Disconnect the wiring plug from the side of the fluid reservoir, then on manual transmission models, pull the clutch master cylinder supply hose from the brake reservoir – be prepared for fluid spillage, and secure the pipe in an upright position **(see illustration)**.
5 Unscrew the retaining Torx pin and separate the reservoir from the master cylinder **(see illustration)**. Examine the condition of the reservoir seals, and renew if necessary.
6 Wipe clean the area around the brake pipe unions on the side of the master cylinder, and

10.2a Release the clips (arrowed) at the front edge of the scuttle trim panel

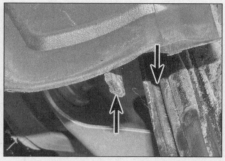

10.2b Note how the scuttle trim panel engages with the extrusion at the base of the windscreen (arrowed)

place absorbent rags beneath the pipe unions to catch any surplus fluid. Make a note of the correct fitted positions of the unions, then unscrew the union nuts and carefully withdraw the pipes. Plug or tape over the pipe ends and master cylinder orifices, to minimise the loss of brake fluid, and to prevent the entry of dirt into the system. Wash off any spilt fluid immediately with cold water.
7 Slacken and remove the two nuts securing the master cylinder to the vacuum servo unit, then withdraw the unit from the engine compartment. If the sealing ring fitted to the rear of the master cylinder shows signs of damage or deterioration, it must be renewed. Discard the retaining nuts, new ones must be fitted.

Overhaul

8 At the time of writing, no parts were

available to overhaul the master cylinder. Check with your MINI dealer, or specialist.

Refitting

9 Remove all traces of dirt from the master cylinder and servo unit mating surfaces and ensure that the sealing ring is correctly fitted to the rear of the master cylinder.
10 Fit the master cylinder to the servo unit. Fit the new master cylinder mounting nuts, and tighten them to the specified torque.
11 Wipe clean the brake pipe unions and refit them to the master cylinder ports, tightening them to the specified torque.
12 Press the mounting seals fully into the master cylinder ports then carefully ease the fluid reservoir into position. Slide the reservoir retaining pin into position and tighten it securely.

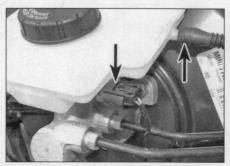

10.4 Disconnect the clutch master cylinder fluid supply hose (where applicable) and the level sensor wiring plug (arrowed)

10.5 Brake master cylinder retaining nuts, pipe unions, and reservoir retaining pin (arrowed)

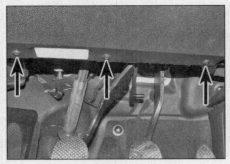

11.1 Undo the screws (arrowed) and remove the panel beneath the steering column

11.2 Pressure pipe retaining clip and switch plug (arrowed)

the clutch hydraulic system as described in Chapter 6.

12 Vacuum servo unit – testing, removal and refitting

Testing

1 To test the operation of the servo unit, depress the footbrake several times to exhaust the vacuum, then start the engine whilst keeping the pedal firmly depressed. As the engine starts, there should be a noticeable 'give' in the brake pedal as the vacuum builds-up. Allow the engine to run for at least two minutes, then switch it off. If the brake pedal is now depressed it should feel normal, but further applications should result in the pedal feeling firmer, with the pedal stroke decreasing with each application.

2 If the servo does not operate as described, first inspect the servo unit check valve as described in Section 13.

3 If the servo unit still fails to operate satisfactorily, the fault lies within the unit itself. Repairs to the unit are not possible – if faulty, the servo unit must be renewed.

Removal

4 Remove the master cylinder as described in Section 10.

5 Carefully prise the vacuum check valve from the servo body.

6 Undo the 3 screws, pull the down the rear edge of the facia panel above the pedals, and disengage it from the retaining clips.

7 Remove the clip and slide out the clevis pin securing the servo pushrod to the brake pedal **(see illustration 11.4)**.

8 Slacken and remove the two nuts securing the servo to the bulkhead **(see illustration)**.

9 Manoeuvre the servo unit out of position, along with its gasket (where fitted). Renew the gasket if it shows signs of damage.

Refitting

10 Refitting is the reverse of removal, noting the following points.
  a) Renew the servo mounting nuts and tighten them to the specified torque.
  b) Refit the master cylinder as described in Section 10 and bleed the complete hydraulic system as described in Section 2.

11.4 Lift the edge (arrowed) and slide off the retaining clip

13 Reconnect the clutch master cylinder supply pipe, level sensor wiring plug, and pressure sensor (where fitted).

14 Refit any components removed to improve access then refill the master cylinder reservoir with new fluid. Bleed the complete hydraulic system as described in Section 2. **Note:** *A hydraulic clutch shares its fluid reservoir with the braking system, and may also need to be bled (see Chapter 6).*

11 Brake pedal – removal and refitting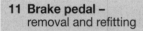

Removal

1 Working inside the driver's footwell, undo the 3 screws and remove the trim panel from above the pedals **(see illustration)**.

2 Disconnect the wiring plug from the clutch master cylinder, then prise out the clip a little, and disconnect the pressure pipe at the connection **(see illustration)**.

3 Disconnect the wiring plug from the brake switch **(see illustration 17.2a)**.

4 Carefully release the securing clip and disconnect the master cylinder pushrod from the brake pedal **(see illustration)**.

5 Pull up the rubber weatherstrip at the front edge, undo the screw and nut at the outer edge, and unclip the cowl panel above the battery. Ensure the cowl seals are not damaged **(see illustrations 10.1a and 10.1b)**.

6 Remove both wiper arms as described in Chapter 12.

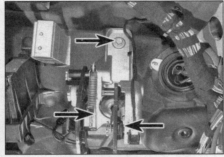

11.10 Pedal bracket retaining bolt/nuts locations (arrowed)

7 Pull up the rubber weather strip, undo the screw and nut at the outer edge, unclip the scuttle panel cowl **(see illustration 10.2a and 10.2b)**.

8 Remove the brake master cylinder reservoir filler cap, and then tighten it down onto a piece of polythene to obtain an airtight seal. This will minimise hydraulic fluid loss.

9 Release the securing clip and disconnect the hydraulic fluid supply pipe from the brake fluid reservoir **(see illustration 10.4)**. Plug or cap the pipe end to prevent further fluid loss and dirt entry.

10 Undo the retaining nuts/bolt and manoeuvre the pedal assembly downwards, and out from the vehicle **(see illustration)**. Discard the nuts – new ones must be fitted. Note that the brake pedal cannot be renewed separately from the pedal assembly.

Refitting

11 Refitting is a reversal of removal. Bleed

12.8 Servo retaining nuts (arrowed)

13 Vacuum servo unit check valve – removal, testing and refitting

Removal

1 Withdraw the valve from its rubber sealing grommet, using a pulling and twisting motion **(see illustration)**. Remove the grommet from the servo.

2 The check valve is only available complete with the vacuum pipe. Trace the pipe along, releasing it from any retaining clips, and separate it at the connection adjacent to the left-hand end of the cylinder head.

Testing

3 Examine the check valve for signs of damage, and renew if necessary. The valve may be tested by blowing through it in both directions. Air should flow through the valve in one direction only – when blown through from the servo unit end of the valve. Renew the valve if this is not the case.
4 Examine the rubber sealing grommet and flexible vacuum hose for signs of damage or deterioration, and renew as necessary.

Refitting

5 Fit the sealing grommet into position in the servo unit.
6 Carefully ease the check valve into position, taking great care not to displace or damage the grommet. Reconnect the vacuum hose, and refit it to the retaining clips.
7 On completion, start the engine and check for air leaks from the check valve-to-servo unit connection.

14 Handbrake – adjustment

1 To check the handbrake adjustment, applying normal moderate pressure, pull the handbrake lever to the fully-applied position, counting the number of clicks emitted from the handbrake ratchet mechanism. If adjustment is correct, there should be 2 clicks before the brakes begins to apply, and no more than 6 before the handbrake is fully applied. If this is not the case, adjust as follows.
2 Squeeze together the sides of the handbrake lever gaiter, and carefully prise it from the centre console (see illustration).
3 Chock the front wheels, then jack up the rear of the vehicle and support it on axle stands (see Jacking and vehicle support).
4 Slacken the adjuster nut on the rod from the equaliser plate (see illustration).
5 Tighten the adjuster nut on the rod until the gap between the lever on the caliper and the stop is 0.5 to 1.5 mm (see illustration).
6 Fully apply the handbrake lever 3 times, and

press the brake pedal down 3 times. Recheck the air gap as described in paragraph 5.
7 Release the lever and check by hand that the rear wheels rotate freely, then check that no more than six clicks are emitted before the handbrake is fully applied.
8 Refit the gaiter, then lower the vehicle to the floor.

15 Handbrake lever – removal and refitting

Removal

1 Remove the rear section of the centre console as described in Chapter 11.
2 Unclip the handbrake warning switch wiring, then undo the four nuts and remove the centre console mounting bracket (see illustrations).

Where applicable, disconnect the wiring plug, undo the two screws and remove the DSC motion sensor.
3 Chock the road wheels to prevent the vehicle moving once the handbrake lever is released.
4 Referring to Section 14, release the hand-brake lever and back off the adjuster nut to obtain maximum freeplay in the cable.
5 Detach both handbrake cables from the equaliser plate (see illustration 16.5).
6 Undo the three nuts and remove the lever assembly (see illustration). Disconnect the handbrake warning switch wiring as the assembly is withdrawn.

Refitting

7 Refitting is a reversal of removal. Tighten the lever retaining nuts to the specified torque, and adjust the handbrake (see Section 14).

13.1 Servo unit check valve (arrowed)

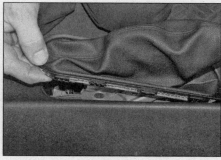
14.2 Squeeze together the sides of the gaiter and unclip it from the console

14.4 Slacken the handbrake adjustment nut (arrowed)

14.5 Use a feeler gauge (arrowed) to set the gap between the lever and stop

15.2a Undo the nuts (arrowed) at the rear of the console…

15.2b …and the nuts (arrowed) each side of the handbrake lever

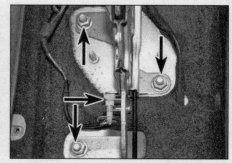
15.6 Handbrake lever retaining nuts and warning switch (arrowed)

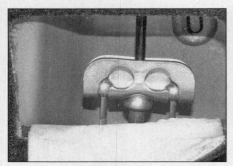

16.5 Slacken the adjuster nut and disengage the cables from the equaliser plate

16 Handbrake cables – removal and refitting

Removal

1 The handbrake cable consists of a left-hand section and a right-hand section connecting the rear brakes to the adjuster mechanism on the handbrake lever rod. The cables can be removed separately.

2 Firmly chock the front wheels, slacken the relevant rear roadwheel bolts, then jack up the rear of the vehicle and support it on axle stands (see *Jacking and vehicle support*). Remove the relevant rear roadwheel.

3 Remove the rear console as described in Chapter 11.

4 Undo the four nuts and remove the console mounting bracket from the floor.

5 Slacken the handbrake adjuster nut sufficiently to be able to disengage the relevant cable end fitting from the equaliser plate **(see illustration)**.

6 Release the cable end fitting from the lever on the brake caliper **(see illustration 5.2c and 5.2d)**.

7 Remove the heat shield above the centre section of the exhaust system.

8 Working inside the vehicle, slide a short length of 12 mm diameter tube over the end of the cable and depress the clips securing the cable outer end fitting to the vehicle body **(see illustration)**.

17.2a Disconnect the stop light switch wiring plug…

16.8 Slide a 12 mm diameter tube over the end of the cable to release the clips securing the cable to the vehicle body (a deep socket will also work)

9 Working underneath the vehicle, note its fitted location, then free the cable from the various retaining clips/brackets along its route, detach the bracket from the subframe and pull the front end of the cable from the opening in the floor. Withdraw the cable from underneath the vehicle

Refitting

10 Refitting is a reversal of the removal procedure, adjusting the handbrake as described in Section 14.

17 Stop-light switch – removal, refitting and adjustment

Removal

1 Remove the driver's side lower facia panel as described in Chapter 11.

2 Disconnect the wiring plug, then pull the switch from the pedal bracket holder **(see illustrations)**.

Refitting and adjustment

3 Depress the brake pedal, then refit the switch to the bracket, inserting it as far as possible.

4 Slowly pull the pedal back to its stop. The switch is now correctly adjusted.

5 Reconnect the wiring plug and refit the trim panel.

17.2b …then pull the switch from the holder

18 Anti-lock braking system (ABS) – general information

ABS is fitted to all models as standard, the system comprises a hydraulic regulator unit and the four roadwheel sensors. The regulator unit contains the electronic control unit (ECU), the hydraulic solenoid valves and the electrically-driven return pump. The purpose of the system is to prevent the wheel(s) locking during heavy braking. This is achieved by automatic release of the brake on the relevant wheel, followed by re-application of the brake.

The solenoid valves are controlled by the ECU, which itself receives signals from the four wheel sensors (front sensors are fitted to the hubs, and the rear sensors are fitted to the caliper mounting brackets), which monitor the speed of rotation of each wheel. By comparing these signals, the ECU can determine the speed at which the vehicle is travelling. It can then use this speed to determine when a wheel is decelerating at an abnormal rate, compared to the speed of the vehicle, and therefore predicts when a wheel is about to lock. During normal operation, the system functions in the same way as a non-ABS braking system.

If the ECU senses that a wheel is about to lock, it closes the relevant outlet solenoid valves in the hydraulic unit, which then isolates the relevant brake(s) on the wheel(s) which is/are about to lock from the master cylinder, effectively sealing-in the hydraulic pressure.

If the speed of rotation of the wheel continues to decrease at an abnormal rate, the ECU opens the inlet solenoid valves on the relevant brake(s), and operates the electrically-driven return pump which pumps the hydraulic fluid back into the master cylinder, releasing the brake. Once the speed of rotation of the wheel returns to an acceptable rate, the pump stops; the solenoid valves switch again, allowing the hydraulic master cylinder pressure to return to the caliper, which then re-applies the brake. This cycle can be carried out many times a second.

The action of the solenoid valves and return pump creates pulses in the hydraulic circuit. When the ABS system is functioning, these pulses can be felt through the brake pedal.

The operation of the ABS system is entirely dependent on electrical signals. To prevent the system responding to any inaccurate signals, a built-in safety circuit monitors all signals received by the ECU. If an inaccurate signal or low battery voltage is detected, the ABS system is automatically shut-down, and the warning light on the instrument panel is illuminated, to inform the driver that the ABS system is not operational. Normal braking should still be available, however.

The MINI is also equipped with additional safety features built around the ABS system. These systems include EBFD (Electronic Brake Force Distribution), which automatically

19.6 Undo the retaining bolt and pull out the front wheel speed sensor

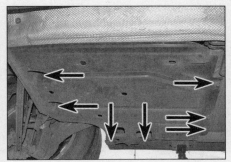

19.14 Undo the fasteners (arrowed) and remove the rear underbody panelling

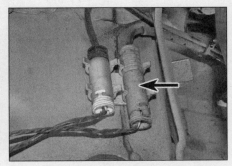

19.15 Disconnect the wheel speed sensor wiring plug (arrowed)

apportions braking effort between the front and rear wheels, and DSC (Dynamic Stability Control) which monitors the vehicles cornering forces and steering wheel angle, then applies the braking force to the appropriate roadwheel to enhance the stability of the vehicle. The DSC motion sensor is fitted beneath the rear centre console, and incorporates both the Yaw rate sensor and the lateral acceleration sensor. The DSC steering angle sensor is fitted to the upper steering column.

If a fault does develop in the any of these systems, the vehicle must be taken to a MINI dealer or suitably equipped specialist for fault diagnosis and repair.

19 Anti-lock braking system (ABS) components – removal and refitting

Regulator assembly

Removal

1 Renewal of the regulator assembly requires access to specialist diagnostic and testing equipment in order to purge air from the system, initialise and code the ECM. Consequently, we recommend this task is entrusted to a MINI dealer or suitably equipped specialist.

Electronic control unit (ECU)

2 The ECU is integral with the regulator assembly, and may not available separately. Check with a MINI dealer or parts specialist. Note that if a new ECU is fitted, it must be programmed using MINI diagnostic equipment. Entrust this task to a MINI dealer or suitably equipped repairer.

Front wheel sensor

Removal

3 Ensure the ignition is turned off.
4 Apply the handbrake, slacken the appropriate front roadwheel bolts, then jack up the front of the vehicle and support securely on axle stands (see *Jacking and vehicle support*). Remove the appropriate front roadwheel.
5 Trace the wiring back from the sensor, releasing it from all the relevant clips and

ties whilst noting its correct routing, and disconnect the wiring connector.
6 Slacken and remove the retaining bolt and withdraw the sensor from the hub carrier **(see illustration)**.

Refitting

7 Ensure that the mating faces of the sensor and the hub carrier are clean, and apply a little anti-seize grease (Staburags NBU 12/K – available from MINI dealers) to the hub carrier hub bore before refitting.
8 Make sure the sensor tip is clean and ease it into position in the hub carrier.
9 Clean the threads of the sensor bolt and apply a few drops of thread-locking compound. Refit the retaining bolt and tighten it to the specified torque.
10 Work along the sensor wiring, making sure it is correctly routed, securing it in position with all the relevant clips and ties. Reconnect the wiring connector.
11 Lower the vehicle and tighten the wheel bolts to the specified torque.

Rear wheel sensor

Removal

12 Ensure the ignition is turned off.
13 Chock the front wheels, slacken the appropriate rear roadwheel bolts, then jack up the rear of the vehicle and support it on axle stands (see *Jacking and vehicle support*). Remove the appropriate roadwheel.
14 Undo the fasteners and remove the rear underbody panelling where applicable **(see illustration)**.

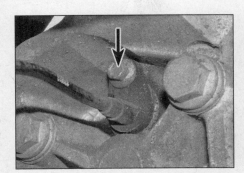

19.16 Rear wheel speed sensor retaining bolt (arrowed)

15 Trace the wiring back from the sensor, releasing it from all the relevant clips and ties whilst noting its correct routing, and disconnect the wiring connector **(see illustration)**.
16 Slacken and remove the retaining bolt and withdraw the sensor **(see illustration)**.

Refitting

17 Ensure that the mating faces of the sensor and the hub are clean, and apply a little anti-seize grease (Staburags NBU 12/K – available from MINI dealers) to the hub bore before refitting.
18 Make sure the sensor tip is clean and ease it into position in the swivel hub.
19 Clean the threads of the sensor bolt and apply a few drops of thread-locking compound. Refit the retaining bolt and tighten it to the specified torque.
20 Work along the sensor wiring, making sure it is correctly routed, securing it in position with all the relevant clips and ties. Reconnect the wiring connector, then lower the vehicle and (where necessary) tighten the wheel bolts to the specified torque.

Dynamic stability control (DSC) yaw rate sensor

21 Remove the centre console as described in Chapter 11.
22 Disconnect the wiring plug from the sensor, then remove it from the mounting bracket **(see illustration)**.
23 When refitting the sensor, tighten the retaining bolts to the specified torque.

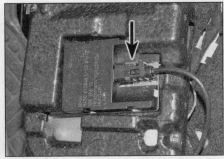

19.22 Disconnect the yaw rate sensor fibre optic plug (arrowed)

Steering angle sensor

24 Position the roadwheels and steering wheel in the straight-ahead position, then engage the steering lock.

25 The sensor is integral with the steering column combination switch assembly. Removal of the switch assembly is described in Chapter 12.

26 Note that is a new sensor/switch assembly is fitted, it must be programmed and calibrated using MINI diagnostic equipment. Entrust this task to a MINI dealer or suitably equipped repairer.

Chapter 10
Suspension and steering

Contents

Degrees of difficulty

Easy, suitable for novice with little experience		Fairly easy, suitable for beginner with some experience		Fairly difficult, suitable for competent DIY mechanic		Difficult, suitable for experienced DIY mechanic		Very difficult, suitable for expert DIY or professional	

Specifications

Front wheel alignment
Toe setting . . . . 0°12' ± 12' toe-in
Camber. . . . . −30' ± 25'
Caster (max difference between left/right) . . . . 30'

Rear wheel alignment
Toe setting . . . . 0°24' ±12' toe-in
Camber. . . . . −1°45' ± 25'

Tyre pressures . . . . See sticker in driver's door aperture

Torque wrench settings

	Nm	lbf ft
Front suspension		
Anti-roll bar clamp bolts....................................	165	122
Anti-roll bar link nuts*....................................	56	41
Driveshaft/hub retaining nut*....................................	182	134
Bearing hub-to-hub carrier*:		
Stage 1....................................	20	15
Stage 2....................................	Angle-tighten a further 90°	
Lower arm inner balljoint*:		
Stage 1....................................	80	59
Stage 2....................................	Angle-tighten a further 90°	
Lower arm outer balljoint:		
To hub carrier*:		
Stage 1....................................	70	52
Stage 2....................................	Angle-tighten a further 90°	
To lower arm*....................................	175	130
Lower arm-to-vehicle body....................................	100	74
Roadwheel bolts....................................	140	103
Suspension strut thrust bearing retaining nut*....................................	64	47
Suspension strut-to-hub carrier pinch-bolt*....................................	100	74
Suspension strut upper mounting nuts*....................................	34	25
Wheel speed sensor bolt....................................	9	6
Rear suspension		
Anti-roll bar clamp bolts....................................	19	14
Anti-roll bar link nuts*....................................	56	41
Control arms-to-trailing arm....................................	100	74
Control arms-to-subframe....................................	100	74
Rear hub/bearing assembly-to-trailing arm....................................	56	41
Reinforcement cross bolts (Convertible only)*:		
Stage 1....................................	56	41
Stage 2....................................	Angle-tighten a further 45°	
Roadwheel bolts....................................	140	103
Shock absorber upper mounting bolts*....................................	56	41
Shock absorber lower mounting bolt....................................	165	122
Shock absorber piston nut*....................................	30	22
Subframe mounting bolts*....................................	100	74
Trailing arm bush/bracket-to-vehicle body....................................	100	74
Trailing arm bush/bracket-to-trailing arm....................................	165	122
Wheel speed sensor bolt....................................	9	6
Steering		
Electric Power Steering motor-to-rack*....................................	24	18
Roadwheel bolts....................................	140	103
Steering column mounting bolts*....................................	35	25
Steering column lower universal joint pinch bolt*....................................	28	21
Steering rack-to-subframe....................................	100	74
Steering wheel....................................	63	46
Track rod end clamp bolt....................................	30	22
Track rod end balljoint-to-hub carrier*....................................	65	47

*Do not re-use

1 General information

The independent front suspension is of MacPherson strut type, incorporating coil springs, integral telescopic shock absorbers, and an anti-roll bar. The struts are attached to steering knuckles at their lower ends, and the knuckles are in turn attached to the lower suspension arm by balljoints. The anti-roll bar is bolted to the rear of the subframe, and is connected to the front suspension struts by links.

The multi-link rear suspension is fully independent with trailing arms attached to the vehicle body, and control arms mounted between the body-mounted subframe and the trailing arms. The gas-pressurised shock absorbers are of the MacPherson type, and are mounted between the vehicle body and the trailing arms. A rear anti-roll bar is fitted to all models.

Both front and rear wheel bearings are integral with the hubs, and no adjustment is possible.

A power steering type rack-and-pinion steering gear is fitted, together with a conventional column and telescopic coupling.

Unlike conventional power steering, assistance is provided by an electric motor attached to the steering rack pinion housing (EPS). This is an energy efficient design as assistance is only provided to the steering rack when required.

When working on the suspension or steering, you may come across nuts or bolts which seem impossible to loosen. These nuts and bolts on the underside of the vehicle are continually subjected to water, road grime, mud, etc, and can become rusted or seized, making them extremely difficult to remove. In order to unscrew these stubborn nuts and bolts without damaging them (or other components), use lots of penetrating oil, and allow it to soak in for a while. Using a wire brush to clean exposed threads will also ease removal of the nut or bolt, and will help to prevent damage to the threads. Sometimes, a sharp blow with a hammer and punch will break the bond between a nut and bolt, but care must be taken to prevent the punch from slipping off and ruining the threads. Using a longer bar or spanner will increase leverage, but never use an extension bar/pipe on a ratchet, as the internal mechanism could be damaged. Actually tightening the nut or bolt slightly first, may help to break it loose. Nuts or bolts which have required drastic measures to remove them should always be renewed. As a general rule, all self-locking nuts (with nylon inserts) should be renewed.

Since most of the procedures dealt with in this Chapter involve jacking up the vehicle and working underneath it, a good pair of axle stands will be needed. A hydraulic trolley jack is the preferred type of jack to lift the vehicle, and it can also be used to support certain components during removal and refitting operations.

⚠️ **Warning: Never, under any circumstances, rely on a jack to support the vehicle while working beneath it. It is not recommended, when jacking up the rear of the vehicle, to lift beneath the rear crossmember.**

2 Front hub carrier – removal and refitting

Removal

1 Slacken the relevant front roadwheel bolts, then jack up the front of the vehicle and support it securely on axle stands. Remove the roadwheel.
2 Have an assistant press the brake pedal, and then slacken and remove the driveshaft nut (see Chapter 8). Discard the nut, a new one must be fitted.
3 Remove the front brake disc as described in Chapter 9.
4 Unscrew the track rod end balljoint nut, and detach the rod from the hub carrier using a conventional balljoint removal tool **(see illustration 22.4)**. Take care not to damage the balljoint seal.
5 Undo the retaining bolt, and remove the wheel speed sensor **(see illustration)**.
6 Remove the lower arm outer balljoint as described in Section 8.
7 Unscrew and remove the pinch-bolt securing the hub carrier assembly to the front suspension strut, noting which way round it is fitted (from the rear) **(see illustration)**. Prise open the clamp a little using a wedge-shaped tool, and release the hub carrier from the strut. If necessary, tap the hub carrier downwards with a soft-headed mallet to separate the two components.

2.5 Wheel speed sensor retaining bolt (arrowed – disc and shield removed for clarity)

Refitting

8 Locate the assembly on the front suspension strut. Insert the pinch-bolt with its head facing the same way as removal, and tighten it to the specified torque.
9 Pull the steering hub carrier assembly outwards, and insert the driveshaft to engage the splines in the hub.
10 Refit the lower arm balljoint into the lower arm, then fit the new nut and tighten it to the specified torque.
11 Refit the brake caliper and brake disc as described in Chapter 9. Refitting the brake hose support bracket to the strut.
12 Refit the wheel speed sensor and tighten the retaining bolt to the specified torque.
13 Reconnect the track rod end balljoint to the hub carrier, and tighten the new nut to the specified torque.
14 Apply a little clean oil to the nut/wheel bearing contact surface, then fit the new driveshaft/hub nut, and tighten to the specified torque, as described in Chapter 8. After tightening, 'stake' the nut as described in Chapter 8.
15 Refit the front wheel, and lower the vehicle to the ground.

3 Front hub and bearings – inspection and renewal

Inspection

1 To check the bearings for excessive wear, apply the handbrake, jack up the front of the vehicle and support it on axle stands (see *Jacking and vehicle support*).
2 Grip the front wheel at the top and the bottom, and attempt to rock it. If excessive movement is noted, it may be that the hub bearings are worn. Do not confuse wear in the driveshaft outer joint or front suspension lower arm balljoint with wear in the bearings. Hub bearing wear will show up as roughness or vibration when the wheel is spun; it will also be noticeable as a rumbling or growling noise when driving. No adjustment of the wheel bearings is possible.
Note: *The front wheel bearings are integral*

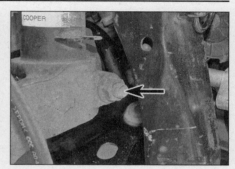

2.7 Remove the pinch bolt (arrowed) at the base of the suspension strut

with the hub assembly, and can only be replaced as a complete assembly.

Renewal

3 Slacken and remove the driveshaft retaining nut as described in 'Driveshaft removal and refitting' in Chapter 8.
4 Remove the relevant front brake disc as described in Chapter 9.
5 Undo the retaining bolt and remove the wheel speed sensor from the hub carrier **(see illustration 2.5)**.
6 Undo the 4 bolts securing the hub assembly to the hub carrier, and detach the assembly **(see illustration)**. No further dismantling is recommended. Discard the bolts – new ones must be fitted.
7 Position the new hub assembly against the hub carrier, then fit and tighten the bolts to the specified torque.
8 Refit the speed sensor to the hub carrier and tighten the retaining bolt to the specified torque.
9 Refit the brake disc and caliper as described in Chapter 9.
10 Apply a little clean oil to the nut/wheel bearing contact surface, then fit the new driveshaft/hub nut, and tighten to the specified torque, as described in Chapter 8. After tightening, 'stake' the nut as described in Chapter 8.
11 Refit the roadwheel, lower the vehicle to the ground and tighten the roadwheel bolts to the specified torque.

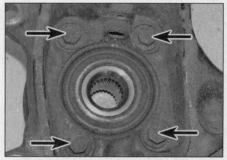

3.6 Front hub assembly retaining bolts (arrowed)

4.2 Pull the brake hose from the bracket on the strut

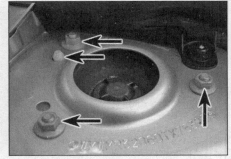

4.3 Insert an Allen key into the end of the shank to counterhold the anti-roll bar link shank (arrowed)

4.6 Strut upper mounting nuts and centring pin (arrowed)

4 Front suspension strut assembly – removal and refitting

Removal

1 Raise the front of the vehicle and support it securely on axle stands (see *Jacking and vehicle support*). Remove the front road wheels.

2 Pull the brake hose from the bracket on the strut **(see illustration)**.

3 Remove the nut from the anti-roll bar link and disconnect it from the strut. Use an Allen key to counterhold the link balljoint shank, or on early models, use a second spanner **(see illustration)**.

3 Release the wheel speed sensor and (where fitted) the brake pad wear sensor wiring from the bracket on the strut.

4 Undo the track rod end nut from the hub carrier, and use a separator tool to detach the track rod end from the hub carrier **(see illustration 22.4)**.

5 Unscrew and remove the pinch-bolt securing the hub carrier assembly to the front suspension strut, noting which way round it is fitted (from the rear). Lever the hub carrier assembly down and release it from the strut **(see illustration 2.7)**. If necessary, tap the carrier downwards with a soft-headed mallet to separate the two components. **Note:** *Support the hub carrier assembly when*

released from the strut, to prevent any damage to the driveshaft/wiring.

6 The upper mounting bearing plate has a centring pin which locates in a corresponding hole in the vehicle body. If this pin is missing, make alignment marks between the mounting studs and the body. This will preserve the camber setting when the assembly is refitted. Support the strut/spring assembly under the wheelarch, then remove the upper mounting nuts **(see illustration)**. Discard the nuts, new ones must be fitted.

7 Lower the suspension strut from under the wheelarch, withdrawing it from the vehicle.

Refitting

8 Refitting is a reversal of removal. Making sure that all the relevant bolts are tightened to their specified torque. **Note:** *The strut pinch bolt/nut must be tightened by rotating the bolt only.*

5 Front suspension strut – overhaul

⚠️ **Warning: Before attempting to dismantle the front suspension strut, a tool to hold the coil spring in compression must be obtained. Do not attempt to use makeshift methods. Uncontrolled release of the spring could cause damage and**

personal injury. Use a high-quality spring compressor, and carefully follow the tool manufacturer's instructions provided with it. After removing the coil spring with the compressor still fitted, place it in a safe, isolated area.

1 If the front suspension struts exhibit signs of wear (leaking fluid, loss of damping capability, sagging or cracked coil springs) then they should be dismantled and overhauled as necessary. The struts themselves cannot be serviced, and should be renewed if faulty; the springs and related components can be renewed individually. To maintain balanced characteristics on both sides of the vehicle, the components on both sides should be renewed at the same time.

2 With the strut removed from the vehicle (see Section 4), clean away all external dirt.

3 Fit the coil spring compressor tools (ensuring that they are fully engaged), and compress the spring until all tension is relieved from the upper mounting **(see illustration)**.

4 Prise off the plastic cap, then hold the strut piston rod with an Allen key, and unscrew the thrust bearing retaining nut with a ring spanner or spark plug type socket with the hexagon section on the outside (or similar) **(see illustrations)**. Discard the nut, a new one must be fitted.

5 Withdraw the top mounting/thrust bearing, dished washer, shim, upper spring cup, rubber spring seat, then slide the damper

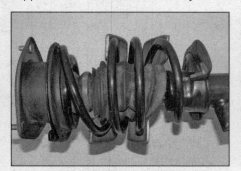

5.3 Fully compress the spring

5.4a Prise off the plastic cap...

5.4b ...then undo the piston nut, counterholding the piston with an Allen key/bit

5.5a Remove the top mounting/thrust bearing...

5.5b ...dished washer...

5.5c ...shim...

body, with the auxiliary damper/gaiter from the compressed spring **(see illustrations)**.

6 Remove the auxiliary damper, gaiter and lower spring pad from the damper body.

7 If a new spring is to be fitted, the original spring must now be carefully released from the compressor. If it is to be re-used, the spring can be left in compression.

8 With the strut assembly now completely dismantled, examine all the components for wear and damage, and check the bearing for smoothness of operation. Renew components as necessary.

9 Examine the strut for signs of fluid leakage. Check the strut piston rod for signs of pitting along its entire length, and check the strut body for signs of damage. Test the operation of the strut, while holding it in an upright position, by attempting to move the piston. It should only be possible to move the piston a very small amount. If it's easy to move or shows little/uneven resistance, or if there is any visible sign of wear or damage to the strut, renewal is necessary.

10 Reassembly is a reversal of dismantling, noting the following points:

a) *Ensure the lower spring pad locating lugs engage correctly with the holes in the damper body flange* **(see illustration)**.

b) *Make sure that the coil spring ends are correctly located in the upper and lower seats before releasing the compressor* **(see illustration)**.

c) *Check that the bearing is correctly fitted to the piston rod seat.*

d) *Tighten the new thrust bearing retaining nut to the specified torque.*

e) *The smaller diameter coil must be fitted against the lower spring seat.*

5.5d ...upper spring cup and seat...

5.5e ...then slide the damper body, auxiliary damper and gaiter from the spring

joint shank as applicable **(see illustration)** Discard the nut – a new one must be fitted.

2 Lower the front subframe as described in Chapter 7A or Chapter 7B.

3 Slacken and remove the four bolts securing

the anti-roll bar clamps to the subframe, then manoeuvre the anti-roll bar from position **(see illustration)**.

4 If required, remove the metal clamp, and prise the rubber bushes from the anti-roll bar.

5.10a Lower spring seat pad locating lugs and holes (arrowed)

5.10b Ensure the ends of the spring are correctly located in the seats

---

6 Front anti-roll bar and links –
removal and refitting

Removal

Anti-roll bar

1 Undo the nut securing the lower end of the links to the anti-roll bar. Use an Allen key to counterhold the balljoint shank or second spanner on the hexagonal section of the ball

6.1 Use an Allen key/bit to counterhold the anti-roll bar link rod joint shank

6.3 Undo the anti-roll bar clamp bolts each side (arrowed)

7.2 Undo the bolt (arrowed) securing the height sensor bracket to the lower arm

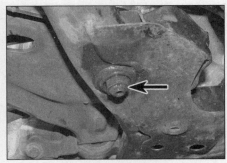

7.4 Slacken the lower arm inner balljoint retaining nut (arrowed)

7.7 Note the fitted position of the lower arm rear bush/mounting

Anti-roll bar links

5 Slacken the relevant front roadwheel bolts, then jack up the front of the vehicle and support it securely on axle stands. Remove the roadwheel.

6 Undo the nuts securing the links to the anti-roll bar and suspension strut. Use an Allen key to counterhold the link's balljoint shanks. On some models, use a second spanner to counterhold the upper balljoint shank **(see illustration 4.3)**.

Refitting

Anti-roll bar

7 When fitting the anti-roll bar bushes make sure they are located correctly on the anti-roll bar, then apply a little Circo Light lubricant (available from MINI dealers) to the outside surface of the bushes, and refit the metal clamps, .

8 Manoeuvre the anti-roll bar into position, and refit the clamps and bolts. Tighten the clamp bolts to the specified torque.

9 Refit the front subframe as described in Chapter 2A.

10 Reconnect the anti-roll bar links and tighten the nuts to the specified torque.

Anti-roll bar links

11 Reconnect the links to the anti-roll bar and suspension strut, then tighten the nuts to the specified torque.

12 Refit the roadwheel and lower the vehicle to the ground.

7 Front suspension lower arm – removal and refitting

Removal

1 Slacken the front roadwheel bolts, raise the front of the vehicle and support it securely on axle stands (see *Jacking and vehicle support*). Remove the front road wheel.

2 If removing the left-hand side lower arm, undo the retaining screw and remove the ride height sensor arm bracket (where fitted) from the lower arm **(see illustration)**.

3 Remove the lower arm outer balljoint as described in Section 8.

4 Slacken the nut securing the lower arm balljoint to the subframe, then strike the balljoint from below to 'break' the taper **(see illustration)**. Note the balljoint end must not be damaged, and the nut must not be re-used. If available, screw MINI tool No. 311040 (mandrel) onto the end of the balljoint to protect it from hammer blows.

5 Lower the front subframe as described in Chapter 7A or Chapter 7B.

6 Undo the bolts securing the front anti-roll bar to the subframe, then manoeuvre the lower arm assembly from place **(see illustration 6.3)**.

7 The lower arm rear bush and mounting assembly must be pressed from the arm, then the bush must be pressed out from, and back into the rear mounting bracket. If a press is available, note the fitted depth and position

of the bush prior to removing the arm/bush to enable refitting **(see illustration)**. If a press is not available, entrust this task to a MINI dealer or suitably equipped specialist.

8 The front/inner balljoint is integral with the lower arm.

Refitting

9 Removal is a reversal of removal, noting the following points:

a) *Press the bush on the rear of the lower arm, to the same depth as the original.*
b) *Replace all self-locking nuts removed.*
c) *Replace the inner balljoint-to-subframe nut.*
d) *Tighten all fasteners to their specified torque where given.*
e) *Have the front wheel alignment checked as described in Section 23.*

8 Front suspension lower arm outer balljoint – renewal

1 Slacken the relevant front roadwheel bolts, then jack up the front of the vehicle and support it securely on axle stands. Remove the roadwheel.

2 Undo the two bolts securing the lower balljoint to the lower arm **(see illustration)**. Discard the nuts, new ones must be fitted.

3 Undo the outer balljoint nut, and use a separator tool to detach the balljoint from the hub carrier **(see illustrations)**. **Note:** *If the separator tool available will not locate correctly*

8.2 Lower arm outer balljoint retaining nuts (arrowed)

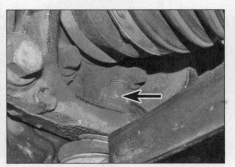

8.3a Lower balljoint-to-hub carrier nut (arrowed)

8.3b If necessary, withdrawn the driveshaft to be able to located the separator tool on the balljoint

on the balljoint, disconnect the steering track rod balljoint from the hub carrier, then undo the nut and pull the hub carrier from the driveshaft a little to increase access for the tool.

4 Secure the new balljoint to the lower arm using new nuts, and tighten them to the specified torque.

5 The remainder of refitting is a reversal of removal. Have the front wheel alignment checked at the earliest opportunity.

9 Rear hub and bearings – inspection and renewal

Inspection

1 The rear hub bearings are non-adjustable.

2 To check the bearings for excessive wear, chock the front wheels, then jack up the rear of the vehicle and support it on axle stands. Fully release the handbrake.

3 Grip the rear wheel at the top and bottom, and attempt to rock it. If excessive movement is noted, or if there is any roughness or vibration felt when the wheel is spun, it is indicative that the hub bearings are worn.

Renewal

4 Remove the rear brake disc (see Chapter 9).

5 Unscrew the ABS sensor retaining bolt, and pull the sensor from place (see illustration).

6 Undo the four mounting bolts and remove the hub and bearing assembly from the hub trailing arm (see illustration).

7 The wheel bearings are integral with the hub and not available separately.

8 Clean the hub seating face on the trailing arm.

9 Position the new hub/bearing assembly against the trailing arm, refit and tighten the bolts to the specified torque.

10 Refit the wheel speed sensor, and tighten the bolt to the specified torque.

11 Refit the rear brake disc as described in Chapter 9.

10 Rear shock absorber – removal and refitting

Removal

1 Chock the front wheels, then jack up the rear of the vehicle and support it on axle stands. Remove the wheels as required.

2 Release the brake hose and wiring harness from the shock absorber bracket.

3 Unscrew and remove the shock absorber lower mounting bolt (see illustration).

4 Undo the two upper mounting bolts, and manoeuvre the shock absorber from place (see illustration).

Refitting

5 Refitting is a reversal of the removal procedure, tightening the mounting bolts to their specified torque. Note: The trailing arm

9.5 ABS sensor retaining bolt (arrowed)

10.3 Rear shock absorber lower mounting bolt (arrowed)

will need to be pushed down a little in order to refit the shock absorber lower mounting bolt. Note: The final tightening of the lower mounting bolt must be carried out with the vehicle weight on the road wheels.

11 Rear shock absorber – overhaul

⚠️ Warning: Before attempting to dismantle the rear suspension strut, a tool to hold the coil spring in compression must be obtained. Do not attempt to use makeshift methods. Uncontrolled release of the spring could cause damage and personal injury. Use a high-quality spring compressor, and carefully follow the tool manufacturer's instructions provided with it. After removing the coil spring with the compressor still fitted, place it in a safe, isolated area.

11.3 Fully compress the coil spring

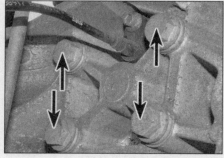

9.6 Rear hub retaining bolts (arrowed)

10.4 Rear shock absorber upper mounting bolts (arrowed)

1 If the suspension struts exhibit signs of wear (leaking fluid, loss of damping capability, sagging or cracked coil springs) then they should be dismantled and overhauled as necessary. The struts themselves cannot be serviced, and should be renewed if faulty; the springs and related components can be renewed individually. To maintain balanced characteristics on both sides of the vehicle, the components on both sides should be renewed at the same time.

2 With the strut removed from the vehicle (see Section 10), clean away all external dirt, then mount in a vice.

3 Fit the coil spring compressor tools (ensuring that they are fully engaged), and compress the spring until all tension is relieved from the upper mounting (see illustration).

4 Hold the strut piston rod with an Allen key, and unscrew the thrust bearing retaining nut with a ring spanner or socket with an external hexagon section (see illustration).

11.4 Counterhold the piston rod with an Allen key/bit

11.5a Remove the concave washer (arrowed)...

11.5b ...foam washer...

dismantled, examine all the components for wear and damage, and check the bearing for smoothness of operation. Renew components as necessary.

8 Examine the strut for signs of fluid leakage. Check the strut piston rod for signs of pitting along its entire length, and check the strut body for signs of damage. Test the operation of the strut, while holding it in an upright position, by moving the piston through a full stroke, and then through short strokes of 50 to 100 mm. In both cases, the resistance felt should be smooth and continuous. If the resistance is jerky, uneven, or if there is any visible sign of wear or damage to the strut, renewal is necessary.

9 Reassembly is a reversal of dismantling, noting the following points:

a) *Make sure that the coil spring narrow end is correctly located in the lower seat, and*

5 Withdraw the concave washer, foam washer, metal bushing, upper mounting plate, foam bush, upper spring seat, spring rubber seat, washer, bump stop, plastic shroud, spring and lower spring rubber seat **(see illustrations)**.

6 If a new spring is to be fitted, the original spring must now be carefully released from the compressor. If it is to be re-used, the spring can be left in compression.

7 With the strut assembly now completely

11.5c ...metal bushing...

11.5d ...upper mounting plate...

11.5e ...foam bush...

11.5f ...upper spring seat/rubber...

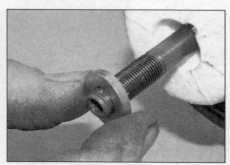

11.5g ...washer...

11.5h ...bump stop...

11.5i ...plastic shroud...

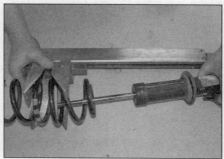

11.5j ...spring...

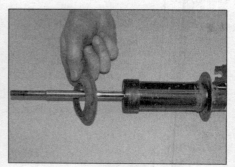

11.5k ...and lower spring seat

the upper spring correctly locates in the upper spring seat **(see illustration)**.

b) Refit the washer above the bump stop with the bevelled inner edge downwards **(see illustration)**.

c) Check that the bearing is correctly fitted to the piston rod seat.

d) Tighten the thrust bearing retaining nut to the specified torque.

12 Rear anti-roll bar, bushes and links – removal and refitting

Removal

1 Slacken the rear roadwheel bolts, then jack up the rear of the vehicle, and support it securely on axle stands (see *Jacking and vehicle support*). Remove both rear roadwheels.

Anti-roll bar

2 Undo the fasteners and remove the left, and right-hand side underbody panelling **(see illustration)**.

3 On convertible models, remove the cross reinforcement **(see illustration)**.

4 Remove both rear shock absorbers as described in Section 10.

5 Undo the nuts securing the anti-roll links to the anti-roll bar and trailing arm. Use an Allen key or second spanner to counterhold the balljoint shank as the nut is slackened **(see illustration)**. Discard the nuts – new ones must be fitted.

6 Undo the nuts/screws and remove the heat shield below the rear axle assembly. It may be necessary to release the exhaust system from the rubber mountings to provide sufficient clearance.

7 Release the metal brake pipes from the clips on the vehicle body in front of the fuel tank.

8 Position a trolley jack under the rear subframe, slacken and remove the four subframe mounting bolts. Discard the bolts – new ones must be fitted.

9 Lower the subframe a maximum of 40 mm.

10 Undo the bolts securing the anti-roll bar clamps to the subframe, and manoeuvre the bar from position **(see illustration)**.

12.5 Insert an Allen key/bit into the end of the balljoint shank to counterhold (arrowed)

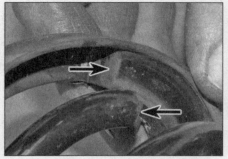

11.9a Ensure the spring end locates against the step in the seat (arrowed)

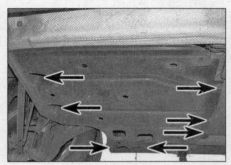

12.2 Undo the fasteners (arrowed) and remove the underbody panelling each side

Bushes

11 Undo the bolts securing the anti-roll bar clamps to the subframe, prise up the metal clamps and remove the bushes **(see illustration 12.10)**.

Links

12 Undo the nuts securing the anti-roll links to the anti-roll bar and trailing arm. Use an Allen key or second spanner to counterhold the balljoint shank as the nut is slackened **(see illustration 12.5)**. Discard the nuts – new ones must be fitted.

Refitting

13 When fitting the bushes to the anti-roll bar, make sure they are located correctly with no lubricant (except water if required).

14 Locate the anti-roll bar on the rear

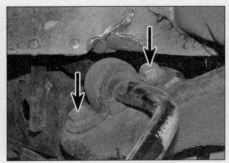

12.10 Rear anti-roll bar clamp bolts (arrowed)

11.9b The bevelled side of the washer locates against the conical shoulder of the piston rod (arrowed)

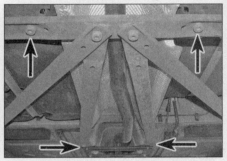

12.3 Undo the convertible models cross reinforcement bolts (arrowed) – outer bolts not shown

subframe, then refit the clamps and tighten the bolts to the specified torque.

15 Lift the subframe and tighten the mounting bolts to the specified torque.

16 The remainder of refitting is a reversal of removal.

13 Rear suspension trailing arm – removal, overhaul and refitting
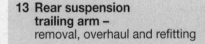

Removal

1 Remove the rear brake disc (see Chapter 9).

2 Undo and remove the nut securing the anti-roll bar link to the trailing arm **(see illustration)**. Use an Allen key or second spanner to counterhold the balljoint shank whilst undoing the nut.

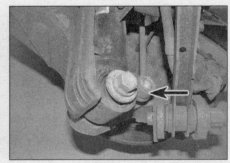

13.2 Disconnect the anti-roll bar link rod (arrowed)

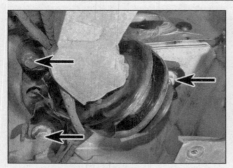

13.7 Undo the bolts (arrowed) securing the trailing arm bracket to the vehicle body

3 Undo the bolt and remove the wheel speed sensor from the trailing arm (see Chapter 9).

4 Mark the position of the lower control arm mounting bolt eccentric washer in relation to the trailing arm, in order to preserve the rear wheel alignment upon reassembly, then slacken and remove the bolts securing the control arms to the trailing arm **(see illustrations 14.5 and 14.6)**.

5 Slacken and remove the lower shock absorber mounting bolt.

6 Detach the wheel speed sensor and brake pad wear sensor cables from the retaining clips on the trailing arm.

7 Make alignment marks between the trailing arm bush mounting plate and the vehicle body to aid refitment, then undo the bolts and manoeuvre the trailing arm from the vehicle **(see illustration)**.

8 If required, undo the four bolts and detach the hub/bearing assembly from the trailing arm.

Overhaul

9 To replace the metal/rubber bush on the trailing arm, undo the retaining bolt and washer **(see illustration)**.

10 At the time of writing, the bush was not available separately from the mounting bracket. If the bush is worn or damaged, the bracket/bush assembly must be renewed as a compete unit.

11 Position the new bracket/bush against the trailing arm, fit the bolt, but only finger-tighten it at this stage. The final tightening of the bolt should be carried out once the wheels are back on the ground and the vehicle normally loaded.

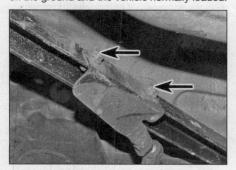

14.5 Undo the bolts (arrowed) and detach the height sensor bracket from the arm

13.9 Unscrew the bolt and slide the mount bush assembly from the trailing arm

Refitting

12 Refitting is a reversal of the removal procedure, noting the following points:

a) Delay fully tightening the control arm, and trailing arm-mounting bolts, until the vehicle wheels are one the ground, and normally loaded. Normally loaded is defined as 68 kg on each front seat, 14 kg in the centre of the luggage compartment, and a full tank of fuel.

b) Align the previously made marks prior to tightening the trailing arm bush mounting bracket bolts

c) The wheel alignment will also require checking, see Section 23.

14 Rear suspension control arms – removal and refitting

Removal

Note: The bushes in the suspension arms cannot be renewed separately; renew the complete arm if there is any wear or damage.

1 Slacken the relevant rear roadwheel bolts, then jack up the rear of the vehicle and support it on axle stands (see Jacking and vehicle support). Remove the relevant roadwheel.

2 Undo the fasteners and remove the rear underbody panelling on the relevant side. On convertible models, undo the bolts and remove the rear cross reinforcement assembly **(see illustration 12.2 and 12.3)**.

3 Remove the spare wheel where applicable.

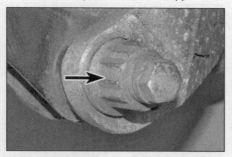

14.6 Make alignment marks between the serrated eccentric nut and the trailing arm (arrowed)

4 Remove the heat shield below the rear axle assembly.

5 If removing the left-hand side upper control arm, undo the bolts and detach the ride-height sensor arm bracket (where fitted) from the arm **(see illustration)**.

6 Prior to removing the lower control arm outer retaining bolt, make alignment marks between the serrated eccentric nut and the trailing arm, to preserve the rear wheel alignment upon refitting **(see illustration)**.

7 Slacken and remove the control arm retaining bolts and manoeuvre the arm from under the vehicle **(see illustration)**. Renew the self-locking nuts.

Refitting

8 Refitting is a reversal of the removal procedure, aligning the previously made marks (lower control arm outer bolt eccentric washer only). Delay fully tightening the control arm mounting bolts, until the vehicle is back on its wheels and normally loaded. Normally loaded is defined as 68 kg on each front seat, 14 kg in the centre of the luggage compartment, and a full tank of fuel.

15 Rear suspension subframe – removal and refitting

Removal

1 Slacken the rear roadwheel bolts, then jack up the rear of the vehicle, and support it securely on axle stands (see Jacking and vehicle support). Remove both rear roadwheels.

2 Remove the rear section of the exhaust system (see Chapter 4A).

3 Remove both handbrake cables as described in Chapter 9.

4 Remove the upper and lower control arms as described in Section 14.

5 Disengage the wheel speed sensor wiring harnesses from the retaining brackets on the subframe.

6 Slacken the union nut, and disconnect the brake hose each side under the subframe. Be prepared for fluid spillage. Plug the ends of the pipes to prevent fluid loss and dirt/water ingress.

7 Undo the bolts securing the anti-roll bar clamps to the subframe **(see illustration 12.10)**.

14.7 Rear control arms inner mounting bolts

8 Place a trolley jack and length of wood under the fuel tank to support it, and undo the two bolts securing the tank retaining straps to the subframe.

9 Undo the four subframe mounting bolts, lower the subframe and manoeuvre it from under the vehicle.

Refitting

10 Refitting is a reversal of the removal procedure, noting the following points:

a) *Tighten all bolts to the specified torque.*

b) *Check, and if necessary have the rear wheel toe setting adjusted.*

16 Steering wheel –
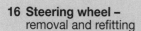
removal and refitting

> ⚠ **Warning:** *All models are equipped with an airbag system. Make sure that the safety recommendations given in Chapter 12 are followed, to prevent personal injury.*

Removal

1 Remove the airbag module (see Chapter 12).

2 Ensure the wheel is in the straight-ahead position, then disconnect the steering wheel switch wiring plugs from the rotary contact unit.

3 Unscrew the retaining bolt from the centre of the steering wheel **(see illustration)**.

4 Remove the steering wheel from the top of the column.

Refitting

5 Make sure that the front wheels are still facing straight-ahead, then locate the steering wheel on the top of the steering column. Align the master splines of the column shaft and steering wheel boss. Note the pin on the rotary contact unit which must locate in the rear of the steering wheel **(see illustration)**.

6 Refit the retaining bolt, and tighten it to the specified torque while holding the steering wheel.

7 Reconnect the wiring connector(s) for the horn and other steering wheel switches (where applicable).

8 Refit the airbag as described in Chapter 12.

16.3 The end of the steering column shaft has a master spline indicated by the factory-made mark (arrowed)

17 Steering column –
removal, inspection and refitting

> ⚠ **Warning:** *All models are equipped with an airbag system. Make sure that the safety recommendations given in Chapter 12 are followed, to prevent personal injury.*

Removal

1 Remove the steering wheel as described in Section 16.

2 Remove the rev counter as described in Chapter 12.

3 Unclip and remove the steering column upper shroud **(see illustration)**.

4 Remove the panel beneath the steering

17.3 Squeeze together the sides and unclip the upper shroud

16.5 The pin on the rotary contact unit (arrowed) must align with the hole in the rear of the steering wheel

column **(see illustration)**. Disconnect the wiring plug as panel is withdrawn.

5 Undo the 4 retaining screws, and remove the steering column lower shroud **(see illustrations)**.

6 Remove the pinch bolt securing the column universal joint to the steering rack pinion **(see illustration)**. Discard the bolt, a new one must be fitted. Note that universal joint will only fit correctly on the steering rack pinion in one place.

7 Note the harness routing, then disconnect the steering column wiring plug(s), and release the wiring harness from any wiring plugs.

8 Undo the 4 bolts and manoeuvre the column assembly from the vehicle **(see illustration)**.

Inspection

9 With the steering lock disengaged, attempt

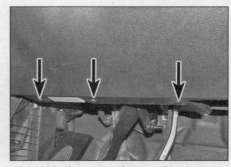

17.4 Undo the screws (arrowed) and remove the panel beneath the steering column

17.5a The steering column lower shroud is secured by screws above (arrowed)...

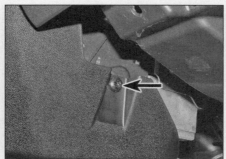

17.5b ...and each side (arrowed)

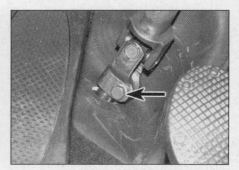

17.6 Remove the steering column universal joint pinch bolt (arrowed)

17.8 Steering column mounting bolts (arrowed)

18.5 Steering column lock wiring plug and shear bolts (arrowed)

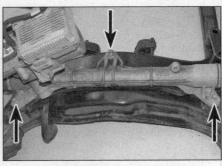

19.5 Steering rack mounting bolts (arrowed)

to move the steering wheel up-and-down and also to the left-and-right without turning the wheel, to check for steering column bearing wear, steering column shaft joint play and steering wheel or steering column being loose. The steering column cannot be repaired, if any faults are detected install a new column.
10 Examine the height adjustment lever mechanism for wear and damage.
11 With the steering column removed, check the universal joints for wear, and examine the column upper and lower shafts for any signs of damage or distortion. Where evident, the column should be renewed complete.

Refitting

12 Refitting is a reversal of removal, noting the following points:
a) *Make sure the wheels are still in the straight-ahead position when the steering column is installed.*
b) *Fit new locking bolts to the steering column mounting bracket.*
c) *Fit new pinch-bolt to the steering column universal joint, which joins to the steering rack.*
d) *Tighten all fasteners to their specified torque where given.*
e) *See Chapter 12 before refitting the airbag.*
f) *If the electronic stability program warning light (if fitted), comes on after installing the steering column the system will need re-configuring at a MINI dealer dedicated test equipment, or at a suitably equipped specialist.*

18 Steering column lock – removal and refitting

1 Disconnect the battery negative lead as described in Chapter 5A.
2 Unclip and remove the steering column upper shroud (see illustration 17.3).
3 Remove the panel trim the steering column (see illustration 17.4). Disconnect the wiring plug as the panel is withdrawn.
4 Undo the 4 retaining screws, and remove the steering column lower shroud (see illustrations 17.5a and 17.5b).
5 Disconnect the wiring plug, then remove

the 2 shear bolts and manoeuvre the lock assembly from place (see illustration).
6 Refitting is a reversal of removal. Tighten the new shear bolts until the heads of the bolts 'shear' off.

19 Power steering rack – removal and refitting

Removal

1 Centralise the steering wheel so that the front wheels are in the straight-ahead position, then disconnect the battery negative lead as described in Chapter 5A.
2 Slacken both front roadwheel bolts, then jack up the front of the vehicle and support it securely on axle stands. Remove both front roadwheels.
3 Unscrew the track rod end nuts, and detach the rods from the hub carriers using a conventional balljoint removal tool (see illustration 22.4). Take care not to damage the balljoint seals.
4 Lower the front subframe as described in Chapter 7A or Chapter 7B.
5 Undo the bolts securing the rack to the subframe, and manoeuvre the rack to the left-hand side, and out from the engine compartment (see illustration).

Refitting

6 Refitting is a reversal of removal, noting the following points:
a) *Tighten all fasteners to their specified torque where given.*

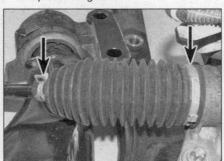

20.2 Release the clips (arrowed) and remove the gaiter

b) *Renew the steering column lower universal joint pinch bolt.*
c) *If a new rack/EPS unit has been fitted, it will need to be programmed using MINI diagnostic equipment. Entrust this task to a MINI dealer or suitably equipped repairer.*
d) *Check the front wheel alignment as described in Section 23.*

20 Power steering gear rubber gaiters – renewal

1 Remove the track rod end and its locknut from the track rod, as described in Section 22. Make sure that a note is made of the exact position of the track rod end on the track rod, in order to retain the front wheel alignment setting on refitting.
2 Release the outer and inner retaining clips, and disconnect the gaiter from the steering gear housing (see illustration).
3 Slide the gaiter off the track rod.
4 Apply grease to the track rod inner joint. Wipe clean the seating areas on the steering gear housing and track rod.
5 Slide the new gaiter onto the track rod and steering gear housing.
6 Fit a new inner and outer retaining clips.
7 Refit the track rod end as described in Section 22.
8 Have the front wheel alignment checked, and if necessary adjusted, at the earliest opportunity (refer to Section 23).

21 Electronic Power Steering (EPS) unit – removal and refitting

Removal

1 Disconnect the battery negative (earth) lead (refer to Chapter 5A).
2 Jack up the front of the vehicle and support it on axle stands (see *Jacking and vehicle support*). Release the fasteners and remove the engine undershield.
3 Remove the air cleaner assembly as described in Chapter 4A or Chapter 4B.
4 Working in the engine compartment, disconnect the wiring plugs from the

EPS (Electronic Power Steering) unit **(see illustration)**.

5 Working underneath the vehicle, undo the bolts securing the EPS unit to the steering rack **(see illustration)**. Discard the bolts, new ones must be fitted.

Manual transmission

6 Remove the EPS unit from above.

Automatic transmission

7 Undo the nuts securing the links to the anti-roll bar, and rotate the anti-roll bar upwards.
8 Unclip the air conditioning refrigerant pipe from the sump.
9 Remove the EPS unit from below.

Refitting

10 Refitting is a reversal of removal, noting the following points.
  a) *Tighten the fasteners to the specified torque where given.*
  b) *Renew the O-ring seal between the EPS unit and the steering rack.*
  c) *Ensure the drive cog of the EPS unit engages correctly with the 'clutch' of the steering rack.*
  d) *If a new EPS unit has been fitted, it must be programmed using MINI diagnostic equipment. Entrust this task to a MINI dealer or suitably equipped repairer.*

22 Track rod end – renewal

Removal

1 Apply the handbrake, then jack up the front of the vehicle and support it on axle stands. Remove the appropriate front roadwheel.
2 Count the number of threads exposed on the inner section of the track rod to aid refitting, then slacken the clamp bolt securing the track rod end to the track rod **(see illustration)**.
3 Unscrew and remove the track rod end balljoint retaining nut.
4 To release the tapered shank of the balljoint from the hub carrier, use a balljoint separator tool **(see illustration)** (if the balljoint is to be re-used, take care not to damage the dust cover when using the separator tool).

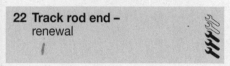

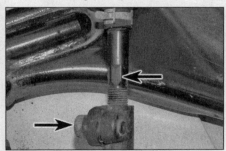

22.2 Slacken the clamp bolt, then unscrew the track rod end, counterholding with a spanner on the hexagonal section (arrowed)

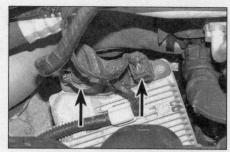

21.4 Working at the rear of the engine, disconnect the EPS unit wiring plugs (arrowed)

5 Unscrew the track rod end from the track rod, counting the number of turns necessary to remove it. If necessary, hold the track rod stationary with using the flats provided.

Refitting

6 Screw the track rod end onto the track rod by the number of turns noted during removal.
7 Engage the shank of the balljoint with the hub carrier, and refit the nut. Tighten the nut to the specified torque. If the balljoint shank turns while the nut is being tightened, use an Allen key to hold the shank or press up on the balljoint. The tapered fit of the shank will lock it, and prevent rotation as the nut is tightened.
8 Tighten the track rod clamp bolt to the specified torque.
9 Refit the roadwheel, and lower the vehicle to the ground.
10 Finally check, and if necessary adjust, the front wheel alignment as described in Section 23.

23 Wheel alignment and steering angles – general information

1 Accurate front wheel alignment is essential to provide positive steering, and to prevent excessive tyre wear. Before considering the steering/suspension geometry, check that the tyres are correctly inflated, that the front wheels are not buckled, and that the steering linkage and suspension joints are in good order, without slackness or wear.

22.4 Use a separator tool to detach the balljoint from the hub carrier

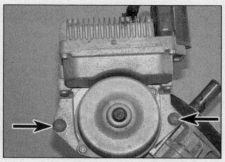

21.5 EPS unit retaining bolts (arrowed)

2 Wheel alignment consists of four factors **(see illustration)**:

Camber is the angle at which the front wheels are set from the vertical, when viewed from the front of the vehicle. 'Positive camber'

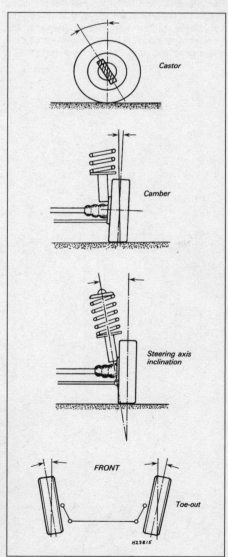

23.2 Wheel alignment and steering angle measurements

is the amount (in degrees) that the wheels are tilted outward at the top of the vertical.

Castor is the angle between the steering axis and a vertical line, when viewed from each side of the car. 'Positive castor' is when the steering axis is inclined rearward at the top.

Steering axis inclination is the angle (when viewed from the front of the vehicle) between the vertical and an imaginary line drawn through the suspension strut upper mounting and the lower suspension arm balljoint.

Toe setting is the amount by which the distance between the front inside edges of the roadwheels (measured at hub height) differs from the diametrically-opposite distance measured between the rear inside edges of the roadwheels.

3 With the exception of the toe setting, all other steering angles are set during manufacture, and no adjustment is possible. It can be assumed, therefore, that unless the vehicle has suffered accident damage, all the pre-set steering angles will be correct. Should there be some doubt about their accuracy, it will be necessary to seek the help of a MINI dealer, as special gauges are needed to check the steering angles.

4 Two methods are available to the home mechanic for checking the toe setting. One method is to use a gauge to measure the distance between the front and rear inside edges of the roadwheels. The other method is to use a scuff plate, in which each front wheel is rolled across a movable plate which records any deviation, or scuff, of the tyre from the straight-ahead position as it moves across the plate. Relatively-inexpensive equipment of both types is available from accessory outlets.

5 Before checking the steering geometry, the vehicle must be loaded to the 'normal' position. To set the vehicle ready for checking, place a 68 kg load on each front seat, a 14 kg load in the luggage compartment, and ensure the fuel tank is full.

6 If, after checking the toe setting using whichever method is preferable, it is found that adjustment is necessary, proceed as follows.

7 Turn the steering wheel onto full-left lock, and record the number of exposed threads on the right-hand track rod. Now turn the steering onto full-right lock, and record the number of threads on the left-hand track rod. If there are the same number of threads visible on both sides, then subsequent adjustment can be made equally on both sides. If there are more threads visible on one side than the other, it will be necessary to compensate for this during adjustment. *After adjustment, there should be the same number of threads visible on each track rod. This is most important.*

8 To alter the toe setting, slacken the clamp bolt on the track rod end **(see illustration 22.2)**, and turn the track rod using the flats provided to achieve the desired setting. When viewed from the side of the car, turning the rod clockwise will increase the toe-in, turning it anti-clockwise will increase the toe-out. Only turn the track rods by a quarter of a turn each time, and then recheck the setting.

9 After adjustment, tighten the clamp bolts. Reposition the steering gear rubber gaiters, to remove any twist caused by turning the track rods.

Chapter 11
Bodywork and fittings

Contents

Degrees of difficulty

Easy, suitable for novice with little experience		**Fairly easy,** suitable for beginner with some experience		**Fairly difficult,** suitable for competent DIY mechanic		**Difficult,** suitable for experienced DIY mechanic		**Very difficult,** suitable for expert DIY or professional	

Specifications

Torque wrench settings	Nm	lbf ft
Facia crossmember bolts (M10).	34	25
Front seat mounting bolts (use thread-locking compound)	36	26
Seat belt bolts*	36	26

Do not re-use

---

1 General information

The bodyshell and underframe on all models feature variable thickness steel. Achieved by laser-welded technology, used to join steel panels of different gauges. This gives a stiffer structure, with mounting points being more rigid, which gives an improved crash performance.

An additional safety crossmember is incorporated between the A-pillars in the upper area of the bulkhead, and the facia and steering column are secured to it. The lower bulkhead area is reinforced by additional systems of members connected to the front

of the vehicle. The body side rocker panels (sills) have been divided along the length of the vehicle by internal reinforcement, this functions like a double tube which increases its strength. All doors are reinforced and incorporate side impact protection, which is secured in the door structure.

All sheet metal surfaces which are prone to corrosion are galvanised. The painting process includes a base colour which closely matches the final topcoat, so that any stone damage is not as noticeable. The front wings are of a bolt-on type to ease their replacement if required.

Automatic seat belts are fitted to all models, and the front seat safety belts are equipped with a pyrotechnic pretension seat belt stack,

which is attached to the seat frame of each front seat. In the event of a serious front impact, the system is triggered and pulls the stalk buckle downwards to tension the seat belt. It is not possible to reset the tensioner once fired, and it must therefore be renewed. The tensioners are fired by an explosive charge similar to that used in the airbag, and are triggered via the airbag control module.

In the UK, central locking is standard on all models. In other countries, it is available on certain models only. In the event of a serious accident, a crash sensor unlocks all doors if they were previously locked.

Many of the procedures in this Chapter require the battery to be disconnected. Refer to Chapter 5A, first.

2 Maintenance – bodywork and underframe

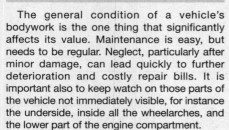

The general condition of a vehicle's bodywork is the one thing that significantly affects its value. Maintenance is easy, but needs to be regular. Neglect, particularly after minor damage, can lead quickly to further deterioration and costly repair bills. It is important also to keep watch on those parts of the vehicle not immediately visible, for instance the underside, inside all the wheelarches, and the lower part of the engine compartment.

The basic maintenance routine for the bodywork is washing – preferably with a lot of water, from a hose. This will remove all the loose solids which may have stuck to the vehicle. It is important to flush these off in such a way as to prevent grit from scratching the finish. The wheelarches and underframe need washing in the same way, to remove any accumulated mud, which will retain moisture and tend to encourage rust. Paradoxically enough, the best time to clean the underframe and wheelarches is in wet weather, when the mud is thoroughly wet and soft. In very wet weather, the underframe is usually cleaned of large accumulations automatically, and this is a good time for inspection.

Periodically, except on vehicles with a wax-based underbody protective coating, it is a good idea to have the whole of the underframe of the vehicle steam-cleaned, engine compartment included, so that a thorough inspection can be carried out to see what minor repairs and renovations are necessary. Steam-cleaning is available at many garages, and is necessary for the removal of the accumulation of oily grime, which sometimes is allowed to become thick in certain areas. If steam-cleaning facilities are not available, there are some excellent grease solvents available which can be brush-applied; the dirt can then be simply hosed off. Note that these methods should not be used on vehicles with wax-based underbody protective coating, or the coating will be removed. Such vehicles should be inspected annually, preferably just prior to Winter, when the underbody should be washed down, and any damage to the wax coating repaired. Ideally, a completely fresh coat should be applied. It would also be worth considering the use of such wax-based protection for injection into door panels, sills, box sections, etc, as an additional safeguard against rust damage, where such protection is not provided by the vehicle manufacturer.

After washing paintwork, wipe off with a chamois leather to give an unspotted clear finish. A coat of clear protective wax polish will give added protection against chemical pollutants in the air. If the paintwork sheen has dulled or oxidised, use a cleaner/polisher combination to restore the brilliance of the shine. This requires a little effort, but such dulling is usually caused because regular

washing has been neglected. Care needs to be taken with metallic paintwork, as special non-abrasive cleaner/polisher is required to avoid damage to the finish. Always check that the door and ventilator opening drain holes and pipes are completely clear, so that water can be drained out. Brightwork should be treated in the same way as paintwork. Windscreens and windows can be kept clear of the smeary film which often appears, by the use of proprietary glass cleaner. Never use any form of wax or other body or chromium polish on glass.

3 Maintenance – upholstery and carpets

Mats and carpets should be brushed or vacuum-cleaned regularly, to keep them free of grit. If they are badly stained, remove them from the vehicle for scrubbing or sponging, and make quite sure they are dry before refitting. Seats and interior trim panels can be kept clean by wiping with a damp cloth. If they do become stained (which can be more apparent on light-coloured upholstery), use a little liquid detergent and a soft nail brush to scour the grime out of the grain of the material. Do not forget to keep the headlining clean in the same way as the upholstery. When using liquid cleaners inside the vehicle, do not over-wet the surfaces being cleaned. Excessive damp could get into the seams and padded interior, causing stains, offensive odours or even rot.
Caution: If the inside of the vehicle gets wet accidentally, it is worthwhile taking some trouble to dry it out properly, particularly where carpets are involved. Do not leave oil or electric heaters inside the vehicle for this purpose.

4 Minor body damage – repair

Repairs of minor scratches in bodywork

If the scratch is very superficial, and does not penetrate to the metal of the bodywork, repair is very simple. Lightly rub the area of the scratch with a paintwork renovator, or a very fine cutting paste, to remove loose paint from the scratch, and to clear the surrounding bodywork of wax polish. Rinse the area with clean water.

Apply touch-up paint to the scratch using a fine paint brush; continue to apply fine layers of paint until the surface of the paint in the scratch is level with the surrounding paintwork. Allow the new paint at least two weeks to harden, then blend it into the surrounding paintwork by rubbing the scratch area with a paintwork renovator or a very fine cutting paste. Finally, apply wax polish.

Where the scratch has penetrated right through to the metal of the bodywork, causing the metal to rust, a different repair technique is required. Remove any loose rust from the bottom of the scratch with a penknife, then apply rust-inhibiting paint to prevent the formation of rust in the future. Using a rubber or nylon applicator, fill the scratch with bodystopper paste. If required, this paste can be mixed with cellulose thinners to provide a very thin paste which is ideal for filling narrow scratches. Before the stopper-paste in the scratch hardens, wrap a piece of smooth cotton rag around the top of a finger. Dip the finger in cellulose thinners, and quickly sweep it across the surface of the stopper-paste in the scratch; this will ensure that the surface of the stopper-paste is slightly hollowed. The scratch can now be painted over as described earlier in this Section.

Repairs of dents in bodywork

When deep denting of the vehicle's bodywork has taken place, the first task is to pull the dent out, until the affected bodywork almost attains its original shape. There is little point in trying to restore the original shape completely, as the metal in the damaged area will have stretched on impact, and cannot be reshaped fully to its original contour. It is better to bring the level of the dent up to a point which is about 3 mm below the level of the surrounding bodywork. In cases where the dent is very shallow anyway, it is not worth trying to pull it out at all. If the underside of the dent is accessible, it can be hammered out gently from behind, using a mallet with a wooden or plastic head. Whilst doing this, hold a suitable block of wood firmly against the outside of the panel, to absorb the impact from the hammer blows and thus prevent a large area of the bodywork from being 'belled-out'.

Should the dent be in a section of the bodywork which has a double skin, or some other factor making it inaccessible from behind, a different technique is called for. Drill several small holes through the metal inside the area – particularly in the deeper section. Then screw long self-tapping screws into the holes, just sufficiently for them to gain a good purchase in the metal. Now the dent can be pulled out by pulling on the protruding heads of the screws with a pair of pliers.

The next stage of the repair is the removal of the paint from the damaged area, and from an inch or so of the surrounding 'sound' bodywork. This is accomplished most easily by using a wire brush or abrasive pad on a power drill, although it can be done just as effectively by hand, using sheets of abrasive paper. To complete the preparation for filling, score the surface of the bare metal with a screwdriver or the tang of a file, or alternatively, drill small holes in the affected area. This will provide a really good 'key' for the filler paste.

To complete the repair, see the Section on filling and respraying.

Repairs of rust holes or gashes in bodywork

Remove all paint from the affected area, and from an inch or so of the surrounding 'sound' bodywork, using an abrasive pad or a wire brush on a power drill. If these are not available, a few sheets of abrasive paper will do the job most effectively. With the paint removed, you will be able to judge the severity of the corrosion, and therefore decide whether to renew the whole panel (if this is possible) or to repair the affected area. New body panels are not as expensive as most people think, and it is often quicker and more satisfactory to fit a new panel than to attempt to repair large areas of corrosion.

Remove all fittings from the affected area, except those which will act as a guide to the original shape of the damaged bodywork (e.g. headlight shells etc). Then, using tin snips or a hacksaw blade, remove all loose metal and any other metal badly affected by corrosion. Hammer the edges of the hole inwards, in order to create a slight depression for the filler paste.

Wire-brush the affected area to remove the powdery rust from the surface of the remaining metal. Paint the affected area with rust-inhibiting paint, if the back of the rusted area is accessible, treat this also.

Before filling can take place, it will be necessary to block the hole in some way. This can be achieved by the use of aluminium or plastic mesh, or aluminium tape.

Aluminium or plastic mesh, or glass-fibre matting, is probably the best material to use for a large hole. Cut a piece to the approximate size and shape of the hole to be filled, then position it in the hole so that its edges are below the level of the surrounding bodywork. It can be retained in position by several blobs of filler paste around its periphery.

Aluminium tape should be used for small or very narrow holes. Pull a piece off the roll, trim it to the approximate size and shape required, then pull off the backing paper (if used) and stick the tape over the hole; it can be overlapped if the thickness of one piece is insufficient. Burnish down the edges of the tape with the handle of a screwdriver or similar, to ensure that the tape is securely attached to the metal underneath.

Bodywork repairs – filling and respraying

Before using this Section, see the Sections on dent, deep scratch, rust holes and gash repairs.

Many types of bodyfiller are available, but generally speaking, those proprietary kits which contain a tin of filler paste and a tube of resin hardener are best for this type of repair. A wide, flexible plastic or nylon applicator will be found invaluable for imparting a smooth and well-contoured finish to the surface of the filler.

Mix up a little filler on a clean piece of card or board – measure the hardener carefully (follow the maker's instructions on the pack), otherwise the filler will set too rapidly or too slowly. Using the applicator, apply the filler paste to the prepared area; draw the applicator across the surface of the filler to achieve the correct contour and to level the surface. As soon as a contour that approximates to the correct one is achieved, stop working the paste – if you carry on too long, the paste will become sticky and begin to 'pick-up' on the applicator. Continue to add thin layers of filler paste at 20-minute intervals, until the level of the filler is just proud of the surrounding bodywork.

Once the filler has hardened, the excess can be removed using a metal plane or file. From then on, progressively-finer grades of abrasive paper should be used, starting with a 40-grade production paper, and finishing with a 400-grade wet-and-dry paper. Always wrap the abrasive paper around a flat rubber, cork, or wooden block – otherwise the surface of the filler will not be completely flat. During the smoothing of the filler surface, the wet-and-dry paper should be periodically rinsed in water. This will ensure that a very smooth finish is imparted to the filler at the final stage.

At this stage, the 'dent' should be surrounded by a ring of bare metal, which in turn should be encircled by the finely 'feathered' edge of the good paintwork. Rinse the repair area with clean water, until all of the dust produced by the rubbing-down operation has gone.

Spray the whole area with a light coat of primer – this will show up any imperfections in the surface of the filler. Repair these imperfections with fresh filler paste or bodystopper, and once more smooth the surface with abrasive paper. Repeat this spray-and-repair procedure until you are satisfied that the surface of the filler, and the feathered edge of the paintwork, are perfect. Clean the repair area with clean water, and allow to dry fully.

The repair area is now ready for final spraying. Paint spraying must be carried out in a warm, dry, windless and dust-free atmosphere. This condition can be created artificially if you have access to a large indoor working area, but if you are forced to work in the open, you will have to pick your day very carefully. If you are working indoors, dousing the floor in the work area with water will help to settle the dust which would otherwise be in the atmosphere. If the repair area is confined to one body panel, mask off the surrounding panels; this will help to minimise the effects of a slight mis-match in paint colours. Bodywork fittings (e.g. chrome strips, door handles etc) will also need to be masked off. Use genuine masking tape, and several thicknesses of newspaper, for the masking operations.

Before commencing to spray, agitate the aerosol can thoroughly, then spray a test area (an old tin, or similar) until the technique is mastered. Cover the repair area with a thick coat of primer; the thickness should be built up using several thin layers of paint, rather than one thick one. Using 400-grade wet-and-dry paper, rub down the surface of the primer until it is really smooth. While doing this, the work area should be thoroughly doused with water, and the wet-and-dry paper periodically rinsed in water. Allow to dry before spraying on more paint.

Spray on the top coat, again building up the thickness by using several thin layers of paint. Start spraying at one edge of the repair area, and then, using a side-to-side motion, work until the whole repair area and about 2 inches of the surrounding original paintwork is covered. Remove all masking material 10 to 15 minutes after spraying on the final coat of paint.

Allow the new paint at least two weeks to harden, then, using a paintwork renovator, or a very fine cutting paste, blend the edges of the paint into the existing paintwork. Finally, apply wax polish.

Plastic components

With the use of more and more plastic body components by the vehicle manufacturers (e.g. bumpers. spoilers, and in some cases major body panels), rectification of more serious damage to such items has become a matter of either entrusting repair work to a specialist in this field, or renewing complete components. Repair of such damage by the DIY owner is not really feasible, owing to the cost of the equipment and materials required for effecting such repairs. The basic technique involves making a groove along the line of the crack in the plastic, using a rotary burr in a power drill. The damaged part is then welded back together, using a hot-air gun to heat up and fuse a plastic filler rod into the groove. Any excess plastic is then removed, and the area rubbed down to a smooth finish. It is important that a filler rod of the correct plastic is used, as body components can be made of a variety of different types (e.g. polycarbonate, ABS, polypropylene).

Damage of a less serious nature (abrasions, minor cracks etc) can be repaired by the DIY owner using a two-part epoxy filler repair material. Once mixed in equal proportions, this is used in similar fashion to the bodywork filler used on metal panels. The filler is usually cured in twenty to thirty minutes, ready for sanding and painting.

If the owner is renewing a complete component himself, or if he has repaired it with epoxy filler, he will be left with the problem of finding a suitable paint for finishing which is compatible with the type of plastic used. At one time, the use of a universal paint was not possible, owing to the complex range of plastics encountered in body component applications. Standard paints, generally speaking, will not bond to plastic or rubber satisfactorily. However, it is now possible to obtain a plastic body parts finishing kit which consists of a pre-primer treatment, a primer and coloured top coat. Full instructions are normally supplied with a kit, but basically, the

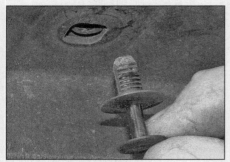

6.3a Prise out the centre pins, lever out the plastic rivets...

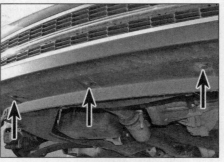

6.3b ...along the underside of the bumper (arrowed)...

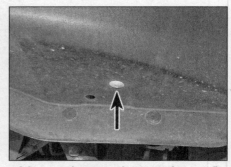

6.3c ...and remove the screw (arrowed) each side

method of use is to first apply the pre-primer to the component concerned, and allow it to dry for up to 30 minutes. Then the primer is applied, and left to dry for about an hour before finally applying the special-coloured top coat. The result is a correctly-coloured component, where the paint will flex with the plastic or rubber, a property that standard paint does not normally posses.

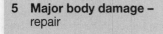

5 Major body damage – repair

Where serious damage has occurred, or large areas need renewal due to neglect, it means that complete new panels will need welding-in; this is best left to professionals. If the damage is due to impact, it will also be necessary to check completely the

alignment of the bodyshell; this can only be carried out accurately by a MINI dealer, using special jigs. If the body is left misaligned, it is primarily dangerous, as the car will not handle properly, and secondly, uneven stresses will be imposed on the steering, suspension and possibly transmission, causing abnormal wear or complete failure, particularly to items such as the tyres.

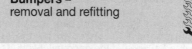

6 Bumpers – removal and refitting

Front bumper cover and bumper carrier

1 Remove the radiator grille (see Section 7).
2 Apply the parking brake, raise the front of the vehicle and support it securely on axle stands (see *Jacking and vehicle support*).

3 Remove the fasteners along the underside of the bumper cover **(see illustrations)**.
4 Release the fasteners and pull the wheelarch liners from the front wing **(see illustration 30.2)**.
5 Release the clips securing the wheelarch outer trim, pull the trim from the wheelarch slightly, and slide the trim forwards from place **(see illustrations 6.12a, 6.12b and 6.12c)**.
6 Undo the 4 retaining bolts at the upper edge of the bumper **(see illustration)**.
7 With the help of an assistant, pull the bumper forwards a little, and disconnect any wiring plugs.
8 Remove the bumper carrier fasteners from each side, then remove the carrier.
9 Refitting is the reverse of the removal procedure. If the absorbing foam bolster became dislodged, properly position it on the reinforcement and secure it with duct tape or industrial adhesive, then refit the bumper cover.

Rear bumper cover and bumper carrier

10 Raise the rear of the vehicle and support it securely on axle stands. Chock the front wheels.
11 Release the fasteners and remove the wheelarch liner each side.
12 Release the fasteners, pull the wheelarch trim from the wing, then release it from the bumper **(see illustrations)**. If equipped, remove the mudguards.

Clubman models

13 Remove the screw each side securing the bumper to the rear wing **(see illustration)**.

6.6 Undo the bolts each side (arrowed) and manoeuvre the bumper forwards

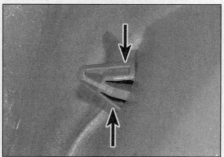

6.12a Squeeze together the sides (arrowed)...

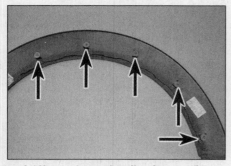

6.12b ...release the clips (arrowed)...

6.12c ...and detach the trims from the wheelarch each side

6.13 Remove the screw (arrowed) each side securing the bumper to the wing

6.14a Undo the 2 screws (arrowed) in the centre...

6.14b ...and the screw (arrowed) each side

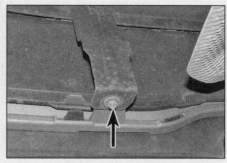

6.15 Undo the screw (arrowed) each side of the heat shield

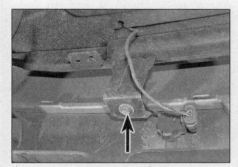

6.16 On Convertible models, reach under and remove the bolt (arrowed) securing the bracket to the bumper

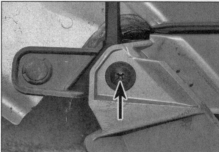

6.17a Remove the screw in the wheelarch area (arrowed)...

6.17b ...and the screw in the tailgate/boot lid aperture (arrowed)

14 Undo the 4 retaining bolts on the underside of the bumper **(see illustrations)**.

Hatchback and Convertible models

15 On models from 08/2010, undo the screw each side on the underside of the bumper, adjacent to the exhaust heat shield **(see illustration)**.
16 On models upto 08/2010, remove the fastener(s) at the lower edge of the rear bumper **(see illustration)**.
17 On all models, undo the screws each side at the upper edge of the bumper. One in the wheelarch area, above the rear wheel, and one in the tailgate/boot lid aperture **(see illustrations)**.

All models

18 With the help of an assistant, pull the bumper rearwards a little, disconnect the wiring plugs, then manoeuvre the bumper from the vehicle. Note the locating peg in the upper, centre of the bumper.
19 Remove the bumper carrier fasteners from each side, then remove the carrier **(see illustration)**.
20 Refitting is the reverse of the removal procedure. If the absorbing foam bolster became dislodged, properly position it on the reinforcement and secure it with duct tape or industrial adhesive, then refit the bumper cover.

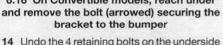
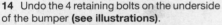

7 Radiator grille –
removal and refitting

1 Press down the clip at each end, and slide

the lower section of the grille forwards **(see illustrations)**.

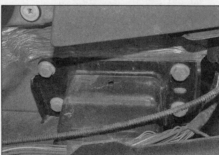

6.19 Undo the bolts each side and remove the bumper carrier

7.1b ...and slide the lower section of the grille forwards

2 Remove the grille upper mounting fasteners **(see illustration)**.

7.1a Press down the clip each side...

7.2 Prise up the centre pins, and lever out the 4 plastic expansion rivets at the upper edge of the grille

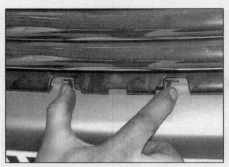

7.3 Press the 4 clips at the lower edge towards the centre and remove the grille

3 Depress the retainers at the bottom of the grille **(see illustration)**, then pull the grille forward and remove it.
4 Refitting is a reversal of the removal procedure.

8 Bonnet – removal, refitting and adjustment

Removal

1 Open the bonnet, undo the 'scrivets' and remove the underbonnet sound insulation panel (where fitted).
2 Disconnect the windscreen washer wiring connector from the bottom of the jets, and disconnect the hose from the junction.
3 Note their fitted positions, and disconnect and other wiring plugs. Trace the wiring loom

9.2 Pull the outer cable from the bracket (arrowed)

10.2 Prise out the pin at the base of the interior release handle trim

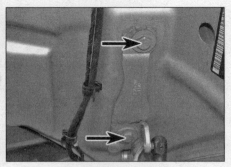

8.5 Undo the bonnet retaining bolts (arrowed) each side

along its route and release it from the retaining clips.
4 Have an assistant support the bonnet, then prise out the clips and disconnect the support struts from balljoints on the bonnet (see Section 18).
5 Make alignment marks between the hinges and the bonnet to aid refitting, unscrew the four bolts, and lift the bonnet from the vehicle **(see illustration)**.

Refitting and adjustment

6 Refitting is a reversal of the removal procedure, noting the following points:
   a) *Position the bonnet hinges within the outline marks made during removal, but if necessary alter its position to provide a uniform gap all round.*
   b) *Adjust the front height by repositioning the bump stops.*

9.4 Open the junction box on the left hand front panel bracket and disconnect the cable

10.3a Carefully prise the trim away from the door to release the clips...

9 Bonnet release cable – removal and refitting

Removal

1 Remove the driver's side sill/footwell kick panel trim as described in Section 26.
2 Pull the outer cable from the lever bracket, then disengage the cable end fitting from the release lever **(see illustration)**.
3 Note it's routing, then trace the cable(s) forward, and release it from any retaining clips.
4 Open the junction box, and disengage the release cable from the coupling **(see illustration)**. Where applicable, undo the nut/scrivets and remove the padded panel from above the junction box.
5 Pull the cable from place.

Refitting

6 Fit the new cable, and secure it in place with the various retaining clips.
7 Engage the cable end fittings with the release lever and junction box coupling, then push the outer cables into place in the support brackets.
8 Check the operation of the bonnet catch/release lever prior to closing the bonnet. There is no adjustment facility for the cables.

10 Door inner trim panel – removal and refitting

Front door

1 Carefully prise the footwell light from the base of the trim panel, and disconnect the wiring plug.
2 Prise out the pin at the base of the interior release handle trim **(see illustration)**. Don't attempt to remove the trim – it comes off with the panel.
3 Using a flat-bladed tool, carefully release the push-on clips around the perimeter of the trim panel **(see illustrations)**.
4 Remove the door inner trim panel. Note the fitted locations of the trim clips, and renew any that are damaged.

10.3b ...and remove the door trim panel

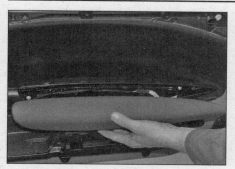

10.5 Pull the armrest from the retaining clips

5 If required, pull the armrest inwards from place to release the retaining clips **(see illustration)**.

6 Refitting is a reversal of the removal procedure.

Rear Club door

7 Undo the 2 screws at the top of the door pillar, and pull away the rubber weatherstrip adjacent to the pillar trim **(see illustration)**.

8 Pull the top edge of the pillar trim panel away from the door and lift it from place **(see illustration)**. Disconnect the airbag warning light wiring plug as the pillar trim panel is withdrawn.

9 Undo the screw at the top of the door trim panel, and the one at the lower rear edge **(see illustrations)**.

10 Using a flat-bladed tool, carefully release the push-on clips around the perimeter of the door trim panel **(see illustrations)**. Note the fitted locations of the trim clips, and renew any that are damaged. Unclip the wiring loom and disconnect the sill light wiring plug as the panel is withdrawn.

11 Refitting is a reversal of the removal procedure.

11 **Door window glass** – removal, refitting, adjustment and initialisation

Door window glass

Removal

1 Remove the door inner trim panel as described in Section 10.

11.2 Pull up the exterior window seal

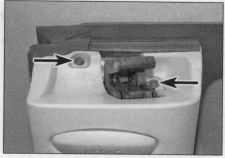

10.7 Undo the screws (arrowed) at the top of the Club door pillar

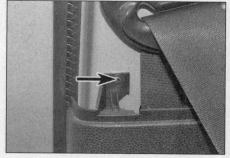

10.9a Undo the screw (arrowed) at the top of the panel...

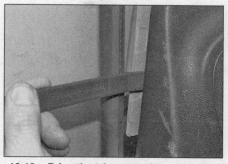

10.10a Prise the trim away from the door to release the clips

2 Carefully prise up and remove the exterior window seal **(see illustration)**.

3 Raise the glass to a height of approximately 75 mm above the door upper edge.

4 Disconnect the cable from the negative terminal of the battery (see Chapter 5A).

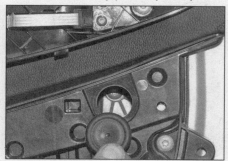

11.5a Remove the plastic covers...

10.8 Note how the base of the pillar trim engages with the lower trim panel

10.9b ...and the one at the lower edge

10.10b Unclip the wiring harness from the door trim panel

5 Remove the access covers, slacken the window securing screws until they become loose, then pull the bolts out again, and unscrew them fully **(see illustrations)**, then lift the glass out of the door. Take care not to drop the window securing screws.

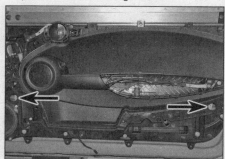

11.5b ...and undo the glass securing screws (arrowed)

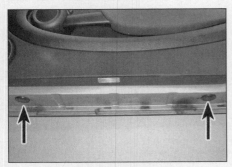

11.9 Prise out the access covers (arrowed) at the base of the door

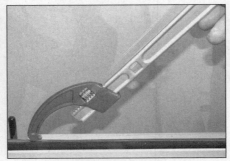

11.10a Insert a slim C-spanner between the glass and door outer skin...

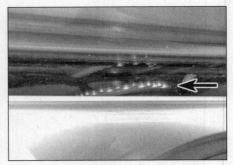

11.10b ...to slacken the knurled adjustment nuts (arrowed)

11.11 Attach masking tape 5.0 mm from the top of the glass, and 4.5 mm from the front edge, halfway up

Installation

6 Refitting is the reverse of the removal procedure. Make sure the glass fits properly with its front and rear brackets, and tighten the screws securely. Do not fit the window exterior seal and door trim panel at this time. Proceed to adjust and initialise the window.

Adjustment

Caution: Do not close the door completely until adjustment has been verified, as glass breakage may result.

Note: *The following procedure assumes that the door is properly adjusted.*

7 Raise the window all the way, then gently close the door so that the latch clicks one notch (don't try to close the door completely).

8 The top of the window should contact the weatherstrip at the top of the door opening when the top of the glass is pushed in with

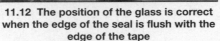
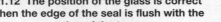
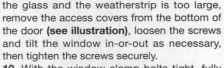

11.12 The position of the glass is correct when the edge of the seal is flush with the edge of the tape

a finger (it shouldn't take much force to make contact).

9 If the glass touches the weatherstrip without pushing the glass in, or if the gap between the glass and the weatherstrip is too large, remove the access covers from the bottom of the door **(see illustration)**, loosen the screws and tilt the window in-or-out as necessary, then tighten the screws securely.

10 With the window clamp bolts tight, fully close the window, then slacken the knurled adjustment nuts (one behind each window clamp bolt) using MINI tool No. 51 3 240 (or a slim C-spanner) so the glass is free to move **(see illustrations)**. Take care not to damage the door paintwork.

11 Attach masking tape 5.0 mm from the top edge of the glass at the front and rear, then another piece of tape 4.5 mm from the front edge halfway up **(see illustration)**.

12 Carefully close the door fully and allow the auto-closing feature to press the glass into its seals. If the position of the glass is correct the edges of the tape will be flush with the edges of the seals **(see illustration)**. If necessary, reposition the glass and recheck. Ideally, use a 'sucker' type tool or double-sided tape/block of wood attached to the glass to facilitate movement.

13 With the glass correctly positioned, tighten the knurled adjustment nuts, then refit the exterior window seal and door trim panel.

Initialisation

14 See Chapter 5A for the initialisation procedure.

Side window glass/regulator – Convertible models only

15 Although removal and refitting of the glass/regulator assembly is possible using common hand tools, after refitting, the position of the glass must be set using MINI special tools (Nos. 51 2 220, and 51 3 240). Without these tools it's not possible to set the position of the glass in relation to the soft-top. If the position of the glass is not correct, damage could result to the glass and/or the soft-top. Consequently, we recommend replacement of the regulator/glass assembly is entrusted to a MINI dealer or suitably equipped repairer.

---

12 Door window regulator and motor – removal and refitting

Removal

1 Remove the door trim panel and armrest (see Section 10).

Motor

2 Disconnect the electrical connector from the motor, then remove the motor retaining screws and detach the motor **(see illustration)**.

3 Refitting is the reverse of removal.

Panel carrier and regulator assembly

4 Remove the window glass (see Section 11).

5 Disconnect the electrical connectors at the front of the carrier **(see illustration)**.

6 Prise out the clips at the rear, move the window cavity seal at each end to one side,

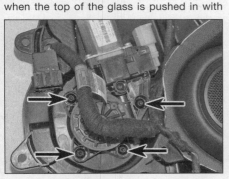

12.2 Window motor retaining screws (arrowed)

12.5 Disconnect the various wiring plugs at the front of the carrier assembly

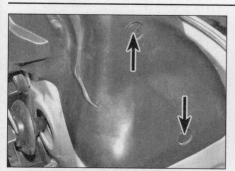

12.6a Prise out the clips (arrowed) at the rear of the cavity seal...

12.6b ...and at the front

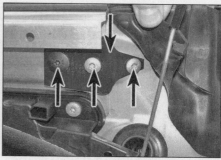

12.6c Undo the screws and remove the holder at the rear (arrowed)...

12.6d ...and the screws/nut (arrowed) at the front

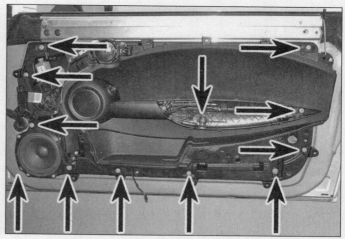

12.7 Remove the remaining fasteners (arrowed)...

then undo the screws/nut at each end of the aluminium strip. Remove the holder from the rear upper edge **(see illustrations)**. Note the metal bracket fitted beneath the retaining nut.

7 Remove the carrier retaining fasteners **(see illustration)**.

8 Pull the carrier up and off the door, then unlatch the cable retainer and detach the cable from the interior release handle **(see illustrations)**.

9 Remove the motor from the carrier **(see illustration 12.2)**, then detach the motor drive from the other side of the carrier by freeing it from the plastic retaining tangs.

10 Detach the cables from any retaining clips, then remove the fasteners and slide the regulator up and off the carrier.

Refitting

11 Refitting is a reversal of the removal procedure, but carry out the adjustment procedure as described in the previous Section.

13 Door handle and lock components – removal and refitting

Exterior handle

1 Remove the door window and carrier assembly as described in Section 12.

2 Detach the cable from the lock/latch assembly **(see illustration)**.

12.8a ...lift the carrier upwards...

12.8b ...prise up the cover...

12.8c ...and detach the cable from the interior handle

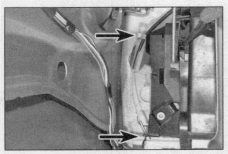

13.2 Detach the cable end fitting from the lever, and release the cable outer from the retaining clip (arrowed)

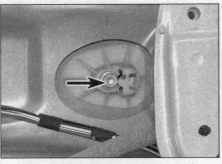

13.3 Undo the screw and remove the plastic mount (arrowed)

13.4a Insert an Allen key through the hole in the door…

13.4b …remove the screw (arrowed) at the rear…

13.4c …then remove the exterior handle

13.8 Pull the lock rod (arrowed) from the lock

3 Remove the screw and detach the plastic mount at the front of the handle **(see illustration)**.

4 Remove the Allen screw at the rear of the door handle, then detach the handle from the door **(see illustrations)**.

5 Refitting is the reverse of the removal procedure.

Lock/latch assembly

6 Remove the door window and carrier assembly as described in Section 12.

7 Remove the exterior door handle as previously described in this Section.

8 Detach the inner door lock rod, then unclip the interior release handle cable from the door frame **(see illustration)**.

9 Remove the lock/latch assembly mounting screws from the end of the door **(see illustration)**.

10 Withdraw the lock/latch assembly and disconnect the electrical connector.

11 Refitting is the reverse of removal. When refitting the lock cylinder actuator rod, ensure the notch in the lock drive aligns with the mark on the casing **(see illustration)**. Apply a little threadlocking compound to the lock retaining screws.

Lock cylinder

12 Remove the door exterior handle as previously described in this Section.

13 Lift the rubber sealing strip at the rear of the door, and undo the screw **(see illustration)**.

14 Remove the lock/latch mounting screws from the end of the door **(see illustration 13.9)**.

15 Lower the door lock/latch a little, and manoeuvre the lock cylinder from place.

16 Refitting is the reverse of removal. When refitting the lock cylinder actuator rod, ensure the notch in the lock drive aligns with the mark on the casing **(see illustration 13.11)**. **Note:** *The lock cylinder retaining screw at the rear edge of the door cannot be fully tightened until the exterior handle has been refitted.*

Striker

17 Using a pencil, mark the position of the striker on the pillar.

13.9 Undo the lock retaining screws (arrowed)

13.11 The notch in the lock drive must align with the mark on the casing (arrowed)

13.13 Lock cylinder retaining screw (arrowed)

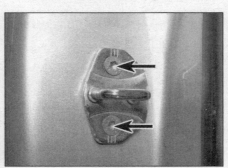

13.18 Striker retaining screws (arrowed)

18 Remove the mounting screws using a Torx key, then remove the striker **(see illustration)**.

19 Refitting is a reversal of the removal procedure, but check that the door lock passes over the striker centrally. If necessary, reposition the striker before fully tightening the mounting screws.

Check strap

20 Remove the door trim panel as described in Section 10.

21 Remove the door speaker from the bottom of the panel carrier assembly.

22 Prise the rubber grommet from the door opening, then remove the mounting screws and withdraw the check strap from the door **(see illustration)**. Guide the check strap out through the speaker opening.

23 Refitting is the reverse of removal.

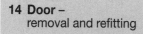

14 Door – removal and refitting

Removal

1 Disconnect the battery negative (earth) lead (Chapter 5A).

2 Unscrew and remove the check strap mounting bolt from the door pillar **(see illustration 13.22)**.

3 Undo the bolt, and pull the wiring connector from the A-pillar, then slide out the locking catch and disconnect the wiring plug.

4 Slacken and remove the retaining screws in the top and bottom hinges.

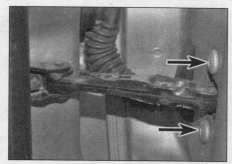

13.22 Check strap retaining screws (arrowed)

5 Carefully lift the door from the hinges.

Refitting

6 Refitting is a reversal of the removal procedure, but check that the door lock passes over the striker centrally. If necessary, reposition the striker.

15 Exterior mirror and glass – removal and refitting

Removal

Mirror

1 Rotate the mirror to expose the mounting screws **(see illustration)**.

2 Undo the Allen screws, and pull the mirror complete from the door. Disconnect the wiring plug as the mirror is withdrawn.

Mirror positioning motor

3 Remove the mirror glass as described in this Section.

4 Release the five clips and remove the front cover from the mirror housing **(see illustration)**.

5 Disconnect the wiring plug, then undo the three screws and remove the motor assembly **(see illustration)**.

Mirror glass

6 Press the top of the mirror glass into the housing, then use a flat-bladed tool to carefully prise the lower edge of the mirror glass from the retaining clips **(see illustration)**.

7 Withdraw the mirror glass and disconnect the wiring connectors for the heated mirrors **(see illustration)**.

Refitting

8 Refitting is a reversal of the removal procedure. Take care not to drop the rubber grommet inside the door panel when removing the mirror, as the interior door trim will have to be removed to retrieve it.

16 Interior mirror – removal and refitting

1 Prise apart the two halves of the mirror base cover, and disconnect the wiring plug **(see illustration)**.

2 Slowly press the mirror assembly forwards to release it from the base. Do not twist the mirror as this may damage the base.

3 Position the mirror base at 45° to the

15.1 Rotate the mirror to access the screws (arrowed)

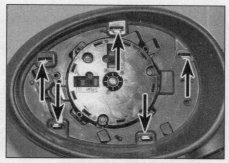

15.4 Release the clips (arrowed) and remove the front cover

15.5 Mirror motor retaining screws (arrowed)

15.6 Push-in the upper edge and carefully prise the lower edge out

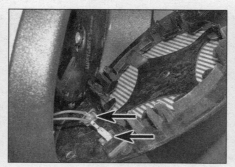

15.7 Disconnect the heated mirror wiring plugs (arrowed)

16.1 Prise apart the halves of the interior mirror base cover

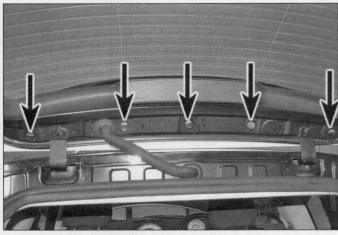

17.1 Undo the fasteners (arrowed) and remove the spoiler from the tailgate

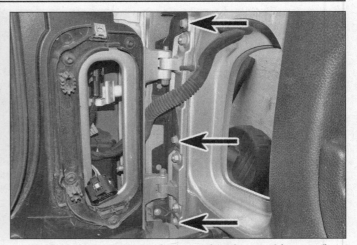

17.10 Undo the screw and remove the trim panel (arrowed)

mounting, then rotate it to the normal position whilst holding the base against the mount. Reconnect the wiring plugs (where applicable) before refitting the mirror.

4 Refit the two halves of the cover.

17 Tailgate/Split doors – removal and refitting

Tailgate

Removal

1 Open the tailgate, prise out the covers, remove the fasteners and remove the spoiler from the top of the tailgate (see illustration).

2 Remove the tailgate trim panels as described in Section 26.

3 Using a small screwdriver, slide off the clip securing the struts to the tailgate (see illustration 18.2). Pull the sockets from the ballstuds, and move the struts downwards.

4 Detach the washer fluid hose and wiring harness connectors.

5 Close the tailgate without allowing it to latch, then, with the help of an assistant and working through the openings previously covered by the spoiler, remove the tailgate mounting nuts.

6 Remove the tailgate, being careful not to damage the paint.

Refitting

7 Refitting is a reversal of the removal procedure, but check that the tailgate is located centrally in the body aperture, and that the striker enters the lock centrally. If necessary, loosen the mounting nuts and reposition the tailgate as required.

Split doors

Removal

8 Remove the relevant rear light unit as described in Chapter 12.

9 Using a small screwdriver, slide off the clip securing the strut to the split door (see illustration 18.2). Pull the socket from the ball-stud, and detach the strut from the door.

10 Undo the 3 retaining screws securing the trim panel to the outer edge of the split door (see illustration).

11 Pull out the holder, and disconnect the split door wiring plugs.

12 Release the wiring harness from the pillar, and feed it out through the aperture.

13 Undo the retaining bolts and detach the split door.

Refitting

14 Refitting is a reversal of the removal procedure, but check that the split doors are located centrally in the body aperture, and that the striker enters the lock centrally.

If necessary, loosen the mounting bolts and reposition the spit doors as required.

18 Support struts – removal and refitting

Tailgate/Bonnet/Split door

1 Have an assistant support the tailgate/ bonnet/split door in its open position.

2 Slide off the spring clips securing the strut to the tailgate/bonnet/split door, then pull the sockets from the ball-studs (see illustration).

3 Refitting is a reversal of the removal procedure, making sure that the strut is fitted the same way up as it was removed. Note that on Clubman models, the left-hand, and right-hand Split door struts are not interchangeable, having different pressures.

Boot lid

4 Remove the boot lid trim panel as described in Section 26.

5 Slide off the spring clips securing the anchor cable to the vehicle body, then pull the sockets from the ball-studs (see illustration).

6 Cut-through the retaining clips, undo the 2 retaining bolts and pull the anchor cable retractor from the boot lid (see illustration).

7 Refitting is a reversal of removal.

18.2 Prise off the support strut spring clip

18.5 Prise off the anchor cable socket retaining clip (arrowed)

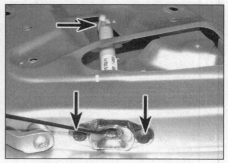

18.6 Undo the retractor retaining bolts, and cut through the clip (arrowed)

19.3a Undo the retaining screws (arrowed)…

19.3b …lit up the lock release assembly and disconnect the wiring plug (arrowed)

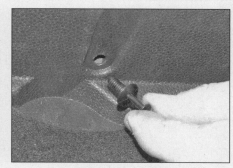

19.4a Prise up the centre pins…

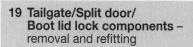

19 Tailgate/Split door/ Boot lid lock components – removal and refitting

Tailgate

Lock release button

1 Disconnect the battery negative lead as described in Chapter 5A.
2 Remove the tailgate lower trim panel as described in Section 26.
3 Remove the 4 screws securing the release button/number plate light assembly from the outside of the hatch. Lift away the assembly and disconnect the wiring plug **(see illustrations)**.

Lock/latch assembly

4 Lift out the luggage compartment floor panel, remove the plastic expansion rivets, and pull the tailgate sill trim panel upwards **(see illustrations)**.
5 Disconnect the electrical connector from the hatch lock assembly.
6 Open the emergency release cable junction box (on models so equipped), then slide the box forwards to detach it from the lock bracket.
7 Make alignment marks between the lock bracket and the vehicle body to aid installation, then remove the two Torx screws and remove the lock assembly **(see illustration)**.
8 Refitting is a reversal of the removal procedure.

Split doors

Exterior handle

9 Remove the door inner trim panel as described in Section 26.
10 Disconnect the wiring plug, then undo the 2 retaining screws and remove the handle from the door **(see illustrations)**.

Lock/latch assembly

Left-hand door
11 Lift out the luggage compartment floor trim panel.
12 Remove the 4 expansion rivets at the lower front edge of the door sill trim panel **(see illustration)**.

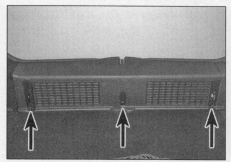

19.4b …and remove the plastic expansion rivets (arrowed)

13 Pull the door sill trim panel upwards to release the retaining clips.
14 Undo the 2 retaining bolts and remove the lock assembly **(see illustration)**. Disconnect the wiring plug as the lock is withdrawn.

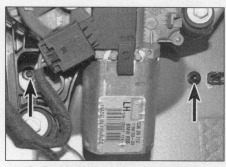

19.10a Undo the screws (arrowed)…

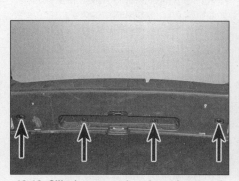

19.12 Sill trim expansion rivets (arrowed)

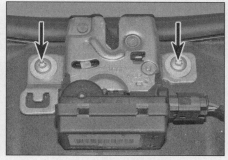

19.7 Tailgate lock retaining screws (arrowed)

15 Refitting is a reversal of removal.
Right-hand door
16 Remove the door inner trim panel as described in Section 26.
17 Undo the retaining bolts and remove the

19.10b …and remove the exterior handle

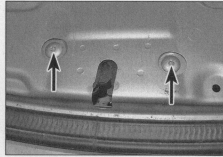

19.14 Left-hand split-door latch retaining bolts (arrowed)

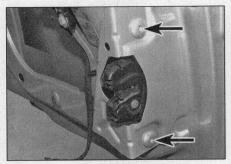

19.17 Right-hand split-door lock retaining bolts (arrowed)

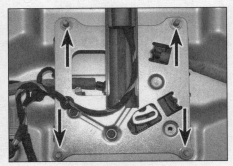

19.20 Undo the nuts (arrowed) and slide the lock assembly from place

19.21 Undo the nut (arrowed) and remove the plastic cover

19.22 Detach the cables from the lock

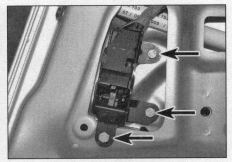

19.25 Outer latch retaining bolts (arrowed)

Tailgate/Split door motors

6 The motor is integral with the tailgate lock. Removal of the lock is described in Section 19.

Refitting

7 In all cases, refitting is a reversal of the removal procedure.

21 Windscreen and fixed windows – removal and refitting

The windscreen and rear window on all models are bonded in place with special mastic, as are the rear side windows. Special tools are required to cut free the old units and fit replacements; special cleaning solutions and primer are also required. It is therefore recommended that this work is entrusted to a MINI dealer or windscreen replacement specialist.

22 Body side-trim mouldings and adhesive emblems – removal and refitting

Removal

1 Body side trims and mouldings are attached either by retaining clips or adhesive bonding. On bonded mouldings, insert a length of strong cord (fishing line is ideal) behind the moulding or emblem concerned. With a sawing action, break the adhesive bond between the moulding or emblem and the panel.
2 Thoroughly clean all traces of adhesive from the panel using methylated spirit, and allow the location to dry.
3 On mouldings with retaining clips, unclip the mouldings from the panel, taking care not to damage the paintwork.

Refitting

4 Peel back the protective paper from the rear face of the new moulding or emblem. Carefully fit it into position on the panel concerned, but take care not to touch the adhesive. When in position, apply hand pressure to the moulding/emblem for a short period, to ensure maximum adhesion to the panel.
5 Replace any broken retaining clips before refitting trims or mouldings.

lock assembly (see illustration). Disconnect the wiring plug as the lock is withdrawn.
18 Refitting is a reversal of removal.

Boot lid lock

19 Remove the boot lid trim panel as described in Section 26.

Lock motor

20 Undo the 4 retaining nuts and slide the lock assembly rearwards from the cable guide (see illustration). Unclip the wiring loom from the mounting plate.
21 Disconnect the lock wiring plug, then undo the nut and carefully remove the plastic cover (see illustration).
22 Unclip the outer cables, and disengage the inner cable end fittings from the lock assembly (see illustration). If required, undo the screws and separate the motor from the mounting plate.
23 Refitting is a reversal of removal.

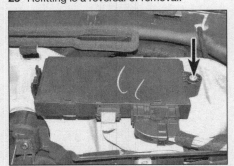

20.3 Car access system control unit retaining bolt (arrowed)

Outer latches

24 Remove the lock motor as previously described in this Section.
25 Undo the 3 retaining bolts and manoeuvre the latch from the boot lid (see illustration).
26 Disconnect the latch wiring plug, and remove the latch. Note that the release cable is integral with the latch.
27 Refitting is a reversal of removal.

20 Central locking system components – removal and refitting

Removal

Car access system control unit

Note: If the module is to be renewed, the new unit must be programmed/coded prior to use. This can only be carried out by a MINI dealer or specialist.

1 Disconnect the battery negative (earth) lead (Chapter 5A).
2 To remove the module, first remove the facia as described in Section 29.
3 Undo the securing bolt, and remove the module (see illustration).
4 Disconnect the wiring multi-plugs as the unit is withdrawn.

Door motors

5 The door lock motor is integral with the door lock. Removal of the door lock is described in Section 13.

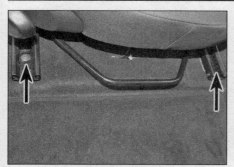

24.3 Front seat runner bolts (arrowed)

24.5 Slide out the locking catch (arrowed) and disconnect the wiring plug beneath the seat

24.7 Rear seat cushion retaining clip (arrowed – seat removed for clarity)

23 Sunroof –
general information and initialisation

General information

1 Due to the complexity of the sunroof mechanism, considerable expertise is needed to repair, renew or adjust the sunroof components successfully. Removal of the roof first requires the headlining to be removed, which is a complex and tedious operation, and not a task to be undertaken lightly. Therefore, any problems with the sunroof should be referred to a MINI dealer or specialist.

2 On models with an electric sunroof, if the motor fails to operate, first check the relevant fuse. If the fault cannot be traced and rectified, then sunroof can be opened and closed manually using an Allen key to turn the motor spindle (a suitable key is supplied with the vehicle tool kit). To gain access to the motor, unclip the reading lights/switch panel/clock console from the headlining. Insert the Allen key into the motor spindle, and move the sunroof to the required position.

3 The water drain tubes are located at each front corner of the sunroof aperture, and are routed behind the A-pillar trim panels, exiting behind each front wheelarch liner.

Initialisation

4 With the battery reconnected, and ignition on, press the sunroof operating switch into the 'tilt' position and hold it there.

5 Once the sunroof has reached the 'fully-tilted' position, hold the switch in that position for approximately 20 seconds.

6 Close the sunroof and release the switch as normal.

24 Seats –
removal and refitting

Removal

Front seat

1 Slide the seat fully forwards.

2 Undo the two rear seat runner bolts.

3 Slide the seat fully rearwards, then undo the two front seat runner bolts **(see illustration)**.

4 On models with electrically-operated or heated seats, or with side airbags, disconnect the battery negative lead, and position the lead away from the battery (see Chapter 5A).

⚠️ *Warning: Where side airbags are fitted, before proceeding, wait a minimum of 5 minutes, as a precaution against accidental firing of the airbag unit. This period ensures that any stored energy is dissipated.*

5 Tilt the seat backwards, and disconnect the various seat wiring multi-plugs from the seat base, noting their fitted positions **(see illustration)**. Remove the seat from the vehicle.

Rear seat cushion

6 Lift the front edge of the seat cushion to release the clips.

7 Press down the centre rear of the cushion to disengage the clip **(see illustration)**. Remove the cushion from the vehicle.

Rear seat backrest

8 Remove the parcel shelf (where fitted – not Convertible models). On Clubman models, remove the centre headrest.

9 Fold the backrest forwards, depress the retaining tab, and lift the backrest out from the central hinge **(see illustration)**.

10 Hold the backrest at an angle of 45 degrees, and pull the backrest from the outer mountings **(see illustration)**.

Refitting

11 Refitting is a reversal of the removal procedure, apply a little thread-locking compound then tighten the mounting bolts to the specified torque where given.

25 Seat belts –
removal and refitting

⚠️ *Warning: Be careful when handling the seat belt tensioning device, it contains a small explosive charge (pyrotechnic device) similar to the one used to deploy the airbag(s). Clearly, injury could be caused if these are released in an uncontrolled fashion. Once fired, the tensioner cannot be reset, and must be renewed. Note also that seat belts and associated components which have been subject to impact loads must be renewed.*

Removal – front seat belt

Hatchback and Clubman models

1 Remove the side panel trim as described in Section 26, or Club door trim panel as described in Section 10.

2 Unscrew the bolt securing the seat belt upper anchorage to the B-pillar or Club door as applicable **(see illustration)**.

3 Unscrew the mounting bolt, and lift seat belt reel unit **(see illustration)**.

24.9 Press the retaining tab (arrowed) across and lift the seat from the central hinge

24.10 Hold the backrest at 45° and pull the outer pin from the slotted socket (arrowed)

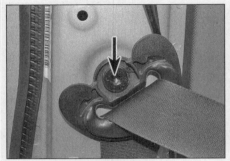

25.2 Front seat belt upper anchorage bolt (arrowed)

25.3 Front seat belt inertia reel bolt (arrowed)

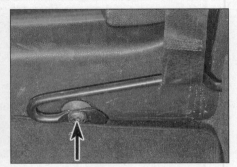

25.4a Front seat belt lower anchorage bolt (arrowed) – Clubman models

25.4b On other models, not the location of the spacer on the belt lower anchorage bolt

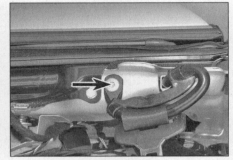

25.6 Undo the bolt (arrowed) securing the deflector bar

25.7 Front seat belt inertia reel bolt (arrowed) – Convertible models

4 Undo the bolt securing the seat belt lower anchorage point **(see illustrations)**.

Convertible models

5 Remove the side panel trim as described in Section 26.

25.10 Rear seat belt inertia reel retaining bolt (arrowed) – Hatchback models

6 Undo the bolt securing the deflector bar at the top of the panel **(see illustration)**.

7 Unscrew the mounting bolt, and lift seat belt reel unit to remove from the base of the pillar **(see illustration)**.

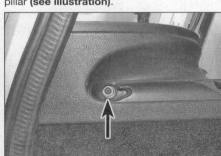

25.12a Undo the screw (arrowed)...

25.12b ...and pull the side capping upwards from the clips

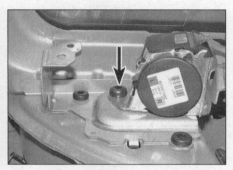

25.14 Rear outer seat belt inertia reel bolt (arrowed) – Clubman models

Removal – rear seat belt

Hatchback models

8 Remove the side trim panel as described in Section 26.

9 Undo the upper and lower seat belt anchorage bolts.

10 Undo the bolt and remove the inertia reel **(see illustration)**.

Clubman models

Outer belts

11 Remove the C-pillar trim as described in Section 26.

12 Undo the retaining screw, and pull the capping on the top of the side panel upwards to release the retaining clips **(see illustrations)**.

13 Undo the seat belt lower anchorage bolt.

14 Undo the retaining bolt and remove the seat belt inertia reel **(see illustration)**.

Centre belt

15 Undo the retaining screw, and carefully slide the inertia reel cover forwards from the headlining **(see illustrations)**.

16 Undo the retaining bolt and remove the seat belt inertia reel **(see illustration)**.

Convertible models

17 Removal of the rear seat belts requires that the roll-over system be triggered. This is only possible using MINI diagnostic equipment. Consequently, we recommend this task is entrusted to a MINI dealer or suitably equipped repairer.

Removal – seat belt stalks

Front seat belt pre-tensioners

18 Remove the relevant front seat as described in Section 24.

⚠️ **Warning: Before proceeding, wait a minimum of 5 minutes, as a precaution against accidental firing of the seat belt tensioner. This period ensures that any stored energy in the back-up capacitor is dissipated.**

19 Undo the screw and remove the pre-tensioner from the seat frame. Release the wiring loom and plug from the clips along its route.

⚠️ **Warning: There is a potential risk of the seat belt tensioning device firing during removal, so it should be handled carefully. Once removed, treat it with care – do not allow use chemicals on or near it, and do not expose it to high temperatures, or it may detonate.**

Rear seat belt stalks

20 The rear seat belt stalks can be removed by removing the rear seat cushion (see Section 24), then lifting the cover (where fitted) and unscrewing the Torx bolt **(see illustration)**.

Refitting

21 Refitting is a reversal of the removal procedure, noting the following points:
a) Use a little thread-locking compound, and tighten the mounting nuts/bolts to the specified torque.
b) Make sure the seat belt reel locating dowel is correctly positioned.

---

26 Interior trim panels – removal and refitting

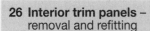

Note: *This section covers the removal and installation of the interior trim panels. It may be necessary to remove an overlapping trim before you can remove the one required. For more information on trim removal, look at relevant Chapters and Sections, where the trims may need to be removed to carry out any other procedures (eg, to remove the steering column you will need to remove the shrouds).*

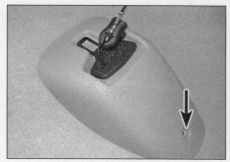

25.15a Undo the screw (arrowed)...

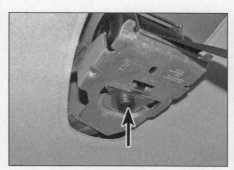

25.16 Centre-rear inertia reel bolt (arrowed)

Removal

Sun visor

Hatchback and Clubman models

1 Prise up the covers, then unscrew the mounting screws and remove the visor **(see illustration)**.
2 Disconnect the wiring for the vanity mirror light, where fitted.

Convertible models

3 Undo the screws and lower the sun visor from place **(see illustration)**.

Passenger grab handle

4 Prise open the covers, then unscrew the mounting screws and remove the grab handle **(see illustration)**.

A-pillar trim

5 On models with head airbags, disconnect the battery as described in Chapter 5A.

25.15b ...and slide the inertia reel cover forwards

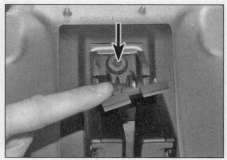

25.20 Lift up the cover to access the centre seat belt stalks

Hatchback and Clubman models

6 Prise out the cover and undo the screw at the top of the pillar trim.
7 Carefully pull the trim inwards from place. Note that the retaining clips are brittle – breakage is likely. Note how the lower edge of the trim engages. Disconnect any wiring plugs as the trim panel is withdrawn.

Convertible models

8 Undo the screws and lower the sun visor from place.
9 Pull the rubber weatherstrip from the vehicle body adjacent to the A-pillar.
10 Unclip the top of the A-pillar trim, then pull it upwards from place. Note how the lower edge engages with the facia **(see illustrations)**. Disconnect any wiring plugs as the trim panel is withdrawn.

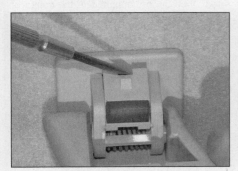

26.1 Prise down the cover to expose the sunvisor screw

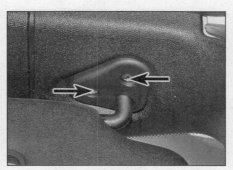

26.3 Sunvisor screws (arrowed) – Convertible models

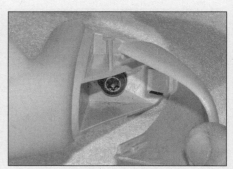

26.4 Prise open the cover to access the grab handle screws

26.10a Pull the top of the A-pillar trim panel inwards

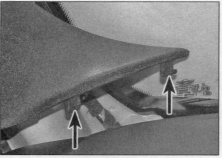

26.10b Note the lugs (arrowed) at the base of the A-pillar trim panel

26.12a Prise out the cover, and undo the B-pillar trim panel screw (arrowed)

26.12b Disconnect the wiring plug as the B-pillar trim panel is removed

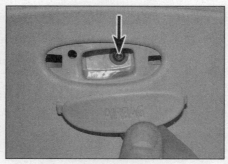

26.14 Prise out the airbag emblem at the top of the C-pillar trim and undo the screw exposed

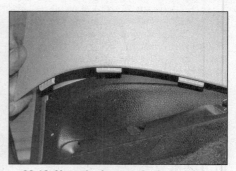

26.16 Note the lugs at the base of the C-pillar trim

B-pillar trim

11 Undo the front seat belt lower anchorage Torx bolt.

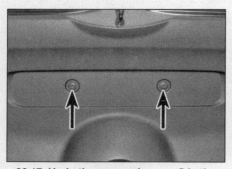

26.17 Undo the screws (arrowed) in the centre of the tailgate panel

26.18 Prise the panel away to release the push-on clips

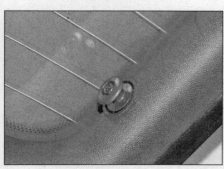

26.19 Remove the parcel shelf support buttons...

26.20 ...and pull the side trims from the tailgate

12 Prise out the cover, and undo the screw at the top of the pillar trim, then pull the panel inwards to release the retaining clips (see illustrations). Where applicable, feed the seat belt through the pillar trim. Unclip the wiring loom as the panel is withdrawn.

C-pillar trim

13 On models with head airbags, disconnect the battery as described in Chapter 5A.
14 Prise out the cover and remove the retaining screw at the top of the pillar trim (see illustration).
15 On hatchback models, if the pillar trim is to be completely removed, undo the seat belt lower anchorage bolt as described in Section 25.
16 Carefully pull the pillar trim towards the centre of the car to release the trim clips (see illustration). When refitting, secure the head airbag (where fitted) to the clip on the trim.

Tailgate trim

17 Remove the warning triangle (where fitted), then undo the screws in the centre of the panel (see illustration).
18 Use a flat-bladed tool to release the push-on clips around the panels perimeter, and remove the panel (see illustration).
19 Remove the screw each side securing the parcel shelf strap buttons (see illustration).
20 Pull the side trims from the tailgate frame (see illustration).
21 Release the clips and pull the upper trim panel from place (see illustration).

Split rear doors trim

22 If removing the left-hand door trim, remove the cover, then make alignment marks between the striker and the door, undo the

26.21 Pull the upper trim from the tailgate

26.22a Remove the rubber cover…

26.22b …mark the position of the striker, undo the screws and remove it

26.24a Release the retaining clips…

26.24b …and remove the split door trim panel

26.25 Work around the edge, releasing the boot lid panel retaining clips

2 retaining bolts and remove the striker **(see illustrations)**.

23 Prise out the courtesy light at the base of the door trim (where fitted), and disconnect the wiring plug.

24 Use a flat-bladed tool to release the push-on clips and remove the door trim **(see illustrations)**.

Boot lid trim

25 Carefully pull the boot lid trim upwards to release the retaining clips around its circumference **(see illustration)**.

Side panel

Hatchback models

26 Remove the rear seats as described in Section 24.

27 Remove the B-pillar and C-pillar trim panels as previously described in this Section.

28 Lift out the luggage compartment floor trim panel.

29 Remove the 3 expansion rivets at the lower front edge of the tailgate sill trim panel **(see illustration 19.3a and 19.3b)**.

30 Pull the tailgate sill trim panel upwards to release the retaining clips.

31 Carefully prise out the luggage compartment light, and disconnect the wiring plug (see Chapter 12).

32 Where fitted, fold the storage closing clip halfway up, open the tabs and remove the surround trim **(see illustration)**.

33 Remove the 5 expansion rivets, and remove the luggage compartment side trim panel **(see illustrations)**. Disconnect any

wiring plugs as the panel is withdrawn. On the left-hand side, the emergency fuel filler flap release cable is detached from the side trim panel through a slot.

26.32 Fold out the tabs and remove the surround trim

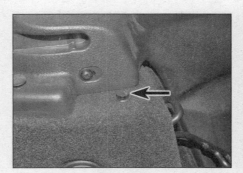

26.33b …and one at the top (arrowed)

34 Undo the 2 screws at the upper edge of the side panel **(see illustrations)**.

35 Pull the side panel inwards to release the retaining clips at lower edge, front edge and

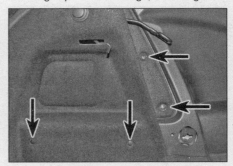

26.33a The luggage compartment side panel is secured by 4 expansion rivets at the side (arrowed)…

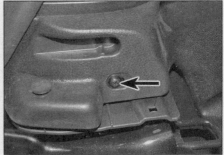

26.34a The side panel is secured by a screw (arrowed) at the rear, upper edge…

26.34b ...and the front upper edge (arrowed)

26.43 Release the clips and remove the luggage floor support

26.44 Undo the screws and remove the luggage anchorages

centre of the panel, then lift it upwards from place. Disconnect any wiring plugs as the panel is withdrawn.

Clubman models

36 Remove the rear seats as described in Section 24.

37 Remove the B-pillar and C-pillar trim panels as previously described in this Section.

38 Lift out the luggage compartment floor trim panel.

39 Remove the 4 expansion rivets at the lower front edge of the split doors sill trim panel **(see illustration 19.12)**.

40 Pull the split doors sill trim panel upwards to release the retaining clips.

41 Remove the luggage compartment roller cover (where fitted).

42 Undo the screw at the rear edge, and pull the capping at the top of the luggage

compartment side panel upwards **(see illustration 25.12a and 25.12b)**.

43 Prise out the clips and remove the luggage compartment floor support **(see illustration)**.

44 Prise away the covers, undo the screws and remove the luggage anchorages **(see illustration)**.

45 Remove the expansion rivets and manoeuvre the luggage compartment side panel from place **(see illustration)**. Disconnect any wiring plugs, and the fuel filler flap release as the panel is withdrawn.

46 If removing the right-hand side panel, undo the bolt securing the seat belt lower anchorage, and pull the slide bar from the locating hole.

47 Remove the expansion rivets, undo the screw, and pull the side panel trim inwards to release the retaining clips at the lower/front edge, then upwards to release the clips along

the upper edge **(see illustrations)**. Disconnect any wiring plugs as the panel is withdrawn.

Convertible models

48 Remove the rear seats as described in Section 24, and fully open the soft top.

49 Pull away the rubber weatherstrip at the front edge and corner, then remove the screw exposed **(see illustration)**.

50 Undo the seat belt lower anchorage bolt.

51 Remove the screw in the upper half of the panel **(see illustration)**.

52 Remove the 2 expansion rivets at the rear edge, then pull the side panel inwards to release the retaining clips, then upwards from place **(see illustration)**. Release any wiring plugs as the panel is withdrawn.

Sill/footwell kick panel trim

53 Pull away the rubber weatherstrip adjacent to the sill trim.

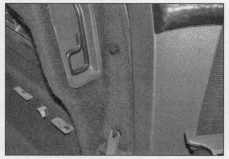

26.45 Prise out the expansion rivets securing the luggage compartment trim panel

26.47a Undo the screw (arrowed) at the front, upper edge...

26.47b ...remove the expansion rivet (arrowed) at the lower edge...

26.47c ... and the rivet (arrowed) at the upper edge

26.49 Pull away the weatherstrip and undo the screw (arrowed)

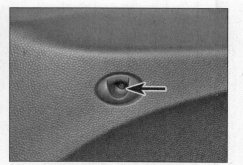

26.51 Remove the screw (arrowed) in the upper half of the side panel

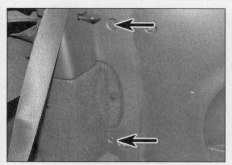

26.52 Remove the plastic expansion rivets (arrowed) at the rear edge of the side panel

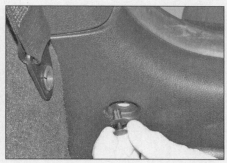

26.55 Prise out the plastic expansion rivet at the rear of the sill trim/kick panel

26.57 Squeeze together the sides of the upper shroud to release the clips (rev counter removed for clarity)

26.59a Undo the screw each side (arrowed)…

26.59b …and the screws (arrowed) at the top of the lower shroud

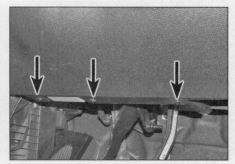

26.60 Drivers lower facia panel screws (arrowed)

54 Undo the seat belt lower anchorage/rail Torx bolt.

55 Remove the plastic expansion rivet, then pull the panel trim horizontally towards the centre of the vehicle to release the push-on clips (**see illustration**). Note that clip breakage is quite likely.

Steering column shrouds

56 Remove the steering wheel as described in Chapter 10.

57 Gently squeeze together the sides of the upper shroud to release the clips, then carefully prise it upwards (**see illustration**). Disconnect the wiring plug as the shroud is withdrawn.

58 Undo the 3 screws and remove the lower facia panel beneath the steering column (**see illustration 26.60**).

59 Press the steering column adjustment lever downwards, undo the 4 screws (2 from the top, 1 each side), and remove the lower shroud (**see illustrations**). Release the wiring harness from any clips as the shroud is withdrawn.

Driver's side lower facia panel

60 Undo the 3 screws at the edge of the panel, and pull down the front edge to release the retaining clips (**see illustration**).

Refitting

61 Refitting is a reversal of the removal procedure. Where seat belt fastenings have been disturbed, make sure that they are tightened to the specified torque. Renew any broken clips as required.

27 Centre console – removal and refitting

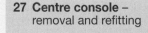

Removal

1 Squeeze together the sides, and unclip the gaiter from around the hand brake lever (**see illustration**).

2 Carefully release the clip each side, remove the end trim from the handbrake lever grip, then release the clips and slide the grip/gaiter from the lever (**see illustrations**).

3 Prise the gear/selector lever gaiter from the console, then pull the lever knob straight up to detach it from the lever (**see illustration**).

27.1 Squeeze together the sides and unclip the handbrake gaiter

27.2a Carefully prise away the end trim…

27.2b …release the clips…

27.2c ...and slide off the grip and gaiter assembly

27.3 Prise up the gaiter

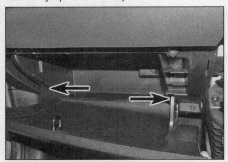

27.5 Undo the screw in the centre and remove the rear cup holder

Don't twist the knob to remove it – damage to the knob will result.

4 On models with a centre armrest, undo the screw each side, unclip the rear covers, undo the retaining screw and pull the cup holder assembly upwards from place.

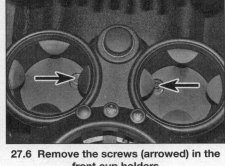

27.6 Remove the screws (arrowed) in the front cup holders

5 On models without a centre armrest, undo the screw and remove the cupholder from the rear of the console **(see illustration)**.
6 Undo the 2 screws at the front, and pull the centre console upwards to release the retaining clips **(see illustration)**.

Disconnect any wiring plugs as the console is withdrawn.

Refitting

7 Refitting is a reversal of the removal procedure.

28 Glovebox – removal and refitting

1 Unclip and withdraw the hinge pins.
2 Open the glovebox, release the guides, and manoeuvre it from place **(see illustration)**.
3 Refitting is a reversal of the removal procedure, making sure that the glovebox/storage tray is located correctly before tightening the screws.

29 Facia – removal and refitting

Removal

1 Disconnect the battery negative (earth) lead (Chapter 5A).
2 Remove the glovebox (see Section 28).
3 Remove the rev counter, steering column switch assembly, facia mounted CD autochanger (where fitted) and central instrument cluster as described in Chapter 12.
4 Carefully prise the panel from the drivers end of the facia **(see illustration)**. Disconnect any wiring plugs as the panels are withdrawn.
5 Undo the 4 retaining screws and remove the air vent cover from the drivers side of the facia **(see illustrations)**.
6 Carefully prise the solar sensor from the facia (where fitted). Disconnect the wiring plug as the sensor is withdrawn.
7 Remove the steering column as described in Chapter 10.
8 Undo the screws and remove the facia storage compartment (where fitted) **(see illustration)**.
9 The upper section of the facia is now secured by 2 screws in the rev counter aperture, 1 screw each side of the central instrument aperture, and 5 screws on the passengers side of the facia **(see**

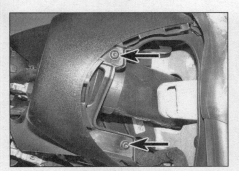

28.2 Unclip the guides (arrowed) and remove the glovebox

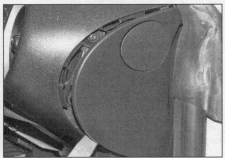

29.4 Prise the panel from the drivers end of the facia

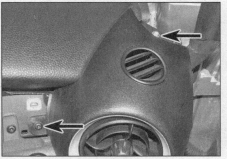

29.5b ...and screw at the top (arrowed)

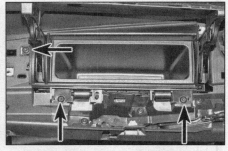

29.8 Undo the screws (arrowed) and remove the storage compartment/CD autochanger (as applicable)

29.5a The air vent cover is secured by screws at the side (arrowed)...

29.9a Remove the screws (arrowed) in the rev counter aperture...

29.9b ...each side of the centre aperture (arrowed)...

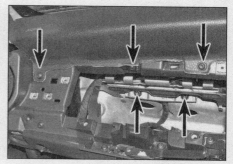

29.9c ...and 5 screws (arrowed) on the passengers side...

29.9d ...then lift upper section of the facia...

illustrations) Undo the screws and, with the help of an assistant, raise the facia panel, then disconnect the passengers airbag wiring plug, and manoeuvre it from the cabin. Feed the solar sensor wiring plug through the aperture as the panel is withdrawn (where applicable).

29.9e ...and disconnect the passengers airbag wiring plug (arrowed)

10 Undo the 4 screws and remove the drivers side outer knee bolster **(see illustrations)**. Disconnect the ignition switch wiring plug as the bolster is withdrawn.

11 Remove the sill/kickpanel each side as described in Section 26.

29.10a Undo the screws above (arrowed)...

12 The lower section of the facia is secured by 6 screws at the passengers end, 4 screws in the centre section, 4 screws to the left of the steering column, and 4 screws at the drivers end **(see illustrations)**. Undo the 2 screws securing the diagnostic plug under the drivers

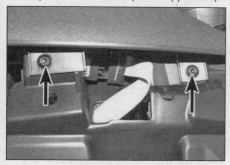

29.10b ...and below the drivers side knee outer bolster

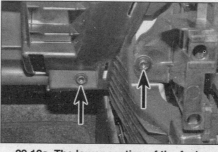

29.12a The lower section of the facia is secured by screws (arrowed) on the passengers side of the centre section...

29.12b ...passengers side upper section (arrowed)...

29.12c ...passengers side lower section (arrowed)...

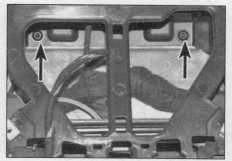

29.12d ...centre, upper section (arrowed)...

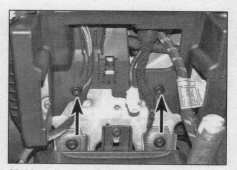

29.12e ...centre, lower section (arrowed)...

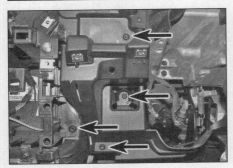

29.12f ...to the left of the steering column aperture (arrowed)...

29.12g ...and at the drivers end (arrowed)

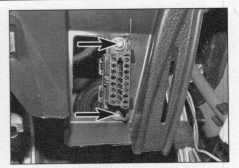

29.12h Diagnostic plug retaining screws (arrowed)

a) *Undo the screw and remove the plastic trim panel at the centre/lower area of the crossmember (see illustration).*
b) *The crossmember is removed along with the attached wiring harnesses. Trace the harnesses to the various wiring plugs, disconnect them, then release the harnesses from any clips as necessary, noting the routing.*
c) *The crossmember is now secured by various bolts/screws (see illustrations). Undo the fasteners, make a final check to ensure all wiring harnesses attached to the crossmember have been disconnected, then with the help of an assistant, manoeuvre the crossmember rearwards, and out from the cabin. Recover the pipe from the evaporator housing to the crossmember (glovebox cooling pipe).*

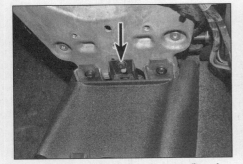

29.13a Undo the screw (arrowed) and remove the panel in the lower, centre of the crossmember

side, and feed the plug through the opening in the facia. With the help of an assistant, manoeuvre the lower section of the facia from the cabin. Note their fitted positions, and

29.13b The crossmember is secured by screws/bolts in the centre, lower area (arrowed)...

disconnect any wiring plugs as the facia is withdrawn.

13 If required, the facia crossmember is removed as follows:

Refitting

14 Essentially, refitting is a reversal of removal. Ensure all wiring harnesses are correctly routed, securely reconnected, and check for correct operation before venturing out onto the roads.

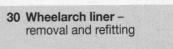

30 Wheelarch liner – removal and refitting

Removal

Front

1 Apply the handbrake. If the wheel is to be removed (to improve access), loosen the wheel nuts. Jack up the front of the vehicle and support it on axle stands. Remove the front wheel.
2 Remove the expansion rivets, undo the nut, undo the screws and manoeuvre the wheelarch liner from place **(see illustration)**.

Rear

3 Chock the front wheels, and engage 1st gear. If the wheel is to be removed (to improve access), loosen the wheel nuts. Jack up the rear of the vehicle and support it on axle stands. Remove the rear wheel.
4 Undo the nuts, remove the expansion rivets,

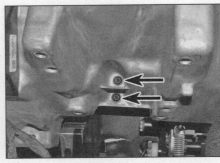

29.13c ...at each end (arrowed)...

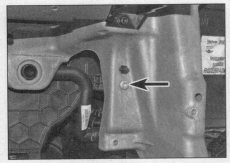

29.13d ...in the steering column aperture (arrowed)...

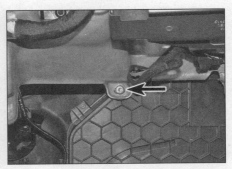

29.13e ...each side of the central aperture (arrowed)...

29.13f ...and to the heater housing on the passengers side (arrowed)

undo the screw at the front underside, and manoeuvre the wheelarch liner from place.

Refitting

5 Refitting is a reversal of the removal procedure. If the wheels were removed, tighten the wheel nuts to the specified torque.

31 Convertible soft-top –
general information,
removal and refitting

General information

1 The soft-top opening/closing mechanism consists of a metal framework operated by hydraulic rams. Pressurised fluid is supplied to the rams from a pump with an integral electric motor. A Convertible top module (CVM) controls the operation of the motor, using information received from various Hall sensors attached to the mechanism. The CVM is also networked to various other control modules in the vehicle. For instance, when the open switch is activated, the CVM sends a signal to the Footwell module, which slightly lowers the front windows prior to the soft-top opening.

2 Although it is possible to renew the fabric covering of the soft-top independently of the frame, the procedure is complex, and requires patience, dexterity and experience to be carried out successfully. Consequently, it's recommended that this task be entrusted to a MINI dealer or suitably equipped/experienced repairer.

3 The hydraulic system is maintenance free, self-bleeding, and filled for life.

4 Should the electrical system fail with the soft-top open, it can be closed manually as follows:

   a) *Remove the luggage compartment light unit as described in Chapter 12.*

   b) *Rotate the screw on the side of the hydraulic motor anti-clockwise 1 ½ turns to release the hydraulic pressure (see illustration).*

   c) *Slide the cover from the top rails forwards to remove it, then unscrew the Allen bolts to release the soft top side rails (see illustration).*

   d) *With the help of an assistant, lift both side rails forwards and up to the windscreen header.*

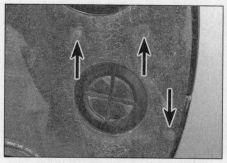

30.2 The wheelarch liners are secured by various fasteners – these are expansion rivets (arrowed). Undo the screw and prise out the rivet

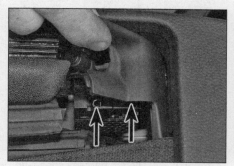

31.4b Slide the cover forwards and slacken the Allen bolts (arrowed)

   e) *Prise off the cover below the sunroof motor, then insert the Allen key from the vehicle toolkit into the centre of the sunroof drive, press the Allen screw upwards and rotate it clockwise to release the soft top locks (see illustration).*

   f) *Manoeuvre the soft-top side rail pins into the corresponding holes in the windscreen header.*

   g) *Press the Allen key upwards and rotate it anti-clockwise until the soft-top is locked.*

Removal

5 With reference to Section 26, remove the rear side trim panels, and the boot lid inner trim panel.

6 Partially close the soft top, stopping the closing operation just before the locks at the

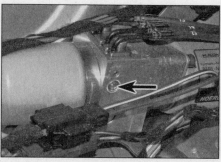

31.4a Working through the light aperture, rotate the screw (arrowed) 1 ½ turns anti-clockwise to release the hydraulic pressure

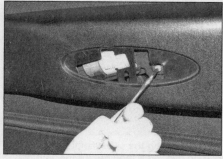

31.4c Press the screw upwards and rotate it clockwise to release the locks

windscreen header engage, then disconnect the battery as described in Chapter 5A.

7 Lift out the luggage compartment floor panel, then remove the 3 plastic expansion rivets and pull up the boot sill trim panel **(see illustrations)**. Disconnect any wiring plugs as the panel is withdrawn.

8 Unlock the Easyload, lift and support the soft top bow **(see illustration)**.

9 Undo the screw each side and manoeuvre the parcel shelf from the luggage compartment **(see illustration)**.

10 Pull the rubber weatherstrip from the sides of the boot lid aperture, then undo the screws and manoeuvre the rear parcel shelf locator panel each side from place **(see illustrations)**. Disconnect the wiring plug from the microswitch in the left-hand panel as it's withdrawn.

31.7a Remove the plastic rivets (arrowed)...

31.7b ...then pull the sill trim panel upwards to release the clips

31.8 Lift the soft top bow and support it with a suitable length of wood

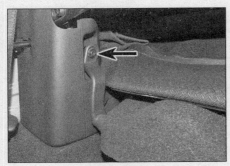

31.9 Undo the screw each side (arrowed) and remove the parcel shelf

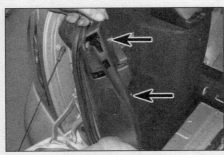

31.10a Undo the screws (arrowed) and remove the parcel shaft locator panel each side

31.10b Disconnect the microswitch wiring plug from the left-hand locator panel

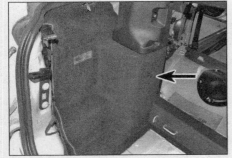

31.11 Prise up the centre pin, lever out the plastic rivet, and manoeuvre the trim panel from place

31.14 Disconnect the wiring plug (arrowed), release the harness clips, and detach the wiring loom from the boot lid

11 Prise out the luggage compartment light, disconnect the wiring plug, then remove the expansion rivet and remove the luggage compartment side trim panel each side **(see illustration)**.

12 In order to minimise any risk of damage to the paintwork, apply masking tape to the tops of the rear wing panels.

13 Trace the hydraulic pipes and release them from any retaining clips. The soft-top is removed complete with hydraulic system still connected.

14 Disconnect the wiring plug, release any wiring harness clips, and detach the wiring loom from the boot lid **(see illustration)**.

15 Undo the 3 bolts securing the hydraulic pump/motor.

16 Disconnect the any wiring plugs that would prevent the soft-top assembly being removed. For instance, the lower plug on the CVM, the plug each side of the hydraulic motor assembly **(see illustration)**.

17 Remove the retaining clip, and detach the fabric cover from the stud each side **(see illustration)**.

18 Remove the frame hinge screw each side **(see illustration)**. When refitting this screw, apply a little locking compound to the threads.

19 With the help of an assistant, raise the side rails slightly, and undo the front pivot bolt each side **(see illustration)**.

20 Undo the 2 nuts each side at the front of the side panel **(see illustration)**.

21 Enlist the help of an additional assistant, and carefully manoeuvre the soft-top assembly upwards and away from the vehicle. Note that the assembly is very heavy!

Refitting

22 Refitting is a reversal of removal. Tighten all retaining bolts/nuts securely, and check for correct operation.

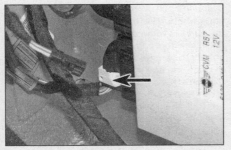

31.16 Pivot over the locking catch (arrowed) and disconnect the lower wiring plug from the CVM

31.17 Remove the clip (arrowed) and pull the fabric from the stud

31.18 Undo the frame hinge screw (arrowed) each side...

31.19 ...the front pivot bolt each side...

31.20 ...and the 2 nuts (arrowed) each side

Chapter 12
Body electrical systems

Contents

Degrees of difficulty

Easy, suitable for novice with little experience | **Fairly easy,** suitable for beginner with some experience | **Fairly difficult,** suitable for competent DIY mechanic | **Difficult,** suitable for experienced DIY mechanic | **Very difficult,** suitable for expert DIY or professional

Specifications

Fuses and relays

Refer to the wiring diagrams at the end of this Chapter, and the information given on the fuse box lid inner.
Note: *Fuse and relay ratings and circuits are liable to change from year to year. Consult the handbook supplied with the vehicle, or consult a MINI authorised repairer, for the latest information.*

Bulbs	Wattage	Type
Direction indicator lights.	21	PY Bayonet
Front foglight	35	H8 Halogen
Headlight Bi-Xenon	35	D1S
Headlight Halogen	60/55	H4
High-level stop-light	LED	
Glovebox	5	Festoon
Ceiling light		
Except Convertible models	6	Wedge
Convertible models.	5	Wedge
Luggage compartment/footwell	5	Wedge
Number plate lights:		
Except Clubman models	5	Festoon
Clubman models	5	Wedge
Rear foglight:		
Except Clubman models	16	Wedge
Clubman models	21	Bayonet

Bulbs (continued)

	Wattage	Type
Stop/tail light:		
Except Clubman models (Tail light is LED from 08.2010)	21	Bayonet
Clubman models:		
Up to 08.2010	21	Bayonet
From 08.2010 (Tail light is LED)	21	Bayonet
Reversing lights:		
Except Clubman models:		
Up to 08.2010	21	Bayonet
From 08.2010	16	Wedge
Clubman models	21	Bayonet
Side repeater direction indicator lights.	5	Wedge
Sidelights	5	Wedge
Vanity light	1.2	Wedge

Torque wrench settings

	Nm	lbf ft
Airbag control unit nuts	8	6
Crash sensor bolt*	8	6
Passengers' airbag nuts*	10	7

Do not re-use

1 General information

⚠ **Warning: Before carrying out any work on the electrical system, read through the precautions given in 'Safety first!' at the beginning of this manual.**

The electrical system is of 12-volt negative earth type. Power for the lights and all electrical accessories is supplied by a silver-calcium battery which is charged by the alternator.

This Chapter covers repair and service procedures for the various electrical components not associated with the engine. Information on the battery, alternator and starter motor can be found in Chapter 5A; the ignition system is covered in Chapter 5B.

All models are fitted with a driver's airbag, which is designed to prevent serious chest and head injuries to the driver during an accident. A similar bag for the front seat passenger is also fitted. The electronic control module for the airbag is located under the centre console inside the vehicle. It contains two frontal impact micro machine sensors, a crash sensor, and a safety sensor. The crash sensor and safety sensor are connected in series, and if they both sense a deceleration in excess of a predetermined limit, the electronic airbag control module will operate the airbag. The airbag is inflated by a gas generator, which forces the bag out of the module cover in the centre of the steering wheel. A sliding contact ring ensures that a good electrical connection is maintained with the airbag at all times as the steering wheel is turned in each direction. There is also a coiled spring, that is able to 'wind-up' and 'unwind' as the steering wheel is turned, maintaining the electronic contact at all times.

As an optional extra, some models can be equipped with side airbags, which are built into the sides of the front seats. The intention of the side airbags is principally to offer greater passenger protection in a side impact. The side airbags are linked to the 'front' airbags, and are also controlled by the electronic control module under the centre console. The side air bags are also controlled by the sensors located under the carpet and sill trims inside the vehicle. Side airbags incorporated into the headlining are also available.

All models are fitted with an ignition immobiliser, which is built into the key and ignition lock.

All models are fitted with a headlight levelling system, which is controlled by a knob on the facia. On position 0, the headlights are in their base position, and on position 5, the headlights are in their maximum inclined angle.

It should be noted that, when portions of the electrical system are serviced, the lead should be disconnected from the battery negative terminal, to prevent electrical shorts and fires. **Caution: When disconnecting the battery for work described in the following Sections, refer to Chapter 5A.**

2 Electrical fault finding – general information

Note: *Refer to the precautions given in 'Safety first!' before starting work. The following tests relate to testing of the main electrical circuits, and should not be used to test delicate electronic circuits (such as engine management systems, anti-lock braking systems, etc), particularly where an electronic control module is used. Also refer to the precautions given in Chapter 5A.*

General

1 A typical electrical circuit consists of an electrical component, any switches, relays, motors, fuses, fusible links or circuit breakers related to that component, and the wiring and connectors which link the component to both the battery and the chassis. To help to pinpoint a problem in an electrical circuit, wiring diagrams are included at the end of this Chapter.

2 Before attempting to diagnose an electrical fault, first study the appropriate wiring diagram, to obtain a complete understanding of the components included in the particular circuit concerned. The possible sources of a fault can be narrowed down by noting if other components related to the circuit are operating properly. If several components or circuits fail at one time, the problem is likely to be related to a shared fuse or earth connection.

3 Electrical problems usually stem from simple causes, such as loose or corroded connections, a faulty earth connection, a blown fuse, a melted fusible link, or a faulty relay (refer to Section 3 for details of testing relays). Visually inspect the condition of all fuses, wires and connections in a problem circuit before testing the components. Use the wiring diagrams to determine which terminal connections will need to be checked in order to pinpoint the trouble-spot.

4 The basic tools required for electrical fault finding include a circuit tester or voltmeter (a 12-volt bulb with a set of test leads can also be used for certain tests); an ohmmeter (to measure resistance and check for continuity); a battery and set of test leads; and a jumper wire, preferably with a circuit breaker or fuse incorporated, which can be used to bypass suspect wires or electrical components. Before attempting to locate a problem with test instruments, use the wiring diagram to determine where to make the connections.

5 To find the source of an intermittent wiring fault (usually due to a poor or dirty connection, or damaged wiring insulation), a 'wiggle' test can be performed on the wiring. This involves wiggling the wiring by hand to see if the fault occurs as the wiring is moved. It should be possible to narrow down the source of the fault to a particular section of wiring. This method of testing can be used in conjunction with any of the tests described in the following sub-Sections.

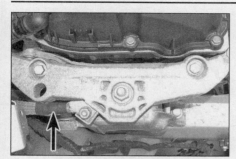

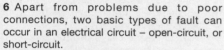

2.22a The main engine earth strap is located on the right-hand mounting (arrowed)

2.22b Other earth connections are in various places, such as the bonnet hinge (arrowed)…

2.22c …front sections of the chassis members (arrowed)…

6 Apart from problems due to poor connections, two basic types of fault can occur in an electrical circuit – open-circuit, or short-circuit.

7 Open-circuit faults are caused by a break somewhere in the circuit, which prevents current from flowing. An open-circuit fault will prevent a component from working.

8 Short-circuit faults are caused by a 'short' somewhere in the circuit, which allows the current flowing in the circuit to 'escape' along an alternative route, usually to earth. Short-circuit faults are normally caused by a breakdown in wiring insulation, which allows a feed wire to touch either another wire, or an earthed component such as the bodyshell. A short-circuit fault will normally cause the relevant circuit fuse to blow.

Finding an open-circuit

9 To check for an open-circuit, connect one lead of a circuit tester or the negative lead of a voltmeter either to the battery negative terminal or to a known good earth.

10 Connect the other lead to a connector in the circuit being tested, preferably nearest to the battery or fuse. At this point, battery voltage should be present, unless the lead from the battery or the fuse itself is faulty (bearing in mind that some circuits are live only when the ignition switch is moved to a particular position).

11 Switch on the circuit, then connect the tester lead to the connector nearest the circuit switch on the component side.

12 If voltage is present (indicated either by the tester bulb lighting or a voltmeter reading, as applicable), this means that the section of the circuit between the relevant connector and the switch is problem-free.

13 Continue to check the remainder of the circuit in the same fashion.

14 When a point is reached at which no voltage is present, the problem must lie between that point and the previous test point with voltage. Most problems can be traced to a broken, corroded or loose connection.

Finding a short-circuit

15 To check for a short-circuit, first disconnect the load(s) from the circuit (loads are the components which draw current from a circuit, such as bulbs, motors, heating elements, etc).

16 Remove the relevant fuse from the circuit, and connect a circuit tester or voltmeter to the fuse connections.

17 Switch on the circuit, bearing in mind that some circuits are live only when the ignition switch is moved to a particular position.

18 If voltage is present (indicated either by the tester bulb lighting or a voltmeter reading, as applicable), this means that there is a short-circuit.

19 If no voltage is present during this test, but the fuse still blows with the load(s) reconnected, this indicates an internal fault in the load(s).

Finding an earth fault

20 The battery negative terminal is connected to 'earth' - the metal of the engine/transmission unit and the vehicle body – and

2.22d …engine compartment chassis members…

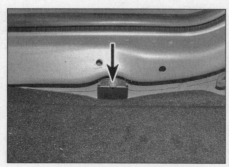

2.22f …under the door sills (arrowed)…

many systems are wired so that they only receive a positive feed, the current returning via the metal of the car body. This means that the component mounting and the body form part of that circuit.

21 Loose or corroded mountings can therefore cause a range of electrical faults, ranging from total failure of a circuit, to a puzzling partial failure. In particular, lights may shine dimly (especially when another circuit sharing the same earth point is in operation), motors (eg, wiper motors or the radiator cooling fan motor) may run slowly, and the operation of one circuit may have an apparently-unrelated effect on another.

22 Note that on many vehicles, earth straps are used between certain components, such as the engine/transmission and the body, usually where there is no metal-to-metal contact between components, due to flexible rubber mountings, etc. **(see illustrations)**.

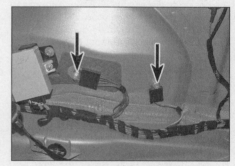

2.22e …left-hand rear side panel (arrowed)…

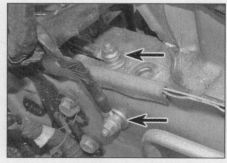

2.22g …behind the transmission mounting (arrowed)

3.1 The main fusebox is located behind the drivers side kick panel

3.2 Engine compartment fuse/relay box

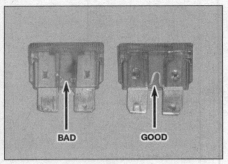

3.3 When a fuse blows, the element between the terminals melts

23 To check whether a component is properly earthed, disconnect the battery (refer to Chapter 5A, Section 4) and connect one lead of an ohmmeter to a known good earth point. Connect the other lead to the wire or earth connection being tested. The resistance reading should be zero; if not, check the connection as follows.

24 If an earth connection is thought to be faulty, dismantle the connection, and clean both the bodyshell and the wire terminal (or the component earth connection mating surface) back to bare metal. Be careful to remove all traces of dirt and corrosion, then use a knife to trim away any paint, so that a clean metal-to-metal joint is made.

25 On reassembly, tighten the joint fasteners securely; if a wire terminal is being refitted, use serrated washers between the terminal and the bodyshell, to ensure a clean and secure connection.

26 When the connection is remade, prevent the onset of corrosion in the future by applying a coat of petroleum jelly or silicone-based grease, or by spraying on (at regular intervals) a proprietary water-dispersant lubricant.

3 Fuses and relays –
testing and renewal

Note: *It is important to note that the ignition switch and the appropriate electrical circuit must always be switched off before any of the fuses (or relays) are removed and renewed. If electrical components/units have to be removed, the battery earth lead must be*

4.3 Pull the decorative strip from the rev counter location

disconnected. When reconnecting the battery, reference should be made to Chapter 5A.

1 Fuses are designed to break a circuit when a predetermined current is reached, in order to protect components and wiring which could be damaged by excessive current flow. Any excessive current flow will be due to a fault in the circuit, usually a short-circuit (see Section 2). The main central fusebox, which also carries some relays, is located behind the drivers side kickpanel in the footwell **(see illustration)**.

2 The auxiliary fusebox is located in the engine compartment **(see illustration)**, against the inner wing next to the air cleaner, and is accessed by unclipping and removing the cover. The auxiliary fusebox also contains some relays.

3 Each circuit is identified by numbers on the main fusebox and on the inside of the auxiliary fusebox cover. Reference to the wiring diagrams at the end of this Chapter will indicate the circuits protected by each fuse. Plastic tweezers are attached to the auxiliary fusebox to remove and refit the fuses and relays. To remove a fuse, use the tweezers provided to pull it out of the holder, then slide the fuse sideways from the tweezers. The wire within the fuse is clearly visible, and it will be broken if the fuse is blown **(see illustration)**.

4 Always renew a fuse with one of an identical rating. Never substitute a fuse of a higher rating, or make temporary repairs using wire or metal foil; more serious damage, or even fire, could result. The fuse rating is stamped on top of the fuse. Never renew a fuse more than once without tracing the source of the trouble.

5 Note that if the vehicle is to be laid up for a long period, there is a 'battery saver'

4.4a Undo the screws (arrowed) above the knee bolster...

relay fitted to the central fusebox to prevent the ancillary electrical components from discharging the battery.

6 Relays are electrically-operated switches, which are used in certain circuits. The various relays can be removed from their respective locations by carefully pulling them from the sockets. Some of the relays in the fuseboxes have a plastic bar on its upper surface to enable the use of the tweezers.

7 If a component controlled by a relay becomes inoperative and the relay is suspect, listen to the relay as the circuit is operated. If the relay is functioning, it should be possible to hear it click as it is energised. If the relay proves satisfactory, the fault lies with the components or wiring of the system. If the relay is not being energised, then either the relay is not receiving a switching voltage, or the relay itself is faulty. (Do not overlook the relay socket terminals when tracing faults.) Testing is by the substitution of a known good unit, but be careful; while some relays are identical in appearance and in operation, others look similar, but perform different functions.

4 Switches –
removal and refitting

Note: *Before removing any electrical switches, disconnect the battery negative (earth) lead (refer to Chapter 5A).*

Removal

Ignition switch

1 Undo the 3 retaining screws at the front edge, then pull down and remove the facia panel above the pedals.

2 Remove the rev counter as described in Section 10.

3 Unclip the decorative strip in front of the rev counter location **(see illustration)**.

4 Undo the 4 screws and remove the knee bolster **(see illustrations)**. Disconnect the ignition switch ribbon wiring plug as the panel is withdrawn.

5 Using a blunt, thin-bladed tool, carefully prise the surround panel from the switch **(see illustrations)**. Take care not to mark the surround panel or bolster as they are easily

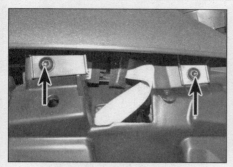

4.4b ...and below (arrowed)

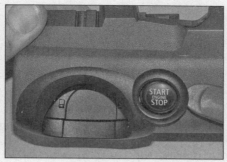

4.5a Carefully prise away...

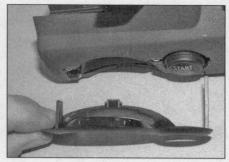

4.5b ...and remove the switch surround panel

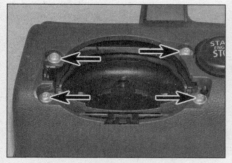

4.6 Switch retaining screws (arrowed)

4.10 Steering column switch cluster clamp screw (arrowed)

4.11 Prise up the clip (arrowed) each side and slide the switch cluster from the column

damaged. Note that damage to the panel retaining clips is likely.

6 Undo the retaining screws and remove the switch **(see illustration)**.

Steering column switch cluster

7 Remove the steering column upper and lower shrouds as described in Chapter 11.

8 Apply a strip of self-adhesive tape to the rotary contact unit on the steering column to prevent its accidental rotation.

9 Disconnect the wiring plugs from the switch cluster.

10 Undo the switch cluster clamp screw **(see illustration)**.

11 Release the clip each side, and slide the switch cluster upwards from the column **(see illustration)**.

12 If a new switch cluster is fitted, it must be programmed/encoded using MINI diagnostic equipment. Entrust this task to a MINI dealer or suitably equipped repairer. **Note:** *If the rotary contact unit has been inadvertently rotated, re-centre it as follows:*

a) *Rotate the contact unit fully anti-clockwise.*

b) *Rotate the contact unit fully clockwise, whilst counting the number of revolutions.*

c) *Turn the unit anti-clockwise half the number of revolutions.*

d) *The centring pin should be at the 6 o'clock position **(see illustration)**.*

Centre console switches

13 Remove the centre console as described in Chapter 11.

14 Undo the retaining screws and remove the relevant switch from the console **(see illustration)**.

Hazard warning switch

15 Remove the central instrument cover as described in Section 10 of Chapter 3 (heater control panel removal).

16 Release the clips and press the hazard

switch from the instrument cover **(see illustration)**.

Door mirror control switches

17 Carefully prise the switch surround from the door trim **(see illustration)**.

4.12 The rotary contact unit centring pin (arrowed) should be in the 6 o'clock position

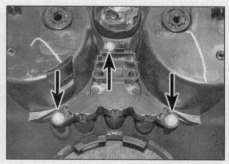

4.14 Centre console switch retaining screws (arrowed)

4.16 Release the clips (arrowed) and remove the hazard warning switch

4.17 Prise the door mirror control switch from the trim panel

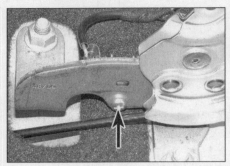

4.26 Handbrake-on warning light switch retaining screw (arrowed)

4.27 Prise the lens at each end of the roof console outwards

4.28a Insert a screwdriver into the slot at each end…

18 Disconnect the multi-plug and withdraw the switch.

Multi-function steering wheel switches

19 Remove the airbag unit as described in Section 21.

20 Undo the retaining screws on the front of the steering wheel, then remove the switches, disconnecting the wiring plugs as they are withdrawn.

Heated rear window switch

21 This switch is integral with the heater control panel. Removal of the panel is described in Chapter 3.

Courtesy light door switch

22 The function of this switch is incorporated into the door lock assembly. See Chapter 11.

Tailgate/door/boot lid opening switch

23 The function of this switch is incorporated into the tailgate lock assembly. See Chapter 11.

4.28b …and release the clips

Facia centre panel switches

24 These switches are integral with the heater control panel. Removal of the panel is described in Chapter 3.

Handbrake-on warning switch

25 Remove the rear centre console as described in Chapter 11.

26 Disconnect the wiring, undo the screw and remove the switch from the handbrake lever bracket **(see illustration)**.

Roof console

27 Carefully prise the lens at each end of the console outwards and remove them **(see illustration)**.

28 Insert a screwdriver into the holes at the front, outer edges, release the clips and lower the front edge of the console **(see illustrations)**. Disconnect the wiring plugs as the console is removed.

Refitting

29 Refitting of all switches is a reversal of the removal procedure.

5 Bulbs (exterior lights) – renewal

1 Whenever a bulb is renewed, note the following points:
a) *Remember that if the light has just been in use, the bulb may be extremely hot.*
b) *Always check the bulb contacts and holder, ensuring that there is clean metal-to-metal contact between the bulb and its live(s) and earth. Clean off any corrosion or dirt before fitting a new bulb.*
c) *Wherever bayonet-type bulbs are fitted, ensure that the live contact(s) bear firmly against the bulb contact.*
d) *Always ensure that the new bulb is of the correct rating and that it is completely clean before fitting it; this applies particularly to headlight/foglight bulbs.*
e) *Do not touch the glass of halogen-type bulbs (headlights, front foglights) with the fingers, as this may lead to rapid blackening and failure of the new bulb; if the glass is accidentally touched, clean it with methylated spirit.*
f) *If renewing the bulb does not cure the problem, check the relevant fuse and relay with reference to the Specifications, and to the wiring diagrams at the end of this Chapter.*

Headlight dipped and main beam – non-Xenon lights

2 At the rear of the headlight unit, release the clip and remove the cover **(see illustration)**.

3 Disconnect the wiring plug from the rear of the bulb **(see illustration)**.

4 Release the retaining clip and remove the bulb. Note how the tab fits in the slot on the rear of the headlight **(see illustrations)**.

5 Refitting is a reversal of the removal procedure.

Bi-Xenon bulbs

Caution! Due to the high voltages supplied to this type of headlights, disconnect the

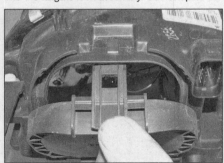

5.2 Unclip the cover at the rear of the headlight

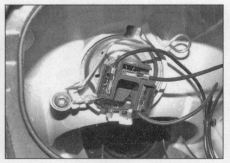

5.3 Pull the wiring plug from the rear of the bulb

5.4a Press the retaining clip downwards to release it…

5.4b ...and remove the bulb

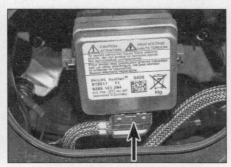

5.7a Disconnect the wiring plug (arrowed)...

5.7b ...rotate the bulb/ignitor anti-clockwise and remove it

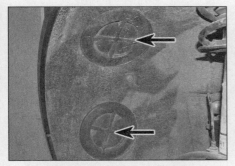

5.9 Side light cover and directional indicator cover (arrowed)

5.10 Rotate the sidelight bulbholder anti-clockwise and pull it from place

5.13 Rotate the inner cover anti-clockwise

battery negative lead is disconnected – refer to Chapter 5A, then operate the headlight switch to dissipate any residual electrical energy.

6 At the rear of the headlight unit, release the clip and remove the cover **(see illustration 5.2).**

7 Disconnect the wiring plug, rotate the bulb/ignitor assembly anti-clockwise and remove it from the rear of the headlight **(see illustrations).** Note that the bulb must not be separated from the ignitor.

⚠ *Warning! Xenon bulbs are highly pressurised – handle them with extreme care.*

8 Fit the new bulb using a reversal of the removal procedure.

Front sidelight

9 In order to access the side light bulbholder, rotate the lower cover in the wheelarch liner anti-clockwise and remove it **(see illustration).**

10 Rotate the bulbholder anti-clockwise and pull it from the rear of the light unit **(see illustration).** Pull the wedge-type bulb from the bulbholder.

11 Fit the new bulb using a reversal of the removal procedure.

Front direction indicator

12 In order to access the side light bulbholder, rotate the upper cover in the wheelarch liner anti-clockwise and remove it **(see illustration 5.9).**

13 Rotate the inner cover anti-clockwise and remove it **(see illustration).**

14 Rotate the bulbholder anti-clockwise, and withdraw it from the light unit **(see illustration).**

15 Twist the bulb anti-clockwise, and remove it from the bulbholder.

16 Fit the new bulb using a reversal of the removal procedure. Note that the bayonet

pins of the bulb are offset – the bulb will only fit correctly into the bulb holder in one position **(see illustration).**

Direction indicator side repeaters

17 Open the bonnet, slide the side repeater/surround assembly forwards, and remove it from the front wing **(see illustration).**

18 Turn the bulbholder anti-clockwise, and disconnect it from the repeater unit **(see illustration).**

19 Pull the wedge-type bulb from the holder.

20 Fit the new bulb using a reversal of the removal procedure.

Front foglight

21 In order to access the foglight bulbholder, rotate the lower cover in the wheelarch liner

5.14 Rotate the indicator bulbholder anti-clockwise and remove it from the headlight

5.16 The directional indicator bulb pins (arrowed) are offset

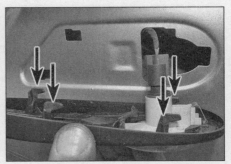

5.17 Slide the side repeater surround forwards to release the hooks (arrowed)

5.18 Rotate the side repeater bulbholder anti-clockwise and pull it from the lens

5.22 Disconnect the front fog light bulb wiring plug (arrowed)

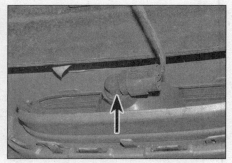

5.24 Rotate the rear foglight bulbholder (arrowed) anti-clockwise – except Clubman models

anti-clockwise and remove it **(see illustration 5.9)**.

22 Disconnect the wiring from the bulb, rotate it anti-clockwise and pull it from the rear of the light unit **(see illustration)**. Note that the bulb is integral with the holder.

23 Fit the new bulb using a reversal of the removal procedure.

Rear foglight – except Clubman models

24 Reach up behind the bumper, turn the bulbholder anti-clockwise to remove from the light unit **(see illustration)**.

25 The foglight bulb is of the wedge type and simply pulls from the bulbholder.

26 Fit the new bulb using a reversal of the removal procedure. Make sure that the light unit is located correctly.

Rear light cluster

Except Clubman models

27 On models upto 08/2010, remove the rear light unit as described in Section 7.

28 On models after 08/2010, release the clips and remove the appropriate access panel from the luggage compartment side panel trim.

29 Rotate the relevant bulbholder anti-clockwise, and pull it from the light unit **(see illustration)**.

30 Depress and twist the appropriate bulb anti-clockwise to remove it from the bulbholder **(see illustration)**.

31 Fit the new bulb using a reversal of the removal procedure.

Clubman models

32 Undo the screw at the top of the rear light

cluster, then pull the light upwards/rearwards from place **(see illustrations)**.

33 Release the retaining clip and remove the bulbholder assembly from the light unit **(see illustration)**.

34 Depress and twist the appropriate bulb anti-clockwise to remove it from the bulbholder.

35 Fit the new bulb using a reversal of the removal procedure.

Number plate light

Except Clubman models

36 Insert a flat-bladed screwdriver in the recess on the right of the number plate light lens, lever the lens to the left, and carefully prise out the light unit **(see illustration)**.

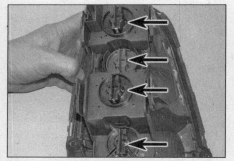

5.29 Rotate the relevant bulbholder anti-clockwise (arrowed)

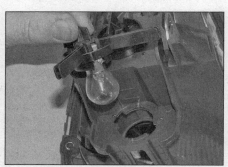

5.30 Depress and twist the relevant bulb anti-clockwise

5.32a Undo the screw (arrowed) at the top of the light unit...

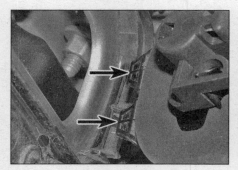

5.32b ...and lift it outwards/upwards. Note the lugs at the base of the light unit (arrowed)

5.33 Release the clip and detach the bulbholder assembly from the light unit

5.36 Insert a screwdriver into the slot and prise down the number plate light

37 Release the festoon-type bulb from the contact springs **(see illustration)**.

38 Fit the new bulb using a reversal of the removal procedure. Make sure that the tension of the contact springs is sufficient to hold the bulb firmly.

Clubman models

39 Insert a flat-bladed screwdriver in the recess on the right of the number plate light, and carefully prise out the light unit.

40 Rotate the bulbholder anti-clockwise and remove it from the light unit **(see illustration)**. Pull the wedge-type bulb from the holder.

41 Fit the new bulb using a reversal of the removal procedure.

High-level stop-light

42 The high-level stop light is an LED unit. If defective, the complete assembly must be replaced as described in Section 7.

6	Bulbs (interior lights) – renewal

1 Whenever a bulb is renewed, note the following points:

a) *Remember that if the light has just been in use, the bulb may be extremely hot.*

b) *Always check the bulb contacts and holder, ensuring that there is clean metal-to-metal contact between the bulb and its live(s) and earth. Clean off any corrosion or dirt before fitting a new bulb.*

c) *Wherever bayonet-type bulbs are fitted,*

5.37 Pull the festoon type bulb from the contacts

ensure that the live contact(s) bear firmly against the bulb contact.

e) *Always ensure that the new bulb is of the correct rating and that it is completely clean before fitting it.*

Ceiling lights

Front (except Convertible models)

2 Prise the lens from place using a small flat-bladed screwdriver **(see illustration)**.

3 Pull the wedge-type bulb from the holder **(see illustration)**.

4 Fit the new bulb using a reversal of the removal procedure.

Front (Convertible models)

5 Remove the roof console as described in Section 4.

6 Rotate the bulbholder anti-clockwise, remove it and pull the capless bulb from the holder **(see illustrations)**.

5.40 Rotate the bulbholder anti-clockwise and pull it from the number plate light

7 Fit the new bulb using a reversal of the removal procedure.

Rear

8 Carefully prise the light lens from place **(see illustration)**.

9 Pull the wedge-type bulb from the holder.

10 Fit the new bulb using a reversal of the removal procedure.

B-pillar

11 The pillar lights are illuminated by LED's. To replace them, begin by removing the B-pillar trim panel as described in Chapter 11.

12 Pull the LED unit from the panel.

13 Refitting is a reversal of removal.

Interior handle illumination

14 These are illuminated by LED's. In order to remove the LED's, remove the relevant door panel as described in Chapter 11. Remove the handle **(see illustration)**.

6.2 Starting at the rear edge, prise the light lens from place

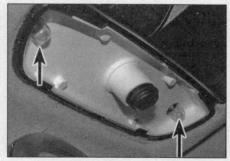

6.3 Pull the wedge bulbs from the holders (arrowed)

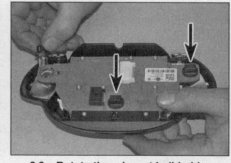

6.6a Rotate the relevant bulbholder (arrowed) anti-clockwise

6.6b Pull the wedge-type bulb from the holder

6.8 Prise the rear interior light lens from place

6.14 Interior release handle retaining screws (arrowed)

6.22 Prise the luggage compartment light from place

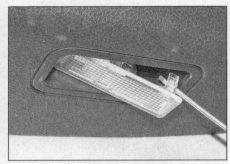

6.25 Split-door light unit

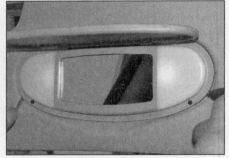

6.28a Prise out the lower edge...

6.28b ...and remove the vanity light/mirror

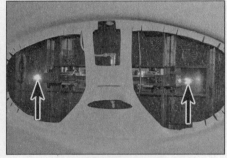

6.29 Pull the wedge-type bulb (arrowed) from place

15 Release the clip and detach the LED from the interior release handle.
16 Refitting is a reversal of removal.

Front door trim panel illumination

17 These are illuminated by LED's. In order to remove them, remove the door trim and armrest as described in Chapter 11.
18 Disconnect the wiring plug, and slide the LED from place.
19 Refitting is a reversal of removal.

Instrument panel illumination and warning lights

20 The instrument panel and warning light are illuminated by LED's. No provision is made for the replacement of these LED's.

Heater control/fan switch illumination

21 The control panel and switches are illuminated by LED's. No provision is made for the replacement of these LED's.

Luggage compartment/footwell/glovebox/Club door lights

22 Carefully prise the light unit from place (see illustration).
23 Pull the wedge type bulb out to remove.
24 Fit the new bulb using a reversal of the removal procedure.

Split door (Clubman models) lights

25 Carefully prise the light unit lens frame from the split door (see illustration).
26 Pull the wedge-type bulb from the holder.
27 Refitting is a reversal of removal.

Vanity lights

28 Fold down the sun visor, and carefully prise the mirror from place, levering at its lower edge as shown (see illustrations).

29 Pull the wedge-type bulb from the holder (see illustration).
30 Refitting is a reversal of removal.

7 Exterior light units – removal and refitting

1 Before removing any light unit, note the following points:
  a) Ensure that the light is switched off before starting work.
  b) Remember that if the light has just been in use, the bulb and lens may be extremely hot.

Headlight unit

2 Open the bonnet, and undo the 4 headlight retaining bolts (see illustration). Make alignment marks between the headlight and the vehicle body to aid refitting.
3 Pull the headlight forwards a little, then disconnect the washer tube (where fitted) and the wiring plug (see illustration).
4 Refitting is a reversal of removal. Check the gap between the headlight and bonnet – reposition the headlight as necessary. Have the headlight alignment checked as described in the next Section.

Xenon control unit

5 Remove the relevant headlight as described previously in this Section.
6 Undo the retaining screws and detach the control unit from the headlight (see illustration). Disconnect the wiring plugs as the control unit is withdrawn.

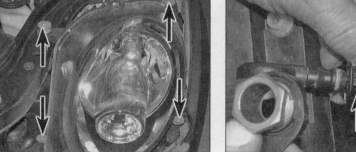

7.2 Headlight retaining bolts (arrowed)

7.3 Squeeze the sides of the collar (arrowed) and disconnect the headlight washer tube

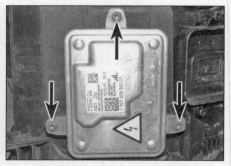

7.6 Xenon control unit screws (arrowed)

7 Refitting is a reversal of removal.

Adaptive headlight control unit

8 Remove the relevant headlight as previously described in this Section.
9 Undo the 4 retaining screws, and carefully pull the control unit from the side of the headlight.
10 Refitting is a reversal of removal. Note that if a new control unit is fitted, it must be programmed/coded using MINI diagnostic equipment. Entrust this task to a MINI dealer or suitably equipped repairer.

Direction indicator side repeaters

11 Open the bonnet, slide the side repeater/surround assembly forwards, and remove it from the front wing (see illustration 5.17).
12 Turn the bulbholder anti-clockwise, and disconnect it from the repeater unit (see illustration 5.18).
13 Refitting is a reversal of the removal procedure.

Front fog/side light

Without headlight cleaning system

14 Remove the wheelarch liner from the relevant side, as described in Chapter 11.
15 Where applicable, undo the retaining nut and move the horn to one side, or undo the fasteners and move the washer reservoir to one side (as applicable).
16 Disconnect the wiring plug from the bulbholders.
17 Undo the 3 screws, and manoeuvre the fog/side light from position (see illustration).
18 Refitting is a reversal of the removal procedure.

With headlight cleaning system

19 Remove the front bumper as described in Chapter 11.
20 Undo the 3 retaining screws and remove the fog/side light.
21 Refitting is a reversal of removal.

Rear foglight

Except Clubman models

22 Reach up behind the bumper, squeeze together the retaining clips, and push the light unit from the bumper (see illustration).

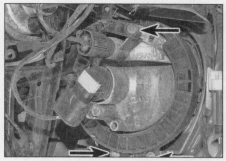

7.17 Front foglight retaining screws (arrowed)

23 Disconnect the wiring connector.
24 Fit the new light unit using a reversal of the removal procedure. Make sure that the light unit is located correctly.

Rear light cluster

All except Clubman models

25 Starting at the top edge, using a blunt, flat-bladed tool, carefully prise the light unit surround trim from place (see illustration).
26 Undo the 3 retaining screws (see illustration).
27 Carefully prise the upper edge of the light unit from the vehicle body, then lift it slightly and manoeuvre it from position. Disconnect the wiring plug as the unit is withdrawn (see illustrations).

All models

28 Fit the new light unit using a reversal of

7.25 Working at the top edge, prise the rear light surround trim from place

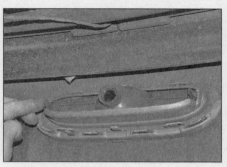

7.22 Release the clip at each end and remove the rear foglight

the removal procedure. Make sure that the light unit is located correctly.

Clubman models

29 Removal of the rear light cluster is described within the bulb replacement procedure – see Section 5.

Number plate light assembly

Clubman models only

30 Removal of the number plate light assembly is described within the bulb replacement procedure – see Section 5.

High-level stop-light

Hatchback models

31 Remove the tailgate upper trim as described in Chapter 11.
32 Undo the 2 retaining screws and remove

7.26 Rear light retaining screws (arrowed)

7.27a Pull the upper edge rearwards a little...

7.27b ...lift the light unit slightly to compress the clip (arrowed) ...

7.27c ...then lift it clear of the lower clips (arrowed)

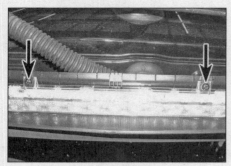

7.32 High-level brake light screws (arrowed) – Hatchback models

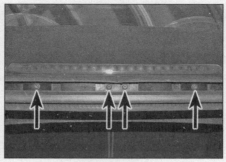

7.34a Undo the screws (arrowed)...

7.34b ...and pull the brake light upwards – Convertible models

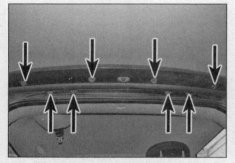

7.36 Undo the screws (arrowed) and lower the trim strip – Clubman models

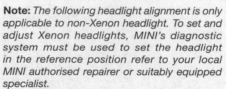

7.37 Release the various clips and disconnect the wiring plug (arrowed)

the light from the tailgate (see illustration). Disconnect the wiring plug as the unit is withdrawn.

33 Fit the new light unit using a reversal of the removal procedure.

Convertible models

34 Open the boot lid, undo the 4 retaining screws, and pull the brake light upwards from place (see illustrations). Disconnect the wiring plug as the unit is withdrawn.

35 Refitting is a reversal of removal.

Clubman models

36 Open the rear split doors, undo the 8 retaining screws, and carefully lower the roof trim strip from place (see illustration).

37 Disconnect the wiring plug, release the clips and detach the light unit from the roof trim strip (see illustration).

38 Refitting is a reversal of removal.

8 Headlight and front foglight beam alignment – checking and adjustment

Note: *The following headlight alignment is only applicable to non-Xenon headlight. To set and adjust Xenon headlights, MINI's diagnostic system must be used to set the headlight in the reference position refer to your local MINI authorised repairer or suitably equipped specialist.*

1 Accurate adjustment of the headlight or front foglight beams is only possible using optical beam-setting equipment. This work should therefore be carried out by a MINI authorised repairer, or other service station with the necessary facilities.

2 Temporary adjustment can be made after renewal of a bulb or light unit, or as

an emergency measure if the alignment is incorrect following accident damage.

3 To adjust the headlight aim, turn the adjustment screws on the back of the headlight unit to make the adjustment (see illustration).

4 To adjust the fog light aim, use a screwdriver to rotate the adjusting screw (see illustration).

5 Before making any adjustments to the settings, it is important that the tyre pressures are correct, and that the vehicle is standing on level ground with no additional load in the vehicle.

6 Bounce the front of the vehicle a few times to settle the suspension. Ideally, somebody of average size should sit in the driver's seat during the adjustment, and the vehicle should have half a tank of fuel.

7 Where a vehicle is fitted with a headlight beam levelling system, set the switch to the 0 position before making any adjustments.

8 Whenever temporary adjustments are made, the settings must be checked and if necessary reset by a MINI authorised repairer or other qualified person as soon as possible.

9 Headlight levelling motor – removal and refitting

It's not possible to dismantle the headlight unit and renew the levelling motor. In the event of a fault the complete headlight unit must be replaced as described in Section 7.

10 Instrument panel – removal and refitting

⚠ Warning: *The instrument panel must be kept in the upright position, to avoid silicone liquid leaking from the gauges.*
Caution! *If the instrument panel is being renewed, the stored configuration data must be loaded into MINI's diagnostic system, and download into the new cluster once fitted. Refer to your local MINI authorised repairer or suitably equipped specialist.*

8.3 Headlamp beam aim adjustment screws (arrowed)

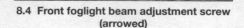

8.4 Front foglight beam adjustment screw (arrowed)

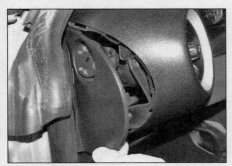

10.4 Prise the panel from the passengers end of the facia

10.5a Pull the panel adjacent to the vent rearwards to release the clips

10.5b On models without a storage compartment, prise the complete panel from place

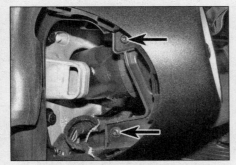

10.6a Undo the screws (arrowed) at the end…

10.6b …and on the right/top (arrowed)…

10.6c …then remove the vent cover

Removal

1 Disconnect the battery negative (earth) lead (refer to Chapter 5A).

Main instrument panel

2 Remove the heater control panel as described in Chapter 3.

3 Remove the passengers side A-pillar trim as described in Chapter 11.

4 Prise the panel from passengers end of the facia **(see illustration)**. Disconnect any wiring plugs as the panel is withdrawn.

5 On models with the facia mounted CD multichanger/storage compartment, carefully prise rearwards the plastic trim panel adjacent to the passenger side air vent **(see illustration)**. On models without a storage compartment, prise the complete trim panel from place **(see illustration)**.

6 Undo the 4 retaining screws and remove the air vent cover from the passengers end of the facia **(see illustrations)**.

7 Undo the 5 retaining screws (3 below, 2 above), and remove the passengers side knee bolster from the facia **(see illustrations)**.

8 Undo the 4 retaining screws and remove the drivers side knee bolster **(see illustrations 4.4a and 4.4b)**.

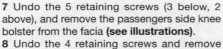

10.7a The passengers knee bolster is secured by screws above (arrowed)…

9 The instrument panel is secured by 5 screws – 1 at the top and 2 each side. Undo the screws and pull the instrument panel rearwards a little **(see illustrations)**. Disconnect the wiring plugs as the panel is withdrawn.

10.7b …and below (arrowed)

10.9a Undo the screw at the top (arrowed)…

10.9b …the 2 screws each side (arrowed)…

10.9c …and remove the main instrument panel with the CD player

10.10 The CD player is secured to the speedometer by 4 screws (arrowed)

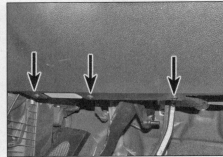

10.11 Undo the screws (arrowed) and remove the drivers side lower facia panel

12 Horn – removal and refitting

1 Remove the right-hand front wheelarch liner as described in Chapter 11.
2 Disconnect the electrical connector(s) from the horn terminal(s).
3 Unscrew the mounting nut(s), and withdraw the horn(s) from under the vehicle.
4 Refitting is a reversal of the removal procedure.

13 Wiper arms – removal and refitting

1 With the wiper(s) parked (in the normal at-rest position), mark the positions of the blade(s) on the windshield, using a wax crayon or strips of masking tape.
2 Lift up the plastic cap from the bottom of the wiper arm, and loosen the nut one or two turns (see illustration).
3 Lift the wiper arm, and carefully release it from the taper on the spindle by moving it from side-to-side. If the wiper arm is stubborn to remove, use a puller (see illustration). On the rear wiper arm fitted to hatchback models where the washer jet is in the centre of the spindle, use a socket under the puller spindle to prevent any damage to the jet (see illustration).
4 Completely remove the nut, and withdraw the wiper arm from the spindle.
5 Installation is a reversal of the removal procedure. Make sure that the arm is installed in the previously-noted position before tightening the nut.

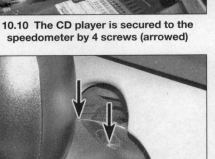

10.12a Rev counter retaining screws (arrowed)

10.12b Disconnect the rev counter wiring plug (arrowed) on the left-hand side of the steering column

Refitting

13 Refitting is a reversal of the removal procedure.

10 If required, undo the 4 screws and detach the speedometer from the CD player/radio (see illustration).

Rev counter

11 Undo the 3 screws at its front edge, and pull down the panel above the pedals (see illustration). Disconnect any wiring plugs as the panel is withdrawn.
12 Fully lower the steering column, undo the two screws and detach the instrument from the column shroud. Disconnect the wiring plug(s) at the left-hand side of the steering column as the instrument is withdrawn (see illustrations). **Note:** *If a new instrument is being fitted, it will need to be 'coded' prior to use. This can only be carried out by a MINI dealer or suitably equipped specialist.*

11 Instrument panel components – removal and refitting

The instrument panel should not be stripped, as no components were available at the time of writing. In the event of a fault, have the vehicles self-diagnosis system interrogated by a MINI dealer or suitably equipped specialist. The instrument panel illumination is provided by LED's, and are not replaceable.

14 Windscreen wiper motor and linkage – removal and refitting

Removal

1 Remove the wiper arms (Section 13).
2 Pull up the rubber weatherstrips, undo the nut and screw each side, and starting with

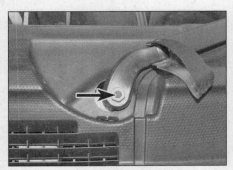

13.2 Lift up the arm cover and slacken the spindle nut (arrowed)

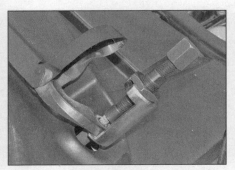

13.3a If necessary, use a puller to remove the wiper arm

13.3b Use a socket as a spacer to protect the washer jet on rear wiper arms

14.2a Pull up the rubber weatherstrip at the rear of the engine compartment…

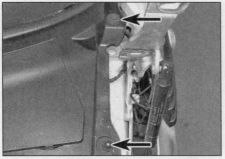

14.2b …undo the nut and screw each side (arrowed)…

14.2c …then pull up the scuttle trim panels above the battery and wiper linkage

the passengers side, pull the cowling panels upwards in the centre, then forward from the windscreen **(see illustrations)**.

3 Remove the wiper linkage and motor mounting fasteners **(see illustration)**.

4 Disconnect the electrical connector and remove the motor and linkage assembly.

5 If required, prise the linkage arms from the crank arm, make alignment marks between the motor spindle and the crank arm, then remove the nut securing the arm to the motor spindle. Remove the three bolts and separate the motor from the linkage **(see illustration)**.

Refitting

6 Refitting is a reversal of the removal procedure, noting the following points:
   a) *Tighten the wiper motor mounting bolts securely.*
   b) *Make sure that the wiper motor is in its 'parked' position before fitting the motor arm, and check that the wiper linkage is in line with the motor arm.*
   c) *Use grease to lubricate the wiper spindle and linkages when re-assembling.*

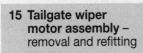

15 Tailgate wiper motor assembly – removal and refitting

Removal

1 Disconnect the battery negative (earth) lead (refer to Chapter 5A).

Hatchback models

2 Remove the tailgate wiper arm as described in Section 13.

3 Remove the tailgate inner trim panel as described in Chapter 11.

4 Disconnect the washer hose and wiring plug from the wiper motor **(see illustration)**.

5 Unscrew the 3 mounting bolts, and remove the wiper motor from inside the tailgate **(see illustration)**.

Clubman models

6 Remove the relevant rear wiper arm as described in Section 13.

7 Remove the relevant split door inner trim panel as described in Chapter 11.

14.2d Release the clips (arrowed) at the front edge of the scuttle trim panel

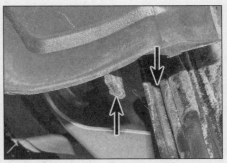

14.2e Note how the scuttle trim panel engages with the extrusion at the base of the windscreen (arrowed)

14.3 Wiper motor and linkage fasteners (arrowed)

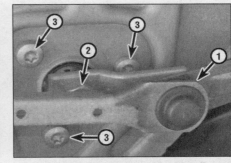

14.5 Wiper motor mounting details

   1 *Linkage arms*
   2 *Crank arm/spindle nut*
   3 *Motor mounting bolts*

15.4 Disconnect the washer hose and wiring plug

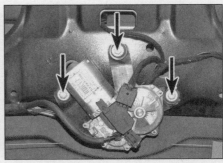

15.5 Tailgate wiper motor mounting bolts (arrowed) – Hatchback models

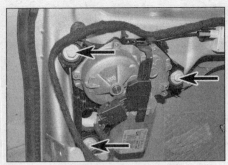

15.8 Rear wiper motor mounting bolts (arrowed) – Clubman models

8 Disconnect the wiring plug, undo the 2 retaining bolts, and manoeuvre the motor assembly from place (see illustration). Check the condition of the spindle sealing grommet, and renew if necessary.

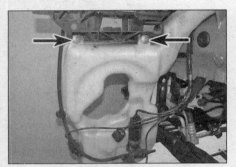

16.4 Washer reservoir mounting fasteners (arrowed)

16.10 Washer fluid pump

16.13b …and push the rear edge from the bonnet

16.3 Prise out the expansion rivet (arrowed) at the top of the reservoir

Refitting

9 Refitting is a reversal of the removal procedure. Make sure that the wiper motor is in its 'parked' position before fitting the wiper arm.

16.8 Pull the washer fluid reservoir level sensor from the rubber grommet

16.13a Push the jet forwards to compress the clip (arrowed)…

16.19 Headlight washer cylinder retaining screws (arrowed)

16 Windscreen/tailgate washer system components – removal and refitting

Removal

Windscreeen/tailgate washer reservoir

1 Remove the left-hand front wheelarch liner as described in Chapter 11.
2 Remove the left-hand headlight as described in Section 7.
3 Remove the plastic fastener securing the top of the reservoir (see illustration).
4 Disconnect the electrical connectors for the fluid level sensor and washer pump. Detach the hoses, then remove the mounting fasteners (see illustration).
5 Carefully prise the bottom of the reservoir up to detach it from its lower mount, then guide the reservoir out.
6 Refitting is the reverse of removal.

Washer reservoir level sensor

7 Remove the left-hand side front wheelarch liner as described in Chapter 11.
8 Disconnect the wiring plug, then pull the sensor from the rubber grommet (see illustration). Be prepared for fluid spillage.

Washer pump

9 Remove the left-hand side front wheelarch liner as described in Chapter 11.
10 Disconnect the wiring plug from the pump, then note their fitted positions and disconnect the hoses from the pump (see illustration).
11 Pull the top of the pump from the reservoir, then pull it up from the rubber grommet. Be prepared for fluid spillage.

Washer jet (windscreen)

12 Disconnect the washer tube from the bottom of the jet, and disconnect the jet heater wiring plug (where fitted).
13 Carefully lever the jet forwards to compress the retaining clip, then push the rear edge from the bonnet, taking care not to damage the paintwork (see illustrations).

Washer jet (rear window)

Hatchback models
14 The jet is integral with the wiper spindle assembly. If faulty, the complete assembly must be renewed.

Clubman models
15 Open the rear split doors, undo the 8 retaining screws and pull the roof trim strip from place (see illustration 7.36). Disconnect the wiring plug and washer hose as the trim strip is withdrawn.
16 Detach the jet from the trim strip.

Headlight washer jet/cylinder (where fitted)

17 Remove the relevant headlight as described in Section 7.
18 Carefully prise the cover from the jet with a small screwdriver.
19 Undo the retaining screws and remove the jet/cylinder assembly (see illustration).

Headlight washer system reservoir

20 The headlight washer jets are supplied with fluid from the windscreen washer fluid reservoir.

Headlight washer pump

21 Remove the left-hand front wheelarch liner as described in Chapter 11.
22 Unclip and disconnect the hose from the pump, and disconnect the wiring plug.
23 Rotate the pump clockwise a little and pull it from the reservoir. Check the condition of the sealing grommet and renew if necessary. Clean the strainer fitted to the pump.

Refitting

24 Refitting is a reversal of the removal procedure, noting the following points:
  a) *In the case of the screen washer jets, press them in firmly until they are fully engaged.*
  b) *After refitting the headlight washer jet, refit the front bumper as described in Chapter 11.*

17 Audio Unit and Car Communication Computer – removal and refitting

Audio unit

1 Remove the main instrument panel as described in Section 10.
2 Undo the screws and separate the speedometer/instrument panel from the audio unit **(see illustration 10.10)**.
3 Refitting is a reversal of removal. If a new unit has been fitted, it must be programmed using MINI diagnostic equipment. Entrust this task to a MINI dealer or suitably equipped repairer.

Car Communication Computer (CCC)

4 Remove the main instrument panel as described in Section 10.
5 Undo the 4 retaining screws, and detach the CCC from the panel **(see illustration)**. Disconnect the wiring plugs as the unit is withdrawn. If a new unit has been fitted, it must be programmed using MINI diagnostic equipment. Entrust this task to a MINI dealer or suitably equipped repairer.

18 Compact disc autochanger – removal and refitting

1 Remove the passengers side A-pillar trim as described in Chapter 11.
2 Prise the panel from passengers end of the facia **(see illustration 10.4)**.
3 Remove the panel adjacent to the air vent **(see illustration 10.5)**.
4 Undo the 4 retaining screws and remove the air vent cover from the passengers end of the facia **(see illustration 10.6a, 10.6b and 10.6c)**.
5 Open the glovebox, undo the 5 retaining screws (3 below, 2 above), and remove the passengers side knee bolster from the facia **(see illustration 10.7a and 10.7b)**.
6 Undo the 3 retaining screws, and slide the CD autochanger from place. Disconnect the wiring plugs as the unit is withdrawn.

Refitting

7 Refitting is a reversal of the removal procedure. If a new unit is fitted, it must be programmed using MINI diagnostic equipment. Entrust this task to a MINI dealer or suitably equipped repairer.

19 Speakers – removal and refitting

Removal

Door bass speaker

1 Remove the front door inner trim panel or luggage compartment side trim panel as described in Chapter 11.
2 Unscrew the four screws, and withdraw the speaker **(see illustration)**.
3 Disconnect the electrical connector on removal of the speaker.

Door mid-range speaker

4 Remove the mirror adjustment switch as described in Section 4.
5 Carefully prise the speaker surround trim from place **(see illustration)**.
6 Undo the 3 screws and remove the speaker

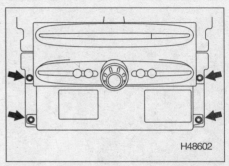

17.5 Car Communication Computer (CCC) retaining screws (arrowed)

(see illustration). Disconnect the wiring plug as the speaker is withdrawn.

Club door mid-range speaker

7 Remove the Club door inner trim panel as described in Chapter 11.
8 Undo the 4 retaining screws and remove the speaker. Disconnect the wiring plug as the speaker is withdrawn.

Rear speakers

9 Remove the side trim panel as described in Chapter 11.
10 Undo the 4 retaining screws and remove the mid-range speaker, or unclip the tweeter as required. Disconnect the wiring plug as the speaker is withdrawn.

A-pillar tweeter

11 Remove the A-pillar trim panel as described in Chapter 11.
12 Release the catches, unclip the wiring harness, and remove the tweeter.

Refitting

13 Refitting is a reversal of the removal procedure.

20 Radio aerial – removal and refitting

Removal

1 If just the aerial mast is to be removed, this can be unscrewed from the base from outside.

19.2 Door bass speaker retaining screws (arrowed)

19.5 Carefully prise the speaker trim away

19.6 Door mid-range speaker retaining screws (arrowed)

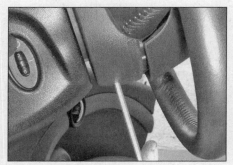

21.2a Insert a T25 Torx screwdriver (or similar diameter rod) into the hole in base of the steering wheel boss...

21.2b ...then push the retaining spring upwards and release the air bag

21.6 Passengers air bag bracket (arrowed)

period ensures that any stored energy in the back-up capacitor is dissipated.

2 Insert a T25 Torx screwdriver (or similar diameter rod) into the hole in the underside of the steering wheel, feeling for the retaining spring wire. Push up on the spring wire with sufficient force to disengage the retaining spring from the airbag unit **(see illustrations)**.

3 Disconnect the electrical connectors for the airbag/horn contact and earth lead **(see illustration)**. Place the airbag in a safe location with the cover facing up as soon as possible. Refitting is the reverse of removal, pushing the airbag unit into place until the retaining spring wires engage with the airbag.

Passenger's airbag

4 Disconnect the battery negative (earth) lead (refer to Chapter 5A).

⚠️ *Warning: Before proceeding, wait a minimum of 5 minutes, as a precaution against accidental firing of the airbag unit. This period ensures that any stored energy is dissipated.*

5 Remove the upper section of the facia as described in Chapter 11.

6 Invert the upper section of the facia, undo the nuts and remove the airbag mounting bracket **(see illustration)**. Discard the nuts, new ones must be fitted.

7 Undo the retaining nuts, and detach the airbag from the facia. Discard the nuts, new ones must be fitted.

8 Refitting is a reversal of removal. Tighten the retaining nuts to the specified torque setting.

Side and side curtain airbags

9 These are not considered to be DIY operations, and should be referred to a MINI authorised repairer.

21.3 Disconnect the air bag/horn contact wiring plug and earth lead (arrowed)

2 Removal of the aerial base requires the headlining at the rear to be lowered. This is a complex task requiring experience and patience to refit the headlining satisfactorily, and is considered beyond the scope of the home mechanic.

Refitting

3 Refitting is a reversal of the removal procedure.

---

21 Airbag units –
removal and refitting

⚠️ *Warning: Handle any airbag unit with extreme care, as a precaution against personal injury, and always hold it with the cover facing away from the body. If in doubt concerning any proposed*

work involving an airbag unit or its control circuitry, consult a MINI authorised repairer or other qualified specialist.

⚠️ *Warning: Stand any airbag in a safe place with the cover uppermost, and do not expose it to heat sources in excess of 100°C.*

⚠️ *Warning: Do not attempt to open or repair an airbag unit, or apply any electrical current to it. Do not use any airbag unit which is visibly damaged or which has been tampered with.*

Driver's airbag

1 Disconnect the battery negative (earth) lead (refer to Chapter 5A).

⚠️ *Warning: Before proceeding, wait a minimum of 5 minutes, as a precaution against accidental firing of the airbag unit. This*

---

22 Airbag control module and crash sensors –
removal and refitting

Removal

1 Disconnect the battery negative (earth) lead (refer to Chapter 5A).

⚠️ *Warning: Before proceeding, wait a minimum of 5 minutes, as a precaution against accidental firing of the airbag unit. This period ensures that any stored energy is dissipated.*

Airbag control module

2 Remove the centre console as described in Chapter 11.

3 Undo the 3 nuts securing control module, noting the earth lead under one of the nuts **(see illustrations)**.

4 Lift the centre console bracket a little, and manoeuvre the control unit from place. Disconnect the wiring plugs from the control unit as it's withdrawn.

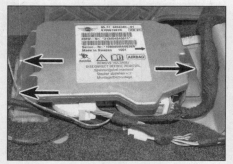

22.3a Air bag control unit retaining nuts (arrowed)

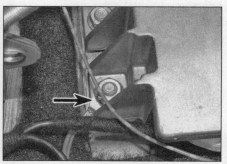

22.3b Note the earth lead (arrowed) under one of the control unit retaining nuts

Side impact sensors

All except Clubman right-hand sensor

5 Remove the rear side trim panel as described in Chapter 11.

6 Undo the retaining screws and slide the sensor downwards from place (see illustration). Discard the screws, new ones must be fitted.

Clubman right-hand sensor

7 Remove the right-hand seat belt inertia reel as described in Chapter 11.

8 Undo the retaining screws and lower the sensor from place. Discard the screws, new ones must be fitted.

Refitting

9 Refitting is a reversal of the removal procedure. Note that if either of these units have been renewed, they may need to be coded/reprogrammed using MINI diagnostic equipment prior to use. Entrust this task to a MINI dealer or suitably equipped specialist.

23 Airbag rotary contact – removal and refitting

The airbag rotary contact unit is integral with the steering column switch assembly. Removal, refitting and re-centring is described in Section 4 of this Chapter.

24 Parking sensor system – general information

Offered as an option, the park reverse aid is an ultrasonic proximity detection system, intended to help avoid rear collisions when reversing.

The system consists of ultrasonic sensors mounted in the rear bumper, a buzzer unit mounted behind the right-hand rear light unit, and an ECU also mounted behind the right-hand rear light unit.

The system is only operational when reverse gear is engaged; changing audible signals warn the driver of impending contact as the car reverses towards an object in its path.

The sensors in the bumper can be unclipped

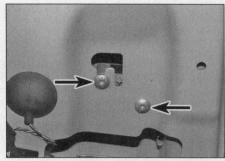

22.6 Side impact sensor retaining screws (arrowed)

25.3 Fuel filler flap motor retaining screws (arrowed) – Convertible and Clubman models

and disconnected once the rear bumper is removed as described in Chapter 11. To remove the buzzer unit/ECU, remove the right-hand rear light unit as described in Section 7, then disconnect the wiring plug(s), undo the nut(s), and remove the buzzer or ECU.

Note: *Caution is required when reversing in heavy rain or similar adverse conditions, as the sensors may not always measure close obstacles accurately. Care must also be taken if a tow bar has been installed.*

25 Fuel filler flap motor – removal and refitting

Clubman and Convertible

1 Open the filler flap, then using a screwdriver,

25.1 Rotate the sleeve (arrowed) 45° anti-clockwise

25.7 Manoeuvre the fuel filler flap motor out through the rear light aperture – Hatchback models

rotate the sleeve 45° anti-clockwise and pull it from place (see illustration).

2 Remove the luggage compartment side panel as described in Chapter 11.

3 Undo the retaining screws and remove the motor (see illustration). Disconnect the wiring plug as the motor is withdrawn.

4 Refitting is a reversal of removal.

Hatchback

5 Remove the left-hand rear light as described in Section 7.

6 Release the catches and remove the access cover from the luggage compartment side trim panel.

7 Disconnect the motor wiring plug, undo the retaining screws and manoeuvre the motor from place (see illustration).

8 Refitting is a reversal of removal.

MINI wiring diagrams

Diagram 1

WARNING: *This vehicle is fitted with a supplemental restraint system (SRS) consisting of a combination of driver (and passenger) airbag(s), side impact protection airbags and seatbelt pre-tensioners. The use of electrical test equipment on any SRS wiring systems may cause the seatbelt pre-tensioners to abruptly retract and airbags to explosively deploy, resulting in potentially severe personal injury. Extreme care should be taken to correctly identify any circuits to be tested to avoid choosing any of the SRS wiring in error.*

For further information see airbag system precautions in body electrical systems chapter.
Note: The SRS wiring harness can normally be identified by yellow and/or orange harness or harness connectors.

Key to symbols

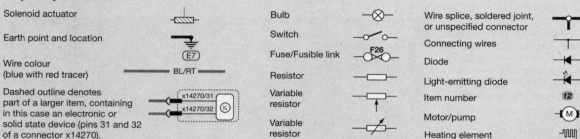

Solenoid actuator	Bulb	Wire splice, soldered joint, or unspecified connector
Earth point and location	Switch	Connecting wires
	Fuse/Fusible link	Diode
Wire colour (blue with red tracer)	Resistor	Light-emitting diode
Dashed outline denotes part of a larger item, containing in this case an electronic or solid state device (pins 31 and 32 of a connector x14270).	Variable resistor	Item number
	Variable resistor	Motor/pump
		Heating element

Battery fusebox 5

Fuse	Rating	Circuit protected
F60	125A	Passenger fusebox fuses F1 - F49
F67	150A	Engine management relay
		Engine fusebox fuses F1 - F10
		Engine fusebox fusible links FL1 - FL12
F68	40A	Engine management
F69	-	Not used

F69 F67 F60 F68

Engine fusebox 6

Fuse	Rating	Circuit protected
FL1	-	Not used
FL2	-	Not used
FL3	-	Not used
FL4	80A	Electric power steering
FL5	-	Not used
FL6	40A	DSC
FL7	50A	Engine management
FL8	-	Not used
FL9	50A	Engine cooling fan
FL10	50A	Heated windscreen
FL11	-	Not used
FL12	30A	DC/DC converter
F1	5A	Engine management
F2	25A	Engine management
F3	20A	Engine management
F4	20A	Engine management
F5	5A	Engine management
F6	25A	DSC
F7	7.5A	Engine management
F8	30/40A	Engine cooling fan
F9	30A	Wash/wipe
F10	15A	Engine management

R1	Engine management relay
R2	Crankcase breather heating relay
R3	Engine cooling fan relay 1
R4	Engine cooling fan relay 2
R5	Wiper on/off relay
R6	Terminal 15 load shedding relay
R7	Wiper setting 1 & 2 relay

Passenger comp. fusebox 7

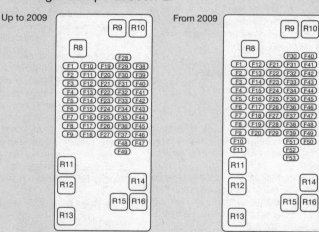

Up to 2009 — From 2009

R8	Headlight washer pump relay
R9	Terminal 15 relay
R10	Heated rear window relay
R11	Air conditioning compressor relay
R12	Windscreen washer pump relay

R13	Rear window wiper relay
R14	Bistable relay
R15	Horn relay
R16	Fuel pump relay
	For fuse ratings see vehicle fusebox lid.

Earth locations

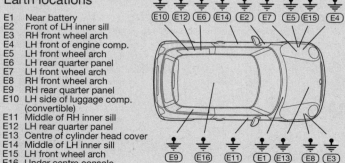

E1	Near battery
E2	Front of LH inner sill
E3	RH front wheel arch
E4	LH front of engine comp.
E5	LH front wheel arch
E6	LH rear quarter panel
E7	LH front wheel arch
E8	RH front wheel arch
E9	RH rear quarter panel
E10	LH side of luggage comp. (convertible)
E11	Middle of RH inner sill
E12	LH rear quarter panel
E13	Centre of cylinder head cover
E14	Middle of LH inner sill
E15	LH front wheel arch
E16	Under centre console

H47574

Colour codes

WS	White	RT	Red
BL	Blue	GN	Green
GR	Grey	VI	Violet
GE	Yellow	SW	Black
BR	Brown	OR	Orange
RS	Pink	TR	Transparent

* Models from 2009

Key to items

1 Battery
2 Battery sensor
3 Starter motor
4 Alternator
5 Battery fusebox
6 Engine fusebox
7 Passenger fusebox
   R15 = horn relay
8 Engine management control unit
9 Car access control unit
10 Electric steering column adjustment unit
11 Stop-start unit
12 Stop light switch
13 Dynamic stability control unit
14 Selector lever position switch
15 Clutch switch (manual trans.)
16 Transmission control unit (auto.trans.)
17 Horn switch
18 Steering column switch unit
19 Horn 1

20 Horn 2
21 Electric steering control unit
22 Electric steering torque sensor

Diagram 2

H47575

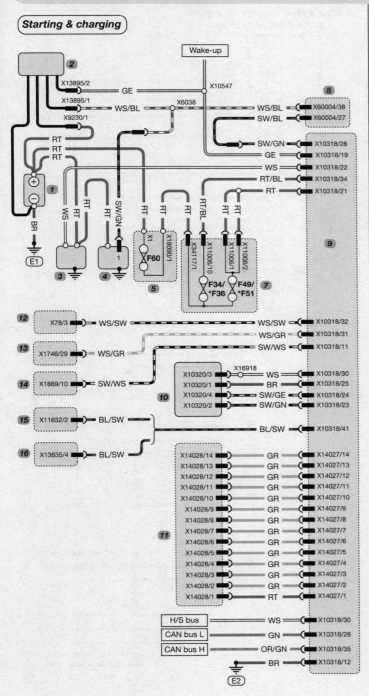

Starting & charging

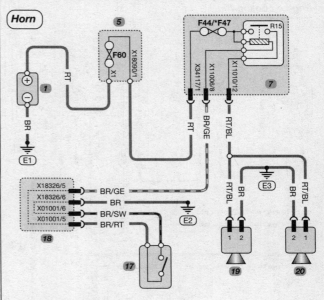

Horn

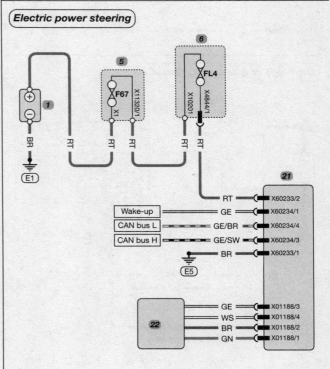

Electric power steering

Colour codes

WS	White	**RT**	Red
BL	Blue	**GN**	Green
GR	Grey	**VI**	Violet
GE	Yellow	**SW**	Black
BR	Brown	**OR**	Orange
RS	Pink	**TR**	Transparent

* Models from 2009

Key to items

1 Battery
5 Battery fusebox
6 Engine fusebox
 R1 = engine management relay
 R3 = engine cooling fan relay 1
7 Passenger fusebox
 R9 = terminal 15 relay
8 Engine management control unit
9 Car access control unit

12 Stop light switch
25 Engine coolant temp. sensor
26 Characteristic map sensor
27 Friction wheel drive
28 Engine cooling fan
29 Front cigar lighter
30 Rear accessory socket
31 Footwell control unit
32 Reversing light switch

33 LH rear light unit
 a = stop light
 b = reversing light
34 RH rear light unit
 a = stop light
 b = reversing light
35 High level stop light

Diagram 3

H47576

Engine cooling fan

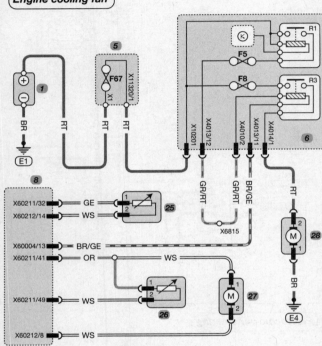

Cigar lighter & accessory socket

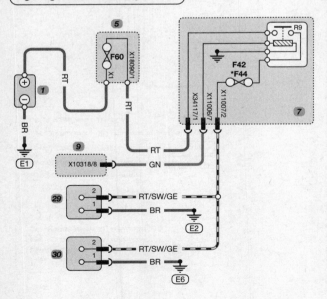

Stop & reversing lights, supply to footwell control unit

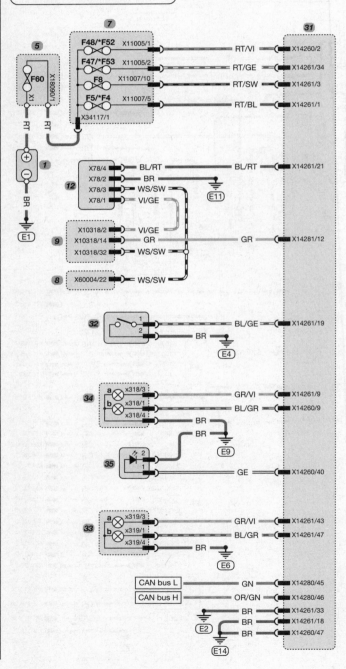

Colour codes

WS	White	RT	Red
BL	Blue	GN	Green
GR	Grey	VI	Violet
GE	Yellow	SW	Black
BR	Brown	OR	Orange
RS	Pink	TR	Transparent

* Models from 2009

Key to items

1 Battery
5 Battery fusebox
7 Passenger fusebox
  R17 = terminal 30 relay
9 Car access control unit
18 Steering column switch unit
31 Footwell control unit
33 LH rear light unit
  c = tail light
  d = direction indicator
34 RH rear light unit
  (c and d as above)
40 LH headlight unit
  a = dip beam
  b = main beam
  c = direction indicator
41 RH headlight unit
  (a and c as above)
42 Rear foglight
43 LH direction indicator side repeater

44 RH direction indicator side repeater
45 LH sidelight/foglight
  a = sidelight
  b = foglight
46 RH sidelight/foglight
  (a and b as above)
47 Hazard warning switch
48 Heater control panel (foglight switch)
49 Boot lid button/number plate light

Diagram 4

H47577

Exterior lighting - side, tail, fog, indicators, hazard, dip & main beam

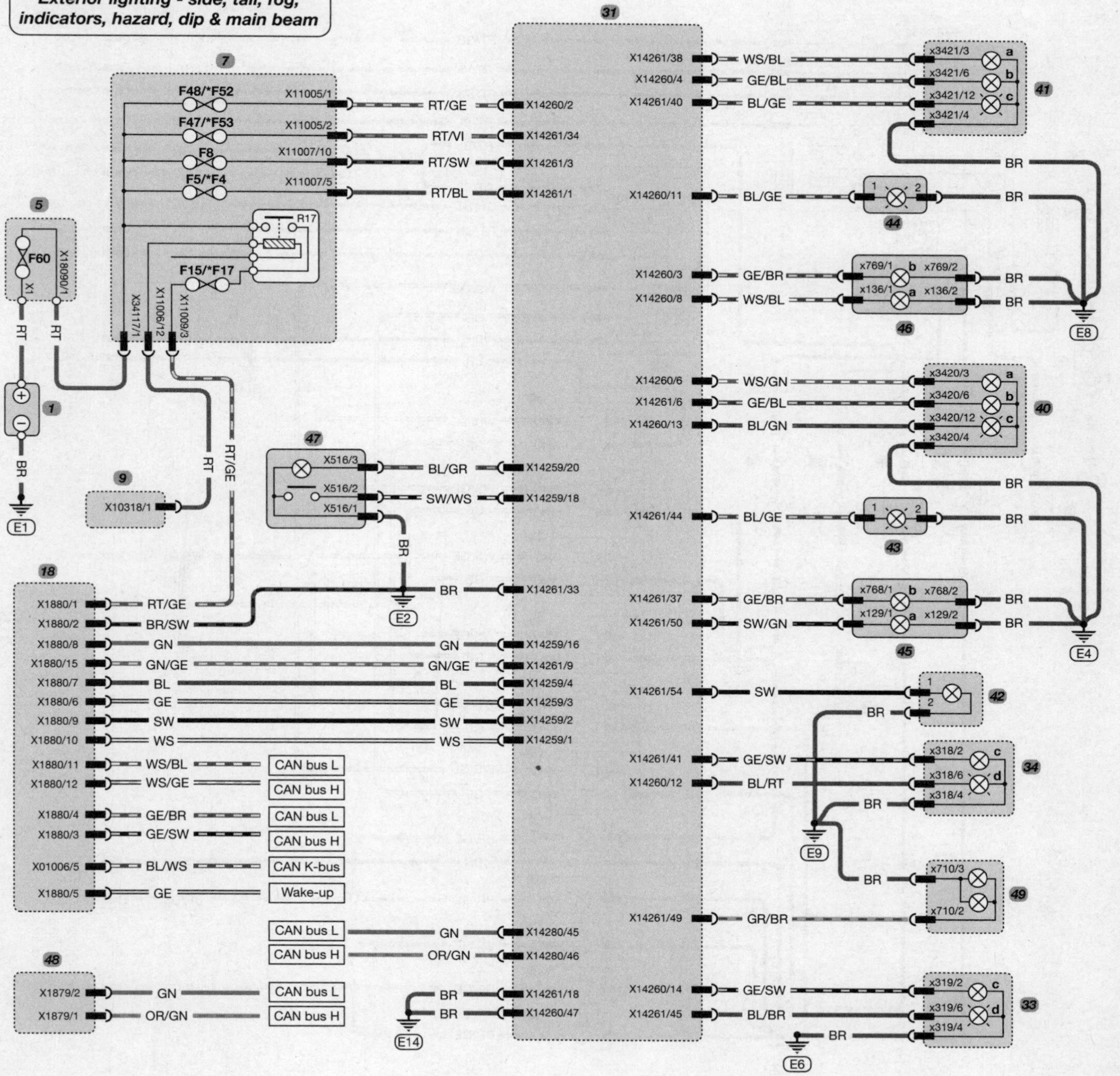

Colour codes

WS	White	RT	Red
BL	Blue	GN	Green
GR	Grey	VI	Violet
GE	Yellow	SW	Black
BR	Brown	OR	Orange
RS	Pink	TR	Transparent

* Models from 2009

Key to items

1 Battery
5 Battery fusebox
7 Passenger fusebox
  R17 = terminal 30 relay
9 Car access control unit
31 Footwell control unit
53 Front interior light
54 Glovebox light
55 LH vanity mirror
56 RH vanity mirror
57 Luggage compartment light
58 Boot lid lid motor
59 LH 'B' pillar ambient lighting
60 RH 'B' pillar ambient lighting
61 Driver's door oddment compartment light
62 Driver's door handle light
63 Passenger's door oddment compartment light
64 Passenger's door handle light
65 Driver's door entrance light
66 Passenger's door entrance light
67 Rear interior light
68 Front LH footwell light
69 Front RH footwell light

Diagram 5

H47578

Interior lighting

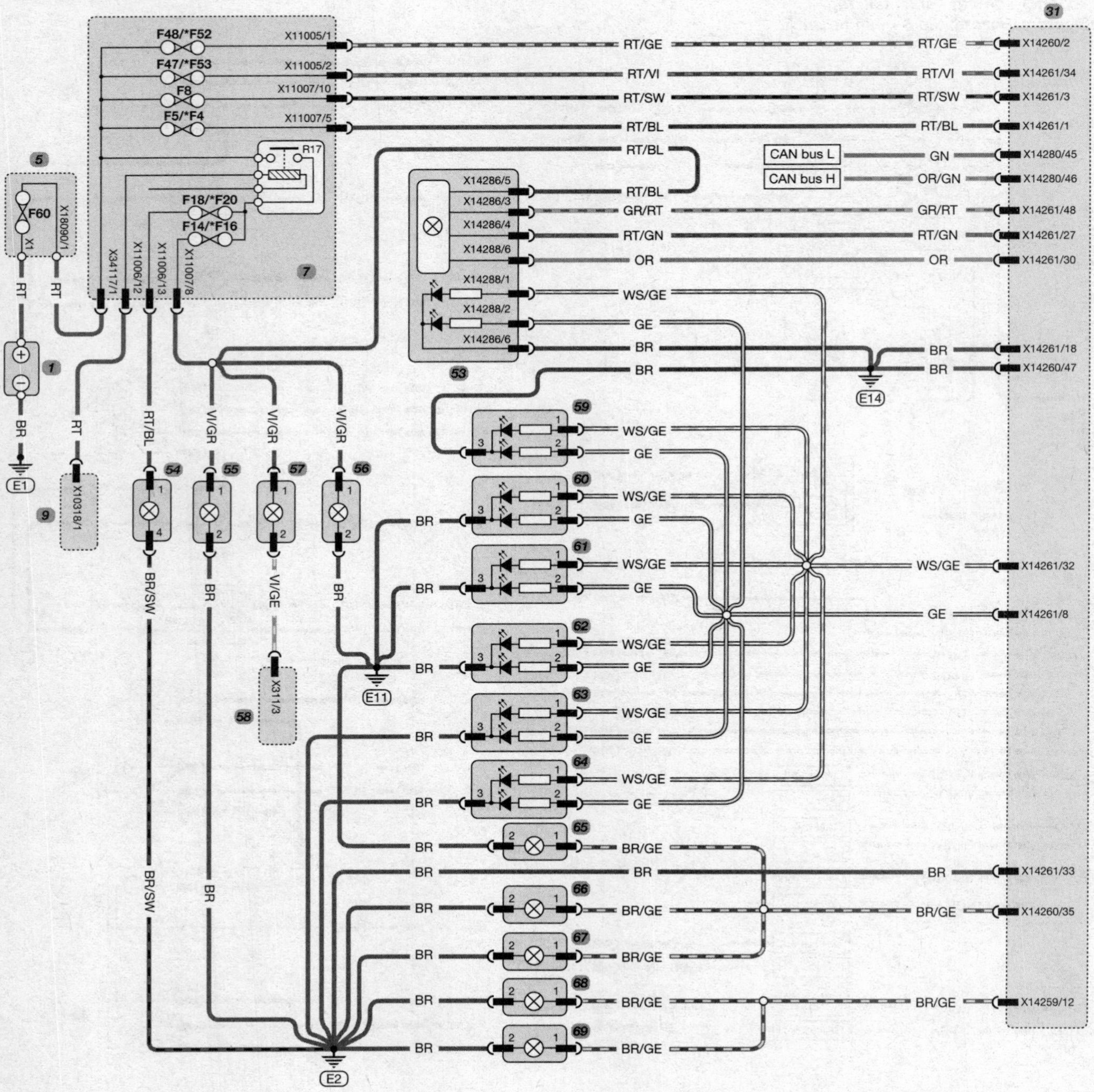

Colour codes

WS	White	**RT**	Red
BL	Blue	**GN**	Green
GR	Grey	**VI**	Violet
GE	Yellow	**SW**	Black
BR	Brown	**OR**	Orange
RS	Pink	**TR**	Transparent

* Models from 2009

Key to items

1 Battery
5 Battery fusebox
6 Engine fusebox
  R5 = wiper on/off relay*
  R7 = wiper setting 1 & 2 relay
7 Passenger fusebox
  R10 = heated rear window relay
  R17 = terminal 30 relay
9 Car access control unit
18 Steering column switch unit
48 Heater control panel
   (heated screen switches)
72 Heated windscreen relay
73 LH heated screen element
74 RH heated screen element
75 Positive rear window filter (if fitted)
76 Negative rear window filter (if fitted)
77 Heated rear window element
78 Front wiper motor
79 Rear wiper motor
80 Rain/light sensor
81 Headlight washer pump
82 Windscreen washer pump
83 Driver's heated washer jet
84 Passenger's heated washer jet

Diagram 6

H47579

Heated screens

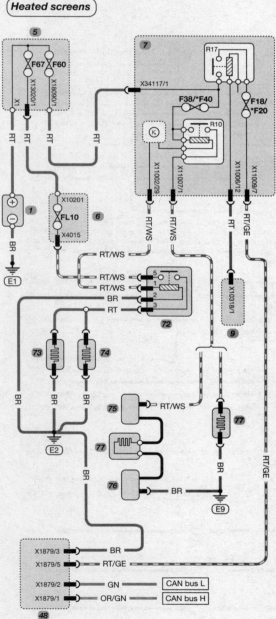

Wash/wipe

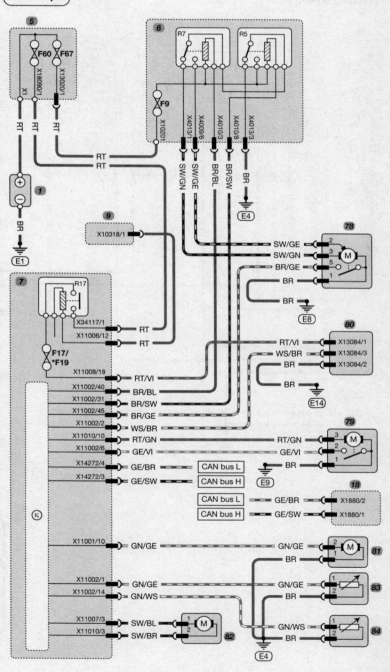

Colour codes

WS	White	RT	Red
BL	Blue	GN	Green
GR	Grey	VI	Violet
GE	Yellow	SW	Black
BR	Brown	OR	Orange
RS	Pink	TR	Transparent

*Models from 2009

Key to items

1 Battery
5 Battery fusebox
7 Passenger fusebox
  R9   = terminal 15 relay
  R11 = a/c compressor relay
  R17 = terminal 30 relay
  R18 = heater blower relay
9 Car access control unit
31 Footwell control unit

48 Heater control panel
86 Fresh/recirculation air flap motor
87 Air distribution flap motor
88 Mixer flap motor
89 Air distribution flap microswitch
90 Heater blower resistors
91 Heater blower motor
92 Compressor clutch
93 Heat exchanger temperature sensor

94 Evaporator temperature sensor
95 Solar sensor
96 Auto air recirculation sensor

Diagram 7

H47580

Heating & ventilation

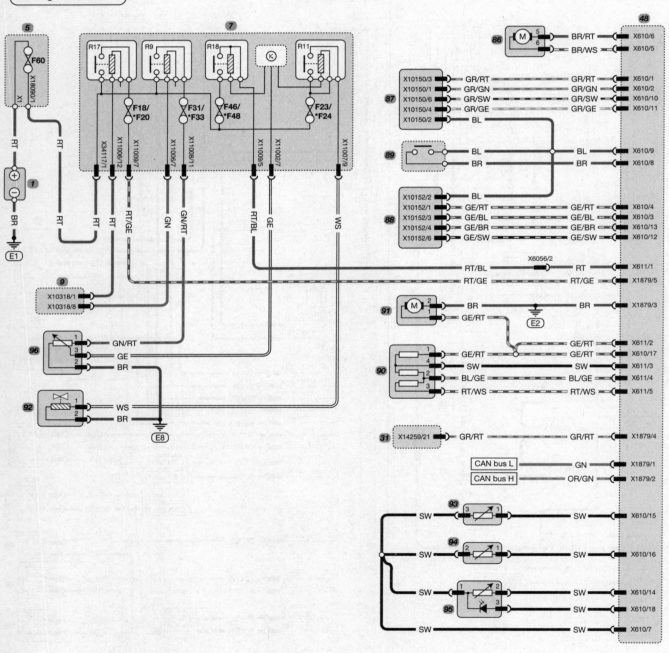

Colour codes

WS	White	**RT**	Red
BL	Blue	**GN**	Green
GR	Grey	**VI**	Violet
GE	Yellow	**SW**	Black
BR	Brown	**OR**	Orange
RS	Pink	**TR**	Transparent

* Models from 2009

Key to items

1 Battery
5 Battery fusebox
7 Passenger fusebox
  R14 = bistable relay
  R17 = terminal 30 relay
98 Instrument cluster control unit
99 Additional instrument cluster
    (Cooper S only)
100 Central information display
101 Outside air temperature sensor

102 Car communication control unit
103 Handbrake switch
104 Low washer fluid switch
105 Fuel pump assembly
  a = LH fuel level sensor
  b = RH fuel level sensor
106 LH front pad wear sensor
107 RH front pad wear sensor

Diagram 8

H47581

Information display with additional instrumentation

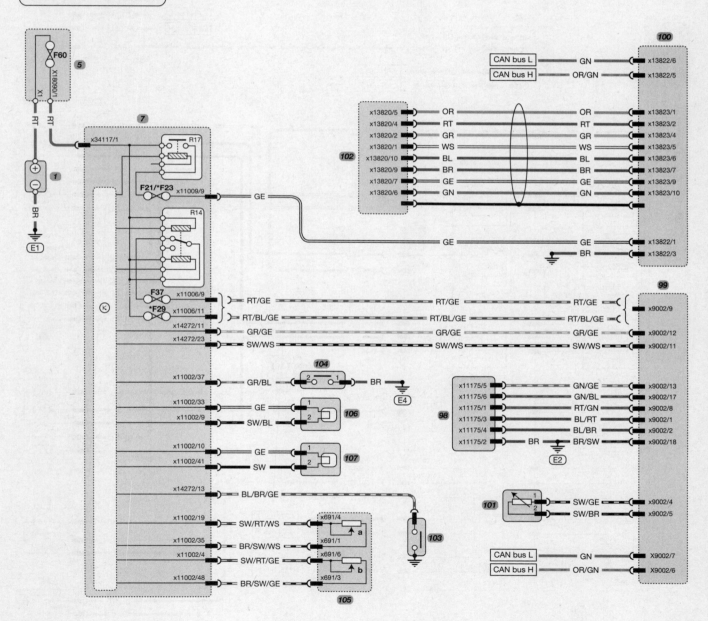

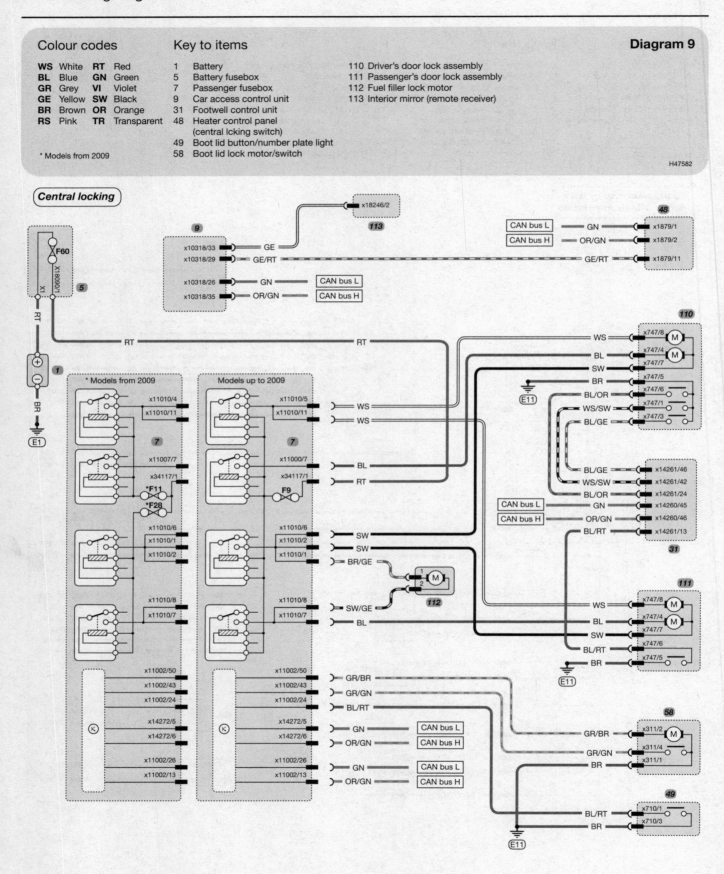

Colour codes

WS	White	**RT**	Red
BL	Blue	**GN**	Green
GR	Grey	**VI**	Violet
GE	Yellow	**SW**	Black
BR	Brown	**OR**	Orange
RS	Pink	**TR**	Transparent

* Models from 2009

Key to items

1 Battery
5 Battery fusebox
7 Passenger fusebox
9 Car access control unit
31 Footwell control unit
48 Heater control panel
   (central lcking switch)
49 Boot lid button/number plate light
58 Boot lid lock motor/switch

110 Driver's door lock assembly
111 Passenger's door lock assembly
112 Fuel filler lock motor
113 Interior mirror (remote receiver)

Diagram 9

H47582

Central locking

Colour codes

WS	White	**RT**	Red
BL	Blue	**GN**	Green
GR	Grey	**VI**	Violet
GE	Yellow	**SW**	Black
BR	Brown	**OR**	Orange
RS	Pink	**TR**	Transparent

* Models from 2009

Key to items

1   Battery
5   Battery fusebox
7   Passenger fusebox
    R9 = terminal 15 relay
    R14 = bistable relay
    R17 = terminal 30 relay
9   Car access control unit
13 Dynamic stability control unit

31 Footwell control unit
48 Heater control panel
    (electric window switches)
116 Driver's window motor
117 Passemger's window motor
118 Sunroof switch
119 Sunroof control unit
121 Mirror fold-in control unit

122 Mirror adjustment switch
123 Driver's mirror assembly
124 Passenger's mirror assembly

Diagram 10

H47583

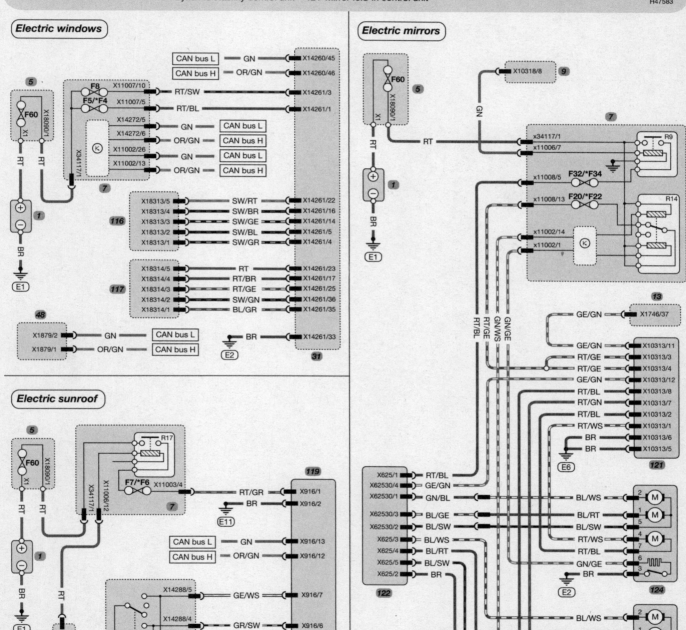

Electric windows

Electric mirrors

Electric sunroof

Dimensions and weights

Note: *All figures are approximate, and may vary according to model. Refer to manufacturer's data for exact figures.*

Dimensions

Overall length:
  Hatchback:
    MINI One, Cooper. . . . . 3699 mm
    Diesel . . . . 3709 mm
    Cooper S. . . . . 3714 mm
  Clubman:
    MINI One, Cooper. . . . . 3937 mm
    Diesel . . . . 3945 mm
    Cooper S. . . . . 3958 mm
  Convertible:
    MINI One, Cooper. . . . . 3699 mm
    Diesel . . . . 3709 mm
    Cooper S. . . . . 3714 mm
Overall width (inc. mirrors) . . . . 1913 mm
Overall height:
  Hatchback . . . . 1407 mm
  Clubman . . . . 1426 mm
  Convertible . . . . 1414 mm
Wheelbase:
  Hatchback and Convertible . . . . 2467 mm
  Clubman. . . . . 2547 mm

Weights

Kerb weight (depending on model) . . . . 1135 kg to 1330 kg
Maximum roof rack load . . . . 75 kg

Fuel economy

Although depreciation is still the biggest part of the cost of motoring for most car owners, the cost of fuel is more immediately noticeable. These pages give some tips on how to get the best fuel economy.

Working it out

Manufacturer's figures

Car manufacturers are required by law to provide fuel consumption information on all new vehicles sold. These 'official' figures are obtained by simulating various driving conditions on a rolling road or a test track. Real life conditions are different, so the fuel consumption actually achieved may not bear much resemblance to the quoted figures.

How to calculate it

Many cars now have trip computers which will

display fuel consumption, both instantaneous and average. Refer to the owner's handbook for details of how to use these.

To calculate consumption yourself (and maybe to check that the trip computer is accurate), proceed as follows.

1. Fill up with fuel and note the mileage, or zero the trip recorder.
2. Drive as usual until you need to fill up again.
3. Note the amount of fuel required to refill the tank, and the mileage covered since the previous fill-up.
4. Divide the mileage by the amount of fuel used to obtain the consumption figure.

For example:

Mileage at first fill-up (a) = 27,903
Mileage at second fill-up (b) = 28,346
Mileage covered (b - a) = 443
Fuel required at second fill-up = 48.6 litres

The half-completed changeover to metric units in the UK means that we buy our fuel

in litres, measure distances in miles and talk about fuel consumption in miles per gallon. There are two ways round this: the first is to convert the litres to gallons before doing the calculation (by dividing by 4.546, or see Table 1). So in the example:

48.6 litres ÷ 4.546 = 10.69 gallons
443 miles ÷ 10.69 gallons = 41.4 mpg

The second way is to calculate the consumption in miles per litre, then multiply that figure by 4.546 (or see Table 2).

So in the example, fuel consumption is:

443 miles ÷ 48.6 litres = 9.1 mpl
9.1 mpl x 4.546 = 41.4 mpg

The rest of Europe expresses fuel consumption in litres of fuel required to travel 100 km (l/100 km). For interest, the conversions are given in Table 3. In practice it doesn't matter what units you use, provided you know what your normal consumption is and can spot if it's getting better or worse.

Table 1: conversion of litres to Imperial gallons

litres	1	2	3	4	5	10	20	30	40	50	60	70
gallons	0.22	0.44	0.66	0.88	1.10	2.24	4.49	6.73	8.98	11.22	13.47	15.71

Table 2: conversion of miles per litre to miles per gallon

miles per litre	5	6	7	8	9	10	11	12	13	14
miles per gallon	23	27	32	36	41	46	50	55	59	64

Table 3: conversion of litres per 100 km to miles per gallon

litres per 100 km	4	4.5	5	5.5	6	6.5	7	8	9	10
miles per gallon	71	63	56	51	47	43	40	35	31	28

Maintenance

A well-maintained car uses less fuel and creates less pollution. In particular:

Filters

Change air and fuel filters at the specified intervals.

Oil

Use a good quality oil of the lowest viscosity specified by the vehicle manufacturer (see *Lubricants and fluids*). Check the level often and be careful not to overfill.

Spark plugs

When applicable, renew at the specified intervals.

Tyres

Check tyre pressures regularly. Under-inflated tyres have an increased rolling resistance. It is generally safe to use the higher pressures specified for full load conditions even when not fully laden, but keep an eye on the centre band of tread for signs of wear due to over-inflation.

When buying new tyres, consider the 'fuel saving' models which most manufacturers include in their ranges.

Driving style

Acceleration

Acceleration uses more fuel than driving at a steady speed. The best technique with modern cars is to accelerate reasonably briskly to the desired speed, changing up through the gears as soon as possible without making the engine labour.

Air conditioning

Air conditioning absorbs quite a bit of energy from the engine – typically 3 kW (4 hp) or so. The effect on fuel consumption is at its worst in slow traffic. Switch it off when not required.

Anticipation

Drive smoothly and try to read the traffic flow so as to avoid unnecessary acceleration and braking.

Automatic transmission

When accelerating in an automatic, avoid depressing the throttle so far as to make the transmission hold onto lower gears at higher speeds. Don't use the 'Sport' setting, if applicable.

When stationary with the engine running, select 'N' or 'P'. When moving, keep your left foot away from the brake.

Braking

Braking converts the car's energy of motion into heat – essentially, it is wasted. Obviously some braking is always going to be necessary, but with good anticipation it is surprising how much can be avoided, especially on routes that you know well.

Carshare

Consider sharing lifts to work or to the shops. Even once a week will make a difference.

Electrical loads

Electricity is 'fuel' too; the alternator which charges the battery does so by converting some of the engine's energy of motion into electrical energy. The more electrical accessories are in use, the greater the load on the alternator. Switch off big consumers like the heated rear window when not required.

Freewheeling

Freewheeling (coasting) in neutral with the engine switched off is dangerous. The effort required to operate power-assisted brakes and steering increases when the engine is not running, with a potential lack of control in emergency situations.

In any case, modern fuel injection systems automatically cut off the engine's fuel supply on the overrun (moving and in gear, but with the accelerator pedal released).

Gadgets

Bolt-on devices claiming to save fuel have been around for nearly as long as the motor car itself. Those which worked were rapidly adopted as standard equipment by the vehicle manufacturers. Others worked only in certain situations, or saved fuel only at the expense of unacceptable effects on performance, driveability or the life of engine components.

The most effective fuel saving gadget is the driver's right foot.

Journey planning

Combine (eg) a trip to the supermarket with a visit to the recycling centre and the DIY store, rather than making separate journeys.

When possible choose a travelling time outside rush hours.

Load

The more heavily a car is laden, the greater the energy required to accelerate it to a given speed. Remove heavy items which you don't need to carry.

One load which is often overlooked is the contents of the fuel tank. A tankful of fuel (55 litres / 12 gallons) weighs 45 kg (100 lb) or so. Just half filling it may be worthwhile.

Lost?

At the risk of stating the obvious, if you're going somewhere new, have details of the route to hand. There's not much point in

achieving record mpg if you also go miles out of your way.

Parking

If possible, carry out any reversing or turning manoeuvres when you arrive at a parking space so that you can drive straight out when you leave. Manoeuvering when the engine is cold uses a lot more fuel.

Driving around looking for free on-street parking may cost more in fuel than buying a car park ticket.

Premium fuel

Most major oil companies (and some supermarkets) have premium grades of fuel which are several pence a litre dearer than the standard grades. Reports vary, but the consensus seems to be that if these fuels improve economy at all, they do not do so by enough to justify their extra cost.

Roof rack

When loading a roof rack, try to produce a wedge shape with the narrow end at the front. Any cover should be securely fastened – if it flaps it's creating turbulence and absorbing energy.

Remove roof racks and boxes when not in use – they increase air resistance and can create a surprising amount of noise.

Short journeys

The engine is at its least efficient, and wear is highest, during the first few miles after a cold start. Consider walking, cycling or using public transport.

Speed

The engine is at its most efficient when running at a steady speed and load at the rpm where it develops maximum torque. (You can find this figure in the car's handbook.) For most cars this corresponds to between 55 and 65 mph in top gear.

Above the optimum cruising speed, fuel consumption starts to rise quite sharply. A car travelling at 80 mph will typically be using 30% more fuel than at 60 mph.

Supermarket fuel

It may be cheap but is it any good? In the UK all supermarket fuel must meet the relevant British Standard. The major oil companies will say that their branded fuels have better additive packages which may stop carbon and other deposits building up. A reasonable compromise might be to use one tank of branded fuel to three or four from the supermarket.

Switch off when stationary

Switch off the engine if you look like being stationary for more than 30 seconds or so. This is good for the environment as well as for your pocket. Be aware though that frequent restarts are hard on the battery and the starter motor.

Windows

Driving with the windows open increases air turbulence around the vehicle. Closing the windows promotes smooth airflow and

reduced resistance. The faster you go, the more significant this is.

And finally . . .

Driving techniques associated with good fuel economy tend to involve moderate acceleration and low top speeds. Be considerate to the needs of other road users who may need to make brisker progress; even if you do not agree with them this is not an excuse to be obstructive.

Safety must always take precedence over economy, whether it is a question of accelerating hard to complete an overtaking manoeuvre, killing your speed when confronted with a potential hazard or switching the lights on when it starts to get dark.

Conversion factors

Length (distance)

Inches (in)	x 25.4	= Millimetres (mm)	x 0.0394	= Inches (in)
Feet (ft)	x 0.305	= Metres (m)	x 3.281	= Feet (ft)
Miles	x 1.609	= Kilometres (km)	x 0.621	= Miles

Volume (capacity)

Cubic inches (cu in; in³)	x 16.387	= Cubic centimetres (cc; cm³)	x 0.061	= Cubic inches (cu in; in³)
Imperial pints (Imp pt)	x 0.568	= Litres (l)	x 1.76	= Imperial pints (Imp pt)
Imperial quarts (Imp qt)	x 1.137	= Litres (l)	x 0.88	= Imperial quarts (Imp qt)
Imperial quarts (Imp qt)	x 1.201	= US quarts (US qt)	x 0.833	= Imperial quarts (Imp qt)
US quarts (US qt)	x 0.946	= Litres (l)	x 1.057	= US quarts (US qt)
Imperial gallons (Imp gal)	x 4.546	= Litres (l)	x 0.22	= Imperial gallons (Imp gal)
Imperial gallons (Imp gal)	x 1.201	= US gallons (US gal)	x 0.833	= Imperial gallons (Imp gal)
US gallons (US gal)	x 3.785	= Litres (l)	x 0.264	= US gallons (US gal)

Mass (weight)

Ounces (oz)	x 28.35	= Grams (g)	x 0.035	= Ounces (oz)
Pounds (lb)	x 0.454	= Kilograms (kg)	x 2.205	= Pounds (lb)

Force

Ounces-force (ozf; oz)	x 0.278	= Newtons (N)	x 3.6	= Ounces-force (ozf; oz)
Pounds-force (lbf; lb)	x 4.448	= Newtons (N)	x 0.225	= Pounds-force (lbf; lb)
Newtons (N)	x 0.1	= Kilograms-force (kgf; kg)	x 9.81	= Newtons (N)

Pressure

Pounds-force per square inch (psi; lbf/in²; lb/in²)	x 0.070	= Kilograms-force per square centimetre (kgf/cm²; kg/cm²)	x 14.223	= Pounds-force per square inch (psi; lbf/in²; lb/in²)
Pounds-force per square inch (psi; lbf/in²; lb/in²)	x 0.068	= Atmospheres (atm)	x 14.696	= Pounds-force per square inch (psi; lbf/in²; lb/in²)
Pounds-force per square inch (psi; lbf/in²; lb/in²)	x 0.069	= Bars	x 14.5	= Pounds-force per square inch (psi; lbf/in²; lb/in²)
Pounds-force per square inch (psi; lbf/in²; lb/in²)	x 6.895	= Kilopascals (kPa)	x 0.145	= Pounds-force per square inch (psi; lbf/in²; lb/in²)
Kilopascals (kPa)	x 0.01	= Kilograms-force per square centimetre (kgf/cm²; kg/cm²)	x 98.1	= Kilopascals (kPa)
Millibar (mbar)	x 100	= Pascals (Pa)	x 0.01	= Millibar (mbar)
Millibar (mbar)	x 0.0145	= Pounds-force per square inch (psi; lbf/in²; lb/in²)	x 68.947	= Millibar (mbar)
Millibar (mbar)	x 0.75	= Millimetres of mercury (mmHg)	x 1.333	= Millibar (mbar)
Millibar (mbar)	x 0.401	= Inches of water (inH₂O)	x 2.491	= Millibar (mbar)
Millimetres of mercury (mmHg)	x 0.535	= Inches of water (inH₂O)	x 1.868	= Millimetres of mercury (mmHg)
Inches of water (inH₂O)	x 0.036	= Pounds-force per square inch (psi; lbf/in²; lb/in²)	x 27.68	= Inches of water (inH₂O)

Torque (moment of force)

Pounds-force inches (lbf in; lb in)	x 1.152	= Kilograms-force centimetre (kgf cm; kg cm)	x 0.868	= Pounds-force inches (lbf in; lb in)
Pounds-force inches (lbf in; lb in)	x 0.113	= Newton metres (Nm)	x 8.85	= Pounds-force inches (lbf in; lb in)
Pounds-force inches (lbf in; lb in)	x 0.083	= Pounds-force feet (lbf ft; lb ft)	x 12	= Pounds-force inches (lbf in; lb in)
Pounds-force feet (lbf ft; lb ft)	x 0.138	= Kilograms-force metres (kgf m; kg m)	x 7.233	= Pounds-force feet (lbf ft; lb ft)
Pounds-force feet (lbf ft; lb ft)	x 1.356	= Newton metres (Nm)	x 0.738	= Pounds-force feet (lbf ft; lb ft)
Newton metres (Nm)	x 0.102	= Kilograms-force metres (kgf m; kg m)	x 9.804	= Newton metres (Nm)

Power

Horsepower (hp)	x 745.7	= Watts (W)	x 0.0013	= Horsepower (hp)

Velocity (speed)

Miles per hour (miles/hr; mph)	x 1.609	= Kilometres per hour (km/hr; kph)	x 0.621	= Miles per hour (miles/hr; mph)

Fuel consumption*

Miles per gallon, Imperial (mpg)	x 0.354	= Kilometres per litre (km/l)	x 2.825	= Miles per gallon, Imperial (mpg)
Miles per gallon, US (mpg)	x 0.425	= Kilometres per litre (km/l)	x 2.352	= Miles per gallon, US (mpg)

Temperature

Degrees Fahrenheit = (°C x 1.8) + 32   Degrees Celsius (Degrees Centigrade; °C) = (°F - 32) x 0.56

It is common practice to convert from miles per gallon (mpg) to litres/100 kilometres (l/100km), where mpg x l/100 km = 282

Spare parts are available from many sources, including maker's appointed garages, accessory shops, and motor factors. To be sure of obtaining the correct parts, it may sometimes be necessary to quote the vehicle identification number. If possible, it can also be useful to take the old parts along for positive identification. Items such as starter motors and alternators may be available under a service exchange scheme – any parts returned should always be clean.

Our advice regarding spare part sources is as follows:

Officially-appointed garages

This is the best source of parts which are peculiar to your car, and are not otherwise generally available (eg, badges, interior trim, certain body panels, etc). It is also the only place at which you should buy parts if the vehicle is still under warranty.

Accessory shops

These are very good places to buy materials and components needed for the maintenance of your car (oil, air and fuel filters, spark plugs, light bulbs, drivebelts, oils and greases, brake pads, touch-up paint, etc). Parts like this sold by a reputable shop are of the same standard as those used by the car manufacturer.

Motor factors

Good factors will stock all the more important components which wear out comparatively quickly and can sometimes supply individual components needed for the overhaul of a larger assembly. They may also handle work such as cylinder block reboring, crankshaft regrinding and balancing, etc.

Tyre and exhaust specialists

These outlets may be independent or members of a local or national chain. They frequently offer competitive prices when compared with a main dealer or local garage, but it will pay to obtain several quotes before making a decision. Also ask what 'extras' may be added to the quote – for instance, fitting a new valve and balancing the wheel are both often charged on top of the price of a new tyre.

Other sources

Beware of parts of materials obtained from market stalls, car boot sales or similar outlets. Such items are not always sub-standard, but there is little chance of compensation if they do prove unsatisfactory. In the case of safety-critical components such as brake pads there is the risk not only of financial loss but also of an accident causing injury or death.

Second-hand components or assemblies obtained from a car breaker can be a good buy in some circumstances, but this sort of purchase is best made by the experienced DIY mechanic.

Vehicle identification numbers

Modifications are a continuing and unpublicised process in vehicle manufacture, quite apart from major model changes. Spare parts manuals and lists are compiled upon a numerical basis, the individual vehicle identification numbers being essential to correct identification of the component concerned.

When ordering spare parts, always give as much information as possible. Quote the vehicle type and year, vehicle identification number (VIN), and engine number, as appropriate.

The vehicle identification number (VIN) is stamped into the right-hand suspension turret in the engine compartment, and is repeated on the model plate affixed to the passengers door central pillar (see illustrations). The model plate also gives vehicle loading details, engine type, and various trim and colour codes.

The engine number is stamped on the left-hand end of the cylinder block.

The transmission identification numbers are located on a plate attached to the top of the transmission casing, or cast into the casing itself.

The Vehicle Identification Number (VIN) is stamped into the right-hand suspension turret in the engine compartment...

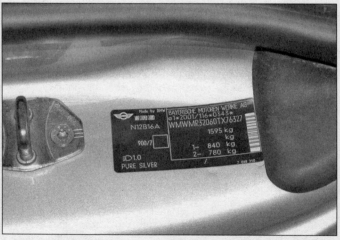

...and is repeated on the model plate attached to the passengers door pillar

Whenever servicing, repair or overhaul work is carried out on the car or its components, observe the following procedures and instructions. This will assist in carrying out the operation efficiently and to a professional standard of workmanship.

Joint mating faces and gaskets

When separating components at their mating faces, never insert screwdrivers or similar implements into the joint between the faces in order to prise them apart. This can cause severe damage which results in oil leaks, coolant leaks, etc upon reassembly. Separation is usually achieved by tapping along the joint with a soft-faced hammer in order to break the seal. However, note that this method may not be suitable where dowels are used for component location.

Where a gasket is used between the mating faces of two components, a new one must be fitted on reassembly; fit it dry unless otherwise stated in the repair procedure. Make sure that the mating faces are clean and dry, with all traces of old gasket removed. When cleaning a joint face, use a tool which is unlikely to score or damage the face, and remove any burrs or nicks with an oilstone or fine file.

Make sure that tapped holes are cleaned with a pipe cleaner, and keep them free of jointing compound, if this is being used, unless specifically instructed otherwise.

Ensure that all orifices, channels or pipes are clear, and blow through them, preferably using compressed air.

Oil seals

Oil seals can be removed by levering them out with a wide flat-bladed screwdriver or similar implement. Alternatively, a number of self-tapping screws may be screwed into the seal, and these used as a purchase for pliers or some similar device in order to pull the seal free.

Whenever an oil seal is removed from its working location, either individually or as part of an assembly, it should be renewed.

The very fine sealing lip of the seal is easily damaged, and will not seal if the surface it contacts is not completely clean and free from scratches, nicks or grooves. If the original sealing surface of the component cannot be restored, and the manufacturer has not made provision for slight relocation of the seal relative to the sealing surface, the component should be renewed.

Protect the lips of the seal from any surface which may damage them in the course of fitting. Use tape or a conical sleeve where possible. Where indicated, lubricate the seal lips with oil before fitting and, on dual-lipped seals, fill the space between the lips with grease.

Unless otherwise stated, oil seals must be fitted with their sealing lips toward the lubricant to be sealed.

Use a tubular drift or block of wood of the appropriate size to install the seal and, if the seal housing is shouldered, drive the seal down to the shoulder. If the seal housing is unshouldered, the seal should be fitted with its face flush with the housing top face (unless otherwise instructed).

Screw threads and fastenings

Seized nuts, bolts and screws are quite a common occurrence where corrosion has set in, and the use of penetrating oil or releasing fluid will often overcome this problem if the offending item is soaked for a while before attempting to release it. The use of an impact driver may also provide a means of releasing such stubborn fastening devices, when used in conjunction with the appropriate screwdriver bit or socket. If none of these methods works, it may be necessary to resort to the careful application of heat, or the use of a hacksaw or nut splitter device. Before resorting to extreme methods, check that you are not dealing with a left-hand thread!

Studs are usually removed by locking two nuts together on the threaded part, and then using a spanner on the lower nut to unscrew the stud. Studs or bolts which have broken off below the surface of the component in which they are mounted can sometimes be removed using a stud extractor.

Always ensure that a blind tapped hole is completely free from oil, grease, water or other fluid before installing the bolt or stud. Failure to do this could cause the housing to crack due to the hydraulic action of the bolt or stud as it is screwed in.

For some screw fastenings, notably cylinder head bolts or nuts, torque wrench settings are no longer specified for the latter stages of tightening, "angle-tightening" being called up instead. Typically, a fairly low torque wrench setting will be applied to the bolts/nuts in the correct sequence, followed by one or more stages of tightening through specified angles.

When checking or retightening a nut or bolt to a specified torque setting, slacken the nut or bolt by a quarter of a turn, and then retighten to the specified setting. However, this should not be attempted where angular tightening has been used.

Locknuts, locktabs and washers

Any fastening which will rotate against a component or housing during tightening should always have a washer between it and the relevant component or housing.

Spring or split washers should always be renewed when they are used to lock a critical component such as a big-end bearing retaining bolt or nut. Locktabs which are folded over to retain a nut or bolt should always be renewed.

Self-locking nuts can be re-used in non-critical areas, providing resistance can be felt when the locking portion passes over the bolt or stud thread. However, it should be noted that self-locking stiffnuts tend to lose their effectiveness after long periods of use, and should then be renewed as a matter of course.

Split pins must always be replaced with new ones of the correct size for the hole.

When thread-locking compound is found on the threads of a fastener which is to be re-used, it should be cleaned off with a wire brush and solvent, and fresh compound applied on reassembly.

Special tools

Some repair procedures in this manual entail the use of special tools such as a press, two or three-legged pullers, spring compressors, etc. Wherever possible, suitable readily-available alternatives to the manufacturer's special tools are described, and are shown in use. In some instances, where no alternative is possible, it has been necessary to resort to the use of a manufacturer's tool, and this has been done for reasons of safety as well as the efficient completion of the repair operation. Unless you are highly-skilled and have a thorough understanding of the procedures described, never attempt to bypass the use of any special tool when the procedure described specifies its use. Not only is there a very great risk of personal injury, but expensive damage could be caused to the components involved.

Environmental considerations

When disposing of used engine oil, brake fluid, antifreeze, etc, give due consideration to any detrimental environmental effects. Do not, for instance, pour any of the above liquids down drains into the general sewage system, or onto the ground to soak away. Many local council refuse tips provide a facility for waste oil disposal, as do some garages. You can find your nearest disposal point by calling the Environment Agency on 08708 506 506 or by visiting www.oilbankline.org.uk.

Note: It is illegal and anti-social to dump oil down the drain. To find the location of your local oil recycling bank, call 08708 506 506 or visit www.oilbankline.org.uk.

The jack available as a MINI accessory should **only** be used for changing the roadwheels in an emergency. When carrying out any other kind of work, raise the vehicle using a heavy-duty hydraulic (or 'trolley') jack, and always supplement the jack with axle stands positioned under the vehicle jacking points. If the roadwheels do not have to be removed, consider using wheel ramps – if wished, these can be placed under the wheels once the vehicle has been raised using a hydraulic jack, and the vehicle lowered onto the ramps so that it is resting on its wheels.

Only ever jack the vehicle up on a solid, level surface. If there is even a slight slope, take great care that the vehicle cannot move as the wheels are lifted off the ground. Jacking up on an uneven or gravelled surface is not recommended, as the weight of the vehicle will not be evenly distributed, and the jack may slip as the vehicle is raised.

As far as possible, do not leave the vehicle unattended once it has been raised, particularly if children are playing nearby.

Before jacking up the front of the car, ensure that the handbrake is firmly applied. When jacking up the rear of the car, place wooden chocks in front of the front wheels, and engage first gear (or P).

When using a hydraulic jack or axle stands, always position the jack head or axle stand head under the relevant rubber lifting blocks. These are situated directly underneath the vehicle jack location holes in the sill – the vehicle can also be raised with a trolley jack positioned under the jacking points on the front subframe **(see illustration)**.

The jack supplied with the vehicle locates in the holes provided in the sill. Ensure that the jack head is correctly engaged before attempting to raise the vehicle.

Never work under, around, or near a raised vehicle, unless it is adequately supported in at least two places.

When jacking or supporting the vehicle at these points, always use a block of wood between the jack head or axle stand, and the vehicle body. It is also considered good practice to use a large block of wood when supporting under other areas, to spread the load over a wider area, and reduce the risk of damage to the underside of the car (it also helps to prevent the underbody coating from being damaged by the jack or axle stand). **Do not** jack the vehicle under any other part of the sill, engine sump, floor pan, subframe, or directly under any of the steering or suspension components.

Never work under, around, or near a raised vehicle, unless it is adequately supported on stands. Do not rely on a jack alone, as even a hydraulic jack could fail under load. Makeshift methods should not be used to lift and support the car during servicing work.

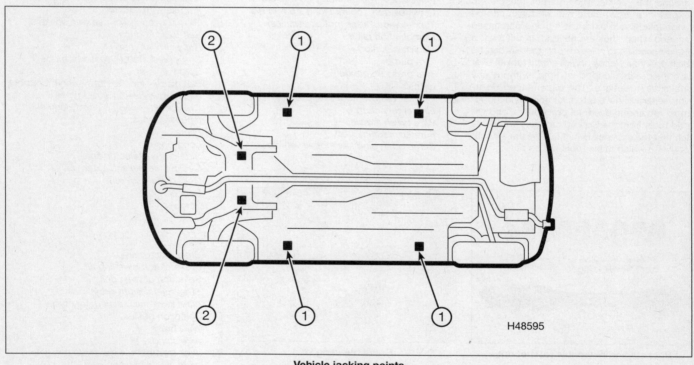

Vehicle jacking points

1   *Sill jacking points*   2   *Front subframe supports*

Tools and working facilities

Introduction

A selection of good tools is a fundamental requirement for anyone contemplating the maintenance and repair of a motor vehicle. For the owner who does not possess any, their purchase will prove a considerable expense, offsetting some of the savings made by doing-it-yourself. However, provided that the tools purchased meet the relevant national safety standards and are of good quality, they will last for many years and prove an extremely worthwhile investment.

To help the average owner to decide which tools are needed to carry out the various tasks detailed in this manual, we have compiled three lists of tools under the following headings: *Maintenance and minor repair, Repair and overhaul,* and *Special.* Newcomers to practical mechanics should start off with the *Maintenance and minor repair* tool kit, and confine themselves to the simpler jobs around the vehicle. Then, as confidence and experience grow, more difficult tasks can be undertaken, with extra tools being purchased as, and when, they are needed. In this way, a *Maintenance and minor repair* tool kit can be built up into a *Repair and overhaul* tool kit over a considerable period of time, without any major cash outlays. The experienced do-it-yourselfer will have a tool kit good enough for most repair and overhaul procedures, and will add tools from the *Special* category when it is felt that the expense is justified by the amount of use to which these tools will be put.

Maintenance and minor repair tool kit

The tools given in this list should be considered as a minimum requirement if routine maintenance, servicing and minor repair operations are to be undertaken. We recommend the purchase of combination spanners (ring one end, open-ended the other); although more expensive than open-ended ones, they do give the advantages of both types of spanner.

- [ ] *Combination spanners:*
  Metric - 8 to 19 mm inclusive
- [ ] *Adjustable spanner - 35 mm jaw (approx.)*
- [ ] *Spark plug spanner (with rubber insert) - petrol models*
- [ ] *Spark plug gap adjustment tool - petrol models*
- [ ] *Set of feeler gauges*
- [ ] *Brake bleed nipple spanner*
- [ ] *Screwdrivers:*
  Flat blade - 100 mm long x 6 mm dia
  Cross blade - 100 mm long x 6 mm dia
  Torx - various sizes (not all vehicles)
- [ ] *Combination pliers*
- [ ] *Hacksaw (junior)*
- [ ] *Tyre pump*
- [ ] *Tyre pressure gauge*
- [ ] *Oil can*
- [ ] *Oil filter removal tool (if applicable)*
- [ ] *Fine emery cloth*
- [ ] *Wire brush (small)*
- [ ] *Funnel (medium size)*
- [ ] *Sump drain plug key (not all vehicles)*

Repair and overhaul tool kit

These tools are virtually essential for anyone undertaking any major repairs to a motor vehicle, and are additional to those given in the *Maintenance and minor repair* list. Included in this list is a comprehensive set of sockets. Although these are expensive, they will be found invaluable as they are so versatile - particularly if various drives are included in the set. We recommend the half-inch square-drive type, as this can be used with most proprietary torque wrenches.

The tools in this list will sometimes need to be supplemented by tools from the *Special* list:

- [ ] *Sockets to cover range in previous list (including Torx sockets)*
- [ ] *Reversible ratchet drive (for use with sockets)*
- [ ] *Extension piece, 250 mm (for use with sockets)*
- [ ] *Universal joint (for use with sockets)*
- [ ] *Flexible handle or sliding T "breaker bar" (for use with sockets)*
- [ ] *Torque wrench (for use with sockets)*
- [ ] *Self-locking grips*
- [ ] *Ball pein hammer*
- [ ] *Soft-faced mallet (plastic or rubber)*
- [ ] *Screwdrivers:*
  Flat blade - long & sturdy, short (chubby), and narrow (electrician's) types
  Cross blade – long & sturdy, and short (chubby) types
- [ ] *Pliers:*
  Long-nosed
  Side cutters (electrician's)
  Circlip (internal and external)
- [ ] *Cold chisel - 25 mm*
- [ ] *Scriber*
- [ ] *Scraper*
- [ ] *Centre-punch*
- [ ] *Pin punch*
- [ ] *Hacksaw*
- [ ] *Brake hose clamp*
- [ ] *Brake/clutch bleeding kit*
- [ ] *Selection of twist drills*
- [ ] *Steel rule/straight-edge*
- [ ] *Allen keys (inc. splined/Torx type)*
- [ ] *Selection of files*
- [ ] *Wire brush*
- [ ] *Axle stands*
- [ ] *Jack (strong trolley or hydraulic type)*
- [ ] *Light with extension lead*
- [ ] *Universal electrical multi-meter*

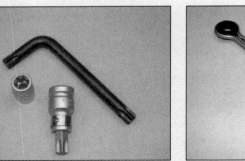

Sockets and reversible ratchet drive

Brake bleeding kit

Torx key, socket and bit

Hose clamp

Angular-tightening gauge

Special tools

The tools in this list are those which are not used regularly, are expensive to buy, or which need to be used in accordance with their manufacturers' instructions. Unless relatively difficult mechanical jobs are undertaken frequently, it will not be economic to buy many of these tools. Where this is the case, you could consider clubbing together with friends (or joining a motorists' club) to make a joint purchase, or borrowing the tools against a deposit from a local garage or tool hire specialist.

The following list contains only those tools and instruments freely available to the public, and not those special tools produced by the vehicle manufacturer specifically for its dealer network. You will find occasional references to these manufacturers' special tools in the text of this manual. Generally, an alternative method of doing the job without the vehicle manufacturers' special tool is given. However, sometimes there is no alternative to using them. Where this is the case and the relevant tool cannot be bought or borrowed, you will have to entrust the work to a dealer.

- ☐ *Angular-tightening gauge*
- ☐ *Valve spring compressor*
- ☐ *Valve grinding tool*
- ☐ *Piston ring compressor*
- ☐ *Piston ring removal/installation tool*
- ☐ *Cylinder bore hone*
- ☐ *Balljoint separator*
- ☐ *Coil spring compressors (where applicable)*
- ☐ *Two/three-legged hub and bearing puller*
- ☐ *Impact screwdriver*
- ☐ *Micrometer and/or vernier calipers*
- ☐ *Dial gauge*
- ☐ *Tachometer*
- ☐ *Fault code reader*
- ☐ *Cylinder compression gauge*
- ☐ *Hand-operated vacuum pump and gauge*
- ☐ *Clutch plate alignment set*
- ☐ *Brake shoe steady spring cup removal tool*
- ☐ *Bush and bearing removal/installation set*
- ☐ *Stud extractors*
- ☐ *Tap and die set*
- ☐ *Lifting tackle*

Buying tools

Reputable motor accessory shops and superstores often offer excellent quality tools at discount prices, so it pays to shop around.

Remember, you don't have to buy the most expensive items on the shelf, but it is always advisable to steer clear of the very cheap tools. Beware of 'bargains' offered on market stalls, on-line or at car boot sales. There are plenty of good tools around at reasonable prices, but always aim to purchase items which meet the relevant national safety standards. If in doubt, ask the proprietor or manager of the shop for advice before making a purchase.

Care and maintenance of tools

Having purchased a reasonable tool kit, it is necessary to keep the tools in a clean and serviceable condition. After use, always wipe off any dirt, grease and metal particles using a clean, dry cloth, before putting the tools away. Never leave them lying around after they have been used. A simple tool rack on the garage or workshop wall for items such as screwdrivers and pliers is a good idea. Store all normal spanners and sockets in a metal box. Any measuring instruments, gauges, meters, etc, must be carefully stored where they cannot be damaged or become rusty.

Take a little care when tools are used. Hammer heads inevitably become marked, and screwdrivers lose the keen edge on their blades from time to time. A little timely attention with emery cloth or a file will soon restore items like this to a good finish.

Working facilities

Not to be forgotten when discussing tools is the workshop itself. If anything more than routine maintenance is to be carried out, a suitable working area becomes essential.

It is appreciated that many an owner-mechanic is forced by circumstances to remove an engine or similar item without the benefit of a garage or workshop. Having done this, any repairs should always be done under the cover of a roof.

Wherever possible, any dismantling should be done on a clean, flat workbench or table at a suitable working height.

Any workbench needs a vice; one with a jaw opening of 100 mm is suitable for most jobs. As mentioned previously, some clean dry storage space is also required for tools, as well as for any lubricants, cleaning fluids, touch-up paints etc, which become necessary.

Another item which may be required, and which has a much more general usage, is an electric drill with a chuck capacity of at least 8 mm. This, together with a good range of twist drills, is virtually essential for fitting accessories.

Last, but not least, always keep a supply of old newspapers and clean, lint-free rags available, and try to keep any working area as clean as possible.

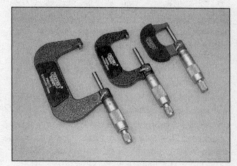

Micrometers

Dial test indicator ("dial gauge")

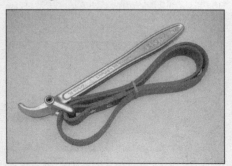

Oil filter removal tool (strap wrench type)

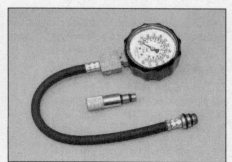

Compression tester

Bearing puller

This is a guide to getting your vehicle through the MOT test. Obviously it will not be possible to examine the vehicle to the same standard as the professional MOT tester. However, working through the following checks will enable you to identify any problem areas before submitting the vehicle for the test.

It has only been possible to summarise the test requirements here, based on the regulations in force at the time of printing. Test standards are becoming increasingly stringent, although there are some exemptions for older vehicles.

An assistant will be needed to help carry out some of these checks.

The checks have been sub-divided into four categories, as follows:

1 Checks carried out **FROM THE DRIVER'S SEAT**

2 Checks carried out **WITH THE VEHICLE ON THE GROUND**

3 Checks carried out **WITH THE VEHICLE RAISED AND THE WHEELS FREE TO TURN**

4 Checks carried out on **YOUR VEHICLE'S EXHAUST EMISSION SYSTEM**

---

1 Checks carried out **FROM THE DRIVER'S SEAT**

Handbrake (parking brake)

☐ Test the operation of the handbrake. Excessive travel (too many clicks) indicates incorrect brake or cable adjustment.

☐ Check that the handbrake cannot be released by tapping the lever sideways. Check the security of the lever mountings.

☐ If the parking brake is foot-operated, check that the pedal is secure and without excessive travel, and that the release mechanism operates correctly.

☐ Where applicable, test the operation of the electronic handbrake. The brake should engage and disengage without excessive delay. If the warning light does not extinguish when the brake is disengaged, this could indicate a fault which will need further investigation.

Footbrake

☐ Depress the brake pedal and check that it does not creep down to the floor, indicating a master cylinder fault. Release the pedal,

wait a few seconds, then depress it again. If the pedal travels nearly to the floor before firm resistance is felt, brake adjustment or repair is necessary. If the pedal feels spongy, there is air in the hydraulic system which must be removed by bleeding.

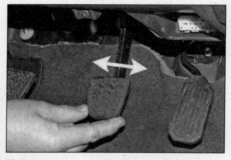

☐ Check that the brake pedal is secure and in good condition. Check also for signs of fluid leaks on the pedal, floor or carpets, which would indicate failed seals in the brake master cylinder.

☐ Check the servo unit (when applicable) by operating the brake pedal several times, then keeping the pedal depressed and starting the engine. As the engine starts, the pedal will move down slightly. If not, the vacuum hose or the servo itself may be faulty.

Steering wheel and column

☐ Examine the steering wheel for fractures or looseness of the hub, spokes or rim.

☐ Move the steering wheel from side to side and then up and down. Check that the steering wheel is not loose on the column, indicating wear or a loose retaining nut. Continue moving the steering wheel as before, but also turn it slightly from left to right.

☐ Check that the steering wheel is not loose on the column, and that there is no abnormal movement of the steering wheel, indicating wear in the column support bearings or couplings.

☐ Check that the ignition lock (where fitted) engages and disengages correctly.

☐ Steering column adjustment mechanisms (where fitted) must be able to lock the column securely in place with no play evident.

Windscreen, mirrors and sunvisor

☐ The windscreen must be free of cracks or other significant damage within the driver's field of view. (Small stone chips are acceptable.) Rear view mirrors must be secure, intact, and capable of being adjusted.

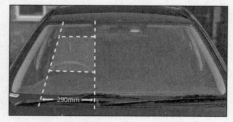

☐ The driver's sunvisor must be capable of being stored in the "up" position.

Seat belts and seats

Note: *The following checks are applicable to all seat belts, front and rear.*

☐ Examine the webbing of all the belts (including rear belts if fitted) for cuts, serious fraying or deterioration. Fasten and unfasten each belt to check the buckles. If applicable, check the retracting mechanism. Check the security of all seat belt mountings accessible from inside the vehicle, ensuring any height adjustable mountings lock securely in place.

☐ Seat belts with pre-tensioners, once activated, have a "flag" or similar showing on the seat belt stalk. This, in itself, is not a reason for test failure.

☐ The front seats themselves must be securely attached and the backrests must lock in the upright position.

Doors

☐ Both front doors must be able to be opened and closed from outside and inside, and must latch securely when closed.

Bonnet and boot/tailgate

☐ The bonnet and boot/tailgate must latch securely when closed.

2 Checks carried out WITH THE VEHICLE ON THE GROUND

Vehicle identification

☐ Number plates must be in good condition, secure and legible, with letters and numbers correctly spaced – spacing at (A) should be 33 mm and at (B) 11 mm. At the front, digits must be black on a white background and at the rear black on a yellow background. Other background designs (such as honeycomb) are not permitted.

☐ The VIN plate and/or homologation plate must be permanently displayed and legible.

Electrical equipment

☐ Switch on the ignition and check the operation of the horn.

☐ Check the windscreen washers and wipers, examining the wiper blades; renew damaged or perished blades. Also check the operation of the stop-lights.

☐ Check the operation of the sidelights and number plate lights. The lenses and reflectors must be secure, clean and undamaged.

☐ Check the operation and alignment of the headlights. The headlight reflectors must not be tarnished and the lenses must be undamaged.

☐ Switch on the ignition and check the operation of the direction indicators (including the instrument panel tell-tale) and the hazard warning lights. Operation of the sidelights and stop-lights must not affect the indicators - if it does, the cause is usually a bad earth at the rear light cluster. Indicators should flash at a rate of between 60 and 120 times per minute – faster or slower than this could indicate a fault with the flasher unit or a bad earth at one of the light units.

☐ Check the operation of the rear foglight(s), including the warning light on the instrument panel or in the switch.

☐ The warning lights must illuminate in accordance with the manufacturer's design. For most vehicles, the ABS and other warning lights should illuminate when the ignition is switched on, and (if the system is operating properly) extinguish after a few seconds. Refer to the owner's handbook.

Footbrake

☐ Examine the master cylinder, brake pipes and servo unit for leaks, loose mountings, corrosion or other damage. If ABS is fitted, this unit should also be examined for signs of leaks or corrosion.

☐ The fluid reservoir must be secure and the fluid level must be between the upper (**A**) and lower (**B**) markings.

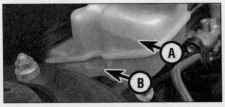

☐ Inspect both front brake flexible hoses for cracks or deterioration of the rubber. Turn the steering from lock to lock, and ensure that the hoses do not contact the wheel, tyre, or any part of the steering or suspension mechanism. With the brake pedal firmly depressed, check the hoses for bulges or leaks under pressure.

Steering and suspension

☐ Have your assistant turn the steering wheel from side to side slightly, up to the point where the steering gear just begins to transmit this movement to the roadwheels. Check for excessive free play between the steering wheel and the steering gear, indicating wear or insecurity of the steering column joints, the column-to-steering gear coupling, or the steering gear itself.

☐ Have your assistant turn the steering wheel more vigorously in each direction, so that the roadwheels just begin to turn. As this is done, examine all the steering joints, linkages, fittings and attachments. Renew any component that shows signs of wear or damage. On vehicles with power steering, check the security and condition of the steering pump, drivebelt and hoses.

☐ Check that the vehicle is standing level, and at approximately the correct ride height.

Shock absorbers

☐ Depress each corner of the vehicle in turn, then release it. The vehicle should rise and then settle in its normal position. If the vehicle continues to rise and fall, the shock absorber is defective. A shock absorber which has seized will also cause the vehicle to fail.

Exhaust system

☐ Start the engine. With your assistant holding a rag over the tailpipe, check the entire system for leaks. Repair or renew leaking sections.

3 Checks carried out **WITH THE VEHICLE RAISED AND THE WHEELS FREE TO TURN**

Jack up the front and rear of the vehicle, and securely support it on axle stands. Position the stands clear of the suspension assemblies. Ensure that the wheels are clear of the ground and that the steering can be turned from lock to lock.

Steering mechanism

☐ Have your assistant turn the steering from lock to lock. Check that the steering turns smoothly, and that no part of the steering mechanism, including a wheel or tyre, fouls any brake hose or pipe or any part of the body structure.
☐ Examine the steering rack rubber gaiters for damage or insecurity of the retaining clips. If power steering is fitted, check for signs of damage or leakage of the fluid hoses, pipes or connections. Also check for excessive stiffness or binding of the steering, a missing split pin or locking device, or severe corrosion of the body structure within 30 cm of any steering component attachment point.

Front and rear suspension and wheel bearings

☐ Starting at the front right-hand side, grasp the roadwheel at the 3 o'clock and 9 o'clock positions and rock gently but firmly. Check for free play or insecurity at the wheel bearings, suspension balljoints, or suspension mount-ings, pivots and attachments.
☐ Now grasp the wheel at the 12 o'clock and 6 o'clock positions and repeat the previous inspection. Spin the wheel, and check for roughness or tightness of the front wheel bearing.

☐ If excess free play is suspected at a component pivot point, this can be confirmed by using a large screwdriver or similar tool and levering between the mounting and the component attachment. This will confirm whether the wear is in the pivot bush, its retaining bolt, or in the mounting itself (the bolt holes can often become elongated).

☐ Carry out all the above checks at the other front wheel, and then at both rear wheels.

Springs and shock absorbers

☐ Examine the suspension struts (when applicable) for serious fluid leakage, corrosion, or damage to the casing. Also check the security of the mounting points.
☐ If coil springs are fitted, check that the spring ends locate in their seats, and that the spring is not corroded, cracked or broken.
☐ If leaf springs are fitted, check that all leaves are intact, that the axle is securely attached to each spring, and that there is no deterioration of the spring eye mountings, bushes, and shackles.

☐ The same general checks apply to vehicles fitted with other suspension types, such as torsion bars, hydraulic displacer units, etc. Ensure that all mountings and attachments are secure, that there are no signs of excessive wear, corrosion or damage, and (on hydraulic types) that there are no fluid leaks or damaged pipes.
☐ Inspect the shock absorbers for signs of serious fluid leakage. Check for wear of the mounting bushes or attachments, or damage to the body of the unit.

Driveshafts (fwd vehicles only)

☐ Rotate each front wheel in turn and inspect the constant velocity joint gaiters for splits or damage. Also check that each driveshaft is straight and undamaged.

Braking system

☐ If possible without dismantling, check brake pad wear and disc condition. Ensure that the friction lining material has not worn excessively, (A) and that the discs are not fractured, pitted, scored or badly worn (B).

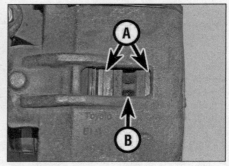

☐ Examine all the rigid brake pipes underneath the vehicle, and the flexible hose(s) at the rear. Look for corrosion, chafing or insecurity of the pipes, and for signs of bulging under pressure, chafing, splits or deterioration of the flexible hoses.
☐ Look for signs of fluid leaks at the brake calipers or on the brake backplates. Repair or renew leaking components.
☐ Slowly spin each wheel, while your assistant depresses and releases the footbrake. Ensure that each brake is operating and does not bind when the pedal is released.

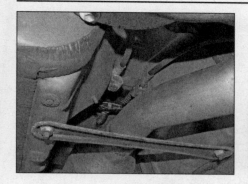

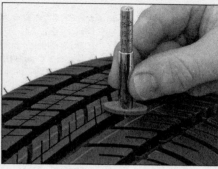

☐ Examine the handbrake mechanism, checking for frayed or broken cables, excessive corrosion, or wear or insecurity of the linkage. Check that the mechanism works on each relevant wheel, and releases fully, without binding.

☐ It is not possible to test brake efficiency without special equipment, but a road test can be carried out later to check that the vehicle pulls up in a straight line.

Fuel and exhaust systems

☐ Inspect the fuel tank (including the filler cap), fuel pipes, hoses and unions. All components must be secure and free from leaks. Locking fuel caps must lock securely and the key must be provided for the MOT test.

☐ Examine the exhaust system over its entire length, checking for any damaged, broken or missing mountings, security of the retaining clamps and rust or corrosion.

Wheels and tyres

☐ Examine the sidewalls and tread area of each tyre in turn. Check for cuts, tears, lumps, bulges, separation of the tread, and exposure of the ply or cord due to wear or damage. Check that the tyre bead is correctly seated on the wheel rim, that the valve is sound and properly seated, and that the wheel is not distorted or damaged.

☐ Check that the tyres are of the correct size for the vehicle, that they are of the same size and type on each axle, and that the pressures are correct.

☐ Check the tyre tread depth. The legal minimum at the time of writing is 1.6 mm over the central three-quarters of the tread width. Abnormal tread wear may indicate incorrect front wheel alignment or wear in steering or suspension components.

☐ If the spare wheel is fitted externally or in a separate carrier beneath the vehicle, check that mountings are secure and free of excessive corrosion.

Body corrosion

☐ Check the condition of the entire vehicle structure for signs of corrosion in load-bearing areas. (These include chassis box sections, side sills, cross-members, pillars, and all suspension, steering, braking system and seat belt mountings and anchorages.) Any corrosion which has seriously reduced the thickness of a load-bearing area (or is within 30 cm of safety-related components such as steering or suspension) is likely to cause the vehicle to fail. In this case professional repairs are likely to be needed.

☐ Damage or corrosion which causes sharp or otherwise dangerous edges to be exposed will also cause the vehicle to fail.

Towbars

☐ Check the condition of mounting points (both beneath the vehicle and within boot/hatchback areas) for signs of corrosion, ensuring that all fixings are secure and not worn or damaged. There must be no excessive play in detachable tow ball arms or quick-release mechanisms.

4 Checks carried out on YOUR VEHICLE'S EXHAUST EMISSION SYSTEM

Petrol models

☐ The engine should be warmed up, and running well (ignition system in good order, air filter element clean, etc).

☐ Before testing, run the engine at around 2500 rpm for 20 seconds. Let the engine drop to idle, and watch for smoke from the exhaust. If the idle speed is too high, or if dense blue or black smoke emerges for more than 5 seconds, the vehicle will fail. Typically, blue smoke signifies oil burning (engine wear); black smoke means unburnt fuel (dirty air cleaner element, or other fuel system fault).

☐ An exhaust gas analyser for measuring carbon monoxide (CO) and hydrocarbons (HC) is now needed. If one cannot be hired or borrowed, have a local garage perform the check.

CO emissions (mixture)

☐ The MOT tester has access to the CO limits for all vehicles. The CO level is measured at idle speed, and at 'fast idle' (2500 to 3000 rpm). The following limits are given as a general guide:

At idle speed – Less than 0.5% CO
At 'fast idle' – Less than 0.3% CO
Lambda reading – 0.97 to 1.03

☐ If the CO level is too high, this may point to poor maintenance, a fuel injection system problem, faulty lambda (oxygen) sensor or catalytic converter. Try an injector cleaning treatment, and check the vehicle's ECU for fault codes.

HC emissions

☐ The MOT tester has access to HC limits for all vehicles. The HC level is measured at 'fast idle' (2500 to 3000 rpm). The following limits are given as a general guide:

At 'fast idle' – Less then 200 ppm

☐ Excessive HC emissions are typically caused by oil being burnt (worn engine), or by a blocked crankcase ventilation system ('breather'). If the engine oil is old and thin, an oil change may help. If the engine is running badly, check the vehicle's ECU for fault codes.

Diesel models

☐ The only emission test for diesel engines is measuring exhaust smoke density, using a calibrated smoke meter. The test involves accelerating the engine at least 3 times to its maximum unloaded speed.

Note: *On engines with a timing belt, it is VITAL that the belt is in good condition before the test is carried out.*

☐ With the engine warmed up, it is first purged by running at around 2500 rpm for 20 seconds. A governor check is then carried out, by slowly accelerating the engine to its maximum speed. After this, the smoke meter is connected, and the engine is accelerated quickly to maximum speed three times. If the smoke density is less than the limits given below, the vehicle will pass:

Non-turbo vehicles: 2.5m-1
Turbocharged vehicles: 3.0m-1

☐ If excess smoke is produced, try fitting a new air cleaner element, or using an injector cleaning treatment. If the engine is running badly, where applicable, check the vehicle's ECU for fault codes. Also check the vehicle's EGR system, where applicable. At high mileages, the injectors may require professional attention.

Engine

- [ ] Engine fails to rotate when attempting to start
- [ ] Engine rotates, but will not start
- [ ] Engine difficult to start when cold
- [ ] Engine difficult to start when hot
- [ ] Starter motor noisy or excessively-rough in engagement
- [ ] Engine starts, but stops immediately
- [ ] Engine idles erratically
- [ ] Engine misfires at idle speed
- [ ] Engine misfires throughout the driving speed range
- [ ] Engine hesitates on acceleration
- [ ] Engine stalls
- [ ] Engine lacks power
- [ ] Engine backfires
- [ ] Oil pressure warning light illuminated with engine running
- [ ] Engine runs-on after switching off
- [ ] Engine noises

Cooling system

- [ ] Overheating
- [ ] Overcooling
- [ ] External coolant leakage
- [ ] Internal coolant leakage
- [ ] Corrosion

Fuel and exhaust systems

- [ ] Excessive fuel consumption
- [ ] Fuel leakage and/or fuel odour
- [ ] Excessive noise or fumes from exhaust system

Clutch

- [ ] Pedal travels to floor – no pressure or very little resistance
- [ ] Clutch fails to disengage (unable to select gears)
- [ ] Clutch slips (engine speed increases, with no increase in vehicle speed)
- [ ] Judder as clutch is engaged
- [ ] Noise when depressing or releasing clutch pedal

Manual transmission

- [ ] Noisy in neutral with engine running
- [ ] Noisy in one particular gear
- [ ] Difficulty engaging gears
- [ ] Jumps out of gear
- [ ] Vibration
- [ ] Lubricant leaks

Automatic transmission

- [ ] Fluid leakage
- [ ] Transmission fluid brown, or has burned smell
- [ ] General gear selection problems
- [ ] Transmission will not downshift (kickdown) with accelerator pedal fully depressed
- [ ] Engine will not start in any gear, or starts in gears other than Park or Neutral
- [ ] Transmission slips, shifts roughly, is noisy, or has no drive in forward or reverse gears

Braking system

- [ ] Vehicle pulls to one side under braking
- [ ] Noise (grinding or high-pitched squeal) when brakes applied
- [ ] Excessive brake pedal travel
- [ ] Brake pedal feels spongy when depressed
- [ ] Excessive brake pedal effort required to stop vehicle
- [ ] Judder felt through brake pedal or steering wheel when braking
- [ ] Brakes binding
- [ ] Rear wheels locking under normal braking

Suspension and steering

- [ ] Vehicle pulls to one side
- [ ] Wheel wobble and vibration
- [ ] Excessive pitching and/or rolling around corners, or during braking
- [ ] Wandering or general instability
- [ ] Excessively-stiff steering
- [ ] Excessive play in steering
- [ ] Lack of power assistance
- [ ] Tyre wear excessive

Electrical system

- [ ] Battery will not hold a charge for more than a few days
- [ ] Ignition/no-charge warning light remains illuminated with engine running
- [ ] Ignition/no-charge warning light fails to come on
- [ ] Lights inoperative
- [ ] Instrument readings inaccurate or erratic
- [ ] Horn inoperative, or unsatisfactory in operation
- [ ] Windscreen wipers inoperative, or unsatisfactory in operation
- [ ] Windscreen washers inoperative, or unsatisfactory in operation
- [ ] Electric windows inoperative, or unsatisfactory in operation
- [ ] Central locking system inoperative, or unsatisfactory in operation

Introduction

The vehicle owner who does his or her own maintenance according to the recommended service schedules should not have to use this section of the manual very often. Modern component reliability is such that, provided those items subject to wear or deterioration are inspected or renewed at the specified intervals, sudden failure is comparatively rare. Faults do not usually just happen as a result of sudden failure, but develop over a period of time. Major mechanical failures in particular are usually preceded by characteristic symptoms over hundreds or even thousands of miles. Those components which do occasionally fail without warning are often small and easily carried in the vehicle.

With any fault finding, the first step is to decide where to begin investigations. Sometimes this is obvious, but on other occasions, a little detective work will be necessary. The owner who makes half a dozen haphazard adjustments or replacements may be successful in curing a fault (or its symptoms), but will be none the wiser if the fault recurs, and ultimately may have spent more time and money than was necessary. A calm and logical approach will be found to be more satisfactory in the long run. Always take into account any warning signs or abnormalities that may have been noticed in the period preceding the fault – power loss, high or low gauge readings, unusual smells, etc – and remember that failure of components such as fuses or spark plugs may only be pointers to some underlying fault.

The pages which follow provide an easy-reference guide to the more common problems which may occur during the operation of the vehicle. These problems and their possible causes are grouped under headings denoting various components or systems, such as Engine, Cooling system, etc. The Chapter and/or Section which deals with the problem is also shown in brackets. Whatever the fault, certain basic principles apply. These are as follows:

Verify the fault. This is simply a matter of being sure that you know what the symptoms are before starting work. This is particularly important if you are investigating a fault for someone else, who may not have described it very accurately.

Don't overlook the obvious. For example, if the vehicle won't start, is there fuel in the tank? (Don't take anyone else's word on this particular point, and don't trust the fuel gauge either). If an electrical fault is indicated, look for loose or broken wires before digging out the test gear.

Cure the disease, not the symptom. Substituting a flat battery with a fully-charged one will get you off the hard shoulder, but if the underlying cause is not attended to, the new battery will go the same way. Similarly, changing oil-fouled spark plugs for a new set will get you moving again, but remember that

the reason for the fouling (if it wasn't simply an incorrect grade of plug) will have to be established and corrected.

Don't take anything for granted. Particularly, don't forget that a 'new' component may itself be defective (especially if it's been rattling around in the boot for months), and don't leave components out of a fault diagnosis sequence just because they are new or recently-fitted. When you do finally diagnose a difficult fault, you'll probably realise that all the evidence was there from the start.

Consider what work, if any, has recently been carried out. Many faults arise through careless or hurried work. For instance, if any work has been performed under the bonnet, could some of the wiring have been dislodged or incorrectly routed, or a hose trapped? Have all the fasteners been properly tightened? Were new, genuine parts and new gaskets used? There is often a certain amount of detective work to be done in this case, as an apparently-unrelated task can have far-reaching consequences.

Engine

Engine fails to rotate when attempting to start

- ☐ Battery terminal connections loose or corroded (see *Weekly checks*)
- ☐ Battery discharged or faulty (Chapter 5A)
- ☐ Broken, loose or disconnected wiring in the starting circuit (Chapter 5A)
- ☐ Defective starter solenoid or ignition switch (Chapter 5A or Chapter 12)
- ☐ Defective starter motor (Chapter 5A)
- ☐ Starter pinion or flywheel ring gear teeth loose or broken (Chapter 2A, Chapter 2B, Chapter 2C or Chapter 5A)
- ☐ Engine earth strap broken or disconnected (Chapter 12)
- ☐ Engine suffering 'hydraulic lock' (eg, from water ingested after traversing flooded roads, or from a serious internal coolant leak) – consult a MINI dealer or specialist for advice
- ☐ Automatic transmission not in position P or N (Chapter 7B)

Engine rotates, but will not start

- ☐ Fuel tank empty
- ☐ Battery discharged (engine rotates slowly) (Chapter 5A)
- ☐ Battery terminal connections loose or corroded (see *Weekly checks*)
- ☐ Ignition components damp or damaged – petrol models (Chapter 1A or 5B)
- ☐ Immobiliser fault, or 'uncoded' ignition key being used (Chapter 12 or *Roadside repairs*)
- ☐ Crankshaft sensor fault (Chapter 4A or 4B)
- ☐ Broken, loose or disconnected wiring in the ignition circuit – petrol models (Chapter 1A or 5B)
- ☐ Worn, faulty or incorrectly-gapped spark plugs – petrol models (Chapter 1A)
- ☐ Preheating system faulty – diesel models (Chapter 5C)
- ☐ Fuel injection system fault (Chapter 4A or 4B)
- ☐ Air in fuel system – diesel models (Chapter 4B)
- ☐ Major mechanical failure (eg, timing chain snapped) (Chapter 2A, 2B, 2C or 2D)

Engine difficult to start when cold

- ☐ Battery discharged (Chapter 5A)
- ☐ Battery terminal connections loose or corroded (see *Weekly checks*)
- ☐ Worn, faulty or incorrectly-gapped spark plugs – petrol models (Chapter 1A)
- ☐ Other ignition system fault – petrol models (Chapter 1A or 5B)
- ☐ Preheating system faulty – diesel models (Chapter 5C)
- ☐ Fuel injection system fault (Chapter 4A or 4B)
- ☐ Wrong grade of engine oil used (*Weekly checks*, Chapter 1A or 1B)
- ☐ Low cylinder compression (Chapter 2A, 2B or 2C)

Engine difficult to start when hot

- ☐ Air filter element dirty or clogged (Chapter 1A or 1B)
- ☐ Fuel injection system fault (Chapter 4A or 4B)
- ☐ Low cylinder compression (Chapter 2A, 2B or 2C)

Starter motor noisy or excessively-rough in engagement

- ☐ Starter pinion or flywheel ring gear teeth loose or broken (Chapter 2A, 2B, 2C or 5A)
- ☐ Starter motor mounting bolts loose or missing (Chapter 5A)
- ☐ Starter motor internal components worn or damaged (Chapter 5A)

Engine starts, but stops immediately

- ☐ Loose or faulty electrical connections in the ignition circuit – petrol models (Chapter 1A or 5B)
- ☐ Vacuum leak at the throttle body or intake manifold – petrol models (Chapter 4A)
- ☐ Blocked injectors/fuel injection system fault (Chapter 4A or 4B)
- ☐ Air in fuel, possibly due to loose fuel line connection – diesel models (Chapter 4B)

Engine idles erratically

- ☐ Air filter element clogged (Chapter 1A or 1B)
- ☐ Vacuum leak at the throttle body, intake manifold or associated hoses – petrol models (Chapter 4A)
- ☐ Worn, faulty or incorrectly-gapped spark plugs – petrol models (Chapter 1A)
- ☐ Uneven or low cylinder compression (Chapter 2A, 2B or 2C)
- ☐ Camshaft lobes worn (Chapter 2A, 2B or 2C)
- ☐ Blocked injectors/fuel injection system fault (Chapter 4A or 4B)
- ☐ Air in fuel, possibly due to loose fuel line connection – diesel models (Chapter 4B)

Engine misfires at idle speed

- ☐ Worn, faulty or incorrectly-gapped spark plugs – petrol models (Chapter 1A)
- ☐ Vacuum leak at the throttle body, intake manifold or associated hoses – petrol models (Chapter 4A)
- ☐ Blocked injectors/fuel injection system fault (Chapter 4A or 4B)
- ☐ Faulty injector(s) – diesel models (Chapter 4B)
- ☐ Uneven or low cylinder compression (Chapter 2A, 2B or 2C)
- ☐ Disconnected, leaking, or perished crankcase ventilation hoses (Chapter 4C)

Engine (continued)

Engine misfires throughout the driving speed range

- [ ] Fuel filter choked (Chapter 1B)
- [ ] Fuel pump faulty, or delivery pressure low – (Chapter 4A or 4B)
- [ ] Fuel tank vent blocked, or fuel pipes restricted (Chapter 4A or 4B)
- [ ] Vacuum leak at the throttle body, intake manifold or associated hoses – petrol models (Chapter 4A)
- [ ] Worn, faulty or incorrectly-gapped spark plugs – petrol models (Chapter 1A)
- [ ] Faulty injector(s) – diesel models (Chapter 4B)
- [ ] Faulty ignition coils – petrol models (Chapter 5B)
- [ ] Uneven or low cylinder compression (Chapter 2A, 2B or 2C)
- [ ] Blocked injector/fuel injection system fault (Chapter 4A or 4B)
- [ ] Blocked catalytic converter/particulate filter (Chapter 4C)
- [ ] Engine overheating (Chapter 3)
- [ ] Fuel tank level low – (Chapter 4A or 4B)

Engine hesitates on acceleration

- [ ] Worn, faulty or incorrectly-gapped spark plugs – petrol models (Chapter 1A)
- [ ] Vacuum leak at the throttle body, intake manifold or associated hoses – petrol models (Chapter 4A)
- [ ] Blocked injectors/fuel injection system fault (Chapter 4A or 4B)
- [ ] Faulty injector(s) – diesel models (Chapter 4B)
- [ ] Faulty clutch pedal switch (Chapter 6)

Engine stalls

- [ ] Vacuum leak at the throttle body, intake manifold or associated hoses – petrol models (Chapter 4A)
- [ ] Fuel filter choked (Chapter 1B)
- [ ] Fuel pump faulty, or delivery pressure low (Chapter 4A or 4B)
- [ ] Fuel tank vent blocked, or fuel pipes restricted (Chapter 4A or 4B)
- [ ] Blocked injectors/fuel injection system fault (Chapter 4A or 4B)
- [ ] Faulty injector(s) – diesel models (Chapter 4B)

Engine lacks power

- [ ] Air filter element blocked (Chapter 1A or 1B)
- [ ] Fuel filter choked (Chapter or 1B)
- [ ] Fuel pipes blocked or restricted (Chapter 4A or 4B)
- [ ] Worn, faulty or incorrectly-gapped spark plugs – petrol models (Chapter 1A)
- [ ] Engine overheating (Chapter 3)
- [ ] Fuel tank level low – diesel models (Chapter 4B)
- [ ] Accelerator position sensor faulty (Chapter 4A or 4B)
- [ ] Vacuum leak at the throttle body, intake manifold or associated hoses – petrol models (Chapter 4A)
- [ ] Blocked injectors/fuel injection system fault (Chapter 4A or 4B)
- [ ] Faulty injector(s) – diesel models (Chapter 4B)
- [ ] Fuel pump faulty, or delivery pressure low – petrol models (Chapter 4A)
- [ ] Uneven or low cylinder compression (Chapter 2A, 2B or 2C)
- [ ] Blocked catalytic converter or particulate filter (Chapter 4C)
- [ ] Brakes binding (Chapter 1A, 1B or 9)
- [ ] Clutch slipping (Chapter 6)
- [ ] Turbocharger fault (Chapter 4)

Engine backfires

- [ ] Vacuum leak at the throttle body, intake manifold or associated hoses – petrol models (Chapter 4A)
- [ ] Blocked injectors/fuel injection system fault (Chapter 4A or 4B)
- [ ] Blocked catalytic converter or particulate filter (Chapter 4C)
- [ ] Ignition coil unit faulty – petrol models (Chapter 5B)

Oil pressure warning light illuminated with engine running

- [ ] Low oil level, or incorrect oil grade (see *Weekly checks*)
- [ ] Faulty oil pressure sensor, or wiring damaged (Chapter 12)
- [ ] Worn engine bearings and/or oil pump (Chapter 2A, 2B, 2C, or 2D)
- [ ] High engine operating temperature (Chapter 3)
- [ ] Oil pump pressure relief valve defective (Chapter 2A, 2B or 2C)
- [ ] Oil pump pick-up strainer clogged (Chapter 2A, 2B or 2C)

Engine runs-on after switching off

- [ ] Excessive carbon build-up in engine (Chapter 2A, 2B, 2C, or 2D)
- [ ] High engine operating temperature (Chapter 3)
- [ ] Fuel injection system fault (Chapter 4A or Chapter 4B)

Engine noises

Pre-ignition (pinking) or knocking during acceleration or under load

- [ ] Ignition timing incorrect/ignition system fault – petrol models (Chapter 1A or 5B)
- [ ] Incorrect grade of spark plug – petrol models (Chapter 1A)
- [ ] Incorrect grade of fuel (Chapter 4A)
- [ ] Knock sensor faulty – petrol models (Chapter 4A)
- [ ] Vacuum leak at the throttle body, intake manifold or associated hoses – petrol models (Chapter 4A)
- [ ] Excessive carbon build-up in engine (Chapter 2A, 2B, 2C, or 2D)
- [ ] Blocked injector/fuel injection system fault (Chapter 4A or 4B)
- [ ] Faulty injector(s) – diesel models (Chapter 4B)

Whistling or wheezing noises

- [ ] Leaking intake manifold or throttle body gasket – petrol models (Chapter 4A)
- [ ] Leaking exhaust manifold gasket or pipe-to-manifold joint (Chapter 4A or 4B)
- [ ] Leaking vacuum hose (Chapter 4A, 4B, 5B or 9)
- [ ] Blowing cylinder head gasket (Chapter 2A, 2B, 2C, or 2D)
- [ ] Partially blocked or leaking crankcase ventilation system (Chapter 4C)
- [ ] Leaking air/turbocharger/intercooler ducts (Chapter 4A or 4B)

Tapping or rattling noises

- [ ] Worn valve gear or camshaft (Chapter 2A, 2B, 2C, or 2D)
- [ ] Ancillary component fault (coolant pump, alternator, etc) (Chapter 3, 5A, etc)

Knocking or thumping noises

- [ ] Worn big-end bearings (regular heavy knocking, perhaps less under load) (Chapter 2D)
- [ ] Worn main bearings (rumbling and knocking, perhaps worsening under load) (Chapter 2D)
- [ ] Piston slap – most noticeable when cold, caused by piston/bore wear (Chapter 2D)
- [ ] Ancillary component fault (coolant pump, alternator, etc) (Chapter 3, 5A, etc)
- [ ] Engine mountings worn or defective (Chapter 2A, Chapter 2B or Chapter 2C)
- [ ] Front suspension or steering components worn (Chapter 10)

Cooling system

Overheating

- ☐ Insufficient coolant in system (see *Weekly checks*)
- ☐ Thermostat faulty (Chapter 3)
- ☐ Radiator core blocked, or grille restricted (Chapter 3)
- ☐ Cooling fan faulty (Chapter 3)
- ☐ Inaccurate coolant temperature sender (Chapter 3)
- ☐ Airlock in cooling system (Chapter 3)
- ☐ Expansion tank pressure cap faulty (Chapter 3)
- ☐ Engine management system fault (Chapter 4A or 4B)
- ☐ Coolant pump failure (Chapter 3)

Overcooling

- ☐ Thermostat faulty (Chapter 3)
- ☐ Inaccurate coolant temperature sender (Chapter 3)
- ☐ Cooling fan faulty (Chapter 3)
- ☐ Engine management system fault (Chapter 4A or 4B)

External coolant leakage

- ☐ Deteriorated or damaged hoses or hose clips (Chapter 1A or 1B)
- ☐ Radiator core or heater matrix leaking (Chapter 3)
- ☐ Expansion tank pressure cap faulty (Chapter 1A or 1B)
- ☐ Coolant pump internal seal leaking (Chapter 3)
- ☐ Coolant pump gasket leaking (Chapter 3)
- ☐ Boiling due to overheating (Chapter 3)
- ☐ Cylinder block core plug leaking (Chapter 2D)

Internal coolant leakage

- ☐ Leaking cylinder head gasket (Chapter 2A, 2B, 2C, or 2D)
- ☐ Cracked cylinder head or cylinder block (Chapter 2D)

Corrosion

- ☐ Infrequent draining and flushing (Chapter 1A or 1B)
- ☐ Incorrect coolant mixture or inappropriate coolant type (see *Weekly checks*)

Fuel and exhaust systems

Excessive fuel consumption

- ☐ Air filter element dirty or clogged (Chapter 1A or 1B)
- ☐ Fuel injection system fault (Chapter 4A or 4B)
- ☐ Engine management system fault (Chapter 4A or 4B)
- ☐ Crankcase ventilation system blocked (Chapter 4C)
- ☐ Tyres under-inflated (see *Weekly checks*)
- ☐ Brakes binding (Chapter 1A, 1B or 9)
- ☐ Fuel leak, causing apparent high consumption (Chapter 1A, 1B, 4A or 4B)

Fuel leakage and/or fuel odour

- ☐ Damaged or corroded fuel tank, pipes or connections (Chapter 4A or 4B)
- ☐ Evaporative emissions system fault – petrol models (Chapter 4C)

Excessive noise or fumes from exhaust system

- ☐ Leaking exhaust system or manifold joints (Chapter 1A, 1B, 4A or 4B)
- ☐ Leaking, corroded or damaged silencers or pipe (Chapter 1A, 1B, 4A or 4B)
- ☐ Broken mountings causing body or suspension contact (Chapter 1A or 1B)

Clutch

Pedal travels to floor – no pressure or very little resistance

- ☐ Air in hydraulic system/faulty master or slave cylinder (Chapter 6)
- ☐ Faulty hydraulic release system (Chapter 6)
- ☐ Clutch pedal return spring detached or broken (Chapter 6)
- ☐ Broken clutch release bearing or fork (Chapter 6)
- ☐ Broken diaphragm spring in clutch pressure plate (Chapter 6)

Clutch fails to disengage (unable to select gears)

- ☐ Air in hydraulic system/faulty master or slave cylinder (Chapter 6)
- ☐ Faulty hydraulic release system (Chapter 6)
- ☐ Clutch disc sticking on transmission input shaft splines (Chapter 6)
- ☐ Clutch disc sticking to flywheel or pressure plate (Chapter 6)
- ☐ Faulty pressure plate assembly (Chapter 6)
- ☐ Clutch release mechanism worn or incorrectly assembled (Chapter 6)

Clutch slips (engine speed increases, with no increase in vehicle speed)

- ☐ Faulty hydraulic release system (Chapter 6)
- ☐ Clutch disc linings excessively worn (Chapter 6)
- ☐ Clutch disc linings contaminated with oil or grease (Chapter 6)
- ☐ Faulty pressure plate or weak diaphragm spring (Chapter 6)

Judder as clutch is engaged

- ☐ Clutch disc linings contaminated with oil or grease (Chapter 6)
- ☐ Clutch disc linings excessively worn (Chapter 6)
- ☐ Faulty or distorted pressure plate or diaphragm spring (Chapter 6).
- ☐ Worn or loose engine or transmission mountings (Chapter 2A, Chapter 2B or Chapter 2C)
- ☐ Clutch disc hub or transmission input shaft splines worn (Chapter 6)

Noise when depressing or releasing clutch pedal

- ☐ Worn clutch release bearing (Chapter 6)
- ☐ Worn or dry clutch pedal bushes (Chapter 6)
- ☐ Worn or dry clutch master cylinder piston (Chapter 6)
- ☐ Faulty pressure plate assembly (Chapter 6)
- ☐ Pressure plate diaphragm spring broken (Chapter 6)
- ☐ Broken clutch disc cushioning springs (Chapter 6)

Manual transmission

Noisy in neutral with engine running

- ☐ Lack of oil (Chapter 7A)
- ☐ Input shaft bearings worn (noise apparent with clutch pedal released, but not when depressed) (Chapter 7A)*
- ☐ Clutch release bearing worn (noise apparent with clutch pedal depressed, possibly less when released) (Chapter 6)

Noisy in one particular gear

- ☐ Worn, damaged or chipped gear teeth (Chapter 7A)*

Difficulty engaging gears

- ☐ Clutch fault (Chapter 6)
- ☐ Worn or damaged gearchange cables (Chapter 7A)
- ☐ Lack of oil (Chapter 7A)
- ☐ Worn synchroniser units (Chapter 7A)*

Jumps out of gear

- ☐ Worn or damaged gearchange cables (Chapter 7A)
- ☐ Worn synchroniser units (Chapter 7A)*
- ☐ Worn selector forks (Chapter 7A)*

Vibration

- ☐ Lack of oil (Chapter 7A)
- ☐ Worn bearings (Chapter 7A)*

Lubricant leaks

- ☐ Leaking driveshaft or selector shaft oil seal (Chapter 7A)
- ☐ Leaking housing joint (Chapter 7A)*
- ☐ Leaking input shaft oil seal (Chapter 7A)*

Although the corrective action necessary to remedy the symptoms described is beyond the scope of the home mechanic, the above information should be helpful in isolating the cause of the condition, so that the owner can communicate clearly with a professional mechanic.

Automatic transmission

Note: *Due to the complexity of the automatic transmission, it is difficult for the home mechanic to properly diagnose and service this unit. For problems other than the following, the vehicle should be taken to a dealer service department or automatic transmission specialist. Do not be too hasty in removing the transmission if a fault is suspected, as most of the testing is carried out with the unit still fitted. Remember that, besides the sensors specific to the transmission, many of the engine management system sensors described in Chapter 4 are essential to the correct operation of the transmission.*

Fluid leakage

- ☐ Automatic transmission fluid is usually brown in colour. Fluid leaks should not be confused with engine oil, which can easily be blown onto the transmission by airflow.
- ☐ To determine the source of a leak, first remove all built-up dirt and grime from the transmission housing and surrounding areas using a degreasing agent, or by steam-cleaning. Drive the vehicle at low speed, so airflow will not blow the leak far from its source. Raise and support the vehicle, and determine where the leak is coming from. The following are common areas of leakage:
  - a) Fluid pan
  - b) Drain or filler plugs.
  - c) Transmission-to-fluid cooler unions (Chapter 7B)

Transmission fluid has burned smell

- ☐ Transmission fluid level low (Chapter 7B)

General gear selection problems

- ☐ Chapter 7B deals with checking the selector cable on automatic

transmissions. The following are common problems which may be caused by a faulty cable or sensor:

- a) *Engine starting in gears other than Park or Neutral.*
- b) *Indicator panel indicating a gear other than the one actually being used.*
- c) *Vehicle moves when in Park or Neutral.*
- d) *Poor gear shift quality or erratic gear changes.*

Transmission will not downshift (kickdown) with accelerator pedal fully depressed

- ☐ Low transmission fluid level (Chapter 7B)
- ☐ Engine management system fault (Chapter 4A or Chapter 4B)
- ☐ Faulty transmission sensor or wiring (Chapter 7B)
- ☐ Faulty selector cable (Chapter 7B)

Engine will not start in any gear, or starts in gears other than Park or Neutral

- ☐ Faulty transmission sensor or wiring (Chapter 7B)
- ☐ Engine management system fault (Chapter 4A or Chapter 4B)
- ☐ Faulty selector cable (Chapter 7B)

Transmission slips, shifts roughly, is noisy, or has no drive in forward or reverse gears

- ☐ Transmission fluid level low (Chapter 7B)
- ☐ Faulty transmission sensor or wiring (Chapter 7B)
- ☐ Engine management system fault (Chapter 4A or Chapter 4B)

Note: *There are many probable causes for the above problems, but diagnosing and correcting them is considered beyond the scope of this manual. Having checked the fluid level and all the wiring as far as possible, a dealer or transmission specialist should be consulted if the problem persists.*

Braking system

Note: *Before assuming that a brake problem exists, make sure that the tyres are in good condition and correctly inflated, that the front wheel alignment is correct, and that the vehicle is not loaded with weight in an unequal manner. Apart from checking the condition of all pipe and hose connections, any faults occurring on the anti-lock braking system should be referred to a MINI dealer or specialist for diagnosis.*

Vehicle pulls to one side under braking

☐ Worn, defective, damaged or contaminated brake pads on one side (Chapter 1A, 1B or 9)
☐ Seized or partially-seized brake caliper piston (Chapter 1A, 1B or 9)
☐ A mixture of brake pad lining materials fitted between sides (Chapter 1A, 1B or 9)
☐ Brake caliper mounting bolts loose (Chapter 9)
☐ Worn or damaged steering or suspension components (Chapter 1A, 1B or 10)

Noise (grinding or high-pitched squeal) when brakes applied

☐ Brake pad friction lining material worn down to metal backing (Chapter 1A, 1B or 9)
☐ Excessive corrosion of brake disc (may be apparent after the vehicle has been standing for some time (Chapter 1A, 1B or 9)
☐ Foreign object (stone chipping, etc) trapped between brake disc and shield (Chapter 1A, 1B or 9)

Excessive brake pedal travel

☐ Faulty master cylinder (Chapter 9)
☐ Air in hydraulic system (Chapter 1A, 1B, 6 or 9)
☐ Faulty vacuum servo unit (Chapter 9)

Brake pedal feels spongy when depressed

☐ Air in hydraulic system (Chapter 1A, 1B, 6 or 9)
☐ Deteriorated flexible rubber brake hoses (Chapter 1A, 1B or 9)

☐ Master cylinder mounting nuts loose (Chapter 9)
☐ Faulty master cylinder (Chapter 9)

Excessive brake pedal effort required to stop vehicle

☐ Faulty vacuum servo unit (Chapter 9)
☐ Faulty vacuum pump – diesel models (Chapter 9)
☐ Disconnected, damaged or insecure brake servo vacuum hose (Chapter 9)
☐ Primary or secondary hydraulic circuit failure (Chapter 9)
☐ Seized brake caliper piston (Chapter 9)
☐ Brake pads incorrectly fitted (Chapter 9)
☐ Incorrect grade of brake pads fitted (Chapter 9)
☐ Brake pad linings contaminated (Chapter 1A, 1B or 9)

Judder felt through brake pedal or steering wheel when braking

Note: *Under heavy braking on models equipped with ABS, vibration may be felt through the brake pedal. This is a normal feature of ABS operation, and does not constitute a fault.*

☐ Excessive run-out or distortion of discs (Chapter 1A, 1B or 9)
☐ Brake pad linings worn (Chapter 1A, 1B or 9)
☐ Brake caliper mounting bolts loose (Chapter 9)
☐ Wear in suspension or steering components or mountings (Chapter 1A, 1B or 10)
☐ Front wheels out of balance (see *Weekly checks*)

Brakes binding

☐ Seized brake caliper piston (Chapter 9)
☐ Incorrectly-adjusted handbrake mechanism (Chapter 9)
☐ Faulty master cylinder (Chapter 9)

Rear wheels locking under normal braking

☐ Rear brake pad linings contaminated or damaged (Chapter 1 or 9)
☐ Rear brake discs warped (Chapter 1A, 1B or 9)

Suspension and steering

Note: *Before diagnosing suspension or steering faults, be sure that the trouble is not due to incorrect tyre pressures, mixtures of tyre types, or binding brakes.*

Vehicle pulls to one side

☐ Defective tyre (see *Weekly checks*)
☐ Excessive wear in suspension or steering components (Chapter 1A, 1B or 10)
☐ Incorrect front wheel alignment (Chapter 10)
☐ Accident damage to steering or suspension components (Chapter 1A or 1B)

Wheel wobble and vibration

☐ Front wheels out of balance (vibration felt mainly through the steering wheel) (see *Weekly checks*)
☐ Rear wheels out of balance (vibration felt throughout the vehicle) (see *Weekly checks*)
☐ Roadwheels damaged or distorted (see *Weekly checks*)
☐ Faulty or damaged tyre (see *Weekly checks*)
☐ Worn steering or suspension joints, bushes or components (Chapter 1A, 1B or 10)
☐ Wheel bolts loose (Chapter 1A or 1B)

Excessive pitching and/or rolling around corners, or during braking

☐ Defective shock absorbers (Chapter 1A, 1B or 10)

☐ Broken or weak spring and/or suspension component (Chapter 1A, 1B or 10)
☐ Worn or damaged anti-roll bar or mountings (Chapter 1A, 1B or 10)

Wandering or general instability

☐ Incorrect front wheel alignment (Chapter 10)
☐ Worn steering or suspension joints, bushes or components (Chapter 1A, 1B or 10)
☐ Roadwheels out of balance (see *Weekly checks*)
☐ Faulty or damaged tyre (see *Weekly checks*)
☐ Wheel bolts loose (Chapter 1A or 1B)
☐ Defective shock absorbers (Chapter 1A, 1B or 10)

Excessively-stiff steering

☐ Seized steering linkage balljoint or suspension balljoint (Chapter 1A, 1B or 10)
☐ Broken or incorrectly-adjusted auxiliary drivebelt (Chapter 1A or 1B)
☐ Incorrect front wheel alignment (Chapter 10)
☐ Steering rack damaged (Chapter 10)

Excessive play in steering

☐ Worn steering column/intermediate shaft joints (Chapter 10)
☐ Worn track rod balljoints (Chapter 1A, 1B or 10)
☐ Worn steering rack (Chapter 10)
☐ Worn steering or suspension joints, bushes or components (Chapter 1A, 1B or 10)

Suspension and steering (continued)

Lack of power assistance

- ☐ Broken or incorrectly-adjusted auxiliary drivebelt (Chapter 1A or 1B)
- ☐ Incorrect power steering fluid level (see *Weekly checks*)
- ☐ Restriction in power steering fluid hoses (Chapter 1A or 1B)
- ☐ Faulty power steering pump (Chapter 10)
- ☐ Faulty steering rack (Chapter 10)

Tyre wear excessive

Tyres worn on inside or outside edges

- ☐ Tyres under-inflated (wear on both edges) (see *Weekly checks*)
- ☐ Incorrect camber or castor angles (wear on one edge only) (Chapter 10)
- ☐ Worn steering or suspension joints, bushes or components (Chapter 1A, 1B or 10)

- ☐ Excessively-hard cornering or braking
- ☐ Accident damage

Tyre treads exhibit feathered edges

- ☐ Incorrect toe-setting (Chapter 10)

Tyres worn in centre of tread

- ☐ Tyres over-inflated (see *Weekly checks*)

Tyres worn on inside and outside edges

- ☐ Tyres under-inflated (see *Weekly checks*)

Tyres worn unevenly

- ☐ Tyres/wheels out of balance (see *Weekly checks*)
- ☐ Excessive wheel or tyre run-out
- ☐ Worn shock absorbers (Chapter 1A, 1B or 10)
- ☐ Faulty tyre (see *Weekly checks*)

Electrical system

Note: *For problems associated with the starting system, refer to the faults listed under 'Engine' earlier in this Section.*

Battery will not hold a charge for more than a few days

- ☐ Battery defective internally (Chapter 5A)
- ☐ Battery terminal connections loose or corroded (see *Weekly checks*)
- ☐ Auxiliary drivebelt worn or incorrectly adjusted (Chapter 1A or 1B)
- ☐ Alternator not charging at correct output (Chapter 5A)
- ☐ Alternator or voltage regulator faulty (Chapter 5A)
- ☐ Short-circuit causing continual battery drain (Chapter 5A or 12)

Ignition/no-charge warning light remains illuminated with engine running

- ☐ Auxiliary drivebelt broken, worn, or incorrectly adjusted (Chapter 1A or 1B)
- ☐ Internal fault in alternator or voltage regulator (Chapter 5A)
- ☐ Broken, disconnected, or loose wiring in charging circuit (Chapter 5A or 12)

Ignition/no-charge warning light fails to come on

- ☐ Broken, disconnected, or loose wiring in warning light circuit (Chapter 5A or 12)
- ☐ Alternator faulty (Chapter 5A)

Lights inoperative

- ☐ Bulb blown (Chapter 12)
- ☐ Corrosion of bulb or bulbholder contacts (Chapter 12)
- ☐ Blown fuse (Chapter 12)
- ☐ Faulty relay (Chapter 12)
- ☐ Broken, loose, or disconnected wiring (Chapter 12)
- ☐ Faulty switch (Chapter 12)

Instrument readings inaccurate or erratic

Fuel or temperature gauges give no reading

- ☐ Faulty gauge sender unit (Chapter 3, 4A or 4B)
- ☐ Wiring open-circuit (Chapter 12)
- ☐ Faulty instrument cluster (Chapter 12)

Fuel or temperature gauges give continuous maximum reading

- ☐ Faulty gauge sender unit (Chapter 3, 4A or 4B)
- ☐ Wiring short-circuit (Chapter 12)
- ☐ Faulty instrument cluster (Chapter 12)

Horn inoperative, or unsatisfactory in operation

Horn operates all the time

- ☐ Horn push either earthed or stuck down (Chapter 12)
- ☐ Horn cable-to-horn push earthed (Chapter 12)

Horn fails to operate

- ☐ Blown fuse (Chapter 12)
- ☐ Cable or connections loose, broken or disconnected (Chapter 12)
- ☐ Faulty horn (Chapter 12)

Horn emits intermittent or unsatisfactory sound

- ☐ Cable connections loose (Chapter 12)
- ☐ Horn mountings loose (Chapter 12)
- ☐ Faulty horn (Chapter 12)

Windscreen wipers inoperative, or unsatisfactory in operation

Wipers fail to operate, or operate very slowly

- ☐ Wiper blades stuck to screen, or linkage seized or binding (Chapter 12)
- ☐ Blown fuse (Chapter 12)
- ☐ Battery discharged (Chapter 5A)
- ☐ Cable or connections loose, broken or disconnected (Chapter 12)
- ☐ Faulty wiper motor (Chapter 12)

Wiper blades sweep over too large or too small an area of the glass

- ☐ Wiper blades incorrectly fitted, or wrong size used (see *Weekly checks*)
- ☐ Wiper arms incorrectly positioned on spindles (Chapter 12)
- ☐ Excessive wear of wiper linkage (Chapter 12)
- ☐ Wiper motor or linkage mountings loose or insecure (Chapter 12)

Wiper blades fail to clean the glass effectively

- ☐ Wiper blade rubbers dirty, worn or perished (see *Weekly checks*)
- ☐ Wiper blades incorrectly fitted, or wrong size used (see *Weekly checks*)
- ☐ Wiper arm tension springs broken, or arm pivots seized (Chapter 12)
- ☐ Insufficient windscreen washer additive to adequately remove road film (see *Weekly checks*)

Electrical system (continued)

Windscreen washers inoperative, or unsatisfactory in operation

One or more washer jets inoperative

☐ Blocked washer jet
☐ Disconnected, kinked or restricted fluid hose (Chapter 12)
☐ Insufficient fluid in washer reservoir (see *Weekly checks*)

Washer pump fails to operate

☐ Broken or disconnected wiring or connections (Chapter 12)
☐ Blown fuse (Chapter 12)
☐ Faulty washer switch (Chapter 12)
☐ Faulty washer pump (Chapter 12)

Washer pump runs for some time before fluid is emitted from jets

☐ Faulty one-way valve in fluid supply hose (Chapter 12)

Electric windows inoperative, or unsatisfactory in operation

Window glass will only move in one direction

☐ Faulty switch (Chapter 12)

Window glass slow to move

☐ Battery discharged (Chapter 5A)
☐ Regulator seized or damaged, or in need of lubrication (Chapter 11)
☐ Door internal components or trim fouling regulator (Chapter 11)
☐ Faulty motor (Chapter 11)

Window glass fails to move

☐ Blown fuse (Chapter 12)
☐ Faulty relay (Chapter 12)
☐ Broken or disconnected wiring or connections (Chapter 12)
☐ Faulty motor (Chapter 11)
☐ Faulty control module (Chapter 11)

Central locking system inoperative, or unsatisfactory in operation

Complete system failure

☐ Remote handset battery discharged, where applicable (Chapter 1)
☐ Blown fuse (Chapter 12)
☐ Defective control module (Chapter 12)
☐ Broken or disconnected wiring or connections (Chapter 12)
☐ Faulty motor (Chapter 11)

Latch locks but will not unlock, or unlocks but will not lock

☐ Remote handset battery discharged, where applicable (Chapter 1)
☐ Faulty master switch (Chapter 12)
☐ Broken or disconnected latch operating rods or levers (Chapter 11)
☐ Faulty control module (Chapter 12)
☐ Faulty motor (Chapter 11)

One solenoid/motor fails to operate

☐ Broken or disconnected wiring or connections (Chapter 12)
☐ Faulty operating assembly (Chapter 11)
☐ Broken, binding or disconnected latch operating rods or levers (Chapter 11)
☐ Fault in door latch (Chapter 11)

Note: *References throughout this index are in the form* "**Chapter number**" • "**Page number**". *So, for example, 2C•15 refers to page 15 of Chapter 2C.*

*Note: References throughout this index are in the form "**Chapter number**" • "**Page number**". So, for example, 2C•15 refers to page 15 of Chapter 2C.*

Note: *References throughout this index are in the form "Chapter number" • "Page number". So, for example, 2C•15 refers to page 15 of Chapter 2C.*

Note: *References throughout this index are in the form* **"Chapter number"** • **"Page number"**. *So, for example, 2C•15 refers to page 15 of Chapter 2C.*

Preserving Our Motoring Heritage

< The Model J Duesenberg Derham Tourster. Only eight of these magnificent cars were ever built – this is the only example to be found outside the United States of America

Almost every car you've ever loved, loathed or desired is gathered under one roof at the Haynes Motor Museum. Over 300 immaculately presented cars and motorbikes represent every aspect of our motoring heritage, from elegant reminders of bygone days, such as the superb Model J Duesenberg to curiosities like the bug-eyed BMW Isetta. There are also many old friends and flames. Perhaps you remember the 1959 Ford Popular that you did your courting in? The magnificent 'Red Collection' is a spectacle of classic sports cars including AC, Alfa Romeo, Austin Healey, Ferrari, Lamborghini, Maserati, MG, Riley, Porsche and Triumph.

A Perfect Day Out

Each and every vehicle at the Haynes Motor Museum has played its part in the history and culture of Motoring. Today, they make a wonderful spectacle and a great day out for all the family. Bring the kids, bring Mum and Dad, but above all bring your camera to capture those golden memories for ever. You will also find an impressive array of motoring memorabilia, a comfortable 70 seat video cinema and one of the most extensive transport book shops in Britain. The Pit Stop Cafe serves everything from a cup of tea to wholesome, home-made meals or, if you prefer, you can enjoy the large picnic area nestled in the beautiful rural surroundings of Somerset.

John Haynes O.B.E., > Founder and Chairman of the museum at the wheel of a Haynes Light 12.

< Graham Hill's Lola Cosworth Formula 1 car next to a 1934 Riley Sports.

The Museum is situated on the A359 Yeovil to Frome road at Sparkford, just off the A303 in Somerset. It is about 40 miles south of Bristol, and 25 minutes drive from the M5 intersection at Taunton.
Open 9.30am - 5.30pm (10.00am - 4.00pm Winter) 7 days a week, *except Christmas Day, Boxing Day and New Years Day*
Special rates available for schools, coach parties and outings Charitable Trust No. 292048

Published in November 2007

A catalogue record for this book is available from the British Library.

ISBN 978 1 84425 452 1

Library of Congress Catalog Card No. 2007931177

Haynes Publishing, Sparkford, Yeovil, Somerset BA22 7JJ, UK

Tel: +44 (0) 1963 442030
Fax: +44 (0) 1963 440001
E-mail: sales@haynes.co.uk
Website: www.haynes.co.uk

Haynes North America, Inc.,
861 Lawrence Drive, Newbury Park,
California 91320, USA

Printed and bound by J.H.Haynes & Co Ltd, Sparkford, Yeovil, Somerset BA22 7JJ, UK

This book is officially licensed by Dorna UK Ltd, commercial rights holder of the British Superbike Championship.

Managing Editor: Louise McIntyre
Design: Carole Bohanan
Sub-editor: Dave Fern
Advertising Sales: David Dew (Motocom)

Author's acknowledgements

Thanks to:

In the pit lane: All the riders, riders' girlfriends and wives, team bosses, technicians, sponsors and PR people (yes, you, Tracie and Mark) in the paddock who put up with me hanging around their pit garages asking the same old stuff week in, week out during the BSB race season. Massive thanks for all your help and for making my life so easy. I said this last year, but truly I can't imagine a better place to work. And, Morgan, do you really call me 'Poison'? Love it man, love it!

In the paddock: Stuart Higgs and his amazingly efficient yet great bunch of MCRCB staff. Dave Fern for all his help in the press office and in subbing this book. Photographers Double Red, Paul Sturman (who still rocks even though he missed the Black Stone Cherry gig – lightweight dude, lightweight), and Paul 'part-time postie pat' Barton. Neil 'Sigma' Spalding for his continued enthusiasm for all things motorcycling, even if he does continue to bang on about bloody slipper clutches. The people at MCN who still manage to keep an old boy like me fired up week in, week out (you know who you are!).

At Haynes: Mark Hughes for trusting me to pull this project off for a second year, Louise McIntyre for organising everything and Carole Bohanan for doing such a bloody brilliant job designing this book yet again.

For my four sons: Joseph the b-baller, lunatic fringe Tyler, plus rockstars Zak and Kel (The Prophesy True – check it out on MySpace!). So proud of all you guys. And to my girlfriend Helen who has helped to keep me sane in this crazy, crazy past year. Love you!

All images supplied by **Double Red**, except for the following:

Paul Barton: page 100

Clive Challinor: pages 95 (bottom), 146/147, 149 (top), 150 (main), 162/163, 166

Martin Heath: Pages 4/5, 90/91

2007
BENNETTS
BRITISH
SUPERBIKES

CONTENTS
BRITISH SUPERBIKE SEASON REVIEW 2007

STUART HIGGS
RACE DIRECTOR, BRITISH SUPERBIKES

WHAT A SHOW!

To say that the 2007 Bennetts British Superbike Championship was a roller-coaster of mixed emotions would be a massive understatement. Keeping the reigns on British Superbikes this year has been one hell of a ride

Optimism was again high last April as the pundits waxed lyrical about the prospect of the best-ever season ahead. Key to this statement was the arrival of the 'young guns' – Leon Camier, Cal Crutchlow and Tom Sykes – and they were to live up to the high expectations set. There was also a welcome return for British Superbikes favourite Chris Walker. These key rider placements alongside the established protagonists set the scene for what promised to be a memorable year.

Pre-season participation levels were again at record numbers across the portfolio of classes, meaning that BSB events would continue to be full to the brim with a highly impressive display.

When the season did get underway, it seemed that the curse of the 2006 weather had been well and truly lifted with glorious events at Brands Hatch and Thruxton. Gregorio Lavilla's display in the first four races was truly masterful but the scrapping pack behind him in those races was the stuff of BSB legend, an incredible show that would surely be any promoter's dream.

As the Championship moved into May, the off-track politics moved up a gear as MCRCB confirmed with the teams and industry the Superbike technical rules for 2008 and beyond. But they weren't quite unanimously accepted as Ducati gave notice of likely issues, a situation that would run for five months. The BSB technical philosophy was clearly flowing into wider areas, the FIM and World Superbikes being on board one minute and going off on their own the next, while the influential Motorcycle Sport Manufacturers Association (MSMA) and, significantly, the American Motorcycle Association (AMA) backed BSB. A carefully worded FIM press release in July suggested the World Superbike Championship would move to more production-based rules by 2010, so maybe the unification of Superbike rules – which would help significantly in economic and sporting areas – still remains a prospect.

Back on track, the summer months proved the most challenging and exhausting of the year. Two separate, desperately tragic accidents claimed the lives of Guy Sanders and Ollie Bridewell, and we all miss their unique personalities. Rider safety is the most important consideration for the MCRCB among the many factors involved in ensuring Britain has a thriving, affordable, motorcycle racing sport. There are many elements involved, including circuit safety, event

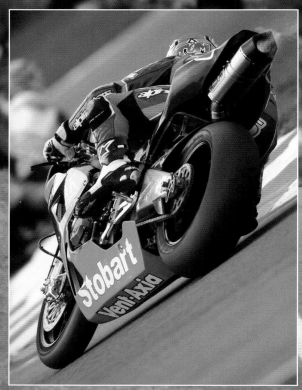

operation safety, machine performance and safety, rider protective clothing and rider technique. In particular circuit safety is continually reviewed and each year safety upgrade changes are made at many circuits as part of the licensing process and continual quest for safety enhancement. Other areas include more technically advanced protective barriers and the highest levels of medical support. In the world of 'Judge and Jury' internet forums, we plot a path by using facts, data and experience – which sadly seems to count for little in ill-informed minds and usually ends up causing more distress.

The appalling 'summer' weather was responsible for causing utter chaos with the events at Knockhill, Mallory Park and Oulton Park, and postponed races were still being placed at the final round at Brands Hatch in October. These situations are pressure enough, but coupled with satisfying the demands of live outside broadcast television takes things to a new level.

Back on track the Championship was drawing to a conclusion but in analysing the season to date it did seem to revolve around which red and white or black and orange bike would win the race. It is always difficult to criticise sporting excellence and domination, and BSB was just going through what football and Formula 1 sees annually.

A deeper investigation brought us back to the tyre debate, which is seemingly the focal point of discussion in many other championships. In canvassing opinion, there was the genuine feeling that for many teams the competition element of the event was over in the first practice session when tyre-allocation choices had been made. Talks of 'pecking orders' prevailed and despite my best attempts to retain open competition to solve the problems, a point had been reached where the greater need of the improvement to the competitive ethos of the Championship was recognised.

The penultimate race of the season at Donington Park marked the start of the 2008 season in anger from the point of view of championship governance, as I'd almost detached myself from outstanding 2007 activities. The key items of business included the 2008 class structure, which aimed to revitalise the event content. Out went the Virgin Media Cup, a five-year success story, to be replaced by a multi-marque, budget-friendly Superstock 600 Championship for riders aged 16 to 25. The National Superstock Cup was also announced to be ceasing, with the world's most radical one-make series coming in instead. The 2008 Yamaha R1 Cup, equipped with 'slick' racing tyres and racing exhausts, was announced and within seven days had attracted 150 expressions of interest from all around the world. These two new series, combined with the flagship existing British and National Championship classes, should

Opposite: BSB 2007: Foreign stars, home-grown heroes, upstart young rookies, factory bikes, awesome racing and glamorous girls.

Whether you were one of the thousands watching it live at the track or among the millions enjoying it on TV, BSB 2007 was one hell of a show

keep TV and trackside audiences entertained as well as providing a logical, budget-sensitive path of progression for riders and teams.

In the same weekend the MCRCB announced that it was pressing ahead with a single-make tyre evaluation, and reaction proved to be very supportive, igniting optimism from teams and riders considering their 2008 options. It blew the rider-transfer market wide open as potential team/tyre company relationships were taken out of play – yet another indicator of the influence of the black, round, rubber things! A decision was expected to be taken in early November, following a tender process, as to who would become the single supplier.

The composition of the 2008 calendar also changes. A more relaxed schedule with no 'back-to-back' race weekends will keep the teams and fans happy, while financial circumstances will mean no trip to the Emerald Isle and as a result the Championship will consist of 12 events.

And so the on-track action came to a conclusion at the venue where it had started six months earlier – Brands Hatch. Everything that is good about British Superbikes was on display on a weekend bathed in sunshine at a race track that sets the standard in facilities and sheer atmosphere. Tears of joy were mixed with tears of relief around the winner's podium, a mark of the pressure that had been endured during the year.

Thoughts quickly turned to 2008 and the technical debate continues to rage in order to ensure that the best teams and riders make the grid. The broader question is also asked, 'How does BSB evolve as a successful sporting property?' Embracing the challenges and opportunities that lie ahead is as daunting as it is exciting. Turning the vision into reality will be the next instalment of BSB.

Enjoy the ride.

HONDA
The Power of Dreams

Champion superbike

Congratulations to Ryuichi Kiyonari on winning his second successive British Superbike championship title on the 14th October 2007. The mighty CBR1000RR Fireblade has given Kiyo and his fellow Honda riders a total of 15 victories from 26 British Superbike races, and it's won eight World Superbike races this season, giving James Toseland and Ten Kate Honda the championship crown. It's also destroyed lap records at the Ulster GP and the Centenary Isle of Man TT this year with Ian Hutchinson and John McGuinness.

Head down to your local Honda dealer today and let the CBR1000RR Fireblade win you over, too.

CBR Fireblade

THE RIDERS

2007 BENNETTS BRITISH SUPERBIKES

BSB 2007 IN FOCUS

All the BSB point scorers summed up in words and numbers, from title-winner Ryuichi Kiyonari, who won nine races and scored 433 points, to the privateers, who scored just one point all season

Incredible! Just like last season, BSB 2007 went to the wire with three riders still in with a shout of the title at the showdown at the final round on the Brands Hatch Indy circuit in October.

Gregorio Lavilla finished the season as he started it, with a race-winning double on the Airwaves Ducati. But Ryuichi Kiyonari secured the title for a second successive season with third and fourth places on the HM Plant Honda after some thrilling racing that typified the 2007 season.

The following pages detail every point-scoring rider in the championship. In addition, there's a tabulated version of the results of all 13 championship rounds plus a look at the Manufacturers' points table as well as the Privateer Cup points.

RYUICHI KIYONARI 1

BORN: 23.09.82
LIVES: Louth
TEAM: HM Plant Honda

To win one BSB title is special. But to win back-to-back BSB titles is something else. Niall Mackenzie was the last rider to achieve that, in 1997, when he won his second of three successive titles.

Ryuichi Kiyonari clinched the 2007 title in the first race of the final round at Brands Hatch. One of only five riders to win races in 2007, he repeated his 2006 achievement by again winning the most races – nine compared to Lavilla's seven, Rea's five, Haslam's four and Byrne's one – to underline once again just how fast he is.

Not only that, but he finished 18 of the 26 races on the podium and only had three DNFs all year, one of them when Cal Crutchlow took him down at Donington. Kiyo's year was one of consistency as well as speed.

After last year's mid-term blip, when the pressure of the impending Suzuki Eight-Hour, got to him and he lost the plot in BSB, this year there was no real sign of weakness.

Kiyo was also more relaxed in 2007 and started to open up to the media. The fans were able to appreciate that this Japanese star isn't just a machine created by HRC but in fact a character in his own right – and a likeable one at that.

But what we also learned was just how hard he worked off the track, as well as on it, in order to secure the title: the countless hours watching DVDs of each race to analyse his faults, walking the tracks with crew chief Adrian Gorst, and the hours spent in the garage when other riders had disappeared back to their motorhomes.

But all the hard work paid off as Kiyo won himself a ride in WSB with Ten Kate Honda, a deal signed with the Dutch team at Croft in the presence of HRC boss Saturo Horiike. If Kiyo gets quickly comfortable with his new bike and new team, the WSB regulars had better watch out.

BH	THR	SILV	OP	Snett	MoP	Kn	OP	MaP	Croft	CP	DP	BH	POINTS
8-5	16-20	25-25	16-25	25-25	11-11	20-16	25-0	25-0	25-25	20-20	0-16	16-13	433

STOPPING POWER

REVOLUTIONARY RCS DESIGN
RATIO CLICK SYSTEM

19mm bore with a dual stroke lever system allowing either 18 or 20mm stroke options complete with folding lever.

HPK – CALIPER & DISC SET

THE RANGE COVERS:
600 / 750 / 1000
Supersport Machines

Aprilia / Ducati / Honda / Kawasaki Suzuki / Triumph / Yamaha

SOLE UK IMPORTER & DISTRIBUTOR

BRAKE COMPONENTS · ORIGINAL EQUIPMENT · CONVERSION · RACING

For further Information Please contact GPR Moto on: T: 08701 600 950 E: sales@gprmoto.com

JONATHAN REA

2

BORN: 02.02.87
LIVES: Ballyclare, Northern Ireland
TEAM: HM Plant Honda

Rea came of age in 2007 when he joined the factory HM Plant Honda team. In 2006 he was fast but inconsistent, largely down to his inexperience. But he adapted very quickly to the Michelin tyres and made good use of his factory bike to become one of BSB's regular front-runners.

He still had the occasional lapse, the most memorable being Mallory, where he refused to back off the throttle and yield to Leon Haslam going into the Bus Stop chicane and crashed.

But otherwise he was fast, winning five races and stepping on the podium 16 times.

His youthful exuberance also shone through in a team not noted for its humour, though he instilled laughter into his side of the garage. His leathers bore the slogan 'The Darkside' – a slap in the face of the critics of the Honda team who slated them for being too focused.

He wasn't afraid to speak out about controversial matters – which occasionally got him a rap across the knuckles by the team management – but he was always engaging and willing to spend time with both media and fans.

He'll be racing for Ten Kate Honda in World Supersport in 2008 and, with the knowledge gained in BSB these past three seasons, shouldn't have a problem becoming a front-runner there.

BH	THR	SILV	OP	Snett	MoP	Kn	OP	MaP	Croft	CP	DP	BH	POINTS
16-20	0-13	20-16	13-11	20-20	13-25	25-25	0-25	20-0	20-20	0-25	11-9	20-20	407

LEON HASLAM

3

BORN: 31.05.83
LIVES: Smalley, Derbyshire
TEAM: Airwaves Ducati

Top Ducati runner in the series and top Dunlop runner. Leon Haslam might take solace from those facts but the truth is he desperately wanted to win the title and will be disappointed to have finished only third.

As in 2006, he was the most consistent finisher, failing to score in just one race all year. He won four races and was on the podium 11 times, and by the end of the year was the hottest property among team managers who would be title contenders in 2008.

But if Haslam was so sought-after come season end and so obviously talented, why didn't he win the title? He came close – and would have been closer still had it not been for a sluggish start to the campaign. But the bottom line was that the Ducati 999 F06 was simply too long in the tooth where it really mattered. No matter how hard Haslam pushed – and he really pushed – the four-cylinder bikes always had the edge on the V-twin on acceleration out of tight corners. Haslam, like Lavilla, spent most of the time playing catch-up on the brakes, although when he did make good starts and had clear track then he was able to take command of a race.

As we went to press it looked likely Haslam would sign for HM Plant Honda, a move that marks him down as a title favourite for the 2008 series.

BH	THR	SILV	OP	Snett	MoP	Kn	OP	MaP	Croft	CP	DP	BH	POINTS
10-13	10-10	10-11	20-20	16-11	25-13	16-20	13-13	16-20	11-10	25-0	25-25	13-11	387

GREGORIO LAVILLA

4

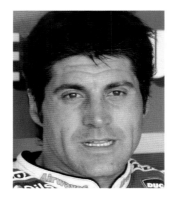

BORN: 29.09.74
LIVES: Narborough and Tarragona
TEAM: Airwaves Ducati

After keeping a low profile and largely being in the shadow of team-mate Leon Haslam's blistering times in pre-season testing, the Spaniard came out guns blazing at the start of the season. He won the first four races, was on the podium at Silverstone and won again at the first Oulton round, but after that his title challenge was blunted by the problems that dogged him in mid-2006: mechanical gremlins and crashes. He bounced back with a series of finishes and recaptured his early-season form with two wins in the final round at Brands. His starts always seemed to hinder him, but his lap times, as ever, were a match for the front-runners. Towards the end of the year he said he wanted to race in WSB again, but then back-tracked and suggested that staying in the UK might not be such a bad way to see out his riding career.

BH	THR	SILV	OP	Snett	MoP	Kn	OP	MaP	Croft	CP	DP	BH	POINTS
25-25	25-25	11-20	25-13	10-0	16-16	9-0	0-6	11-9	10-13	9-16	13-11	25-25	368

SHANE BYRNE

5

BORN: 10.12.76
LIVES: Spain
TEAM: Stobart Vent Axia Motorsport Honda

After being the whipping boy for Rizla Suzuki's lack of success in 2006, Shakey really showed what he could achieve in the right team and on the right bike. And the privateer Stobart Honda team showed what could be achieved with a bike built in-house. Okay, it wasn't perhaps the all-round package of the factory Hondas but it wasn't far away as the charismatic Shakey proved several times, not only when he ran up front but also when he fought his way through from the back. His never-say-die attitude, grit and determination really showed this year. The real high came at Mallory when he gave the team its first win since 2004, but the celebrations were subdued after the tragedy of Friday morning practice when Ollie Bridewell lost his life. But Shakey had other great rides and was on the podium ten times in all.

BH	THR	SILV	OP	Snett	MoP	Kn	OP	MaP	Croft	CP	DP	BH	POINTS
13-3	13-16	0-0	10-16	0-16	20-20	13-11	20-16	25-16	7-9	13-0	16-10	10-0	293

TOM SYKES

6

BORN: 19.08.85
LIVES: Huddersfield
TEAM: Stobart Vent Axia Motorsport Honda

The Grinner had an almost permanent smile on his face throughout his successful rookie season on a superbike. He didn't create any major headlines in pre-season testing but got on with the job of learning how to ride the Stobart Honda and how to set it up. Early season, he continued to plug away with consistent top-six finishes, but as the season wore on he just got faster and faster, finishing on the podium for the first time at Croft where he racked up two third-place finishes. His first BSB victory eluded him but he qualified pole and was battling for lead on more than one occasion, eventually finishing with two second places at Donington. Not only that, his ever-smiling, sometimes goofy, characteristics won him a huge number of fans and his positive approach to the job also won him big praise from team boss Paul Bird. Definitely outstanding in his rookie season.

BH	THR	SILV	OP	Snett	MoP	Kn	OP	MaP	Croft	CP	DP	BH	POINTS
9-11	11-9	9-10	11-10	13-13	0-9	10-13	0-10	10-13	16-16	16-11	20-20	0-9	279

CHRIS WALKER

7

BORN: 25.03.72
LIVES: Nottingham
TEAM: Rizla Suzuki

The Stalker came back to BSB on a hiding to nothing. Shane Byrne had ridden his heart out on the Rizla Suzuki and came away with very little to show for it. Walker did likewise. After seven years away from BSB, it was a tall order. The bike was finicky. He had to adapt from low-grip WSB Pirellis back to super-sticky Dunlops. And he had to relearn the tracks, many of them with subtle changes since his last time in BSB. Walker stuck to his task but copped the same flak as Shakey the previous season when results were hard to come by. His untidy style didn't help in taming the unwieldy Suzuki but he could never be faulted for his 100% effort, both on the bike and off it with the fans. But despite his efforts, Walker was often outpaced and way before the end of the season the writing was on the wall regarding his future with the team.

BH	THR	SILV	OP	Snett	MoP	Kn	OP	MaP	Croft	CP	DP	BH	POINTS
11-8	7-0	16-13	0-7	7-0	7-0	11-10	16-8	13-10	8-6	8-10	10-13	9-10	225

Pts 37

DEAN THOMAS 17

BORN: 04.01.73
LIVES: Wakefield
TEAM: Samsung Suzuki
It was never going to be an easy season running on a limited budget but he showed flashes of his old self, scoring points in several races on what was effectively an ex-Rizla 'bitza' bike.

Pts 31

JAMES HAYDON 18

BORN: 02.11.74
LIVES: Berkhamsted
TEAM: Hawk Kawasaki
Started with Virgin Yamaha but only scored one point before being discarded. Then Hawk Kawasaki signed him late in the year and he was immediately on the pace of other Kawasaki runners.

Pts 28

TOMMY BRIDEWELL 19

BORN: 06.08.88
LIVES: Devizes
TEAM: NB Suzuki
A tough baptism, stepping up from supersport, but he quickly got to grips with it and scored some promising results. Then, of course, brother Ollie sadly lost his life at Mallory.

Pts 27

TRISTAN PALMER 20

BORN: 17.08.82
LIVES: Nuneaton
TEAM: Tena for Men THR Racing
Called in after team owner Michael Howarth broke his leg, Palmer was an immediate hit on the bike, winning both Cup races on his debut at Silverstone en route to that title.

Pts 23

CHRIS MARTIN 21

BORN: 24.01.81
LIVES: York
TEAM: Red Viper Racing
After winning the BSB Cup competition in 2006 (and scoring an impressive 29 points in the BSB series itself), Martin didn't manage to score as many points as in the previous season.

Pts 23

PETER HICKMAN 22

BORN: 08.04.87
LIVES: Alford
TEAM: Hawk Colchester Kawasaki
A traumatic season after such a promising 2006 on the Hawk bike – a dramatic loss of confidence after a crash at Silverstone meant he lost his ride, to be replaced by Haydon.

Pts 16

IAN HUTCHINSON 23

BORN: 12.08.79
LIVES: Bingley
TEAM: Bike Animal Honda
Deputised for the injured Leon Camier in the final two rounds but found it tough to race a superbike on short circuits – even though he's a star on the roads.

Pts 14

SEAN EMMETT 24

BORN: 04.02.70
LIVES: Weybridge
TEAM: Samsung Suzuki
Once a leading light in BSB, started with PR Branson but parted company early in the year; later thrown a lifeline by old buddy Enzo di Clemente after Dean Thomas was injured.

Pts 14

HUDSON KENNAUGH 25

BORN: 12.01.81
LIVES: South Africa
TEAM: Virgin Yamaha
A leading contender in the National Superstock series when Virgin Yamaha signed him to replace Haydon, but he failed to live up to expectations and returned to superstock.

Pts 13

AARON ZANOTTI 26

BORN: 18.06.81
LIVES: Loughborough
TEAM: SMT Yamaha
Difficult first year in BSB on ex-Virgin Yamaha. Switched to Hydrex Honda for final two races in readiness for a full season on an ex-Harris bike with SMT in 2008.

GUY MARTIN 27

Pts 8

BORN: 04.11.82
LIVES: Kirmington
TEAM: Hydrex Honda
Only did a handful of BSB meetings and was never able to realise the potential on the short circuits that he displayed so brilliantly on the roads.

STUART EASTON 28

Pts 8

BORN: 21.07.84
LIVES: Dalbeattie
TEAM: Isilon MSS Discovery
Didn't initially want to ride the team's Kawasaki ZX-10 as well as his supersport bike when Rutter signed off sick, but went well at Knockhill considering his lack of BSB seat time.

MARTY NUTT 29

Pts 8

BORN: 06.12.78
LIVES: Castle Rock, Coleraine
TEAM: Nutt Travel Yamaha
Won five Cup races with the ex-Virgin Yamaha and as a consequence earned himself a 'works' ride on the Virgin bike at Donington and Brands Hatch.

TOM TUNSTALL 30

Pts 5

BORN: 21.06.78
LIVES: Huddersfield
TEAM: Hardinge Ice Valley Honda
After supersport, the bucking bronco of a superbike seemed to take Tunstall rather by surprise, but he rode consistently in the second half of the Cup competiton.

MALCOLM ASHLEY 31

Pts 4

BORN: 15.11.69
LIVES: Stoke Golding
TEAM: MAR Kawasaki
Another consistent finisher in the Cup competition, though he narrowly missed out on podiums through most of the second half of the season.

JAMES BUCKINGHAM 32

Pts 4

BORN: 03.07.84
LIVES: Ilfracombe
TEAM: Quay Garage Honda
Came back after serious ankle injury at Knockhill in 2006 but struggled to find his old form with the same Honda he raced last year – though still a Cup class title contender.

CAMERON DONALD 33

Pts 2

BORN: 28.09.77
LIVES: Claudy, Northern Ireland
TEAM: Uel Duncan Honda
Scored points at the Thruxton round but only did a couple of meetings before being sidelined by a collarbone injury at the North West 200.

JON KIRKHAM 34

Pts 2

BORN: 16.11.84
LIVES: Ockbrook, Derby
TEAM: Jentin Yamaha
Concentrated on Superstock this year but rode the Jentin Yamaha at Donington in place of injured Simon Andrews and scored two points.

PAUL BARRON 35

Pts 1

BORN: 02.11.81
LIVES: Dublin, Ireland
TEAM: PBM Racing Yamaha
MRO Powerbike champion in 2006, the Dubliner found life very challenging in BSB on his ex-Virgin Yamaha and scored just a single point.

DAVID JOHNSON 36

Pts 1

BORN: 16.04.82
LIVES: Hinckley
TEAM: PR Branson Honda
Took over vacant PR Branson Honda ride following Sean Emmett's departure from the team, which just didn't live up to expectations after a great 2006 season.

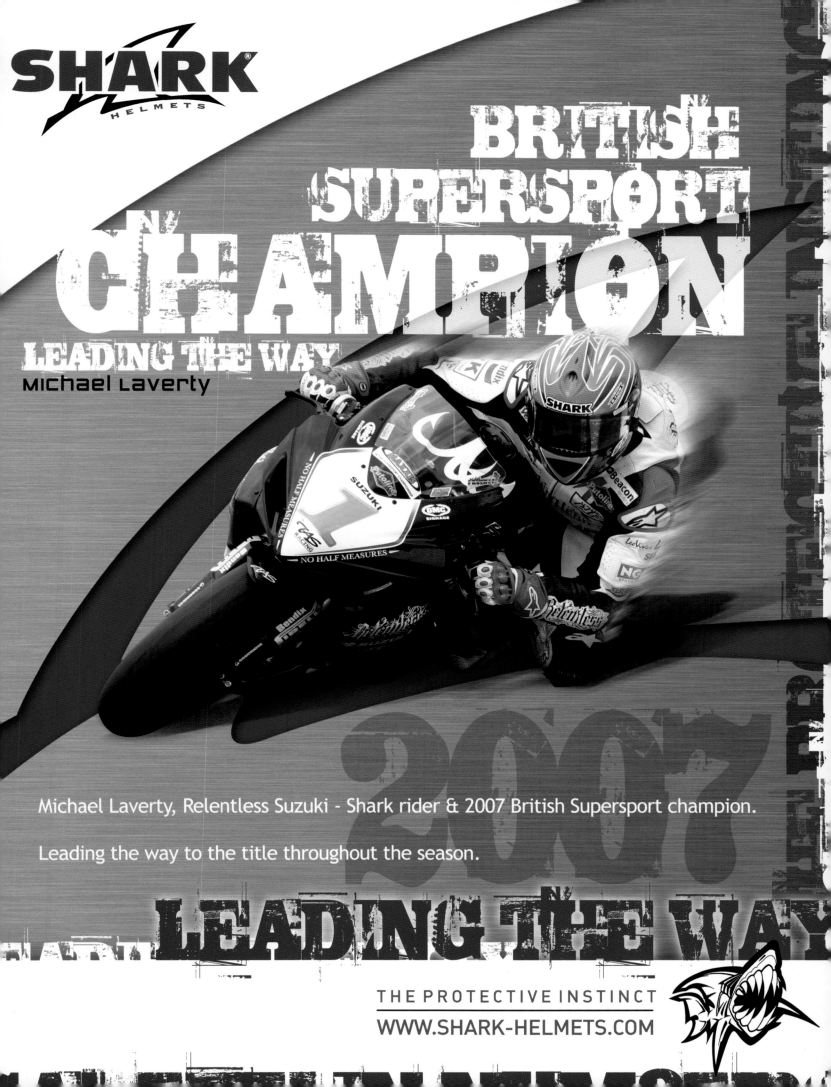

Haynes books

From rider biographies to motorcycle marque histories, you can trust Haynes to have it covered.

Check out our website at **www.haynes.co.uk** to order books and to view our online catalogue.

All Haynes publications are available through bookshops, car accessory stores and mail order outlets.

Haynes Publishing, Sparkford, Yeovil, Somerset BA22 7JJ, UK
Tel: **+44 (0) 1963 442030** Fax: **+44 (0) 1963 440001**
E-mail: **sales@haynes.co.uk** Website: **www.haynes.co.uk**

By Gary Pinchin
£19.99 HARDBACK

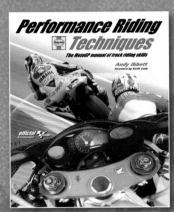

By Andy Ibbott
£19.99 HARDBACK

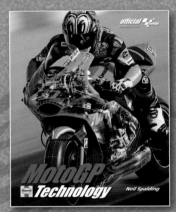

By Neil Spalding
£25.00 HARDBACK

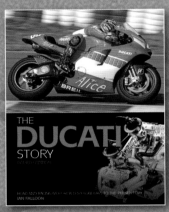

By Ian Falloon
£25.00 HARDBACK

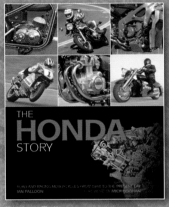

By Ian Falloon
£25.00 HARDBACK

By Gary Pinchin
£19.99 HARDBACK

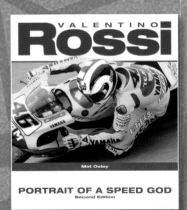

By Mat Oxley
£19.99 HARDBACK

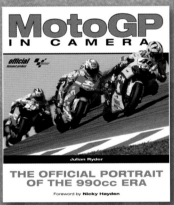

By Julian Ryder
£30.00 HARDBACK

By Julian Ryder
£19.99 HARDBACK

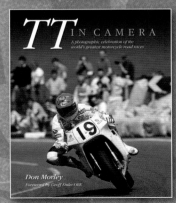

By Don Morley
£30.00 HARDBACK

By Mac McDiarmid
£8.99 PAPERBACK

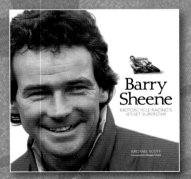

By Michael Scott
£25.00 HARDBACK

By Paul Sample
£14.99 HARDBACK

RIZLA SUZUKI
SUZUKI GSX-R1000 K7

Les Pearson has worked as crew chief for Yukio Kagayama and Shane Byrne at Rizla Suzuki, and for Michel Rutter at HM Plant Honda. This season he was reunited with Chris Walker. The pair of them previously worked at Suzuki seven years ago in BSB, and with Shell Honda in 500GPs in 2001. Here's what he had to say about development of this year's K7 GSX-R1000

"Engine-wise we started off as we were in 2006. We focused on valve control which, in the past, was a Suzuki Achilles heel due to (inferior) component quality and we experienced a couple of failures last year – which could have been attributed to the cam shape.

Chris had one 2007 engine with stock valve-train components but we built others following a valve spring control programme and now run stock exhaust valve springs – but from a GSX-R600 – and a Yoshimura inlet spring.

All Cal's engines run with Yoshimura STRR cam, inlet spring, stock exhaust spring, valve and retainer plus Yoshimura collets, which have proved totally reliable.

Power-wise, until we built the 2008 supersport-spec engine in the second half of the season in preparation for next year's new rules, everything stayed the same as 2006, although we worked on the mapping to improve the delivery.

We developed the slipper clutch in-house and have uprated that. But we built a prototype to test before the end of the year with ramps, but we're using steel bars instead of steel balls. Honda's slipper clutch only has ramps, so with our ball and ramp system there's less friction. But the problem is that it returns too fast so the bike still tends to back into corners, no matter how much we play with the engine management. The idea behind the prototype is to make it return slower, with a smoother transition to drive to stop it backing in. Cal, however, didn't have any problems on corner entry, mainly because he uses combined engine-braking strategies, using electronics as well as the slipper clutch.

Chassis-wise the biggest problem we've had is

that it's a brand new bike and we have two new riders, neither of whom rode the old bike to understand what it should feel like [Walker came from WSB and a bike with traction control and Pirellis, while Crutchlow was in supersport].

Yukio, Shakey and Chris have all said the GSX-R1000 feels too stiff, that it bounces off bumps. But that's when the bike is capable of doing the lap times.

Our main emphasis this year has been on the rear linkage – to give the riders that contact feel with the tyre on the road. We have a factory link, which Chris prefers, and our Crescent link, which Cal runs. We also made our own bracket, where the link mounts to the swing-arm to give us more options. Chris uses the factory bracket and Cal uses ours.

At Donington we tested four types of set-up: what they run in AMA, what they run in WSB and the two different set-ups of our riders. The AMA setting really takes some believing. On its wheels the bike is 20mm higher than Chris's and 37mm higher than Cal's! The WSB and BSB settings are more ballpark to what you'd expect. Even despite the height differences, our riders run different head angles, swing-arm pivot positions and linkages.

In some ways the Suzuki is the most adjustable bike in the paddock – and that can sometimes work against us. When JR [John Reynolds], Yukio and Shakey rode the GSX-Rs they had the caster kicked out and the rear up. The new bike seems to work best with a steeper caster and the rear down. It's very different to the old bike anyway with the engine in a different position and the frame around the engine being much stiffer."

SWING-ARM PIVOT
The rules say the swing-arm pivot point must remain stock so Suzuki have an advantage since the stock pivot is adjustable – and the aftermarket Yoshimura kit pivot offers even more adjustment. Rizla's own adjuster allows them to move the pivot point down by 4mm and forward and back by 4mm. Rizla can keep the stock pivot pin whereas Yamaha, with no adjustment in stock form, had to go to a smaller pivot pin to obtain any adjustment. Walker runs his pivot in the stock position, whereas Crutchlow is down 4mm to gain more pro squat – so under acceleration it doesn't push the rear end up.

ENGINE MANAGEMENT
Motec software is continually being updated and moved on quite a lot this year to give Rizla more scope for controllability. Biggest change this year was a new stepper servo which lets air into the engine when braking to reduce the engine braking effect.

Above: Rizla use Ohlins gas forks and Brembo radial calipers.

Below: Steering head had adjustable inserts; both riders had different settings.

SHOCK
The Ohlins TTX Shock has 16 settings and both riders worked with that to settle on a spec that suited them. Crutchlow had more rebound and compression that Walker, though the spring rates were the same.

ENGINE OIL
Motorex came up with new 0W40 oil to allow the team to run a slower oil pump. The oil is thinner when cold but the same viscosity when hot. According to the team, it's worth 1.5bhp compared with using the normal oil pump! It's a small percentage when the bike is already putting out over 200bhp but a few little improvements like that can add up and you start seeing a big difference. And those small gains will become even more important next year when the more stringent supersport rules come into play.

STEERING HEAD
The steering-head angle was stock but with adjustable inserts to allow the team to adjust up to plus or minus one degree in caster and plus or minus 3mm forward and back. For comfortable front-end feel, Crutchlow ran half a degree but zero mm, and Walker ran minus half a degree with 3mm forward.

FORKS
Both Rizla bikes have customer Ohlins forks. Crutchlow ran the same fork settings all year as does Walker but his have five millimetres less travel than Cal's (125mm to 130mm). According to the team, Walker struggled to find a good setting that works into and out of a corner. If he was happy with it on the way in, then it didn't feel good on the way out – and vice versa but he's always been very aggressive on the brakes so it was difficult to find a good balance.

ENGINE
Rizla were the first team to build and race an engine to the new 2008 BSB regulations, which rule out aftermarket pistons and rods and restrict camshaft design to be more in keeping with supersport-tune. Concern was raised in the paddock about using stock pistons and con-rods, but Rizla had no failures in their new engine, which produced more torque than the 2007 open-spec engine and only marginally less top end – which the team reckon they will have got back by the start of next year by fine-tuning the fuel and ignition mapping and having a new exhaust pipe design.

ABOUT THE TEAM

It was always going to be a tough season. Stepping up from British Supersport to develop from scratch a bike from a factory that has a reputation for not really having the resources to fund a superbike programme as well as their MotoGP project.

In other words, MSS Kawasaki were largely on their own. The plan was for the team to tap into the experience of Akira, the French engine tuner, who were the engine partners to WSB team PSG-1.

But PSG-1, along with anyone else who has run superbike ZX-10s, has always been fighting an uphill battle against the better-developed Honda, Ducati and Suzuki factory bikes.

It didn't help when the bikes arrived late. MSS were on the back foot from the start and initially went testing with a stock engine. And they didn't get the much-vaunted Akira engines until late in the season – and when one finally did arrive, it wasn't the big leap everyone had hoped for. Ray Stringer's engines, which the team had been using, produced just as much mid-range and more top end.

Signing Rutter, a vastly experienced rider and one with a lot of technical know-how, appeared a coup. MSS hoped he could speed the development progress but his pursuit of perfection frustrated the team. When things are right Rutter can be an awesome rider with clinical precision on the track. When they aren't, sadly, he's often an also-ran. And the bike needed a lot of work. The team went to massive lengths, even to the point of running Dunlop MotoGP-spec tyres at some events, but the frustrations became obvious and morale dropped to an all-time low at Croft – though the arrival of Jack Valentine to oversee garage operations during a race weekend (he wasn't a full-time manager as such) lifted the team at the end of the season. But that in part was down to a new arrival in the other side of the garage.

It was no coincidence that when Stuart Easton – struggling on the team's supersport bike – was injured, replacement rider James Webb injected fresh impetus to the team with his 'let-me-at-'em' approach, which spread across the other side of the garage.

The bottom line, though, was that the team lacked experience and testing this year. When they tested, it was usually on a Friday of a race meeting and that always left them playing catch-up.

MSS ISILON KAWASAKI ZX-10

ENGINE	
Engine builder	Ray Stringer, MSS and Akira
Pistons	N/A (Stringer), Pistal (Akira)
Rods	Arrow steel (Stringer), unspecified titanium (Akira)
Valves	Stock (Stringer), N/A (Akira)
Cams	Kent Cams (Stringer), Akira (Akira)
Gearbox	Kawasaki kit
Clutch	Stock
Exhaust	Arrow
Engine management	Motec M880
Engine oil	Elf
CHASSIS	
Forks	Showa
Shock	Showa
Swing-arm	Stock modified
Brake discs	Brembo 320mm
Brake calipers	Brembo MotoGP spec
Wheels	Marchesini
Tyres	Dunlop
ANCILLARIES	
Radiator	Stock top rad, Fabrication Techniques extension
Bars	DBR
Levers	Brembo
Pegs	MSS
Bodywork	F-Hot (lower than stock)
Paint	Padded Cell

MSS ISILON
KAWASAKI ZX-10

Matt Proud has worked with MSS for several years. As well as building all the team's supersport engines in-house, he is also Michael Rutter's crew chief

"Because the whole project came together so late and the bike only turned up just before Spain, we ran stock engines initially in testing at Guadix, with the aim of going to Akira engines for the start of the season.

But when it looked like that wasn't going to happen straight away, Ray Stringer built engines for us for the first round at Brands Hatch and we continued to use them all season. We're on out fourth Stringer-spec engine now.

We also started the season with a stock airbox and ran that for the first three rounds, then went to a huge carbon airbox, made in-house using the base of the fuel tank as the lid. One round later we got a WSB airbox [from PSG-1] with various velocity stacks to try.

Direct factory support has varied through the year. We get information but little in the way of hardware, so a lot of development has been done in-house.

We've had just the one Akira engine which we first raced at Croft. There's not much difference in the Akira engines on top end compared to Ray's but they have maybe a bit more mid-range. But Ray's latest-spec engine was as strong as the Akira one throughout the range and had different porting and combustion chamber.

Stringer uses Arrow rods. He started the season with titanium and then went to steel. The heavier steel rods make for a better power deliver with the increased inertia softening the power delivery.

Ray started with kit pistons and then went to Perfect Bore. He also uses stock valve gear, with uprated exhaust valve springs, and gets Kent cams to make the camshafts to his spec. Akira internals include titanium rods, Pistal pistons and different cams.

We opted to run Showa suspension and have worked closely with Ken Sommerton of K-Tech. We modified the stock swing-arm for length to give us more adjustability and to increase the width to accept the Marchesini wheels. We've also added the usual captive nuts and so on to make wheel-changing easy. We only have one linkage, the standard one, which seems to work fine. The rules say you can't modify the swing-arm pivot so we've got a smaller pivot pin, which gives us one millimetre of adjustment up and down.

Rutter likes the front end of this bike. He's got a lot of confidence in it [which he didn't have in his final year on the HM Plant bike or the Stobart Honda until late in the season in 2006]. What he doesn't like is the way the bike wheelies everywhere. The wheelbase is short and if we run it long the steering is too slow and it becomes a big heavy motorcycle.

We've been on a big learning curve this year but the goal has been to learn about the engine management system and we've concentrated on the fuelling to give the bike a nice user-friendly throttle response and keep Michael happy."

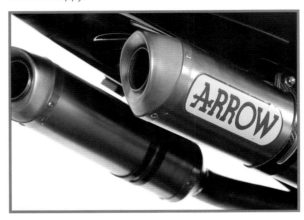

Above: MSS developed exhaust system in conjunction with Arrow, and swing-arm was modified stock

Below: Most of the team's season was run with an engine tuned by Ray Stringer

EXHAUST
MSS worked closely with Arrow, who made pipes specifically for the team. They've had two different sets of head pipes from the Italian company, but the tailpipe has remained the same.

SWING-ARM
MSS used a standard swing-arm that had been lengthened and had captive nuts, etc, added for quick wheel changes. The arm was also widened to accept the Marchensini race wheels.

GEARBOX
MSS use a kit Kawasaki gearbox with four ratio options per gear. They alter the gearbox from track to track. To change the gearbox means splitting the cases but the team can do this for both bikes in an evening. The problem they've had this year is that they have no experience to tap into in order to judge the optimum ratios for each track.

THUMB BRAKE
This is Rutter's anti-wheelie system! The MSS Kawasaki has no traction control, no wheelie control, no anti-spin – so keeping the bike under control when braking into corners, balancing the bike mid-corner and then getting good drive off the corners is all down to good mapping and Rutter's sensitive right hand – and left thumb.

FORKS
MSS opted to go the Showa route with Rutter having used them at HM Plant in 2005/2006 and suspension experts K-Tech helping to promote the product in the UK and working closely to speed development. One thing Rutter liked about the ZX-10 was the front-end feel.

ENGINE
The team started with Ray Stringer engines, expecting the Akira support (for which MSS had to pay handsomely) to come on line – but that didn't arrive until late in the season so the team largely stuck with the British tuner who proved more than up to the job. What the team lacked, though, was the full traction control electronics package that some of their rivals were running.

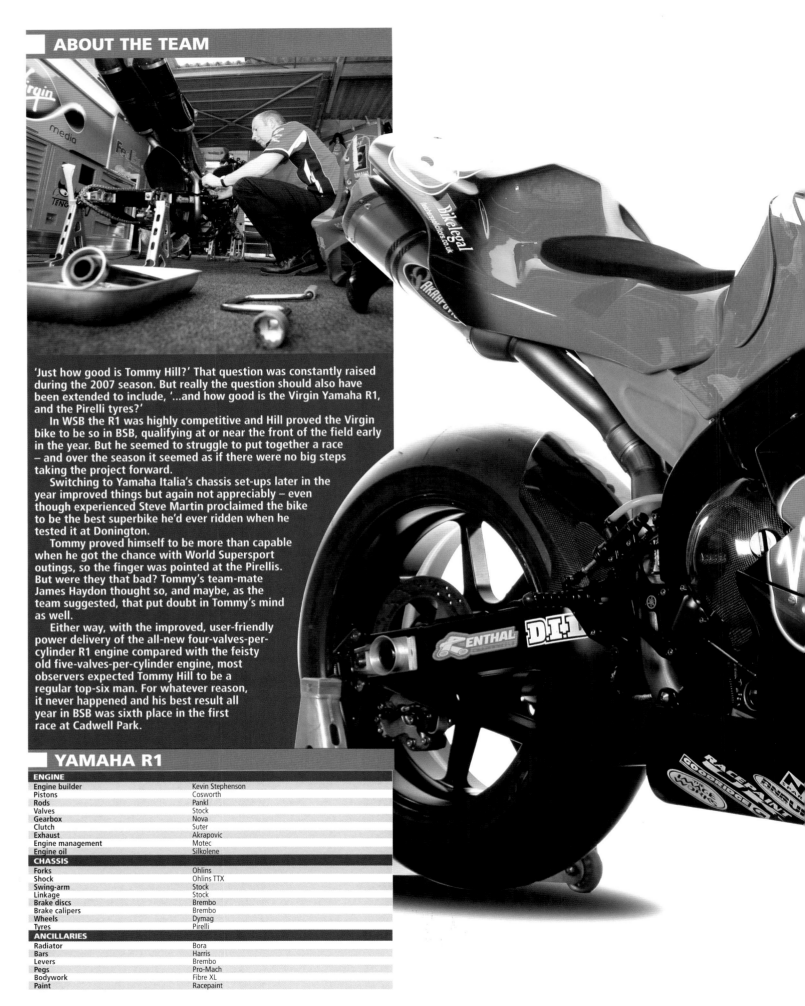

ABOUT THE TEAM

'Just how good is Tommy Hill?' That question was constantly raised during the 2007 season. But really the question should also have been extended to include, '...and how good is the Virgin Yamaha R1, and the Pirelli tyres?'

In WSB the R1 was highly competitive and Hill proved the Virgin bike to be so in BSB, qualifying at or near the front of the field early in the year. But he seemed to struggle to put together a race – and over the season it seemed as if there were no big steps taking the project forward.

Switching to Yamaha Italia's chassis set-ups later in the year improved things but again not appreciably – even though experienced Steve Martin proclaimed the bike to be the best superbike he'd ever ridden when he tested it at Donington.

Tommy proved himself to be more than capable when he got the chance with World Supersport outings, so the finger was pointed at the Pirellis. But were they that bad? Tommy's team-mate James Haydon thought so, and maybe, as the team suggested, that put doubt in Tommy's mind as well.

Either way, with the improved, user-friendly power delivery of the all-new four-valves-per-cylinder R1 engine compared with the feisty old five-valves-per-cylinder engine, most observers expected Tommy Hill to be a regular top-six man. For whatever reason, it never happened and his best result all year in BSB was sixth place in the first race at Cadwell Park.

YAMAHA R1

ENGINE	
Engine builder	Kevin Stephenson
Pistons	Cosworth
Rods	Pankl
Valves	Stock
Gearbox	Nova
Clutch	Suter
Exhaust	Akrapovic
Engine management	Motec
Engine oil	Silkolene
CHASSIS	
Forks	Ohlins
Shock	Ohlins TTX
Swing-arm	Stock
Linkage	Stock
Brake discs	Brembo
Brake calipers	Brembo
Wheels	Dymag
Tyres	Pirelli
ANCILLARIES	
Radiator	Bora
Bars	Harris
Levers	Brembo
Pegs	Pro-Mach
Bodywork	Fibre XL
Paint	Racepaint

VIRGIN MEDIA OPTOMA LOANS
YAMAHA R1

Kev Stephenson is in charge of Virgin Yamaha's engine development and was already underway with the team's 2008-spec engines before the 2007 season had finished. He took time out to talk through Virgin's BSB season.

"Our bike arrived late, not until after Christmas. To start with we ran the engine completely stock on the dyno to see where we stood. The new bike is better in respect of the four-valve head: while it makes good power, it's also very useable. Tommy said that the five-valve head engine was always hectic but he loved the new engine.

At the first Croft test we thought we had it cracked. He loved the way it was so user-friendly. And in the dry we were only just off our best laps times even though it was the middle of winter!

All our engine development is done in-house. Yamaha Italia have helped with chassis set-up and we tried a kit generator from Yamaha France but neither helped with engine work. We were third or fourth quickest in the Snetterton BSB test at the start of the season but then we went to Brands Hatch and struggled for grip all weekend. Tommy put too much pressure on himself and slipped off in practice, and we were on the back foot from there. And then we had a crank snap.

We were a bit despondent because testing had gone so well for us, so we went to Thruxton with the power softened off and Tommy got pole. That lifted us but he struggled for grip in the races when the track temperature went up.

We went to Silverstone and Tommy was again on the pace with Lavilla looking for a tow off him, but again he struggled when racing.

The problem again was not having anyone to push Tommy along. Haydon didn't get on with the Pirellis and that seemed to put doubt in Tommy's mind. Despite that he's been faster at every track this year – but so has everyone else.

Chassis-wise we made a smaller swing-arm pivot pin and that gave us adjustment of 2.5mm up and 2.5mm down. We run a stock linkage. Yamaha Italia use pretty close to stock on their WSB bike.

Mid-season we got some chassis set-up information from the factory Yamaha Italia WSB team. Tommy had run the bike low at the rear and high on the front, but there was more rear right up and front right down – more how you'd expect it. Steve Martin tested the bike for us at Donington in WSB trim and said it felt awesome. Tommy tried it at Knockhill but wasn't comfortable, but then we tried again at Croft and he went faster.

But that brought fresh problems. Because the settings were so radically different, we had no base to work from, so each meeting it cost us time to perfect it.

Apart from Martin riding at Donington and in the Brands WSB round, Tommy bore all the development work and it's turned out quite a frustrating year for everyone because in testing we were so competitive and it didn't work out in the season.

In the last two months of the season we started work on the 2008 engine in the new supersport-spec trim. We used info from this year but built it to the new rules using stock parts and were only 5bhp down on the 2007-spec engine. We're confident we can get that back with fine tuning of the engine management system over the winter.

The biggest thing for us, though, was to evaluate the stock rods to check the reliability."

Yamaha Italia WSB settings meant jacking the rear and lowering the front to improve handling – the opposite to the way Tommy Hill had run the first half of the year

CHASSIS SET-UP
Tommy Hill ran almost two-thirds of the races with the machine balance biased to the rear, but Virgin Yamaha dropped the front down and raised the rear after taking advice from WSB team Yamaha Italia. Steve Martin gave it the thumbs-up after testing it at Donington, but it wasn't until after Knockhill that Hill was confident enough to race with it.

TYRES
While the majority of their rivals ran Dunlops, apart from HM Plant Honda who were on Michelins, Virgin Yamaha continued for a second season on Pirellis. The big problem for the team this year was the very strict rules on the number of tyres used, so they were restricted on how much new Pirelli product they could evaluate. Finding the best race tyre became something of a compromise on some race weekends.

SWING-ARM
Virgin Yamaha neatly side-stepped the 'stock swing-arm pivot' rule by machining a smaller-diameter swing-arm pivot pin which gave them 2.5mm of adjustment up and down, without modifying the frame.

ENGINE
Virgin's 2007 engine had Cosworth pistons and Pankl rods, but in the last couple of rounds they also ran a 2008-spec engine for Marty Nutt in order to evaluate the stock rods and pistons in real-world racing, to test reliability of the components as well as assessing performance. The first engine built was just 5bhp down on the 2007 machine.

Bike Animal livery replaced Red Bull Rookies livery. Tom Larsen, the 2006 crew chief with Karl Harris, swapped places with Chris Pike, who went with Jonathan Rea to the HM Plant team. Leon Camier was signed to ride.

Camier benefitted from having Larsen, who had factory team experience and helped the rookie work methodically through an intensive pre-season testing programme. Testing is almost the wrong word because what Camier needed more than anything was seat time on a superbike to get a good handle on how the bike and team worked.

Testing could not have gone better and Camier came out guns blazing and shocked everyone, including himself, with second and third places in the first race at Brands Hatch. He largely maintained the impressive momentum until the weather turned bad – and that's when he started to slide.

Taking the wrong direction in set-up then hurt them later and that one-bike curse hit them several times, once when a gearbox was assembled wrongly and he missed most of qualifying, and also after a crash at Mallory Park through no fault of his own.

Camier and the Bike Animal crew had just picked up the game again when he crashed heavily cresting the Mountain, at Cadwell Park, and badly broke his leg, ending his season early.

HONDA CBR1000RR FIREBLADE

ENGINE	
Engine builder	N/A
Pistons	HRC
Rods	HRC
Valves	HRC
Gearbox	HRC
Clutch	HRC
Exhaust	Akrapovic
Engine management	HRC
Engine oil	Castrol
CHASSIS	
Forks	Showa
Shock	Showa
Swing-arm	HRC kit
Brake discs	Brembo 320mm
Brake calipers	Brembo
Wheels	Marchesini or Enki (made to HRC design)
Tyres	Dunlop
ANCILLARIES	
Radiator	HRC
Bars	Honda Racing
Levers	Honda Racing
Pegs	Brembo
Bodywork	C-Tech
Paint	Pray Bay, Immingham

BIKE ANIMAL
HONDA CBR1000RR FIREBLADE

Tom Larsen was more than a crew chief when he guided Karl Harris to the British Supersport title. He was more like a mentor and continued to work with him for two seasons in BSB. This year he's carried out that same crew chief/mentor role with Leon Camier and this is what he had to say about the season

"When we went testing we used Jonny Rea's 2006 settings as a starting point and they were pretty similar to the HM Plant bike I worked on. Then we went all around the houses, trying stuff, and figured out what worked.

We used what we had learned for the first three races of the year, apart from fork-spring changes and maybe 0.5mm on geometry, and we were racing for the podium places. Then we did some development and tried forks from HM Plant. We could have any of their 2006 chassis stuff but that doesn't necessarily work with this year's tyres or our rider. But we were trying to improve and stuck with the '06 forks until Croft, when we finally went back to our original set-up.

We had tried all types of Showa stuff, looking for some variations that might help. The advantage would have been to make the bike turn better but the drawback was that it hindered initial turn-in and stopping. The fork action [of the '06 kit] was smooth and to a higher level than we had to start with, but to maximise that the rider had to push a lot harder and that was a scary thing to try and do on initial turn-in when the feel was not so good.

Going back to the original set-up meant the bike didn't absorb the bumps so well and we've sacrificed some mid-corner speed, but Leon liked the feel. Our engine is the same spec as the factory bikes started with in 2006. Compared with 2007 factory spec, our engine is actually stronger mid-range but drops off at the end.

Tyre development has been unbelievable this year and that's been the big thing for Leon – adapting to the tyres. We started off on the same N-Techs as everyone and the bike felt balanced. Then we went to the STQ [the new Dunlops which are specially built to take up to five compounds] but it felt stiffer, so we tried to alter the bike to accommodate that.

Initially Leon didn't like the way they felt and even now goes better when the tyres have lost grip and give more feedback. With new tyres, he says there's so much grip it pushes the front. There have been times when you could say that having only one bike hurt us, but we work with what we've got. It's no problem.

Leon was having a good season until he hurt himself. He understands how to ride it and how to start it. Apart from the guys who have won races, he's the only guy racing to win. He's clever and I've really enjoyed working with him. There's a lot of satisfaction working with a kid who gives it 100%."

ABOUT THE TEAM

With the arrival of MSS Kawasaki as the 'official' Kawasaki team in BSB, Stuart Hicken's small but experienced team were out of the limelight. But on the race track there wasn't much to choose between Scott Smart (and late in the season James Haydon) and MSS rider Michael Rutter, which tended to suggest that the ZX-10 was not such an easy to beast to set up or ride.

Hicken admitted as such: "I think if you look where we were in 2004 and 2005, when we were running up front, that's when we had a good starting product. I'm sure if we were running a Honda we'd be in the top six. We've put more work into this year's bike than any bike in all my years of racing – all on a limited budget. If I were running the teams just above us in the points, and some below us, I'd be ashamed to be beaten by us.

"To get us to the next level, I think me and my team could improve if I'm being honest. Where we are with the bike currently, though, I think we're doing better than both PSG-1 in WSB and MSS in BSB. The bike is finicky because it's 50/50 and it's very difficult to set up. That's why we went radical in the last couple of rounds."

Hawk may not have had a huge budget but Hicken didn't scrimp on development, enlisting Ray Stringer to concentrate on engine tuning. The team also had the support of Italian suspension company Bitubo (on Peter Hickman's and then Haydon's side of the garage) while Smart's bike had full Ohlins.

Hawk had to let Hickman go when he suffered a massive loss of confidence after a crash early in the year at Silverstone and struggled to find the form he had shown in 2006. Haydon was drafted into the team and rode well despite missing a huge chunk of the season. He was able to run the pace of team-mate Scott Smart and Rutter from his first race on the Bitubo-suspended bike, at Cadwell.

KAWASAKI ZX-10

ENGINE	
Engine builder	Ray Stringer/Hawk Kawasaki
Pistons	Kawasaki kit
Rods	Arrow titanium
Valves	Stock
Gearbox	Nova
Clutch	Stock
Exhaust	Akrapovic
Engine management	Motec
Engine oil	Rock Oil
CHASSIS	
Forks	Ohlins (Smart), Bitubo (Haydon)
Shock	Ohlins (Smart), Bitubo (Haydon)
Swing-arm	Modified stock
Brake discs	Brembo
Linkage	Stock
Brake calipers	Brembo
Wheels	Dymag
Tyres	Dunlop
ANCILLARIES	
Radiator	N/A
Bars	Hawk Kawasaki
Levers	Hawk Kawasaki
Pegs	Hawk Kawasaki
Bodywork	Chase Race Paint

HAWK
KAWASAKI ZX-10

Stuart Hicken, who raced for a dozen years before turning his skills to suspension and chassis preparation, then team management, talks about the workings of his privately owned equipe

"We've done a lot of engine development this year and in conjunction with Ray Stringer we've built all the engines in our own workshop. Our engines use titanium rods and Kawasaki two-ring pistons. Camshafts are made by Kent Cams but to our specification. The state of engine tune is largely down to Ray. We've gone from 186bhp at the end of last year to 205bhp this year, and a lot of that is down to camshaft design and exhaust port work.

We also have a new airbox, designed by ourselves, which uses the tanks as the lid and the sides of the frames as its sides, so it's not physically possible to get the airbox any bigger.

We have different gearbox ratios from Nova. We've no cassette gearbox so it's important to have a gearbox that works everywhere.

We use a stock Kawasaki slipper clutch but we don't rely on that because it gives too much slip for Smartie, so we control the slippage with the engine management. We've done a lot of work with the Motec engine management, and use its traction-control and engine-braking facilities, but it's taken a lot of hard work all year to perfect it. We started working on engine-braking systems last year and I'm sure you noticed the big flame-outs on the way into corners. We were chucking fuel in to stop the bike backing in so much. Well, that's gone now as we've improved on the system.

When James joined us, one thing he complained about was how difficult it was to get the bike to transfer weight. It was 50/50 but now it's slightly biased to the front. We achieved that by running a 35mm longer swing-arm – and used it for the first time at Donington. We're still running a stock swing-arm and our own quick-release ends but the arm is now longer, and stronger.

Scott never complained about rear grip before, neither did James, but now we've given them more front grip (and reduced the bike's propensity for wheelies). Scott has run Ohlins all year while James is on Bitubo, a small Italian company who are dead keen and have been to several BSB rounds this year to help out.

We've had no problems with Dunlop all year. My team has been with them for years and while we're maybe not on the same rubber as the top Honda and two Ducatis, we're not complaining about the service we get. We've even been given MotoGP tyres to try: some work on our circuits and some don't.

Everything we've done with this bike to get it to work, though, won't be possible in 2008 because of the new rules."

ABOUT THE TEAM

What a turbulent year for Jentin Racing. They struggled with money and missed races. They went with a new engine tuner who never lived up to expectations. But then it all came good when Lloyds British suddenly agreed to back the team, not just as a short-term fix but in a deal that will give Jentin Racing real stability through until the end of the 2008 season.

Jentin parted company with Mountune, a car racing firm who came to bikes with great intentions but failed to grasp the intricacies of motorcycle road racing engine tuning compared to the car field in which they are undoubted experts.

Back into the frame came Race Techniques, one of the most unsung engine-tuning companies in the business, and suddenly everything looked rosy for Jentin.

The team were forced to start the year with 'old faithful', the bike James Ellison used to win them the 2004 BSB Privateer Cup. Mountune were handling the engine build for the 2007 bike but that never lived up to expectations. Then the money problems hit and everything was on hold. Lloyds British came in and helped to get the project back on the tracks but just when the team had turned a corner in engine, and chassis, development, rider Simon Andrews broke his collarbone at Cadwell Park. Jon Kirkham deputised for him at Donington but the team were hoping to re-sign Andrews for 2008.

JENTIN LLOYDS BRITISH R1

ENGINE	
Engine builder	Race Techniques
Pistons	Yamaha race kit
Rods	Arrow titanium
Cams	Piper, to Race Techniques spec
Valves	Stock
Gearbox	Yamaha race kit
Clutch	STM
Exhaust	Arrow
Engine management	Motec
Engine oil	Shell Advance
CHASSIS	
Forks	Ohlins 2006 customer spec
Shock	Ohlins TTX
Swing-arm	Harris Performance
Brake discs	Brembo
Linkage	Stock
Brake calipers	Brembo
Wheels	Dymag
Tyres	Dunlop
ANCILLARIES	
Radiator	Bora
Bars	Harris Performance
Levers	Harris Performance
Bodywork	Race Products
Paint	Spray Tech

JENTIN LLOYDS BRITISH
YAMAHA R1

Bernie Toleman, a former world endurance racer in his own right, is the figurehead of the small but enthusiastic West Country-based Jentin Racing team. He's helped keep the team rolling, even when times were hard, but now, with Lloyds British backing, he can plan ahead. This is how development went in 2007

"We started the year with a 2004 bike that was virtually unchanged from the year before. We put a TTX shock in it and that was about the extent of the changes. We already had 2006 forks and had fitted a thumb brake for Simon when he rode the bike last year.

We never wanted to start the season with the 2004 bike but it ran so well so we kept it as it was until the 2007 bike was ready. But it wasn't until the second Oulton round that we were able to run the 2007 R1 for the first time, though we didn't race it until Cadwell Park.

The 2007 R1 finished the season with a Race Techniques head, using their camshaft made by Piper but to their specs. We use Yamaha kit parts, pistons, springs and gearbox but prefer to use Arrow titanium rods. I'm opposed to the supersport rules next year because we have to use stock rods, which I don't agree with on safety grounds. In the long term it's going to cost the teams more anyway because you'll have to rebuild engines more frequently with standard rods. Titanium rods you can virtually fit and forget.

We've used various slipper clutches, Suter and STM, and are still experimenting. Historically we have used STM but we tried a Suter clutch at Donington.

We run Motec electronics and dash, supplied by Steve Hurst of GWR Motorsport, who also builds our looms. We don't run any traction control, launch control or anti-wheelie, but all are in development for 2008.

We use customer Ohlins 2006-spec forks in the new bike but will go to the TTX fork in 2008. We already have a TTX shock, but run a stock Yamaha linkage.

We work closely with Harris Performance and use their yokes, swing-arm and sub-frame plus bars and footrests.

Simon likes the 2007 chassis and found it a lot more user-friendly after the 2004 bike – to the point that he started refusing to ride the '04 at all! I don't think you can point to any one thing that's made such a difference, it's just a lot of small changes in the '07 that have added to a big improvement in the overall package."

ABOUT THE TEAM

The Hydrex Honda team moved up a gear in 2007 and, as Karl Harris showed at Oulton in July when he finished second in race two, their bike had more than enough potential to be competitive.

Sadly, after going so well in pre-season testing, Harris lacked consistency and wasn't seriously in contention on a sufficiently regular basis to figure in the championship. But it's difficult to pin down whether that was down to the rider not performing at the highest level or the tyres.

The team's technical co-ordinator, Mick Shanley, explained: "Karl is quicker in some places than he was on the factory bike last year. At Oulton, for example, he was never out of the top four in race two and finished second."

Maybe that was the story? At many tracks Harris clearly wasn't on the pace as strongly as he was at his beloved Oulton Park, and the truth is that the BSB front-runners moved up a step in 2007.

Some of that could be attributed to tyres. Certain teams did development work for Dunlop which meant they got the very latest equipment. Hydrex wasn't one of them – but Shanley reckons they still got the good stuff – if only occasionally.

He said: "Everyone's talking about who gets what tyres this year. We get decent rubber here and there. Karl is on 2006 lap-record rubber – it's just that the guys at the front are pushing so hard and have taken it to another level."

Whatever the reason, it was a frustrating time for team owner Shaun Muir and the rest of the Hydrex crew, especially when the team was so competitive on the roads with Guy Martin.

HONDA CBR1000RR FIREBLADE

ENGINE	
Engine builder	Chris Mehew
Pistons	Pistal
Rods	Stock
Valves	HRC kit
Gearbox	HRC kit
Clutch	STM
Exhaust	Micron
Engine management	Motec M880
Engine oil	Putoline
CHASSIS	
Forks	Showa 45mm A-kit Evolution
Shock	Showa kit
Swing-arm	HRC kit
Brake discs	Brembo
Linkage	2005 stock, 2006 stock, 2007 SMR
Brake calipers	Brembo
Wheels	PVM
Tyres	Dunlop
ANCILLARIES	
Radiator	Febur
Bars	Fabrications Techniques
Levers	Brembo
Bodywork	G-Meiner
Pegs	SMR
Paint	Local bodyshop

HYDREX
HONDA CBR1000RR FIREBLADE

Former GP technician and current Hydrex Honda technical co-ordinator Mick Shanley summed up Karl Harris's 2007 season

"With Karl joining us from the factory-backed HM Plant Honda team, it was important for him to get a feel for our bike early on and tell us how it compared with the HRC bike.

We met before the pre-season testing to talk over what Karl was looking for from our bike. After all, he'd ridden the BLD Dunlop bike in 2005 as well as the HRC bike last year, so he had a good idea of what to expect and how the Honda felt on Dunlops and Michelins.

He said our bike was so easy to ride compared to the factory bike and that ours had smooth power and a forgiving chassis. That was promising but that was early on.

Glen Richards rode for us up to the end of 2006 and he wanted the engine softer and softer to make it easier to ride. But Karl was very different and wanted more and more horsepower.

With the improvements in our electronics we could give him as much as he wanted and then used things like anti-spin, anti-wheelie and air-bleed electronics to make the bike more user-friendly.

Glen had a version of all this in 2006 but with Karl we've pushed it more and he's more up for experimenting with new ideas. We've not been able to do stuff like that on the dyno. You need to alter different things depending on the circuit and conditions. It's a case of trawling data to find trends and adjust accordingly.

With Karl it's important not to take too much of the feel away but we have had to tailor the way the bike delivers its power from track to track to suit him. With the wide variety of tracks in BSB, it could always be that way.

As for engine spec, we have all the power stuff like big cams back in it now and we're where we finished 2005 with Glen. We've improved on the power but it's about as far as you'd want to push the current Blade engine.

Outright power is no longer an issue for anyone anyway. We've all got in excess of 200bhp so now it's a case of how you use it. We've given Karl the grunt but we've kept it sweet with traction control. He's said the thing is an animal if he turns off the electronics.

Chassis-wise, Glen always wanted the bike set up with everything on the front so it steered like crazy. As soon as we tested Karl immediately said the bike had too much steering and not enough rear grip.

This year we've got Xavier Mounoz Labrador with us at several races from Pro Shock in Spain to help with the Showa suspension development. He was my factory technician in Grands Prix for two years and has helped us so much in the past couple of seasons."

ABOUT THE TEAM

After all the worry and strife last year within the Stobart camp, things have been turned around dramatically – or that's how it looks. But according to the team there was 'nothing wrong with the bike last year', and signing Shane Byrne and Tom Sykes has proved that.

The bike is essentially the same as the one Rutter and Laverty raced in 2006 but has been refined in lots of areas, especially the electronics. The team claim that they had that all in place last year but Rutter preferred not to use it, because he wanted to get the mechanical grip sorted first to avoid masking any potential problems with the bike – but you can't hide the fact that Stobart Honda with Shakey and Sykes have been the only non-factory team to rattle the likes of HM Plant Honda and Airwaves Ducati this year.

Shakey gave the team their first win since 2004 when he won at Mallory, and he had some other great rides, especially his last-to-sixth run at Donington on his spare bike. Sykes stuck the bike on pole and was consistently a front-runner – impressive considering it was his rookie season.

It all proved the effectiveness of the bike from 'the little team up north', as owner Paul Bird likes to throw into conversation. Not bad considering there were only four full-time staff doing development work on the bikes between races.

Next year there's a new Honda to develop. It took Stobart three years to get the current one right but that was building a race bike from a roadster, something they had little experience of as they ran Ducati factory bikes before. And they had to learn their way around the complex Magneti Marelli system and all of its electronic aids. With all that experience tucked away, developing the new bike won't take half as long.

HONDA CBR1000RR FIREBLADE

ENGINE	
Engine builder	FW Developments/Phil Borley
Pistons	HRC kit
Rods	HRC kit
Valves	HRC kit
Gearbox	Unspecified Formula One-based partner
Clutch	STM
Exhaust	Arrow
Engine management	Magneti Marelli
Engine oil	Motul
CHASSIS	
Forks	Ohlins TTX 42mm
Shock	Ohlins K-Tech modified
Swing-arm	KR 2006-spec
Brake discs	Brembo
Linkage	Stobart Honda
Brake calipers	Brembo
Wheels	N/A
Tyres	Dunlop
ANCILLARIES	
Radiator	N/A
Bars	Renthals
Levers	Brembo
Bodywork	N/A
Paint	N/A

STOBART VENT AXIA
HONDA CBR1000RR FIREBLADE

Stuart Bland is the long-serving Stobart Honda Team Co-ordinator. So who better to ask about this year's bike?

"The bike is not that different to last year's, yet the team was slated for a lack of results, which was pretty frustrating. We knew it was right at the end of last year and this year we've just perfected all the stuff we had in place before.

The main work has been in improving the Magneti Marelli electronics package, including the dash. You can't miss the distinctive popping and banging off the throttle from our bike and that is down to the engine-braking system. We had it last year but (Michael) Rutter refused to use it so (Michael) Laverty developed it. Both our riders have used it all year. Maybe GSE (Airwaves Ducati) are the only ones using full traction control.

It's debatable whether you need traction control if you have good tyres and we've certainly had some great support from Dunlop this year and have as good a selection of tyres as anyone in the BSB paddock. Our riders have the option to run three different maps, adjustable from a switch on the handlebars. We also have anti-wheelie electronics.

We use kit engine parts plus that we've developed ourselves with FW Development. The gearbox is made to our spec by an F1 company and we run an STM slipper clutch. There's also a new Arrow exhaust. We had several updates but the biggest came for Croft with a distinctive and brand new muffler shape.

We also ran a new Motul engine oil this year, developed specifically from MotoGP technology, the Rossi link if you like!

Chassis-wise we have Ohlins TTX 42mm forks that are the same as those used in MotoGP. We also have a K-Tech-modified Ohlins shock – I'd say it's now 20% Ohlins and 80% K-Tech. We're running the same KR swing-arm as in 2006 but we have a selection of new linkages.

Both our current riders run similar set-ups – you could change one to suit the other in less than ten minutes, although sometimes they prefer different linkage ratios.

We have some trick new Renthal bars this year that are calibrated to make adjustment easier.

Shakey just got on and rode the bike. At Cadwell he was a second off the pace throughout the first race, then picked up six-tenths in race two. The difference: "I bit the screen," according to him.

The trick has been to get the front traction good. If he's happy with that, he's confident all round. He rides the front so hard and leans on it so much, even as he's turning in. Traction was a bit inconsistent in the wet but the more updates we've had, the better it has got."

ABOUT THE TEAM

During the winter the team owner, the mysterious 'Tony G', sold the Vivaldi potato brand and instead opted to promote the Naturally Best side of his business. Hence the team becoming known as Team NB, although the familiar cream and burgundy livery remained.

Team Manager Norris Farrow was allowed to retain the team's hardware and was given a budget for the season, and was permitted to restructure the team as he saw fit. That entailed slimming it down to a more manageable two-man effort with Wiltshire-based brothers Ollie and Tommy Bridewell, the latter getting his first season on a superbike.

After a steady build-up in pre-season testing and some consistent finishes early in the year, things started looking up for a team that had developed beyond recognition from the previous season.

Tommy broke into the top ten a couple of times, running with riders with far more experience. And Ollie overcame some early-season blues to match his brother's early success. Ollie really shone in the wet meetings that characterised the middle of the season, coming eighth and 10th at Knockhill and scoring two ninth places at Oulton.

Then suddenly Ollie was gone, killed in a crash during wet practice on Friday morning at Mallory Park.

It wasn't until Donington that Tommy finally decided to ride again. It was a difficult time for him. Not only was he having to deal with racing for the first time without his brother, but he'd been off a bike since July.

Now Tommy and Farrow's team have the winter to recoup and make some tough decisions on their futures.

SUZUKI GSX-R1000 K6

ENGINE	
Engine builder	Team NB
Pistons	Stock
Rods	Stock
Valves	Stock
Gearbox	Suzuki kit
Clutch	Stock
Exhaust	Yoshimura
Engine management	Motec M880
Engine oil	Maxima
CHASSIS	
Forks	Ohlins
Shock	Ohlins
Swing-arm	Fabrications Techniques
Brake discs	Brembo
Linkage	AMA Yoshimura
Brake calipers	Brembo
Wheels	Dymag
Tyres	Pirelli WSB 2007 spec
ANCILLARIES	
Radiator	Stock
Bars	Team NB
Pegs	Team NB
Levers	Brembo
Bodywork	CS Carbon
Paint	Heathrow

TEAM NB
SUZUKI GSX-R1000 K6

Norris Farrow was Fred Merkel's crew chief and team manager when the American won back-to-back WSB titles in 1988 and '89 with Rumi Honda. Farrow was also Aaron Slight's long-serving crew chief on the Castrol Honda team. Now he runs Team NB (_née_ Vivaldi) and reflects on the team's 2007 performances

"Between 2006 and 2007 we simplified our engine spec, ironically more in line with the new 2008 regulations than 2007. We've gone from running expensive hardware to more stock internals and even use the genuine Suzuki road bike valve springs.

We ran Carillo rods in 2006 and there's not a lot of difference between them and the stock stuff. We've got stock pistons but we've modified the crowns [not permitted in the 2008 supersport-spec regs]. What we did with the compression ratio and cam timing was the main change in engine character for this year.

We've improved the power delivery by making big inroads with electronics. At the start of the year we had no traction control, no anti-spin. We had the facility all along but only started to use it at Snetterton, but realised then we needed more time to make it work properly.

We got on top of it, though, even if Ollie and Tom didn't like the feel initially. Because of their inexperience they didn't understand how to maximise it. Basically, you're de-tuning the engine and they didn't like that at all. But they needed more confidence to open the throttle earlier. By the time that they were on it, the engine wasn't driving like it should have been. We were developing it well, then the bad weather kicked in so we never got it fully dialled in.

In the wet we lacked grip [possibly due to the production-spec Pirellis]. We won in the wet with Scott Smart at Donington in 2006 but had nothing like the same success in the four wet races this year.

Chassis-wise we've not veered much from the 2006 set-up. We had a Fabrications Techniques swing-arm in '06 but went away from that. The stock arm had more adjustment so Scott (Smart) tried that but wasn't sure if it was any better. So now we're back to the Fab Tech arm with more adjustment built into it.

Forks are 2006 Ohlins with exactly the same valving as last year. We have a customer-spec Ohlins shock which is more Honda-based than Suzuki and has Ohlins-spec valving."

SUFFER FOR YOUR ART. NO HALF MEASURES.

THE RACES

KIYO BREAKS LAVILLA'S STREAK

Reigning Champion Ryuichi Kiyonari finds his form at Silverstone to halt the Ducati star's unbeaten run

Previous pages: Kiyonari fought back at Silverstone with two wins, but Lavilla kept the series lead with fifth and second places

Opposite: Though Leon Haslam was sore from a high-speed get-off in practice, he still got into the top six in both races. Shakey Byrne, though, had a disastrous weekend

Below: Chris Walker scored his first podium of the season on the Rizla Suzuki with a third place in race one behind Jonathan Rea

Silverstone put everything back into perspective. Gregorio Lavilla's unbeaten four-win streak was impressive enough but he came within inches of being beaten by Ryuichi Kiyonari in the second race at Thruxton.

But at Silverstone it was finally Kiyo's turn to taste the winner's champagne again. He qualified on pole, his first since Silverstone 2005, and dominated both races. Lavilla had a tyre issue in race one but normal service was resumed in race two when he finished second – and it looked like a serious case of 2006 revisited!

It would have been no surprise if BSB paddock experts and the fans on the other side of the fence were wondering when a British rider might actually win a race again!

Leon Haslam was second at one stage in race two but was punted off the track by Shane Byrne. That Haslam was even on a bike was testament to his guts and determination. He crashed at 174mph in practice at Maggots on Friday and was black and blue down his back and left thigh after clouting the high Silverstone kerbs twice as he slid across the track.

The meeting was also the occasion Rizla Suzuki finally found form with Chris Walker finishing third in race one and fourth in race two, but only after the team had carried out an unscheduled test day at Oulton Park – and then made some drastic last-minute changes to the bike on race day at Silverstone to finally give Walker a package he could race with.

RACE ONE

It was a frantic first lap. Jonathan Rea took the lead from Kiyonari, Byrne and Haslam, who moved up to third coming out of Copse, and then Walker chopped across Shakey's Stobart Honda going into Becketts for fourth. Haslam took the lead at the Hairpin with a cool out-braking effort, and then Walker pushed Rea even further back into the chicane after Rea had held up the Suzuki in the previous corner.

Lavilla was back in sixth but everyone expected him to be calm and collected and mount one of his usual charges through the field. Sure enough, on the second lap he took Shakey but by now Kiyo was up to third having passed Walker going into the chicane. A lap later Shakey slid off at the Hairpin.

Lap eight and Kiyo was in front, going on the inside

on the brakes into the chicane, and he simply pulled the pin after that. His lead on lap 12 was 2.3s, on lap 13 it was 3.13s and on lap 14 it was 4.46s, but behind him Walker had passed Haslam at the chicane and Lavilla pushed his team-mate back into the clutches of Leon Camier and Rea.

On lap 17 it all started to go bad for Airwaves Ducati. As Rea's rear Michelin came in, the Dunlops started to lose grip. Rea went second at Copse, and Lavilla dropped back further to come under pressure from Camier and Haslam.

In the last four laps Kiyo stretched his lead to almost eight seconds from Rea, who in turn was a comfortable second from a charging Walker and Camier, with Lavilla and Haslam struggling in fifth and sixth. Airwaves team boss Colin Wright later openly admitted that the problem was the team making the wrong choice of tyres and not in any way the fault of Dunlop.

Kiyo gave his usual bland post-race commentary: "Race not easy but pleasing result. Very enjoyable. Maybe I had good tyre. I had good gap to Gregorio. I need to win more races."

Rea's ride was probably the best feature of the race and showed just how smart the kid is. It would have been so easy to panic early in the race and push to the point of crashing trying to keep on the pace.

Rea said: "I knew the rear tyre would be slow to come in and I got a bit beaten up by some of the more experienced riders early on. Maybe it's time I should start some of the rough manoeuvres they make so they know I'm not a soft touch. But once it was up to temperature I gained my composure and my confidence grew.

HAYDON'S LAST RIDE FOR VIRGIN YAMAHA?

It was painfully obvious that James Haydon's position within the Virgin Media Yamaha team was in jeopardy. He was 17th and 16th at Brands, 17th in both races at Thruxton, and 15th and 16th at Silverstone.

Haydon was around two seconds off the pace at Silverstone. Even though there was a glimmer of hope during practice, where he found over a second in one session, he never improved on that and word got out via the World Superbike paddock that team boss Rob McElnea had invited Andrew Pitt to replace Haydon at Silverstone – but the Aussie had a prior commitment in the World Supersport race the same weekend.

Haydon simply struggled to find any confidence in the Pirellis. The tyre company even came up with a new, stiffer front in the Oulton test a week prior to Silverstone, and Tommy Hill tested it and said he thought it would suit Haydon because it felt so like a Dunlop. According to Hill, the normal Pirellis do move around but still have fantastic grip.

So it was no surprise that three days after the Silverstone race Virgin revealed that Haydon had injured his shoulder in a mountain bike crash during training and would not ride for at least two races. They announced that 26-year-old South African Hudson Kennaugh would take his place. He was running second in the National Superstock points on a Raceways Yamaha at the time.

So why weren't Virgin Yamaha up-front about the true situation? McElnea said: "It's not the kind of publicity you want, announcing that you've sacked a rider. But we couldn't carry on as we were. We opted to give Hudson a big chance. He was only in Superstock to try and get noticed. And we were looking for someone who was hungry and had no preconceptions about the tyres or the bike."

"I think it was the best race I've ever ridden – I was riding with real heart to get back up there. We could have gone with a tyre that comes in earlier but then it might not go race distance. The tyre we used was actually last year's race tyre."

Camier had turned around a tough qualifying, when he struggled to get his head around how best to sort the bike, and finished fourth. He said: "This weekend is the first time I've ridden the bike and not gone forwards each time we've made changes. It wasn't until I got with Kiyo in the race for a while that I actually started to piece the whole jigsaw together."

RACE TWO

Kiyonari led the second race from Shakey, Haslam, Walker and Rea, but Haslam took Shakey for second and Walker moved him back to fourth in the complex but then ran in too hot into the hairpin and Shakey was back into third.

Tommy Hill was making life hard on himself, too, overshooting Becketts, and he dropped to ninth.

With hopefully the correct tyre choice for race two, Lavilla was back on the charge again, passing Walker for fourth at the hairpin on the fourth lap.

On lap six Shakey ran into Luffield too hard, looking for a way by Haslam, then realised the Ducati wasn't

getting the drive that he expected and tagged its rear tyre as he tried to avoid contact. The move punted Haslam on to the infield while Shakey was flicked off his Honda for his second DNF of the day.

Haslam managed to keep his bike on two wheels but dropped from second place to sixth behind Rea. Haslam said: "He must have been in there miles too fast and knocked me out of second place. I was pushing too hard after that and wouldn't have caught anyone back up because I'd used my tyre – plus I was struggling in the lefts with my bruised leg so I was losing out each time in the final sector through the complex."

That meant Kiyo now led from Lavilla, with a gap to Walker and Camier. Lap eight saw Lavilla set a new lap record at 1m 25.49s, as the gap dropped from 3.00s to 2.64s. It came down again the next lap to 2.4s but Kiyo responded to his pit board and it was back to 2.58s at lap ten, the halfway stage.

Behind them Walker had been a little slow into the Hairpin on lap nine and Camier let off his brakes and drove ever so smoothly under him to take third place.

By the 11th lap, though, Rea was charging again as his tyres really started working at their best. Camier had a whiff of closing down Lavilla at the same time but pushed that little bit too hard, got into Priory a little hot and just ran out on to the really bumpy section of track, enough to wash the front – and down he went. It was his first crash since joining the Bike Animal Honda team, including throughout all of testing!

Camier said: "I saw Greg coming back to me and thought, 'keep going', but I made a tiny mistake and went down. It's a bit bumpy in there and, to be honest, I was pushing hard. I was on the edge but I was also lapping seven-tenths faster in the race than I'd gone in practice on a race tyre."

Rea took Walker for third at Bridge on lap 12 and with 9.3s to make up on Lavilla in seven laps, the questions were being asked whether he could do enough to sneak second. Sadly it was a moot point as Paul Barron and Tom Tunstall both went down in a cloud of oil smoke on the 14th lap after Steve Plater's AIM Yamaha broke a con-rod. As the race had gone two-thirds distance and there was clearly a large slick of oil down, the race was red-flagged and the result called.

Rea said: "First lap my tyre wasn't up to temperature again and it spun out on me in the first turn and I got a bit duffed up again."

Kiyo, therefore, took the second race from Lavilla, with Rea having to be content with third place. Walker was fourth with Haslam fifth ahead of Tom Sykes and Cal Crutchlow.

Kiyo didn't have a lot to say but his crew chief Adrian Gorst helped out and revealed that it was a new, stiffer front tyre that helped Kiyonari overcome his jittery start to the season.

Gorst said: "We had tyre issues at Thruxton and spent the qualifying session doing a race run to try and sort it out. That's why Kiyo qualified so badly – which hurt him in the race.

"But here Michelin came up with a new front and we've got some different suspension settings to allow him to pass on the brakes again. That's what has been hurting him – the tyre was moving around too much for his liking before. His forte is getting people on the brakes and he's not been able to do that until this weekend."

Above: Things started to improve for Rizla Suzuki, with Chris Walker getting on the podium with third place in race one and following that with fourth place in race two

Opposite: Leon Haslam had a fraught weekend. First a crash in practice, then a wrong tyre choice in race one, and then Shakey Byrne nailing him at the chicane in race two

TYPICAL GREGORIO GUTS AND GLORY

Lavilla wins one, spins one and then stages one of his spellbinding fightbacks

Of all the places BSB visits, Oulton Park is the one where you know you'll see some really memorable racing. It's all to do with the rolling Cheshire landscape and fantastic circuit layout with its vast array of corner types. There are so many places to pass, so many options to suit all sorts of riding styles and bike characteristics.

There are so many good things about Oulton: the full-throttle bravery needed out of Cascades to line up a move at Island, the possibility to run deep into Shell Oils Corner to go under someone, the do-or-die chicanes at Brittens and Hizzy's, the rapid approach to today's considerably safer Druids (thanks to Jonathan Palmer's willingness to create a much safer run-off than previous Oulton owners said was possible), and the glorious multi-line Old Hall where you can really see who's late on the brakes.

Airwaves Ducati team boss Colin Wright was musing over Oulton's delights during a lull in Friday's practice day and said: "Oulton has seen great races for GSE Racing: 2000 was probably the most memorable for different reasons.

"First came the epic scrap between Neil Hodgson and Chris Walker [then on Suzuki] for the lead. Both went off, Hodgson rejoined to finish 11th, Walker was 13th.

Suzuki protested and Hodgson was given a 36s penalty which dropped him down the field to 14th, one place behind Walker. So we appealed and Neil was reinstated in fourth place and Walker was dropped to 14th.

"Then came Hodgson's win from the back of the grid. James Haydon had stalled his Suzuki on the line at Silverstone and took ages to get it sorted out, so everyone agreed to a rule change where if a rider stalled on the grid and caused a delay he'd have to go to the back of the grid.

"I agreed because our riders had never stalled a bike on the grid. So what happens in the next race at Oulton? Hodgson stalls it, so he starts from the back of the grid. He was eighth on the third lap and came through the field to win the race."

Little did Wright know just how memorable the first BSB race of the day would be in 2007, with both of his riders involved in a fairing-bashing scrap for the win!

RACE ONE

Ryuichi Kiyonari got the lead into Old Hall from pole man Gregorio Lavilla. Tom Sykes made the most of his first time on the front row in a superbike race to grab third on the Stobart Honda followed by Leon Haslam,

Previous pages: Lavilla leads Haslam in race one, but Kiyo broke the Airwaves Ducati domination in race two

Below: Tommy Hill had been on pole at Silverstone but was 13th on the grid at Oulton – and struggled all weekend

who passed Sykes out of the first turn to claim third. Leon Camier also made a good start after struggling in qualifying, but Jonathan Rea was back in 11th.

By the fourth lap Kiyo, Lavilla, Haslam and Camier (having set the fastest lap at that stage) had broken clear of the bunch led by Sykes, Shane Byrne, Cal Crutchlow, Rea, Karl Harris and Michael Rutter.

Lavilla made his move for the lead at Lodge and Kiyo had no resistance. It took until the 12th lap for Kiyo to come back at the Ducati rider, using the power of his Honda to pass along the start/finish straight, but it was only a brief spell in front as Lavilla soon stuffed him on the inside at Cascades to take control.

It became a Ducati 1–2 when Haslam took Kiyo before the end of the lap, and then a lap later he got in front for the first time, getting into Lodge later on the brakes with the rear tyre hovering mid-air and stepped out sideways. Lavilla had to lift to avoid a clash and Kiyo closed right in on the Spaniard.

On the penultimate lap Lavilla ran into Shell Oils at what looked to most to be a little too fast. Haslam obviously was pushing on too because he was inches off the apex and Lavilla sniffed a gap. He let his brakes off to run his bike in so hard that Haslam this time had no option but to lift and run wide.

The move was so hard it left some of his front Dunlop rubber on the inside of Haslam's fairing. No team orders then!

On the final lap Haslam tried to go under Lavilla at Old Hall but Lavilla kept the faith, and stayed on the gas on the outside of the corner to just maintain his advantage and from there rode the most defensive last lap you'll ever see to clinch his fifth win of the season.

The first thing Lavilla did when he reached the winner's enclosure was to run over and give Haslam a big hug: "Sorry mate," he said, referring to his forceful Hairpin move, but there was no need to apologise.

Haslam was all smiles, probably just happy to be back in the thick of the action.

Haslam told Lavilla: "I went into Old Hall so fast I was thinking, 'shit, if I'm in this fast, he's in even faster – and you still got by'."

"I know, I was right out on the ripples," Lavilla told Haslam, and then added: "I desperately wanted to pass Leon at the hairpin but going in there I was very fast – too fast. I braked so hard trying not to touch him, so hard my back wheel lifted off the ground. Luckily, he was a bit wide and I could let my brakes off and get through. It was a great race, everyone was slipping and sliding."

Haslam said: "Greg apologised. He lost his braking point and left his tyre mark on my fairing, but that was just racing."

But with a typical tongue-in-cheek remark that has a little bite to it, Haslam added: "It was a bit harsh, to be fair, but I've got all season to repay him!"

Kiyo had the best seat in the house to watch the action but, as usual, was keeping most of his thoughts to himself. All he could muster for the media at the end of the race was: "They are both very good riders. There was a lot of fighting. I hope I can do better next time."

Behind the leading three, Rea staged another late charge to claim fourth ahead of Sykes and Byrne.

RACE TWO

The weather had been threatening rain all day and drizzle just before the start of race two saw the usual panic in the pits, with everyone hedging bets on which way the conditions were going. Ultimately the race was declared dry and everyone started on slicks.

As the pack set off, Camier was swallowed up with the Bike Animal Honda doing a good impression of a pogo-stick as the rider tried to cope with a grabby clutch.

Above: Up for the Cup, James Buckingham leads Tom Tunstall and Malcolm Ashley in the privateer scrap

■ REA'S CHANCE DISCOVERY

All through testing and in the first three rounds of the season, Jonathan Rea privately admitted he lacked that last little bit of confidence to really commit to corners on the HM Plant Honda.

It took a quiet evening meal with his crew chief Chris Pike, mulling over the first three races of the year, to come up with the solution.

Rea said: "We were just chatting things over and I suddenly realised why I was having the problem. For some reason I wasn't releasing the front brake so I couldn't get the bike to turn in. I was stopping myself too much when

I just needed more confidence to commit to the corners. I was stopping the bike and squirting it."

To give Rea more confidence to turn in, Pike went softer on the fork setting and lifted the front end too. He explained: "It steered much better after the changes – which isn't what you would expect. The problem was that he was holding the brake right to the apex and when he let go of the lever, the front forks rebounded and upset the balance of the bike as he turned in. Now he's able to release the brake early and when he starts to accelerate the bike is still turning."

Rea finished fourth and fifth in the races and

said: "In the first race I pushed hard after a bad start and got arm pump. My trainer, Dan Roberts, did a good job getting me back in shape for the second race but I still didn't get away well. The conditions were a bit dodgy and I got beat up in the first turn again and as a couple of guys banged into me, I lifted and three more came by.

"I gave it everything, though, at the end of the race and was really pleased to set the fastest lap of the race right there on the penultimate lap."

GREG'S DISASTER, KIYO'S DOUBLE

Lavilla's Snetterton jinx came back to haunt him as Kiyonari sped to a double victory and the points lead

It all seemed a touch too much *déjà vu* for Gregorio Lavilla. The championship leader arrived at Snetterton fearing it would be a big ask of the Airwaves Ducati to match the Honda grunt out of Sear and Russell, the two corners leading on to the long straights. But after some dramatic gearing changes to his bike, he appeared happy and confident throughout the three free practice sessions and qualified a strong third.

Then, just as in 2006, when he low-sided at the exit of Coram when the forks bottomed out in practice, he could only finish sixth in race one and then went down at The Esses in race two. Lavilla's Snetterton jinx, which had seen him finish only two races in four attempts prior to this year, hit home again.

It all turned pear-shaped in Sunday morning warm-up when he crashed with just over a minute of the session to go. He was unhurt but suddenly the gloss was taken off what looked like the potential for some good damage-limitation in the races.

Things didn't get any better in race one when he ran off the track while charging to catch the leading bunch, and then his bike suddenly stopped running in race two.

Lavilla could only watch Ryuichi Kiyonari take his second win of the day and assume control of the championship, 11 points ahead of the luckless Spaniard.

Lavilla said: "First race my brake lever was back to the bar in the first few laps and I thought maybe I'll crash if I push too hard and I lost positions. I lost the front at Riches and had to go on the grass. After that I lost my rhythm. Then in the second race, one minute the bike was fine and then it felt like it was out of fuel. It wasn't, but that was the feeling. The bike just stopped."

RACE ONE

Jonathan Rea qualified second to Shane Byrne and made no mistake at the start, as he had in previous rounds, to grab the holeshot from Leon Haslam, Kiyonari, Chris Walker and Byrne, who quickly got past the Rizla biker and set off after the leading trio. Also well-placed were Tom Sykes, Lavilla and Tommy Hill, while Cal Crutchlow led the increasingly impressive Tommy Bridewell, Michael Rutter, Scott Smart and the rest of the pack.

Five laps into the race Shakey was touring, looking down at the back end of the machine. He'd just latched

Previous pages: HM Plant Honda assumed control at Snetterton – and double race winner Kiyo took the championship lead for the first time in the year

Below: Gregorio Lavilla hits the deck in race two, handing his championship lead to arch-rival Kiyo

on to the back of Rea, Haslam and Kiyonari when he ran a little wide exiting Sear and on to the 'marbles' (the dirty outer edge of the race track). A stone had been flicked up by one of his tyres and smashed off the rear wheel speed sensor. With no data from the rear wheel, the computer assumed the bike was at rest and reconfigured itself into launch mode.

With Byrne out of the race, Stobart's hopes rested with Sykes, who was having another brilliant ride in fourth place, holding Hill, Lavilla, Walker, Crutchlow and Tommy Bridewell at bay.

On lap six Lavilla went by Hill at the end of the back straight, and Crutchlow picked off Walker at the same spot. Lavilla posted the fastest race lap on lap seven and went ahead of Sykes on lap 11, the same lap on which Kiyonari made his bid for the lead.

Lavilla continued to charge and on lap 15 put in a 1m 04.77s lap when everyone was still running in the 1:05 bracket, but two laps later he miscued going into Riches and was forced to take to the grass. He managed to save the impending crash but lost around eight seconds and dropped to sixth behind Sykes and Leon Camier, who had come from the back of the grid (see panel, next page) but it was too late in the race for the Spaniard to make up any places.

Lavilla said: "My brake lever was back to the handlebar in the first laps so I lost position and once I was in traffic it was hard to pass. When I finally got some clear track I could do the times, but I lost the front end in the first corner and had to go on the grass. After that I didn't have a good feeling and lost my rhythm."

Up front Kiyonari was under pressure from his team-mate Rea but held on to take his fourth win of the season, while Haslam dropped off the pace at a rate of seven-tenths a lap in the closing half-dozen laps.

Kiyo said: "These points were very important. I thought maybe before we arrive this could be good track for us. I hoped to win but I made mistake in qualifying so only fifth on grid. Good to race with Jonny though. He uses a very different riding style to me, he has faster corner speed but I pick up bike early and go full throttle. He's also smoother on braking. I'm very ragged."

Rea said: "I couldn't get the drive off corners and I don't know why. I made a good start and felt comfortable but Kiyo got the lead early on when he got out of Sears better than me and passed me down the back straight.

Haslam said: "I knew it would be hard here. I could make it up in the corners but lost down the straight."

Sykes was fourth, continuing his amazing form, and Camier was an astounding fifth from the back row.

Top: Chris Walker's job at Rizla Suzuki was on the line after two ninth places at Snetterton

Above: Shakey Byrne gave Stobart Honda something to shout about when he claimed pole – he hit problems in race one but bounced back with third in race two

■ CAMIER'S TWO FIFTH PLACES FROM THE BACK ROW

Leon Camier's disastrous qualifying session on Saturday highlighted how crucial it is to have two bikes. He did his out-lap on the Bike Animal Honda but then pulled in before completing his first flying lap to complain there was something wrong with the gearbox, which had been rebuilt between sessions with new ratios.

The team quickly diagnosed the fault but the pit garage shutters came down to end Camier's day because there had been an error in the gearbox reassembly and it wasn't going to be fixed in the 50-minute qualifying session.

Thanks to a promoter's option clause in the regulations, Camier was permitted to start from the back of the grid and kept his head to thread through the traffic and pick up fifth place in race one and sixth in race two.

The team were over the moon not just with the results, but the maturity he showed.

Tom Larsen, his crew chief, said: "We're really pleased with the way he conducted himself out there. It would have been all too easy for a rider of his limited experience to push too hard and throw it down the road. He rode smart again."

Camier said: "It wasn't so much starting from the back that worried me, though that was going to be hard enough, it was the fact that I missed a whole session of set-up again [just as at Oulton when he had brake problems and missed a big chunk of one session]. That's the worst thing.

"It was a good learning experience because I was pushing so hard that I used my tyres, changing my style to suit. I ended up braking in different places because I was getting so much movement from the front tyre. I did the braking sat up and then slapped it on its side, where normally I'd have used a lot more corner speed."

Lack of practice hampered Leon Camier's efforts on the Bike Animal Honda but he still managed two top-six finishes

KIYO WRAPS IT UP

Ryuichi Kiyonari clinches his second successive BSB title after finishing third in the first race at Brands

In a repeat of the 2006 season, BSB went to Brands Hatch in October for a three-rider showdown for the title. And just like last year, Ryuichi Kiyonari wrapped it up in the first race with a relatively safe ride to third place.

Last year's final round was on the long circuit and Kiyo suffered a 120mph crash in practice. Then the races were held in changeable conditions and the title was decided when the first race was stopped prematurely, robbing the fans of any real excitement.

This year the races were held on the tight Indy circuit and it was pretty much a formality that Kiyo, with a 37-point lead over HM Plant Honda team-mate Jonathan Rea and a 41-point lead over Leon Haslam, would take the crown.

But that didn't stop a whopping 40,000 crowd turning out over a warm, autumnal weekend – that was only 5,000 down on WSB at the height of summer and with Brit James Toseland a title contender. The spectators weren't disappointed by the close-fought action with Gregorio Lavilla finishing the season as he started it by winning both races on the Airwaves Ducati.

Rea was second in both races to retain second place in the points ahead of Haslam, while Cal Crutchlow won huge applause when he finished third in the second race – his first-ever BSB podium finish.

RACE ONE

Lavilla sat on pole from Tom Sykes, Rea and Shane Byrne, while Kiyo was on the second row along with Cal Crutchlow, Haslam (who had been hampered by a problem with the idle motor that helps with the engine braking system) and Karl Harris. But it was Rea who grabbed the holeshot into Paddock from Kiyo, Sykes, Lavilla, Haslam and Crutchlow.

It takes just over 45s to do a quick lap of the Brands Indy circuit and so the laps were rattled off fast and furiously. It's also a difficult track to overtake on and it took Lavilla until the eighth lap to make an attempt on Sykes on the inside of Clearways – a bold move. The corner is a long, long right-hander and the part of the curve where the Spaniard chose to pass is where everyone hugs the inside line before drifting to the edge of the track on the exit to get the run down the start-finish straight.

Lavilla set a new lap record on lap nine to peg the gap to Rea and Kiyo up front, but the safety car was mobilised on the tenth lap when Sykes low-sided at Graham Hill Bend. He was okay but his bike burst into flames and the marshals had a long jog with heavy extinguishers to quell the blaze. It seemed to take an age before the fire was out but thankfully the only real damage to the bike was to the wiring loom.

Previous pages: Kiyo celebrates with his team at Brands. He indicates 'number one – twice'

Below: Tom Sykes, leading here, wasn't able to round out an otherwise great season on the Stobart Honda as he couldn't run the race tyre for which the bike was set up. Cal Crutchlow, behind him, finished his rookie BSB year with a podium in race two

Even while the safety car was out, there was another crash when Martin Jessopp went down, an ignominious end to his first ride on a Stobart Honda, now in Riders colours in readiness for the 2008 season.

Once racing resumed on lap 12, Lavilla set to work on the two Hondas, finally picking off Kiyo at Paddock with a move that started all the way back at Clearways with a big effort to get good drive out of the fast right.

It took until lap 20 before Lavilla took the lead, again using his signature move on the inside at Clearways, this time making Rea lift up to avoid a clash.

Lavilla said: "It was important for me to show that I can ride as I know. The race showed I can be fast on my own with this bike but it is very difficult to run with other bikes because we lose out on acceleration. After last time when I did all my passing at Paddock I had to invent a new place to pass but it was

very difficult to make it through safely each time."

Lavilla didn't back off once he got into the lead and gradually, tenths at a time, he eked out an advantage that saw him cross the line 2.44s ahead of Rea at the finish – a huge gap considering the length of the course and how competitive things had been early in the race.

Rea said: "Congratulations to Kiyo. He's been that bit stronger than me all year. Today we had some set-up problems which I hope to sort for the second race."

Behind them, though, the action continued with Shakey up to sixth on lap 22 and knocking on the door for fifth, having recovered from a bad start that saw him down in ninth on the first lap. On lap 23 he passed Crutchlow, dropping down Paddock Hill, but the Rizla rider fought back, scuttling past on the brakes into Druids to secure what would be fifth place at the finish.

Haslam wasn't happy with fourth place behind

Opposite: Gregorio Lavilla was in no mood for messing at Brands, winning both races with some stunning passes at Clearways

Below left: Chris Walker's disappointing BSB season almost ended prematurely with this sorry mess after he had crashed in practice. Amazingly Walker raced on Sunday despite barely being able to walk

Below right: Shakey sends a message to his dad, who was hospitalised suffering from lung cancer at the time of the final round

Above: The results might not have been as fiery as his Hawk Kawasaki afterburners, but James Haydon was just happy to be back in the mix to regain his old confidence on Dunlops after a terrible start to the year with the Pirelli-shod Virgin Yamaha

Below: HM Plant finished one-two in the championship – the '4' on Rea's bike just needed to be changed to a '2'. Kiyo, of course, already had the 'Number 1' plate from last year!

Kiyo and kept pushing ever closer until he ran wide at Paddock on the 28th lap and then had to fend off Crutchlow at the line.

Kiyo's third place give him the title and he said: "I'm so happy. Thank you very much everybody [who helped me win this]. I push every lap but I was also thinking of the championship. I got a great start and push but not too much – too easy to crash. Also if relax too much – too easy to crash. So, very difficult race but now I'm happy."

Haslam looked exasperated at the end of the race. He said: "We had a problem with the idle system all weekend so the tickover was high and pushing me into corners. We didn't realise it though and made some

chassis changes to get it steering better. Then we made some improvements in the fuelling for the race so the geometry was wrong. I was losing it big-style in the early part of corners when I was trying to get drive."

RACE TWO

Rea took the lead again as the field thundered down Paddock Hill for the start of the second race, with Kiyo, Shakey, Lavilla, Sykes and Haslam chasing.

The race was into the sixth lap when Lavilla pulled off another move at Clearways, this time to pass Shakey for third – just as the safety car was scrambled because James Buckingham's Quay Garages Honda had expired in a huge plume of smoke as he turned down Paddock.

BENNETTS BRITISH SUPERBIKE CHAMPIONSHIP

	RIDER	TOTAL	R1	R2	R3	R4	R5	R6	R7	R8	R9	R10	R11	R12	R13	R14	R15	R16	R17	R18	R19	R20	R21	R22	R23	R24	R25	R26
1	Ryuichi KIYONARI	433	8	5	16	20	25	25	16	25	25	25	11	11	20	16	25			25	25	25	20	20		16	16	13
2	Jonathan REA	407	16	20		13	20	16	13	11	20	20	13	25	25	25		25	20		20	20		25	11	9	20	20
3	Leon HASLAM	387	10	13	10	10	10	11	20	16	11	25	13	16	20	13	13	16	20	11	10	25		25	25	13	11	
4	Gregorio LAVILLA	368	25	25	25	25	11	20	25	13	10		16	16	9			6	11	9	10	13	9	16	13	11	25	25
5	Shane BYRNE	293	13	3	13	16			10	16		16	20	20	13	11	20	16	25	16	7	9	13		16	10	10	
6	Tom SYKES	279	9	11	11	9	9	10	11	10	13	13		9	10	13		10	10	13	16	16	16	11	20	20		9
7	Chris WALKER	225	11	8	7		16	13		7	7	7	7		11	10	16	8	13	10	8		8	10	10	13	9	10
8	Leon CAMIER	199	20	16	20	11	13		8	8	11	10	9	10		9	10	11	8	5	9	11						
9	Cal CRUTCHLOW	152			9		5	9	9		8		8	5			11		7	11	13	3	11	13				11	16
10	Tommy HILL	138	7		8	6	8	8	6	9	9	9	6	7	3		8		9	7	6		10	9					3
11	Karl HARRIS	121	2	10	6	7	7	4	7		3	1	10	8	6	8		20		3	5					6			8
12	Michael RUTTER	118	6	9	5	8	6	7	1	3	5							9		8	3	8	5	6	7	8	8	6
13	Scott SMART	95			2	5		2	5		2	8	4	6				9	5	6	6	2	5	6	4	9		5	4
14	Ollie BRIDEWELL	56		1		3	5	3	5		6		5	8	6	7	7												
15	Steve PLATER	51		2	3	3					1			4		4						3	7	6	7	6	5		
16	Simon ANDREWS	49	5	7				4	2	4								5	4	4	7					7			
17	Dean THOMAS	37		6		2	3		6		3	2	3					4	2		4	2							
18	James HAYDON	31			1																7	8	8						7
19	Tommy BRIDEWELL	28	4		1		4	6	2	4	6																	1	
20	Tristan PALMER	27											1		2	5	4	3		1	3	4	1	2	1				
21	Chris MARTIN	23					1		2	5							1	1	1		4	5		3					
22	Peter HICKMAN	23	1	4	4	4					2			3	3	2													
23	Ian HUTCHINSON	16																					5	5	4	2			
24	Sean EMMETT	14									7	7																	
25	Hudson KENNAUGH	14							4	3		4	3																
26	Aaron ZANOTTI	13							5										2			2	4						
27	Guy MARTIN	8			1		1						6																
28	Stuart EASTON	8								1		2	5																
29	Marty NUTT	8								1		1							3		3								
30	Tom TUNSTALL	5									2	2							1										
31	Malcolm ASHLEY	4									4																		
32	James BUCKINGHAM	4									1					1		2											
33	Cameron DONALD	2			2																								
34	Jon KIRKHAM	2																					2						
35	Paul BARRON	1											1																
36	David JOHNSON	1																	1										

BRITISH SUPERBIKE CUP

	RIDER	TOTAL	R1	R2	R3	R4	R5	R6	R7	R8	R9	R10	R11	R12	R13	R14	R15	R16	R17	R18	R19	R20	R21	R22	R23	R24	R25	R26
1	Tristan PALMER	426					25	25	20	20		16	25	20	25	25	25	25	25				25	25	25	25	25	25
2	James BUCKINGHAM	373	25	25	25				25	25	20	20	9		9		11		13	13	16	20	25	20	20	16		
3	Tom TUNSTALL	332	20	20	16	20				16	10	11	20	13	13		11	20	11	16	16	16	16	16	20	20	16	
4	Malcolm ASHLEY	322	16		11	16	16	20	16	16	13	13	10	11	11	16	20		10	13	13	13	13	13	13		13	16
5	Marty NUTT	261		20	25					25	25	25	20	16	20	11	16	13		25	20							
6	Paul BARRON	147		13	13	20		13			16	20	16	25						11								
7	Neil FAULKER	90		9	10	13	16				11													11			20	
8	Lee JACKSON	40																	20	20								
9	Brian McCORMACK	37									13	13							11									
10	Ryan FARQUHAR	21			10	11																						
11	Ryan RAINEY	21																				10	11					

BRITISH MANUFACTURERS CUP

	RIDER	TOTAL	R1	R2	R3	R4	R5	R6	R7	R8	R9	R10	R11	R12	R13	R14	R15	R16	R17	R18	R19	R20	R21	R22	R23	R24	R25	R26
1	Honda	591	20	20	20	20	25	25	25	25	25	20	25	25	25	25	25	25	25	25	20	25	20	20	20	20	20	
2	Ducati	507	25	25	25	25	11	20	25	20	16	11	25	16	16	20	13	13	16	20	11	13	25	16	25	25	25	
3	Suzuki	263	11	8	9		16	13	9	7	8	7	8	5	11	10	16	8	13	11	13	6	11	13	10	13	11	16
4	Yamaha	180	7	7	8	6	8	8	6	9	9	9	6	7	4	4	8	1	9	7	6	7	10	9	6	7	7	5
5	Kawasaki	169	6	9	5	8	6	7	5	3	5	8	4	6	2	5	9	6	8	3	8	7	9	8	9	8	8	7

Lightly we turned, through wet woods blossom-hung,
Into the open. Down the supernal roads,
With plumes a-tossing, purple flags far flung,
Rank upon rank, unbridled, unforgiving,
Thundered the black battalions of the Gods.

RUPERT BROOKE - 1908

CONGRATULATIONS
TO MICHAEL LAVERTY

AND THE ENTIRE RELENTLESS SUZUKI BY TAS TEAM
ON WINNING THE 2007 BRITISH SUPERSPORT TITLE.

⟨ NO HALF MEASURES ⟩

ENERGY ✱ STAMINA ✱ FOCUS ✱ DRIVE

THE RACES
2007 MAXXIS BRITISH SUPERSPORT CHAMPIONSHIP

Established names: Michael Laverty, Dennis Hobbs, Jamie Robinson, John McGuinness. Young guns: Ian Lowry, Billy McConnell, Tom Grant, Ian Hutchinson. Laverty won the war but British Supersport was always full of fairing-bashing battles and dramatic incidents

BRANDS HATCH ROUND **13**

McConnell wins final battle

With Michael Laverty already having wrapped up the title at Donington, the focus of attention at Brands Hatch was on whether Ian Lowry could defend his second place in the championship and make it a 1–2 for the Relentless by TAS Suzuki team, or whether Dennis Hobbs could pull something out of the bag on the Padgetts Honda to overhaul him.

But it was Billy McConnell who wanted the glory. He overhauled John McGuinness and early leader Dennis Hobbs to take the lead on the fourth lap and led it the rest of the way until Aaron Walker crashed on the 23rd lap, causing the race to be red-flagged and the points awarded.

It was McConnell's second win of the year but, more important, it completed a strong end-of-season run for the Virgin Yamaha rider with podium finishes (including the two wins) in the final four races of the year.

McConnell said: "I got my best start all year and I'm really happy. The boys said 'go out to win' today and this is a payback to them and our sponsors for everything they've put into the team this year."

Behind McConnell, Hobbs was pushing hard. Though he reduced a 1.19s deficit to just three tenths of a second in the closing stages, he was robbed of any chance of putting a move on the Yamaha rider when the race was ended prematurely by the red flag.

With Lowry finishing sixth, however, Hobbs had to be content with third place overall, just six points down on the Irishman in the final reckoning.

"I was lining up Billy for a go on the last lap but then it got stopped. I've got to thank Padgetts for everything they've done for me in the past two years. And my Grandad's in hospital suffering from cancer so I'd like to dedicate this result to him. I'd like to have won for him but I did my best today."

It was already announced prior to the race weekend that Hobbs had signed to ride for the Centurion Honda team in the 2008 British Supersport series.

Hobbs' team-mate McGuinness didn't have so much luck at Brands. He was running third close behind Hobbs in the early stages but was adjudged to have jumped the start and was awarded a ride-through penalty.

Clearly angered by the decision, McGuinness said: "All that achieved was to rob the fans of a race. I didn't gain any advantage at the start so why penalise me?"

Laverty gained from McGuinness pulling in on the tenth lap, shortly after he'd completed his ride-through penalty. He finished third and said: "I think I could have picked up the pace in the closing stages to have won that. We had some problems in practice so we were guessing on a tyre but I would have given it a go there."

Laverty raced in 2005 and 2006 with Stobart Honda but is destined to return to BSB in 2008 with Relentless by TAS on a new Suzuki GSX-R1000. He said: "This year's been great for the team but next year we're in BSB and I'm really looking forward to the new challenge."

Below: Billy McConnell finished his and Virgin Yamaha's season on a high note

SUPERSPORT RESULTS
2007 MAXXIS BRITISH SUPERSPORT CHAMPIONSHIP

ROUND 1 BRANDS HATCH

	No	Rider	Team Entry	Time	Gap	MPH	Best
1	2	Michael LAVERTY	Suzuki - Relentless Suzuki by TAS	13:01.199		84.83	1:30.004
2	77	Jamie ROBINSON	Honda - Margal / BykerBabe	13:01.722	0.523	84.77	1:29.978
3	5	Ian LOWRY	Suzuki - Relentless Suzuki by TAS	13:01.903	0.704	84.75	1:30.112
4	33	Aaron WALKER	Honda - TJW Racing	13:05.284	4.085	84.39	1:30.567
5	3	Stuart EASTON	Kawasaki - Isilon MSS Discovery Kawasaki	13:05.574	4.375	84.35	1:30.548
6	6	John McGUINNESS	Honda - Padgetts Motorcycles	13:06.035	4.836	84.31	1:30.191
7	47	Richard COOPER	Yamaha - AIM Racing	13:06.706	5.507	84.23	1:30.844
8	99	Steven NEATE	Honda - Angel Racing	13:07.405	6.206	84.16	1:30.380
9	88	Ian HUTCHINSON	Honda - Bike Animal Honda	13:07.623	6.424	84.14	1:30.475
10	27	James WESTMORELAND	Honda - Centurion Racing	13:08.335	7.136	84.06	1:30.497
11	20	Daniel COOPER	Honda - Centurion Racing	13:09.778	8.579	83.91	1:30.752
12	31	Sam OWENS	Honda - Premier Motorsport	13:10.285	9.086	83.85	1:30.933
13	75	Craig FITZPATRICK	Yamaha - BLDS	13:14.113	12.914	83.45	1:31.478
14	94	Jack KENNEDY	Honda - TAG Racing	13:14.125	12.926	83.45	1:31.372
15	94	Ben WYLIE	Yamaha - Wylie & Holland Racing	13:14.369	13.170	83.42	1:31.734
16	70	Tom GRANT	Yamaha - Virgin Media Yamaha	13:16.846	15.647	83.16	1:30.254
17	13	Gary MAY	Yamaha - Powerbiking Yamaha	13:16.925	15.726	83.15	1:32.168
18	14	Christian ELKIN	Honda - BBR Racing	13:20.723	19.524	82.76	1:32.052
19	72	James WEBB	Kawasaki - Team Buff Kawasaki	13:21.711	20.512	82.66	1:32.930
20	42	Guy SANDERS	Kawasaki - Gearlink Racing	13:22.649	21.450	82.56	1:32.898
21	17	Ian LOUGHER	Honda - Team Blackhorse	13:23.189	21.990	82.50	1:33.264
22	96	Paul YOUNG	Triumph - Paul Young Racing	13:23.311	22.112	82.49	1:32.922
23	8	Brian CLARK	Yamaha - Tamworth Yamaha Racing	13:29.883	28.684	81.82	1:33.702
24	69	Anthony HINTON	Yamaha - NST Yamaha	13:30.188	28.989	81.79	1:33.702
25	67	Glynn THOMAS	Honda - JJR	13:34.657	33.458	81.34	1:34.659
26	21	Alex LOWES	Honda - Double Vision Racing	13:50.328	49.129	79.81	1:33.555

ROUND 2 THRUXTON

	No	Rider	Team Entry	Time	Gap	MPH	Best
1	2	Michael LAVERTY	Suzuki - Relentless Suzuki by TAS	26:12.443		102.47	1:17.835
2	77	Jamie ROBINSON	Honda - Margal / BykerBabe	26:20.365	7.922	101.95	1:18.220
3	4	Billy McCONNELL	Yamaha - Virgin Media Yamaha	26:25.161	12.718	101.65	1:18.387
4	27	James WESTMORELAND	Honda - Centurion Racing	26:26.934	14.491	101.53	1:18.580
5	3	Stuart EASTON	Kawasaki - Isilon MSS Discovery Kawasaki	26:27.014	14.571	101.53	1:18.664
6	88	Ian HUTCHINSON	Honda - Bike Animal Honda	26:27.356	14.913	101.50	1:18.393
7	40	Martin JESSOPP	Ducati - Riders Racing	26:30.309	17.866	101.32	1:18.604
8	20	Daniel COOPER	Honda - Centurion Racing	26:45.399	32.956	100.36	1:18.971
9	24	Jack KENNEDY	Honda - TAG Racing	26:46.591	34.148	100.29	1:19.084
10	21	Alex LOWES	Honda - Double Vision Racing	26:47.013	34.570	100.26	1:18.644
11	42	Guy SANDERS	Kawasaki - Gearlink Racing	26:49.361	36.918	100.12	1:19.417
12	33	Aaron WALKER	Honda - TJW Racing	26:55.957	43.514	99.71	1:19.332
13	94	Ben WYLIE	Yamaha - Wylie & Holland Racing	26:56.132	43.689	99.70	1:19.975
14	96	Paul YOUNG	Triumph - Paul Young Racing	26:56.412	43.969	99.68	1:19.887
15	75	Craig FITZPATRICK	Yamaha - BLDS	26:56.939	44.496	99.65	1:19.941
16	8	Brian CLARK	Yamaha - Tamworth Yamaha Racing	27:08.210	55.767	98.96	1:20.284
17	13	Gary MAY	Yamaha - Powerbiking Yamaha	27:08.411	55.968	98.95	1:20.306
18	54	Jack GROVES	Yamaha - Kingswood Moto-Sport	27:09.184	56.741	98.90	1:20.219
19	11	Matt LAYT	Yamaha - BPM Yamaha/Scott & Scott	27:25.832	1:13.389	97.90	1:20.908
20	67	Glynn THOMAS	Honda - JJR	27:30.234	1:17.791	97.64	1:21.381
21	46	John ROBB	Honda - NEAT Ltd	27:30.361	1:17.918	97.63	1:21.079
22	9	Jack WRIGHT	Kawasaki - Hawk Kawasaki Juniors	27:30.431	1:17.988	97.63	1:21.419
23	58	Conor O'BRIEN	Honda - Arkwood Honda	27:30.917	1:18.474	97.60	1:21.524
24	16	Craig SPROSTON	Honda - CS Racing	27:31.743	1:19.300	97.55	1:21.123

ROUND 3 SILVERSTONE

	No	Rider	Team Entry	Time	Gap	MPH	Best
1	25	Dennis HOBBS	Honda - Padgetts Motorcycles	27:36.571		86.55	1:29.164
2	5	Ian LOWRY	Suzuki - Relentless Suzuki by TAS	27:40.085	3.514	86.37	1:29.376
3	2	Michael LAVERTY	Suzuki - Relentless Suzuki by TAS	27:41.635	5.064	86.29	1:29.193
4	88	Ian HUTCHINSON	Honda - Bike Animal Honda	27:46.758	10.187	86.03	1:29.659
5	70	Tom GRANT	Yamaha - Virgin Media Yamaha	27:48.737	12.166	85.92	1:29.761
6	6	John McGUINNESS	Honda - Padgetts Motorcycles	27:50.429	13.858	85.84	1:29.645
7	4	Billy McCONNELL	Yamaha - Virgin Media Yamaha	27:54.958	18.387	85.60	1:29.117
8	40	Martin JESSOPP	Ducati - Riders Racing	27:58.594	22.023	85.42	1:29.842
9	3	Stuart EASTON	Kawasaki - Isilon MSS Discovery Kawasaki	27:59.666	23.095	85.36	1:30.091
10	47	Richard COOPER	Yamaha - AIM Racing	28:03.669	27.098	85.16	1:30.596
11	31	Sam OWENS	Honda - Premier Motorsport	28:04.840	28.269	85.10	1:30.858
12	24	Jack KENNEDY	Honda - TAG Racing	28:05.334	28.763	85.08	1:30.793
13	27	James WESTMORELAND	Honda - Centurion Racing	28:07.260	30.689	84.98	1:30.642
14	42	Guy SANDERS	Kawasaki - Gearlink Racing	28:11.360	34.789	84.77	1:30.733
15	37	James HILLIER	Kawasaki - Gearlink Racing	28:14.087	37.516	84.64	1:31.174
16	96	Paul YOUNG	Triumph - Paul Young Racing	28:14.894	38.323	84.60	1:30.998
17	75	Craig FITZPATRICK	Yamaha - BLDS	28:15.388	38.817	84.57	1:31.132
18	14	Christian ELKIN	Honda - BBR Racing	28:16.549	39.978	84.51	1:31.023
19	99	Steven NEATE	Honda - Angel Racing	28:16.783	40.212	84.50	1:30.927
20	21	Alex LOWES	Honda - Double Vision Racing	28:16.858	40.287	84.50	1:30.759
21	20	Daniel COOPER	Honda - Centurion Racing	28:19.322	42.751	84.38	1:31.191
22	56	John CROCKFORD	Suzuki - Crescent Performance Suzuki	28:20.658	44.087	84.31	1:31.063
23	13	Gary MAY	Yamaha - Powerbiking Yamaha	28:22.713	46.142	84.21	1:31.499
24	12	Sam LOWES	Honda - Double Vision Racing	28:28.779	52.208	83.91	1:31.423
25	78	Alan O'CONNOR	Honda - Team MFC Racing	28:36.974	1:00.403	83.51	1:32.349
26	76	Ross WALTER	Triumph - Interserve Racing	28:42.577	1:06.006	83.24	1:32.929

ROUND 4 OULTON PARK

	No	Rider	Team Entry	Time	Gap	MPH	Best
1	25	Dennis HOBBS	Honda - Padgetts Motorcycles	26:52.676		96.14	1:40.007
2	5	Ian LOWRY	Suzuki - Relentless Suzuki by TAS	26:53.350	0.674	96.10	1:40.058
3	2	Michael LAVERTY	Suzuki - Relentless Suzuki by TAS	26:54.370	1.694	96.04	1:40.229
4	42	Guy SANDERS	Kawasaki - Gearlink Racing	27:05.975	13.299	95.36	1:40.436
5	6	John McGUINNESS	Honda - Padgetts Motorcycles	27:14.048	21.372	94.88	1:41.242
6	70	Tom GRANT	Yamaha - Virgin Media Yamaha	27:14.159	21.483	94.88	1:41.190
7	31	Sam OWENS	Honda - Premier Motorsport	27:17.901	25.225	94.66	1:41.084
8	96	Paul YOUNG	Triumph - Paul Young Racing	27:19.230	26.554	94.59	1:41.546
9	77	Jamie ROBINSON	Honda - Margal / BykerBabe	27:22.972	30.296	94.37	1:41.449
10	3	Stuart EASTON	Kawasaki - Isilon MSS Discovery Kawasaki	27:23.096	30.420	94.36	1:41.386
11	18	Guy MARTIN	Honda - Hydrex Honda	27:23.501	30.825	94.34	1:41.471
12	37	James HILLIER	Kawasaki - Gearlink Racing	27:24.326	31.650	94.29	1:41.576
13	99	Steven NEATE	Honda - Angel Racing	27:26.012	33.336	94.20	1:41.692
14	47	Richard COOPER	Yamaha - AIM Racing	27:29.679	37.003	93.99	1:41.959
15	94	Ben WYLIE	Yamaha - Wylie & Holland Racing	27:32.273	39.597	93.84	1:41.942
16	14	Christian ELKIN	Honda - BBR Racing	27:33.003	40.327	93.80	1:42.071
17	20	Daniel COOPER	Honda - Centurion Racing	27:33.075	40.399	93.79	1:42.225
18	27	James WESTMORELAND	Honda - Centurion Racing	27:35.077	42.401	93.68	1:41.884
19	48	Joe DICKINSON	Honda - Trucklinks Racing	27:35.557	42.881	93.65	1:41.815
20	75	Craig FITZPATRICK	Yamaha - BLDS	27:35.885	43.209	93.63	1:42.169
21	12	Sam LOWES	Honda - Double Vision Racing	27:43.968	51.292	93.18	1:42.752
22	21	Alex LOWES	Honda - Double Vision Racing	27:55.994	1:03.318	92.51	1:42.702
23	30	Jamie HAMILTON	Kawasaki - Longshot Racing KGR	28:18.303	1:25.627	91.30	1:44.694
24	16	Craig SPROSTON	Honda - CS Racing	28:21.557	1:28.881	91.12	1:44.710
25	69	Anthony HINTON	Yamaha - NST Yamaha	28:23.164	1:30.488	91.03	1:45.079
26	54	Jack GROVES	Yamaha - Kingswood Moto-Sport	28:23.385	1:30.709	91.02	1:44.585

ROUND 5 SNETTERTON

	No	Rider	Team Entry	Time	Gap	MPH	Best
1	5	Ian LOWRY	Suzuki - Relentless Suzuki by TAS	22:58.589		101.93	1:08.069
2	2	Michael LAVERTY	Suzuki - Relentless Suzuki by TAS	22:58.845	0.256	101.91	1:08.171
3	25	Dennis HOBBS	Honda - Padgetts Motorcycles	22:58.924	0.335	101.90	1:08.308
4	4	Billy McCONNELL	Yamaha - Virgin Media Yamaha	23:04.609	6.020	101.49	1:08.417
5	77	Jamie ROBINSON	Honda - Margal / BykerBabe	23:12.083	13.494	100.94	1:08.958
6	96	Paul YOUNG	Triumph - Paul Young Racing	23:13.019	14.430	100.87	1:08.807
7	42	Guy SANDERS	Kawasaki - Gearlink Racing	23:13.710	15.121	100.82	1:08.859
8	27	James WESTMORELAND	Honda - Centurion Racing	23:13.764	15.175	100.82	1:08.655
9	6	John McGUINNESS	Honda - Padgetts Motorcycles	23:15.213	16.624	100.71	1:08.969
10	70	Tom GRANT	Yamaha - Virgin Media Yamaha	23:15.246	16.657	100.71	1:08.890
11	20	Daniel COOPER	Honda - Centurion Racing	23:20.944	22.355	100.30	1:09.081
12	88	Ian HUTCHINSON	Honda - Bike Animal Honda	23:21.263	22.674	100.28	1:09.190
13	31	Sam OWENS	Honda - Premier Motorsport	23:21.392	22.803	100.27	1:09.427
14	99	Steven NEATE	Honda - Angel Racing	23:26.042	27.453	99.94	1:09.515
15	14	Christian ELKIN	Honda - BBR Racing	23:27.863	29.274	99.81	1:09.374
16	37	James HILLIER	Kawasaki - Gearlink Racing	23:27.957	29.368	99.80	1:09.607
17	94	Ben WYLIE	Yamaha - Wylie & Holland Racing	23:28.599	30.010	99.76	1:09.439
18	75	Craig FITZPATRICK	Yamaha - BLDS	23:29.688	31.099	99.68	1:09.269
19	48	Joe DICKINSON	Honda - Trucklinks Racing	23:29.906	31.317	99.66	1:09.619
20	10	Liam LYON	Yamaha - Seton Tuning	23:51.998	53.409	98.13	1:10.678
21	33	Aaron WALKER	Honda - TJW Racing	24:04.105	1:05.516	97.30	1:10.055
22	58	Conor O'BRIEN	Honda - Arkwood Honda	23:04.618	1 lap	96.41	1:11.077
23	26	Ben HANDLEY	Honda - A1 Plant Haulage Racing	23:15.326	1 lap	95.67	1:12.246
24	67	Glynn THOMAS	Honda - JJR / RS Securtity / BMC M/c's	23:47.466	1 lap	93.52	1:12.740

ROUND 6 MONDELLO PARK

	No	Rider	Team Entry	Time	Gap	MPH	Best
1	25	Dennis HOBBS	Honda - Padgetts Motorcycles	15:22.686		76.43	1:41.039
2	77	Jamie ROBINSON	Honda - Margal / BykerBabe	15:27.369	4.683	76.04	1:42.093
3	5	Ian LOWRY	Suzuki - Relentless Suzuki by TAS	15:27.490	4.804	76.03	1:41.970
4	6	John McGUINNESS	Honda - Padgetts Motorcycles	15:29.257	6.571	75.89	1:42.045
5	3	Stuart EASTON	Kawasaki - Isilon MSS Discovery Kawasaki	15:30.935	8.249	75.75	1:42.211
6	70	Tom GRANT	Yamaha - Virgin Media Yamaha	15:36.768	14.082	75.28	1:43.001
7	75	Craig FITZPATRICK	Yamaha - BLDS	15:45.400	22.714	74.59	1:43.808
8	27	James WESTMORELAND	Honda - Centurion Racing	15:46.990	24.304	74.46	1:43.824
9	40	Martin JESSOPP	Ducati - Riders Racing	15:47.029	24.343	74.46	1:43.692
10	31	Sam OWENS	Honda - Premier Motorsport	15:49.054	26.368	74.30	1:44.418
11	88	Ian HUTCHINSON	Honda - Bike Animal Honda	15:49.256	26.570	74.29	1:44.452
12	48	Joe DICKINSON	Honda - Trucklinks Racing	15:50.084	27.398	74.22	1:44.132
13	96	Paul YOUNG	Triumph - Paul Young Racing	15:51.758	29.072	74.09	1:44.569
14	33	Aaron WALKER	Honda - TJW Racing	15:52.249	29.563	74.05	1:44.600
15	20	Daniel COOPER	Honda - Centurion Racing	15:52.872	30.186	74.00	1:44.757
16	68	Declan SWANTON	Honda - McKenny Racing	16:07.311	44.625	72.90	1:45.860
17	16	Craig SPROSTON	Honda - CS Racing	16:08.442	45.756	72.81	1:46.164
18	22	Jonny BUCKLEY	Yamaha - Module Road & Race	16:08.900	46.214	72.78	1:45.685
19	8	Brian CLARK	Yamaha - Tamworth Yamaha Racing	16:09.448	46.762	72.74	1:46.096
20	4	Billy McCONNELL	Yamaha - Virgin Media Yamaha	16:11.649	48.963	72.57	1:41.209
21	26	Ben HANDLEY	Honda - A1 Plant Haulage Racing	16:26.115	1:03.489	71.51	1:47.420
22	76	Ross WALTER	Triumph - Interserve Racing	16:26.438	1:03.752	71.49	1:48.083
23	63	Mick DALY	Honda - Co Ordit Racing	16:30.284	1:07.598	71.21	1:47.785
24	67	Glynn THOMAS	Honda - JJR / RS Securtity / BMC M/c's	17:05.016	1:42.330	68.80	1:49.491